"*POJOs in Action* provides good coverage of the current EJB 3.0 and POJO discussions in the developer community. The book is easy to read and has lots of good examples. It provides a complete discussion of the subject matter, from the basic data definitions to the implications on the client-side: I haven't seen another book that takes this approach, so it definitely fills a niche.

"The author describes some technologies as being unsuitable for most situations, but sticks to his guns and maintains the philosophy of providing the user with a choice, describing each possible solution in depth, despite previous assertions that a particular solution may be sub-optimal. This reflects the realities in a developer's world, where we are often forced to use technologies that we might not have chosen ourselves: this support is A Good Thing.

"Compared to Martin Fowler's *Enterprise Architecture Patterns*, which provides a generalized description of the enterprise, this book attempts to present the solutions to the situations Fowler describes. While much of the information can be found elsewhere, including the websites for the technologies as well as Fowler's book, the combination of focused information and the explicit samples makes *POJOs in Action* much more than the sum of its parts. It isn't merely a duplication of what's available elsewhere: it carefully explains the technologies with plenty of sample code, in a consistent style."

BRENDAN MURRAY
Senior Software Architect
IBM

POJOs in Action

DEVELOPING ENTERPRISE APPLICATIONS
WITH LIGHTWEIGHT FRAMEWORKS

CHRIS RICHARDSON

MANNING
Greenwich
(74° w. long.)

For online information and ordering of this and other Manning books, please visit www.manning.com. The publisher offers discounts on this book when ordered in quantity. For more information, please contact:

Special Sales Department
Manning Publications Co.
209 Bruce Park Avenue   Fax:(203) 661-9018
Greenwich, CT 06830   email: manning@manning.com

Manning Publications Co.   Copyeditor: Liz Welch
209 Bruce Park Avenue   Typesetter: Gordan Salinovic
Greenwich, CT 06830   Cover designer: Leslie Haimes

ISBN 1932394583

Printed in the United States of America

2 3 4 5 6 7 8 9 10 – VHG – 10 09 08 07 06

To my mum, my dad, and my grandparents
Thank you for everything

—C. R.

brief contents

contents

Back in 1999, I enthusiastically embraced J2EE and started developing applications with servlets, JSP pages, and EJBs. Even though I was an uncritical fan of those frameworks, I found that I could simplify development by using what came to be known as "Plain Old Java Objects" (POJOs). For example, in the presentation tier I wrote servlets that delegated to POJOs. And in the business tier I wrote session beans that delegated to POJOs and entity beans that extended POJOs. Using POJOs enabled me to test my code without having to wait for it to be deployed in the server. Because POJOs were not directly supported by the servlet and EJB frameworks, however, I had to jump through a few hoops to use them.

Ironically, it wasn't until after writing an article describing some of those hoops that I started to use lightweight frameworks which support POJOs directly. A couple of reader comments were along the lines of "Why bother with entity beans—why not use an object/relational mapping framework instead? It's a lot simpler." Another reader suggested using Hibernate and another suggested JDO, which were two technologies that I was only vaguely aware of. After experimenting with them for a couple of weeks, I realized that they made persisting objects a lot easier. I found I could develop and test most of the business logic outside of the server. I was hooked!

Hibernate and JDO replaced entity beans, but what to do about those pesky session beans? They need to be deployed in a server, which slows down development. The solution came in the form of the Spring framework. I'd read a few articles about Spring, but its significance did not sink in until I went to TheServer-Side.com's Java Symposium (TSSJS) 2004. For the three days I was there, I was indoctrinated in the joys of dependency injection, Spring, and aspect-oriented programming (AOP). I realized that I could replace the session beans with Spring-managed POJOs. I started using Spring right away and immediately found that I could do most development without going near a server. And if a server was required, I could mostly use lightweight servers such as a Jetty. The impact on development was remarkable. All of the benefits of agile development became readily accessible to me.

Somewhere along the way, I decided to write this book to share what I had learned. My goal is to teach other developers simpler and faster ways to write enterprise Java applications. I also want to contribute to the Java community from whom I had learned a lot by reading all of those books, articles, and blogs. Originally, this book was going to cover EJBs, JDO, and Hibernate. I had planned to write about how to use POJOs and EJBs together. But when I discovered that a pure POJO and lightweight framework design was a much better approach for many enterprise Java applications, I decided to write a book that focused on POJOs.

Writing this book has been an "interesting" experience, to put it mildly. It has occupied all of my spare time for so long that I've worn out my desk chair and occasionally I'm surprised that I have three children instead of two. (When did that happen?) Along the way I've learned a lot. I've been challenged to think hard about what works and what doesn't. I hope that in this book you will find simpler and faster ways to develop your enterprise Java applications.

acknowledgments

I love deadlines. I like the whooshing sound they make as they fly by.
—Douglas Adams

Many deadlines whooshed by as I labored on this book in my downstairs office for far longer than anyone could possibly imagine. Despite the missed deadlines, Manning publisher Marjan Bace refused to give up on me. I'm grateful to him for his determination to see this book published and for pushing me to complete it.

There are also several others at Manning Publications whom I wish to thank, especially Jackie Carter for doing an excellent job as my developmental editor. The hours we spent discussing the chapters forced me to clarify my thoughts and made me a better writer. I'd like to thank Doug Bennett for the final round of development editing that brought the book over the finish line. And many thanks to the rest of the *POJOs in Action* production team: project manager Mary Piergies, copyeditor Liz Welch, review editor Karen Tegtmayer, design editor Dottie Marsico, cover designer Leslie Haimes, webmaster Ian Shigeoka, proofreader Elizabeth Martin, publicist Helen Trimes, and typesetter Gordan Salinovic.

I am very grateful to the numerous reviewers who provided valuable feedback and helped improve the manuscript: Ara Abrahamian, Muhammad Ashikuzzaman, Robert Benson, Michael Caro, Neal Ford, Peter George, Ajay Govindarajan, Jack Herrington, Olivier Jolly, Gavin King, Michael Koziarski, Patrick Linskey, Ron Lichty, John D. Mitchell, Tony Morris, Brendan Murray, J. B. Rainsberger, Norman Richards, Anne Rosset, Russ Rufer, Jon Skeet, Chris Smith, David Tinker,

Luigi R. Viggiano, David Vydra, Doug Warren, Meghan Ward, Miles Woodroffe, and Oliver Zeigermann.

I would like to thank a number of reviewers in particular. Sincere thanks to Azad Bolour for both the time he spent reviewing the book face to face and for the tea and cheese he provided during those reviews, and to Jennifer Shi, who graciously spent part of her vacation reviewing the draft manuscript. I'd also like to thank the technical reviewers, Brendan Murray, Olivier Jolly, and Oliver Zeigermann who proofread the final text and code shortly before the book went to press. Any errors that remain are entirely my responsibility.

I'm also very grateful to many of the people I have worked with over the years developing enterprise Java applications. I'd like to thank my former colleagues at BEA, including Ajay Ailawahdi, Ashok Anand, Durai Kalaiselvan, Georgia McNamara, Dave Robinson, Scott Shaw, Sushil Shukla, and Kumar Sundararaman. Many thanks to my former colleagues at Insignia Solutions, Inc: Mainak Datta, Paul Edmonds, Ajay Govindarajan, Anne Rosset, Daniel Huang, Bidyut Pattanayak, Senthil Saivam, and Harold Scanlon. Much of this book is a result of the experience I gained while working with them. They were the guinea pigs as I experimented with new and better frameworks for building applications.

Finally, many thanks to my family and friends for their support. Extra special thanks to Brian and Mariann for keeping my family company while I worked on the book. I'd like to thank my children, Janet, Thomas, and Ellie, for providing constant laughter and joy—and a reason to take a break from writing. Last, and most important, I would like to thank my wife Laura for her constant love, encouragement, and support. Without her, I would never have finished this book.

about this book

POJOs in Action is a practical guide to using POJOs and lightweight frameworks to develop the back-end logic of enterprise Java applications. These technologies are important because they dramatically simplify how you build an application's business and persistence tiers. This book covers key lightweight frameworks: Spring, JDO, Hibernate, and iBATIS. It also covers EJB 3, which embraces POJOs and some of the characteristics of lightweight frameworks.

In this book you will learn how to apply test-driven development and object design to enterprise Java applications. It illustrates how to develop with POJOs and lightweight frameworks using realistic use cases from a single example application that is used throughout the book. It even implements the same use case using multiple approaches so that you can see the essential differences between them.

A key message of *POJOs in Action* is that every technology has both benefits and drawbacks. This book will teach you when to use—and when not to use—each of the frameworks. For example, although the emphasis is on the Spring framework and POJOs, this book also describes when it makes sense to use EJBs. It explains when to use an object-oriented design and an object/relational mapping (ORM) framework and when to use a procedural design and SQL directly. This sets *POJOs in Action* apart from many other books that blindly advocate the use of their favorite framework.

Enterprise Java frameworks are constantly evolving. While I was writing this book, all of the frameworks I describe had several releases. EJB 3 appeared, albeit in draft form. And between the time this book is printed and the time you read it, some enterprise Java frameworks will have evolved further yet. But the good news is that this book will remain relevant. POJOs and nonintrusive lightweight frameworks are here to stay.

Regardless of how the frameworks evolve, there are some key concepts that will not change. First, it's vital that you objectively evaluate the pros and cons of a framework and not be swayed by clever marketing. Second, POJOs and nonintrusive frameworks are a good thing. You want to avoid coupling your business logic to an infrastructure framework, especially if it slows down the edit-compile-debug cycle. Third, testing is essential. If you don't write tests, then you can't be sure that your application works. And you must be able to write tests, so designing for testability is also important. Finally, as Albert Einstein said, "Everything should be made as simple as possible, but not simpler."

Roadmap

This book consists of four parts. Part 1 is an overview of POJOs and lightweight frameworks and the key design decisions you must make when developing an enterprise Java application. It begins with chapter 1, which introduces the concepts of POJOs and lightweight frameworks. It's here you will learn about the key differences between POJO design and an old-style EJB 2 design. This chapter describes the benefits of an object-oriented design. You will explore the design of a simple application that persists POJOs with Hibernate and makes them transactional with Spring.

Chapter 2 describes the design decisions that you must make when developing the back-end logic of an enterprise Java application. Some decisions are between lightweight frameworks and EJBs. Other decisions are between particular lightweight frameworks, such as whether to access the database using an ORM framework or to execute SQL directly using iBATIS. There are also decisions that you need to make regardless of which technology you use, such as how to organize the business logic and handle database concurrency. This chapter provides an overview of design decisions you must make along with the options available to you. We also introduce the example application and its use cases that appear throughout the book as we explore the design options.

Part 2 describes one simple yet very effective approach to designing enterprise Java applications. It's an approach that's applicable to many enterprise Java applications. The design implements the business logic with an object-oriented domain model. It persists objects with an ORM framework such as JDO or Hibernate, and it encapsulates the business logic with a POJO façade instead of an EJB session façade. Because of its many benefits, including ease of development and testing, it's the approach I prefer to use whenever possible.

The first step in applying this design is to develop a domain model. A domain model is an excellent way to tackle the complex business logic found in many enterprise Java applications. Chapter 3 describes how to implement business logic using a POJO domain model. You will learn about the structure of domain models and the benefits and drawbacks of using one. We explain how you can identify the domain model's classes, fields, and relationships by analyzing the application's requirements and talking with the business experts. We then show you how to implement domain services and entities using test-driven development techniques. You will learn how to use mock objects to test the domain model without the database, which simplifies testing considerably. This chapter uses the Place Order use case from the example application to illustrate how to develop a domain model

Once you have developed a domain model, you need to persist it. Usually, the best way to do that is to use an ORM framework, which transparently maps your objects to the database. Chapter 4 provides an overview of ORM frameworks. In this chapter you will learn the strategies for overcoming the impedance mismatch between a database schema and domain model. We describe how to map a domain model's classes, fields, and relationships to a database schema, and we list the key features of an ORM framework. You will learn effective testing strategies for a persistence layer. The chapter introduces Hibernate and JDO, which are two popular ORM frameworks, and describes how to use the Spring ORM classes to implement the application classes that access the database.

JDO is an ORM standard from Sun, and at the time of this writing version 2 of the specification was close to completion. Chapter 5 explains how to use JDO 2 to persist the domain model developed in chapter 3. We describe issues you will encounter and the decisions you must make when using JDO. You will learn how to persist objects with JDO and how to implement domain model repositories (data access objects) using Spring's JDO support classes. We explain how to test a JDO persistence layer effectively and list some of the ways you can improve the performance of a JDO application.

Chapter 6 describes how to persist a domain model developed earlier in chapter 3 using Hibernate, an extremely popular open source framework. You will learn about the various issues and limitations you will encounter when using Hibernate. We explain how to implement repositories with Spring's Hibernate support classes. In addition, you will learn how to test a Hibernate persistence layer effectively and examine some of the ways you can improve the performance of a Hibernate application.

Encapsulating the business logic is the final step in this process. The standard EJB approach is to use an EJB session façade and to return DTOs to the presentation tier. But developing EJBs and writing DTOs can be pretty tedious. Fortunately, there is a better way. Chapter 7 describes how to encapsulate the business logic with a POJO façade, which is a lot easier to develop and test. You will learn how the Spring framework provides a much more convenient way to have declarative security and transactions. Moreover, you'll learn how to use what are known as detached JDO and Hibernate objects to return data to the presentation tier and thereby eliminate the need to write many DTOs.

The approach described in part 2 is an effective way to design business logic and access the database. But it's not the only way. Part 3 offers alternative approaches to designing the business and persistence tiers of an enterprise application. Chapter 8 describes how you can dispense with the façade if the business and presentation tiers are running in the same JVM. Although exposing the domain model to the presentation tier might sound like heresy, doing so has its benefits. Since there is no façade, there is less code to write and maintain. It also avoids some of the potential problems with using detached objects. But as you will discover, in order to use this approach you must solve some tricky database connection and transaction management issues.

I'm a great fan of implementing the domain logic using an object-oriented design and persisting the objects using an ORM framework. But sometimes it doesn't make sense to use this approach. In chapter 9 you will learn when you should consider implementing the business logic using a procedural design. We describe how to develop a procedural business logic starting from a use case and how to structure it in a way that makes it easier to maintain. You will learn how to access the database using Spring's iBATIS support classes.

Dissatisfaction with EJB motivated the Java community to adopt alternative frameworks such as Spring, Hibernate, and JDO. In response, EJB has evolved and embraced many POJO and lightweight framework concepts. Chapter 10 takes a look at EJB 3 and compares it with JDO, Hibernate, and Spring. You will explore the benefits and drawbacks of EJB 3. We describe how to use EJB 3 to persist the domain model developed earlier in chapter 2 and expose some significant limitations. We also look at implementing the session façade developed in chapter 7 as an EJB 3 session bean. You will learn how to use EJB 3 dependency injection to assemble an application. This chapter also explains how to integrate EJB 3 and Spring dependency injection.

Part 4 of this book looks at some important database-related issues that you must address when developing an enterprise Java application. It begins with chapter 11, which examines implementing search screens that let the user enter search criteria and page through the matching results. Implementing search screens can be challenging. The application must be able to efficiently query the database and allow the user to page through a large result set. It must also dynamically generate queries in a maintainable way. In this chapter, you will learn how to implement dynamic paged queries using iBATIS, JDO, and Hibernate, and when you might want to use Hibernate and JDO native SQL queries.

You also have to deal with database concurrency. Enterprise applications have multiple users and background tasks, which means that sometimes multiple database transactions will attempt to access the same data simultaneously. In chapter 12, you will learn how to handle concurrent accesses at the database transaction level. We describe how to handle database concurrency in iBATIS, JDO, and Hibernate applications, and how AOP can provide a simple way to recover from database concurrency failures.

Chapter 13 extends the concepts described in chapter 12 to handle database concurrency across a sequence of transactions. Many web applications have edit-style use cases that allow users to edit data in the database. The code that implements these use cases typically requires one database transaction to read the data and another to update. In chapter 13, you will learn how to handle database concurrency in edit-style use cases. We describe the various options and detail their respective benefits and drawbacks.

Who should read this book?

If you are a developer or architect who has mastered the basics of enterprise Java development and you want to learn how to use POJOs and lightweight frameworks effectively, this book is for you.

Code conventions

All source code in listings or in text is in a `fixed-width font like this` to separate it from ordinary text. We make use of Java and XML but we try to adopt a consistent approach. Class and method names, XML elements, and attributes in text are presented using this same font.

In many cases, the original source code has been reformatted: we've added line breaks and reworked indentation to accommodate the available page space in the book. In rare cases even this was not enough, and listings include line-continuation markers. Additionally, comments have been removed from the listings. Where appropriate, we've also cut implementation details that distract rather than help tell the story, such as JavaBean setters and getters, and import statements.

Code annotations accompany many of the listings, highlighting important concepts. In some cases, numbered bullets link to explanations that follow the listing.

UML diagrams

This book uses some simple UML class diagrams and sequence diagrams to describe designs visually. You don't need to know UML to understand these diagrams, but if you're interested, see www.uml.org/ for more information.

Downloads

The complete source code for this book is freely available from www.manning.com/crichardson. There you will find complete instructions on how to install and run each of the examples. The download package contains the source code as well as instructions for accessing the external dependencies, development environment, and build scripts.

Software requirements

The examples in this book depend on the frameworks shown in table 1. This table lists the version that we used and where you can download it. With the exception of Kodo JDO, all of the frameworks are open source.

Table 1   Frameworks used in this book

Framework	Version	URL
Hibernate	3.0	www.hibernate.org
Spring	1.2.3	www.springframework.org
Kodo JDO (commercial)	3.3	www.solarmetric.com
JBoss EJB 3	Beta	www.jboss.org
iBATIS	2.0.6	http://ibatis.apache.org
HSQLDB	1.7.2	www.hsqldb.org/
JMock	1.0.1	www.jmock.org
JUnit	3.8.1	www.junit.org
JPOX JDO	1.1 beta4	www.jpox.org

For the latest information on the dependencies, check out www.manning.com/crichardson.

Author Online

Purchase of *POJOs in Action* includes free access to a private web forum run by Manning Publications where you can make comments about the book, ask technical questions, and receive help from the author and from other users. To access the forum and subscribe to it, point your web browser to www.manning.com/crichardson. This page provides information on how to get on the forum once you are registered, what kind of help is available, and the rules of conduct on the forum.

Manning's commitment to our readers is to provide a venue where a meaningful dialogue between individual readers and between readers and the author can take place. It is not a commitment to any specific amount of participation on the part of the author, whose contribution to the book's forum remains voluntary (and unpaid). We suggest you try asking the author some challenging questions, lest his interest stray!

The Author Online forum and the archives of previous discussions will be accessible from the publisher's website as long as the book is in print.

About the author

Chris Richardson is a developer, architect, and mentor with over 20 years of experience. He runs a consulting company that helps development teams become more productive and successful by adopting POJOs and lightweight frameworks. Chris has been a technical leader at a variety of companies, including Insignia Solutions and BEA Systems. Chris holds a BA and MA in computer science from the University of Cambridge in England. He lives in Oakland, California, with his wife and three children.

about the title

By combining introductions, overviews, and how-to examples, the *In Action* books are designed to help learning and remembering. According to research in cognitive science, the things people remember are things they discover during self-motivated exploration.

Although no one at Manning is a cognitive scientist, we are convinced that for learning to become permanent it must pass through stages of exploration, play, and, interestingly, re-telling of what is being learned. People understand and remember new things, which is to say they master them, only after actively exploring them. Humans learn *in action*. An essential part of an *In Action* guide is that it is example-driven. It encourages the reader to try things out, to play with new code, and explore new ideas.

There is another, more mundane, reason for the title of this book: our readers are busy. They use books to do a job or solve a problem. They need books that allow them to jump in and jump out easily and learn just what they want just when they want it. They need books that aid them in action. The books in this series are designed for such readers.

about the cover illustration

The figure on the cover of *POJOs in Action* is a "Hombre de Sierra Leone," a man from the African country of Sierra Leone. The illustration is taken from a Spanish compendium of regional dress customs first published in Madrid in 1799. The book's title page states:

> *Coleccion general de los Trages que usan actualmente todas las Nacionas del Mundo des-ubierto, dibujados y grabados con la mayor exactitud por R.M.V.A.R. Obra muy util y en special para los que tienen la del viajero universal*

which we translate, as literally as possible, thus:

> *General collection of costumes currently used in the nations of the known world, designed and printed with great exactitude by R.M.V.A.R. This work is very useful especially for those who hold themselves to be universal travelers*

Although nothing is known of the designers, engravers, and workers who colored this illustration by hand, the "exactitude" of their execution is evident in this drawing. The "Hombre de Sierra Leone" is just one of many figures in this colorful collection. Their diversity speaks vividly of the uniqueness and individuality of the world's towns and regions just 200 years ago. This was a time when the dress codes of two regions separated by a few dozen miles identified people uniquely as belonging to one or the other. The collection brings to life a sense of isolation and distance of that period-and of every other historic period except our own hyperkinetic present.

Dress codes have changed since then and the diversity by region, so rich at the time, has faded away. It is now often hard to tell the inhabitant of one continent from another. Perhaps, trying to view it optimistically, we have traded a cultural and visual diversity for a more varied personal life. Or a more varied and interesting intellectual and technical life.

We at Manning celebrate the inventiveness, the initiative, and, yes, the fun of the computer business with book covers based on the rich diversity of regional life of two centuries ago, brought back to life by the pictures from this collection.

Part 1

Overview of POJOs
and lightweight frameworks

In part 1, you'll get an overview of developing with plain old Java objects (POJOs) and lightweight frameworks such as Spring, Hibernate, and JDO. In chapter 1, "Developing with POJOs: faster and easier," we'll explore the basics of POJOs and lightweight frameworks and how they differ from Enterprise JavaBeans. As the title implies, you'll see how POJOs and lightweight frameworks make development easier and faster. We'll look at a simple design that uses Hibernate for persistence and the Spring framework for transaction management and application assembly.

In chapter 2, "J2EE design decisions," we'll look at some of the key decisions that you must make when developing enterprise Java applications, including when to use the POJO approach. You'll learn about the different ways you can organize and encapsulate business logic, access databases, and handle database concurrency. The options described in this chapter are explored in detail in the rest of the book. You'll see an example of how a project team might go about making these design decisions for their application. This chapter also introduces the example application that is used throughout the book.

Developing with POJOs: faster and easier

This chapter covers

- Comparing lightweight frameworks and EJBs
- Simplifying development with POJOs
- Developing an object-oriented design
- Making POJOs transactional and persistent

Sometimes you must use a technology for a while in order to appreciate its true value. A few years ago I had to go out of the country on a business trip, and I didn't want to risk missing episodes of my favorite show. So, rather than continuing to struggle with the timer function on my VCR, I bought a TiVo box. At the time I thought it was simply going to be a much more convenient and reliable way to record programs. The TiVo box certainly made it easy to record a show, but before long it completely changed how I watched television. In addition to being able to pause live TV, I was able to watch my favorite shows when I wanted and without commercials.

I had a similar experience with plain old Java objects (POJOs), Hibernate, and Spring. I was part of a team developing a server product that had a "classic" Enterprise JavaBeans (EJB) architecture: the business logic consisted of session beans and entity beans. EJB definitely helped by handling infrastructure issues such as transaction management, security, and persistence—but at a high price. For example, we endured long edit-compile-debug cycles caused by having to deploy the components in the application server. We also jumped through all kinds of hoops in order to implement a domain model with entity beans. But somehow we accepted all of this pain as normal.

The final straw was when we were faced with having to support the product on two application servers. Rather than endure the lack of portability of EJB container-managed persistence (CMP) we decided to be adventurous and use a portable persistence mechanism that I was hearing a lot about: Hibernate. Hibernate worked the same way on both application servers and eliminated the need to maintain two separate but equivalent sets of EJB CMP deployment descriptors. But before long we discovered other, much more important benefits of Hibernate. It enabled us to implement a more elaborate POJO domain model in the next version of the product. It sped development by allowing the domain model to be tested without an application server or a database. And soon after we discovered the Spring framework, which enabled us to create a more loosely coupled architecture consisting of easy-to-test POJO services. In hindsight, it's amazing that we accomplished as much as we did with the old architecture.

POJOs in Action describes how POJOs and lightweight technologies such as Spring, Hibernate, and Java Data Objects (JDO) make it easier and faster to develop testable and maintainable applications. You will learn how object-oriented design goes hand in hand with POJOs and how to endow POJOs with the characteristics that enterprise applications require, such as transactions and persistence. It describes how to use Spring for transaction management and Hibernate, JDO, EJB 3, and iBATIS for persistence.

Much of this book focuses on alternatives to EJBs because they frequently offer better characteristics: good object-oriented design, testability, less complexity, easier maintenance, and a raft of other benefits. However, it's important to remember that EJBs are sometimes the right tool for the job, which is why chapter 10 is about using EJB 3. The key is to be conscious of the options and to make explicit informed decisions rather than slavishly following dogma.

1.1 The disillusionment with EJBs

This book isn't a screed about why you shouldn't use "traditional" Java 2 Enterprise Edition (J2EE) architecture and design. It is sometimes the best tool for the job, and later on in this book I describe when you should use it. However, today many developers use it for applications for which it is ill suited. Let's briefly review the history of EJBs and discover why the Java development community's initial enthusiasm for them has turned into disillusionment. After that, I will describe an alternative approach to designing an enterprise Java application that uses POJOs.

1.1.1 A brief history of EJBs

EJB is the Java standard architecture for writing distributed business applications. It's a framework that provides a large number of useful services and handles some of the most time-consuming aspects of writing distributed applications. For example, EJB provides declarative transactions, which eliminate the need to write transaction management code. The EJB container automatically starts, commits, and rolls back transactions on behalf of the application. Automatically handling transactions was a huge innovation at the time and is still a vital service. In addition, business logic implemented using EJBs can participate in distributed transactions that are started by a remote client. EJBs also provide declarative security, which mostly eliminates the need to write security code, which is another common requirement handled by the application server. Entries in the bean's deployment descriptor specified who could access a particular bean.

EJB version 1.0 was released in 1998. It provided two types of enterprise beans: session beans and entity beans. Session beans represent either stateless services or a stateful conversation with a client. Entity beans represent data in a database and were originally intended to implement business objects. EJB 1.0 fulfilled its mandate by insulating the application developer from the complexities of building distributed enterprise systems. EJB 2 refined the EJB programming model. It added message-driven beans (which process Java Message Service, or JMS, messages) as well as enhanced entity beans to support relationships managed by the container. The evolution continues in EJB 3 (described later in this chapter), which simplifies the programming model considerably by enabling POJOs to be EJBs.

1.1.2 A typical EJB 2 application architecture

Let's look at an example of a typical EJB 2 application architecture. Imagine that you work for a bank and you have to write a service to transfer money between two accounts. Figure 1.1 shows how you might use EJB to implement the money transfer service.

The business logic consists of the TransferService EJB and data access objects (DAOs). The TransferService EJB is a session bean that defines the interface that the business logic exposes to the presentation tier. It also implements the business logic.

The TransferService EJB calls the AccountDAO to retrieve the two accounts, and performs any necessary checks and other business logic. For example, it verifies that fromAccount contains sufficient funds and will not become overdrawn. The TransferService EJB calls AccountDAO again to save the updated accounts in the database. It records the transfer by calling TransactionDAO. The TransferService

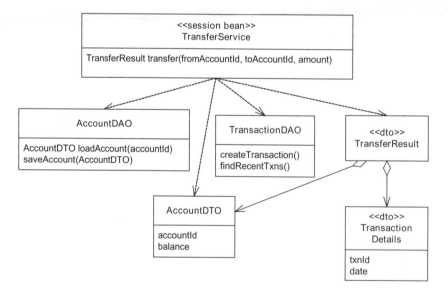

Figure 1.1 The money transfer service implemented using a typical EJB-based design

EJB returns a `TransferResult`, which is a DTO that contains the `AccountDTOs` and their recent transactions. It is used by the presentation tier to display a web page to the customer.

The DAOs, which are implemented using JDBC, provide methods for accessing the database. This application could also use entity beans instead of DAOs to access the database. That is, after all, the role of entity beans within the J2EE architecture. However, for reasons I describe later, EJB 2 entity beans have several drawbacks and limitations. As a result, many J2EE applications use DAOs instead of EJB 2 entity beans.

The class design and their relationships are simple. I haven't shown the XML deployment descriptors, which are used to configure the EJB, but `Transfer-Service` is ready to be invoked remotely and to participate in distributed transactions. But despite its apparent simplicity (and sometimes because of it), several serious problems lurk within.

1.1.3 *The problems with EJBs*

Like many other Java developers, I enthusiastically adopted EJBs and spent several years writing applications whose design was similar to the one you just saw. I was so excited about using the new standard that I thought nothing of abandoning the object-oriented design skills I'd spent the previous decade learning. I was more than happy to write lots of code and XML configuration files just to do the simplest things. I found ways to pass the time while my code deployed. After all, isn't enterprise application development meant to be challenging?

It is certainly true that some aspects of developing enterprise applications are challenging, such as complex and changing requirements and the need to scale and have high throughput and availability. However, while EJB solves some problems with developing enterprise applications, it does not live up to one of its key goals: making it easy to write applications. Ironically, in order to be a competent EJB developer you need to know how to solve problems that are caused by EJB. An excellent book that tackles the shortcomings of EJB is *Bitter EJB* by Bruce Tate [Tate 2003]. Other books address the complexity of building effective EJB applications, such as *Core J2EE Patterns* [Alur 2003] and *EJB Design Patterns* [Marinescu 2002], which contains patterns to help make sense of EJB and solutions to problems rather than patterns for improving the design of software.

Although these books help developers grapple with EJB and learn how to use it effectively, they don't directly address the two fundamental problems with EJBs. The first is that EJBs encourage developers to write procedural-style applications. The second problem is that the cumbersome nature of the development process when using EJBs doesn't allow developers to take advantage of many of the best practices used for "normal" Java development.

The shortcomings of procedural design

There are two main ways to organize business logic: procedural or object-oriented. The procedural approach organizes the code around functions that manipulate separate simple data objects. In procedural architectures, data structures are populated, passed as parameters to functions, and returned to the caller. The relationship between the data and the operations is very loosely defined, and wholly maintained by the developer. Prior to object-oriented languages, this style of programming dominated software development, and was featured in C, Pascal, and other languages.

By contrast, the object-oriented approach organizes code around objects that have state and behavior and that collaborate with other objects. The data structures and operations are defined in one language construct, co-locating the data and the operations on the data. The relationship (and state) between the data and the operations is maintained by the language. An object-oriented design is easier to understand, maintain, extend, and test than a procedural design.

Despite the benefits of an object-oriented design, most J2EE applications, including the one shown in figure 1.1, are written in a procedural style. In our example, all of the business logic is concentrated in the `TransferService` EJB, which consists of the `transfer()` method and possibly one or more helper methods. None of the objects manipulated by the `TransferService` EJB implement any business logic. These objects exist to provide plumbing and services to the `TransferService` EJB. The DAOs are wrappers around JDBC, and the remaining objects (including the entity beans) are simple data objects. Even though this business logic is written in Java, which is an object-oriented language, this design fits the definition of procedural code exactly.

The procedural design style isn't a problem if the business logic is simple, but business logic has a habit of growing in complexity. As the requirements change and the business logic has to implement new features, the amount of code in the EJB steadily increases. For example, in order to add a new kind of overdraft policy you would have to add yet more code to the `TransferService` EJB to implement that new policy. Even if each enhancement only adds a few lines of code, EJBs that started out quite simple over time can grow into large complex beasts, such as the ones that I encountered on one early J2EE project that were each many hundred of lines of code.

EJBs like these that contain large amount of code cause several problems. The lack of modularity makes them difficult to understand and maintain because it's hard to find your way around long methods and large classes. They can be extended to support new requirements only by adding more code, which makes the problem worse. Complex EJBs are also very difficult to test because they lack the subcomponents to test in isolation. But if this procedural design style has these problems, why is it so common in J2EE application?

Why J2EE encourages developers to write procedural code

There are a couple of reasons why J2EE developers often write procedural-style code rather than developing an object model. One reason is that the EJB specification makes it seductively easy. Although the specification does not force you to write this type of code, it lays down a path of least resistance that encourages stateless, procedural code. When implementing new behavior, you don't have to worry about identifying classes and assigning responsibilities as you would if you were designing a real object model. Instead, you can write a new session bean method or add code to an existing one.

The second reason why J2EE developers write procedural-style code is that it is encouraged by the EJB architecture, literature, and culture, which place great emphasis on EJB components. EJB 2 components are not suitable for implementing an object model. Session beans and message-driven beans are monolithic, heavyweight classes that cannot be used to implement a fine-grained object model. Nor can they represent business objects that are stored in a database. The best way to use them in an application is to encapsulate an object model: the *Session Façade* and *Message Façade* patterns.

EJB 2 entity beans, which are intended to represent business objects, have numerous limitations that make it extremely difficult to use them to implement a persistent object model. This is why I didn't use them in our earlier example. EJB 2 entity beans support some kinds of relationships, but not inheritance. Entity beans do not support recursive calls or "loopback" calls, which are common in an object model and occur when object A calls object B, which calls object A. We'll discuss other limitations of entity beans in a moment. Entity beans have so many limitations that it's amazing that developers have used them successfully. This is a fundamental problem with the preferred J2EE architecture. Each framework creates a path of least resistance for its use. It is possible to diverge from the path, but it goes against the grain of the framework and takes a great deal of effort. The path of least resistance in J2EE and EJB leads inexorably toward procedural code.

As a result, it has been difficult to do any true object-oriented development in a J2EE application. Furthermore, this procedural design style is so ingrained in the J2EE culture that it has even carried over into newer, non-EJB ways of developing J2EE applications. Some developers still view persistent objects simply as a means to get data in and out of the database and write procedural business logic. They develop what Fowler calls an "anemic domain model" [Fowler Anemic]. Just as anemic blood lacks vitality, anemic object models only superficially model the problem and consist of classes that implement little or no behavior

The pain of EJB development

Another problem with EJBs is that development and testing are painfully tedious for the following reasons:

- *You must deal with annoyingly long edit-compile-debug cycles*—Because EJBs are server-side components, you must deploy them in the EJB container, which is a time-consuming operation that interrupts your train of thought. Quite often the time to redeploy a component crosses the 10-second threshold, at which point you might be tempted to do something else, like surf the Web or IM a friend. The impact on productivity is particularly frustrating when doing test-driven development, where it is desirable to run the tests frequently, every minute or two. Test-driven development and unit testing are common best practices for Java development made difficult by the infrastructure required when developing EJBs.

- *You face a lack of separation of concerns*—EJB often forces you to solve several difficult problems simultaneously—business logic design, database schema design, persistence mapping, etc.—rather than allowing you to work on one problem at a time. Not only is this mentally overwhelming but it also adds to the already long edit-compile-debug cycle. When you change a class, you might have to update the database schema before you can test your changes.

- *You must write a lot of code to implement an EJB*—You must write a home interface, a component interface, the bean class, and a deployment descriptor, which for an entity bean can be quite complex. In addition, you must write a number of boilerplate bean class methods that are never actually called but that are required by the interface the bean class implements. This code isn't conceptually difficult, but it is busywork that you must endure.

- *You have to write data transfer objects*—A data transfer object (DTO) is a dumb data object that is returned by the EJB to its caller and contains the data the presentation tier will display to the user. It is often just a copy of the data from one or more entity beans, which cannot be passed to the presentation tier because they are permanently attached to the database. Implementing the DTOs and the code that creates them is one of the most tedious aspects of implementing an EJB.

Developing EJBs can be a slow, mind-numbing process. While you can get used to it and find ways to occupy your time while waiting for components to deploy, it isn't a good way to develop software. As I mentioned earlier, the nature of J2EE development with EJB precludes many of the best practices common in other types of Java development. Because the components must run in the application server in order to access the services it provides, an incremental development strategy that frequently executes the edit-compile-debug cycle is difficult. Eventually, many enterprise Java developers have become painfully aware of these limitations and have started to ask questions: Does the development I'm doing require all these services for which I'm paying such a high price? Is this the right tool for the job?

1.1.4 EJB 3 is a step in the right direction

The EJB standard isn't frozen in amber. The designers of the specifications at Sun listen to developers and are modifying the EJB specification accordingly. The main goal of the newest EJB 3 standard is to simplify EJB development. It addresses some of the perceived problems and issues with the current specification:

- EJBs are POJOs, there is a lot less boilerplate code to write, and the code is less coupled to the application server environment.
- EJB 3 entity beans are intended to be the standard Java persistence mechanism and run in both J2EE and J2SE environments.
- EJB 3 supports the use of Java 5 annotations instead of difficult-to-write deployment descriptors to specify such things as transaction attributes, security attributes, and object/relational mapping.
- Entity beans support inheritance (finally!), making it possible to implement a true object model.
- EJB 3 also has reasonable defaults for much of the deployment information, so there is a lot less of it to write.
- EJB 3 entity beans can be used to return data to the presentation tier, which eliminates the need to write DTOs.

EJB 3 still has limitations. For example, it forces components into three categories—session beans, entity beans, and message-driven beans—even though in a typical object model there are classes that do not fall into one of these three categories. As a result, many classes are unable to use the services provided by the EJB 3 container. Also, the June 2005 public draft of the specification still had only limited support for collection classes. In addition, there is no guarantee that the EJB 3 containers will provide fast and painless deployment of EJBs. As a result, EJB 3 still appears to be inferior to the lightweight technologies such as JDO, Hibernate, and Spring that I describe later in this chapter.

Despite its limitations, it is extremely likely that EJB 3 will be widely used for the simple reason that it is part of the J2EE standard. It is also important to remember that EJB is an appropriate implementation technology for two types of applications:

- Applications that use distributed transactions initiated by remote clients
- Applications that are heavily message-oriented and need message-driven beans

But for many other applications superior alternatives exist that are considerably easier to use. The remainder of this book focuses on those alternatives: POJOs and lightweight technologies such as Spring, Hibernate, and JDO.

1.2 Developing with POJOs

Long before the EJB 3 specification was written, some developers disillusioned with EJB started to look for alternative frameworks. POJOs are an especially compelling alternative to EJBs. A POJO is simply a Java object that does not implement any special interfaces such as those defined by the EJB framework. The name was coined by Fowler, Rebbecca Parsons, and Josh MacKenzie [Fowler POJO] to give regular Java objects an exciting-sounding name. Later in this section you will see how this simple idea has some surprisingly important benefits.

However, POJOs by themselves are insufficient. In an enterprise application you need services such as transaction management, security, and persistence, which were previously provided by the EJB container. The solution is to use the increasingly popular so-called "lightweight" frameworks that replace some "heavyweight" parts of the J2EE stack. They do not completely replace the J2EE stack but can be used in combination with some parts of it to provide important enterprise services.

The four lightweight frameworks that I describe in this book are Hibernate, JDO, iBATIS, and Spring. Except for JDO, which is a specification, they are open source projects, which have helped drive the adoption of POJOs and lightweight frameworks by the community. Hibernate and JDO are persistence frameworks, which map POJOs to a relational database. They are layered on top of JDBC and significantly increase developer productivity. iBATIS is also layered on top of JDBC, but it maps POJOs to SQL statements and is a very convenient way to execute SQL statements. The Spring framework has a wide range of features that make it easier to use than EJB, including the equivalent of container-managed transactions for POJOs.

An important feature of these technologies is that they are nonintrusive. Unlike EJBs, they provide transactions and persistence without requiring the application classes to implement any special interfaces. Even when your application's classes are transactional or persistent, they are still POJOs, which means that you continue to experience the benefits of POJOs that I describe in this chapter.

Some excellent books are available that describe these frameworks in depth: *Hibernate in Action* [Bauer 2005], *Spring in Action* [Walls 2005], *iBATIS in Action* [Begin, forthcoming], and *Java Data Objects* [Russell 2003]. You do not need to read these books to understand and benefit from this book. But to apply what you learn here you do need to read them to learn the details.

In this section I will provide an overview of how to use POJOs and lightweight frameworks to redesign the money transfer service and make it easier to develop, test, and maintain. This new design is object-oriented POJO-based instead of a procedural EJB-based. It accesses the database using a persistence framework that is layered on top of JDBC instead of using JDBC directly. The business logic is encapsulated by a POJO façade instead of a session bean, and transactions are managed by the Spring framework instead of the EJB container. The business logic returns real business objects to the presentation tier instead of DTOs. The application is assembled by passing a component's dependencies as setter or constructor arguments instead of the component using Java Naming and Directory Interface (JNDI) lookups. Because the design is object-oriented and uses these lightweight technologies, it is much more developer-friendly than the EJB version we saw earlier.

Table 1.1 summarizes the differences between the two designs.

Table 1.1 Comparing classic EJB and POJO approaches

	Classic EJB approach	**POJO approach**
Organization	Procedural-style business logic	Object-oriented design
Implementation	EJB-based	POJOs
Database access	JDBC/SQL or Entity beans	Persistence framework
Returning data to the presentation tier	DTOs	Business objects

Table 1.1 Comparing classic EJB and POJO approaches *(continued)*

	Classic EJB approach	POJO approach
Transaction management	EJB container-managed transactions	Spring framework
Application assembly	Explicit JNDI lookups	Dependency injection

Don't worry if you are not familiar with all of these terms. In this section, I'll examine each difference and explain and justify the POJO approach. You will see how to develop business logic using the POJO approach. I use the money transfer application from section 1.1.2 as an example.

1.2.1 Using an object-oriented design

Rather than structuring the money transfer example around methods such as `transfer()` and its helper methods, the code should be structured around an object model, which is a collection of classes that typically corresponds to real-world concepts. For example, in the money transfer application, the object model consists of classes such as `Account`, `OverdraftPolicy`, and `BankingTransaction`. In addition, there is a `TransferService` that coordinates the transfer of money from one account to another. Figure 1.2 shows the design.

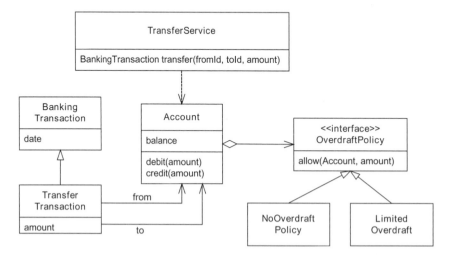

Figure 1.2 An object model for the money transfer application

An `Account` maintains its balance and has an `OverdraftPolicy`, which determines what happens when the account is about to become overdrawn. `OverdraftPolicy` is an example of a *Strategy* pattern [Gang of Four] and there are two implementations of `OverdraftPolicy`: one for each type of real-world policy. Better yet, an `Overdraft-Policy` could encapsulate a rules engine and thereby enable the business rules for overdrafts to be changed dynamically. `TransferTransaction`, which is a subclass of `BankingTransaction`, records the transfer of money between two accounts.

Using an object-oriented design has a number of benefits. First, the design is easier to understand and maintain. Instead of consisting of one big class that does everything, it consists of a number of small classes that each have a small number of responsibilities. In addition, classes such as `Account`, `BankingTransaction`, and `OverdraftPolicy` closely mirror the real world, which makes their role in the design easier to understand.

Second, our object-oriented design is easier to test: each class can and should be tested independently. For example, we could write unit tests for `Account` and for each implementations of `OverdraftPolicy`. In comparison, an EJB can only be tested by calling its public methods, for example, `transfer()`, which is a lot more difficult. You can only test the complex functionality exposed by the public methods rather than test the simpler pieces of the design.

Finally, the object-oriented design in figure 1.2 is easier to extend because it can use well-known design patterns, such as the Strategy pattern and the *Template Method* pattern [Gang of Four]. Adding a new type of overdraft policy simply requires defining a new subclass of `OverdraftPolicy`. By contrast, extending an EJB-style procedural design usually requires changing the core code, and rewriting or chaining procedure calls together.

As you can see, our object-oriented design has some important benefits. But it is essential to know when it is not a good choice. Later in this book I describe how to decide between procedural and object-oriented approaches.

1.2.2 Using POJOs

Once you break free of the constraints imposed by the EJB 2 programming model, implementing the object model shown in figure 1.2 is easy. Java provides all of the necessary features, including fine-grained objects, relationships, inheritance, and recursion. It is straightforward to implement expressive object models like this one using POJOs and thus benefit from improved maintainability and testability. Java is an object-oriented language, so it is foolish not to use its capabilities.

As a bonus, POJOs have these other important benefits:

- *Easier development*—There is less cognitive load because rather than being forced to think about everything—business logic, persistence, transactions etc.—at once you can instead focus on one thing at a time. You can first design and implement the business logic and then, once that is working, you can deal with persistence and transactions.

- *Faster development*—You can develop and test your business logic outside of the application server and without a database. You do not have to package your code and deploy it in the application. Also, you do not have to keep the database schema constantly in sync with the object model or spend time waiting for slow-running database tests to finish. Tests can run in a few seconds and development can happen at the speed of thought—or at least as fast as you can type!

- *Improved portability*—You are not tied to a particular implementation technology. The cost of switching to the next generation of Java technology is minimized because you have to rewrite only a small amount of code, if any.

I was genuinely surprised by how POJOs changed how I went about development because I'd become so accustomed to the cumbersome EJB approach. As with the TiVo box I described earlier, I had to use them before I appreciated their true value. But now I couldn't imagine reverting to the old way of working. Of course, you still need to handle persistence and transactions, which is where lightweight frameworks come in.

1.2.3 Persisting POJOs

When the time comes to persist the POJOs that implement the business logic, there are some powerful object/relational mapping frameworks to choose from. The main ones are JDO, which is a standard from Sun, and Hibernate, which is an extremely popular open source framework. In addition, the specification for EJB 3 entity beans appears to be potentially quite powerful.

Transparent persistence with JDO and Hibernate

JDO and Hibernate provide transparent persistence, which means that the classes are unaware that they are persistent. The application just needs to call the persistence framework APIs to save, query, and delete persistent objects. The persistence framework automatically generates the SQL statements that access the database using an object/relational mapping, which is defined by XML documents or Java 5 annotations. The object/relational mapping specifies how classes map to tables, fields map to columns, and relationships map to either foreign keys or join tables. JDO and Hibernate can also run outside of the application server, which means that you can test your persistent business logic without deploying it in a server. You can, for example, simply run tests from within your integrated development environment (IDE).

Encapsulating the calls to the persistence framework

Even though Hibernate and JDO provide transparent persistence, some parts of an application must call the JDO and Hibernate APIs to save, query, and delete persistent objects. For example, `TransferService` must call the persistence framework to retrieve the accounts and create a `BankingTransaction`. One approach is for `TransferService` to call the persistence framework APIs directly. Unfortunately, this would couple `TransferService` directly to the persistence framework and the database, which makes development and testing more difficult.

A better approach is to encapsulate the Hibernate or JDO code behind an interface, as shown in figure 1.3. The persistence framework, which in this example is

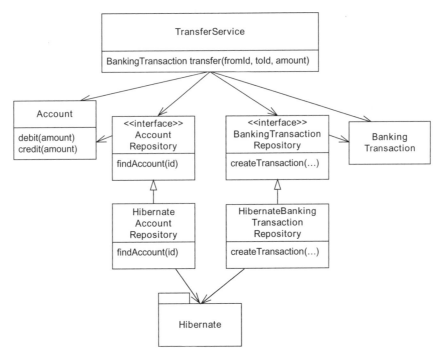

Figure 1.3 **Using repositories to encapsulate the persistence framework hides the persistence details from the rest of the application.**

Hibernate, is encapsulated by the repository classes. Each repository consists of an interface and a Hibernate implementation class and is responsible for one type of object. The JDO implementation would be similar.

In this example, repositories call the Hibernate APIs to access the database. `AccountRepository` finds accounts and `BankingTransactionRepository` creates `BankingTransactions`. The `TransferService` is written in terms of the `Account-Repository` and `BankingTransactionRepository` interfaces, which decouples it from the persistence framework and the database. By the intelligent use of interfaces, you can avoid coupling your domain logic to a particular persistence framework. This will enable you to test the domain model without the database, which simplifies and accelerates testing. It also enables you to use a different persistence framework if your needs change. For example, changing this application from Hibernate to JDO or even EJB 3 is simply a matter of changing the concrete classes that access the persistence framework. It's a generally accepted observation that loosely coupled applications are easier to maintain and test, and you will see examples of how to do this throughout this book.

1.2.4 *Eliminating DTOs*

Another way to improve a J2EE application is to eliminate the DTOs, also known as value objects. A DTO is a simple object consisting of only fields (i.e., no behavior) and is used to return data from the business tier to the presentation tier. An EJB application uses DTOs because EJB 2 entity beans cannot be efficiently accessed by the presentation tier. Each call to an entity bean might be a remote call and/or a separate database transaction. As a result, they must only be accessed by the session façade, which copies data from them into DTOs. The trouble with using DTOs, however, is that they and the code that creates them are extremely tedious to develop and can sometimes be a significant portion of a J2EE application. Hibernate, JDO, and EJB 3 objects do not have this limitation and can be accessed directly by the presentation tier. As a result, we eliminate many or all of the DTOs in an application.

Returning domain objects to the presentation tier

There are a couple of ways to return Hibernate, JDO, and EJB 3 objects to the presentation tier. One option is for the business tier to return objects that are still persistent. This can be simpler to implement but requires the presentation tier to manage database connections, which is sometimes neither desirable nor possible. I will describe this option in more detail in chapter 8.

Another approach, which is described in detail in chapter 7, is for the business tier to return detached objects. A detached object is a previously persistent object that is no longer connected to the database. Instead of copying values from a persistent object into a DTO, the business tier detaches the object and returns it to the persistent tier. This approach eliminates the need for DTOs while keeping all database accesses in the business tier.

Different persistence frameworks handle detached objects in different ways. In Hibernate and EJB 3, objects are automatically detached but the application must ensure that all of the objects required by the presentation tier are loaded, which can sometimes require extra calls to the persistence framework. In JDO 2.0 an application must explicitly detach the required objects by calling a JDO API.

Using a façade to retrieve and detach domain objects

An important design decision is determining which class will be responsible for calling the persistence framework to retrieve and detach the objects required by the presentation tier. For example, the money transfer business logic must retrieve the recent transactions and detach them along with the account objects. You could make this the responsibility of the `TransferService`, but doing so would make it more complicated and couple it to the needs of the presentation tier. Moreover, because the business tier must sometimes call the persistent framework to ensure that the domain objects can be returned to the presentation tier, making the `TransferService` call the detachment logic would mix together pure business logic with infrastructure details.

Unless the service is very simple and contains little or no business logic, a better option is to retrieve and detach the required objects in a separate class— `TransferFacadeImpl`. As figure 1.4 shows, `TransferFacadeImpl` implements the `TransferFacade` interface, which specifies the methods that can be called by the business logic's client and plays a role similar to that of an EJB component interface. It returns a `TransferResult` that contains the domain objects.

Like the EJB we saw earlier, `TransferFacade` defines a `transfer()` method that returns a `TransferResult`. It calls `TransferService` and `TransactionRepository`, and creates `TransferResult`. As you can see, `TransferResult` is the only DTO in this example. The rest of the objects returned to the presentation tier are domain objects. Later in chapter 7, we look at a more elaborate example of a façade.

1.2.5 Making POJOs transactional

Let's review what we have done so far. We replaced a procedural design with an object-oriented design, replaced entity beans with POJOs plus a persistence framework (either Hibernate or JDO), and eliminated DTOs. Because of these changes,

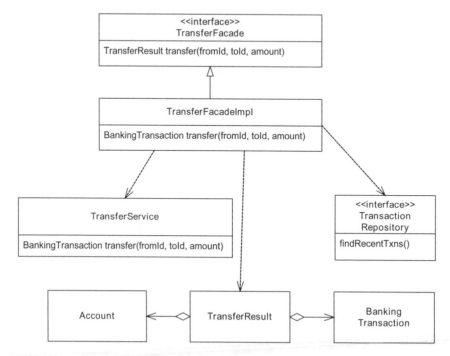

Figure 1.4 The design of `TransferFacade`, which encapsulates the business logic and detaches objects

we have a design that is easier to understand, maintain, and extend. In addition, the edit-compile-debug cycle is extremely short. We now have an application where most of the code is sufficiently modular that you can write unit tests. We haven't yet discussed how to eliminate the `TransferService` EJB. Even though it is a simple class that calls the object model classes, development slows down considerably any time we have to change it because of the deployment requirement. Let's see what we can do about that.

Although session beans support distributed applications, the main reason they are used in many applications is because they provide container-managed transactions. The EJB container automatically starts a transaction when a business method is invoked and commits the transaction when the method returns. It rolls back the transaction if a `RuntimeException` is thrown. Container-managed transactions are extremely useful. They free you from writing error-prone code to manually manage transactions. Consequently, if you want to replace session beans with POJOs, you should use an equally convenient mechanism to manage transactions. This naturally takes us to the Spring framework.

Managing transactions with Spring

There are several lightweight mechanisms for making POJOs transactional. One very popular framework that provides this capability is Spring. Spring is a powerful J2EE application framework that makes it significantly easier to develop enterprise Java applications. It provides a large number of features, and I'm only going to provide a brief overview of a few of them in this chapter. For more information see *Spring in Action* [Walls 2005].

The Spring framework provides an extremely easy-to-use mechanism for making POJOs transactional that works in a similar way to container-managed transactions. Spring will automatically begin a transaction when a POJO method is invoked and commit the transaction when the method returns. It can also roll back a transaction if an error occurs. Spring can manage transactions using the application server's implementation of the Java Transaction API (JTA) if the application accesses multiple resources such as a database and JMS. Alternatively, Spring can manage transactions using the persistence framework or JDBC transaction management APIs, which are simpler and easier to use because they do not require an application server.

When using the Spring framework, we can make a POJO transactional by defining it as a Spring bean, which is simply an object that is instantiated and managed by Spring. Defining a Spring bean requires only a few lines of XML. The XML is similar to a deployment descriptor and configures Spring's lightweight container, which is a sophisticated factory for constructing objects. Each entry in the XML file defines the configuration of a Spring bean, which includes its name, its POJO implementation class, and a description of how to instantiate and initialize it. An application obtains a bean by calling the Spring bean factory with the name and expected type of the bean:

```
BeanFactory beanFactory = …
TransferFacade tf = (TransferFacade)
    beanFactory.getBean("TransferFacade", TransferFacade.class);
```

This code fragment calls the `BeanFactory.getBean()` method with `Transfer-Facade` as the name of the bean and `TransferFacade` as the expected class. The bean factory will throw an exception if a bean with that name does not exist or is of a different type.

As well as being a highly configurable way to instantiate objects, a Spring bean factory can be configured to return a proxy instead of the original object. A proxy, which is also known as an interceptor, is an object that masquerades as the original object. It executes arbitrary code before and after invoking the original object. In an enterprise Java application, interceptors can be used for a number of purposes, including security, database connection management, and transaction management.

In this example application, we can configure the Spring bean factory to wrap Transfer-Facade with a proxy that manages transactions. To do that, we must define several beans, including those shown in figure 1.5. This diagram shows the TransferFacade bean, along with PlatformTransactionManager, TransactionInterceptor, and BeanNameAutoProxy-Creator, the Spring classes that make Transfer-Facade transactional.

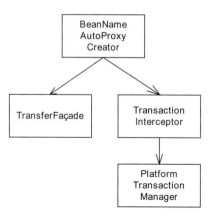

Figure 1.5 The Spring bean definitions required to make TransferFacade transactional

The BeanNameAutoProxyCreator bean wraps TransferFacade with a TransactionInterceptor, which manages transactions using the PlatformTransactionManager. The PlatformTransactionManager in this example is implemented by the HibernateTransactionManager class, which uses the Hibernate Transaction interface to begin, commit, and roll back transactions. Listing 1.1 shows an excerpt from the XML configuration file that defines these beans.

Listing 1.1 Configuring Spring transaction management

```
<beans>

<bean id="TransferFacade"        ◁————————❶ Define the
     class="TransferFacadeImpl">            TransferFacade
...
</bean>

<bean id="PlatformTransactionManager"        Define the Hibernate ❷
     class="org.springframework.orm.    PlatformTransactionManager
          ➥ hibernate3.HibernateTransactionManager">    ◁————
...
</bean>

                              ❸ Define the
<bean id="TransactionInterceptor"    ◁———  TransactionInterceptor
     class="org.springframework.transaction.
          ➥ interceptor.TransactionInterceptor">
     <property name="transactionManager"
             ref="PlatformTransactionManager"/>
     <property name="transactionAttributeSource"
             value="*=PROPAGATION_REQUIRED"/>
</bean>
```

```
<bean id="BeanNameAutoProxyCreator"                         Apply the
   class="org.springframework.aop.framework.             TransactionInterceptor
          autoproxy.BeanNameAutoProxyCreator">    4     to the TransferFacade
    <property name="beanNames">
        <idref bean="TransferFacade"/>
    </property>
    <property name="interceptorNames">
        <list>
            <idref bean="TransactionInterceptor"/>
        </list>
    </property>
</bean>

</beans>
```

Let's take a closer look at this listing:

1 This defines a bean called `TransferFacade`, which is implemented by the `Transfer-FacadeImpl` class.

2 This defines a bean called `PlatformTransactionManager`, which is implemented by the `HibernateTransactionManager` class that manages transactions using the Hibernate API.

3 This defines a bean called `TransactionInterceptor`, which is implemented by the `TransactionInterceptor` class that makes an object transactional. `Transaction-Interceptor` intercepts calls to the object and calls a `PlatformTransactionManager` to begin, commit, and roll back transactions. It has a `transactionManager` property, which specifies which `PlatformTransactionManager` to use, and a `transaction-AttributeSource` property, which specifies which methods to make transactional. In this example, all method calls are configured to be transactional.

4 This defines a bean called `BeanNameAutoProxyCreator`, which wraps `Transfer-Facade` with `TransactionInterceptor`. It has an `interceptorNames` property, which specifies the list of interceptors to apply, and a `beanNames` property, which specifies the beans to wrap with interceptors.

These bean definitions arrange for the bean factory to wrap `TransferFacade` with `TransactionInterceptor`. When the presentation tier invokes what it thinks is `TransferFacade`, `TransactionInterceptor` is invoked instead. The sequence of events is shown in figure 1.6.

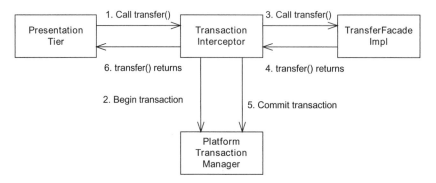

Figure 1.6   Using Spring interceptors to manage transactions

Let's look at the sequence of events:

1   The presentation tier calls `TransferFacade` but the call is routed to `Trans-actionInterceptor`.

2   `TransactionInterceptor` begins a transaction by calling `PlatformTransactionManager`, which begins a transaction using either the JTA provided by the application server or the transaction management API provided by the persistence framework.

3   `TransactionInterceptor` invokes the real `TransferFacadeImpl`.

4   The call to `TransferFacadeImpl` returns.

5   `TransactionInterceptor` commits the transaction by calling `PlatformTransactionManager`.

6   The call to `TransactionInterceptor` returns.

In step 5 `TransactionInterceptor` could also roll back the transaction if the `TransferMoney` service threw an exception. By default, `TransactionInterceptor` emulates EJBs and rolls back a transaction if a `RuntimeException` is thrown. However, you can write rollback rules that specify which exceptions should cause a transaction to be rolled back. Using rollback rules simplifies the application and decouples it from the transaction management APIs by eliminating code that programmatically rolls back transactions. This is one example of how the Spring framework is more flexible than an EJB container.

Another benefit of using Spring is that you can test your transactional POJOs without deploying them in the application server. Because code that uses JDO or Hibernate can also be tested within your IDE, you can often do a lot of development without ever starting up an application server. In fact, I often find that the only time I need to use one is when developing code that uses a service such as JMS that is provided by the application server. Even when working on the presentation tier I'm able to use a simpler web container such as Jetty. This is yet another example of how lightweight frameworks make your life as a developer easier.

The role of AOP in the Spring framework

The technology underlying Spring's transaction management mechanism is known as Aspect-Oriented Programming (AOP). AOP is a declarative mechanism for changing the behavior of an application without requiring any modification to the application itself. You write rules that specify new code to be executed when methods are called and, in some cases, fields are accessed or objects instantiated. In this example the `BeanNameAutoProxyCreator` arranged for the `Transaction-Interceptor` to be executed whenever the `TransferFacade` was called without any code changes. AOP is not limited to transaction management, and in this book you will see examples of interceptors that implement security, manage database connections, and automatically retry transactions.

I'm using the Spring AOP implementation in this book for the simple reason that it provides the AOP interceptors for managing transactions, JDO, and Hibernate connections. It is important to remember that the techniques described in this book will work equally as well with other lightweight containers such as PicoContainer [PicoContainer], and other AOP mechanisms like AspectJ [Laddad 2003]. However, as of this writing, Spring provides the best implementation of the features required by enterprise applications such as the Food to Go application, which is the example application used throughout the rest of this book.

The Spring framework is one example of a growing number of technologies that are compelling alternatives to EJBs. Using Spring AOP provides the same benefits of using EJB session beans but also allows you to use POJOs for your problem domain. An EJB container provides a large number of services, including transaction management. But is it worth compromising the design of the application to take advantage of these services—especially if you can implement them using a technology such as Spring in an à la carte fashion?

1.2.6 Configuring applications with Spring

Most applications consist of multiple components that need to access one another. A traditional J2EE application uses JNDI as the mechanism that one component uses to access another. For example, the presentation tier uses a JNDI lookup to obtain a reference to a session bean home interface. Similarly, an EJB uses JNDI to access the resources that it needs, such as a JDBC `DataSource`. The trouble with JNDI is that it couples application code to the application server, which makes development and testing more difficult. The Spring framework provides POJOs with a much easier-to-use mechanism called *dependency injection*, which decouples application components from one another and from the application server.

Dependency injection is another powerful feature of Spring's bean factory. Spring beans can be configured to depend on other beans, and when Spring instantiates a bean, it will pass to it any required beans, instantiating them if necessary. Two main types of dependency injection are used with Spring: constructor injection and setter injection. With constructor injection, the container passes the required objects to a component's constructor; with setter injection, the container passes the required objects by calling setters.

Dependency injection was used earlier to wire together the Spring beans—`TransactionInterceptor`, `PlatformTransactionManager`, and `BeanNameAutoProxy-Creator`—that provide transaction management. It can also be used to wire together application components. In the money transfer example, we can configure the `TransferFacade` bean to depend on `TransferService` and `Transfer-Service` to depend on `HibernateAccountRepository` and `HibernateBanking-TransactionRepository`:

```
<beans>

...
<bean id="TransferFacade"
    class="TransferFacadeImpl">
  <constructor-arg ref="TransferService"/>
</bean>

<bean id="TransferService"
    class=" TransferServiceImpl">
  <constructor-arg ref="AccountRepository"/>
  <constructor-arg ref="BankingTransactionRepository"/>
</bean>
...
</beans>
```

The first bean definition specifies that `TransferFacadeImpl`'s constructor take a `TransferService` as a parameter. The second bean definition specifies that `Trans-ferServiceImpl`'s constructor be passed `AccountRepository` and `BankingTrans-actionRepository`. When Spring instantiates `TransferFacade`, it will also instantiate `TransferService`, `HibernateAccountRepository`, and `HibernateBankingTrans-actionRepository`. See the online source code, which can be downloaded from http://www.manning.com/crichardson, for the definition of the `Hibernate-AccountRepository`, `HibernateBankingTransactionRepository`, and `Hibernate-ObjectDetacher`, along with the configuration of the Hibernate `SessionFactory` and the JDBC `DataSource`.

Dependency injection is an extremely easy way to configure an application. Instead of using an object containing code to look up its dependencies, they are automatically passed in by the bean factory. It doesn't have to call any application server APIs. In chapter 7, I'll show how dependency injection is a useful way of decoupling components from one another and the application server environment.

1.2.7 *Deploying a POJO application*

As I mentioned earlier, one of the great things about POJOs and lightweight frameworks is that you can do a lot of development without going near an application server. Eventually, however, you do need to deploy the application. An application that uses Spring for transaction management and Hibernate or JDO for persistence can often be deployed in a simple web container-only server such as Jetty, Tomcat, or WebLogic Express, as shown in figure 1.7.

The application is simply packaged as a web archive file (WAR) and deployed in the server's web container. It would use either a JDBC connection pool provided by

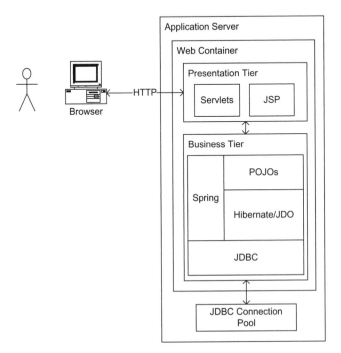

Figure 1.7
Deploying a POJO application in a web container

the application server or an open source implementation such as DBCP [DBCP]. If the application needed to be clustered for scalability and reliability, then it would use the clustering feature of the web container.

An application only needs to be deployed in a full-blown application server (e.g., WebLogic Server or JBoss) if it requires those parts of the J2EE stack such as JTA or JMS that are not provided by the web container or some third-party software. You might also want to deploy your application in a particular server if you wanted to use a vendor-specific feature. For example, some application servers have sophisticated security and management capabilities. Only some applications have these requirements, and if you break the dependency on EJBs by using POJOs and lightweight technologies, you can often deploy an application in a simpler and, in some cases, cheaper server.

1.2.8   POJO design summary

Let's review the design of the money transfer service that uses a POJO object model, Spring for transaction management and dependency injection, and Hibernate for persistence. The design, which is shown in figure 1.8, has more components than the EJB-based design described earlier in section 1.1.2. However, this more modular design is easier to understand, test, and extend than the original version. Each class has a small number of well-defined and easy-to-understand responsibilities. The use of interfaces for the repositories simplifies testing by allowing the real implementations of the repositories to be replaced with stubs. OverdraftPolicy enables the design to be extended to support new types of overdrafts without requiring modifications to existing code.

The core of the business logic consists of object model described earlier in section 1.2.1 and includes classes such as Account and OverdraftPolicy. The AccountRepository and BankingTransactionRepository classes encapsulate the Hibernate APIs. AccountRepository defines a method for retrieving accounts, and BankingTransactionRepository provides a method for creating transactions. TransferService is a simple service that looks up the accounts by calling Account-Repository and calls credit() and debit() on them. It also creates a Banking-Transaction to record the transfer.

TransferFacade is a simple wrapper around TransferService that retrieves the data required by the presentation tier. This functionality could be implemented by TransferService, but implementing it in a separate class keeps Transfer-Service focused on transferring money and away from the presentation tier and the details of detaching objects. TransferFacade is wrapped with a Spring Trans-actionInterceptor that manages transactions.

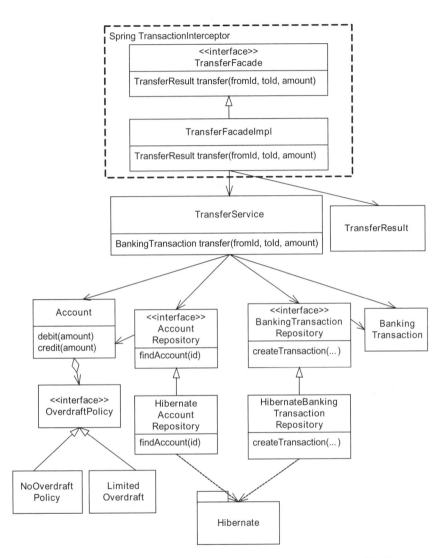

Figure 1.8   Money transfer service implemented with POJOs, Hibernate, and Spring

I have omitted some of the details, but I hope you can see what you can accomplish with POJOs and lightweight frameworks such as Spring. By using Spring, we have the functionality we formerly needed from the EJB container. By using POJOs, we also have a design and structure of code that is impossible if we use the heavyweight J2EE application server and all its services. Using the lighter weight tools allows us to improve the structure, maintainability, and testability of our code.

1.3 Summary

Building enterprise Java applications with a simple technology—POJOs—in conjunction with lightweight frameworks such as Spring, Hibernate, and JDO has some surprising benefits. You have the freedom to develop expressive object models rather than being forced down a procedural path. You get the benefits of EJB, such as declarative transaction management and security, but in a much more developer-friendly form. You can work on your core business logic without being distracted by enterprise "issues" such as transaction management and persistence. You can develop and test your code without being slowed down by deployment. As a bonus, because the lightweight frameworks are noninvasive you can readily take advantage of new and improved ones that will inevitably be developed.

In the next chapter we look at the design decisions you need to make when using them to develop an enterprise application.

J2EE design decisions

This chapter covers

- Encapsulating the business logic
- Organizing the business logic
- Accessing the database
- Handling database concurrency

Now that you have had a glimpse of how POJOs and lightweight frameworks such as Spring and JDO make development easier and faster, let's take a step back and look at how you would decide whether and how to use them. If we blindly used POJOs and lightweight frameworks, we would be repeating the mistake the enterprise Java community made with EJBs. Every technology has both strengths and weaknesses, and it's important to know how to choose the most appropriate one for a given situation.

This book is about implementing enterprise applications using design patterns and lightweight frameworks. To enable you to use them effectively in your application, it provides a decision-making framework that consists of five key questions that must be answered when designing an application or implementing the business logic for an individual use case. By consciously addressing each of these design issues and understanding the consequences of your decisions, you will vastly improve the quality of your application.

In this chapter you will get an overview of those five design decisions, which are described in detail in the rest of this book. I briefly describe each design decision's options as well as their respective benefits and drawbacks. I also introduce the example application that is used throughout this book and provide an overview of how to make decisions about its architecture and design.

2.1 Business logic and database access decisions

As you saw in chapter 1, there are two quite different ways to design an enterprise Java application. One option is to use the classic EJB 2 approach, which I will refer to as the heavyweight approach. When using the heavyweight approach, you use session beans and message-driven beans to implement the business logic. You use either DAOs or entity beans to access the business logic.

The other option is to use POJOs and lightweight frameworks, which I'll refer to as the POJO approach. When using the POJO approach, your business logic consists entirely of POJOs. You use a persistence framework (a.k.a., object/relational mapping framework) such as Hibernate or JDO to access the database, and you use Spring AOP to provide enterprise services such as transaction management and security.

EJB 3 somewhat blurs the distinction between the two approaches because it has embraced POJOs and some lightweight concepts. For example, entity beans are POJOs that can be run both inside and outside the EJB container. However, while session beans and message-driven beans are POJOs they also have heavyweight behavior since they can only run inside the EJB container. So, as you can see, EJB 3 has both heavyweight and POJO characteristics. EJB 3 entity beans are part of the lightweight approach whereas session beans and message-driven beans are part of the heavyweight approach.

Choosing between the heavyweight approach and the POJO approach is one of the first of myriad design decisions that you must make during development. It's a decision that affects several aspects of the application, including business logic organization and the database access mechanism. To help decide between the two approaches, let's look at the architecture of a typical enterprise application, which is shown in figure 2.1, and examine the kinds of decisions that must be made when developing it.

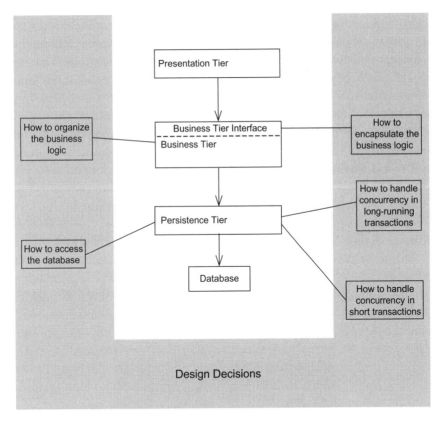

Figure 2.1   A typical application architecture and the key business logic and database access design decisions

The application consists of the web-based presentation tier, the business tier, and the persistence tier. The web-based presentation tier handles HTTP requests and generates HTML for regular browser clients and XML and other content for rich Internet clients, such as Ajax-based clients. The business tier, which is invoked by the presentation tier, implements the application's business logic. The persistence tier is used by the business tier to access external data sources such as databases and other applications.

The design of the presentation tier is outside the scope of this book, but let's look at the rest of the diagram. We need to decide the structure of the business tier and the interface that it exposes to the presentation tier and its other clients. We also need to decide how the persistence tier accesses databases, which is the main source of data for many applications. We must also decide how to handle concurrency in short transactions and long-running transactions. That adds up to five decisions that any designer/architect must make and that any developer must know in order to understand the big picture.

These decisions determine key characteristics of the design of the application's business and the persistence tiers. There are, of course, many other important decisions that you must make—such as how to handle transactions, security, and caching and how to assemble the application—but as you will see later in this book, answering those five questions often addresses these other issues as well.

Each of the five decisions shown in figure 2.1 has multiple options. For example, in chapter 1 you saw two different options for three of these decisions. The EJB-based design, which was described in section 1.1, consisted of procedural code implemented by a session bean and used JDBC to access the database. In comparison, the POJO-based design, which was described in section 1.2, consisted of an object model, which was mapped to the database using JDO and was encapsulated with a POJO façade that used Spring for transaction management.

Each option has benefits and drawbacks that determine its applicability to a given situation. As you will see in this chapter, each one makes different trade-offs in terms of one or more areas, including functionality, ease of development, maintainability, and usability. Even though I'm a big fan of the POJO approach, it is important to know these benefits and drawbacks so that you can make the best choices for your application.

Let's now take a brief look at each decision and its options.

2.2 Decision 1: organizing the business logic

These days a lot of attention is focused on the benefits and drawbacks of particular technologies. Although this is certainly very important, it is also essential to think about how your business logic is structured. It is quite easy to write code without giving much thought to how it is organized. For example, as I described in the previous chapter it is too easy to add yet more code to a session bean instead of carefully deciding which domain model class should be responsible for the new functionality. Ideally, however, you should consciously organize your business logic in the way that's the most appropriate for your application. After all, I'm sure you've experienced the frustration of having to maintain someone else's badly structured code.

The key decision you must make is whether to use an object-oriented approach or a procedural approach. This isn't a decision about technologies, but your choice of technologies can potentially constrain the organization of the business logic. Using EJB 2 firmly pushes you toward a procedural design whereas POJOs and lightweight frameworks enable you to choose the best approach for your particular application. Let's examine the options.

2.2.1 Using a procedural design

While I am a strong advocate of the object-oriented approach, there are some situations where it is overkill, such as when you are developing simple business logic. Moreover, an object-oriented design is sometimes infeasible—for example, if you do not have a persistence framework to map your object model to the database. In such a situation, a better approach is to write procedural code and use what Fowler calls the *Transaction Script* pattern [Fowler 2002]. Rather than doing any object-oriented design, you simply write a method, which is called a transaction script, to handle each request from the presentation tier.

An important characteristic of this approach is that the classes that implement behavior are separate from those that store state. In an EJB 2 application, this typically means that your business logic will look similar to the design shown in figure 2.2. This kind of design centralizes behavior in session beans or POJOs, which implement the transaction scripts and manipulate "dumb" data objects that have very little behavior. Because the behavior is concentrated in a few large classes, the code can be difficult to understand and maintain.

The design is highly procedural, and relies on few of the capabilities of object-oriented programming (OOP) languages. This is the type of design you would create if you were writing the application in C or another non-OOP language.

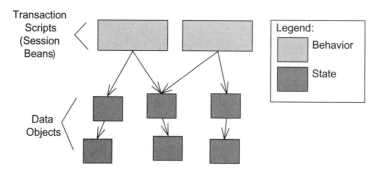

Figure 2.2   The structure of a procedural design: large transaction script classes and many small data objects

Nevertheless, you should not be ashamed to use a procedural design when it is appropriate. In chapter 9 you will learn when it does make sense and see some ways to improve a procedural design.

2.2.2   *Using an object-oriented design*

The simplicity of the procedural approach can be quite seductive. You can just write code without having to carefully consider how to organize the classes. The problem is that if your business logic becomes complex, then you can end up with code that's a nightmare to maintain. Consequently, unless you are writing an extremely simple application you should resist the temptation to write procedural code and instead develop an object-oriented design.

In an object-oriented design, the business logic consists of an object model, which is a network of relatively small classes. These classes typically correspond directly to concepts from the problem domain. For example, in the money transfer example in section 1.2 the POJO version consists of classes such as `TransferService`, `Account`, `OverdraftPolicy`, and `BankingTransaction`, which correspond to concepts from the banking domain. As figure 2.3 shows, in such a design some classes have only either state or behavior but many contain both, which is the hallmark of a well-designed class.

As we saw in chapter 1, an object-oriented design has many benefits, including improved maintainability and extensibility. You can implement a simple object model using EJB 2 entity beans, but to enjoy most of the benefits you must use POJOs and a lightweight persistence framework such as Hibernate and JDO. POJOs enable you to develop a rich domain model, which makes use of such features as inheritance and loopback calls. A lightweight persistence framework enables you to easily map the domain model to the database.

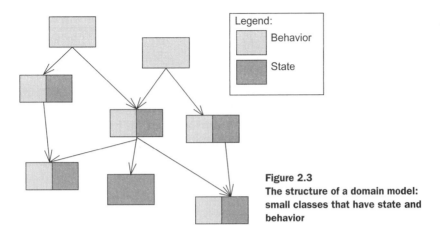

Figure 2.3
The structure of a domain model:
small classes that have state and
behavior

Another name for an object model is a domain model, and Fowler calls the object-oriented approach to developing business logic the *Domain Model* pattern [Fowler 2002]. In chapter 3 I describe one way to develop a domain model and in chapters 4-6 you will learn about how to persist a domain model with Hibernate and JDO.

2.2.3 *Table Module pattern*

I have always developed applications using the Domain Model and *Transaction Script* patterns. But I once heard rumors of an enterprise Java application that used a third approach, which is what Martin Fowler calls the *Table Module* pattern. This pattern is more structured than the Transaction Script pattern, because for each database table it defines a table module class that implements the code that operates on that table. But like the Transaction Script pattern it separates state and behavior into separate classes because an instance of a table module class represents the entire database rather individual rows. As a result, maintainability is a problem. Consequently, there is very little benefit to using the Table Module pattern, and so I'm not going to look at it in anymore detail in this book.

2.3 *Decision 2: encapsulating the business logic*

In the previous section, I covered how to organize the business logic. You must also decide what kind of interface the business logic should have. The business logic's interface consists of those types and methods that are callable by the presentation tier. An important consideration when designing the interface is how much of the business logic's implementation should be encapsulated and therefore not visible to the presentation tier. Encapsulation improves maintainability because by hiding the business logic's implementation details it can prevent changes to it affecting the presentation tier. The downside is that you must typically write more code to encapsulate the business logic.

You must also address other important issues, such as how to handle transactions, security, and remoting, since they are generally the responsibility of the business logic's interface code. The business tier's interface typically ensures that each call to the business tier executes in a transaction in order to preserve the consistency of the database. Similarly, it also verifies that the caller is authorized to invoke a business method. The business tier's interface is also responsible for handling some kinds of remote clients.

Let's consider the options.

2.3.1 EJB session facade

The classic-J2EE approach is to encapsulate business logic with an EJB-based session façade. The EJB container provides transaction management, security, distributed transactions, and remote access. The façade also improves maintainability by encapsulating the business logic. The coarse-grained API can also improve performance by minimizing the number of calls that the presentation tier must make to the business tier. Fewer calls to the business tier reduce the number of database transactions and increase the opportunity to cache objects in memory. It also reduces the number of network round-trips if the presentation tier is accessing the business tier remotely. Figure 2.4 shows an example of an EJB-based session façade.

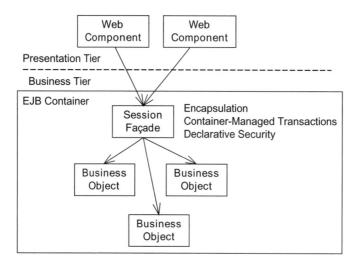

Figure 2.4
Encapsulating the business logic with an EJB session façade

In this design, the presentation tier, which may be remote, calls the façade. The EJB container intercepts the calls to the façade, verifies that the caller is authorized, and begins a transaction. The façade then calls the underlying objects that implement the business logic. After the façade returns, the EJB container commits or rolls back the transaction.

Unfortunately, using an EJB session façade has some significant drawbacks. For example, EJB session beans can only run in the EJB container, which slows development and testing. In addition, if you are using EJB 2, then developing and maintaining DTOs, which are used to return data to the presentation tier, is tedious and time consuming.

2.3.2 *POJO façade*

For many applications, a better approach uses a POJO façade in conjunction with an AOP-based mechanism such as the Spring framework that manages transactions, persistence framework connections, and security. A POJO facade encapsulates the business tier in a similar fashion to an EJB session façade and usually has the same public methods. The key difference is that it's a POJO instead of an EJB and that services such as transaction management and security are provided by AOP instead of the EJB container. Figure 2.5 shows an example of a design that uses a POJO façade.

The presentation tier invokes the POJO façade, which then calls the business objects. In the same way that the EJB container intercepts the calls to the EJB

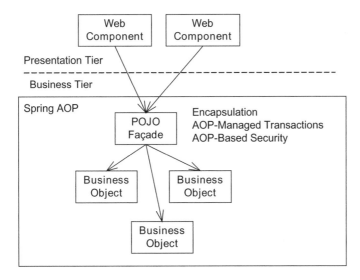

Figure 2.5
Encapsulating the business logic with a POJO façade

façade, the AOP interceptors intercept the calls to the POJO façade and authenticate the caller and begin, commit, and roll back transactions.

The POJO façade approach simplifies development by enabling all of the business logic to be developed and tested outside the application server, while providing many of the important benefits of EJB session beans such as declarative transactions and security. As an added bonus, you have to write less code. You can avoid writing many DTO classes because the POJO façade can return domain objects to the presentation tier; you can also use dependency injection to wire the application's components together instead of writing JNDI lookup code.

However, as you will see in chapter 7 there are some reasons not to use the POJO façade. For example, a POJO façade cannot participate in a distributed transaction initiated by a remote client.

2.3.3 *Exposed Domain Model pattern*

Another drawback of using a façade is that you must write extra code. Moreover, as you will see in chapter 7, the code that enables persistent domain objects to be returned to the presentation tier is especially prone to errors. There is the increased risk of runtime errors caused by the presentation tier trying to access an object that was not loaded by the business tier. If you are using JDO, Hibernate, or EJB 3, you can avoid this problem by exposing the domain model to the presentation tier and letting the business tier return the persistent domain objects back to the presentation tier. As the presentation tier navigates relationships between domain objects, the persistence framework will load the objects that it accesses, a technique known as *lazy loading*. Figure 2.6 shows a design in which the presentation tier freely accesses the domain objects.

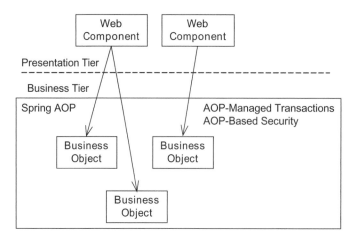

Figure 2.6
Using an exposed
domain model

In the design in figure 2.6, the presentation tier calls the domain objects directly without going through a façade. Spring AOP continues to provide services such as transaction management and security.

An important benefit of this approach is that it eliminates the need for the business tier to know what objects it must load and return to the presentation tier. However, although this sounds simple you will see there are some drawbacks. It increases the complexity of the presentation tier, which must manage database connections. Transaction management can also be tricky in a web application because transactions must be committed before the presentation tier sends any part of the response back to the browser. Chapter 8 describes how to address these issues and implement an exposed domain model.

2.4 Decision 3: accessing the database

No matter how you organize and encapsulate the business logic, eventually you have to move data to and from the database. In a classic J2EE application you had two main choices: JDBC, which required a lot of low-level coding, or entity beans, which were difficult to use and lacked important features. In comparison, one of the most exciting things about using lightweight frameworks is that you have some new and much more powerful ways to access the database that significantly reduce the amount of database access code that you must write. Let's take a closer look.

2.4.1 What's wrong with using JDBC directly?

The recent emergence of object/relational mapping frameworks (such as JDO and Hibernate) and SQL mapping frameworks (such as iBATIS) did not occur in a vacuum. Instead, they emerged from the Java community's repeated frustrations with JDBC. Let's review the problems with using JDBC directly in order to understand the motivations behind the newer frameworks. There are three main reasons why using JDBC directly is not a good choice for many applications:

- *Developing and maintaining SQL is difficult and time consuming*—Some developers find writing large, complex SQL statements quite difficult. It can also be time consuming to update the SQL statements to reflect changes in the database schema. You need to carefully consider whether the loss of maintainability is worth the benefits.

- *There is a lack of portability with SQL*—Because you often need to use database-specific SQL, an application that works with multiple databases must have multiple versions of some SQL statements, which can be a maintenance nightmare. Even if your application only works with one database in production, SQL's lack of portability can be an obstacle to using a simpler and faster in-memory database such as Hypersonic Structured Query Language Database Engine (HSQLDB) for testing.

- *Writing JDBC code is time consuming and error-prone*—You must write lots of boilerplate code to obtain connections, create and initialize `Prepared-Statements`, and clean up by closing connections and prepared statements. You also have to write the code to map between Java objects and SQL statements. As well as being tedious to write, JDBC code is also error-prone.

The first two problems are unavoidable if your application must execute SQL directly. Sometimes, you must use the full power of SQL, including vendor-specific features, in order to get good performance. Or, for a variety of business-related reasons, your DBA might demand complete control over the SQL statements executed by your application, which can prevent you from using persistence frameworks that generate the SQL on the fly. Often, the corporate investment in its relational databases is so massive that the applications working with the databases can appear relatively unimportant. Quoting the authors of *iBATIS in Action,* there are cases where "the database and even the SQL itself have outlived the application source code, or even multiple versions of the source code. In some cases, the application has been rewritten in a *different language,* but the SQL and database remained largely unchanged." If you are stuck with using SQL directly, then fortunately there is a framework for executing it directly, one that is much easier to use than JDBC. It is, of course, iBATIS.

2.4.2 Using iBATIS

All of the enterprise Java applications I've developed executed SQL directly. Early applications used SQL exclusively whereas the later ones, which used a persistence framework, used SQL in a few components. Initially, I used plain JDBC to execute the SQL statements, but later on I often ended up writing mini-frameworks to handle the more tedious aspects of using JDBC. I even briefly used Spring's JDBC classes, which eliminate much of the boilerplate code. But neither the home-grown frameworks nor the Spring classes addressed the problem of mapping between Java classes and SQL statements, which is why I was excited to come across iBATIS.

In addition to completely insulating the application from connections and prepared statements, iBATIS maps JavaBeans to SQL statements using XML descriptor files. It uses Java bean introspection to map bean properties to prepared statement placeholders and to construct beans from a `ResultSet`. It also includes support for database-generated primary keys, automatic loading of related objects, caching, and lazy loading. In this way, iBATIS eliminates much of the drudgery of executing SQL statements. As you will see in several chapters, including chapter 9, iBATIS can considerably simplify code that executes SQL statements. Instead of writing a lot of low-level JDBC code, you write an XML descriptor file and make a few calls to iBA-TIS APIs.

2.4.3 *Using a persistence framework*

Of course, iBATIS cannot address the overhead of developing and maintaining SQL or its lack of portability. To avoid those problems you need to use a persistence framework. A persistence framework maps domain objects to the database. It provides an API for creating, retrieving, and deleting objects. It automatically loads objects from the database as the application navigates relationships between objects and updates the database at the end of a transaction. A persistence framework automatically generates SQL using the object/relational mapping, which is typically specified by an XML document that defines how classes are mapped to tables, how fields are mapped to columns, and how relationships are mapped to foreign keys and join tables.

EJB 2 had its own limited form of persistence framework: entity beans. However, EJB 2 entity beans have so many deficiencies, and developing and testing them is extremely tedious. As a result, EJB 2 entity beans should rarely be used. What's more, as I describe in chapter 10 it is unclear how some of their deficiencies will be addressed by EJB 3.

The two most popular lightweight persistence frameworks are JDO[JSR12][JSR243], which is a Sun standard, and Hibernate, which is an open source project. They both provide transparent persistence for POJO classes. You can develop and test your business logic using POJO classes without worrying about persistence, then map the classes to the database schema. In addition, they both work inside and outside the application server, which simplifies development further. Developing with Hibernate and JDO is so much more pleasurable than with old-style EJB 2 entity beans.

Several chapters in this book describe how to use JDO and Hibernate effectively. In chapter 5 you will learn how to use JDO to persist a domain model. Chapter 6 looks at how to use Hibernate to persist a domain model. In chapter 11 you will learn how to use JDO and Hibernate to efficiently query large databases and process large result sets.

In addition to deciding how to access the database, you must decide how to handle database concurrency. Let's look at why this is important as well as the available options.

2.5 Decision 4: handling concurrency in database transactions

Almost all enterprise applications have multiple users and background threads that concurrently update the database. It's quite common for two database transactions to access the same data simultaneously, which can potentially make the database inconsistent or cause the application to misbehave. In the `TransferService` example in chapter 1, two transactions could update the same bank account simultaneously, and one transaction could overwrite the other's changes; money could simply disappear. Given that the modern banking system is not backed by gold, nor even paper, but just supported by electronic systems, I'm sure you can appreciate the importance of transaction integrity.

Most applications must handle multiple transactions concurrently accessing the same data, which can affect the design of the business and persistence tiers.

Applications must, of course, handle concurrent access to shared data regardless of whether they are using lightweight frameworks or EJBs. However, unlike EJB 2 entity beans, which required you to use vendor-specific extensions, JDO and Hibernate directly support most of the concurrency mechanisms. What's more, using them is either a simple configuration issue or requires only a small amount of code.

The details of concurrency management are described in chapters 12 and 13. In this section, you will get a brief overview of the different options for handling concurrent updates in database transactions, which are transactions that do not involve any user input. In the next section, I briefly describe how to handle concurrent updates in longer application-level transactions, which are transactions that involve user input and consist of a sequence of database transactions.

2.5.1 Isolated database transactions

Sometimes you can simply rely on the database to handle concurrent access to shared data. Databases can be configured to execute database transactions that are, in database-speak, isolated from one another. Don't worry if you are not familiar with this concept; it's explained in more detail in chapter 12. For now the key thing to remember is that if the application uses fully isolated transactions, then the net effect of executing two transactions simultaneously will be as if they were executed one after the other.

On the surface this sounds extremely simple, but the problem with these kinds of transactions is that they have what is sometimes an unacceptable reduction in performance because of how isolated transactions are implemented by the database. For this reason, many applications avoid them and instead use what is termed optimistic or pessimistic locking, which is described a bit later.

Chapter 12 looks at when to use database transactions that are isolated from one another and how to use them with iBATIS, JDO, and Hibernate.

2.5.2 *Optimistic locking*

One way to handle concurrent updates is to use optimistic locking. Optimistic locking works by having the application check whether the data it is about to update has been changed by another transaction since it was read. One common way to implement optimistic locking is to add a version column to each table, which is incremented by the application each time it changes a row. Each UPDATE statement's WHERE clause checks that the version number has not changed since it was read. An application can determine whether the UPDATE statement succeeded by checking the row count returned by PreparedStatement.executeUpdate(). If the row has been updated or deleted by another transaction, the application can roll back the transaction and start over.

It is quite easy to implement an optimistic locking mechanism in an application that executes SQL statements directly. But it is even easier when using persistence frameworks such as JDO and Hibernate because they provide optimistic locking as a configuration option. Once it is enabled, the persistence framework automatically generates SQL UPDATE statements that perform the version check. Chapter 12 looks at when to use optimistic locking, explores its drawbacks, and shows you how to use it with iBATIS, JDO, and Hibernate.

Optimistic locking derives its name from the fact it assumes that concurrent updates are rare and that instead of preventing them the application detects and recovers from them. An alternative approach is to use pessimistic locking, which assumes that concurrent updates will occur and must be prevented.

2.5.3 *Pessimistic locking*

An alternative to optimistic locking is pessimistic locking. A transaction acquires locks on the rows when it reads them, which prevent other transactions from accessing the rows. The details depend on the database, and unfortunately not all databases support pessimistic locking. If it is supported by the database, it is quite easy to implement a pessimistic locking mechanism in an application that executes SQL statements directly. However, as you would expect, using pessimistic locking in a JDO or Hibernate application is even easier. JDO provides pessimistic locking as a configuration option, and Hibernate provides a simple programmatic API for locking objects. Again, in chapter 12 you will learn when to use pessimistic locking, examine its drawbacks, and see how to use it with iBATIS, JDO, and Hibernate.

In addition to handling concurrency within a single database transaction, you must often handle concurrency across a sequence of database transactions.

2.6 Decision 5: handling concurrency in long transactions

Isolated transactions, optimistic locking, and pessimistic locking only work within a single database transaction. However, many applications have use cases that are long running and that consist of multiple database transactions which read and update shared data. For example, one of the use cases that you will encounter later in this chapter is the Modify Order use case, which describes how a user edits an order (the shared data). This is a relatively lengthy process, which might take as long as several minutes and consists of multiple database transactions. Because data is read in one database transaction and modified in another, the application must handle concurrent access to shared data differently. It must use the *Optimistic Offline Lock* pattern or the *Pessimistic Offline Lock* pattern, two patterns described by Fowler [Fowler 2002].

2.6.1 Optimistic Offline Lock pattern

One option is to extend the optimistic locking mechanism described earlier and check in the final database transaction of the editing process that the data has not changed since it was first read. You can, for example, do this by using a version number column in the shared data's table. At the start of the editing process, the application stores the version number in the session state. Then, when the user saves their changes, the application makes sure that the saved version number matches the version number in the database.

In chapter 13 you will learn more about when to use Optimistic Offline Lock pattern and how to use it with iBATIS, JDO, and Hibernate. Because the Optimistic Offline Lock pattern only detects changes when the user tries to save their changes, it only works well when starting over is not a burden on the user. When implementing use cases such as the Modify Order use case where the user would be extremely annoyed by having to discard several minutes' work, a much better option is to use the Pessimistic Offline Lock.

2.6.2 *Pessimistic Offline Lock pattern*

The Pessimistic Offline Lock pattern handles concurrent updates across a sequence of database transactions by locking the shared data at the start of the editing process, which prevents other users from editing it. It is similar to the pessimistic locking mechanism described earlier except that the locks are implemented by the application rather than the database. Because only one user at a time is able to edit the shared data, they are guaranteed to be able to save their changes. In chapter 13 you will learn more about when to use Pessimistic Offline Lock pattern, examine some of the implementation challenges, and see how to use it with iBATIS, JDO, and Hibernate.

Let's review the five design decisions. These decisions and their options are summarized in table 2.1. In the rest of the book you will learn more about each option, examining in particular its benefits and drawbacks and how to implement it.

Table 2.1   The key business logic design decisions and their options

Decision	Options
Business logic organization	Domain Model pattern Transaction Script pattern Table Module pattern
Business logic encapsulation	EJB Session Façade pattern POJO Façade pattern Exposed Domain Model pattern
Database access	Direct JDBC iBATIS Hibernate JDO
Concurrency in database transactions	Ignore the problem Pessimistic locking Optimistic locking Serializable isolation level
Concurrency in long-running transactions	Ignore the problem Pessimistic Offline Lock pattern Optimistic Offline Lock pattern

Now that you have gotten an overview of the business logic and database access design decisions, let's see how a development team applies them.

2.7 Making design decisions on a project

In this section you will see an example of how a development team goes about making the five design decisions I introduced in this chapter. It illustrates the kind of decision-making process that you must use when choosing between the POJO approach and the heavyweight approach. The team in this example is developing an application for a fictitious company called Food to Go Inc. I describe how the developers make decisions about the overall design of the Food to Go application and decisions about the design of the business logic for individual use cases.

2.7.1 Overview of the example application

Before seeing how the team makes decisions, let's first review some background information about the problem the team is trying to solve, and the application's high-level architecture. This will set the stage for a discussion of how a development team can go about making design decisions. Food To Go Inc. is a company that delivers food orders from restaurants to customers' homes and offices. The founders of Food to Go have decided to build a J2EE-based application to run their business. This application supports the following kinds of users:

- *Customers*—Place orders and check order status
- *Customer service reps*—Handle phone enquiries from customers about their orders
- *Restaurants*—Maintain menus and prepare the orders
- *Dispatchers*—Assign drivers to orders
- *Drivers*—Pick up orders from restaurants and deliver them

The company has put together a team consisting of five developers: Mary, Tom, Dick, Harry, and Wanda. They are all experienced developers who will jointly make architectural decisions in addition to implementing the application. The businesspeople and the development team kick off the project by meeting for a few days to refine the requirements and develop a high-level architecture.

The requirements

After a lot of discussion, they jointly decide on the following scenario to describe how an order flows through the system. The sequence of events is as follows:

1 The customer places the order via the website.

2 The system sends the order (by fax or email) to the restaurant.

3 The restaurant acknowledges receipt of the order.

4 A dispatcher assigns a driver to the order.

5 The system sends a notification to the assigned driver.

6 The driver views the assigned order on a cell phone.

7 The driver picks up the order from the restaurant and notifies the system that the order has been picked up.

8 The driver delivers the order to the customer and notifies the system that the order has been delivered.

In addition to coming up with a scenario that captures the vision of how the application will ultimately work, the developers and businesspeople also break down the application's requirements into a set of use cases. Given that Food to Go has limited resources, the team has decided to use an iterative and incremental approach to developing the application. They have decided to defer the implementation of use cases for dispatches and drivers to later iterations and to tackle the following use cases in the first iteration:

- *Place Order*—Describes how a customer places an order
- *View Orders*—Describes how a customer service representative can view orders
- *Send Orders to Restaurant*—Describes how the system sends orders to restaurants
- *Acknowledge Order*—Describes how a restaurant can acknowledge receipt of an order
- *Modify Order*—Describes how a customer service representative can modify an order

These use cases are used throughout this book to illustrate how to develop enterprise Java applications with POJOs and lightweight frameworks. I describe each of these use cases in a bit more detail later in this chapter, but let's first look at the application's high-level architecture.

The application's architecture

In the kickoff meeting, the team also sketches out the application's high-level architecture, which is shown in figure 2.7. This diagram shows the application's main components and its actors. It has the standard three-layer architecture consisting of the web-based presentation, business, and database access tiers. As you would expect, the application stores its data in a relational database.

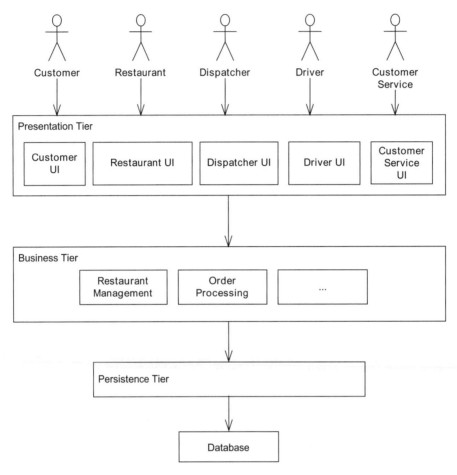

Figure 2.7 High-level architecture of the Food to Go application

The application has a web-based presentation tier that implements the user interface (UI) for the users. The application's business tier consists of various components that are responsible for order management and restaurant management.
The application's persistence tier is responsible for accessing the database. The
design of the presentation tier is outside the scope of this book, and so we are
going to focus on the design of the business and persistence tiers. Let's see how
the team makes some critical design decisions.

2.7.2 *Making high-level design decisions*

After identifying some requirements and sketching out a high-level architecture, the team needs to make the high-level design decisions that determine the overall design of the application. In this section, we consider each of the five design decisions that we described earlier and show how a development team might make those decisions. You will learn about the kind of process that you must use when designing your application.

Organizing the business logic

The business logic for this application is responsible for such tasks as determining which restaurants can deliver to a particular address at the specified time, applying discounts, charging credit cards, and scheduling drivers. The team needs to choose between an object-oriented approach or a procedural approach. When making this decision, the team first considers the potential complexity of the business logic. After reviewing the use cases, the team concludes that it could become quite complex, which means that using an object-oriented approach and developing a domain model is the best approach. Even though it is simpler, using a procedural approach to organize the business logic would lead to maintenance problems in the future.

The team also briefly looks at the issue of whether they could use a persistence framework to access the database. Unlike when developing some past applications, they are not constrained by a legacy schema or the requirement to use SQL statements maintained by a database administrator (DBA). Consequently, they are free to use a persistence framework and to implement the business logic using a domain model. However, they also decide that some business logic components can use a procedural approach if they must access the database in ways that are not supported by the persistence framework.

Encapsulating the business logic

In the past the team used EJB-based session façades to encapsulate the business logic and provide transaction management and security. EJB session façades worked reasonably well except for the impact they have on the edit-compile-debug cycle. Eager to avoid the tedium of deploying EJBs, the team is ready to adopt a more lightweight approach. Mary, who has just returned from the TSS Java Symposium 2005, where she spent three days hearing about POJOs, dependency injection, lightweight containers, AOP, and EJB 3, convinces the rest of the team to use the Spring framework instead of EJBs.

Having decided to use Spring, the team must now decide between using POJO façades and the exposed domain model. After spending a lot of time discussing these two options, they decide that the exposed domain model approach is too radical and that they are more comfortable using a POJO façade.

Accessing the database

Because the team has decided to use a domain model, it must pick a persistence framework. It would simply be too much work to persist the domain model without one. On its last project, the team used EJB CMP because, despite its glaring deficiencies, it was at that time the most mature solution. JDO was still in its infancy and the team had not yet heard of Hibernate. However, that was quite some time ago, and since then the team members have all read a few articles about JDO and Hibernate and decide that they are powerful and mature technologies. They are excited that they do not have to use entity beans again. After an animated discussion, the team picks JDO because its company prefers to use standards that are supported by multiple vendors. It hopes, however, to use Hibernate on some other project in the future.

Handling concurrent updates

The Food to Go application, like many other enterprise applications, is a *multiuser* application, which means that multiple transactions will access the same data concurrently. For example, two transactions could attempt to update the same order simultaneously. Therefore, it's essential to have a concurrency strategy. After reviewing the three options—isolated database transactions, optimistic locking, and pessimistic locking—the team picks optimistic locking because they have had experience with it and know that it performs well. Moreover, it is supported by JDO, which means that using it involves a simple configuration option.

Handling offline concurrency

Some of the application's use cases, such as the Modify Order use case, are long-running application transactions where data read in one database transaction is updated in another database transaction. In order to prevent two users from editing the same order simultaneously and overwriting each other's changes, it's important to implement an offline concurrency mechanism. The Optimistic Offline Lock pattern is easier to implement, especially because the application can leverage the optimistic locking mechanism provided by the persistence framework. However, the team decides to use the Pessimistic Offline Lock pattern for the `Order` class because users would be frustrated if they could not save the changes that they made to an order.

Summary of the high-level decisions

The team has made a number of key design decisions. They have decided that the business logic must be primarily organized using a JDO-based domain model, and encapsulated using POJO façades that use detached domain objects as DTOs. Finally, they have decided to use optimistic locking as the database-level concurrency mechanism, the Optimistic Offline Lock pattern as the default offline locking mechanism, and the Pessimistic Offline Lock pattern when necessary. However, these decisions are not completely set in stone, and they agree to revisit them as more is discovered about the application during development. Table 2.2 summarizes the architectural choices and options available to the developers.

Table 2.2   Architectural decisions

Decision	Options
Business logic organization strategy	Domain model with transaction scripts where necessary
Business logic encapsulation strategy	POJO façade
Persistence strategy	JDO for the domain model
Online concurrency strategy	Optimistic locking
Offline concurrency strategy	Optimistic Offline Lock pattern Pessimistic Offline Lock pattern (if required)

Table 2.2 shows the default design decisions the team made when implementing each component of the application. However, a developer working on a particular use case can use a different approach if it is absolutely necessary. For example, she might discover that the business logic for a use case needs to execute SQL directly instead of JDO in order to achieve the necessary performance. Let's look at examples of the decisions that are made when developing individual use cases.

2.7.3   Making use case–level decisions

Mary, Tom, Dick, Harry, and Wanda are each responsible for analyzing one use case and determining the most appropriate option for each design decision. Naturally, they have to work within the constraints imposed by the architecture that they have defined. In addition, even though some business logic components are specifically for a single use case, others are shared by multiple use cases and so it is essential that the developers collaborate closely.

In this section we show how a developer might go about designing the business logic for a use case and direct you to the chapters that will teach you how to implement the chosen options. It's important to remember, however, that the decisions made by each developer in this section are only one of several different ways to implement the use case. Consequently, we also point you to the chapters that describe how to implement alternative approaches. Let's look at each of the use cases and see which options the developer's pick.

The Place Order use case

Mary is responsible for implementing the Place Order use case:

> The customer enters the delivery address and time. The system first verifies that the delivery time is in the future and that at least one restaurant serves the delivery information. It then updates the pending order with the delivery information, and displays a list of available restaurants.
>
> The customer selects a restaurant. The system updates the pending order with the restaurant and displays the menu for the selected restaurant.
>
> The customer enters quantities for each menu item. The system updates the pending order with the quantities and displays the updated pending order.
>
> The customer enters payment information (credit card information and billing address). The system updates the pending order with the payment information and displays the pending order with totals, tax, and charges.
>
> The customer confirms that she wants to place the order. The system authorizes the credit card, creates the order, and displays an order confirmation, which includes the order number.

As you can see, the business logic for this use case is fairly complex, and so it makes sense to implement it using a domain model that is persisted with JDO. Database concurrency isn't an issue because this use case does not update any shared data. The pending order is data that is private to a single user's session and the order, which is shared data, is not updated in this use case once it has been created. After analyzing the use case, Mary makes the decisions shown in table 2.3. In chapter 4, you will learn how to develop a domain model for the Place Order use case; chapter 5 shows you how to persist it with JDO. In chapter 6, we describe

Table 2.3   Mary's decisions

Strategy	Decision	Rationale
Business logic organization	Domain Model pattern	The business logic is relatively complex. There does not appear to be any queries that cannot be handled by the JDO query language.
Database access	JDO	Using the Domain Model pattern.
Concurrency	None	This use case does not update shared data. The order is created at the end of the use case. The pending order is session state and is only updated by this session.

how to persist that domain model with Hibernate, and in chapter 9 you will see
how to implement the same business logic using a procedural approach.

The View Orders use case

Tom is responsible for implementing the View Orders use case:

> The customer service representative enters the search criteria. The system dis-
> plays the orders that match the search criteria. The customer service representa-
> tive can cancel or modify an order.

Tom analyzes this use case and concludes that a key issue is that the order table
will contain a large number of rows and will need to be denormalized for efficient
access. In addition, the queries will need to be heavily tuned and make use of Ora-
cle-specific features. Consequently, Tom decides that he needs to use SQL queries
to retrieve the orders. Table 2.4 summarizes his decisions.

Table 2.4   Tom's decisions

Strategy	Decision	Rationale
Business logic organization	Transaction Script pattern	Simple business logic. Uses iBATIS.
Database access	iBATIS	Heavily optimized SQL queries using Oracle-specific features. Database schema denormalized for efficient access.
Concurrency	None	This use case does not update shared data.

In chapter 11, you will learn about the different ways to implement this use case.

The Send Orders to Restaurant use case

Dick is responsible for implementing the Send Orders to Restaurant use case:

> *X* minutes before the scheduled delivery time, the system either emails or faxes the order to the restaurant.

The business logic for this use case is fairly simple. Dick determines that he can implement this use case using a single database transaction, which finds the orders that need to be sent, sends them to the restaurant, and updates the orders. He also decides that even though the business logic is simple, it fits with the existing domain model. Table 2.5 summarizes his decisions.

Table 2.5   Dick's decisions

Strategy	Decision	Rationale
Business logic organization	Domain Model pattern	Even though the business logic is simple, it fits with the existing domain model.
Database access	JDO	Using the Domain Model pattern.
Concurrency	Optimistic locking	The use case updates orders, which consist of shared data in a single transaction.
Offline concurrency	None	The use case is a single transaction.

Dick forgets that the Order class needs to use an offline locking pattern.

Chapter 12 looks at the different ways of implementing this use case.

The Acknowledge Order use case

Harry is responsible for implementing the Acknowledge Order use case:

> The system displays an order that has been sent to the restaurant. The restaurant's order taker accepts or rejects the order. The system displays a confirmation page. The restaurant's order taker confirms that he or she accepts or rejects the order. The system changes the state of the order to "ACCEPTED" or "REJECTED."

Harry determines that the business logic for this use case is quite simple and that he can implement it using the Domain Model pattern. He decides that he must use an offline locking pattern because this use case uses two database transactions: one to read the order, and another to change the status of the order. Table 2.6 lists the design decisions that Harry makes.

Table 2.6   Harry's decisions

Strategy	Decision	Rationale
Business logic organization	Domain Model pattern	Even though the business logic is simple, it fits with the existing domain model.
Database access	JDO	Using the Domain Model pattern.
Concurrency	Optimistic locking	The use case updates orders, which are shared data.
Offline concurrency	Optimistic Offline Lock pattern	The use case reads the order in one transaction and updates it in another. The cost and probability of starting over is small.

Harry also forgets that the Order class needs to use an offline locking pattern.

Chapter 13 looks at the different ways of implementing this use case.

The Modify Order use case

Finally, Wanda is responsible for implementing the Modify Order use case:

> The customer service representative selects the order to edit. The system locks and displays the order. The customer service representative updates the quantities and the delivery address and time. The system displays the updated order. The customer service representative saves his changes. The system updates and unlocks the order.

After analyzing the use case, Wanda makes the following decisions. Because the business logic is complex, she decides to implement it using the Domain Model pattern. Furthermore, Wanda thinks that she can reuse a lot of the pending order code from the Place Order use case.

Wanda also decides that she must use an offline concurrency pattern since the business logic consists of multiple database transactions. Because it would be very inconvenient for the user to start over if some other user changed the order while she was editing it, Wanda decides to use the Pessimistic Offline Lock pattern. Table 2.7 summarizes Wanda's decisions.

Table 2.7 Wanda's decisions

Strategy	Decision	Rationale
Business logic organization	Domain Model pattern	Complex business logic.
Database access	JDO	Using the Domain Model pattern.
Concurrency	Optimistic locking	The use case updates orders, which consist of shared data.
Offline concurrency	Pessimistic Offline Lock pattern	The use case reads the order in one transaction and updates it in another. The cost of starting over is high.

Wanda plans to meet with Dick and Harry to reconcile their respective concurrency requirements.

Chapter 13 looks at the different ways of implementing this use case.

2.8 Summary

This chapter describes how the task of designing the business and persistence tiers can be broken down into five main design decisions: organizing business logic; encapsulating business logic; accessing the database; handling database transaction-level concurrency; and handling concurrency in long-running transactions. Each decision has multiple options, and each option has benefits and drawbacks that determine whether it makes sense in a particular situation.

These decisions play a critical role in helping you decide between a POJO approach and a heavyweight EJB 2 approach. Some decisions have POJO options and heavyweight options. For example, you can encapsulate the business logic with a POJO façade or an EJB session façade. Other decisions have options that are made easier by using the POJO approach. For example, as we described in chapter 1, the heavyweight approach favors business logic that is organized procedurally, whereas the POJO approach enables you to use an object-oriented design.

Now that we have reviewed the design decisions and their options, let's examine each one in depth. In the next chapter, we first look at how to implement business logic using the Domain Model pattern.

A simpler, faster approach

Part 1 described some important design decisions you must make and each of their different options. In part 2, you will learn about a combination of options that is a particularly effective way to design applications with POJOs and lightweight frameworks.

One of the great things about POJOs and lightweight frameworks is that they enable you to tackle complex business logic using an object-oriented design. In chapter 3, you will see how to implement the business logic as a domain model, which is also known as an object model. You will learn how to develop a domain model using a test-driven approach and mock objects.

Once you have developed a domain model, you invariably need to persist it. In chapter 4, you will learn how to persist a domain model using an object/relational mapping (ORM) framework. You will examine the key features of an ORM framework and learn strategies for testing a persistence layer effectively.

Chapters 5 and 6 describe how to persist the domain model we developed in chapter 3 using two popular ORM frameworks. Chapter 5 discusses JDO, and chapter 6 explores the issues you must solve when persisting a domain model with Hibernate.

In chapter 7, you will learn how to encapsulate the business logic with a POJO façade instead of the traditional EJB session façade. This chapter describes how to manage transactions with the Spring framework, and you will also see how to detach JDO and Hibernate objects so that they can be returned to the presentation tier.

Using the Domain
Model pattern

This chapter covers

- Organizing business logic as a domain model
- Implementing a domain model with POJOs
- Using a test-driven approach
- Testing with mock objects

Programming languages and techniques evolve as developers discover new and better ways to build applications. In the 1990s, it was generally accepted that a good way to tackle the complexity of applications was to use object-oriented (OO) design techniques. Then, the end of that decade saw the arrival of Enterprise Java-Beans (EJBs). Before using EJBs, I spent over a decade developing applications in a variety of OO languages, including Common Lisp, C++, and Java. But OO design became a lot less important and a lot more difficult when doing EJB development. Even though many early enterprise Java applications were quite complex and could have benefited from using an OO approach, there were, as I described in chapter 1, cultural and technical obstacles to using such a strategy. Fortunately, Java technologies have evolved to sweep those obstacles aside. By developing with POJOs and lightweight frameworks, you can use OO design techniques in your enterprise Java applications.

This chapter describes the Domain Model pattern, which organizes the business logic as a domain model. A domain model is an object model of the application's problem domain, which identifies the problems that the application is trying to solve. The Domain Model pattern is important because it offers all of the benefits of object-oriented development, including improved maintainability and extensibility.

In this chapter, you will learn how a domain model fits into the application's architecture and its relationship with the presentation tier and the persistence framework. I also describe the structure of the domain model and show how to decouple it from the database and other external components so that it can be developed and tested more easily. You will learn how to develop a POJO domain model using test-driven development techniques. Throughout this chapter I use the domain model for the Place Order use case as an example.

3.1 Understanding the Domain Model pattern

The Domain Model pattern implements the business logic using good old-fashioned object-oriented analysis and design techniques (OOAD). This pattern uses OOAD to build an object model—the domain model—that is both a description of the problem domain and a blueprint for the design of the business logic. An object model consists of classes corresponding to concepts from the problem domain, which can make it easier to understand. Moreover, as I have mentioned previously, an object model is an excellent way to tackle complex business logic.

Business logic that is implemented using the Domain Model pattern is structured very differently than the traditional EJB design. Rather than the business logic being concentrated in a few, large classes, a domain model consists of many relatively small classes that have both state and behavior. For example, as you will see later in this chapter, the domain model for the Food to Go application consists of classes such as `Order`, `Restaurant`, and `MenuItem`.

An important issue when using the Domain Model pattern is how to access the database. Many of domain model classes are persistent and correspond to data in the database. Unless the domain model is extremely simple, the application must use an object/relational mapping (ORM) framework to persist the objects. In chapters 4-6 you will learn how to persist a domain model with Hibernate and JDO, which are two popular ORM frameworks, and chapter 10 will show you how to persist the domain model with EJB 3.

Let's now look at how a domain model fits into the overall application architecture and its relationship with the presentation tier and persistence framework; after that we will look at the structure of the domain model.

3.1.1 *Where the domain model fits into the overall architecture*

In an application where the business logic is organized using the Domain Model pattern, the domain model is the core of the business tier. Consider, for example, the application shown in figure 3.1, which consists of a presentation tier, a business tier, and a persistence framework. As this diagram shows, the domain model is invoked by either the presentation tier or by a façade that encapsulates the business tier.

The presentation tier handles HTTP requests from the user's browser by calling the domain model either directly or indirectly via a façade, which as I described in the previous chapter is either a POJO or an EJB. Each request results in one or more domain model methods being called. These methods perform various business logic operations, including retrieving and validating data, performing calculations, and updating the database.

The persistent domain objects are unaware that they are persistent. They are transparently mapped to the database by the persistence framework. Only a few of the domain model classes (which are called *repositories*, as you will see later in this chapter) explicitly call the persistence framework to create, find, and delete persistent objects. As a result, we can develop almost the entire domain model without having to worry about persistence. The domain model consists of POJOs, and any calls to the persistence framework are hidden behind interfaces. In the next chapter we will look at the topic of persistence in more detail, but for now let's examine the structure of the domain model.

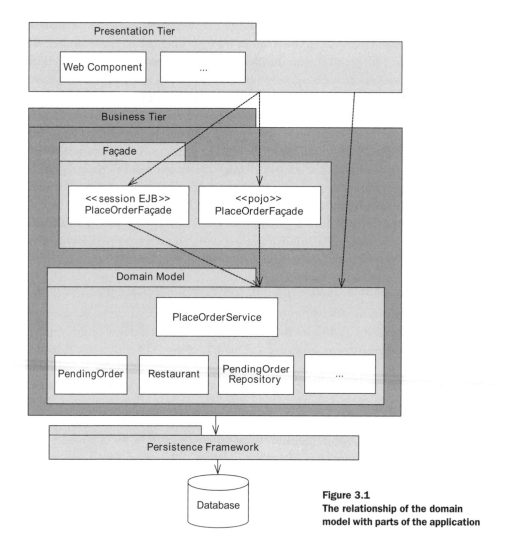

Figure 3.1
The relationship of the domain
model with parts of the application

3.1.2 *An example domain model*

A domain model consists of a network of interconnected objects, many of which have both state and behavior. As well as storing data, a domain model object usually implements the business logic that operates on that data. Most of the classes in a typical domain model are specific to the application's problem domain. A banking application's domain model contains classes such as Account and Transaction whereas the Food to Go application's domain model contains classes such as Order and Restaurant. It's always helpful to see an example, so let's focus on part of the domain model for the Food to Go application, which is shown in figure 3.2.

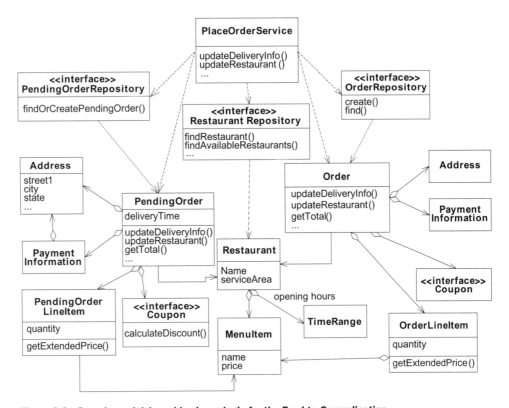

Figure 3.2   Domain model–based business logic for the Food to Go application

There are lots of details on this diagram, but let's focus on the important classes. The key classes are as follows:

- `PlaceOrderService`: Defines methods that correspond to steps of the Place Order use case and update domain model objects.

- `PendingOrder`: This application's shopping cart. `PendingOrder` has a delivery time attribute and a delivery address, a collection of line items, an associated restaurant, and a coupon. Each line item has a quantity attribute and an associated `MenuItem`.

- `Restaurant`: Represents a restaurant that prepares food for delivery. A restaurant has a name attribute and one or more menu items available for delivery, a geographic service area (which consists of a set of ZIP codes), and opening hours.

- `MenuItem`: Describes a menu item and has a name, a description, and a price.

- `TimeRange`: Consists of a day of the week, as well as the start and end time.

- `Order`: Represents an order that is created at the end of the Place Order use case. Like `PendingOrder` it has a delivery address, line items, and a restaurant, and it can also have a coupon. In theory we could have used the `Order` class to represent both the order being entered and the placed order, but this would have made the application more complex. Using two separate classes simplifies the design.

- `Coupon`: Represents a discount that can be applied to an order. Coupons are identified by a code and are valid only for a specified time period. The `Coupon` class is another example of the Strategy pattern. Like the `OverdraftPolicy` you saw in chapter 1, it is an interface and has several implementations—one for each kind of coupon.

- `PendingOrderRespository`: Defines methods for finding and creating `PendingOrders`.

- `OrderRepository`: Defines methods for finding and creating orders.

- `RestaurantRepository`: Defines methods for finding restaurants.

There are also some other classes such as the `Address` class, which represents an address, and `PaymentInformation`, which stores payment information.

This is a pretty simple domain model, but it still has quite a few classes. A complete domain model for an enterprise application would contain a great many more. Finding your way around a large domain model can be a lot easier if you know the roles the different classes play.

3.1.3 Roles in the domain model

Even though domain models from different problem domains are wildly different, the classes can be categorized by their role in the domain model. Identifying the role that a class plays can make it easier to name the class and help with the designing the domain model. As you will see, a class's role implies certain kinds of responsibilities and relationships with other classes in the domain model. Understanding these roles will help you develop your own domain model.

There are several different naming conventions for roles. My favorite scheme is based on the one in *Domain-Driven Design* [Evans 2003] and has the following roles:

- *Entities*—Objects with a distinct identity

- *Value objects*—Objects with no distinct identity

- *Factories*—Define methods for creating entities

- *Repositories*—Manage collections of entities and encapsulate the persistence framework
- *Services*—Implement responsibilities that can't be assigned to a single class and encapsulate the domain model

Let's now look at each of these roles.

Entities

Entities are objects that have a distinct business identity that is separate from the values of their attributes. Two entities are different even if the values of their attributes are the same and cannot be used interchangeably. Identifying entities is important because they often correspond to real-world concepts and are central to the domain model. Examples of entities in this application are `PendingOrder`, `Order`, and `Restaurant`.

Value objects

Value objects are objects that are primarily defined by the value of their attributes. They are often immutable, which means that once they are created they cannot be updated. Two instances whose attributes have the same values can be used interchangeably. Examples of value objects in this domain model include `PaymentInformation` and `Address`.

Factories

A Java application creates objects by using the `new` operator. Sometimes, using the `new` operator directly is sufficient, but if you need to instantiate a complex graph of objects or you need to vary the types of the objects that are created, then you might need to use a factory. A *factory* defines methods for creating entities. It encapsulates the mechanism that instantiates a graph of objects and connects them together, which simplifies the client code.

Repositories

Repositories manage collections of entities and define methods for finding and deleting entities. They can also play the role of factories if the factory code is simple. A repository encapsulates the persistence framework and consists of an interface and an implementation class. The interface defines the methods that can be called by the repository's client, and the implementation class implements the interface by calling the persistence framework. Because the persistence framework is encapsulated behind an interface, you can focus on developing the business logic without being slowed down or distracted by database issues.

Services

The fifth and final kind of objects that are found in a domain model are *services*, which implement the workflow of the application. These classes are the driving force of the application, with the methods that fulfill a use case. Generally, services include behaviors that cannot be assigned to a single entity and consist of methods that act on multiple objects. An example of a service in this domain model is `PlaceOrderService`, which defines methods corresponding to the steps of the Place Order use case.

A service consists of an interface and an implementation class. It is invoked by the domain model's client, which is either the façade or the presentation tier. A service method rarely implements a significant amount of business logic. Instead, a typical service method retrieves objects using a repository and then delegates to them. For example, `PlaceOrderService` calls `RestaurantRepository` and `PendingOrderRepository` and mostly delegates to `PendingOrder`.

The methods defined by a domain model service are very similar to those defined by a session façade or a POJO façade. The methods usually correspond to the steps of the use case. However, a service, unlike a façade, doesn't deal with such things as performing transactions, gathering the data that must be returned to the presentation tier, detaching objects, and all of the other things that the façade has to deal with. Instead, it just focuses on pure business logic. Keeping the service separate from the façade is useful because you can work on the service and the rest of the domain model without worrying about "plumbing" and other infrastructure issues. In fact, as you will see in the next section, the service is a good place to start when implementing a domain model.

3.2 *Developing a domain model*

Now that you have seen what a domain model is and how it fits in to the overall architecture of an application, let's take a step back and see how to go about developing one from scratch. The process of developing a domain model takes the application's requirements, which are typically use cases or stories, and creates an executable and tested domain model. There are many ways to develop a domain model, and you could very well have your own preferred strategy. In this section I'm going to describe a simple, informal approach that has worked well for me in the past. It's an approach that you can use to develop a domain model for your application.

3.2.1 *Identifying classes, attributes, and relationships*

Designing a domain model, like many other software design activities, requires both a solid understanding of the problem domain as well as a certain amount of creativity, experience, and common sense. A good way to start is by talking to the businesspeople who understand the problem domain and by analyzing the use cases. Quite often the nouns that are used when describing the problem domain suggest class names. *Applying UML and Patterns* [Larman 2004] offers an in-depth discussion of how to identify classes, their attributes, and associations.

Not surprisingly, in the case of the example application, the Food to Go businesspeople and the Place Order use case both use terms such as Order, Restaurant, Menu Item, Coupon, Address, and Payment Information, which are all plausible classes. Furthermore, we know from past experience that this application requires a shopping cart concept, which means that we need some classes to accumulate information about the order. Analyzing the domain and applying a small amount of creativity yields the domain model shown in figure 3.3.

This domain model is a simplified version of the one you saw earlier in figure 3.2. In this version of the domain model, the classes only have attributes and relationships; the methods have not yet been identified. Furthermore, this domain model only defines entities such as `PendingOrder` and `Restaurant` and value objects such as `Address` and `TimeRange`. It does not define `PendingOrderRepository`, `RestaurantRepository`, `OrderRepository`, or `PlaceOrderService`. Although it would be reasonable to assume the existence of those classes, we will instead identify them as we determine the behavior for the domain model classes in the next section.

3.2.2 *Adding behavior to the domain model*

So far, the classes in the domain model have only attributes and associations. This is certainly a necessary first step, but we need to bring the domain model to life by adding behavior. To determine their behavior, we must identify their responsibilities and collaborations. The *responsibility* of a class is what the class does, knows, or decides and is fulfilled by one or more methods. The domain model in figure 3.1 describes what each class knows because it defines attributes and associations. What it doesn't describe are responsibilities that concern what each class does or decides. The *collaborations* of a class are the other classes that it invokes in order to fulfill its responsibilities. The domain model in figure 3.1 outlines some of the possible collaborations because it describes associations between classes. However, as we will see, many more are waiting to be discovered.

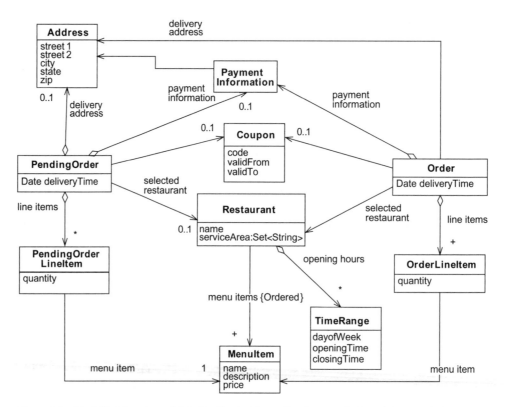

Figure 3.3 The initial domain model for the Food to Go application, consisting of classes, their attributes, and associations

So how to do we go about determining the responsibilities and collaborations? Many books have been written about OO design that describe a variety of techniques ranging from the more formal, UML-based responsibility driven design [Wirfs-Brock 2002] to the less formal, code-based test-driven development [Beck 2002]. In this chapter I am going to describe my favorite approach, which consists of the following steps:

1   Identify the requests that the application must handle by analyzing the requirements (use case, or story) or UI design.

2   Determine the interface (types and methods) that the domain model must expose in order to enable the presentation tier and the business tier's façades to handle those requests.

3 Implement the interface using a test-driven approach by considering each request in turn.

Let's first look at each one of these steps and then see how they are applied.

Identifying requests

The first step in adding behavior to the domain model is to identify the requests that the application must process and determine how it responds to them. When the application receives a request from its client, it must process the request and send back the appropriate response. For example, in a web application, when a user performs some action such as filling in a form or making a selection by clicking on a link, their browser sends an HTTP request and the application sends back an HTML page. The presentation tier handles requests by directly or indirectly calling the domain model, which performs the calculations, updates the database, and retrieves the required data. Consequently, we can determine the interface—types and methods—that the domain model must expose by analyzing the requests.

We can identify the requests that the application must process by analyzing either the UI design or the application's use cases or stories. The UI design specifies the user's actions, such as form submissions and mouse clicks, and clearly specifies the requests that must be processed by the application. Use cases often define a sequence of requests. For example, consider the Place Order use case that you first saw in chapter 2:

The customer enters the delivery address and time. The system first verifies that the delivery time is in the future and that at least one restaurant serves the delivery information. It then updates the pending order with the delivery information, and displays a list of available restaurants.

The customer selects a restaurant. The system updates the pending order with the restaurant and displays the menu for the selected restaurant.

The customer enters quantities for each menu item. The system updates the pending order with the quantities and displays the updated pending order.

The customer enters payment information (credit card information and billing address). The system updates the pending order with the payment information and displays the pending order with totals, tax, and charges.

The customer confirms that she wants to place the order. The system authorizes the credit card, creates the order, and displays an order confirmation, which includes the order number.

Each paragraph of the use case consists of two parts. The first part describes the user performing an action such as entering values or making a selection and corresponds to an HTTP request in a web-based application. The Place Order use case implies that the application has to process the following requests:

- *Enter delivery info*—The customer enters the delivery information.
- *Select restaurant*—The customer selects a restaurant.
- *Update quantities*—The customer enters quantities of menu items.
- *Check out*—The customer indicates that they are done entering quantities.
- *Enter payment information*—The customer enters the payment information.
- *Place order*—The customer confirms that they want to place the order.

The second part of each paragraph in the use case describes the application's response to the request. The application response can be described by a set of responsibilities. For example, the application processes the *enter delivery info* request by:

- Verifying that the delivery time is in the future and that at least one restaurant serves the delivery information
- Updating the pending order with the delivery information
- Displaying a list of available restaurants.

The application's responsibilities fall into two main categories. The first kind of responsibility is one that *verifies* or *validates* user input, *calculates* values, and *updates* the database. Typically either services or entities must define methods to fulfill these responsibilities. The second kind of responsibility is one that *displays* values. Although the presentation tier is responsible for displaying data, the domain model is responsible for providing the data. Typically, either entities or repositories must define methods that return the required data. Each responsibility corresponds to one or more domain model methods, and so the first step in implementing a responsibility is to define the methods and assign them to classes.

Identifying methods

Once we have determined the requests and how the application responds to each one, the next step is to determine what methods the domain model classes must provide in order to make this possible. As we saw in figure 3.1, when the application handles a request, the domain model's client—a façade or presentation tier—makes one or more calls to the domain model to validate the request, perform calculations, and update the database. It also calls the domain model to get the data that it displays to the user. To begin the process of writing the business logic, we must identify the methods that are called by the domain model's client and determine its parameters, its return type, and the class to which it belongs.

For each request, we typically define a service method that does the bulk of the work, including validating the request, performing calculations, and updating the database. We also define other entity and repository methods that return data to display. To see how to do this, let's identify the methods that the domain model classes must define to handle the *enter delivery info* request. The Food to Go application processes this request in two steps. First, it must verify that delivery information and update PendingOrder. Second, it must display the list of available restaurants. Let's consider each responsibility in turn.

The first responsibility belongs to the business tier because it consists of *verifying* user input based on the available set of restaurants, which are presumably stored in the database and *updating* PendingOrder, which is a domain object. The domain model's client could call PendingOrder directly to verify and store the delivery information. But as I described earlier, a domain model service is a better choice to handle this request because it provides superior encapsulation and moves more logic into the domain model, which simplifies the domain model's client.

This domain model does not have any services, so we need to define one. The simplest thing to do is define a service for the Place Order use case called PlaceOrderService. It has an updateDeliveryInfo() method, which verifies that the delivery information is served by at least one restaurant and updates the PendingOrder:

```
public interface PlaceOrderService {
  PlaceOrderServiceResult updateDeliveryInfo(String pendingOrderId,
                                             Address deliveryAddress,
                                             Date deliveryTime);
  …
}

public class PlaceOrderServiceResult {
  private int statusCode;
  private PendingOrder pendingOrder;
  …
}
```

This code takes the pendingOrderId and delivery information as parameters. The pendingOrderId parameter is the primary key of PendingOrder in the database, and is stored by the presentation tier in either HttpSession or the browser. The deliveryAddress and deliveryTime parameters contain the values entered by the user.

The `updateDeliveryInfo()` method returns a `PlaceOrderServiceResult` that contains a status code and `PendingOrder`. The status code indicates the outcome of verifying the delivery information. This method returns `PendingOrder` because it is needed by caller. It is, for example, displayed by the presentation tier.

The other responsibility when processing the *enter delivery info* request is displaying the list of available restaurants. This responsibility primarily belongs to the presentation tier because it consists of *displaying* data. However, the domain model must provide a way to find the available restaurants. Finding the available restaurants is a database query, which is encapsulated by a repository.

Because we are finding restaurants, it makes sense to add a `RestaurantRepository` to the domain model and make it responsible for retrieving the list of available restaurants. We define a `findAvailableRestaurants()` method that takes the delivery information as a parameter and returns the list of restaurants that serve it:

```
public interface RestaurantRepository {
       List findAvailableRestaurants(Address deliveryAddress,
                                      Date deliveryTime);
   ...
}
```

In addition, since the presentation tier displays each restaurant's name and type, the `Restaurant` class must define getters that return these values:

```
public class Restaurant {
  public String getName() { ... }
  public String getType() { ... }
  ...
}
```

The `getName()` method returns the name of the restaurant and the `getType()` method returns its type.

The presentation tier or the façade first calls the `PlaceOrderService` to update the `PendingOrder` and then calls `RestaurantRepository` to retrieve the available restaurants. `PlaceOrderService` doesn't return the list of available restaurants because, if it did, it would be tightly coupled to the UI design. It is better to decouple services from the UI and let the domain model's client make extra calls to the domain model to get the data that it needs to display. The façade or the presentation tier calls the domain model service to update the domain model and calls repositories to get the data that is displayed to the user. It is important to remember that the domain model is invoked via local calls, and so there is no overhead associated with multiple calls.

As you can see, we can analyze a use case and identify the methods that are called by the domain model's client. We can use this process to analyze the other steps of the Place Order use case and identify additional methods. Once you have identified these methods, the next step is to implement them.

Implementing methods using test-driven development

At this point in the development process, we have identified methods specified by the `PlaceOrderService` and `RestaurantRepository` interfaces and some simple getters defined by the `Restaurant` class. We now need to implement these methods. There are several ways to go about this. My favorite approach is to use test-driven development [Beck 2002], which is an informal, code-centric, and incremental development technique. When using test-driven development, you first write automated unit test cases for the new functionality. You then write the code that implements the functionality and makes the tests pass.

For example, when using test-driven development to implement a service method such as `PlaceOrderService.updateDeliveryInfo()`, you begin by writing one or more test cases. Each test calls the method with a particular combination of arguments and verifies that it correctly updates `PendingOrder` and returns the expected result. After writing the tests, you then implement the service method and make them pass. The output of test-driven development is working and tested code and automated test cases. In addition to ensuring that the code works, the tests document the expected behavior of the application.

In order to successfully use test-driven development, you need a development environment that provides immediate feedback to small changes. The process of writing a test and making it pass happens many times a day. *Refactoring*, a process that improves the design and that we describe in a moment, also consists of making small changes and testing them. As a result, it is common to go through the edit-compile-debug cycle every couple of minutes or even less. You can't wait for EJBs to deploy or for the database to be rebuilt if you want to be productive. As you can see, test-driven development and lightweight technologies work well together.

The importance of refactoring your code

Test-driven development is very different from development techniques that involve a lot of up-front design because the design incrementally evolves as more tests are written. But one risk of evolving a design is that you could end up with an unstructured mess. To prevent this from happening, it's important to periodically refactor the code.

Refactoring is a process that improves the design without changing its behavior and is done once the tests for the new functionality pass. Examples of refactoring techniques include extracting duplicated code into a method and introducing a superclass that implements common behavior. A good way to refactor code is to make a series of small changes and run the tests after every change. Refactoring is an essential part of test-driven development that will help you develop a well-designed application. For more information about refactoring, please see Fowler [Fowler 1999].

The benefits of using JUnit

While it is certainly possible to write the tests from scratch, it's rarely a good idea. A much better approach is to use a testing framework such as JUnit [JUnit], which provides classes that make it easier to write and run tests. It handles exceptions and reports test failures; provides methods for making assertions about the outcome of calling a method; and enables you to organize tests into a hierarchy of test suites. In addition, IDEs such as Eclipse [Eclipse] provide a GUI for running JUnit tests. There are also various JUnit extensions that provide additional features such as JMock, which I discuss a bit later. For more information about JUnit, please see *JUnit in Action* [Massol 2003] and *JUnit Recipes* [Rainsberger 2004].

Simplifying and speeding up tests with mock objects

I'm a big fan of test-driven development and believe that rigorous automated testing is essential if you want to successfully develop software without chaos and long nights spent tracking down bugs. But writing tests can be difficult because of all the setup code you must write. Moreover, if you have written a lot of tests they can take a very long time to run, especially if they access a database. On a couple projects that I've worked on, as more and more tests were written, it eventually took over 30 minutes to run them. This might not sound like a long time, but it was a big source of frustration that slowed down development because everyone was required to run the tests prior to checking in their changes.

The main reason why a class's tests can be difficult to write and slow to execute is because of its collaborators. Most classes are not standalone and instead collaborate with one or more other classes. For example, later on you will see how `Place-OrderService` calls several other domain model classes, including `PendingOrder`, `RestaurantRepository`, and `PendingOrderRepository`. Collaboration is generally a good thing because it keeps the class small. It is also essential if the class must access external resources such as a database, because in order to do that, it must use other classes such as those provided by JDBC. But collaboration can make testing difficult:

- *Top-down development and testing is tricky*—You must implement the collaborators before you can write any of a class's unit tests. This, for example, makes it impossible to develop and test a service before such as `PlaceOrderService` before implementing the domain model classes that it calls. We are forced to immediately dive into the details of the domain model.

- *Creating and initializing the collaborators makes a class's tests more complicated*— Some objects require complex initialization in order to get them into the correct state for a test. For example, if we wanted to test the scenario where `PlaceOrderService.updateDeliveryInfo()` is called with the ID of a pending order that has already been placed, we would have to call multiple methods on a `PendingOrder` to get it into the "Placed" state. This makes writing tests a lot more difficult.

- *Collaborators introduce undesirable coupling*—For example, using real implementations of the repositories would couple the domain model to the database and force us to address persistence issues. This is more complexity than we should tackle at this point. Furthermore, the overhead of accessing the database slows down the tests.

Fortunately, we can solve this problem by using *mock objects.* A mock object is a fake implementation that is used solely for testing. A test will configure a mock object to expect certain method calls and to return predetermined values. The mock object will throw an exception if its expectations are not met. By using mock objects, we simulate a domain object's collaborators without having to implement them. Also, by mocking repositories, we do not have to deal with persistence issues and can write tests that run without database. Using mock objects allows us to simplify otherwise complex object interactions, enabling us to focus on one piece of the application at a time.

If the class that you want to test invokes a collaborator via an interface, then one way to implement a mock object is to simply define a fake class that implements that interface. A test case for `PlaceOrderService`, which uses the `RestaurantRepository` interface, could define a dummy class that implements the `RestaurantRepository` interface, whose methods return test values. Although this approach works well in very simple cases, writing the fake classes can easily become pretty tedious. Moreover, you can only use this approach if there is an interface to implement.

A much better way to implement mock objects is to use mock object testing frameworks. Not only do they make it easier to write tests, but they also support mocking of concrete classes. There are several mock object testing frameworks, including EasyMock [EasyMock] and jMock [jMock]. EasyMock and jMock are both extensions to JUnit, and provide classes for creating and configuring mock objects.

Let's look at a simple example of how to use jMock, which is my personal favorite since it appears to be a little more flexible than the others. Imagine you needed to write a test for `PlaceOrderService.updateRestaurant()`, which calls `RestaurantRepository.findRestaurant()`. Instead of hand-coding a fake `RestaurantRepository`, you use jMock to create a mock `RestaurantRepository` and configure it to expect its `findRestaurant()` method to be called. jMock will throw an exception if either some other method was called unexpectedly or the expected method was not called. Listing 3.1 shows an excerpt of a test case for `PlaceOrderService` that does this.

Listing 3.1   An example of a test case that uses jMock

```
public class PlaceOrderServiceTests
          extends MockObjectTestCase {        ◁────────❶
  private Mock mockRestaurantRepository;
  private Restaurant restaurant;
  private PlaceOrderService service;

  public void setUp() {
    mockRestaurantRepository =
        new Mock(RestaurantRepository.class);     ◁────────❷
    RestaurantRepository restaurantRepository =   ◁────────❸
      (RestaurantRepository)mockRestaurantRepository.proxy();
    service =
      new PlaceOrderServiceImpl(restaurantRepository);   ◁────────❹
     restaurant = new Restaurant();
  }

  public void testUpdateRestaurant_good() throws Exception {
    mockRestaurantRepository.expects(once())
      .method("findRestaurant")                     ❺
      .with(eq(restaurantId))
      .will(returnValue(restaurant));

    PlaceOrderServiceResult result
      = service.updateRestaurant(      ◁────────❻
          pendingOrderId,
          restaurantId);
  ...
    }
  ...
```

❶ `PlaceOrderServiceTests` extends `MockObjectTestCase`, which is provided by jMock.

❷ The `setUp()` method creates the mock `RestaurantRepository`.

❸ It gets the jMock-created proxy, which implements the `RestaurantRepository` interface.

❹ The `setUp()` method creates the `PlaceOrderServiceImpl`, passing the proxy to its constructor.

❺ The `testUpdateRestaurant_good()` method configures the mock `Restaurant-Repository` to expect its `findRestaurant()` method to be called with a particular `restaurantId` and to return the test `Restaurant`.

❻ The test calls the service method, which then calls the mock restaurant.

The two key classes provided by jMock are `Mock` and `MockObjectTestCase`. The `Mock` class is used to create a mock object that behaves as if it is an instance of the class or interface passed to the `Mock` class's constructor. A test case can access the mock object by calling `proxy()` and downcasting the result to the correct type. The expectations for the mock are defined by calling various methods on the `Mock` class, including the `Mock.expects()` method. A mock object will throw an exception if a method is called unexpectedly. In addition, a test case can verify that all of the expected methods were called by calling `Mock.verify()`, which will throw an exception if any were not.

`MockObjectTestCase` is a subclass of the JUnit `TestCase` that is used for writing mock object tests. It provides convenience methods such as `eq()` and `return-Value()` that are used for configuring expectations. In addition, it automatically calls `verify()` on any fields of type `Mock` and verifies that all methods were called as expected.

Using a mock object framework such as jMock enables you to implement a domain model in a top-down fashion starting from the service and repository interface methods that are derived from the requirements. After implementing one domain model class and testing it with mock objects, we will have identified the methods that its collaborators must implement. We can then repeat the process for each of those classes. We write tests for each of their methods and use mock objects for their collaborators. This process is repeated until all of the classes and methods have been implemented. At the end of the process, we have an executable and tested domain model consisting of POJOs. Let's look at an example of how this is done.

3.3 *Implementing a domain model: an example*

In this section you will see an example of how the techniques described in the previous section can be used to develop a domain model. I show how to do this by developing the methods that are called to handle the *enter delivery information* request. I first implement the `PlaceOrderService`'s `updateDeliveryInfo()` method we identified earlier. After that, I show how to implement a `PendingOrder` method, which is called by `updateDeliveryInfo()`. The end result is working and tested `PlaceOrderService` and `PendingOrder` methods that verify the delivery information and update `PendingOrder`. The required repository methods are also identified. By studying this small example, you will learn an effective way to develop and test a domain model. Since the repository methods call the persistence framework, we won't implement those until chapters 4-6.

3.3.1 *Implementing a domain service method*

`PlaceOrderService`, which is a domain model service, has an `updateDelivery-Info()` method that is invoked when the user enters the delivery information. This method has the following signature:

```
public interface PlaceOrderService {
    PlaceOrderServiceResult updateDeliveryInfo(String pendingOrderId,
                        Address deliveryAddress,
                        Date deliveryTime);
}
```

Its parameters consist of `pendingOrderId`, which is the primary key of `PendingOrder` in the database, and the `deliveryAddress` and `deliveryTime` parameters, which specify the delivery information. It returns a `PlaceOrderServiceResult`, which consists of a status code and `PendingOrder`.

When `updateDeliveryInfo()` is invoked, `PlaceOrderService` retrieves `PendingOrder` or creates one if it does not exist. It then does one of the following:

- If the delivery time is in the future and the delivery information is served by at least one restaurant, `PlaceOrderService` updates `PendingOrder` with the new delivery information. It returns a `PlaceOrderServiceResult` containing a successful status code and `PendingOrder`.

- If the delivery address and time are not served by any restaurant or the delivery time is not in the future, `PlaceOrderService` leaves `PendingOrder` unchanged. It returns a `PlaceOrderServiceResult` containing a status code indicating failure and `PendingOrder`.

The test for the first scenario calls updateDeliveryInfo() with valid delivery information and verifies that it updates PendingOrder. Each of the tests for the other scenario calls updateDeliveryInfo() with invalid delivery information and verifies that it returns an error code and leaves the PendingOrder unchanged. When doing test-driven development we write tests for each of these scenarios and use them to drive the design of PlaceOrderService. Let's look at the test for the first scenario.

Writing a test

Listing 3.2 shows a JUnit-based test case for the successful scenario. This test case calls updateDeliveryInfo() with valid delivery information and verifies that it returns the expected result. Because it is a unit test, it doesn't need to use Spring to construct the service. It simply instantiates PlaceOrderServiceImpl using new, invokes a method, and verifies that it returns the correct result.

Listing 3.2 The valid delivery information test case

```
public class PlaceOrderServiceTests extends TestCase {

    private PlaceOrderService service;

    public void setUp() throws Exception {          ①  Creates
        service = new PlaceOrderServiceImpl();             PlaceOrderServiceImpl
    }

    public void testUpdateDeliveryInfo_Valid() throws Exception {
        Address deliveryAddress =
                makeGoodDeliveryAddress();          ②  Creates
        Date deliveryTime = makeGoodDeliveryTime();      test data

        String pendingOrderId = null;

        PlaceOrderServiceResult result =
            service.updateDeliveryInfo(             ③  Calls the
                pendingOrderId,                         service
                deliveryAddress,
                deliveryTime);

        PendingOrder pendingOrder = result.getPendingOrder();

        assertTrue(result.isSuccess());
        assertEquals(                               ④  Verifies the
            deliveryAddress,                            outcome
            pendingOrder.getDeliveryAddress());
        assertEquals(deliveryTime,
                pendingOrder.getDeliveryTime());
    }
```

Let's take a closer look:

1 The setup() method creates PlaceOrderServiceImpl.

2 The test method calls makeGoodDeliveryAddress() and makeGoodDeliveryTime(), which are helper methods that create the test delivery information.

3 The test method calls the service.

4 The test method verifies that the call to the service succeeds and that the delivery information was stored in the pending order.

Let's look at what needs to be done to get this test to compile and pass.

Implementing the method

After writing a test case, the next step is to write some code to make it compile and pass. We need to define the PlaceOrderServiceImpl class and write an update-DeliveryInfo() method. To write this method, we need to determine which of its responsibilities it handles directly and which it handles by calling other objects. If you carefully examine the description of the method given earlier, you will see that it has four key responsibilities:

1 Finds or creates the PendingOrder

2 Verifies that the delivery time is in the future and that the delivery information is served by at least one restaurant

3 Updates PendingOrder

4 Creates PlaceOrderServiceResult

Let's look at each one of these responsibilities in turn, beginning with how PlaceOrderService finds or creates PendingOrder. Earlier in this chapter I described how repositories are responsible for creating and finding entities. Consequently, PlaceOrderService must call a PendingOrderRepository to find or create Pending-Order. PendingOrderRepository has a findOrCreatePendingOrder() method that returns PendingOrder.

The business logic implemented by this method validates the delivery information by checking that the delivery time is in the future and by calling a repository to verify that there is at least one restaurant in the database that serves the delivery information. PlaceOrderService could be responsible for validating the delivery information and then updating PendingOrder by calling setters. However, this is not a very robust design since PendingOrder should be responsible for ensuring the validity of its state. A better approach is for PendingOrder to have an updateDeliv-eryInfo() method that verifies the delivery information and updates PendingOrder.

PlaceOrderService can handle the fourth responsibility itself by instantiating PlaceOrderServiceResult. PendingOrder just needs to return a status code indicating whether or not the delivery information was valid.

Now that we have figured out how these responsibilities are assigned, let's look at the code for the updateDeliveryInfo() method. Listing 3.3 shows the Place-OrderServiceImpl class and its updateDeliveryInfo() method.

Listing 3.3 PlaceOrderServiceImpl

```
public class PlaceOrderServiceImpl implements PlaceOrderService {

  private PendingOrderRepository pendingOrderRepository;

  public PlaceOrderService(PendingOrderRepository repository) {   ◄─┐
    this.pendingOrderRepository = repository;                       Takes
  }                                        PendingOrderRepository parameter ❶

  public PlaceOrderServiceResult updateDeliveryInfo(
    String pendingOrderId,
    Address deliveryAddress,
    Date deliveryTime) {
    PendingOrder pendingOrder =
      pendingOrderRepository
      .findOrCreatePendingOrder(   ◄──── ❷  Gets PendingOrder from
  pendingOrderId);                            PendingOrderRepository
    boolean success =
      pendingOrder.updateDeliveryInfo(   ◄──── ❸  Invokes
                  deliveryAddress,                 PendingOrder
                  deliveryTime);
    return new PlaceOrderServiceResult(success, pendingOrder);   ◄──┐
  }                                                            Creates
}                                              PlaceOrderServiceResult ❹
```

Here's what this code does:

❶ PlaceOrderServiceImpl is configured with PendingOrderRepository via constructor injection. It has a constructor that takes PendingOrderRepository as a parameter, and stores it in a field. Later in chapter 7 you will see how the Spring framework is used to instantiate and configure PlaceOrderServiceImpl.

❷ The updateDeliveryInfo() method calls PendingOrderRepository to get Pending-Order.

❸ This method invokes `PendingOrder`.

❹ The `updateDeliveryInfo()` method creates and returns a `PlaceOrderService-Result` that contains the status and the `PendingOrder`.

`PlaceOrderService` collaborates with the `PendingOrderRepository` and `Pending-Order` classes. Implementing the `PendingOrder` and `PendingOrderRepository` classes at this stage would be a distraction from implementing `PlaceOrderService`. If we implemented the `PendingOrder` class we would have to dive into the details of the business logic, and if we implemented `PendingOrderRepository` we would have to deal with ORM issues. A better approach for the tests is for the `Place-OrderService` to use mock object implementations.

To do this with jMock, however, we do need to at least define the `PendingOrder-Repository` interface and write a stub implementation of `PendingOrder`. The `Pend-ingOrderRepository` interface defines the `findOrCreatePendingOrder()` method:

```
public interface PendingOrderRepository {
    PendingOrder findOrCreatePendingOrder(String pendingOrderId);
}
```

The `PendingOrder` class defines a stub for the `updateDeliveryInfo()` method, which we will fill in later:

```
public class PendingOrder {
    public boolean updateDeliveryInfo(Address deliveryAddress,
                                      Date deliveryTime) {
      return false;
    }
}
```

The stub for the `updateDeliveryInfo()` method returns `false`.

Finishing the test

We've written the `updateDeliveryInfo()` method and defined the `PendingOrder-Repository` interface and `PendingOrder` class, but at this point we need to revise the test we wrote earlier. It no longer compiles because `PlaceOrderServiceImpl`'s constructor now expects to be passed a `PendingOrderRepository`. In addition, the test must create and configure mocks for `PendingOrder` and `PendingOrderRepository`. The mock `PendingOrderRepository` expects to have its `findOrCreatePending-Order()` method called and returns a mock `PendingOrder`. `PendingOrder` expects to have its `updateDeliveryInfo()` method called. Listing 3.4 shows the updated test.

Listing 3.4 Test case using mock objects

```
public class PlaceOrderServiceTests
         extends MockObjectTestCase {          ◁———————❶ Extends
                                                         MockObjectTestCase
  private Mock mockPendingOrder;
  private Mock mockPendingOrderRepository;

  private PendingOrder pendingOrder;
  private String pendingOrderId;
  private Date goodDeliveryTime;
  private Address goodDeliveryAddress;
  private PlaceOrderService service;

  public void setUp() throws Exception {
    mockPendingOrderRepository =
      new Mock(PendingOrderRepository.class);

    PendingOrderRepository pendingOrderRepository =
      (PendingOrderRepository)
        mockPendingOrderRepository.proxy();          ❷ Creates
    service = new PlaceOrderServiceImpl                 mock objects
      (pendingOrderRepository);

    mockPendingOrder =
          new Mock(PendingOrder.class);
    pendingOrder =
       (PendingOrder)
          mockPendingOrder.proxy();

    goodDeliveryAddress = new Address(…);
    goodDeliveryTime = new Date();

    pendingOrderId = "pendingOrderId";
  }

  public void testUpdateDeliveryInfo_Good() throws Exception {

    mockPendingOrderRepository
      .expects(once())
      .method("findOrCreatePendingOrder")
      .with(eq(pendingOrderId))
      .will((returnValue(pendingOrder)));          ❸ Configures
                                                      mock objects
    mockPendingOrder
      .expects(once())
      .method("updateDeliveryInfo")
      .with(eq(goodDeliveryAddress),
            eq(goodDeliveryTime))
      .will((returnValue(true)));
```

```
PlaceOrderServiceResult result =
  service.updateDeliveryInfo(
    pendingOrderId,
    goodDeliveryAddress,
    goodDeliveryTime);
```
❹ **Invokes the service**

```
assertTrue(result.isSuccess());

PendingOrder returnedPendingOrder =
  result.getPendingOrder();
assertSame(pendingOrder,
           returnedPendingOrder);
  }

}
```
❺ **Verifies the result**

Let's look at what this test does:

❶ The test case class extends the jMock `MockObjectTestCase` class, which automatically verifies that the mock object's expectations are met.

❷ The `setup()` method creates the mock `PendingOrderRepository`, the mock `PendingOrder`, and `PlaceOrderService`.

❸ The test defines the expectations for the mocks and their return values. The mock `PendingOrderRepository` expects to have `findOrCreatePendingOrder()` called with the delivery information and returns the mock `PendingOrder`. The mock `PendingOrder` expects to have `updateDeliveryInfo()` called with the delivery information. It returns `true` to indicate that the delivery information was valid and that `PendingOrder` was updated.

❹ After configuring the expectations, the test calls `PlaceOrderService.updateDeliveryInfo()`.

❺ The test then asserts that the call succeeds and verifies that `PlaceOrderService` returned the mock `PendingOrder`. It no longer verifies that `PendingOrder` contains the correct delivery information because it assumes that `PendingOrder.updateDeliveryInfo()` behaves correctly.

As you can see, this method and its tests are relatively simple because like most service methods it simply invokes other domain model objects. By using mocks for those objects, we can develop and test `PlaceOrderService` without having to get into their implementation details.

3.3.2 *Implementing a domain entity method*

We have implemented our first method, and it's tested and working! But we still have more to do. While implementing `PlaceOrderService.updateDelivery-Info()`, we determined that it delegates to `PendingOrder`, which is a domain model entity, and calls its `updateDeliveryInfo()` method. This method validates the delivery information and updates `PendingOrder`. It returns a boolean value that indicates whether the delivery information was valid. Let's look at how to implement this method.

Writing a test

As before, we start off by writing a test. Listing 3.5 shows a simple test for this method that calls it with valid delivery information. It uses `RestaurantTestData`, which isn't shown, to create some test data.

Listing 3.5 PendingOrderTests

```java
public class PendingOrderTests extends TestCase {

    private Date goodDeliveryTime;
    private Address goodDeliveryAddress;
    private PendingOrder pendingOrder;

    protected void setUp() throws Exception {
        super.setUp();
        pendingOrder = new PendingOrder();          ◁———❶ Creates the
        goodDeliveryAddress =                                PendingOrder
            RestaurantTestData.ADDRESS1;
        goodDeliveryTime =
            RestaurantTestData.
            ➥ makeGoodDeliveryTime();
    }

    public void testUpdateDeliveryInfo_good() throws Exception {
        boolean result =
            pendingOrder.updateDeliveryInfo(      ❷ Calls
                goodDeliveryAddress,                 updateDeliveryInfo()
                goodDeliveryTime);

        assertTrue(result);
        assertSame(goodDeliveryAddress,           ❸ Verifies
            pendingOrder.getDeliveryAddress());      the outcome
        assertSame(goodDeliveryTime,
            pendingOrder.getDeliveryTime());
    }

}
```

The test case calls `PendingOrder.updateDeliveryInfo()` with valid delivery information and verifies that it updates `PendingOrder` and returns `true`.

Implementing the method

Because `PendingOrder` already defines a stub method, this test compiles without a problem. But in order for it to pass, we need to replace the stub with a real implementation that validates the delivery information and updates `PendingOrder`.

`PendingOrder` first checks that the delivery information is at least one hour in the future by using the Java `Calendar` class. It then queries the database to validate the delivery information. *The simplest approach is to encapsulate this query within* `RestaurantRepository` *and* define an `isRestaurantAvailable()` method. The `updateDeliveryInfo()` method calls `isRestaurantAvailable()` and stores the delivery information if it returns `true`:

```
public class PendingOrder {

  private Date deliveryTime;
  private Address deliveryAddress;

  public boolean updateDeliveryInfo(
    Address deliveryAddress,
    Date deliveryTime) {

    Calendar earliestDeliveryTime = Calendar.getInstance();
    earliestDeliveryTime.add(Calendar.HOUR, 1);
    if (deliveryTime.before(earliestDeliveryTime.getTime()))
      return false;

    //How to access this?
    RestaurantRepository restaurantRepository = …;

    if (restaurantRepository
      .isRestaurantAvailable(deliveryAddress, deliveryTime)) {
      this.deliveryAddress = deliveryAddress;
      this.deliveryTime = deliveryTime;
      return true;
    } else
      return false;
  }
}
```

One important design issue, which we haven't resolved, is how `PendingOrder` accesses `RestaurantRepository`. Let's look at how to do this.

Options for accessing a repository

Repositories are mainly used by the domain services, but they are also invoked by some entities such as `PendingOrder`. To invoke a method on a repository object, the caller must obviously have a reference to the object. Earlier you saw how the repositories were passed as constructor parameters to `PlaceOrderService`. However, for the reasons that I describe next, it is not always possible to do this with domain model entities. Let's explore the problem and the various solutions.

The most convenient approach is to pass the repositories to entities as constructor parameters in this same way that they are passed to services. This enables the entities to be initialized using the lightweight container's constructor injection mechanism. Passing repositories as constructor parameters is a lot simpler than passing repositories around as method parameters and does not have the drawbacks of using singletons, as I describe a bit later. However, using this approach to initialize entities is not straightforward because unlike services, which are typically instantiated by the lightweight container, entities are created by the persistence framework when it loads them from the database.

By default, a persistence framework creates objects directly using the class's default constructor, and it's not possible to pass in any required objects. Some (but not all) persistence frameworks have a configurable object instantiation mechanism that allows an application to control how objects are instantiated. The application can configure the persistence framework to create objects using a lightweight container that injects the dependencies. For an example of using constructor injection with Hibernate, see http://hibernate.org/182.html [Hibernate injection]. However, because this approach is not universally available I am not going to use it in this book.

Another option is to implement repositories using static methods and variables. You could, for example, implement a repository as a singleton or a `Thread-Local`. This approach works with any persistence framework and does not require the repositories to be passed around, which can sometimes make the code too complicated. The problem with static methods and variables is that they make code harder to test. For example, they prevent you from using an alternative implementation such as a mock object because you cannot redirect a static method call or variable access to a different class. They also introduce hidden dependencies because the code depends on static variables that must be initialized. Consequently, static methods and variables are best avoided.

Given that only some persistence frameworks allow you to use constructor injection to initialize entities and that using static methods and variables has some serious drawbacks, it often makes sense to pass repositories as method parameters. It avoids the problems of using singletons and does not rely on proprietary persistence framework features. The one drawback of adopting this approach, however, is that it can have a ripple effect through the code. We might have to change many methods to take repositories as parameters in order to pass them from the services, which obtain them via constructor injection, to the methods that use them.

In this example, passing `RestaurantRepository` to `PendingOrder` requires only minor changes. We just need to change `PlaceOrderService` (in listing 3.3) to pass `RestaurantRepository` as an argument to `PendingOrder.updateDeliveryInfo()`, which in turn requires `PlaceOrderService`'s constructor to take it as a parameter. Listing 3.6 shows the `PendingOrder.updateDeliveryInfo()` method.

Listing 3.6   PendingOrder

```
public class PendingOrder {

  private Date deliveryTime;
  private Address deliveryAddress;

  public boolean updateDeliveryInfo(
    RestaurantRepository restaurantRepository,
    Address deliveryAddress,
    Date deliveryTime) {

    Calendar earliestDeliveryTime = Calendar.getInstance();
    earliestDeliveryTime.add(Calendar.HOUR, 1);
    if (deliveryTime.before(earliestDeliveryTime.getTime()))
      return false;

    if (restaurantRepository
      .isRestaurantAvailable(deliveryAddress, deliveryTime)) {
      this.deliveryAddress = deliveryAddress;
      this.deliveryTime = deliveryTime;
      return true;
    } else
      return false;
  }
}
```

This method calls the `RestaurantRepository.isRestaurantAvailable()` method and, if it succeeds, updates `PendingOrder` with the delivery information.

In order to get this class to compile, we need to define the `isRestaurantAvailable()` method:

```
public interface RestaurantRepository {
  boolean isRestaurantAvailable(Address deliveryAddress,
      Date deliveryTime)
  ...
}
```

This method returns true if there is at least one restaurant that serves the specified delivery information. We also have to change PlaceOrderService to take RestaurantRespository as a constructor parameter and pass it to PendingOrder and change its tests to use a mock RestaurantRepository.

Revising the test

After writing PendingOrder's method, we only have one thing left to do. We must go back to its test and change it to create and configure the required mock objects. This test, which is shown in listing 3.7, creates and configures a mock RestaurantRepository and passes it as an argument to the call to updateDeliveryInfo().

Listing 3.7   Tests for the updateDeliveryInfo() method

```
public class PendingOrderTests extends MockObjectTestCase {

    private Date goodDeliveryTime;
    private Address goodDeliveryAddress;
    private RestaurantRepository restaurantRepository;
    private Mock mockRestaurantRepository;
    private PendingOrder pendingOrder;

    protected void setUp() throws Exception {
        super.setUp();
        pendingOrder = new PendingOrder();

        goodDeliveryAddress = RestaurantTestData.ADDRESS1;
        goodDeliveryTime =
            RestaurantTestData.
                ➥ makeGoodDeliveryTime();

        mockRestaurantRepository =
            new Mock(RestaurantRepository.class);
        restaurantRepository =
            (RestaurantRepository) mockRestaurantRepository.proxy();
    }

    public void testUpdateDeliveryInfo_good() throws Exception {

        mockRestaurantRepository
            .expects(once())
            .method("isRestaurantAvailable")
            .with(eq(goodDeliveryAddress),
                eq(goodDeliveryTime))
            .will(returnValue(true));

        boolean result =
            pendingOrder.updateDeliveryInfo(
                restaurantRepository,
```

Creates PendingOrder and test data

Creates mock Restaurant

Configures expectations

Calls updateDeliveryInfo()

```
        goodDeliveryAddress,     △ Calls
        goodDeliveryTime));       │ updateDeliveryInfo()

    assertTrue(result);
    assertSame(
      goodDeliveryAddress,
      pendingOrder.getDeliveryAddress());       Verifies
    assertSame(                                 the outcome
      goodDeliveryTime,
      pendingOrder.getDeliveryTime());

  }

}
```

The test case configures the mock RestaurantRepository to expect its isRestaurantAvailable() method to be called and return true. It verifies that PendingOrder.updateDeliveryInfo() stores the delivery information stored in PendingOrder and returns true.

3.3.3 Summary of the design

So far we have only scratched the surface of the design, but by taking the *enter payment information* request, writing a couple of tests, and implementing some methods, we have already started to flesh out the domain model for the Place Order use case.

As figure 3.4 shows, we have partially implemented and tested several classes and methods. We have written the PlaceOrderService.updateDeliveryInfo() and PendingOrder.updateDeliveryInfo() methods. We have also identified some repository methods: PendingOrderRepository.findOrCreatePendingOrder(), RestaurantRepository.isRestaurantAvailable(), and RestaurantRepository.findAvailableRestaurants().

Of course, there is a lot more work to do. For example, we need to write some more tests for PlaceOrderService.updateDeliveryInfo() and PendingOrder.updateDeliveryInfo(), including ones that call those methods with invalid delivery information. There are also all the other requests to implement. After each minicycle of test writing and implementation, we move closer and closer to the domain model shown at the beginning of this chapter. To see the complete domain model, visit the book's website.

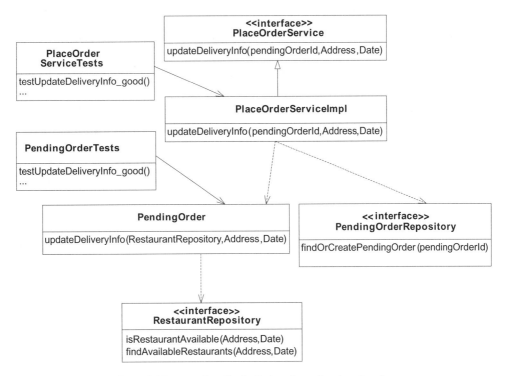

Figure 3.4 The domain model types and methods that we have developed so far

3.4 *Summary*

The Domain Model pattern organizes the business logic as a domain model, which is an object model of the application's problem domain. The domain model classes are invoked by either directly by the presentation tier or indirectly via a POJO façade or a session façade. Each request handled by the presentation tier typically results in one or more calls to domain model objects. The domain objects validate user input, perform calculations, and access the database.

This pattern has all the benefits of the OO paradigm. For example, the business logic is easier to maintain because responsibilities are distributed among the classes of the object model rather than being concentrated in a few large classes. It is also easier to extend because the domain model can use Gang of Four patterns, such as the Strategy and Template Method patterns. The Domain Model pattern is typically the best way to design complex business logic.

An effective way to develop a domain model is to first analyze the use cases and talk to the customer to create the initial domain model, which consists primarily of the classes and their attributes and associations. Then analyze the requirements to identify the methods that the domain model must expose to its client. After that, implement those methods using a test-driven development process.

To avoid dealing with persistence issues, it is usually a good idea to use mock objects to simulate the database access code. This enables you to focus on getting the business logic right. It also speeds up the tests for the domain model classes by eliminating the overhead of the database. At some point, of course, you have to map the persistent objects to the database and implement the database access code. The next chapter shows you how to do this.

Overview of persisting a domain model

This chapter covers

- Mapping a domain model to the database
- Accessing the database with an ORM framework
- Using Spring's ORM support classes
- Testing a persistence layer

When my son was younger, he liked to play with a toy that involved matching shapes with the corresponding holes. At first, he struggled to put the right shape in the right hole. It took him a while to realize that it's impossible put a round peg into a square hole. But eventually, he developed good shape recognition and matching skills and was able to master the game.

When developing enterprise Java applications, we have to do the equivalent of putting a round peg into a square hole. Because object databases never became a mainstream technology, we must store objects in a relational database. When processing a request, an application has to move domain objects between the JVM and the database. It must load an object from the database before invoking any of its methods or accessing any of its fields, and it must save the object back to the database if it has been modified. Persisting objects is a remarkably challenging problem because of the significant differences between a domain model and a database schema—the so-called impedance mismatch.

Persisting a domain model is made even more difficult by the need to do it without the classes knowing that they are persistent. The term for this is *transparent persistence*, and it's important because it simplifies development considerably. It enables classes to be POJOs and decouples them from the database. In contrast, EJB 2.0 entity beans are an example of nontransparent persistence and you know about their problems. However, as you will learn in this chapter, implementing transparent persistence is difficult because objects and databases are accessed in very different ways.

In this chapter you will learn why using an ORM framework is much better than trying to solve these problems yourself. I explain how to map the classes and relationships of an object model to a database schema. I describe the key features of ORM frameworks and provide an overview of JDO and Hibernate, which are two popular options. You will learn how to effectively test a persistent domain model and see some repository design techniques that make testing easier.

4.1 *Mapping an object model to a database*

If you have developed a domain model such as the one shown in figure 4.1, then you must map its classes and their fields to tables and columns in the database.

But how do you map a network of interconnected objects to a database schema, which has a flat structure consisting of tables and columns? Important OO concepts such as inheritance have no corresponding database equivalent. The rich set of relationships between objects doesn't map easily into the foreign key relationships between tables. Object identity and lifecycle also don't translate

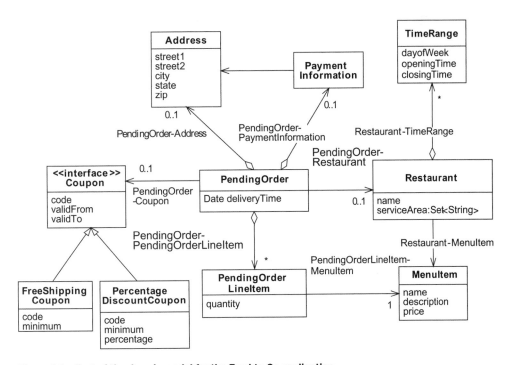

Figure 4.1   Part of the domain model for the Food to Go application

in a straightforward way into the database concepts. As a result, deciding how each object, field, and relationship in the domain model is stored in the database is a difficult problem. In this section, you will learn how.

4.1.1 Mapping classes

The central concept in a domain model is, of course, the class, which describes the structure and behavior of its instances or objects. There are three main ways to map a class to a database schema:

- Map a class to its own table.
- Map a class to some other class's table.
- Map a class to multiple tables.

Let's look at each one.

Map a class to its own table

The simplest approach is to define a table for the class and map the class's simple fields (e.g., those of type int, String, and Date) to table columns. For example, the PendingOrder class from the Food to Go application has fields such as state and deliveryTime:

```
public class PendingOrder {
    private int state;
    private Date deliveryTime;
    …
}
```

This class and its simple fields can be mapped to the PENDING_ORDER table:

```
CREATE TABLE PENDING_ORDER (
    PENDING_ORDER_ID NUMBER(10),
    STATE NUMBER(5)
    DELIVERY_TIME DATE,
    …
)
```

The PendingOrder class is mapped to the PENDING_ORDER table, whose primary key is PENDING_ORDER_ID. The class's simple fields are mapped to columns of this table. For example, the deliveryTime field maps to the DELIVERY_TIME column.

Map a class to its parent's table

Another way to map a class to a database schema is to map it to some other class's table. This approach, also called the *Embedded Value* pattern [Fowler 2002], is often used to persist a simple value object that is a child of a parent object. The fields of the child are mapped to the columns of the parent object's table. For example, the PendingOrder class has a deliveryAddress field, which is a reference to an Address object:

```
public class PendingOrder {
    private Address deliveryAddress;
    …
}

public class Address {
    private String street1;
    private String street2;
    private String city;
    private String state;
    private String zip;
    …
}
```

The `Address` class could be mapped to its own table, as I describe a bit later, but it is simpler and more efficient to map its fields to PENDING_ORDER:

```
CREATE TABLE PENDING_ORDER (
  PENDING_ORDER_ID NUMBER(10),
  STATE NUMBER(5)
  DELIVERY_TIME DATE,
  DELIVERY_STREET1 VARCHAR2(50),
  DELIVERY_STREET2 VARCHAR2(50),
  DELIVERY_CITY VARCHAR2(50),
  DELIVERY_STATE VARCHAR2(2),
  DELIVERY_ZIP VARCHAR2(10),
...
)
```

The PENDING_ORDER table has columns such as DELIVERY_STREET1 and DELIVERY_CITY that store the delivery address fields.

This approach simplifies the database schema by reducing the number of tables. It also improves performance by reducing the number of joins required to retrieve data. For example, the application can retrieve a `PendingOrder` and its delivery address by only querying the PENDING_ORDER table.

Map a class to multiple tables

We will usually map a class to either its own table or to its parent's table. But sometimes, you need to map a class to multiple tables. This is useful when you're mapping an object model to a legacy schema. It can also be used to improve performance when a class has a large number of attributes. Instead of mapping the class to a single table with a large number of columns, the less frequently used attributes can be mapped to a separate table, which is queried only when necessary.

Now that we have explored how to map classes and their simple fields to the database, let's look at mapping relationships.

4.1.2 *Mapping object relationships*

We have seen that simple fields are easily mapped to table columns. However, mapping the other fields that represent relationships between objects is a little more complicated. There are several kinds of relationships between objects, including one-to-one, many-to-one, one-to-many, and many-to-many. Let's see how to map each one.

Mapping one-to-one and many-to-one relationships

One-to-one and many-to-one relationships are implemented by fields that reference the other object. For example, the `PendingOrder`-`Address` relationship from figure 4.1, which is a one-to-one relationship, is implemented by the `delivery-Address` field, which references an `Address` object and the `PendingOrder-Restaurant` relationship, which is a many-to-one relationship, is implemented by a restaurant field, which references a `Restaurant`:

```
public class PendingOrder {
    private Address deliveryAddress
    private Restaurant restaurant;
...
```

The `PendingOrder.restaurant` field represents a many-to-one relationship because multiple pending orders can be for the same restaurant. The `Pending-Order.deliveryAddress` field represents either a one-to-one relationship where each address belongs to a single `PendingOrder` or a many-to-one relationship where each `Address` is shared by many `PendingOrders`.

There are a couple of ways of mapping a one-to-one relationship. One option is to use the Embedded Value pattern described earlier and map the child object to the parent object's table. The other option is for the referenced class to have its own table. For example, the delivery address for a `PendingOrder` can be stored in its own table as follows:

```
CREATE TABLE PENDING_ORDER (
    PENDING_ORDER_ID NUMBER(10),
    DELIVERY_TIME DATE
    ...
)

CREATE TABLE  DELIVERY_ADDRESS
   PENDING_ORDER_ID NUMBER(10),
   DELIVERY_STREET1 VARCHAR2(50),
   DELIVERY_STREET2 VARCHAR2(50),
   DELIVERY_CITY VARCHAR2(50),
   DELIVERY_STATE VARCHAR2(2),
   DELIVERY_ZIP VARCHAR2(10),
   ...
```

The delivery address is stored in the DELIVERY_ADDRESS table, whose primary key is `PENDING_ORDER_ID`.

A many-to-one relationship is mapped by the referencing object's table having a foreign key to the referenced object's table. For example, the `PendingOrder-Restaurant` relationship from figure 4.1 can be mapped by the PENDING_ORDER table having a foreign key to the RESTAURANT table:

```
CREATE TABLE PENDING_ORDER (
   ...
   RESTAURANT_ID NUMBER(1),
```

```
      CONSTRAINT P_ORDER_RESTAURANT_FK
      FOREIGN KEY(RESTAURANT_ID)
      REFERENCES RESTAURANT(RESTAURANT_ID),
      ...
 )

CREATE TABLE RESTAURANT (
  RESTAURANT_ID NUMBER PRIMARY KEY,
  ...
 )
```

In this example, the `Restaurant` class is mapped to the RESTAURANT table, whose primary key is RESTAURANT_ID. The `restaurant` field of the `PendingOrder` class is mapped to the RESTAURANT_ID column of the PENDING_ORDER table. It is a foreign key to the RESTAURANT table.

Mapping one-to-many relationships

Java classes don't just have fields that store simple values and references to other objects. They also have collection fields such as lists, maps, sets, and fields that store arrays. These collection and array fields implement one-to-many and many-to-many relationships. A relationship called A-B is one-to-many when each B object is only referenced by a single A object. The Food to Go domain model contains several examples of one-to-many relationships. For instance, the `Pending-Order.lineItems` field implements the `PendingOrder-PendingOrderLineItem` relationship in figure 4.1, which is a one-to-many relationship:

```
public class PendingOrder {
  private List lineItems; /* List<PendingOrderLineItem> */
  ...
}
```

A one-to-many relationship is usually mapped using a foreign key in the referenced class's table. We can, for instance, map the `PendingOrder lineItems` field using a foreign key in the PENDING_ORDER_LINE_ITEM table:

```
CREATE TABLE PENDING_ORDER_LINE_ITEM (
  ...
  PENDING_ORDER_ID NUMBER(10)
  LINE_ITEM_INDEX NUMBER(10) NOT NULL,
  CONSTRAINT P_ORD_LINE_ITEM_ORDER_FK
    FOREIGN KEY(PENDING_ORDER_ID)
    REFERENCES PENDING_ORDER(PENDING_ORDER_ID)
```

The PENDING_ORDER_LINE_ITEM table has a PENDING_ORDER_ID column, which is a foreign key to the PENDING_ORDER table. In addition, because lists are ordered, the PENDING_ORDER_LINE_ITEM table has a LINE_ITEM_INDEX column, which stores the position of the line item in the list.

One-to-many relationships are often *whole-part* relationships, which are relationships where the part cannot exist independently of the whole. A part must be deleted if either the whole is deleted or the part is no longer associated with the whole. Examples of whole-part relationships in the Food to Go domain model are PendingOrder-PendingOrderLineItem and Restaurant-MenuItem. A line item or menu item cannot exist independently of its PendingOrder or Restaurant. As I describe later, it is extremely useful if an ORM framework directly supports whole-part relationships.

Mapping many-to-many relationships

A relationship called A-B is many-to-many when a B object can be referenced by multiple A objects. For example, if a customer could use multiple coupons when placing an order, then PendingOrder-Coupon relationship would be many-to-many instead many-to-one. A PendingOrder could have multiple coupons and a coupon could be used by multiple PendingOrders:

```
public class PendingOrder {
  private List coupons;
  …
}

public class Coupon {
  …
}
```

A many-to-many relationship is mapped using a join table that has foreign keys to both classes' tables. The PendingOrder-Coupon relationship can be mapped as follows:

```
CREATE TABLE PENDING_ORDER (
    PENDING_ORDER_ID,
…
)

CREATE TABLE COUPON (
    COUPON_ID
…
)

CREATE TABLE PENDING_ORDER_COUPON (
  PENDING_ORDER_ID
  COUPON_ID
)
```

The `PendingOrder-Coupon` relationship is represented by the PENDING_ORDER _COUPON table. This table has foreign keys to both the PENDING_ORDER table and the COUPON table, which stores the coupons. A one-to-many relationship can also be mapped using a join table, although this approach is used less often because the foreign key mapping we just described is simpler and faster.

4.1.3 *Mapping inheritance*

Inheritance is another kind of relationship between classes. This fundamental object-oriented concept is widely used in domain models. For example, the Food to Go domain model has the `Coupon` hierarchy shown in figure 4.2.

In this example, a `PendingOrder` and an `Order` can have a `Coupon`, which is an interface that encapsulates how to calculate a discount on an order that satisfies some minimum value. Each concrete implementation of the `Coupon` interface implements a different algorithm. The `FreeShippingCoupon` class provides free shipping on orders, and the `PercentageDiscountCoupon` class provides a percentage discount. Because relational databases do not directly support inheritance, an application must map an inheritance hierarchy to one or more tables.

Three main ways exist to map an inheritance hierarchy to a relational schema:

- Single table per inheritance hierarchy
- Table per class
- Table per concrete class

Let's look at each one of these in turn.

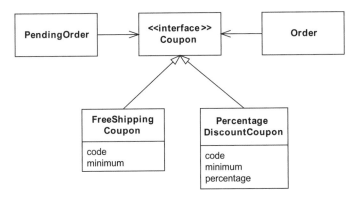

Figure 4.2 **The** `Coupon` **inheritance hierarchy from the Food to Go domain model**

Table per hierarchy

One ORM approach is to map all of the classes in an inheritance hierarchy to a single table. For example, we can map the Coupon hierarchy to the COUPON table as follows:

```
CREATE TABLE COUPON (
  CODE VARCHAR2(30),
  COUPON_TYPE VARCHAR2(100),
  MINIMUM NUMBER(10,2),
  PERCENT_DISCOUNT NUMBER(5,2),
  ...
);
```

The COUPON table has columns that store the fields of all three classes:

- CODE: Stores the coupon code from the FreeShippingCoupon and Percentage-DiscountCoupon classes
- MINIMUM: Stores the minimum quantity from the FreeShippingCoupon and PercentageDiscountCoupon classes
- PERCENT_DISCOUNT: Stores the percentage discount from PercentageDiscountCoupon

It also has a COUPON_TYPE column, which is a discriminator column that stores the type of each coupon.

This approach has the following benefits:

- It uses the minimum number of SQL statements and joins to access and manipulate objects because they are stored in a single table. Finding objects requires a SELECT statement that references a single table, and updating and creating objects requires a single INSERT or SELECT statement.
- A reference to a superclass is simply mapped as a foreign key to a single table. For example, the PendingOrder-Coupon relationship is mapped to a foreign key from the PENDING_ORDER to the COUPON table.

This approach has the following drawbacks:

- A row can have unused columns because only those columns that correspond to one subclass's fields are used. This can potentially result in inefficient storage utilization and unnecessary traffic between the application and the database. It can prevent you from defining the correct database schema constraints. For example, the DISCOUNT_PERCENTAGE column is only used in those rows that represent instances of PercentageDiscountCoupon, and so we cannot define the DISCOUNT_PERCENTAGE column as NOT NULL.

- Each time we define a new subclass that requires new columns, we must modify this table.

Table per class

If you want to avoid those problems, you can instead map each class to its own table. In this example we use three coupon tables, one for each class:

```
CREATE TABLE COUPON (
  COUPON_ID NUMBER(10) NOT NULL,
  CODE VARCHAR2(30) NOT NULL,
  COUPON_TYPE VARCHAR2(100) NOT NULL,
  MINIMUM NUMBER(10,2) NOT NULL,
  );

CREATE TABLE PERCENT_DISCOUNT_COUPON (
  COUPON_ID NUMBER(10) NOT NULL,
  DISCOUNT_PERCENTAGE NUMBER(5,2),
  CONSTRAINT COUPON_PK
    PRIMARY KEY(COUPON_ID),
  CONSTRAINT PERCENT_DISCOUNT_COUPON_FK
    FOREIGN KEY(COUPON_ID)
    REFERENCES COUPON(COUPON_ID)
);

CREATE TABLE FREE_SHIPPING_COUPON (
  COUPON_ID NUMBER(10) NOT NULL,
  CONSTRAINT COUPON_PK
    PRIMARY KEY(COUPON_ID)
  CONSTRAINT FREE_SHIPPING_COUPON_FK
    FOREIGN KEY(COUPON_ID)
    REFERENCES COUPON(COUPON_ID)
);
```

The COUPON table contains a row for each coupon. The PERCENT_DISCOUNT table contains the percentage discount coupons and its primary key column, COUPON_ID, is a foreign key to the COUPON table. Similarly, the FREE_SHIPPING_COUPON table contains the free shipping coupons and its primary key is also a foreign key to the COUPON table.

This approach has the following benefits:

- It does not result in unused columns, which minimizes space utilization and enables columns, such as DISCOUNT_PERCENTAGE, to have the appropriate NOT NULL definition.

- References to a superclass are simply mapped to a foreign key reference to a single table.

- It enables new subclasses to be added without having to modify existing tables.

The main drawback of this approach is that it requires multiple SQL statements to update and delete entities. It also requires SQL statements to use multiway joins. For example, when the application creates a FreeShippingCoupon, it must insert a row into the COUPON and FREE_SHIPPING_COUPON tables; when it loads a Coupon, it must either use a SQL SELECT statement that does a join with all three tables or execute multiple SELECT statements.

Table per concrete class

The third and final option is to define a table for each concrete class, that is, each class that is not an abstract class or an interface. In the Coupon hierarchy example, we define the tables for the PercentageDiscountCoupon and FreeShippingCoupon classes:

```
CREATE TABLE PERCENT_DISCOUNT_COUPON (
  COUPON_ID NUMBER(10) NOT NULL,
  CODE VARCHAR2(30) NOT NULL,
  MINIMUM NUMBER(10,2) NOT NULL,
  DISCOUNT_PERCENTAGE NUMBER(5,2),
  CONSTRAINT COUPON_PK
    PRIMARY KEY(COUPON_ID),
)

CREATE TABLE FREE_SHIPPING_COUPON (
  COUPON_ID NUMBER(10) NOT NULL,
  CODE VARCHAR2(30) NOT NULL,
  MINIMUM NUMBER(10,2) NOT NULL,
  CONSTRAINT COUPON_PK
    PRIMARY KEY(COUPON_ID)
)
```

Each table has columns corresponding to fields for the class and its superclasses. This approach has the following benefits:

- Creating or saving instances only requires a single INSERT or UPDATE statement.
- There are no unused columns, and the application can define the correct constraints.

There are, however, numerous drawbacks:

- References to a superclass are difficult to map to the database schema. For example, in order to represent the PendingOrder-Coupon relationship, PENDING_ORDER would need foreign keys to the PERCENT_DISCOUNT _COUPON and FREE_SHIPPING_COUPON tables.

- Querying for an abstract superclass can be inefficient because the application must either execute a SQL SELECT statement for each table or use the SQL UNION operator, which is only supported by some databases and can be inefficient.

- Maintenance is more difficult since columns correspond to fields in superclasses are duplicated in each table. If you add a field to a superclass, you have to add a column to multiple tables.

My preference is to use the table-per-hierarchy approach whenever possible, and it is the approach used by the examples in this book. However, you should use the table-per-class approach if the table-per-hierarchy approach would result in too many unused or null columns.

Deciding how the domain model maps to the database schema is one part of solving the impedance mismatch between the object-oriented and relational worlds. You must also deal with object lifecycle and identity issues.

4.1.4 *Managing object lifecycles*

In addition to mapping a domain model to the database, you have to deal with the impact of persistence on an object's lifecycle. Let's first look at the lifecycle of a nonpersistent Java object. A Java object comes into existence when the application calls new or invokes a constructor via reflection. After creating an object, the application can then invoke its methods and access its fields. Because Java has a garbage collector, an application does not explicitly destroy an object. Instead, the application stops referencing the object, which is eventually destroyed by the garbage collector.

The creation and destruction of a persistent object needs to be handled differently because the database is involved. When a persistent object is created, the application must execute a SQL INSERT statement to insert a row. Similarly, in order to delete a persistent object the application must execute a SQL DELETE statement to remove the row from the database. As I describe in a moment, an ORM framework will often persist and delete persistent objects automatically. Sometimes, however, an application must persist and delete an object by calling an ORM framework API.

4.1.5 *Persistent object identity*

Persistence does not just affect an object's lifecycle. Another issue to consider when mapping a domain model to a database schema is dealing with the identity of persistent objects. A persistent object has both Java identity and database identity, which are two very different concepts. Java defines the == operator, which returns true if the two operands reference the same object. In the database, the identity of a row is its primary key, which is a column or set of columns that uniquely identifies a row in table. Two objects in a relational database are the same if they map to the same row in the same table.

The differences between Java identity and database identity impact the application in a number of ways. Usually, an application must assign a primary key to a persistent object. The primary key can sometimes be a natural key, which is a value that has a business meaning, such as a social security number. However, because even a social security number can change, it is almost always better to use a surrogate key, which is a unique value generated by the application or database. The application typically stores the primary key in the object for easy access. This, of course, requires each persistent class to define a field to store it.

Also, when processing a request the application must ensure there is only a single in-memory instance of a persistent object in order to guarantee that the database identity matches the Java identity. Otherwise, if there were two copies of the same persistent object in memory the application would behave incorrectly. Correctly managing the identity of persistent objects is tricky, and as you will see in the next section, one of the main benefits of using an ORM framework is that it is handled automatically.

4.2 Overview of ORM frameworks

Now that you seen the different ways of mapping a domain model to a database schema, let's tackle the problem of getting objects in and out of the database. Each request handled by the application results in one or more calls to the business tier, which accesses, instantiates, updates, and deletes domain objects. Because these objects are persistent, the application must execute SELECT statements to load them from the database and execute INSERT, UPDATE, and DELETE statements to update the database to reflect the changes made to them.

If the domain model is extremely simple and used in a very straightforward way, you might be able to persist it yourself using JDBC or iBATIS. For example, writing the code to load and save an individual domain object using either of these technologies is not difficult. But imagine how much database access code you would have to write to persist a large domain model. It could be overwhelming. It would be like trying to demolish an iceberg with an ice pick. In addition, the database access code has to solve some challenging problems. Let's examine those challenges and see why you don't want to solve them yourself.

4.2.1 *Why you don't want to persist objects yourself*

There are three main challenges when trying to persist objects. One is enabling the application to navigate relationships between domain objects while minimizing the number of objects loaded from the database. When an object is loaded, the database access code does not know which related objects will be later accessed by the application. Loading all of the objects that might be accessed is extremely inefficient because an object graph (which is the set of objects that are accessible from the root object) can be quite large. The database access code must instead implement a mechanism called lazy loading that loads objects on demand, when they are first accessed.

The second major challenge is writing back to the database only those objects that have been modified. An application might load a large number of objects and yet only modify a few of them. It would be extremely inefficient to save all objects regardless of whether they have changed. It would also be unreasonable and error-prone for the application to remember the modified objects. The database access code must keep track of which objects need to written back to the database.

Also, as I mentioned earlier, the database access code must preserve object identity by ensuring that there is a single in-memory instance of a persistent object when processing a request. It must keep track of every object that is loaded by maintain a map between primary keys and objects—the so-called *Identity Map* pattern [Fowler 2002]. The database access code must look in the map before loading an object from the database. This is certainly not difficult to do, but it adds additional complexity to the database access code.

As you can envisage, database access code that implements features such as lazy loading and change tracking can become extremely complex. Most applications must use an ORM framework, which handles these and a myriad of other issues.

4.2.2 *The key features of an ORM framework*

An ORM framework solves the difficult problem of storing objects in a relational database. You tell the framework how your domain model maps to the database schema, and it takes care of getting your objects in and out of the database. This enables you to focus on solving your business problems rather than writing lots of low-level database access code.

The key features of an ORM framework are as follows:

- *Declarative mapping between the object model and database schema*—Describes how the object model's classes, attributes and relationships are mapped to database table and columns and used by the ORM framework to generate SQL statements

- *An API for creating, reading, updating, and deleting objects*—Called by the domain model's repositories to manipulate persistent data

- *A query language*—Used to efficiently find persistent objects that satisfy search criteria

- *Support for transactions*—Maintains data integrity and handles concurrent updates

- *Lazy and eager loading*—Optimizes performance by controlling when objects are loaded

- *Caching*—Improves performance by minimizing database accesses

- *Detached objects*—Enables persistent objects to be passed between the presentation tier and the business tier

Before looking at these features in detail, let's first see how an ORM framework fits in with the rest of the application. Figure 4.3 shows that the framework is invoked by the POJO façade and the repositories.

The POJO façade calls the ORM framework to manage transactions and detach and attach objects. The repositories call it to create, find, and delete persistent objects such as `PendingOrder` and `Restaurant`. The framework accesses the database using SQL statements generated from the declarative mapping information. Let's now look at each of main features of an ORM framework.

Declarative mapping between the object model and schema

An ORM framework lets you specify how your domain model maps to your database schema using the mapping options described earlier in section 4.1. You typically define the mapping using XML, although some O/R frameworks also allow you to use Java 5 annotations. The mapping document or annotations specify how classes map to tables, how fields or JavaBean properties map to columns, and how relationships map to foreign keys or join tables. The ORM framework uses this mapping information to generate the SQL statements that load, save, update, and delete persistent objects.

The ORM framework provides transparent persistence. The persistent classes are rarely aware that they are persistent. Quite often you only need to add a field that stores the persistent identity. They do not have to implement any special

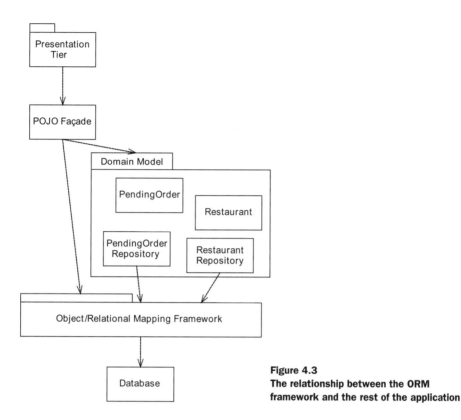

Figure 4.3
The relationship between the ORM
framework and the rest of the application

interfaces or call any ORM framework APIs. Later you will see that the repositories are the only domain model classes that call the ORM framework API to create, find, and delete persistent objects.

An API for creating, loading, and deleting objects

In addition to providing a declarative mapping mechanism, an ORM framework provides an API for creating, loading, and deleting persistent objects. These APIs are invoked by the domain model repositories, as shown in figure 4.3. A repository instantiates a persistent object using new and calls an ORM framework API method to save it in the database. It loads an object by calling an ORM framework API method, with a class and object ID as arguments. If the object is not already loaded, the framework queries the database and loads the object. The framework will also lazily load an object when the application navigates to it. An application deletes a persistent object by calling the ORM framework API, which deletes it from the database.

The application does not explicitly call an API method to save an updated object. Instead, the ORM framework tracks which objects have been changed by the application and automatically updates the database. Moreover, some ORM frameworks automatically save or delete an object without the application calling an API method. They automatically save a nonpersistent object in the database if it is referenced by another persistent object. An application only needs to save top-level "root" objects that are not referenced by any other persistent objects. Similarly, some ORM frameworks can be configured to automatically delete a child object when its parent is deleted or when it is no longer referenced by its parent.

Query language

In addition to loading objects individually, an application often needs to execute queries that find all matching objects. To do this, it uses the ORM framework's query language. A query is expressed in terms of objects, their attributes, and relationships. The query language supports sorting and aggregate functions such as `sum()`, `min()`, and `max()`. When called by a repository to execute a query, the ORM framework translates the query into a SQL `SELECT` statement that retrieves the objects. Some ORM frameworks also allow the application to retrieve objects using a SQL query, which is useful when it needs to use database-specific SQL features.

Support for transactions

An application must usually update a database using transactions in order to preserve data integrity. Transactions (which are described in more detail in chapter 12) ensure, among other things, that if the application fails partway through updating the database the already made changes will be undone. An ORM framework supports transactions in a couple of ways. It is integrated with the JTA, which enables it to be used by applications that update multiple resources, such as a database and JMS, at the same time. An ORM framework also has an API for managing transactions directly. The API provides methods for beginning, committing, and rolling back a transaction. An application can use this transaction management API instead of JTA if it accesses a single database using the ORM framework.

Lazy and eager loading

As we will see in later chapters, the business tier typically handles a request by first calling the ORM framework to explicitly load one or more "root" objects and then navigating to other objects by traversing relationships starting from the root objects. For instance, the example application loads a `PendingOrder` and then navigates to its line item and its restaurant. An important way to improve performance is to optimize the loading of objects by using the right balance of lazy and eager loading.

Lazy loading occurs when the ORM framework loads objects on-demand, when they are first accessed by the application. It is a key technique for improving performance since it limits the amount of data that will be loaded. The opposite of lazy loading is *eager* loading, which consists of loading multiple related objects with a single SELECT statement instead of using multiple SELECT statements.

One way the ORM framework could allow an application to traverse relationships starting from a root object would be to load all accessible objects up front. In the case of a pending order, the framework could also load the pending order's line items, its restaurant, and its menu items just in case the application navigates to those objects. However, this can be inefficient because an application typically only needs a few of what could be a large number of objects. To avoid this overhead, the ORM framework loads objects lazily, when they are first accessed by the application.

To understand the importance of lazy loading, consider the following. I once ported an application from EJB 2.0 entity beans, which use lazy loading, to Hibernate 2.0, which uses eager loading by default. The performance of the application dropped from N transactions per second to $1/N$ transactions per second because of the excessive eager loading done by Hibernate. Once I configured all of the classes to be lazily loaded, the throughput went back to N transactions per second.

Even though lazy loading is essential, eagerly loading related objects that will be navigated to can often improve performance. For example, if the application needs a pending order, its line items, and its restaurant, then it can load all of those objects with a single SELECT statement. Because those objects are accessed by the application, this approach is a lot more efficient than lazily loading one object at a time.

The SQL statement that retrieves rows from multiple tables can use either an inner (regular) join or an outer join. An outer join is useful because, unlike a regular join, it will return rows even if one or more of the tables contain no matching rows. For example, a SQL statement that uses an outer join will still return the rows from the PENDING_ORDER table even if a pending order has a null foreign key to a restaurant or has no line items. In comparison, a regular join will not return any rows.

The challenge, however, with using eager loading is that different requests often access different parts of the object graph. For example, one request might use the pending order and its restaurant, and another might use the pending order and its line items. It can be tricky to ensure that only the required objects are eagerly loaded by each request. In chapters 5 and 6, I explain how you can configure JDO and Hibernate to do this.

Object caching

Earlier I described how an ORM framework must maintain a map of primary keys and objects to ensure that only one copy of an object is loaded. The map acts also as a cache and improves performance by eliminating database accesses. When loading an object, the persistence framework can check the cache before accessing the database. By default, an ORM framework caches objects for either the duration of a request or the duration of a transaction. It can also be configured to cache objects for longer, which can sometimes improve performance considerably. For example, the application can keep read-only objects in a process-level cache and so rarely have to go to the database. An application can also cache data that is updated, but this can be tricky if the application is running on a cluster or the database is updated by another application.

Detached objects

One of the most tedious parts of developing a classic J2EE application is writing the DTOs, which contain a copy of the data stored in the entity beans that implement the domain objects and are returned to the presentation tier. Fortunately, we no longer need to copy data into DTOs because one of the exciting features of modern ORM frameworks is what are called detached objects.

A *detached object* is one that is no longer persistent but that contains data from the database and keeps track of its persistent identity. The business tier (usually the POJO façade) can return a detached object to its client instead of creating a DTO, which means that you need to write a lot less code.

What's more, detached objects make it easier to write edit-style use cases, which are use cases that allow the user to edit data from the database. The presentation tier can update one or more detached objects to reflect a user's changes. Then when the user saves the changes, the presentation tier passes the modified detached objects back to the business tier. The business tier (usually the POJO façade) reattaches them by calling the ORM framework, which updates the database. See chapter 13 for an example of such a use case.

4.2.3 Benefits and drawbacks of using an ORM framework

Using an ORM framework has several benefits and drawbacks. Let's look at each one.

Improved productivity

One important benefit of using an ORM framework is improved productivity. You have significantly less code to write. The framework takes care of generating and executing the SQL statements, which means you can focus on developing the business logic. In addition, development, testing, and maintenance are easier because the business logic is decoupled from the database.

Improved performance

Using an ORM framework also improves performance. The framework caches objects, which reduces the number of database accesses. In addition, features such as eager loading mean that the persistence framework can generate SQL statements that are often much more efficient than those hand-written by developers. Furthermore, unlike a developer, an ORM framework can do this consistently.

Improved portability

In addition to increasing productivity and performance, an ORM framework increases portability across databases. The framework takes care of generating the database-specific SQL statements, and migrating from one database to another is usually as simple as setting a configuration parameter. In comparison, writing portable SQL by hand is extremely difficult.

Sometimes you must use SQL directly

Despite the benefits of an ORM framework, using SQL directly is sometimes the only way to get good performance. You can use database-specific features such as optimizer hints or Oracle's CONNECT feature to improve the performance of queries. In addition, SQL lets you insert, delete, or update a large number of rows with a single SQL statement. For example, an INSERT statement such as the following inserts the results of querying one table into another table:

```
INSERT INTO DESTINATION_TABLE
    SELECT …
    FROM SOURCE_TABLE
    WHERE …
```

In comparison, an ORM framework would typically have to perform the following steps:

1 Execute a query, which returns a set of objects that are mapped to SOURCE_TABLE.

2 Create objects that are mapped to DESTINATION_TABLE.

3 Save those objects.

This would be very inefficient if the query returned a large number of rows. As well as transferring the data from the database to the application and back again, there is also the overhead of manipulating the Java objects.

You might still have to use SQL even if there are no significant performance benefits. Consider the policies laid down by your DBA. He might require you to maintain your application's SQL statements in separate files so that he can tune them. Or, your DBA might require your application to access the database using stored procedures. Consequently, you cannot let the ORM framework generate SQL for you.

Some ORM frameworks provide support for executing SQL statements directly. Hibernate and JDO allow you to write native SQL queries. In addition, Hibernate lets you specify the SQL statements to use for creating, updating, and deleting individual objects. Hibernate and some JDO implementations provide some support for stored procedures. Hibernate also supports certain kinds of bulk updates and deletes. But, even though these features are extremely useful, sometimes you must execute SQL statements using either JDBC or iBATIS.

ORM limitations

ORM frameworks are not all-powerful. They have limitations that can prevent you from mapping your domain model to a database schema in exactly the way you want it to be done. This can be particularly challenging when you're working with a legacy schema. For example, a common performance optimization is to eliminate joins by denormalizing the schema and storing the first N items of a one-to-many relationship in the parent table. In this kind of situation, you typically have to mirror the database structure in the domain model, which makes the code more complicated.

You might also design a domain model that cannot be mapped to the desired database schema. If this happens, you must change either the domain model or the database schema. For example, I once worked on an application that had a class hierarchy of embedded objects that I wanted to map to the parent object's table. The ORM framework did not support this mapping, and so I had to map the class hierarchy to its own table. In this instance, this limitation was only a minor issue because I had control over the database schema. But if the database schema had been fixed, I would have needed to change the domain model.

Despite their limitations, ORM frameworks are an extremely useful technology in many applications. They significantly increase productivity of developers by reducing the amount of database access code that must be rewritten. Moreover, they often increase the performance and portability of an application.

4.3 *Overview of JDO and Hibernate*

Now that we have looked at the key features of an ORM framework, let's examine Hibernate and JDO, which are two popular ORM frameworks that provide a rich set of features. Hibernate is a widely used open source project. Hibernate 1.0 was released in 2002, and as of this writing, Hibernate 3.1 is in beta. JDO is a standard (JSR-012 and JSR-243) that has both commercial and open source implementations. The JDO 1.0 specification was also released in 2002, and as of this writing, the JDO 2.0 specification is nearing release.

In this section I review what Hibernate and JDO provide in terms of the seven ORM framework features I described in the previous section. Chapter 10 describes the O/R mapping capabilities in EJB 3.

4.3.1 *Declarative mapping between the object model and the schema*

JDO and Hibernate define the O/R mapping using XML documents. Historically, Hibernate provided a much richer set of O/R mapping features than most of the early JDO implementations. However, over time JDO implementations improved considerably. JDO 1.0 implementations developed a rich set of ORM extensions, and the newer JDO 2.0 standard incorporated many of those extensions and now provides a rich object/relational mapping. As a result, today Hibernate and JDO are fairly comparable in terms of the object/relational mapping features they provide.

One key difference between JDO and Hibernate is that JDO only supports mapping fields to the database schema whereas Hibernate supports mapping either fields or JavaBean-style properties. Usually, you only need to map fields, but occasionally it is useful to map JavaBean properties instead. For example, the getter can calculate the value that is stored in the database, and a setter can initialize nonpersistent fields.

JDO and Hibernate let you map your objects to an existing schema. Alternatively, Hibernate and many JDO implementations can generate the database schema from the O/R mapping. This is extremely useful because it eliminates the need to maintain the data definition language (DDL) files that define the database schema. It also increases the portability of the application because Hibernate and JDO will generate the database-specific DDL. Later I describe how this can be useful when testing with an in-memory database. However, even though this feature is extremely convenient you cannot always use it. For example, you might have to use database-specific schema definition features that are not supported by the ORM framework. Also, the database schema is often owned and maintained by a separate group, such as the DBAs.

4.3.2 API for creating, reading, updating, and deleting objects

The Hibernate and JDO APIs are quite similar and consist of interfaces that play the following roles:

- A connection factory interface for creating connections
- A connection interface, which represents a connection to the database and provides methods for creating, loading, and deleting persistent objects
- A query interface for executing queries
- A transaction interface for managing transactions

Table 4.1 shows the interfaces provided by Hibernate and JDO that play these roles.

Table 4.1 The key JDO and Hibernate interfaces

Role	JDO	Hibernate
Connection factory	PersistenceManagerFactory	SessionFactory
Connection	PersistenceManager	Session
Query	Query	Query
Transaction	Transaction	Transaction

The repositories in the example application call the connection and query interfaces to create, find, and delete persistence objects. The POJO façade calls the connection factory to create a connection, the transaction interface to manage transactions, and the connection interface to detach and attach objects.

In chapters 5 and 6 we will see that the business tier typically uses a single connection while handling a request from the presentation tier. It creates a connection at the start of each request and closes the connection at the end of handling the request. A Hibernate application creates a `Session` by calling `SessionFactory.openSession()`, and a JDO application creates a `PersistenceManager` by calling `PersistenceManagerFactory.makePersistenceManager()`. The application can then use `Session` or `PersistenceManager` to create, load, or delete objects; create a query; and access the transaction interface.

Table 4.2 shows the key methods defined by the `Session` and `PersistenceManager` interfaces.

Table 4.2   Examples of JDO `PersistenceManager` and Hibernate `Session` methods

	Hibernate `Session`	**JDO `PersistenceManager`**
Making an object persistent	save()	makePersistent()
Loading an object	load()	getObjectById()
Deleting an object	delete()	deletePersistent()
Creating a query	createQuery() createNamedQuery()	newQuery() newNamedQuery()
Accessing the transaction object	beginTransaction()	currentTransaction()
Closing the connection	close()	close()

As you can see, `Session` and `PersistenceManager` define methods with very similar purposes. For example, the `save()` and `makePersistent()` methods persist an object, and the `load()` and `getObjectById()` methods load the specified instance. There are also methods for creating queries, accessing the transaction object, and closing the connection.

4.3.3   *Query language*

Hibernate and JDO provide several options for executing queries. An application can use either *object queries*, which are queries expressed in terms of objects, or *SQL native queries*, which are written in SQL. JDO and Hibernate provide a textual query language for writing object queries. In addition, Hibernate has what are called *criteria queries*, which are nontextual queries.

Object queries

Object queries are the easiest to use because they take full advantage of the ORM framework. JDO and Hibernate each have a textual query language for object queries. JDO object queries are written in JDO Query Language (JDOQL), whose syntax is based on Java expressions; Hibernate provides Hibernate Query Language (HQL), whose syntax is similar to SQL. JDOQL and HQL queries usually return persistent objects, but you can also write *projection queries*, which return DTOs and other values.

Native SQL queries

Although we mainly use object queries, native SQL queries are useful when you need to use database-specific features to get good performance. JDO and Hibernate provide an API for executing a SQL query and will construct a collection of objects from the result set. JDO native SQL queries can return either persistent objects or DTOs, whereas Hibernate SQL queries can return only persistent objects.

Executing JDOQL, HQL, and SQL queries

JDOQL, HQL, and SQL queries are executed using the `Query` interface. A JDO application creates a query by calling a `PersistenceManager` method, and a Hibernate application creates a query by calling a `Session` method. The method that creates the query takes as a parameter either the query string or the name of the query that is defined in the ORM document. The application can then call various setters to define various aspects of the query. A JDO application executes the query by calling `Query.execute()`, which returns a list of persistent objects or values. A Hibernate application executes a query by calling either `Query.list()`, which returns a list, or `Query.scroll()`, which returns a `ScrollableResults` that allows the application to navigate through the underlying JDBC `ResultSet`.

Hibernate criteria queries

In addition to HQL and SQL queries, Hibernate has criteria queries, which are object queries that are defined using objects rather than a textual query language. Later in chapter 11 you will see how Hibernate criteria queries are extremely useful when constructing queries dynamically since they avoid the need to write messy code that concatenates query fragment strings.

4.3.4 Support for transactions

The fourth of the seven ORM framework features is transaction management. Hibernate and JDO provide a `Transaction` interface, which allows an application to explicitly manage transactions. A JDO application obtains a `Transaction` object by calling `PersistenceManager.currentTransaction()`. The application begins a transaction by calling `Transaction.begin()`, commits a transaction by calling `Transaction.commit()`, and roll backs a transaction by calling `Transaction.rollback()`. Similarly, a Hibernate application accesses a `Transaction` object by calling `Session.beginTransaction()`, which begins a transaction. The application can commit a transaction by calling `Transaction.commit()` or roll back a transaction by calling `Transaction.rollback()`. Later in chapter 7, you will see how the

Spring framework provides AOP interceptors that call the transaction management APIs on behalf of the application.

In addition, JDO and Hibernate provide JTA integration. A Hibernate `Session` or JDO `PersistenceManager` that is opened within a JTA transaction will automatically participate in the transaction.

4.3.5 *Lazy and eager loading*

By default, JDO and Hibernate load objects lazily, but you can configure them to load objects eagerly. The details differ by framework but they provide roughly equivalent functionality.

Configuring eager loading in JDO

You configure eager loading in JDO by using fetch groups. A JDO fetch group specifies a graph of interconnected objects and is defined in the XML mapping document. When an application loads an object or executes a query, it can identify the objects to eagerly load by specifying one or more active fetch groups.

You can use fetch groups to configure eager loading in one of two ways:

- Statically configure a relationship to be always loaded.
- Activate particular fetch groups at runtime to dynamic control which relationships to eagerly load.

For more information on JDO fetch groups, see chapter 5.

Configuring eager loading in Hibernate

Hibernate provides two ways to configure eager loading. You can specify in the O/R mapping which relationships should be eagerly loaded. This approach is useful when a relationship is always traversed by the application. Alternatively, you can use a Hibernate query with what is termed a *fetch join* to specify which objects should be eagerly loaded by a query. By using different queries at runtime, you can dynamically control which objects are eagerly loaded when handling a request. See chapter 6 for more information about Hibernate and eager loading.

4.3.6 *Object caching*

Hibernate and JDO cache objects, albeit with some minor differences. By default, Hibernate caches objects in the `Session` for the lifetime of the session, which can span multiple transactions, and JDO caches objects in the `PersistenceManager` for the duration of a transaction. However, this difference is not usually that important because a Hibernate application typically uses a single `Session` and transaction per request and a JDO application uses a single `PersistenceManager` and transaction per request.

In addition to caching objects in the Hibernate `Session` or the JDO `PersistenceManager`, most implementations support process-level caching, which can often significantly improve the performance of an application. Some implementations also provide a query cache, which sometimes increases performance. Let's see how those mechanisms work.

Process-level caching

Applications often access the same set of objects repeatedly, and so you can improve performance by caching those objects across transactional boundaries. Hibernate and some JDO implementations can be configured to cache objects for longer than a single request or transaction in a process-level cache. The ORM framework looks in the process-level cache for an object after looking in the `Session` or `PersistenceManager`-level cache. If the object is in the process-level cache, the ORM framework does not need to access the database, which often improves the performance of the application significantly.

It is important to turn off eager loading for any cached objects since that bypasses the cache and fetches them from the database. For example, if a restaurant was eagerly loaded with its referencing pending order, the persistence framework would never look in the process-level cache for the restaurant. Using lazy loading ensures that the persistence framework will look in the process-level cache.

There are some important issues to consider when using a process-level cache, such as what objects to cache and how to handle updates to cached objects. The process-level cache is typically highly configurable. You can usually control which classes are stored in the cache, how many objects should be cached, and for how long. It is best suited to storing frequently accessed but rarely modified objects. For example, in the Food to Go application, restaurants, menu items, and other restaurant-related objects are frequently accessed but rarely change; thus, it makes sense to cache those objects in the process-level cache to avoid loading them repeatedly from the database.

One challenge with using a process-level cache is handling updates to cached objects. This isn't an issue if a single-server application updates the database using the persistence framework since the framework updates the process-level cache. There are, however, a couple of ways in which the objects in the cache can become out of date. First, in a clustered application one cluster member can update objects that are stored in another cluster member's cache. Second, the database can be updated without using the persistence framework by either a module written in JDBC or by a different application. In most applications you need to arrange for the process-level cache to load the changed objects from the database in order to prevent the application from working with old data.

There are three ways to do this:

- *Periodically invalidate cached objects*—If the application can tolerate slightly stale data, then you can configure the process-level cache to periodically invalidate cached objects and force the latest copies to be loaded from the database.

- *Broadcast change notifications*—If the application is clustered, then you can configure the persistence framework running in each application that makes up the cluster to broadcast change notifications so that other cluster members know to invalidate cached copies of the changed objects.

- *Programmatically invalidate cached objects*—If the application has bypassed the persistence framework and updated the database using some other mechanism such as JDBC, you can programmatically invalidate cached objects and force them to be reloaded. This approach can only be used by applications that are aware of the process-level cache.

Cached objects that are updateable should typically use optimistic locking (see chapter 12) because that will prevent the application from blindly overwriting changes in the database. If a transaction updates a cached object that had already been changed in the database, the optimistic locking failure will cause the transaction to be rolled back. The persistence framework will remove the stale data from the cache, and the application can retry transaction with the latest version of the data.

Despite the complication of handling updated objects, a process-level cache is an extremely useful way to improve the performance of an application that uses a persistence framework.

Query caching

Hibernate and some JDO implementations also provide a query cache, which stores the primary keys of the objects found by a query. When it executes a query, the ORM framework looks in the query cache for the result before accessing the database. If the query cache contains the results of the query, the framework then looks up the objects in the process-level cache. A query cache can sometimes improve performance but is only useful for read-only data because the ORM framework flushes all cached queries that involve a modified table.

4.3.7 *Detached objects*

The last of the seven ORM framework features is detached objects. Hibernate objects are automatically detached when their Session is closed. The application simply has to ensure that the objects that it needs are loaded before the Session is closed. It can either eagerly load or navigate to the objects that it needs. Although this sounds simple, as you will see in chapter 7 this can sometimes require extra code in the façade, which encapsulates the business logic, to traverse the object graph and force objects to be loaded. The application can reattach those objects to a new Session and Hibernate will update the database with the changes.

Detached objects are a new feature in JDO 2.0. There are three ways to detach objects in JDO 2.0. One option is to configure the PersistenceManager to behave the same way as a Hibernate Session and to automatically detach objects when it is closed. Another option is to serialize the JDO objects. The third option is to explicitly detach objects by invoking the PersistenceManager. This option gives the application the most control over which objects are detached because the objects to detach are specified using a fetch group. The PersistenceManager returns nonpersistent, detached copies of the specified objects. An application can later reattach those objects to a different PersistenceManager. The JDO implementation will update the database with the changes.

4.3.8 *Hibernate vs. JDO*

As you can see, at a high level JDO and Hibernate provide an equivalent set of features. Hibernate and the various JDO implementations are constantly improving, so no single product has the lead for very long. Many of the controversial differences are mostly inconsequential. Also, benchmarks such as TORPEDO [TORPEDO] show that the performance is similar. So how do you choose between them?

Some important nontechnical issues differentiate JDO and Hibernate. From the outset Hibernate has been an open source project, which has contributed greatly to its incredible popularity. Budget-constrained organizations and other open source projects have been able to download and use it. In comparison, JDO is a standard with multiple implementations. Until recently the main JDO implementations were commercial implementations, whose licensing fees discouraged some organizations from using JDO. However, today there are open source JDO implementations such as JPOX [JPOX]. In addition, some organizations want to avoid being dependent on a product that is available from a single source and thus use a standards-based product that is available from multiple vendors.

Some technical issues differentiate JDO and Hibernate. For example, JDO implementations support other data sources, including Lightweight Directory Access Protocol (LDAP) and object databases. Throughout the rest of the book you will see several subtle yet important issues that differentiate JDO and Hibernate.

It is also worth remembering that JDO and Hibernate are nonintrusive technologies; the persistent classes have no dependencies on JDO or Hibernate APIs. Consequently, switching to a different ORM framework can be straightforward because the only classes that need to be rewritten are the repositories.

4.4 Designing repositories with Spring

Now that you have gotten an overview of Hibernate and JDO, let's look at how to design the repositories, which provide methods for creating, finding, and deleting persistent objects. They are the only part of the domain model that call Hibernate or JDO to do this. The persistent classes are unaware that they are persistent since JDO and Hibernate provide transparent persistence. Because of the similarity of the JDO and Hibernate APIs, we can use the same approach to implement the JDO and Hibernate repositories. In this section, you will learn how to use Spring to simplify the implementation of the repository and how to design the repositories in a way that makes them easier to test.

4.4.1 Implementing JDO and Hibernate repositories

A *repository* consists of an interface, which specifies the public methods, and an implementation class, which calls the persistence framework. Because the persistence framework-specific classes are encapsulated behind interfaces, the rest of the domain model classes are decoupled from both the persistence framework and the database. This is an excellent example of using interfaces to create more decoupled applications, where implementation details "plug into" the interfaces that define the behavior. Furthermore, as we saw in chapter 3, it enables the domain model classes to be tested using mock repositories.

A repository implementation class calls the Connection or the Query interface to manipulate persistent data. The repository uses the Connection interface to create, load, and delete persistent objects. It uses the Query interface to execute queries that load multiple objects. However, as you will see in this section, rather than calling the persistence framework APIs directly the repository implementation classes use the Spring framework's ORM support classes.

4.4.2 Using the Spring ORM classes

In chapter 1, I explained that one of the key benefits of using Spring is that it makes implementing Hibernate and JDO applications considerably easier. One reason why it simplifies application development is because, as you will see in chapters 7 and 8, it provides AOP interceptors and filters for opening and closing JDO and Hibernate connections and managing transactions. Another reason why Spring makes development easier is it provides the `JdoTemplate` and `Hibernate-Template` classes, which are easy-to-use wrappers around the JDO and Hibernate APIs. These ORM template classes implement the boilerplate code that's required when using a persistence framework and significantly simplify the implementation of repositories. In order to see the benefit of using Spring's ORM template classes, let's first look an example of a repository that does not use them.

Using Hibernate without a Spring HibernateTemplate

Listing 4.1 shows an example Hibernate repository method, which loads an object by calling `Session.load()`. It uses `SessionFactoryUtils`, which is a Spring framework helper class that defines various static methods for managing Hibernate `Ses-sions` and mapping exceptions. The repository method calls `SessionFactory-Utils.getSession()` to get a `Session` and `SessionFactoryUtils.releaseSession()` to release the `Session`. The method uses a `try/catch/finally` to map the `Hibernate-Exception` to a Spring data access exception and to ensure that `release-Session()` is always called.

> **Listing 4.1   HibernatePendingOrderRepositoryImpl**

```
public class HibernatePendingOrderRepositoryImpl
    implements PendingOrderRepository {
  private SessionFactory sessionFactory;

  public HibernatePendingOrderRepositoryImpl(
      SessionFactory sessionFactory) {
    this.sessionFactory = sessionFactory;
  }

  public PendingOrder findOrCreatePendingOrder(String pendingOrderId) {
    if (pendingOrderId != null)
      return findPendingOrder(pendingOrderId);
    else
      return createPendingOrder();
  }

  public PendingOrder findPendingOrder(String pendingOrderId) {
    Session session =
```

```
            SessionFactoryUtils.getSession(        ❶ Boilerplate
                    sessionFactory, true);            code
        try {

          return (PendingOrder)                     ❷ Code that loads
           session.load(PendingOrder.class,            the object
              new Integer(pendingOrderId));

        } catch (HibernateException e) {
          throw SessionFactoryUtils.
            ➥ convertHibernateAccessException(e);   ❸ More
        } finally {                                     boilerplate
          SessionFactoryUtils.releaseSession(session,
              sessionFactory);
        }
    }

    public PendingOrder createPendingOrder() {
      ...
    }
}
```

Let's take a closer look at this listing:

❶ The first piece of boilerplate code calls `SessionFactoryUtils.getSession()` to get a `Session` for the specified `SessionFactory`. This method will return the `Session` that has been opened and bound to the thread by a Spring AOP interceptor or filter. If there isn't an existing `Session`, the `true` argument tells `getSession()` to open a new `Session`. This feature enables the repository to work both inside the application and in a unit-testing environment.

❷ The `Session.load()` method loads the specified object.

❸ The second piece of boilerplate code consists of a `catch` clause and a `finally` clause. The `catch` clause calls `SessionFactoryUtils.convertHibernateAccessException()` to convert the Hibernate-specific `HibernateException` to a generic Spring data access exception. A Spring data access exception is an unchecked exception that enables the higher levels of the application to treat all data access exceptions uniformly. The `finally` clause calls `SessionFactoryUtils.releaseSession()`, which closes the `Session` if it was opened by the call to `SessionFactoryUtils.getSession()`. The `releaseSession()` method does nothing if `getSession()` returned an already open `Session`.

As you can see, in addition to the single call to `Session.load()` there are several lines of boilerplate code to manage the `Session` and map the `HibernateException`.

This code is certainly simple, but it is potentially error-prone and can add significantly to the size of the application. In addition, the calls to static methods complicate testing. You cannot use mock objects, which enable the code to be tested independently of the database, and are extremely useful when the repository contains complex code.

Using the Spring template classes

Using Spring's ORM template classes can significantly simplify the implementation of a repository. They take care of obtaining and releasing a connection and map persistence framework-specific exceptions to Spring data access exceptions. The template classes also provide convenience methods that mirror the methods defined by the Connection and Query interfaces. As result, many repository methods become one-liners. For example, here is the HibernatePendingOrderRepositoryImpl we looked at earlier rewritten to use the HibernateTemplate class:

```
public class HibernatePendingOrderRepositoryImpl extends
    HibernateDaoSupport implements PendingOrderRepository {

  public HibernatePendingOrderRepositoryImpl(
      HibernateTemplate template) {
    setHibernateTemplate(template);
  }
  …
  public PendingOrder findPendingOrder(String pendingOrderId) {
    return (PendingOrder)getHibernateTemplate().
          load(PendingOrder.class,
                new Integer(pendingOrderId));
  }
  …
}
```

Here, HibernatePendingOrderRepositoryImpl implements the PendingOrderRepository interface and extends HibernateDaoSupport, which is a Spring support class that stores a HibernateTemplate and provides the setHibernateTemplate() and getHibernateTemplate() methods. HibernatePendingOrderRepositoryImpl defines a constructor that stores the template parameter by calling setHibernateTemplate(). The findPendingOrder() method gets the template by calling getHibernateTemplate(). This method calls HibernateTemplate.load(), which gets the Hibernate Session, calls Session.load(), and then closes the Session if required.

As you can see, findPendingOrder() is extremely simple because HibernateTemplate hides all of the calls to SessionFactoryUtils and eliminates the need to use a try/catch/finally. HibernateTemplate takes a SessionFactory as a constructor argument. `HibernateTemplate` is typically instantiated by Spring's bean factory and passed by dependency injection to the repositories that need it.

Using an ORM template class also facilitates testing. The repository methods that call a convenience method can be tested with a mock template object. A test case can construct a repository passing in a mock template object and verify that the expected method is called.

Despite these advantages, you cannot always use the convenience methods because they do not expose all of the functionality of the persistence framework's APIs.

4.4.3 *Making repositories easier to test*

A repository must call the persistence framework APIs directly if the ORM template does not expose the functionality that it needs. It could use the `SessionFactory-Utils` and `PersistenceManagerFactoryUtils` classes to obtain a connection, but code that uses those classes is more difficult to test because it can't be tested with mock objects. A better approach is to use an ORM template class to execute what Spring refers to as a callback.

The trouble with anonymous callback classes

A Spring callback object is an instance of a class that implements a callback interface. It has a method that is passed a persistence framework connection as a parameter, and it can manipulate persistent objects. The simplest way to execute a callback with an ORM template class is to use an anonymous class. For example, the `RestaurantRepository`'s `findRestaurants()` method could use the `JdoTemplate` to execute a callback that uses the `Query` interface directly:

```
public class JDORestaurantRepositoryImpl extends JdoDaoSupport
    implements RestaurantRepository {

  public List findRestaurants(final Address deliveryAddress,
      final Date deliveryTime) {
    JdoTemplate jdoTemplate = getJdoTemplate();
    return (List) jdoTemplate.executeFind(new JdoCallback() {
      public Object doInJdo(PersistenceManager pm) {
        Map parameters = makeParameters(deliveryAddress,
                        deliveryTime);
        Query query = pm.newQuery(Restaurant.class);
        query.declareVariables("TimeRange tr");

        ...

        return query.executeWithMap(parameters);
      }
    });
  }
```

```
    private Map makeParameters(Address deliveryAddress,
        Date deliveryTime) {
      Map params = new HashMap();
      params.put("zipCode", deliveryAddress.getZip());
      …
      return params;
    }
  }
```

In this example, `JdoTemplate.executeFind()` is passed a callback that is an instance of an anonymous class. The callback has a `doInJdo()` method, which takes a `PersistenceManager` as a parameter. It creates and executes a `Query` calling methods such as `declareVariables()` that are not supported by the `JdoTemplate`. Behind the scenes, the template class obtains a connection, invokes the callback, and then releases the connection. Using a template class to execute a callback is a lot easier than using a `SessionFactoryUtil` or `PersistenceManagerFactoryUtil` directly because you do not have to write `try/catch/finally` blocks.

However, the callback-based API with instances of anonymous classes also complicates testing. For example, because the `findRestaurants()` contains a fair amount of code, it makes sense to use some mock object tests rather than testing it directly against the database. A mock object test would want to verify that it invokes `JdoTemplate.executeFind()` correctly. Unfortunately, it would be difficult to define a mock object expectation that does this because `executeFind()` is passed an instance of anonymous class.

Using named callback classes

A better approach, which improves testability, is to use a named callback class that has an `equals()` method. The repository instantiates the callback class, passing the query's parameters to its constructor, and executes it using the template. The `equals()` method returns `true` if the two callback objects have the same parameters. This class enables a mock object expectation to verify that the template is invoked with the correct callback. The expectation uses the `equals()` methods to compare the actual and expected callbacks. `MyExampleCallback` is an example of such a callback. It implements the `JdoCallback` interface and defines an `equals()` method that returns `true` if the delivery information in the two objects is the same:

```
class MyExampleCallback implements JdoCallback {
  private final Address deliveryAddress;

  private final Date deliveryTime;
```

```
public MyExampleCallback(Address deliveryAddress,
    Date deliveryTime) {
  this.deliveryAddress = deliveryAddress;
  this.deliveryTime = deliveryTime;
}

public boolean equals(Object other) {
  if (other == null)
    return false;
  if (!(other instanceof MyExampleCallback))
    return false;
  MyExampleCallback x = (MyExampleCallback) other;
  return deliveryAddress.equals(x.deliveryAddress)
      && deliveryTime.equals(x.deliveryTime);
}


public Object doInJdo(PersistenceManager pm) {
  Map params = makeParameters(deliveryAddress,
      deliveryTime);
  Query query = pm.newQuery(Restaurant.class);
  query.declareVariables("…");
  query.declareImports("…");
  return query.executeWithMap(params);
}

private Map makeParameters(Address deliveryAddress,
  Date deliveryTime) {

  return…;
}
}
```

❶ Saves delivery information

❷ Tests for equality

❸ Executes the query

Let's take a closer look at `MyExampleCallback`:

❶ The constructor takes the delivery information as parameters and stores it in a field.

❷ The `equals()` method returns `true` if the delivery information is the same in both callbacks.

❸ The `doInJdo()` method executes the query.

And here is an example of a repository that uses it:

```
public class JDORestaurantRepositoryImpl extends JdoDaoSupport
    implements RestaurantRepository {

  public JDORestaurantRepositoryImpl(JdoTemplate jdoTemplate) {
    setJdoTemplate(jdoTemplate);
  }
```

```
    public List findRestaurants(Address deliveryAddress,
        Date deliveryTime) {
      JdoTemplate jdoTemplate = getJdoTemplate();
      return (List) jdoTemplate.executeFind(
            new MyExampleCallback(deliveryAddress,
                                  deliveryTime));
    }
  }
```

This version of the findRestaurants() method instantiates a MyExampleCallback, passing the delivery address and time as constructor parameters. It then executes the callback using JdoTemplate.

Because MyExampleCallback has an equals() method, it is easy to test find-Restaurants() with a mock JdoTemplate that expects to be called with a particular MyExampleCallback object:

```
  public void testFindRestaurants() {
      expectedMyExampleCallback = new MyExampleCallback(…)

    mockJdoTemplate.expects(once())
          .method("executeFind")
          .with(eq(expectedMyExampleCallback))
          .will(returnValue(expectedRestaurants));

    JdoTemplate jdoTemplate =
          (JdoTemplate)mockJdoTemplate.proxy();

    RestaurantRepository r =
          new JDORestaurantRepository(jdoTemplate);

    List restaurants = r.findRestaurants(…);
      …
  }
```

This test creates a MyExampleCallback containing the expected values. The mock JdoTemplate verifies that executeFind() is called with a MyExampleCallback that is equal to the expected one. In chapters 5 and 6 you will see more examples of repositories that have been implemented with this approach.

We have now seen an overview of the key ORM concepts and the capabilities of JDO and Hibernate. The next step is testing an application's persistence layer.

4.5 *Testing a persistent domain model*

Every six months, Anne-Marie, who is my dental hygienist, gives me the same lecture on the importance of flossing. And each time, I half-heartedly promise that I will make more of an effort—but I never keep that promise. Some developers treat testing in the same way I treat flossing: It's a good idea but they either do it with great reluctance or not at all.

Nevertheless, testing is a key part of the software development process, and just as flossing prevents dental decay, testing prevents software decay. The persistent layer, like most other application components, is not immune to decay and so requires testing. You need to write tests that verify that the domain model is mapped correctly to the database and that the queries used by the repositories work as expected. There are two main challenges when testing a persistent domain model. The first challenge is writing tests that detect the ORM-specific bugs. These bugs are often caused by inconsistencies between the domain model, the ORM document, and the database schema. For example, one common mistake is to forget to define the mapping for a newly added field, which can cause subtle bugs. Database constraints are another common problem that prevents the application from creating, updating, or deleting persistent objects. It's essential to have tests for the persistent domain model that catch these and other issues.

The second challenge is effectively testing the persistent domain model while minimizing the amount of time it takes for the tests to run. The test suite for the O/R mapping of a large domain model can take a long time to execute. Not only are there a large number of tests but also a test that accesses the database can take much longer to run than a simple object test. Although some database testing is unavoidable, it's important to find ways to do testing without it.

In this section you will learn about the different kinds of ORM bugs and how to write tests to detect them. I describe which aspects of the O/R mapping must be tested against the database and which other aspects can be tested without a database in order to minimize test execution time. You will see example tests that use the strategies described here in chapters 5 and 6.

4.5.1 *Object/relational testing strategies*

A variety of bugs can lurk in the O/R mapping, including the following:

- Missing mapping for a field
- References to nonexistent tables or columns
- Database constraints that prevent objects from being inserted, updated, or deleted
- Queries that are invalid or that return the wrong result
- Incorrect repository implementation

Many bugs are caused by the domain model, ORM documents, and the database schema getting out of sync. For example, it is easy to change the domain model by adding a new field or renaming an existing one and then forgetting to add or update the O/R mapping for that field, which specifies how it is stored in the database. Some ORM frameworks will generate an error message if the O/R mapping for a field is undefined, but others (including Hibernate) will silently allow a field to be nonpersistent, which can cause subtle and hard-to-find bugs. It is also quite easy to forget to update the database schema when defining the mapping for a field.

Some bugs are easily caught, such as those detected by the ORM framework at startup. For instance, Hibernate complains about missing fields, properties, or constructors when the application opens a `SessionFactory`. Other kinds of bugs require a particular code path to be executed. An incorrect mapping for a collection field can remain undetected, for example, until the application tries to access the collection. Similarly, bugs in queries are often not detected until they are executed. In order to catch these kinds of bugs, we must thoroughly test the application.

One way to test a persistence layer is to write tests that run against the database. For example, we can write tests that create and update persistent objects and call repository methods. Yet one problem with this kind of testing is that the tests take a while to execute even when using an in-memory database such as HSQLDB. Another problem is that they can fail to detect some bugs, such as a missing mapping for a field. And writing them can be a lot of work.

A more effective and faster approach is to use several kinds of tests that test each part of the persistence layer separately. Some kinds of tests run against the database and others run without the database. The tests that run against the database are:

- Test that create, update, and delete persistent objects
- Tests for the queries that are used for the repositories
- Tests that verify that the database schema matches the object/relational mapping

There are also tests that don't use the database:

- Mock object tests for the repositories
- Tests that verify the O/R mapping by testing the XML mapping documents

Next we'll look at these different kinds of tests, beginning with those that run against the database.

4.5.2 *Testing against the database*

Tests that run against the database are an essential part of testing the persistent domain model even though they take a relatively long time to execute. There are two kinds of database-level tests. The first kind verifies that persistent objects can be created, updated, and deleted. The second kind verifies the queries that are used by the repositories. Let's look at each approach.

Testing the persistent objects

One goal of testing the persistent domain model is to verify that persistent objects can be saved in the database. A simple approach is to write a test that creates a graph of objects and saves it in the database. The test doesn't attempt to verify that the database tables contain the correct values and instead fails only if an exception is thrown by the ORM framework. This kind of test is a relatively easy way to find basic ORM bugs, including missing mappings for a class and missing database columns. It also verifies that the database constraints allow new objects to be inserted into the database. However, even though this kind of test is a good way to start, it does not detect other common ORM bugs, such as constraint violations that occur when objects are updated, added, or deleted.

We can catch those types of bugs by writing more elaborate tests that update and delete persistent objects. As well as saving an object in the database, a test loads the object, updates it, and saves it back. A test can also delete the object. For example, a test for PendingOrder could consist of the following steps:

1　Create a PendingOrder and save it.

2　Load it, update the delivery information, and save it.

3　Load it, update the restaurant, and save it.

4　Load it, update the quantities, and save it.

5　Load it, update the quantities, and save it (again to test deleting line items).

6　Load it, update the payment information, and save it.

7　Delete the PendingOrder.

This testing approach verifies that the database can store all states of an object and detects problems with database constraints when creating or destroying associations between objects. Each step of the test consists of a database transaction that uses a new persistence framework connection to access the database. Using a new transaction and connection each time ensures that objects are really persisted in the database and loaded again. It also makes sure that deferred constraints, which are not checked until commit time, are satisfied. The downside of this approach is that it changes the database, which requires each test to initialize the database to a known state.

We could also enhance the tests to verify that an object's fields are mapped correctly by validating the contents of the database tables. After inserting the object graph into the database, the test verifies that the database contains the expected rows and column values. A test can verify the contents of the database by using to JDBC to retrieve the data. Alternatively, it could use DbUnit [DbUnit], which is a JUnit extension, to compare the database tables against an XML file that contains the expected values. However, although this approach is more thorough it is extremely tedious to develop and maintain these kinds of tests. In addition, the tests don't detect a missing mapping for a newly added field or property. Consequently, a much better way to test that classes and field/properties are mapped correctly is, as I describe later, to test the ORM document directly.

Tests that insert, update, and delete persistent objects are extremely useful, but they can be challenging to write. One reason is because some objects have lots of states that need to be tested. Another reason for the complexity is the amount of setup often required. Tests may have to create other persistent objects that are referenced by the object being tested. For example, in order to persist a `Pending-gOrder` and its line items, the test has to initialize the database with `Restaurant` and `MenuItems`. In addition, an object's public interface doesn't usually allow its fields to be set directly and so a test must call a sequence of business methods with the correct arguments, which can involve even more setup code. As a result, it can be challenging to write good persistence tests.

The other drawback with this approach is that executing the tests can be slow because of the number of times the database is accessed. Each persistent class can have multiple tests that each consists of multiple steps. Each step makes multiple calls to the ORM framework, which executes multiple SQL statements. Consequently, these tests usually take too long to be part of the unit tests suite and instead should be part of the functional tests.

Even though these persistent object tests can be difficult to write and can take a significant amount of time to execute, they are an important part of the test suite for a domain model. If necessary you can always start off by writing tests that just save objects in the database and over time add tests that update and delete objects.

Testing queries

We need to write database-level tests for some of the queries that are used by the repositories. One basic way to test the queries is to execute each query once and ignore the result. This quick and easy approach can catch lots of basic errors and is often all you need to do for simple queries.

For more complex queries, it is usually important to detect bugs in the logic of the query such as using < instead of <=. To catch these kinds of bugs, we need to write tests that populate the database with test data, execute the query, and verify that it returns the expected objects. Unfortunately, these kinds of tests are time consuming to both write and execute.

There are a couple of ways a test can execute a query. One option is to execute the query directly using the Spring and Hibernate APIs. The other option is to execute the query indirectly by invoking the repository. Which of these options is better depends on various factors, including the complexity of the repository. If the repository is fairly simple, then it can be easier to test the query by calling the repository because it is straightforward to execute the query with a particular set of arguments. If the repository is more complex, then testing the queries directly can be easier.

To be able to test a query independently of the repository that executes it, the query must be stored separately from the repository. The easiest way to accomplish this is to use named queries that are defined in the mapping document. Both Hibernate and JDO 2.0 let you define queries in the XML mapping document and provide an API for executing them by name. In addition to keeping the queries separate from the repositories, it is a lot more manageable to define multiline queries in an XML document than it is to do so in Java code by concatenating multiple strings. Alternatively, if you are using an ORM framework that doesn't support named queries, such as a JDO 1.x implementation, then you should store the queries in a properties file. Once you have done this, the queries can be tested separately.

Verifying that the schema matches the mapping

Unless the schema is generated from the O/R mapping, it is possible for the mapping and the schema to get out of sync. It is quite easy, for example, to forget to add a new column to a table after defining the mapping for a field. Consequently, we must write tests that verify that the database schema matches the O/R mapping.

One way to test the database schema is to extract the table and column names from the mapping document and use the JDBC metadata APIs to verify that every table and column exists in the database schema. This kind of test executes fairly quickly because it makes relatively few calls to the database. However, the one drawback is that you have to write a lot of code to implement this kind of test.

A much easier option that you can use some with ORM frameworks such as Hibernate is the ORM framework's schema generation feature. Some ORM frameworks provide an API to generate a SQL script that adds the missing tables and columns to the database schema. It is extremely easy to write a test that generates the script and fails if it contains SQL commands to add tables or columns.

Using an in-memory database

A great way to speed up database-level tests is to use an in-memory SQL database such as HSQLDB [HSQLDB]. An in-memory database runs in the application's JVM and is a lot faster than a regular database because there is no network traffic or disk access. Because the ORM framework insulates application code from many aspects of the database, some aspects of using an in-memory database are very straightforward. To configure the ORM framework to use the in-memory database, you typically have to specify the appropriate JDBC driver and other settings. Once you have done this, the ORM framework will automatically generate the correct SQL statements.

One challenge when using an in-memory database is ensuring that its schema is identical to the production database's schema. This isn't a problem if the ORM framework generates the database schema. However, if the production database schema is maintained separately, then its definition might not be compatible with the in-memory database. It could, for example, use vendor-specific data types and other features. In order to use an in-memory database, you will need to use a different schema definition or generate its schema from the ORM. In either case, there is no guarantee that the in-memory database has the same schema as the production database. As a result, an in-memory database is only useful for certain kinds of tests. You could, for example, use an in-memory database to test the queries.

Another issue with using an in-memory database is that although it is faster than a regular database, the tests can still be much slower than simple object tests. This is because calling the ORM framework and accessing the database simply involves a lot of overhead. In addition, initializing the database to the correct state at the start of a test and verifying its state at the end can make the tests more complicated. Consequently, in order to minimize test execution time and complexity it is important to test as much as possible without the database.

4.5.3 Testing without the database

Testing against the database is certainly important, but a lot of testing can be done without the database. We can verify that the O/R mapping correctly maps classes and fields to tables and columns without even opening a database connection. We can also test the repositories using mock objects. Let's take a closer look.

Verifying the mapping document

JDO and Hibernate define the O/R mapping using an XML document. We can write tests that verify that the mapping document correctly specifies the mapping from classes, fields, and relationships to tables, columns, and foreign keys. For example, it is quite easy to write a test that verifies that a class is mapped to a particular table and that all of its fields are mapped to columns of that table. This kind of test is extremely useful since it fails whenever you forget to map a newly defined field. With a little bit more effort we could also write a test that verifies that each field is mapped to the correct column.

One straightforward way to implement this kind of test is to use XmlUnit [XmlUnit], which is a JUnit extension for testing XML documents. A test for the ORM can use XmlUnit to make assertions about the contents of the document. For example, a test can verify that the PendingOrder class is mapped to the PENDING_ORDER table using the following code:

```
class PendingOrderMappingTests extends XMLTestCase {

  public void testMapping() throws Exception {
    Document mappingDocument = …;
    assertXpathEvaluatesTo("PENDING_ORDER",
        "hibernate-mapping/class[@name='PendingOrder']/@table",
        mappingDocument);
    …
  }
}
```

The test case extends XMLTestCase, which is provided by XmlUnit. It calls assertXpathEvaluatesTo(), which is an XmlUnit method that throws an exception if the specified XPath expression does not evaluate to the expected value. The XPath expression used by this particular test retrieves the value of the table attribute of a <class> element that is a child of <hibernate-mapping> and has a name attribute whose value is PendingOrder. The test could also call to assertXpathEvaluatesTo() to verify that each field is mapped to the correct column. It is also valuable to use reflection to get the names of all of the fields and verify that each field is mapped.

You can use XmlUnit to test the O/R mapping for a variety of ORM frameworks. The one drawback is that writing the XPath expressions can be tricky. A better option, which can be used with some ORM frameworks, is to get the O/R mapping metadata from the ORM framework. Some ORM frameworks provide an API, which returns Java objects that describe the mapping. An ORM test can then make assertions about the objects. This approach does not require detailed knowledge about the structure of the mapping document but does require the ORM framework to expose the necessary APIs. I describe how to write ORM tests in more detail in chapters 5 and 6.

Mock object testing of repositories

We could test a repository using database-level tests. For example, one way to test a repository method that executes a query is to populate data with test objects, call the method, and verify that it returns the expected objects. The problem with this approach is that it tests several things simultaneously: the repository, any queries that it executes, and the O/R mapping. The test needs a lot of setup and executes slowly. A better approach, which reduces the number of test cases and database accesses, is to test the repository using mock objects and to test the queries against the database separately.

Consider, for example, the `PendingOrder.createPendingOrder()` method, which creates a `PendingOrder` in the database. One way to test this method is to write a test that calls it and then verifies that it inserted a row into the PENDING_ORDER table. However, if you have written tests for the object/relational mapping, then you can safely assume that `HibernateTemplate.save()` or `JdoTemplate.makePersistent()` will work as expected. The repository test does not need to verify that a `PendingOrder` will be inserted into the PENDING_ORDER table when the repository calls `save()` or `makePersistent()`. We can therefore simplify and speed up the repository test by using a mock object for `HibernateTemplate` or `JdoTemplate` and verifying that the repository calls `save()` or `makePersistent()` as expected. We can use a similar approach to test other repository methods.

4.5.4 Overview of ORMUnit

In order to make it easier to write tests for the O/R mapping and persistent objects, I've written a simple JUnit extension called ORMUnit. It provides several base classes that extend `JUnitTestCase`:

- `HibernateMappingTests`: For testing a Hibernate object/relational mapping
- `JDOMappingTests`: For testing a JDO object/relational mapping
- `HibernatePersistenceTests`: For testing Hibernate objects and queries
- `JDOPersistenceTests`: For testing JDO objects and queries

`HibernateMappingTests` and `JDOMappingTests` simplify the task of testing the object/relational mapping. They provide methods for making assertions about the mapping and for verifying that it matches the database schema. For example, they make it easy to write a test that verifies that all of a class's fields are mapped to the database.

`JDOPersistenceTests` and `HibernatePersistenceTests` make it easier to write tests for persistent objects and queries. They take care of opening and closing the `PersistenceManager` and `Session`; create the `HibernateTemplate` and `JdoTemplate`; and provide methods for managing transactions. In chapters 5 and 6 you will see examples of tests that use these classes.

Automated testing is an important tool for ensuring that the application works correctly. It's something that we all need to do regularly (along with flossing). But when we are developing an application we also need to consider performance. Let's now look at how to optimize the performance of an application that uses JDO and Hibernate.

4.6 *Performance tuning JDO and Hibernate*

The database is often the bottleneck in an enterprise application, and to achieve good performance it's essential to tune the persistence layer and minimize the number of calls to the database. We saw in section 4.3 that JDO and Hibernate provide two main ways of improving performance. One way is to use eager loading and to load related objects using a single `SELECT` statement. The other way is to use process-level caching of objects and queries. An application can use both eager loading and a process-level caching, but as you will see later on in this section, using a process-level cache affects how you use eager loading.

I begin this section by describing the SQL statements that Hibernate or JDO application will use during the execution of an example use case without doing any performance tuning. You will then see how eager loading can be used to optimize performance. Finally, I describe how to use a process-level cache to optimize performance. This section doesn't get into the details of optimizing performance when using a particular framework. For that, please see chapter 5, which describes how to optimize performance with JDO, and chapter 6, which describes how to improve performance of a Hibernate application.

4.6.1 *Without any tuning*

Let's begin by considering what happens during the Place Order use case when the user enters the payment information. The application first calls `PlaceOrderService` to validate the payment information and update the pending order. It then displays the pending order, its restaurant, and its line items on the confirmation screen. By default, JDO and Hibernate will load all objects lazily, which means that the call to `PlaceOrderService` will load only the `PendingOrder`. The restaurant or the line items will not be loaded until the application navigates to them. As a result, the application executes several SQL SELECT statements:

```
select … from PENDING_ORDER po
        where po.PENDING_ORDER_ID=?
select … from RESTAURANT r
        where r.RESTAURANT_ID=?
select … from PENDING_ORDER_LINE_ITEM li
        where li.PENDING_ORDER_ID=?
select … from MENU_ITEM mi
        where mi.MENU_ITEM_ID=?
select … from MENU_ITEM mi
        where mi.MENU_ITEM_ID=?
…
```

The first SQL statement is executed when PlaceOrderService loads PendingOrder. The next two SQL statements are executed when the application navigates from PendingOrder to its restaurant and line items. The remaining SQL statements are executed as the application navigates from each line to its menu item. This might not seem like a lot of SQL statements, but imagine if the application is handling tens or hundreds of requests per second. Let's look at how eager loading can used to improve performance.

4.6.2   Configuring eager loading

There are two ways to use configure eager loading for a relationship. One option is to *statically* configure eager loading, which means that a related object will always be loaded with its referencing object. The other option is to *dynamically* configure eager loading and only load related objects when handling some requests. In order to know which relationships need to be eagerly loaded and to determine whether to do it statically or dynamically, we must identify the relationships that are traversed while handling each kind of request.

There are a few methods of determining which relationships are traversed when handling each request. One is to look at the code and see what relationships it traverses. Another is to run the application with logging enabled and examine the SQL statements that are executed. Alternatively, the persistence framework might have a tool that provides this information. Once you have done this analysis, you will know which relationships are always traversed and which relationships are only traversed by some requests.

As you can see in figure 4.4, if we analyze the Place Order use we will find that the application always traverses the PendingOrder-Restaurant and PendingOrder-Line-MenuItem relationships and only sometimes traverses other relationships such as Restaurant-MenuItem and PendingOrder-PendingOrderLineItem.

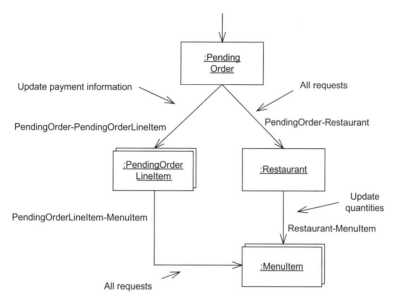

Figure 4.4   The relationships traversed by each request in the Place Order use case

The application only traverses the `Restaurant-MenuItem` relationship when handling the update quantities requests and only traverses `PendingOrder-PendingOrderLineItem` when handling some requests, such as updating payment information.

Once we have determined when each relationship is traversed, we can then configure eager loading for some of them. We can statically configure eager loading for those relationships that are always traversed and dynamically configure eager loading for the other relationships. However, we do not want to blindly use eager loading because that can sometimes reduce performance. For example, eagerly loading two one-to-many relationships will create a result set containing the Cartesian product of both relationships. If the result set is extremely large, then it is usually better to load one of the relationships lazily. It's important to use eager loading carefully and do a lot of performance testing.

Let's see how to configure eager loading for the Place Order use case.

Configuring eager loading statically
If we statically configure eager loading for the `PendingOrder-Restaurant` and `PendingOrderLineItem-MenuItem` relationships, then the persistence framework will always load the related objects. It will always load the pending order's restaurant with the

pending order and load a line item's menu item with the line item. This means, for example, that when the application handles a request to update the payment information, the persistence framework will execute the following SQL statements:

```
select …
from PENDING_ORDER po
      left outer join RESTAURANT r
          on po.RESTAURANT_ID=r.RESTAURANT_ID
where po.PENDING_ORDER_ID=?

select …
from PENDING_ORDER_LINE_ITEM li
     left outer join MENU_ITEM mi
          on li.MENU_ITEM_ID=mi.MENU_ITEM_ID
where li.PENDING_ORDER_ID=?
```

The first statement does a join between the PENDING_ORDER and RESTAURANT tables and the second does a join between the PENDING_ORDER_LINE_ITEM and MENU_ITEM tables. This is considerably more efficient than what we achieved with the default settings. By making only two small changes to the ORM document we were able to replace several SELECT statements with two SELECT statements. However, we can do even better by configuring eager loading dynamically.

Configuring eager loading dynamically

By dynamically configuring eager loading for each request, we can often get the persistence framework to load more objects with each SELECT statement. For example, with the update payment information request we can configure the persistence framework to eager load the PendingOrder-PendingOrderLineItem relationship in addition to the PendingOrder-Restaurant and PendingOrderLineItem-MenuItem relationships. The persistence framework will then execute a single SQL SELECT statement that does a join between the PENDING_ORDER, RESTAURANT, PENDING_ORDER_LINE_ITEM, and MENU_ITEM tables.

```
select *
from FTGO_PENDING_ORDER po
  left outer join FTGO_RESTAURANT r
    on po.RESTAURANT_ID=r.RESTAURANT_ID
  left outer join FTGO_PENDING_ORDER_LINE_ITEM li
    on po.PENDING_ORDER_ID=li.PENDING_ORDER_ID
  left outer join FTGO_MENU_ITEM mi
    on li.MENU_ITEM_ID=mi.MENU_ITEM_ID
where po.PENDING_ORDER_ID=?
```

As you can see, by using eager loading we have replaced several SELECT statements with a single SELECT statement. The details of how you dynamically configure eager loading depend on the persistence framework, and I will describe the process in chapters 5 and 6.

Eager loading is only one of the ways to optimize the performance of a JDO or Hibernate application. Another way to improve performance is to reduce database accesses by using a process-level cache.

4.6.3 *Using a process-level cache*

Eager loading improves performance by loading related objects with a single SELECT statement. In contrast, process-level caching improves performance by eliminating SELECT statements entirely by retrieving objects from the process-level cache instead of the database. To use a process-level cache, we must first determine which objects to keep in the cache. In this example, the restaurant-related classes—Restaurant, MenuItem, and TimeRange—are rarely updated and thus are good candidates for process-level caching. We would then configure the persistence framework to cache those objects, which I describe how to do in chapters 5 and 6.

Once we have decided which objects to cache, the next step is to optimize object loading by configuring eager loading as described in the previous section. When doing this, however, it is important to lazily load relationships from non-cached objects to cached objects. Otherwise, the application would bypass the cache and load the objects from the database.

For example, when handling the update payment information request only the PendingOrder-PendingOrderLineItem relationship should be loaded eagerly. The other relationships, such as PendingOrder-Restaurant and PendingOrderLineItem-MenuItem, must be loaded lazily to ensure that the restaurants and menu items are retrieved from the process-level cache. The persistence framework would use a SQL statement that does a join between the PENDING_ORDER and PENDING_ORDER_LINE_ITEM tables:

```
select *
from FTGO_PENDING_ORDER po
  left outer join FTGO_PENDING_ORDER_LINE_ITEM li
  on po.PENDING_ORDER_ID=li.PENDING_ORDER_ID
where po.PENDING_ORDER_ID=?
```

The other objects would be retrieved from the process-level cache when the application navigates to them.

4.6.4 *Using the query cache*

So far, we have optimized the loading of a pending order and its related objects by caching the restaurants and using queries with fetch joins. We also need to consider improving the performance of the query that finds the available restaurants. One option is to use the query cache. Enabling caching for this query might improve performance because JDO or Hibernate will then try to get the results of the query from the query cache instead of executing a SQL statement. However, because there are potentially many combinations of values for the query's parameters—for example, ZIP code and delivery time—it is unclear whether there would be any benefit. We would have to analyze the running application to determine whether there is any benefit. The query cache can improve performance of other queries significantly.

By using eager loading, process-level caching, and query caching, you can often significantly improve the performance of your application. The details depend on which persistence framework your application uses. You will learn about those in the next two chapters, but before that we must look at the details of the example schema.

4.7 *The example schema*

We have now had an overview of ORM and looked at how to write tests and optimize the performance of a persistence layer. The next step is to learn how to persist a domain model using Hibernate and JDO. Because I'm going to use the Food to Go domain model as an example, it will be helpful to look at the database schema that the application uses. The schema, which is shown in figure 4.5, is quite similar to the domain model you saw in chapter 3.

It uses many of the ORM techniques you saw earlier in section 4.1. Each of the main classes in the domain model—PendingOrder, PendingOrderLineItem, Order, OrderLineItem, Coupon, Restaurant, and MenuItem—has a corresponding table. The Restaurant-MenuItem and PendingOrder-PendingOrderLineItem relationships, which are one-to-many relationships, are represented by foreign keys in the MENU_ITEM and PENDING_ORDER_LINE_ITEM tables, respectively.

Similarly, the PendingOrder-PendingOrderLineItem, which is a many-to-one relationship, is represented by a foreign key in the PENDING_ORDER_LINE_ITEM table. A restaurant's ZIP codes—which in Java is a collection of strings and corresponds to a many-to-many relationship between restaurants and ZIP codes—is represented by the join table RESTAURANT_ZIP_CODE, which has foreign keys to both the RESTAURANT and ZIP_CODE tables.

In the following chapters, this schema is used to illustrate some of the challenges you will face when trying to Hibernate or JDO to persist a domain model.

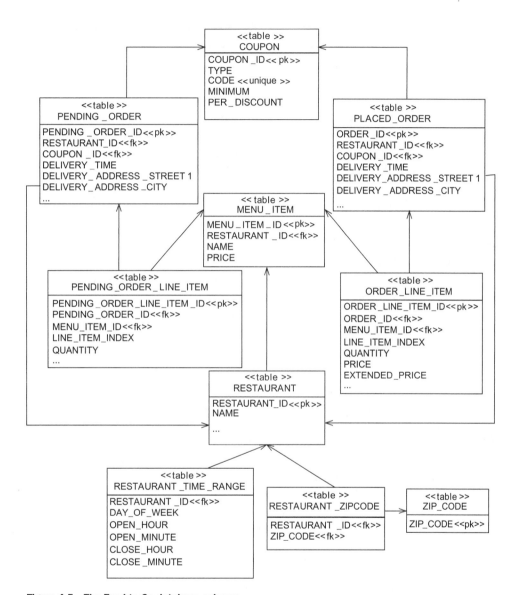

Figure 4.5   The Food to Go database schema

4.8 Summary

Business logic that is implemented using the Domain Model pattern consists of a fine-grained web of interconnected objects. Many of those objects are persistent, which means that when the application handles a request it must transfer objects to and from the database. Storing domain objects in a database is a remarkably difficult problem. One reason is that any OO concepts such as inheritance have no equivalent database concept. Another challenge is implementing transparent persistence, which means that persistent objects are unaware that they are persistent.

Persisting a domain model almost always requires an ORM framework because it is simply too difficult to do yourself with JDBC. An ORM framework provides features such as declarative object/relational mapping; an API for creating, finding, updating, and deleting persistent objects; a query language; caching to improve performance; and support for transactions. Two popular ORM frameworks are JDO and Hibernate, which despite their numerous differences provide a comparable set of features.

Because JDO and Hibernate provide transparent persistence, the only domain model classes that call the persistence framework APIs to create, find, and delete persistent objects are the repositories, which define methods for these tasks. We can use the Spring ORM template classes, which are wrappers around the ORM framework APIs, to significantly simplify the implementation of these classes. Most repository methods are easy to test one-liners that call a template class convenience method.

It is important to test the persistent classes and repositories because a variety of bugs are caused by the domain model, the object/relational mapping, and the database schema getting out of sync. Effective testing requires using a combination of different kinds of tests. Some tests (such as those that verify that persistent objects can be created, updated, deleted, and queried) must use the database. However, because testing with a database is slow, it's important to test as much of the persistence layer as possible without it.

Now that you have learned about ORM concepts and the basics of Hibernate and JDO, the next chapters examine those ORM frameworks in more detail, starting with JDO.

Persisting a domain model with JDO 2.0

This chapter covers

- Persisting objects with JDO
- Testing a JDO persistence layer
- Using Spring's JDO support classes
- Tuning a JDO application

Now that you have gotten an overview of ORM framework concepts in JDO and Hibernate, let's look at how you can persist a domain model with JDO 2.0. As we saw in chapter 4, JDO provides mostly transparent persistence for POJOs. Most classes are unaware that they are persistent, and JDO supports the natural Java programming style, including inheritance and recursive calls between objects. In addition, because JDO can be used both inside and outside an application server, you can develop and test business logic without having to first deploy it, which accelerates development.

Of course, no technology is perfect; JDO has various shortcomings that must be accommodated when you're developing an application. In this chapter we describe the decisions you must make and the workarounds you must use when developing with JDO. You will learn how to persist domain objects with JDO and implement domain model repositories using Spring and JDO. This chapter also explains how to optimize performance in a JDO application by using eager loading and caching. We will use the Food to Go domain model developed in chapter 3 as an example.

For more detailed information about JDO, see *Java Data Objects* [Russell 2003].

5.1 *JDO issues and limitations*

JDO is one of those technologies that has never received a huge amount of attention and hype. Although it was the first standard for Java transparent persistence, it has always has been overshadowed by Hibernate. And, to make matters worse, politics led the EJB 3 expert group (JSR-220) to define a totally new standard for Java transparent persistence instead of using JDO. But JDO is an excellent ORM technology that has multiple commercial and open source implementations. The trend is for those implementations to also support EJB 3, and as developers inevitably run into EJB 3's limitations (see chapter 10), it's likely they will find their way to JDO.

JDO provides a flexible ORM mechanism that makes it straightforward to persist a typical domain model. It supports all of the ORM features I described in chapter 4, including relationships, embedded value objects, and inheritance. You rarely need to make significant changes to your domain model in order to persist it unless, of course, you are working with a legacy schema that has some quirky features (such as denormalized columns). Making a domain model persistent is usually only a matter of writing the XML metadata that defines how it maps to the database schema and perhaps adding ID fields to classes.

You must, however, decide which kind of JDO object identity to use for each of the classes in the domain model. In addition, you need to work around a limitation of how interfaces are mapped to the database.

5.1.1 *Configuring JDO object identity*

An object's persistent identity identifies it in the database. One important decision you must make when persisting a domain model with JDO is what kind of object identity to use for each class. JDO provides three different kinds:

- *Application identity*—Persistent identity is managed by the application and is stored in an object's field or fields.

- *Datastore identity*—Persistent identity is managed by the database and is not stored in an object's field.

- *Nondurable identity*—Objects have a unique identity in memory but not in the database.

Nondurable identity is intended for specialized situations such as log files whose table does not have a primary key. Because it isn't appropriate for most databases applications, I will not spend more time discussing it. See the JDO specification for more information about nondurable identity.

For each class in your application, you must decide whether to use datastore identity or application identity. You can use a different type of identity for each class in the domain model. The only constraint is that all classes in an inheritance hierarchy must use the same type of identity.

Let's look at how application identity and datastore identity work and their benefits and drawbacks.

Application identity

With application identity, an object's persistent identity consists of the values of one or more of the object's fields. These primary key field or fields are mapped to the primary key column or columns of the class's table. An object's persistent identity is generated by either the application or the JDO implementation, which is usually the simplest approach.

Here is an example of how to use application identity with the `PendingOrder` class:

```
class PendingOrder {
    private int id;

    public int getId() { return id; }
}

<class name="PendingOrder"
    identity-type="application">
    <field name="id"
```

```
        primary-key="true" value-strategy="native" />
    ...
</class>
```

This example shows part of the `PendingOrder` class and an excerpt of its XML metadata. To use application identity with the `PendingOrder` class we must add an ID field to store the primary key. It usually makes sense to also define a getter so that the rest of the application can access the ID. This example configures the JDO identity of the `PendingOrder` class using the following attributes:

- The `identity-type="application"` attribute specifies that you want to use application identity.

- The `primary-key="true"` attribute specifies that the `PendingOrder.id` field will store the primary key.

- The `value-strategy="native"` attribute tells the JDO implementation to pick the most suitable identifier generation strategy based on the underlying database.

When the application calls `PersistenceManager.makePersistent()` to save a newly created `PendingOrder` object, the JDO implementation will generate the primary key using one of a variety of key generation mechanisms, including database sequences and auto-increment columns, and store it in the ID field.

The application can also assign values to the primary key field(s) before calling `PersistenceManager.makePersistent()`. This can be useful when you're mapping a domain model to a legacy schema that uses a natural primary key instead of a surrogate primary key. If necessary, either the application can implement its own key-generation mechanism or it can call JDO to generate a primary key value.

A class that uses application identity must have an object ID class, which defines fields corresponding to the names of the class's primary key fields. An application loads an existing object with a particular primary key by passing an instance of the object ID class that contains the primary key to a method, such as `getObjectById()`. If a class has a single primary key field, which is termed *single field identity*, then the application uses one of the built-in single field identity primary key classes. However, if the class has multiple primary key fields, then the application defines a custom object ID class.

Here is an example of how an application would retrieve a `PendingOrder` with an ID of 555 when using application identity:

```
String idString = "555";
IntIdentity objectId = new IntIdentity(PendingOrder.class, idString);
PendingOrder p = (PendingOrder)pm.getObjectById(objectId);
```

This example first constructs an instance of the IntIdentity class, which is a built-in JDO single field identity class, and then calls getObjectById(), which returns PendingOrder.

An important benefit of application identity is that the application can easily access an object's persistent identity because it is stored in the object. This benefit is especially important in web applications, which store object identifiers between requests in the HttpSession or the browser by embedding them in cookies, URLs, or hidden form fields. For example, the Food to Go application stores the identity of a PendingOrder in the HttpSession and embeds restaurant IDs in URLs on the page that displays the list of available restaurants. Because the object identifier is stored in the object, the presentation tier can get the object identifiers by calling a getter on the detached object returned by the business tier.

Another benefit of application identity is that the object's identity is almost always a simple value such as an integer or a short string. This makes it straightforward to embed the object identifier in a URL or hidden field. In comparison, when using datastore identity the string form of an object identifier is too long to embed in a URL.

Application identity is also useful in applications that use a mixture of JDO and JDBC/iBATIS code. Because the JDO identity is the database primary key, you can write JDO and JDBC/iBATIS code that exchanges primary keys. For example, you can write JDBC/iBATIS code that executes a query and gets back some primary keys and then uses JDO APIs to retrieve objects. Conversely, you can pass the persistent identity of a JDO object to JDBC/iBATIS code, which then executes a stored procedure.

The main drawback of using application identity is that because a primary key usually has no meaning in the domain model, you must add a primary key field to each class that uses application identity. Typically, however, the benefits of using application identity outweigh the drawback of having to make some minor changes to the domain model. If an application needs to access the persistent identity of an object in its class, you should use application identity. On the other hand, if you cannot add a primary key field to a class because you do not have access to its source code, then you must use datastore identity.

Datastore identity

The other JDO identity mechanism is datastore identity, in which an object's persistent identity is managed entirely by the JDO implementation. The O/R mapping for a class specifies the primary key column(s) but does not map them to any of the class's fields. Instead, the persistent identity of any in-memory JDO objects is maintained by PersistenceManager. The JDO implementation generates a persistent identity using a variety of mechanisms, including database sequences and auto-increment columns, but does not store the identity in the object.

Here is an example of using datastore identity with the `PendingOrder` class:

```
<class name="PendingOrder" identity-type="datastore" >
    <datastore-identity strategy="native"
              column="PENDING_ORDER_ID"/>
    ...
</class>
```

Because we are using datastore identity, we do not add a primary key field to the `PendingOrder` class. This example configures the JDO identity of the `Pending-Order` class as follows:

- The `identity-type="datastore"` attribute specifies that the `Pending-Order` class uses datastore identity. Note, however, that because `datastore` is the default value of this attribute (if no field is flagged with `primary-key="true"` within this class mapping), this can be omitted.

- The `<datastore-identity>` element configures the datastore identity. The `column="PENDING_ORDER_ID"` attribute specifies that `PENDING_ORDER_ID` is the primary key column. The `strategy="native"` attribute tells the JDO implementation to use the most appropriate primary key generation mechanism for the underlying database.

As you can see, the primary key column is not mapped to a field in the object. An application must call `JDOHelper.getObjectId(object)` to get the identity of an object. This method returns an instance of an implementation-specific object ID class. The application can convert an object ID to a string by calling `toString()`. It could then, for example, store that string ID in the `HttpSession` or store it in the browser in a cookie, or hidden field, or as a URL parameter.

Later on, the application can convert a string obtained in this way back to an object ID by calling `PersistenceManager.newObjectIdInstance()`. Here is an example of how an application would retrieve a `PendingOrder` with a particular ID when using datastore identity:

```
HttpServletRequest request = ...;
String idString = request.getParameter("pendingOrderId");
Object objectId = pm.newObjectIdInstance(PendingOrder.class,
                    idString);
PendingOrder p = (PendingOrder)pm.getObjectById(objectId);
```

The `newObjectIdInstance()` method returns an instance of an object ID class, which is then passed to `getObjectId()`. Note that, unlike this code snippet, a real application would get `pendingOrderId` from the `HttpServletRequest` and pass it to the business tier rather than calling the JDO APIs directly.

The main benefit of JDO datastore identity is that you do not have to add a primary key field to a class. This simplifies the domain model and enables you to persist classes that don't have a primary key field. It works well when the application never needs to access an object's persistent identity.

Datastore identity makes it difficult for the application to access and manipulate an object's persistent identity. The first problem is that the application must call `JDOHelper.getObjectId(object)` to get the object identifier, which clutters the code with calls to JDO. This makes the presentation tier more complicated because it would have to call this method to get the identity of a detached object instead of simply asking the object. It also breaks encapsulation because the presentation tier needs to know that the business tier uses JDO. You could avoid this problem by having the business tier call `getObjectId()` and return a DTO containing the object and its ID to the presentation tier, but that requires extra DTO classes.

Another problem with datastore identity is that the JDO object ID string is too long to be embedded within a web page. The ID string is usually the fully qualified class name concatenated with the primary key. If the application embedded these values in URLs, the result would be ugly, hard-to-read URLs.

The third problem with datastore identity is that the persistent identity is different than the database primary key, which makes it very difficult to write JDO and JDBC/iBATIS code that works together. In order to convert between a primary key and a datastore identity, you would have to write code that relied on the vendor-specific format of the JDO object ID string.

Using datastore identity is certainly worthwhile because you don't have to add an ID field to your domain objects. However, because of its drawbacks you should only use it for objects whose persistent identity is never accessed by the application. Examples of classes in the Food to Go domain model that can use datastore identity are `PendingOrderLineItem`, `MenuItem`, and `TimeRange` because their primary keys are never used. For other classes you should use application identity and add primary key fields.

Adding primary key fields is only one of the changes you must make to your domain model. You might also need to make some changes when persisting class hierarchies.

5.1.2 *Persisting interfaces*

Persisting a class hierarchy is generally straightforward because JDO supports each of the mapping schemes described in chapter 4. A class can be mapped to its superclass's table or to its subclasses' tables, or it can have its own table. However, one tricky problem is mapping interfaces such as Coupon. As figure 5.1 shows, the Coupon interface is implemented by the FreeShippingCoupon and Percentage-DiscountCoupon classes.

We need to map the Coupon interface and its implementation classes to the COUPON table and map the many-to-one relationships Order-Coupon and Pending-Order-Coupon to foreign keys in the PLACED_ORDER and PENDING_ORDER tables. Unfortunately, JDO does not allow this to be done directly by mapping an interface

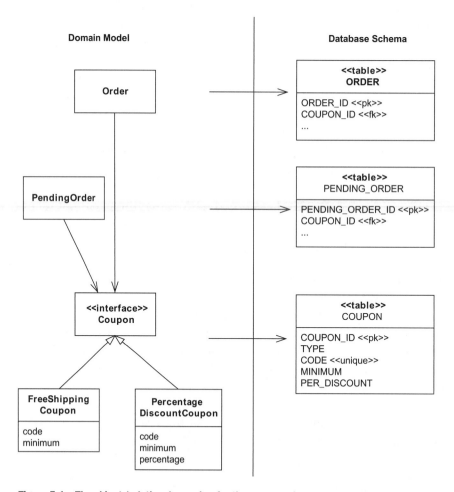

Figure 5.1 The object/relational mapping for the Coupon classes

to a table in the same way as a class. You must instead change the class hierarchy by introducing a common superclass that implements the interface and then map it to the database table.

For example, to persist the Coupon hierarchy we define an AbstractCoupon-Impl class that implements the Coupon interface. The concrete Coupon classes such as FreeShippingCoupon and PercentageDiscountCoupon extend this class:

```
interface Coupon {..};
class AbstractCouponImpl implements Coupon {…};
class FreeShippingCoupon extends AbstractCouponImpl {…};
class PercentageDiscountCoupon extends AbstractCouponImpl {…};
```

Once we have made these changes to the domain model, we can then define the XML metadata for the O/R mapping for the Coupon class hierarchy. Here is an excerpt of the XML metadata that defines the mapping for the AbstractCoupon-Impl and FreeShippingCoupon classes:

```
<class name="AbstractCouponImpl" table="COUPON" >
  <implements name="net.chrisrichardson.foodToGo.domain.Coupon"/>
  <inheritance strategy="new-table">
   <discriminator strategy="value-map">
     <column name="COUPON_TYPE"/>
   </discriminator>
  </inheritance>
</class>

<class name="FreeShippingCoupon" persistence-capable-superclass=
➥ "net.chrisrichardson.foodToGo.domain.AbstractCouponImpl">
  <inheritance strategy="superclass-table">
    <discriminator value="FREE_SHIP"/>
  </inheritance>
  <field name="minimum">
    <column name="FREE_SHIP_MINIMUM" allows-null="true"/>
  </field>
</class>
```

The <implements> element specifies that the AbstractCouponImpl class implements the Coupon interface. This tells the JDO implementation that any field of type Coupon is really a reference to an instance of this class or one of its subclasses.

The <inheritance> element of the AbstractCouponImpl specifies that the AbstractCouponImpl class has its own table called COUPON and that the COUPON_TYPE column stores the type of the coupon. The <inheritance> element of the FreeShippingCoupon class specifies that the FreeShippingCoupon is mapped to the COUPON table and that its type code is FREE_SHIP. The mapping for PercentageDiscountCoupon would be defined in a similar way.

In most cases this is a simple change with only a minimal impact on the domain model. It is also common to have such an abstract class already in place. However, it's a shame that we need to introduce an abstract class because interfaces are such a fundamental OO concept.

Let's now look at the JDO enhancer tool and its impact on the edit-compile-debug cycle.

5.1.3 *Using the JDO enhancer*

Cirque du Soleil's Mystere at Treasure Island in Las Vegas is my favorite performance of all time. The clowns and acrobats perform one breathtaking act after another. They appear to defy gravity and do things that do not seem humanly possible. Making it look so effortless requires a tremendous amount of hard work, countless backstage people, and large amounts of technology.

Implementing persistence transparently is also a difficult problem. In order to make it seem effortless, ORM frameworks such as JDO must perform "behind the scenes" magic to implement features such as lazy loading and change tracking. Consider, for example, what happens when the application executes the following code snippet that loads a `PendingOrder` and navigates to its restaurant:

```
String idString = "555";
IntIdentity objectId = new IntIdentity(PendingOrder.class, idString);
PendingOrder p = (PendingOrder)pm.getObjectById(objectId);
String restaurantName p = p.getRestaurant().getName()
```

The JDO implementation must provide the illusion that the `Restaurant` object is in memory even when it is loaded lazily. The JDO implementation must also keep track of changes to objects so that it can update the database.

There is more than one way to implement transparent persistence, but the approach taken by most JDO implementations is to use a bytecode enhancer. The *bytecode enhancer* is a tool that must be run on the persistent classes and any classes that directly access their fields. It reads the XML metadata defining the object/relational mapping and changes the bytecodes in each class file to implement features such as lazy loading and change tracking. The enhancer, which was mandatory in JDO 1.0, became optional in JDO 2.0, but it is likely that it will continue to be the way JDO implementations provide transparent persistence. One of its valuable benefits is that JDO objects, unlike Hibernate objects, work with `instanceof` and can be downcasted.

One drawback of using the enhancer is that it's an extra step in the edit-compile-debug cycle. Before the application or its tests can be executed, you must run the bytecode enhancer, either from within your IDE or by using Ant, on any newly compiled class files. This can be a problem when you're working within an IDE such as Eclipse, which incrementally compiles files when you save them. Some JDO vendors provide an Eclipse plug-in that automatically enhances class files, but some only do so during a full rebuild. As a result, a test will sometimes fail because it attempts to persist an object whose class has not been enhanced. You must then manually run the enhancer, which can be frustrating. However, I believe that this is a small price to pay for objects that support `instanceof` and downcasting.

Now that we have looked at some of the issues with using JDO, let's see how to use it to persist a domain model class and implement repositories.

5.2 *Persisting a domain model class with JDO*

You now should have a good understanding of the issues you will encounter and the decisions you must make when using JDO to persist to a domain model. In this section, we'll use JDO to persist the `PendingOrder` class. You will see examples of the tests that you will need to write when using a test-driven approach to persisting your own domain model with JDO. We'll describe the minor changes, such as adding an ID field, that you must make to some classes in order to be able to persist them, and we'll show the JDO object/relational mapping for the `PendingOrder` class.

5.2.1 *Writing JDO persistence tests with ORMUnit*

The first step in the process of making a class persistent is to write some tests that verify the correctness of the object/relational mapping and make sure that instances of the class can be saved, updated, and deleted. Ironically, writing these tests usually takes longer than making the classes persistent. There are also lots of details to discuss, so bear with me through this discussion.

To make writing JDO persistence tests easier, ORMUnit provides three base classes: `JDOMappingTests`, `JDOSchemaTests`, and `JDOPersistenceTests`. As figure 5.2 shows, each class extends JUnit `TestCase`. You use `JDOMappingTests` and `JDOSchemaTests` to write tests for the object/relational mapping and `JDO-PersistenceTests` to write tests that create, find, update, and delete persistent JDO objects.

`JDOMappingTests` and `JDOSchemaTests` delegate to a strategy class that implements the `JDOMappingStrategy` interface and uses the vendor-specific APIs to test the object/relational mapping. `JDOPersistenceTests` is implemented using the standard JDO APIs. Let's first look at these classes and then see how to use them.

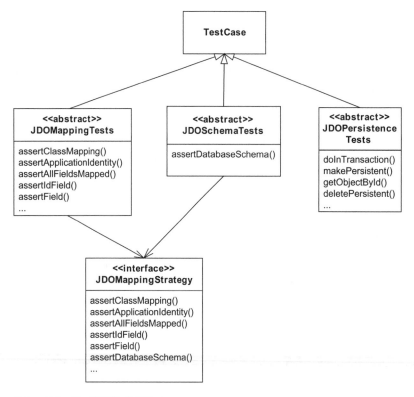

Figure 5.2   The ORMUnit JDO classes

Overview of JDOMappingTests

JDOMappingTests is a base class for writing tests that verify the ORM defined by the XML metadata. It defines methods for making assertions about the mapping, including the following:

- assertClassMapping(): Verifies that the class is mapped to the specified table
- assertApplicationIdentity(): Verifies that the class uses application identity
- assertAllFieldsMapped(): Verifies that all the fields of a class are mapped
- assertIdField(): Verifies that the class's ID field is mapped to the specified column
- assertField(): Verifies that a field is mapped to the specified columns

JDO does not define a standard way to access the O/R mapping, and so each method delegates to a vendor-specific implementation of `JDOMappingTestsStrategy`:

```
public abstract class JDOMappingTests extends TestCase {
  JDOMappingTestsStrategy strategy;

  protected void assertClassMapped(Class type, String table) {
    strategy.assertClassMapping(type, table);
  }

  protected void assertAllFieldsMapped() {
    strategy.assertAllFieldsMapped();
  }
  ...
}
```

Let's now look at `JDOSchemaTests`, which also delegates to a `JDOMappingTests-Strategy`.

Overview of JDOSchemaTests

In addition to testing the O/R mapping, you must verify that the database schema matches the mapping. `JDOSchemaTests` is a base class for writing this kind of test. It defines an `assertDatabaseSchema()` method, which fails if the mapping references tables or columns that are missing from the database schema. Because the JDO specification does not provide a standard API for doing this, `JDOSchemaTests` delegates to vendor-specific implementation of the `JDOMappingTestsStrategy`:

```
public class JDOSchemaTests  extends TestCase {

  JDOMappingTestsStrategy strategy;

  protected void assertDatabaseSchema() throws Exception {
    strategy.assertDatabaseSchema();
  }
  ...
}
```

The `assertDatabaseSchema()` method simply delegates to the corresponding method defined by the `JDOMappingTestsStrategy`. Let's see how this works.

JPOXMappingStrategy

ORMUnit encapsulates the vendor-specific APIs behind the `JDOMappingTests-Strategy` interface. There is a separate implementation of this interface for each JDO implementation. Listing 5.1 shows an excerpt from the JPOX implementation of `JDOMappingStrategy`. The methods that make assertions about the O/R mapping use JPOX's metadata classes. They call the JPOX `MetaDataParser`, which is a class that parses XML metadata files, instantiates metadata objects, and stores them in a `MetaDataManager` class that acts as a repository of the metadata. ORMUnit can then use the information contained in the metadata objects to make assertions about the object/relational mapping. Similarly, the `assertData-baseSchema()` method calls `SchemaTool.validateSchema()`, which is a JPOX class that reads the XML mapping data and throws an exception if tables or columns are missing from the database schema.

Listing 5.1   JPOXMappingStrategy

```
public class JPOXMappingStrategy implements
    JDOMappingTestsStrategy {

  private MetaDataManager mdm;
  private ClassMetaData cmd;
  private final String jdoProperties;
  private final String[] metadataFiles;

  public JPOXMappingStrategy(String jdoProperties,
      String[] metadataFiles) throws Exception {
    this.jdoProperties = jdoProperties;
    this.metadataFiles = metadataFiles;
    mdm = createMetaDataManager();     ◁——❶ Gets
  }                                         the JDO metadata

  private MetaDataManager createMetaDataManager()
                                throws Exception {
    mdm = new MetaDataManager();
    for (int i = 0; i < metadataFiles.length; i++) {
      String fileName = metadataFiles[i];
      FileInputStream fis = new FileInputStream(fileName);
      FileMetaData fmdUtil =
          MetaDataParser.parseMetaDataStream(fis,
                               true, mdm, fileName);
      fis.close();
    }
    return mdm;
  }

  private void assertClassMapped(Class type, String table) {
    cmd = mdm.getMetaDataForClass(type);
    assertEquals(table, cmd.getTable());     ◁——❷ Verifies the
  }                                                class mapping

  protected void assertDatabaseSchema()
      throws FileNotFoundException, IOException, Exception {
    FileInputStream fis =
```

```
                  new FileInputStream(jdoProperties);
      System.getProperties().load(fis);
      fis.close();                                          ③ Verifies the
      String[] args = metadataFiles;                          database schema
      SchemaTool.validateSchemaTables(args, false);
  }

  ...
}
```

Let's take a closer look at this listing:

① The constructor calls `createMetaDataManager()`, which creates a `MetaData-Manager` and iterates through the list of JDO metadata files, calling the `MetaDataParser` on each one.

② The `assertClassMapping()` method gets the class's metadata from the `MetaDataManager` and verifies that it is mapped to the expected table.

③ The `assertDatabaseSchema()` method loads the JDO properties file into `System.getProperties()`. It then calls `SchemaTool.validateSchemaTables()`, passing the list of JDO metadata files. `SchemaTool.validateSchemaTables()` uses the system properties to open a database connection and verifies that the database schema matches the JDO metadata files.

Now that we have seen how these test classes work, let's look at `JDOPersistence-Tests`.

Overview of JDOPersistenceTests

ORMUnit also defines the `JDOPersistenceTests` class, which extends JUnit `TestCase` and makes it easier to write tests for persistent objects. It defines `setUp()` and `tearDown()` methods that implement the boilerplate code of a JDO persistence test such as configuring a `PersistenceManagerFactory` and opening and closing a `PersistenceManager`. It also provides convenience methods for manipulating persistent data and managing transactions, such as:

■ `doInTransaction()`: Executes the callback method within a JDO transaction and ensures that the same `PersistenceManager` is used throughout. It does this using a Spring `TransactionTemplate` that is configured to use a `JdoTransactionManager`.

■ `makePersistent()`: Saves an object by calling `JdoTemplate.makePersistent()`.

- `getObjectById()`: Loads a persistent object by calling `JdoTemplate` `.getObjectById()`.

- `deletePersistent()`: Deletes a persistent object by calling `JdoTemplate` `.deletePersistent()`.

These methods make it easier to write tests for persistent objects. See this book's online source code for the details of the class.

5.2.2 *Testing persistent JDO objects*

Now that you have seen an overview of ORMUnit's JDO classes, we'll look at writing tests for the JDO persistence layer using the testing strategy described in earlier chapter 4. There are three different sets of tests. The first set of tests verifies we have correctly implemented the O/R mapping, an excerpt of which is shown in figure 5.3. These tests verify, for example, that the `PendingOrder` class is mapped to the PENDING_ORDER table and that each of its fields is mapped to a column of that table.

The second set of tests verifies that the database schema matches the O/R mapping. The tests verify that every table and column referenced by the mapping exists in the database schema. The third set of tests verifies that persistent pending orders can be saved, queried, updated, and deleted. The next section explains how to implement these tests for the `PendingOrder` class.

Verifying the O/R mapping

The first test we must write is one that verifies that the `PendingOrder` class is mapped correctly to the database. Here is a simple test for the `PendingOrder` class:

```
public class FoodToGoDomainMappingTests extends JDOMappingTests {

  public void testSimple() throws Exception {
    assertClassMapped(PendingOrder.class, "PENDING_ORDER");
    assertAllFieldsMapped();
  }
```

The test extends the ORMUnit class `JDOMappingTests`. It calls `assertClass-Mapped()` to verify that `PendingOrder` is mapped to the PENDING_ORDER table and then calls `assertAllFields()` to verify that all of `PendingOrder`'s fields are mapped to the database.

This test only verifies that each field is mapped to the database. If you need to verify that each field is mapped to the correct column, then you can write a more elaborate test that calls methods such as `assertField()`. Here's an example:

```
public class FoodToGoDomainMappingTests extends JDOMappingTests {

  public void test() throws Exception {
    assertClassMapped(PendingOrder.class, "PENDING_ORDER");
    assertApplicationIdentity();

    assertIdField("id", "PENDING_ORDER_ID");
    assertField("deliveryTime", "DELIVERY_TIME");
    assertManyToOneField("restaurant", "RESTAURANT_ID");

    assertAllFieldsMapped();
  }
```

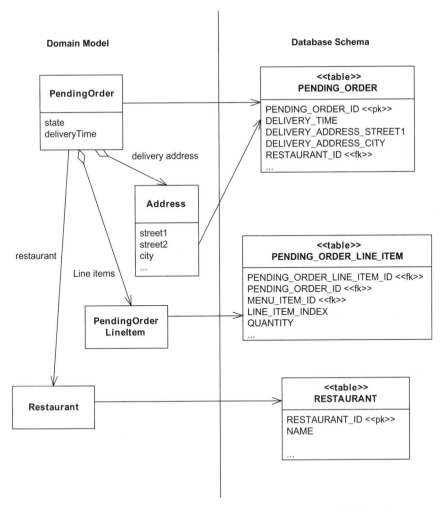

Figure 5.3   Part of the object/relational mapping for the Food to Go domain model

This test verifies that the `PendingOrder` class uses application identity and that the ID field is mapped to the `PENDING_ORDER_ID` column. It also verifies the `restaurant` field is mapped to a foreign key column called `RESTAURANT_ID`. Writing this test can take a while, but it is a lot easier than verifying the contents of the database.

I often find it useful to first write some very simple tests that verify that the class is mapped to the right table and that all of its fields are mapped to the database. This initial step detects many common problems. I then expand the tests over time to verify the correct mapping for each field.

Verifying that the schema matches the mapping

The second kind of test that you need to write is one that verifies that the database schema matches the O/R mapping. ORMUnit makes it easy to verify that the database schema matches the O/R mapping:

```
public class JDOFoodToGoSchemaValidationTests extends
    JDOSchemaTests {

  public void test() throws Exception {
    assertDatabaseSchema();
  }
}
```

This test calls `assertDatabaseSchema()`, which we described earlier, to verify that there are no missing columns. It will catch common mistakes such as defining the O/R mapping for a new field without adding the corresponding column to the schema. Because it checks that the database schema matches the O/R mapping for all classes, we only need to write it once.

Now that we have written tests to verify that the O/R mapping and the database schema, let's look at writing tests that persist JDO objects.

Verifying that objects can be created, queried, updated, and deleted

The third and final kind of tests is one that verifies that the `PendingOrder` can be created, queried, updated, and deleted. A good way to begin is to write a test that simply saves the `PendingOrder` in the database and then write more elaborate tests later. Here is a test for `PendingOrder` that does just that:

```
public class JDOPendingOrderPersistenceTests extends
    JDOPersistenceTests {

  public void testPendingOrderSimple() throws Exception {

    doWithTransaction(new TxnCallback() {
      public void execute() throws Exception {
        PendingOrder po = new PendingOrder();
```

```
            makePersistent(po);
            int poId = po.getId();
        }
    });
}
```

JDOPendingOrderPersistenceTests extends JDOPersistenceTests, which is an ORMUnit class. The test instantiates a PendingOrder and saves it in the database by calling makePersistent(), which is defined by JDOPersistenceTests and calls JdoTemplate.makePersistent().

A more thorough test would create a PendingOrder, update it, and delete it. Listing 5.2 shows an example of such a test. This creates a PendingOrder, updates it in different ways, and then deletes it. Each step of the test is a separate database transaction that creates, deletes, and updates objects in the database.

Listing 5.2 JDOPendingOrderPersistenceTests

```
public class JDOPendingOrderPersistenceTests extends
    JDOPersistenceTests {

  private String poId;

  private String restaurantId;

  public void testPendingOrder() throws Exception {

    createPendingOrder();

    createRestaurant();

    updateDeliveryInformation();

    updateRestaurant();

    updateQuantities();

    changeQuantities();

    deletePendingOrder();

  }

  private void createPendingOrder() {        ◄———❶ Creates and saves
    doWithTransaction(new TxnCallback() {            PendingOrder
      public void execute() throws Exception {
        PendingOrder po = new PendingOrder();
        makePersistent(po);
        poId = po.getId();
```

```
        }
      });
    }
    private void createRestaurant() {          ◁——————② Creates and
      doWithTransaction(new TxnCallback() {              saves a Restaurant
        public void execute() throws Exception {
          Restaurant restaurant = RestaurantMother
              .makeRestaurant();
          makePersistent(restaurant);
          restaurantId = restaurant.getId();
        }
      });
    }

    private void updateDeliveryInformation() {  ◁——————③ Updates
      doWithTransaction(new TxnCallback() {              PendingOrder's
        public void execute() throws Exception {         delivery info
          PendingOrder po = loadPendingOrder();
          assertNull(po.getDeliveryAddress());
          Date deliveryTime = RestaurantMother
              .makeDeliveryTime();
          Address deliveryAddress = new Address("1 High St", null,
              "Oakland", "CA", "94619");
          JDORestaurantRepositoryImpl restaurantRepository =
            new JDORestaurantRepositoryImpl(getJdoTemplate());
          int updateDeliveryInfoResult = po
              .updateDeliveryInfo(restaurantRepository,
                  deliveryAddress, deliveryTime, true);
          assertEquals(PlaceOrderStatusCodes.OK,
              updateDeliveryInfoResult);
        }
      });
    }

    private PendingOrder loadPendingOrder() {
     return (PendingOrder) getObjectById(
         PendingOrder.class, poId);
    }

    private void updateRestaurant() {          ◁——————④ Updates
      doWithTransaction(new TxnCallback() {            PendingOrder's restaurant
        public void execute() throws Exception {
          PendingOrder po = loadPendingOrder();
          Restaurant restaurant = (Restaurant) getObjectById(
              Restaurant.class, restaurantId);
          boolean updateRestaurantResult = po
              .updateRestaurant(restaurant);
          assertTrue(updateRestaurantResult);
        }
      });
    }
```

```
private void updateQuantities() {        <────●5  Updates
                                                  PendingOrder's line items
  doWithTransaction(new TxnCallback() {
    public void execute() throws Exception {
      PendingOrder po = loadPendingOrder();
      po.updateQuantities(new int[] { 1, 2 });
    }
  });
}

private void changeQuantities() {        <────●6  Changes
  doWithTransaction(new TxnCallback() {            PendingOrder's line items
    public void execute() throws Exception {
      PendingOrder po = loadPendingOrder();
      po.updateQuantities(new int[] { 0, 2 });
    }
  });
}

private void deletePendingOrder() {      <────●7  Deletes
  doWithTransaction(new TxnCallback() {            PendingOrder
    public void execute() throws Exception {
      PendingOrder po = loadPendingOrder();
      deletePersistent(po);
    }

  });
}

}
```

The testPendingOrder() method calls several helper methods that implement the steps of the test. Let's look at the details:

●1 The createPendingOrder() method creates a PendingOrder and persists it.

●2 The createRestaurant() method creates and saves a Restaurant, which is used by the test.

●3 The updateDeliveryInformation() method loads PendingOrder and calls PendingOrder.updateDeliveryInfo().

●4 The updateRestaurant() method loads PendingOrder and the Restaurant that was created earlier and calls PendingOrder.updateRestaurant(), which creates an association from the PendingOrder to the Restaurant.

●5 The updateQuantities() method calls PendingOrder.updateQuantities(), which creates line items.

❻   The `changeQuantities()` method changes the line item quantities, which deletes the existing line items and creates new ones.

❼   The `deletePendingOrder()` method deletes the `PendingOrder`, which should also delete the line items.

This test corresponds to one possible scenario in the lifetime of a pending order. In order to thoroughly test the `PendingOrder` class, we would also need to write other tests, such as one that calls `updatePaymentInfo()` with a `Coupon`. Although developing these tests can be time consuming, they are an important part of the test suite for JDO persistence layer. As with the O/R mapping tests, you can start off by writing a simple test that creates and saves a `PendingOrder` and then add more comprehensive tests over time. Let's look at what we have to do in order to get these tests to pass.

5.2.3   *Making a class persistent*

Developing the persistence tests is, in some ways, the most challenging and time-consuming part of making a class persistent. Getting them to pass is comparatively easy. To do that, we must make some changes to the `PendingOrder` class and write the JDO XML metadata files that define its object/relational mapping.

Modifying the class

We need to modify the `PendingOrder` in order to be able to persist it. Because we have decided to use application identity, we have to add an ID field, which stores the primary key, and a getter that returns its value. Here are the changes:

```
public class PendingOrder {
   private int id;

   private int getId() {
     return id;
   }
}
   ...
```

The rest of the class is unchanged.

Defining the O/R mapping

The final step in persisting the `PendingOrder` class is writing the JDO XML metadata that maps the `PendingOrder` class to the database schema and specifies various aspects of the class, including the JDO identity type and how to generate the primary key. Some JDO implementations provide GUI tools that help with this, but it is fairly easy to do by hand.

The JDO XML metadata specifies the persistence information and ORM metadata. The persistence information describes the persistent classes, each class's JDO identity type, and which fields are persistent. The ORM metadata describes how the domain model maps to the database schema. You can put the persistence information and ORM metadata together in a .jdo file or you can put the mapping in a separate .orm file. Most of the time you will want to put the metadata in a single file, but separate files are useful if, for example, you want to map a domain model to different database schemas.

The JDO XML metadata can be for either a single class or for one or more packages. If it is for a single class, the name of the name of the XML metadata file is <class-Name>.jdo. If the metadata is for one or more packages, it is called package.jdo. JDO defines a set of search rules for locating metadata files. You can, for example, put a package.jdo file in a class path directory corresponding to the package name, such as net/chrisrichardson/foodToGo/domain, or in a class path directory corresponding to a partial package name, such as net/chrisrichardson/foodToGo.

Listing 5.3 shows an excerpt of the JDO metadata for the `PendingOrder` class.

Listing 5.3   XML metadata for the PendingOrder class

```
<jdo>
...
    <class name="PendingOrder"
         table="PENDING_ORDER"                    ❶ Configures
         identity-type="application" >              class mapping

        <field name="id" primary-key="true"
             value-strategy="native">             ❷ Configures id as
          <column name="PENDING_ORDER_ID"/>          primary key field
        </field>

        <field name="deliveryTime">               ❸ Maps
         <column name="DELIVERY_TIME" jdbc-type="TIMESTAMP"/>   deliveryTime
        </field>                                      field


        <field name="deliveryAddress"
             default-fetch-group="true">
          <embedded
           null-indicator-column="DELIVERY_STREET1">   ❹ Maps
            <field name="street1">                        deliveryAddress field
              <column name="DELIVERY_STREET1"/>
            </field>
            <field name="street2">
              <column name="DELIVERY_STREET2"/>
            </field>
```

```
      <field name="city">
        <column name="DELIVERY_CITY"/>
      </field>
      <field name="state">
        <column name="DELIVERY_STATE"/>        ❹ Maps
      </field>                                     deliveryAddress field
      <field name="zip">
        <column name="DELIVERY_ZIP"/>
      </field>
    </embedded>
  </field>

  <field name="restaurant">                    ❺ Maps
    <column name="RESTAURANT_ID"                   restaurant field
          target="RESTAURANT_ID"/>
  </field>

  <field name="lineItems">
    <collection
        element-type="PendingOrderLineItem"
        dependent-element="true"/>            ❻ Maps
    <element>                                    lineItems field
        <column name="PENDING_ORDER_ID"
          allows-null="false"/>
    </element>
    <order column="LINE_ITEM_INDEX"/>
  </field>
...
</class>
...
</jdo>
```

Let's look at the details of the mapping:

❶ This maps the `PendingOrder` class to the PENDING_ORDER table and specifies that it uses application identity.

❷ This section specifies that `id` is the primary key field and that primary keys should be generated using a database-approach mechanism.

❸ This maps simple fields such as `deliveryTime` to columns of the PENDING_ORDER table.

❹ This section maps the fields of `deliveryAddress` to the columns of the PENDING_ORDER table. The `null-indicator-column` specifies that if the DELIVERY_STREET1 column is `null`, then `deliveryAddress` is `null`.

⑤ This maps the restaurant field to the RESTAURANT_ID column, which is a foreign key column that references the RESTAURANT table.

⑥ The lineItems field is defined to be a collection of PendingOrderLineItem objects. The dependent-element="true" attribute specifies that line items should be deleted when removed from the line items collection or when the pending order is deleted. The <element> element specifies that the lineItems field is mapped to the PENDING_ORDER_ID foreign key column of Pending-OrderLineItem's table (i.e., PENDING_ORDER_LINE_ITEM). The allows-null="false" attribute specifies that the column cannot be null. The <order> element specifies that the position of the line item in the list is stored in the LINE_ITEM_INDEX column of the PENDING_ORDER_LINE_ITEM table.

The metadata for the other domain classes is similar. Once you have written the JDO XML metadata for a domain model, you must run the JDO implementation's bytecode enhancer to modify the class files. Once you do, the application will be able to persist instances of those classes in the database and the tests we wrote earlier will pass.

At this point, you know how to persist domain objects; the next step is to write the repositories.

5.3 *Implementing the JDO repositories*

One part of persisting a domain model with JDO is defining the O/R mapping and writing the tests to verify that it works. We must also implement the repositories, which define methods for creating, finding, and deleting persistent domain objects and are the only domain model classes that call the JDO APIs to manipulate persistent objects.

If you are using test-driven development, you begin the process of implementing a repository by writing some tests for the repository. We saw in chapter 4 that there are two kinds of tests that you need to write for a repository. First are mock object tests that verify that the repository calls the JDO and Spring APIs correctly. Mock objects are an effective way to directly test the functionality implemented by the repository independently of the persistence framework and the database. Second, you need database tests for the queries that are executed by the repository. These tests execute the queries against a database populated with test data and verify that they return the correct results. Once you have written the tests, you then write the code for the repository and get the tests to pass.

This section shows how to do this for the RestaurantRepository.find-AvailableRestaurants() method, which finds the restaurants that serve a given delivery address and time using the Spring and JDO APIs. First, we write some mock object tests for `RestaurantRepository`. After that we write the method and get the mock objects test to pass. Finally, we write some database tests for the JDO query that is executed by `RestaurantRepository` to find the restaurants.

5.3.1 *Writing a mock object test for findRestaurants()*

The mock objects test for `findRestaurants()` uses mock objects to verify that it calls the Spring and JDO APIs correctly. But to know which objects to mock we must decide how `findRestaurants()` executes the query. It can use either a named query or a query that is embedded in the code. In this particular case it makes sense to use a named query because, as you will see shortly, the query is too large to embed inside Java code. It would be spread over several lines of code, which would be messy.

Executing a named query using a callback class

A repository could execute a query by calling the JDO APIs directly, but it is usually much easier to use the `JdoTemplate` class. It implements boilerplate code that you would otherwise have to write and provides a number of convenience methods. However, at the time of this writing one limitation of the `JdoTemplate` class is that it lacks a convenience method for executing named queries with parameters. We must instead use it to execute a `JdoCallback` that creates and executes the named query. Even though this requires more code than calling a convenience method, it is still simpler than using the JDO APIs directly because the `JdoTemplate` takes care of opening and closing the `PersistenceManager` and mapping exceptions thrown by JDO to Spring data access exceptions.

The most straightforward and commonly used way to use a `JdoTemplate` to execute a `JdoCallback` is to use an anonymous class. But one big problem with using an anonymous callback is that it's impossible for a mock `JdoTemplate` to verify that `execute()` is called with the correct `JdoCallback` object. A better approach is to use a named `JdoCallback` class that implements the `equals()` method because we would then be able to configure a mock `JdoTemplate`.

To implement the `findRestaurants()` method, we can define a `JdoCall-back` class called `ExecuteNamedQueryWithMapCallback` whose constructor takes as parameters the name of the query and the `Map` containing the query's parameters. This class, shown in listing 5.4, creates the named query and returns the result of executing it by calling `Query.executeWithMap()`. It has an `equals()` method that returns `true` if the query names and parameters are the same in the two objects.

Listing 5.4 ExecuteNamedQueryWithMapCallback

```
public class ExecuteNamedQueryWithMapCallback implements
    JdoCallback {

  private String queryName;

  private Map parameters;

  private Class type;

  public ExecuteNamedQueryWithMapCallback
             (String queryName,        ◁──────── ❶ Creates ExecuteNamedQuery
                     Map parameters,                WithMapCallback
                     Class type) {
    this.queryName = queryName;
    this.parameters = parameters;
    this.type = type;
  }

  public boolean equals(Object other) {   ◁──────── ❷ Tests for
    if (other == null)                                 equality
      return false;
    if (!(other instanceof ExecuteNamedQueryWithMapCallback))
      return false;

    ExecuteNamedQueryWithMapCallback x =
      (ExecuteNamedQueryWithMapCallback) other;

    return queryName.equals(x.queryName)
        && parameters.equals(x.parameters)
        && type.equals(x.type);
  }

  public int hashCode() {
    return queryName.hashCode()
        ^ parameters.hashCode()
        ^ type.hashCode();
  }

  public Object doInJdo(PersistenceManager pm)   ◁──────── ❸ Executes the
      throws JDOException {                                    named query
    Query query = pm.newNamedQuery(type, queryName);
    return query.executeWithMap(parameters);
  }
}
```

Let's take a closer look at `ExecuteNamedQueryWithMapCallback`:

❶ The constructor takes the class, the query name, and the query parameters as parameters and stores them in fields.

❷ The equals() method returns true if the type, the query name, and the query parameters of the two objects are the same.

❸ The doInJdo() method, which is invoked by the JdoTemplate with a PersistenceManager, creates the named query and executes it.

Although this seems like a lot of code to do something so simple, it's important to remember that this class is reusable and it makes the repository easier to test. Let's see how.

Writing the mock object test

Once we have defined the ExecuteNamedQueryWithMapCallback class, we can then write a mock object test for findRestaurants(). This test configures a mock JdoTemplate to expect its execute() method to be called with an instance of the class that contains the expected query name and query parameters. Listing 5.5 shows the mock object test for findRestaurants() that does this.

Listing 5.5   JDORestaurantRepositoryImplTests

```
public class JDORestaurantRepositoryImplTests extends
    MockObjectTestCase {

  private Mock mockJdoTemplate;

  private JDORestaurantRepositoryImpl repository;

  private static final int EXPECTED_MINUTE = 6;

  private static final int EXPECTED_HOUR = 5;

  private static final int EXPECTED_DAY_OF_WEEK = 3;

  Address deliveryAddress;

  Date deliveryTime;

  public void setUp() {        ◁────── ❶ Creates mock objects
    mockJdoTemplate =                     and test data
      new Mock(JdoTemplate.class);
    repository = new JDORestaurantRepositoryImpl(
        (JdoTemplate) mockJdoTemplate.proxy(), null);
    restaurant = new Restaurant();
    deliveryTime = makeDeliveryTime(EXPECTED_DAY_OF_WEEK,
        EXPECTED_HOUR, EXPECTED_MINUTE);
```

```
    deliveryAddress = new Address("1 somewhere", null,
        "Oakland", "CA", "94619");
}

private Date makeDeliveryTime(int dayOfWeek, int hour,
    int minute) {
  Calendar c = Calendar.getInstance();
  c.set(Calendar.DAY_OF_WEEK, dayOfWeek);
  c.set(Calendar.HOUR_OF_DAY, hour);
  c.set(Calendar.MINUTE, minute);
  return c.getTime();
}

public void testFindAvailableRestaurants() {
  List expectedRestaurants = Collections      ◁──────❷ Creates result
      .singletonList(new Restaurant());                  of query

  ExecuteNamedQueryWithMapCallback          ❸ Creates expected
      expectedCallback =                       callback
          makeExpectedCallback();

  mockJdoTemplate.expects(once())
      .method("execute")                    ❹ Configures
      .with(eq(expectedCallback))              expectations
      .will(returnValue(
              ➥ expectedRestaurants));

  List foundRestaurants = repository           ❺ Calls repository
      .findAvailableRestaurants(deliveryAddress,   and checks result
          deliveryTime);
  assertEquals(expectedRestaurants, foundRestaurants);
}

private ExecuteNamedQueryWithMapCallback makeExpectedCallback() {
  String queryName = "Restaurant.findAvailableRestaurants";
  Map parameters = new HashMap();
  parameters.put("zipCode", deliveryAddress.getZip());
  parameters.put("day", new Integer(EXPECTED_DAY_OF_WEEK));
  parameters.put("hour", new Integer(EXPECTED_HOUR));
  parameters.put("minute", new Integer(EXPECTED_MINUTE));

  Class type = Restaurant.class;

  ExecuteNamedQueryWithMapCallback expectedCallback
      = new ExecuteNamedQueryWithMapCallback(type,
                                             queryName,
                                             parameters);
  return expectedCallback;
}
}
```

Let's look at the details:

❶ The setup() method creates the mock JdoTemplate, the JdoRestaurant-Repository, and the delivery information that is used for the test.

❷ The testFindAvailableRestaurants() method creates the list of restaurants that is returned by ExecuteNamedQueryWithMapCallback and that should be returned by the repository.

❸ This calls makeExpectedCallback() to create the ExecuteNamedQueryWith-MapCallback that should be passed to the JdoTemplate. The makeExpected-Callback() method creates an ExecuteNamedQueryWithMapCallback that specifies the Restaurant class, the Restaurant.findAvailableRestaurants query, and the query's parameters, which consist of the delivery information's ZIP code, day of the week, hour, and minute.

❹ The testFindAvailableRestaurants() method configures the mock JdoTem-plate to expect its execute() method to be called with an ExecuteNamedQuery-WithMapCallback and to return the list of restaurants.

❺ This calls findAvailableRestaurants() and verifies that it returns the expected list of restaurants.

5.3.2 Implementing JDORestaurantRepositoryImpl

The next step is to write the JDORestaurantRepositoryImpl class and the findRestaurants() method. This will be easy since we had to decide how it worked in order to write the test. Listing 5.6 shows the JDORestaurantReposi-tory class, which uses the JdoTemplate class to execute an instance of the Exe-cuteNamedQueryWithMapCallback class.

Listing 5.6   The JDORestaurantRepository class

```
public class JDORestaurantRepositoryImpl extends JdoDaoSupport
    implements RestaurantRepository {

    public JDORestaurantRepositoryImpl            ❶ Creates
            (JdoTemplate jdoTemplate) {              JDORestaurantRepositoryImpl
        setJdoTemplate(jdoTemplate);
    }

    public List findAvailableRestaurants(Address deliveryAddress,
        Date deliveryTime) {
        Calendar c = Calendar.getInstance();
        c.setTime(deliveryTime);                  ❷ Creates
        int dayOfWeek =                             parameters
```

```
                    c.get(Calendar.DAY_OF_WEEK);
    int hour = c.get(Calendar.HOUR_OF_DAY);
    int minute = c.get(Calendar.MINUTE);

    Map parameters = new HashMap();
    parameters.put("zipCode",                    ➋ Creates
                deliveryAddress.getZip());          parameters
    parameters.put("day",
                    new Integer(dayOfWeek));
    parameters.put("hour",
                    new Integer(hour));
    parameters.put("minute",
                    new Integer(minute));

    ExecuteNamedQueryWithMapCallback
        callback =                                ➌ Creates
        new ExecuteNamedQueryWithMapCallback(       callback
            Restaurant.class,
            "Restaurant.findAvailableRestaurants", parameters);

    return (List)
        getJdoTemplate().execute(callback);    ◁──── ➍ Executes
}                                                      callback
```

JDORestaurantRepositoryImpl implements RestaurantRepository and extends JdoDaoSupport, which is a Spring-provided support class that includes convenience methods such as setJdoTemplate() and getJdoTemplate(). Let's look at the details:

➊ The constructor takes a JdoTemplate as a parameter and calls setJdoTemplate().

➋ The findRestaurants() method uses a Calendar to get the day of week, hour, and minute from the delivery time and then creates a Map containing the query parameters.

➌ The findRestaurants() method instantiates an ExecuteNamedQueryWithMapCallback object, passing the name of the query, the restaurant class, and the query parameters to its constructor.

➍ It calls JdoTemplate.execute() to execute the ExecuteNamedQueryWithMapCallback object.

As you can see, implementing a repository using JDO is quite easy. The only complication was the requirement to define a named JdoCallback class in order to make the findAvailableRestaurants() method easier to test.

5.3.3 *Writing the query that finds the restaurants*

So far we have implemented the `findAvailableRestaurants()` method and written a test that verifies that it executes the named query correctly. The final step is to implement the JDO query that it uses to finds the available restaurants. Because it is a named query, it is defined in the XML metadata for the `Restaurant` class:

```
<class name="Restaurant" table="RESTAURANT" ...>
...
  <query name="Restaurant.findAvailableRestaurants">
      <![CDATA[
      select
      where serviceArea.contains(zipCode)
        && timeRanges.contains(tr)
        && (tr.dayOfWeek == day
          && (tr.openHour < hour
              || (tr.openHour == hour
                  && tr.openMinute <= minute))
          && (tr.closeHour > hour
              || (tr.closeHour == hour
                  && tr.closeMinute > minute))
        )
      variables TimeRange tr
      parameters String zipCode, int day, int hour, int minute
      ]]>
  </query>
</class>
```

This query takes a ZIP code, a day of the week, an hour, and a minute as parameters. It finds all restaurants whose `serviceArea` field contains the specified ZIP code and whose `timeRanges` field contains a `TimeRange` for the specified day of the week, hour, and minute.

5.3.4 *Writing tests for a query*

Unless a query is extremely simple, it is usually worthwhile to write tests for it. Let's look at one way to test the query that finds the available restaurants. This query's `where` clause contains several relational operators, and so it is important to test with various combinations of test data. Each of the tests for this query, some of which are shown in listing 5.7, initializes the database with test data, invokes the query with a particular set of arguments, and verifies that it returns the expected results. The test class extends the ORMUnit class `JDOPersistenceTests` and uses the `RestaurantMother` helper class to construct the test restaurant.

Listing 5.7 JDORestaurantRepositoryQueryTests

```
public class JDORestaurantRepositoryQueryTests extends
    JDOPersistenceTests {

  private JDORestaurantRepositoryImpl repository;

  private String restaurantId;

  protected void setUp() throws Exception {
    super.setUp();
    repository = new JDORestaurantRepositoryImpl(
        getJdoTemplate());
    initializeDatabase();    ◁————————❶
  }

  private void initializeDatabase() {
    doWithTransaction(new TxnCallback() {

      public void execute() throws Throwable {
        deletePersistent(Order.class);
        deletePersistent(PendingOrder.class);
        deletePersistent(Restaurant.class);
        Restaurant r = RestaurantMother
            .makeRestaurant(RestaurantTestData.GOOD_ZIP_CODE);
        makePersistent(r);
        restaurantId = r.getId();
      }
    });
  }

  private void findAvailableRestaurants(final int dayOfWeek,    ◁————————❷
      final int hour, final int minute, final String zipCode,
      final boolean expectRestaurants) throws Exception {

    doWithTransaction(new TxnCallback() {

      public void execute() throws Throwable {
        Date deliveryTime = makeDeliveryTime(dayOfWeek,
            hour, minute);
        Address deliveryAddress = new Address(
            "1 Good Street", null, "Good Town", "CA",
            zipCode);

        Collection availableRestaurants = repository
            .findAvailableRestaurants(deliveryAddress,
                deliveryTime);
        if (expectRestaurants)
          assertFalse(availableRestaurants.isEmpty());
        else
          assertTrue(availableRestaurants.isEmpty());
```

```
        }
      });

    public void testFindAvailableRestaurants()    ◄────── ❸
                       throws Exception {
      findAvailableRestaurants(Calendar.TUESDAY, 19, 0,
          RestaurantTestData.GOOD_ZIP_CODE, true);
    }

    public void testFindAvailableRestaurants_closedDay()    ◄────── ❹
        throws Exception {
      findAvailableRestaurants(Calendar.MONDAY, 19, 0,
          RestaurantTestData.GOOD_ZIP_CODE, false);
    }

    public void testFindAvailableRestaurants_badZipCode()    ◄────── ❺
        throws Exception {
      findAvailableRestaurants(Calendar.MONDAY, 19, 0,
          RestaurantTestData.BAD_ZIP_CODE, false);
    }

  }
```

Here's a closer look at JDORestaurantRepositoryQueryTests:

❶ The setUp() method initializes the database by deleting existing restaurants and inserting a test restaurant.

❷ The findAvailableRestaurants() method, which is a helper method called by the tests, executes the query with the parameters and verifies the result.

❸ The testFindAvailableRestaurants_good() method executes the query with delivery information that is served by a restaurant.

❹ The testFindAvailableRestaurants_closedDay() method executes the query with delivery information for a day that is not served by any restaurants.

❺ The testFindAvailableRestaurants_badZipCode() method executes the query with a ZIP code that is not served by any restaurants.

This class would also define tests for various boundary conditions such as a delivery time that is equal to the opening time of a restaurant and a delivery time that is equal to its closing time.

Although these tests can be time consuming to write and execute, they are extremely useful because they verify that the query behaves correctly.

Once you've written the XML metadata, made the necessary changes to the domain model classes, implemented the repositories, and written the tests, you will have a persistent domain model. You will then be able to integrate it with the presentation tier to create a working application. However, before your application goes into production it is quite likely that you will have to improve performance by using eager loading and caching.

5.4 *JDO performance tuning*

A wise software developer once said, "First, make it work, then make it work right, and finally make it work fast." The tests that we have written should ensure that it works right, and so now we turn our attention to how to make it work fast. We saw in chapter 4 that lazy loading, eager loading, process-level caching, and query caching are important mechanisms for improving the performance of an application that uses an ORM framework. They reduce the load on the database, which is often the bottleneck in an enterprise application.

It is important to achieve the correct balance between lazy and eager loading. Lazy loading minimizes the number of objects the application loads from the database by only loading objects that are actually accessed. Eager loading minimizes the number of trips to the database by retrieving multiple related objects at a time. By using the right combination of eager and lazy loading, you can often improve the performance of an application.

Process-level caching is another way to improve the performance of an application. It reduces the number of database accesses by caching frequently accessed objects in memory. Before accessing the database, the JDO implementation first checks in the process-level cache. Using a process-level cache can often improve the performance of an application significantly. In this example application, it makes sense to cache the restaurant-related classes—`Restaurant`, `MenuItem`, and `TimeRanges`—because they are frequently accessed but rarely updated. An application can use a combination of eager loading and process-level caching. However, relationships from objects that are not cached to those that are should not be eagerly loaded because that would bypass the cache.

Query caching is an extension of the process-level caching mechanism. The query cache stores the IDs of the objects returned by a query. When the JDO implementation is called by the application to execute in the query, it looks in the query cache before accessing the database. If the query is in the cache, the JDO implementation then retrieves the objects from the process-level cache. For some queries in some applications, this can improve performance significantly.

In this section you will learn how to use eager loading, process-level caching, and query caching in a JDO application. We describe how to use JDO fetch groups to configure eager loading. You will learn how to use AOP to separate the code that configures the eager loading from the code the core business logic. We discuss how to use process-level caching and query caching in one popular JDO implementation, and use the Place Order use case as an example.

5.4.1 *Using fetch groups to optimize object loading*

JDO, like most other ORM frameworks, uses lazy loading by default. You configure eager loading by using either JDO fetch groups or an implementation-specific mechanism. A JDO fetch group, which is associated with a class, describes the structure of an object graph whose root object is an instance of that class. It specifies the objects and their fields that should be loaded when the application executes a JDO query or loads an instance. There are two ways to eagerly load a related object using fetch groups. The simpler of the approaches is to add the field that references the object to what is called the *default fetch group*. The other approach is to define a *custom fetch group*. Let's look at each strategy.

Using default fetch groups

Every persistent JDO class has a default fetch group, which contains the fields that the JDO implementation loads by default. By default, this group contains the class's primitive fields, the date fields, string fields, and fields whose type is a number wrapper class. As a result, the JDO implementation will only load those fields that contain simple values and any referenced objects will be loaded lazily. However, an easy way to eagerly load an object is to add the field that references it to the default fetch group.

For example, the application always traverses the `PendingOrder-Restaurant` and `PendingOrderLineItem-MenuItem` relationships in the Food to Go Domain model. It makes sense, therefore, to add the corresponding fields to the default fetch group. The default fetch group is configured in the XML metadata. For example, this is how you would add the `PendingOrder.restaurant` field to the default fetch group:

```
<class name="PendingOrder" identity-type="application">
   ...
    <field name="restaurant" default-fetch-group="true">
   ...
</class>
```

The default-fetch-group="true" attribute specifies that the restaurant field is a member of the PendingOrder's default fetch group. A JDO implementation typically loads a PendingOrder by executing a SELECT table that does a join between the PENDING_ORDER and RESTAURANT tables. The PendingOrderLineItem-MenuItem is configured in a similar fashion. Once we have configured the fetch groups, the JDO implementation will load the related objects using a SQL join.

Adding a field to the default fetch group is a useful way to improve performance if the relationship is always traversed when the referencing object is loaded. However, if different requests traverse different relationships, then the default fetch group mechanism isn't all that useful. We must instead use custom fetch groups to dynamically control eager loading.

Using custom fetch groups to optimize object loading

A custom fetch group is defined in the XML metadata for a class and specifies one or more of the class's fields and possibly one or more other fetch groups. An application tells JDO to eagerly load the relationships specified by a custom fetch group by activating the fetch group programmatically. For example, when handling the update payment information request the application needs to eagerly load the pending order's lineItems and their menu items in addition to its restaurants. It can do this using the following custom fetch group:

```
<class name="PendingOrder" identity-type="application">
  ...
 <fetch-group name="PendingOrder.withLineItems">
  <field name="lineItems"/>
   </fetch-group>
  ...
</class>
```

Note that because the PendingOrder.restaurant and PendingOrderLineItem.menuItem fields already belong to the default fetch group, they do not need to be specified in the custom fetch group.

Once you have defined a custom fetch group, you can use it to eagerly load those objects by writing code to add it to the PersistenceManager's active fetch groups, which control which objects and fields are loaded. By default, the "default" fetch group is the only active fetch group, which is how fields that belong to the default fetch group are loaded. However, if there is an active fetch group that contains a field that is a reference to another object, the JDO implementation will eagerly load that object in addition to any objects referenced by fields in the default fetch group.

To configure the active fetch groups, you use a `FetchPlan`, which is accessed by calling `PersistenceManager.getFetchPlan()`. You can, for example, call `FetchPlan.addGroup()` to add a fetch group to the active fetch groups for the `PersistenceManager`:

```
PersistenceManager pm = …;
FetchPlan fp = pm.getFetchPlan();
fp.addGroup("PendingOrder.withLineItems");
```

In this example, adding the fetch group we defined earlier to the set of active fetch groups causes the `PersistenceManager` to load the pending order, its restaurant, its line items, and their menu items. Fetch groups are mostly a hint to the JDO implementation when loading objects, but it is likely that a good JDO implementation would honor them.

Optimizing object loading in Kodo JDO

One of the challenges with using a new standard is that the implementations sometimes lag behind. At the time of this writing, I didn't have access to a JDO implementation that supported the JDO 2 custom fetch group mechanism; therefore, I needed to use a vendor-specific mechanism to dynamically configure eager loading. But even though it is nonstandard, it illustrates the kinds of things you will be able to do with JDO 2 fetch groups once they are supported.

Kodo JDO 3.3 provides a couple of ways to dynamically configuring eager loading. It provides custom fetch groups that are similar to those supplied by JDO 2 but less flexible because a field can only belong to either the default fetch group or to at most one custom fetch group. As a result, you cannot define multiple fetch groups that have fields in common, which makes them quite difficult to use.

Fortunately, Kodo JDO also has a per-field fetch configuration mechanism that lets you explicitly specify the fields that should be loaded eagerly. This mechanism is more flexible than its custom fetch groups because you can specify an arbitrary set of fields. To use this feature, you must downcast the `PersistenceManager` to a `KodoPersistenceManager` and get its `FetchConfiguration`, which is similar to the `FetchPlan` class discussed earlier. This class provides methods for specifying the fields that should be loaded by its `PersistenceManager`. Here is an example of how to arrange for the `PendingOrder`'s line items and restaurant to be eagerly loaded:

```
PersistenceManager pm = …;
KodoPersistenceManager kpm = (KodoPersistenceManager)pm;
FetchConfiguration fc = pm.getFetchConfiguration();
fc.addField("net.chrisrichardson.foodToGo.PendingOrder.lineItems");
fc.addField("net.chrisrichardson.foodToGo.PendingOrder.restaurant");
```

The call to `FetchConfiguration.addField()` tells Kodo JDO to eagerly load the `PendingOrder`'s line items and restaurant.

To dynamically configure object loading, the application must call `FetchConfiguration.addField()` with the required fields prior to calling `PersistenceManager.getObjectById()`. For the Place Order use case, one option is for the `PendingOrderRepository` to define multiple versions of the `findPendingOrder()` method that calls `FetchConfiguration.addField()` with the appropriate fields. For example, the `findPendingOrderWithLineItemsAndRestaurant()` method, which is called by `PlaceOrderService.updatePaymentInformation()`, would add the `PendingOrder.lineItems` and `PendingOrder.restaurant` fields to the active fields using code similar to that shown earlier.

However, the trouble with this approach is that it requires changing the domain model. Although some objects are loaded because they are required by the business logic, other objects are loaded because they are needed by the UI. It is undesirable to couple the core business logic to the UI design because we might have to repeatedly change the business logic to reflect changes to the UI. Furthermore, it also makes the domain model less reusable. To avoid these problems, we have to separate the business logic from the code that configures object loading. Let's see how to do this.

Using AOP to dynamically configure eager loading

We can use a Spring AOP interceptor to separate the business logic from the code that configures object loading. The interceptor, which intercepts requests to the business logic, adds the fields that must be eagerly loaded to the `FetchConfiguration`. Listing 5.8 shows the `KodoFetchGroupInterceptor`, which is a Spring AOP interceptor that configures the `FetchConfiguration` based on the method that is invoked. When the interceptor is invoked, it uses the method name to determine which fields to add to the `FetchConfiguration`. The set of fields to use for a given method invocation is specified by the map that is passed to the interceptor's constructor. The key of each map entry is the name of a service method, and the value is a list of fully qualified field names.

Listing 5.8   KodoFetchGroupInterceptor

```
public class KodoFetchGroupInterceptor
               implements MethodInterceptor {
    private PersistenceManagerFactory pmf;

    private Map fetchGroupConfig;
```

```
public KodoFetchGroupInterceptor(PersistenceManagerFactory pmf,
    Map fetchGroupConfig) {
  this.pmf = pmf;
  this.fetchGroupConfig = fetchGroupConfig;
}

public Object invoke(MethodInvocation methodInvocation)
    throws Throwable {
  PersistenceManager pm = PersistenceManagerFactoryUtils
      .getPersistenceManager(pmf, false);
  KodoPersistenceManager kpm = (KodoPersistenceManager) pm;

  FetchConfiguration fetchConfiguration = kpm
      .getFetchConfiguration();
  String[] originalFetchGroups = fetchConfiguration
      .getFetchGroups();
  String[] originalFields = fetchConfiguration.getFields();

  try {
    configureFetchGroups(methodInvocation.getMethod()
        .getName(), kpm, fetchConfiguration);
    return methodInvocation.proceed();
  } finally {
    fetchConfiguration.clearFetchGroups();
    fetchConfiguration.addFetchGroups(originalFetchGroups);
    fetchConfiguration.clearFields();
    fetchConfiguration.addFields(originalFields);

    PersistenceManagerFactoryUtils
        .closePersistenceManagerIfNecessary(pm, pmf);
  }
}

private void configureFetchGroups(String methodName,
    KodoPersistenceManager kpm,
    FetchConfiguration fetchConfiguration) {
  List fieldNames = getFieldNames(methodName);
  if (fieldNames != null) {
    for (Iterator it = fieldNames.iterator(); it
        .hasNext();) {
      String fieldName = (String) it.next();
      fetchConfiguration.addField(fieldName);
    }
  }
}

private List getFieldNames(String methodName) {
  List fieldNames = (List) fetchGroupConfig
      .get(methodName);
  if (fieldNames == null)
    fieldNames = (List) fetchGroupConfig.get("*");
```

- ❶
- ❷
- ❸
- ❹
- ❺
- ❻
- ❼
- ❽
- ❾

```
        return fieldNames;
    }
}
```

Unlike other examples you've seen, the `KodoJDOFetchGroupInterceptor` does not use a `JdoTemplate` to execute a `JdoCallback` because `MethodInvocation.proceed()` is declared to throw a `Throwable` whereas a `JdoCallback` can only throw a `JDOException`. Let's look at the details:

❶ Its constructor takes a `PersistenceManagerFactory` and a `Map` as parameters and saves them.

❷ The `invoke()` method gets the `PersistenceManager` bound to the thread;

❸ saves the original active fields; **❹** calls `configureFetchGroups()` to configure them; **❺** calls `proceed()` to invoke the original method; **❻** restores the `FetchConfiguration` to its original state; **❼** and closes the `PersistenceManager` if necessary.

❽ The `configureFetchGroups()` method gets the list of field names.

❾ If the list is non-null, it iterates through calling `FetchConfiguration.addField()`.

Listing 5.9 show the Spring bean definitions that configure the `KodoFetchGroupInterceptor` and applies it to the `PlaceOrderService`.

Listing 5.9 Configuring the KodoFetchGroupInterceptor

```
<beans>
...
  <bean id="FetchGroupInterceptor"
    class="net.chrisrichardson.foodToGo.util.jdo.kdo.fetchGroups.
        ➥ KodoFetchGroupInterceptor">
    <constructor-arg ref="myPersistenceManagerFactory" />
    <constructor-arg>
      <map>
        <entry key="updateQuantities">
          <list>
            <value>
              net.chrisrichardson.foodToGo.domain.
                  ➥ PendingOrder.restaurant
            </value>
            <value>
              net.chrisrichardson.foodToGo.domain.
                  ➥ PendingOrder.lineItems
```

```
            </value>
            <value>
              net.chrisrichardson.foodToGo.domain.
                  ➦ Restaurant.menuItems
            </value>
          </list>
        </entry>
        <entry key="updatePaymentInformation">
          <list>
            <value>
              net.chrisrichardson.foodToGo.domain.
                  ➦ PendingOrder.restaurant
            </value>
            <value>
              net.chrisrichardson.foodToGo.domain.
                  ➦ PendingOrder.lineItems
            </value>
          </list>
        </entry>
      </map>
    </constructor-arg>
  </bean>

  <bean id="PlaceOrderFieldProxyCreator"
    class="org.springframework.aop.framework.autoproxy.
                      ➦ BeanNameAutoProxyCreator">
    <property name="beanNames">
      <list>
        <idref bean="PlaceOrderService" />
      </list>
    </property>
    <property name="interceptorNames">
      <list>
        <idref bean="FetchGroupInterceptor" />
      </list>
    </property>
  </bean>
  ...

</beans>
```

The `FetchGroupInterceptor` bean creates and configures a `KodoFetch-GroupInterceptor`. One parameter is the `PersistenceManagerFactory`, which is defined elsewhere, and the other is a map that specifies the fields to eagerly load when a method is invoked. The map is constructed by the `<map>` element constructs. Each `<entry>` element constructs a map entry with the method as a key and a list of field names as the value, and each `<list>` element constructs a list of field names. `PlaceOrderFieldProxyCreator` applies the `KodoFetch-GroupInterceptor` to the `PlaceOrderService`.

Each time the `PlaceOrderService` is called, the `KodoFetchGroupInterceptor` will add the specified fields to the `FetchConfiguration`, which will cause them to be eagerly loaded. If the UI design changes and requires different fields to be loaded, you will just need to edit the Spring bean definition and not modify any code.

You will be able to configure JDO 2.0 fetch groups using a similar AOP-based approach. Instead of configuring individual fields, the interceptor will use the JDO 2.0 APIs to configure the active fetch groups. Eager loading is only one way to improve performance. Another option is to use process-level caching.

5.4.2 *Using a PersistenceManagerFactory-level cache*

By default, a JDO implementation only caches objects in `PersistenceManager`. It looks in the `PersistenceManager` cache before loading an object from the database. In addition to ensuring that there is at most one in-memory representation of a persistent object, the cache improves performance by reducing database accesses. However, the `PersistenceManager` cache is flushed when a transaction ends, which means that the next time the application accesses an object the JDO implementation has to load it from the database. In a JDO application, you can often improve performance significantly by caching frequently accessed but rarely modified objects in the `PersistenceManagerFactory`-level cache, which is JDO's way of providing process-level caching.

Overview of the PersistenceManagerFactory-level cache

The JDO implementation looks in the `PersistenceManagerFactory`-level cache after checking the `PersistenceManager` cache but before accessing the database. This cache is not flushed when a transaction commits and consequently contains objects accessed by multiple transactions. Enabling the `PersistenceManagerFactory`-level cache can often increase performance significantly by reducing the number of database accesses.

The JDO specification does not define the detailed behavior of the `PersistenceManagerFactory`-level cache or how to configure it. You must typically configure the cache by using a combination of vendor-specific `PersistenceManagerFactory` properties and XML metadata. For example, the Kodo JDO `PersistenceManagerFactory` cache is enabled using the following `PersistenceManagerFactory` properties:

```
kodo.DataCache: true
kodo.RemoteCommitProvider: sjvm
```

The kodo.DataCache property enables the PersistenceManagerFactory-level cache and also specifies the cache configuration, such as its size and how long cached items should remain in the cache. You can also configure multiple caches with different configurations. The kodo.RemoteCommitProvider property specifies how to broadcast change invalidation messages to other cluster members when objects are modified. A value of sjvm is used in a single JVM configuration.

When Kodo's PersistenceManagerFactory-level cache is enabled, all classes will be cached by default. You can configure caching behavior for individual classes, however, using metadata extensions. The data-cache extension specifies whether instances of this class should be cached and which cache to use. The data-cache-timeout extension specifies how long an instance should be cached; a timeout of -1 means indefinitely. Here is an example:

```
<class name="Restaurant" identity-type="application">
    ...
    <extension vendor-name="kodo"
        key="data-cache-timeout"
        value="3600000"/>
    ...
</class>
```

This metadata specifies that the Restaurant class should be cached for at most one hour.

Kodo JDO, like other JDO implementation, also provides methods for evicting objects from the PersistenceManagerFactory-level cache. An application removes an single object from the cache by calling DataCache.remove() and removes a collection of objects by calling DataCache.removeAll(). An application often needs to evict stale objects from the cache if it updates the database by using, for example, iBATIS or JDBC.

Using the PersistenceManagerFactory-level cache

To cache only the restaurant-related classes—Restaurant, MenuItem, and TimeRange—in the Kodo JDO PersistenceManagerFactory-level cache, we would enable the cache and disable caching for the other domain model classes, such as PendingOrder and PendingOrderLineItem. We would also have to turn off any eager loading of the restaurant-related classes to ensure that the PersistenceManagerFactory-level cache is used. Kodo would then just load the pending order and its line items using a single SQL statement. The JDO implementation retrieves the restaurant and menu item objects referenced by the pending order and its line items from the `PersistenceManagerFactory`-level cache when the application navigates to them.

5.4.3 Using a query cache

The `PersistenceManagerFactory`-level cache optimizes the loading of individual objects but, by default, queries still go to the database. To improve query performance, some JDO implementations also provide a query cache that caches the results of a query and avoids the need to execute a SQL `SELECT` statement. The query cache is used in conjunction with the `PersistenceManagerFactory`-level cache. It caches the IDs of the objects returned by the query, which are then used to find the objects in the `PersistenceManagerFactory`-level cache. A query is dropped from the cache when an instance of a class that is accessed by the query is modified.

Overview of the query cache

The details of the query cache depend on the JDO implementation. For example, the Kodo JDO query cache is enabled by default if the data cache is enabled but can be disabled by setting the `kodo.QueryCache PersistenceManagerFactory` property to `false`. If the query cache is enabled, it can be turned off for a `Persistence-Manager` by calling `KodoPersistenceManager.setQueryCacheEnabled(false)` and turned off for a query by calling `KodoQuery.setQueryCacheEnabled-(false)`. You also need to remember that the query cache is ignored in some situations. For example, the query cache is not used during pessimistic transactions (see chapter 12 for a description of pessimistic transactions) because Kodo JDO must go to the database to lock the rows.

Using the query cache for the Place Order use case

For the Place Order use case, the queries that could be cached are those executed by `RestaurantRepository.isRestaurantAvailable()` and `findAvailable-Restaurants()`. However, there are potentially many combinations of values for each query's parameters – `zipCode`, and `deliveryTime`—so it is unclear whether caching them would be advantageous. We would have to analyze the running application to determine whether there is any benefit.

5.5 Summary

JDO 2.0 is a standard ORM framework that is comparable in power to Hibernate. It provides mostly transparent persistence for POJOs, and a typical domain model can be mapped to the database without significant changes. In the example domain model, we just needed to insert an abstract class into an inheritance hierarchy.

One important decision you need to make when persisting a class is whether to use application identity or datastore identity. With application identity, an object's persistent identity corresponds to the database primary key and is stored in its primary key field or fields, which makes it readily accessible. With datastore identity, an object's persistent identity is managed by the JDO implementation and is not stored in the object. You don't need to add primary key fields to the domain model, but it makes accessing the primary key of an object more difficult.

JDO provides a straightforward API for manipulating persistent data, which is made even easier to use by Spring's `JdoTemplate` class. Many repository methods can call a `JdoTemplate` method and never need to call the JDO APIs directly. Those methods that do need to call the JDO APIs use the `JdoTemplate` to execute a `JdoCallback`. To enable testing with mock objects, the repository methods must used a named `JdoCallback` class instead of the commonly used anonymous `JdoCallback`.

JDO provides several features for improving the performance of an application. You can use fetch groups to configure eager loading. A fetch group is specified in the XML metadata and defines the structure of an object graph to eagerly load. A key feature of fetch groups is that they enable you to use a Spring AOP interceptor to dynamically configure eagerly loading for each request without having to change the code. JDO also provides a `PersistanceManagerFactory`-level cache, which caches objects across transaction boundaries. In addition, some JDO implementations provide a query cache, which caches the results of a query. It is important to remember, however, that because JDO is a standard, the quality and features of each specific implementation determine performance.

Now that you have seen how to persist a POJO domain model with JDO, the next chapter examines how to do the same thing with Hibernate.

Persisting a domain model with Hibernate 3

195

Hibernate is an extremely popular open source, ORM framework. It provides mostly transparent persistence for POJOs as well as a rich set of ORM options. Hibernate can run inside an application server or in a two-tier environment (which accelerates development by enabling Hibernate-based business logic to be developed and tested outside of the application server). However, like every technology Hibernate has its strengths and weaknesses. In this chapter, you will learn how to leverage Hibernate's strengths and how to work around its weaknesses.

We describe how use Hibernate 3.0 to persist a domain model using the Food to Go domain model from chapter 3 as an example. You will learn how Hibernate implements each of the main ORM concepts described in chapter 4, including its mapping features and API. We describe how to map the domain model to a database schema and the changes that we must make to accommodate Hibernate's limitations. You will learn how to implement domain model repositories with the Hibernate API and the Spring framework. We also explain how to effectively test a Hibernate-based persistence layer.

For more detailed information about Hibernate, see *Hibernate in Action* [Bauer 2005].

6.1 Hibernate ORM issues

Hibernate is the de facto standard for Java transparent persistence. This is because it's free, it's well documented, and it works. You can download it and install it without having to make a case for spending thousands of dollars in development licenses. The excellent documentation means that getting started is relatively painless. Also, other than a few quirks here and there, it works as advertised. As a result, Hibernate is widely used.

Because Hibernate provides a powerful and flexible ORM mechanism, persisting a typical domain model is mostly straightforward. However, there are still some Hibernate-specific issues to resolve. In this section and the next one, we describe those issues and explore the different options. Let's first look at some of the decisions you must make when defining the O/R mapping for a domain model.

6.1.1 Fields or properties

A persistence framework such as Hibernate must read and write the object's state when it transfers the object to and from the database. An object's state consists of the values of its fields, but sometimes it is useful to encapsulate the state with Java Bean-style properties. Hibernate, unlike JDO, can map either fields or Java Bean-style properties to the database schema. If the O/R mapping is defined in terms of fields, Hibernate accesses the fields directly when loading and saving objects. Alternatively, if the mapping is defined using properties, Hibernate calls getters and setters. Table 6.1 lists the pros and cons of each option.

Table 6.1 Pros and cons of mapping fields and properties

	Pros	Cons
Properties	Encapsulation Accessors can transform values It's the default	Must define accessors (but they can be private)
Fields	No need to define accessors—especially setters	Less encapsulation Not the default, so that mapping becomes more verbose

Hibernate's O/R mapping uses the <property> element to map either a field or a property to a column, which can be confusing at first. For example, you can map the price property of a MenuItem using this:

```
class MenuMenu {
…
  public double getPrice() {…};
  private void setPrice(double newPrice) {…};
…
}

<class name="MenuItem" …>
…
  <property name="price" column="PRICE"/>
…
</class>
```

Hibernate calls accessors when it loads and saves a MenuItem. It calls the get-Price() getter when it saves a MenuItem and will call the setPrice() setter when it loads a MenuItem. Note that accessors can be private if necessary.

Alternatively, you can map the price field using this:

```
class MenuMenu {
  private double price;
…
}

<class name="MenuItem" …>
…
  <property name=" price" column="PRICE" access="field"/>
…
</class>
```

The `access` attribute specifies that the price is a field rather than a property. Hibernate will read and write the `price` field, which can be private, directly without calling an accessor.

You can avoid having to specify an `access` attribute for every property by defining the default in the `<hibernate-mapping>` element:

```
<hibernate-mapping
  default-access="field">
  …
<class name="MenuItem" …>
…
  <property name="price" column="PRICE"/>
…
</class>
```

Because the `default-access` attribute has the value of `field`, the `<property>` element refers to the field rather than the property.

Mapping properties is useful in some situations, such as when an object needs to initialize some nonpersistent fields or transform the persisted value. However, except in those rare situations I would recommend mapping fields. Since Hibernate's purpose is to store the state of an object in the database schema, I have found no benefit in hiding that state from Hibernate with accessors. Moreover, many objects have getters for their state but do not define setters. For example, the `PendingOrder` class has a `getDeliveryAddress()` method but does not define a `setDeliveryAddress()` method. Its client must instead call `updateDeliveryInfo()`, which validates its arguments. There is little value in defining a private `setDeliveryAddress()` method for Hibernate's exclusive use. Even though it is generally considered to be bad practice to access an object's fields directly, this is a situation where it is perfectly acceptable.

6.1.2 *Hibernate entities and components*

When we're using Hibernate, an important part of defining the O/R mapping for a domain model is to determine which classes are entities and which are components. This distinction is important because Hibernate maps entities and components to the database in slightly different ways. A Hibernate entity is a standalone object whose lifecycle is independent of the lifecycle of any other object that references it. This is similar to but not quite the same as the domain model entity concept you learned about in chapter 3.

In contrast, a Hibernate component is an object that is part of some other parent object and that is persisted and deleted with its parent. A component is also deleted when it is no longer associated with its parent object. Hibernate components are important for two reasons:

- You can use a component to map an object to its parent object's table.
- You can use a collection of components to efficiently persist a unidirectional one-to-many relationship that is mapped using a foreign key.

To determine whether a domain model class should be a Hibernate entity or a component, you must carefully analyze the relationships that it has with other classes. A class that is associated with only one other class and whose lifecycle is dependent on that other class is a good candidate to be a component. On the other hand, classes that have an independent existence or that are referenced by multiple classes should be mapped as entities. Figure 6.1 is a UML class diagram that shows some of the classes and relationships in the Food to Go domain model.

In this example, domain model classes such as PendingOrder, Restaurant, and Order are clearly Hibernate entities. They are objects whose lifetime is independent of any other objects. On the other hand, classes such as Address and PaymentInformation are components because they are simple value objects with

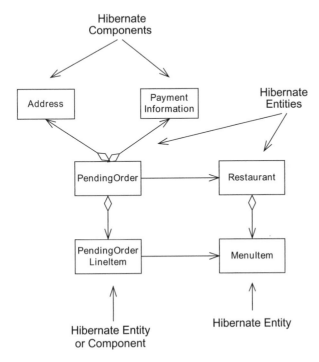

Figure 6.1
The Hibernate entities and components in part of the Food to Go domain model

no distinct identity and stored in their parent object's table. The lifetime of each `PendingOrderLineItem`, `OrderLineItem`, and `MenuItem` object is dependent on its parent. `PendingOrderLineItem` and `OrderLineItem` could be either entities or components, but `MenuItem` needs to be an entity because it is referenced by `Pending-OrderLineItem`, `OrderLineItem`, and `Restaurant`.

Later in this section, we'll describe these choices in more detail when we look at how to define the O/R mapping for the various relationships in the domain model.

6.1.3 Configuring object identity

A persistent object has a persistent identity, which is the primary key of the corresponding row the database table. The persistent identity usually consists of a single value, which maps to a primary key column. A class can also have a composite key consisting of multiple properties that map to multiple table columns, but we don't describe this feature here. In the Hibernate O/R mapping for a class, you can specify various aspects of its persistent identity, including the primary key column, whether it is maintained in the object, and whether the application or Hibernate generates the persistent identity. Let's look at an example.

An example of how to configure the identity

A class's persistent identity is configured using the `<id>` and `<generator>` elements in the mapping document:

```
<class name="PendingOrder" table="PENDING_ORDER">
    <id name="id" column="PENDING_ORDER_ID">
      <generator class="native"/>
    </id>
  ...
</class>
```

In this example the `<id>` and `<generator>` elements specify the following information about the persistent identity of the `PendingOrder` class:

- The `PENDING_ORDER_ID` column is the primary key for the PENDING_ORDER table.
- The `PendingOrder.id` field stores the persistent identity.
- Hibernate should generate persistent identifiers using a database-specific mechanism such as an Oracle sequence or an identity column.

Now that you have seen an example, let's look at the decisions you must make when configuring Hibernate object identity.

Generating persistent identifiers

First you must pick an identifier-generation strategy. Hibernate, like JDO, can generate the persistent identifier for your objects, or it can allow your application to generate them. Application-generated persistent identifiers are useful when the application needs precise control over the object's primary key. For example, one common reason to use application-assigned identifiers is if you are working with a legacy schema that uses a natural key as the primary key. In this situation, the application must assign a primary key value to an object before calling `Session.save()`.

Most of the time, however, it is a lot more convenient to let Hibernate generate an object's persistent identity, especially because it is good practice to use surrogate instead of natural keys. You also have less code to write. Hibernate provides several identifier-generation strategies, including Oracle sequences, identity columns, and Unique Universal Identifier (UUID) generation algorithms. The best approach is to configure Hibernate to use the native generation strategy, as illustrated by the earlier example. Hibernate picks the most appropriate strategy for the database. For example, Hibernate uses sequences for an Oracle database and identity columns for an HSQLDB database. Native generation is extremely useful because it enables the O/R mapping to be portable across databases. You can, for example, test against HSQLDB and then deploy on Oracle without changing the O/R mapping document.

Using identifier properties

In addition to deciding how to generate identifiers, you must determine whether you need to define an identifier property in which to store them. The class must have an identifier property if it uses an application-generated primary key because it must be able to assign a value to the property before saving the object. An identifier property is optional if Hibernate is responsible for generating identifiers. If an object has an identifier property, Hibernate assigns the generated identifier to it when the object is saved.

As we described in chapter 5 when comparing JDO datastore identity and application identity, the main benefit of identifier properties is that they make an object's persistent identity readily available to the rest of the application. They are extremely useful when the business tier returns domain objects to the presentation tier, which typically embeds object identifiers in URLs or hidden fields or stores them as part of the session state. If an object has an identifier property, the presentation tier can easily get an object's identifier. However, if an object does not have an identifier property, either the business tier or presentation tier must get an object's identity by calling `Session.getIdentity()` with the object as a parameter, which is much less convenient.

The downside of using identifier properties is that because they are usually surrogate keys that are not part of the domain model. For example, none of the classes in the Food to Go domain model developed in chapter 3 has an identifier property. Consequently, if you want to use identifier properties you must add them to the domain model classes. However, this is usually worthwhile for those objects whose identity is accessed by the application.

Mapping one-to-many relationships

An important part of defining the O/R mapping for a domain model is mapping relationships to the database schema. Hibernate's rich ORM features makes this mostly straightforward. However, one tricky area is defining the mapping for unidirectional one-to-many relationships such as `PendingOrder-PendingOrderLineItem` and `Restaurant-MenuItem`. In the domain model, these relationships are implemented by a collection of child objects in the parent object, and in the database they are represented by a foreign key from the child table to the parent table. Because of the way Hibernate handles this kind of relationship, you must sometimes choose between using suboptimal SQL or changing the domain model and database schema. Hibernate provides two ways to define the mapping for this kind of relationship. Let's look at the details of each approach and its respective benefits and drawbacks.

Using entity collections

One approach is to map the one-to-many relationship as a collection of Hibernate entities. For example, we saw in section 6.1.1 that the `MenuItem` class must be mapped as a Hibernate entity because it is referenced by multiple classes. This means that we must map the `Restaurant-MenuItems` relationship as an entity collection:

```
<class name="Restaurant" table="RESTAURANT">
...
   <list name="menuItems"
       cascade="all,delete-orphan">
     <key column="RESTAURANT_ID" not-null="true"/>
     <index column="MENU_ITEM_INDEX"/>
     <one-to-many class="MenuItem"/>
   </list>
</class>

<class name="MenuItem" table="MENU_ITEM">
...
   <property name="name" column="NAME"/>
```

```
<property name="price" column="PRICE"/>
</class>
```

This mapping specifies that the `menuItems` field is an ordered list of `MenuItem` entities. The `<key>` element specifies that the foreign key in `MENU_ITEM` is `RESTAURANT_ID`, and the `not-null` attribute tells Hibernate that the foreign key cannot be `null`. It is usually important to specify `not-null="true"` because otherwise Hibernate initially will not supply a value for a foreign key such as the `RESTAURANT_ID` column, which typically has a `NOT NULL` constraint. The `<index>` element specifies that the column that Hibernate uses to store the position of `MenuItem` in the list be called `MENU_ITEM_INDEX`.

The `cascade="all,delete-orphan"` attribute specifies that menu items should be saved or deleted at the same time as the restaurant and that a menu item should be deleted when it is removed from the `menuItems` collection. This means, for example, that the application can construct a restaurant and its menu items and then save them by calling `save()` on the restaurant. Hibernate will automatically save the menu items as well. Later, in section 6.1.5, we describe the `cascade` attribute in more detail.

Here is the definition of the MENU_ITEM table:

```
CREATE TABLE MENU_ITEM(
  MENU_ITEM_ID NUMBER(10) NOT NULL,
  RESTAURANT_ID NUMBER(10) NOT NULL,
  MENU_ITEM_INDEX NUMBER(10) NOT NULL,
  NAME VARCHAR(50) NOT NULL,
  PRICE NUMBER(5, 2) NOT NULL,
)
```

The `MENU_ITEM_ID` column is the surrogate primary key and the `RESTAURANT_ID` column is a foreign key to the RESTAURANT table.

As you can see, defining the mapping is straightforward. Hibernate will automatically delete a child when either the parent is deleted or the child is removed from the collection. Furthermore, the child table can be referenced by classes other than its parent.

But one drawback of using an entity collection is that Hibernate persists a newly created child using two SQL statements rather than one:

```
insert
   into MENU_ITEM (VERSION, NAME, PRICE, RESTAURANT_ID,
          MENU_ITEM_INDEX, MENU_ITEM_ID)
   values (?, ?, ?, ?, ?, ?)

update MENU_ITEM
  set RESTAURANT_ID=?, MENU_ITEM_INDEX=?
  where MENU_ITEM_ID=?
```

First, Hibernate executes a SQL INSERT statement that inserts the MenuItem into the MENU_ITEM table. Then, for no obvious reason, Hibernate executes a SQL UPDATE statement that sets the MENU_ITEM_INDEX and RESTAURANT_ID foreign keys to the parent's row. Luckily, the overhead of the extra statement is insignificant because the example application rarely creates menu items.

In most applications, inserts are relatively infrequent when compared to reads, so it's unlikely that this quirky behavior will cause a performance problem. But one workaround is to make the relationship bidirectional and have the child maintain a reference to the parent and a field that stores its position in the list. In this example, a MenuItem would maintain a reference to its Restaurant and an index field. But one problem with using a bidirectional relationship is that the domain model classes must contain extra code to set the fields in the child object. Another problem is that bidirectional relationships introduce cyclic dependencies into the design, which degrades maintainability. Also, it might not be possible to modify a third-party class library to make the association bidirectional.

Despite these drawbacks, you must use an entity collection if the child is referenced by multiple objects or if you need to use a surrogate key in the child table. In other situations, however, using a component collection can be a better approach.

Using component collections

Another way to implement a one-to-many relationship is as a component collection, which avoids the problem of the extra SQL statements. For example, we have seen how PendingOrderLineItem can be mapped as either a component or an entity because it is only referenced by a PendingOrder. We could, therefore, map the PendingOrder-PendingOrderLineItem as a component collection instead of an entity collection. We do this by using the <composite-element> element within the <list> element:

```
<class name="PendingOrder" table="PENDING_ORDER">

<list name="lineItems"
  table="PENDING_ORDER_LINE_ITEM"
  cascade="all">

<key column="PENDING_ORDER_ID"/>
<index column="LINE_ITEM_INDEX"/>
<composite-element
    class="PendingOrderLineItem">
  <property name="quantity" column="QUANTITY"/>
  <many-to-one
      name="menuItem"
      column="MENU_ITEM_ID"
```

```
        cascade="none" />
  </composite-element>

</list>
...
</class>
```

This mapping specifies that the `lineItems` property is a collection of `Pending-OrderLineItem` components that is stored in the PENDING_ORDER_LINE_ITEM table. Notice that because `PendingOrderLineItem` is mapped as a component it does not have a separate `<class>` mapping.

Here is the definition of the PENDING_ORDER_LINE_ITEM table:

```
CREATE TABLE PENDING_ORDER_LINE_ITEM (
   QUANTITY NUMBER(10) NOT NULL,
   PENDING_ORDER_ID NUMBER(10) NOT NULL,
   LINE_ITEM_INDEX NUMBER(10) NOT NULL,
   MENU_ITEM_ID NUMBER(10),
 )
```

The `PENDING_ORDER_ID` column is a foreign key to the PENDING_ORDER table, and the `MENU__ITEM_ID` column is a foreign key to the MENU_ITEM table. Notice that this table does not have a surrogate primary key. Instead, the primary key consists of the `PENDING_ORDER_LINE_ITEM_ID` and `LINE_ITEM_INDEX` columns.

A benefit of using component collections is that Hibernate persists a newly created child by executing a single `INSERT` SQL statement. There are, however, a couple of limitations. The child table cannot use a surrogate key, which means, for example, that Hibernate will not set a surrogate primary key column to a generated value. If the table must have a surrogate key—in order to comply with database schema design guidelines, for instance—the application must use a trigger to initialize the primary key.

Another important limitation of component collections is that the child class can only be referenced by its parent. Because of this restriction, we cannot use a component collection for the `Restaurant-MenuItem` relationship since menu items are also referenced by pending order line items and order line items. We can, however, use component collections for the `PendingOrder-PendingOrderLineItem` and `Order-OrderLineItem` relationships because line items are referenced only by their parent.

6.1.4 *Using the cascade attribute*

In chapter 4 we saw that an ORM framework must participate in the creation and destruction of a persistent object in order to update the database. For example, when the application creates a restaurant and its menu items, Hibernate must update the database. Similarly, when the application wants to delete a restaurant and its menu items, it must call Hibernate to delete them from the database. Simply using the new operator to create an object or relying on the garbage collector to delete an object is insufficient.

Hibernate provides a couple of ways of doing this. One option is for an application to explicitly call save() to save a persistent object and delete() to delete a persistent object. We would, for example, call save() or delete() on the restaurant and each of its menu items. The other option is to configure Hibernate to automatically persist an object when it is referenced by an already persistent object and delete an object when either its referencing object is deleted or it becomes unassociated from its parent object. We can, for example, configure Hibernate to automatically save the restaurant's menu items when the restaurant is saved and to delete the menu items when the restaurant is deleted. Not only does automatically invoking operations such as save and delete on related objects preserve the consistency of the database, but it also means that you have to write a lot less code.

You can control what happens on a per-relationship basis by specifying a value for the cascade attribute of an association-mapping element, which describes how the relationship is mapped to the database schema. The cascade attribute is a comma-separated list of values that correspond to the names of certain Session methods. It specifies whether a method that is invoked on the parent object should recursively propagate to the child objects. For example, a value of save-update specifies that save() should also save the children, and a value of delete specifies that delete() should delete the children. The possible values for the cascade attribute include:

- none: The application must explicitly save or delete the referenced object and is the default value unless overridden by the default-cascade attribute of the <hibernate-mapping> element.

- save-update: Hibernate will automatically save the referenced object when it is associated with a referencing object that is already persistent or when the referencing object is saved.

- all: Hibernate will automatically save and delete the referenced object with the referencing object.

- delete: Hibernate will delete the children when the parent is deleted.

- delete-orphan: This value is used for collections and specifies that an object is automatically deleted when it is removed from the collection.

You need to carefully determine the most appropriate cascade setting for each relationship on a case-by-case basis. Mostly you will want use the default cascade value of none for many-to-one and many-to-many relationships and a value of either all or all,delete-orphan for one-to-many relationships. For example, a value of all,delete-orphan is appropriate for the Restaurant-MenuItem relationship because a menu item should be saved when associated with a restaurant and deleted when either its restaurant is deleted or it is no longer associated with its restaurant. Conversely, a value of none is appropriate for the PendingOrder-Restaurant relationship because the restaurant's lifecycle is independent of any pending orders that reference it.

6.1.5 *Persisting interfaces*

Inheritance is an important OO concept and is widely used in domain models. Persisting a class hierarchy is generally straightforward because Hibernate supports each of the mapping schemes described in chapter 4. It even lets you persist interfaces, which means, for example, that you can define a mapping for the PendingOrder-Coupon relationship. However, persisting an interface is tricky if you want the classes in the hierarchy to have an identifier property. Unlike a class, which can define private accessors for the identifier property or a private identifier and a public getter, an interface must define public accessors, which is not a desirable approach because of the lack of encapsulation.

For example, if we want the classes in the Coupon hierarchy to have an identifier property the Coupon interface must define a getId() and a setId() method:

```
public interface Coupon {
   int getId();
   void setId(int id);
   ...
}
```

Any of the Coupon's clients could call the getId() and setId() methods, which is less than ideal. Moreover, the classes that implement this interface are required to define accessors, which is extra code that must be written.

One way to improve encapsulation is to insert an abstract class into the hierarchy that implements the interface and defines the id field. The other classes in the hierarchy are changed to extend the abstract class. The O/R mapping persists this class instead of the interface. Although you do not need to change the type of any of the fields that reference the interface, their association mapping elements must have a class attribute that defines the property type to be the abstract class. This is a good way to persist interfaces, but because Java lacks support for multiple inheritance there are situations where it conflicts with existing uses of inheritance.

Luckily, the Coupon hierarchy is extremely simple and so we do not have this problem. To persist these classes, we would define an AbstractCouponImpl class that implements the Coupon interface. The concrete coupon classes such as Free-ShippingCoupon extend this class. Here is part of the O/R mapping document for the Coupon class hierarchy:

```
<class  name="AbstractCouponImpl"
    table="COUPON">
...
  <discriminator column="COUPON_TYPE" />

  <subclass
    name="FreeShippingCoupon"
    discriminator-value="FREE_SHIP">
    <property name="code" column="CODE"  />
    <property name="minimum" column="MINIMUM"  />
  </subclass>
...
</class>
```

This mapping specifies that the AbstractCouponImpl class is mapped to the COUPON table and the <discriminator> element specifies that the discriminator column, which stores the type of the coupon, is called COUPON_TYPE. The <subclass> element specifies that the FreeShippingCoupon subclass of Coupon is mapped to the same table. The discriminator-value attribute of the <subclass> element specifies that the discriminator value for the FreeShippingCoupon is FREE_SHIP. The <property> elements map the fields of the FreeShippingCoupon class to the COUPON table.

The <many-to-one> for the PendingOrder.coupon field has the class="Abstract-CouponImpl" attribute:

```
<class name="PendingOrder" table="PENDING_ORDER">
...
    <many-to-one name="coupon"
        class="AbstractCouponImpl" column="COUPON_ID"
            />
...
</class>
```

This attribute specifies that the PendingOrder.coupon field is really a reference to an AbstractCouponImpl even though its type is Coupon. This approach eliminates the need to add accessors for the identifier property to the Coupon and improves encapsulation.

6.2 Other Hibernate issues

In addition to these O/R mapping issues, there are other issues with Hibernate that can make writing applications difficult.

6.2.1 Exception handling

One potential problem with how Hibernate handles errors is that when it encounters an error, it throws a `HibernateException` and leaves the `Session` in a potentially inconsistent state. According to the Hibernate documentation, the application must close the `Session` immediately, which can sometimes make recovering from exceptions unnecessarily complicated if the application wants to continue using the `Session`. For more information, see chapter 8, which describes how to recover from errors in an application that uses an exposed domain model. Fortunately, this isn't a problem when using a POJO façade because the application uses a new `Session` each time the façade is called.

6.2.2 Lazy loading and inheritance hierarchies

As we saw in chapter 4, lazy loading is an important feature of an ORM framework. Hibernate provides a couple of ways to do lazy loading. The simpler approach is to use Hibernate's proxy-based mechanism, which is enabled by default in Hibernate 3. When using proxies, a reference to a lazily loaded object is actually a reference to a proxy that will load the real object the first time one of its methods is called. The trouble with proxies is that, as we describe a bit later, they break code that uses `instanceof` or downcasting, which are two important features of the Java language.

Alternatively, if your application needs objects to use `instanceof` and downcasting, then you can use lazy property loading. This mechanism works by loading objects only when the property that references them is first accessed. The drawback of lazy property loading is that it is less convenient because you must run a bytecode enhancer that modifies the classes to intercept references to properties. In addition, Hibernate can generate suboptimal SQL to load an object referenced by a lazily loaded property. Let's look at the details of these two mechanisms.

Using proxies with instanceof and downcasting

Let's imagine that you are writing some presentation tier code to display a pending order and that how you display a coupon depends on its actual class. You will probably write some code similar to this:

```
Coupon coupon = pendingOrder.getCoupon();
if (coupon instanceof PercentageDiscountCoupon) {
  PercentageDiscountCoupon percentageCoupon =
              (PercentageDiscountCoupon)coupon;
  ...
}
else if (coupon instanceof FreeShippingCoupon) {
  FreeShippingCoupon freeShippingCoupon =
              (FreeShippingCoupon)coupon;
  ...
}
...
```

This code will certainly work with regular Java objects, but it won't work when the application uses Hibernate proxies to implement lazy loading. If Hibernate lazily loads a Coupon, then PendingOrder.getCoupon() will return a proxy rather than the real Coupon. Unfortunately, the trouble with proxies is that they do not work correctly with instanceof and do not support downcasting. A Coupon proxy will never appear to be an instance of FreeShippingCoupon or PercentageDiscountCoupon, and so neither call to instanceof will return true. Certainly, using instanceof is generally not considered to be good style, but it is useful in cases such as this.

An application can work around this problem by calling Hibernate.get-Class(), which is a static method that returns an object's true class:

```
Class trueClass = Hibernate.getClass(coupon);
if (PercentageDiscountCoupon.class.isAssignableFrom(trueClass))  {
  ...
}
```

The trouble with this solution is that it pollutes application code with calls to Hibernate APIs.

The other problem with proxies is that it is not possible to downcast a reference to a proxy. The downcasts in the previous code will fail if the Coupon is a proxy. The workaround described in the Hibernate manual is to use parallel hierarchy of interfaces and downcast to an interface instead of a concrete class:

```
interface ICoupon {..};
interface IPercentageDiscountCoupon extends Coupon {…};

if (PercentageDiscountCoupon.
    isAssignableFrom(Hibernate.getClass(coupon)))  {
  IPercentageDiscountCoupon percentageCoupon =
              (IPercentageDiscountCoupon)coupon;
  ...
}
```

This, of course, requires changes to the domain model, which runs counter to the idea of transparent persistence.

Using lazy property loading

The other way to lazily load related objects is to use Hibernate's lazy property fetching mechanism, which was introduced in Hibernate 3. This mechanism lets you specify that a property should be loaded only when it is first accessed instead of when the object is loaded. Its primarily purpose is to improve performance by loading large fields only when absolutely necessary. It uses a bytecode enhancer to instrument the Java class files. You can use lazy property fetching to lazily load related objects without using proxies and thereby solve the problem with instanceof and downcasting. However, as you will see later it has some important drawbacks and using lazy property fetching is rarely worthwhile.

To lazily load a related class, you must configure the `<many-to-one>` or `<one-to-one>` association element that references the class to use lazy loading. You must also disable proxying for the referenced class. For example, you can lazily load a `PendingOrder`'s coupon by configuring the `PendingOrder`'s coupon property with `lazy="true"`. Here is an excerpt from the O/R mapping document for the `PendingOrder` and `Coupon` classes that does this:

```
<class name="PendingOrder" table="PENDING_ORDER">
...
    <many-to-one name="coupon"
            class="AbstractCouponImpl"
            column="COUPON_ID"
            lazy="true"
            fetch="select"
            />
...
</class>

<class  name="AbstractCouponImpl"
    lazy="false"
    table="COUPON">

...
```

The `lazy="true"` attribute of the `<many-to-one>` element specifies that the `coupon` property should only be loaded when it is first accessed. The `fetch="select"` prevents Hibernate from eagerly loading the `Coupon` using an outer join. The `lazy="false"` attribute of the `<class>` element for the `AbstractCouponImpl` class tells Hibernate to not use a proxy for this class.

When Hibernate loads a `PendingOrder`, it will neither load the `Coupon` nor create a proxy for it. A `Coupon` will only be loaded when the application accesses the coupon field. Hibernate will instantiate the appropriate subclass of Coupon and the application will be able to use instanceof and downcasting.

Using lazy property fetching to implement lazy loading of related objects has two main drawbacks. First, it is a lot less convenient than using proxies because you have to run the bytecode enhancer, which is an extra step in the edit-compile-debug cycle.

Second, it is less efficient because lazily loaded properties are retrieved from the database one at time, Moreover, Hibernate can use inefficient SQL to load each property. For example, when loading a coupon Hibernate uses an additional SQL statement that loads the COUPON_ID foreign key column from the PENDING_ORDER table. Here are the SQL statements that Hibernate uses to load the PendingOrder and its Coupon:

```
select pendingord0_....
  from PENDING_ORDER pendingord0_
    where pendingord0_.PENDING_ORDER_ID=?

select pendingord_.COUPON_ID as COUPON11_1_
  from PENDING_ORDER pendingord_
    where pendingord_.PENDING_ORDER_ID=?

select abstractco0_...
    from COUPON abstractco0_
    where abstractco0_.COUPON_ID=?
```

The first SQL SELECT statement retrieves all of the columns from the PENDING_ORDER table except for the COUPON_ID column, which is the foreign key to the COUPON table. The second statement, which is executed when the application accesses the coupon property, retrieves the COUPON_ID foreign key column. The third SQL SELECT statement loads the coupon. In comparison, if Hibernate was configured to use proxies it would only use two SQL SELECT statements, one for the PendingOrder and another for the Coupon.

Because of these problems, it is usually much better to use Hibernate's proxy-based mechanism for lazily loading and to work around the problems with instanceof and downcasting.

6.3 *Persisting a domain model class using Hibernate*

We have now seen the issues and challenges you will face when using Hibernate to persist a domain model, so let's look at an example. In this section, we implement the Hibernate O/R mapping for the PendingOrder class from the Food to Go domain model. It illustrates some of the typical issues that you will encounter when persisting a domain model class with Hibernate. You will also learn how to implement some of the testing techniques described in chapter 4, including how to write tests that use the Hibernate metadata APIs to validate the O/R mapping. In the following section, we show how to implement a domain model repository using Hibernate.

The `PendingOrder` class is a good example of a domain model entity. To persist this class we will need to use a variety of Hibernate's ORM features. The `Pending-Order` class has simple fields such as `deliveryTime` and `state` that need to be mapped to columns of the PENDING_ORDER table. It has also has fields that reference embedded value objects such as `paymentInformation` and `deliveryAddress` that must also be mapped to columns in the PENDING_ORDER table. It also has references to persistent objects stored in other tables, including `PendingOrderLine-Items`, `Restaurant`, and `Coupon`. The reference to a `Coupon` is a polymorphic reference because `Coupon` is an interface.

But before getting into the details of writing the O/R mapping for this class, let's first look at how to write tests that verify that the persistent `PendingOrder` objects can be created, loaded, updated, and deleted.

6.3.1 *Writing Hibernate persistence tests with ORMUnit*

Because we are using test-driven development, the first step in the process of making the `PendingOrder` class persistent is to write some tests using the testing strategies described in chapter 4. There are three different kinds of tests that we need to write for a class such as `PendingOrder`:

1 Tests that verify that the O/R mapping correctly maps the `PendingOrder` class to the database schema. This includes making sure that all fields that should be persistent are mapped to the database.

2 Tests that verify that instances of the `PendingOrder` class can be created, loaded, updated, and deleted. Sometimes, for example, incorrectly defined database constraints prevent objects from being persisted.

3 Tests that verify that the tables and columns referenced by the `Pending-Order`'s O/R mapping exist.

The ORMUnit test framework, which we introduced in chapter 4, provides `Hibernate-MappingTests`, `HibernateSchemaTests`, and `HibernatePersistenceTests`, which are base classes that make it easier to write Hibernate persistence tests. Let's see how to use these classes.

HibernateMappingTests

HibernateMappingTests is the base class for writing tests for the O/R mapping. It provides methods for making assertions about the O/R mapping, including:

- assertClassMapping(): Verifies that the class is mapped to the specified table
- assertAllFieldsMapped(): Verifies that all of the fields of a class are mapped
- assertIdField(): Verifies that the class's id field is mapped to the specified column
- assertField(): Verifies that a field is mapped to the specified columns

HibernateMappingTests call the Hibernate metadata APIs to find out about the O/R mapping. The Hibernate metadata API exposes the O/R mapping as Java objects. A test obtains the O/R metadata for a class by calling getClassMapping() on the Configuration object that constructs the SessionFactory.

```
Configuration cfg = …;
PersistentClass classMapping =
   cfg.getClassMapping(PendingOrder.class.getName());
```

This method takes a Java class as a parameter and returns a PersistentClass object that describes its O/R mapping. The Hibernate metadata APIs are only documented in the JavaDoc and not the manual, but they appear to be relatively stable. The only issues with using them is that the tests must call Configuration.openSessionFactory() in order to ensure that Hibernate completely initializes the metadata. This can sometimes result in a database connection being opened, which can slow down the tests slightly.

Here is an excerpt of the source code for HibernateMappingTests that shows how assertClassMapping() verifies that the class is mapped to the specified table:

```
public abstract class HibernateMappingTests extends TestCase {

  private static Configuration cfg;
  private PersistentClass classMapping;
  private Class type;

  protected void assertClassMapping(Class type, String tableName) {
    this.type = type;
    classMapping = cfg.getClassMapping(type);
    assertEquals(tableName, classMapping.getTable().getName());
  }
  …
}
```

The `assertClassMapping()` method gets the class mapping for the specified class from the `Configuration`, which was constructed by the `setUp()` method (not shown). It saves both the type and the class mapping in fields for use by other methods. It calls `assertEquals()` to verify that the class is mapped to the specified table.

HibernateSchemaTests

To verify that the database schema matches the O/R mapping we can use `HibernateSchemaTests`, which is shown in listing 6.1. It provides an `assertDatabase-Schema()` method that checks for missing tables and columns by using Hibernate to generate a SQL script from the mapping that adds any missing tables and tables. The method throws an exception if the generated script contains SQL commands that would change the schema.

Listing 6.1 HibernateSchemaTests

```
public abstract class HibernateSchemaTests extends TestCase {

  public void assertDatabaseSchema() throws Exception {          Generates
    String[] script = generateScript();              <───────     script
    List differences = getSignificantDifferences(script);
    assertTrue(differences.toString(),
               differences.isEmpty());      <────────┐ Fails if tables or
  }                                                   │ columns added

  private String[] generateScript() throws Exception {
    Configuration cfg = getConfiguration();
    SessionFactory sessionFactory = cfg.buildSessionFactory();
    Session session = sessionFactory.openSession();
    try {
      Dialect dialect = getDatabaseDialect();
      DatabaseMetadata dbm = new DatabaseMetadata(session      Generates
         .connection(), dialect);                              DDL script
      String[] script = cfg.generateSchemaUpdateScript(
         dialect, dbm);
      return script;
    } finally {
      session.close();
    }
  }

  protected Dialect getDatabaseDialect() throws Exception {
    return (Dialect)Class.forName(
       getConfiguration().getProperty(
          "hibernate.dialect"))
       .newInstance();
  }

  private List getSignificantDifferences(String[] script) {
```

```
    List differences = new ArrayList();
    for (int i = 0; i < script.length; i++) {
      String line = script[i];
      if (line.indexOf("add constraint")      Removes unimportant
                    == -1)                     commands
        differences.add(line);
    }
    return differences;
  }

  protected Configuration getConfiguration()
                  throws HibernateException {
    …
    return cfg;
  }
}
```

The assertDatabaseSchema() method first calls Configuration.generateSchema-
UpdateScript() to generate the script. It then finds any significant differences by
ignoring DDL commands to add constraints. It fails if it encounters any DDL commands that add tables or columns.

HibernatePersistenceTests

In addition to HibernateMappingTests and HibernateSchemaTests, ORMUnit
defines the HibernatePersistenceTests class, which extends JUnit TestCase and
makes it easier to write tests for persistent objects. It defines setUp() and tear-
Down() methods that implement the boilerplate code of a Hibernate persistence
test and provides methods for manipulating persistent data and managing transactions, including:

- doInTransaction(): Executes the callback method within a Hibernate transaction and ensures that the same Session is used throughout. It does this
  using a Spring TransactionTemplate that is configured to use a Hibernate-
  TransactionManager.

- save(): Saves an object by calling HibernateTemplate.save().

- load(): Loads a persistent object by calling HibernateTemplate.load().

- delete(): Deletes a persistent object by calling HibernateTemplate.delete().

See this book's online source code for the details of the class. Let's now look at
some tests that use ORMUnit.

6.3.2 *Testing persistent Hibernate objects*

This section explores the persistence tests you need to write for the `PendingOrder` class. Even though ORMUnit makes it easier to write tests, it can still be time consuming to develop thorough persistence tests. Consequently, we describe how to start off with a simple test and then add more elaborate ones.

Verifying the O/R mapping

We need to write tests that verify that the O/R mapping correctly maps the `PendingOrder` class to the PENDING_ORDER table. We must verify that each persistent class is mapped to the correct table and that each field is mapped to the correct database column, foreign key, or join table. A good way to do this is to write tests for the ORM documents using the Hibernate version of ORMUnit, which verifies the O/R mapping by using Hibernate metadata APIs. This approach is much easier than using DbUnit to verify the contents of the database. The tests also run much faster.

Here is a very simple O/R mapping test for the `PendingOrder` class. `FoodToGoHibernateMappingTests` extends the ORMUnit `HibernateMappingTests` class and defines a `testPendingOrderMapping()` method, which make basic assertions about the `PendingOrder` class's O/R mapping:

```
public class FoodToGoHibernateMappingTests extends
    HibernateMappingTests {

  public void testPendingOrderMapping() throws SQLException,
      HibernateException {
    assertClassMapping(PendingOrder.class, "PENDING_ORDER");
    assertAllFieldsMapped();
  }
  …
```

This test verifies that the `PendingOrder` class is mapped to the PENDING_ORDER table and that all of its fields are mapped to the database. It detects the common problem of forgetting to define the mapping for a newly added field.

This simple test is a good start, but sometimes it is useful to write a test that verifies that each field is mapped correctly to the database. Here is a more elaborate test that makes assertions about the O/R mapping for each field of the `PendingOrder` class:

```
public class FoodToGoHibernateMappingTests extends
    HibernateMappingTests {

  public void testPendingOrderMapping() throws SQLException,
      HibernateException {

    assertClassMapping(PendingOrder.class,
                       "PENDING_ORDER");

    assertIdField("id", "PENDING_ORDER_ID");
    assertField("state", "STATE");

    assertManyToOneField("restaurant",
                        "RESTAURANT_ID");

    assertComponentField("deliveryAddress");
    ComponentFieldMapping deliveryAddress =
                getComponentFieldMapping("deliveryAddress");
    deliveryAddress.assertAllFieldsMapped();

    assertCompositeListField("lineItems");
    CompositeListFieldMapping lineItems =
        getCompositeListFieldMapping("lineItems");
    lineItems.assertTable("PENDING_ORDER_LINE_ITEM");
    lineItems.assertForeignKey("PENDING_ORDER_ID");
    lineItems.assertIndexColumn("LINE_ITEM_INDEX");
    lineItems.assertField("quantity", "QUANTITY");
    lineItems.assertManyToOneField("menuItem", "MENU_ITEM_ID");
    lineItems.assertAllFieldsMapped();

    // PaymentInformation
    // Coupon
    // …
    assertAllFieldsMapped();
  }
```

❶ Verifies table mapping

❷ Verifies simple field mapping

❸ Verifies association

❹ Verifies delivery address

❺ Verifies line items

❻ Verifies that all fields are mapped

Let's look at the details:

❶ `testPendingOrderMapping()` verifies that the `PendingOrder` class is mapped to the correct table.

❷ This method verifies `PendingOrder`'s simple value fields are mapped correctly.

❸ `testPendingOrderMapping()` verifies the mapping for the `PendingOrder-Restaurant` association.

❹ This method verifies the mapping for delivery address, which is an embedded value object.

⑤ `testPendingOrderMapping()` verifies the mapping for the line items.

⑥ This method verifies that all fields are mapped by calling `assertAllFieldsMapped()`.

As you can see, writing a comprehensive test for the mapping requires a lot of work, but sometimes it is worthwhile. Let's now look at how to verify that the schema matches the O/R mapping.

Verifying that the schema matches the mapping

Another part of testing the O/R mapping is verifying the existence of all of the database tables and columns that it references. Of course, if the schema is automatically generated from the O/R mapping then we don't have to do this. However, in many applications the schema is maintained separately and so can potentially be inconsistent with the O/R mapping. ORMUnit makes it easy to verify that the database schema matches the O/R mapping:

```
public class FoodToGoSchemaTests extends HibernateSchemaTests {

  public void test() throws Exception {
    assertDatabaseSchema();
  }
}
```

This test calls `assertDatabaseSchema()`, which was described earlier, to verify that there are no missing columns. It will catch common mistakes such as defining the O/R mapping for a new field without adding the corresponding column to the schema. Because it can check that the schema matches the O/R mapping for all classes, we only need to write it once.

Now that we have written tests for the O/R mapping, let's look at how to write tests that create, find, update, and delete persistent objects.

Writing persistence tests

We are almost done with the tests. The last set of tests we must write are those that create, update, and delete `PendingOrders`. These tests are necessary because sometimes incorrectly defined constraints can prevent objects from being persisted and associations from being formed and destroyed. Consequently, it is useful to write tests that take a persistent object through its lifecycle.

Because writing these kinds of tests can be time consuming, you might want to start off with a really simple test such as the following, which creates and saves a `PendingOrder`:

```
public class HibernatePendingOrderPersistenceTests extends
    HibernatePersistenceTests {
```

```
    public void testPendingOrder() {
      PendingOrder po = new PendingOrder();
      save(po);
    }
  }
```

A simple test will typically catch some basic O/R mapping problems. However, you will usually want to write a more elaborate test that also updates the persistent object and possibly deletes it. Listing 6.2 shows a test that takes a `PendingOrder` through its lifecycle, which creates and destroys relationships with other objects, including restaurants and line items. It consists of the following steps:

1   Create a `PendingOrder` and save it.

2   Load `PendingOrder`, update delivery information, and save it.

3   Load `PendingOrder`, update the restaurant, and save it.

4   Load `PendingOrder`, update quantities, and save it.

5   Load `PendingOrder`, update quantities, and save it (again to test deleting line items).

6   Load `PendingOrder`, update payment information, and save it.

7   Delete `PendingOrder`.

Each step is executed within a transaction that keeps a Hibernate `Session` open so objects can be loaded lazily.

Listing 6.2   HibernatePendingOrderPersistenceTests

```
public class HibernatePendingOrderPersistenceTests extends
    HibernatePersistenceTests {

  private RestaurantRepository restaurantRepository;
  private String pendingOrderId;
  private String restaurantId;

  protected Properties getSessionFactoryProperties() {
    return new Properties();
  }

  public void setUp() throws Exception {
    super.setUp();
    restaurantRepository =
      new HibernateRestaurantRepositoryImpl(     ◁────────●❶ Creates Hibernate
                    getHibernateTemplate());                  RestaurantRepositoryImpl

    delete(PendingOrder.class);      ❷ Initializes
    delete(MenuItem.class);              database
```

```
    delete(Restaurant.class);
    Restaurant r =
      RestaurantMother.makeRestaurant();
    save(r);
    restaurantId = r.getId();
}

public void testSimple() throws Exception {

    createPendingOrder();

    updateDeliveryInfo();

    updateRestaurant(restaurantId);

    updateQuantities1();

    updateQuantities2();

    updatePaymentInfo();

    deletePendingOrder();
}

private void createPendingOrder() {
    PendingOrder po = new PendingOrder();
    save(po);
    pendingOrderId = po.getId();
}

private void updateDeliveryInfo() {
    doWithTransaction(new TxnCallback() {
      public void execute() throws Exception {
        Date deliveryTime = makeDeliveryTime();
        Address deliveryAddress = new Address("1 High St",
            null, "OAKLAND", "CA", "94619");

        PendingOrder po = (PendingOrder) load(PendingOrder.class,
                          pendingOrderId);

        boolean updateDeliveryInfoResult =
         po.updateDeliveryInfo(
            restaurantRepository,
            deliveryAddress,
            deliveryTime,);

        assertTrue(updateDeliveryInfoResult);
      }
    });
}
```

2 Initializes database

3 Calls helper methods

4 Creates PendingOrder

5 Updates PendingOrder's delivery info

```
private Date makeDeliveryTime() {
  Calendar c = Calendar.getInstance();
  c.set(Calendar.DAY_OF_WEEK, Calendar.TUESDAY);
  c.set(Calendar.HOUR_OF_DAY, 19);
  c.add(Calendar.DAY_OF_MONTH, 7);
  return c.getTime();
}

private void updateRestaurant(final String restaurantId) {
  doWithTransaction(new TxnCallback() {
    public void execute() throws Exception {
      PendingOrder po =
          (PendingOrder) load(PendingOrder.class,
                              pendingOrderId);
      Restaurant r =
          (Restaurant)load(Restaurant.class, restaurantId);

      boolean updateRestaurantResult = po
          .updateRestaurant(r);
      assertTrue(updateRestaurantResult);
    }
  });
}
private void updateQuantities1() {
  doWithTransaction(new TxnCallback() {
    public void execute() throws Exception {
      PendingOrder po =
          (PendingOrder) load(PendingOrder.class,
                              pendingOrderId);
      po.updateQuantities(new int[] { 1, 2 });
    }
  });
}

private void updateQuantities2() {
  doWithTransaction(new TxnCallback() {
    public void execute() throws Exception {
      PendingOrder po = (PendingOrder) load(PendingOrder.class,
                          pendingOrderId);
      po.updateQuantities(new int[]
                          {0, 3 });
    }
  });
}

private void updatePaymentInfo() {
  doWithTransaction(new TxnCallback() {
    public void execute() throws Exception {
      PendingOrder po = (PendingOrder) load(PendingOrder.class,
                          pendingOrderId);
      PaymentInformation paymentInfo =
```

6 Updates its restaurant

7 Updates its line items

8 Updates its line items again

```
                           PendingOrderTestData.PAYMENT_INFORMATION;
              po.updatePaymentInformation(paymentInfo, null);   ⟵──────⑨ Updates
            }                                                              payment info
          });
      }

      private void deletePendingOrder() {
        doWithTransaction(new TxnCallback() {
          public void execute() throws Exception {
            PendingOrder po = (PendingOrder)load(PendingOrder.class,
                              pendingOrderId);

            delete(po);   ⟵──────┐     Deletes
          }                     ⑩    PendingOrder
        });
      }

   }
```

`HibernatePendingOrderPersistenceTests` extends `HibernatePersistenceTests`.
Let's look at the details:

① The `setup()` method creates a `HibernateRestaurantRepositoryImpl`.

② The `setup()` method deletes existing data and inserts a restaurant.

③ The `testSimple()` method calls a sequence of helper methods.

④ The `createPendingOrder()` method creates a `PendingOrder` and calls `save()`, which
is a method defined by `HibernatePersistenceTests` that calls `Hibernate.save()`.

⑤ The `updateDeliveryInfo()` method updates the `PendingOrder` with delivery information. It first calls `load()`, which is a method defined by `HibernatePersisten-
ceTests` that calls `Hibernate.load()`, and then calls `updateDeliveryInfo()`.

⑥ The `updateRestaurant()` method loads the pending order and calls `Pending-
Order.updateRestaurant()`.

⑦ The `updateQuantities()` method loads the pending order and updates the line
item quantities.

⑧ The `updateQuantities()` method loads the pending order and deletes one of the
line items.

⑨ The `updatePaymentInformation()` method loads the pending order and updates
the payment information.

⑩ The `deletePendingOrder()` method loads the pending order and deletes it.

This test corresponds to one possible scenario in the lifetime of a `PendingOrder`. In order to thoroughly test `PendingOrder`, we would also need to write other tests, such as one that calls `updatePaymentInfo()` with a `Coupon`. Developing these tests can be time consuming, but they are an important part of the test suite for Hibernate persistence layer. As with the O/R mapping tests, you can start off by writing a simple test that creates and saves a `PendingOrder` and then add more comprehensive tests over time. Let's look at what we have to do in order to get these tests to pass.

6.3.3 *Making a class persistent*

We have written the tests and thus have put behind us what is often the most difficult part of persisting a class. To get these tests to pass, we have to make some minor changes to the `PendingOrder` class and write the O/R mapping document.

Changing the class

To be able to persist a class, you typically have to make a few changes to accommodate Hibernate's requirements. For example, a class must have a default constructor. Also, you usually have to add a field to store the object's persistent identity, and some classes require a version field for optimistic locking. In addition, as described in *Hibernate in Action* [Bauer 2005], you must—in certain situations—implement `equals()` and `hashCode()` methods. Furthermore, even though Hibernate provides a rich set of O/R mapping features, you sometimes have to make changes to work around its limitations.

Fortunately, we only need to make some minor changes to the `PendingOrder` class. The class already has a default constructor, and does not require a version field because its session state is accessed by just one user. As a result, we only have to add an `id` field and a getter for accessing it:

```
public class PendingOrder {
  private int id = -1;

  private int getId() {
    return id;
  }
  ...
```

The rest of the class is unchanged and it's still a POJO. As you can see, this is a very simple change, which is one of the really nice things about using an ORM framework such as Hibernate.

Defining the O/R mapping

Now that we have made that simple change to `PendingOrder`, the other thing we must do is to write the O/R mapping document, which describes how its fields and relationships map to the database schema. Let's first examine how the `Pending-Order` class, its fields, and its relationships are mapped to the database schema; after that we'll look at the Hibernate mapping document.

In chapter 4 we described how the `PendingOrder` class is mapped to the PENDING_ORDER table. The `id` field is mapped to the `PENDING_ORDER_ID` column, which is the table's primary key. Its simple fields are mapped to columns of this table. The `state` field is mapped to the `STATE` column, and the `deliveryTime` field is mapped to the `DELIVERY_TIME` column.

The `deliveryAddress` and `paymentInformation` fields reference embedded value objects, and so the fields of the `Address` and `PaymentInformation` objects are mapped to the columns of the PENDING_ORDER table. For example, the `street1` field of the `Address` object is mapped to the `DELIVERY_STREET1` column of the PENDING_ORDER table.

The `PendingOrder-PendingOrderLineItem` relationship is an ordered, unidirectional, one-to-many relationship. In addition, a `PendingOrderLineItem` must be deleted when its `PendingOrder` is deleted or when it is no longer associated with a `PendingOrder`. We saw in section 6.1.1 that Hibernate provides two ways to map this kind of relationship: as an entity collection or as a component collection. Because the line items are only referenced by `PendingOrder`, we can use a component collection, which is slightly more efficient because Hibernate uses fewer SQL statements. `PendingOrderLineItems` are mapped to the PENDING_ORDER_LINE_ITEM table, which has a foreign key to the PENDING_ORDER table, and a `LINE_ITEM_INDEX` column that stores the position of the line item.

The `PendingOrder-Restaurant` and `PendingOrder-Coupon` relationships are unidirectional, many-to-one relationships. The PENDING_ORDER table has a `RESTAURANT_ID` column, which is a foreign key to the RESTAURANT table, and a `COUPON_ID` column, which is a foreign key to the COUPON table.

Listing 6.3 shows PendingOrder.hbm.xml, which is the O/R mapping document for `PendingOrder`. PendingOrder.hbm.xml must be accessible at runtime and is often located in the same directory of the class and on the class path. In chapter 7, we will look at how to create a `SessionFactory` that uses PendingOrder.hbm.xml.

226 | **CHAPTER 6**
Persisting a domain model with Hibernate 3

Listing 6.3 PendingOrder.hbm.xml

```xml
<hibernate-mapping>
...
  <class name="PendingOrder"                    ❶ Configures
         table="PENDING_ORDER">                    class mapping

    <id name="id" column="PENDING_ORDER_ID"
                 unsaved-value="-1">
      <generator class="native">                 ❷ Configures
        <param name="sequence">                     primary key field
        ➥ UNIQUE_ID_SEQUENCE</param>
      </generator>
    </id>

    <property name="deliveryTime"
              column="DELIVERY_TIME"             ❸ Maps simple
         type="timestamp"/>                         fields

    <property name="state" column="STATE" />

    <component name="deliveryAddress">
      <property name="street1"
                column="DELIVERY_STREET1"/>
      <property name="street2"
                column="DELIVERY_STREET2"/>      ❹ Maps
      <property name="city"                         deliveryAddress
                column="DELIVERY_CITY"/>
      <property name="state"
                column="DELIVERY_STATE"/>
      <property name="zip"
                column="DELIVERY_ZIP"/>
    </component>

    <many-to-one name="restaurant"               ❺ Maps
         column="RESTAURANT_ID"                     restaurant field
         class="Restaurant"/>

    <list name="lineItems"
        table="PENDING_ORDER_LINE_ITEM"
        cascade="all">
      <key column="PENDING_ORDER_ID"/>
      <index column="LINE_ITEM_INDEX"/>
      <composite-element                          ❻ Maps
          class="PendingOrderLineItem">             lineItems field
        <property name="quantity"
                  column="QUANTITY"/>
        <many-to-one name="menuItem"
                  column="MENU_ITEM_ID"/>
      </composite-element>
    </list>
```

```
<many-to-one name="Coupon"
        class="AbstractCouponImpl"
        column="COUPON_ID"/>
```
**❼ Maps
coupon field**

```
   ...
   </class>
...
<hibernate-mapping>
```

Let's look at the details:

❶ The `<class>` element specifies that the `PendingOrder` is mapped to the PENDING_ORDER table.

❷ The `<id>` element defines the primary key property and its column.

❸ The `deliveryDate` and `state` fields are mapped to columns.

❹ The mapping for the `deliveryAddress` field uses the `<component>` mapping. The `<property>` elements nested within the `<component>` element map the fields of the `Address` to columns of its PENDING_ORDER table. The mapping for the payment information field is similar.

❺ The `PendingOrder-Restaurant` relationship is mapped using a `<many-to-one>` element.

❻ The `PendingOrder-PendingOrderLineItems` relationship is mapped as a component collection by using a `<list>` element that contains a `<composite-element>`, as described in section 6.1.1.

❼ The `PendingOrder-Coupon` relationship is mapped using a `<many-to-one>` element.

Note that the relationship mappings in this example use the default setting for eager/lazy loading and so Hibernate will lazily load related classes such as `Restaurant`, `Coupon`, and `PendingOrderLineItem`. In section 6.5 you will see how to configure eager loading to improve performance.

After adding the `id` field to the `PendingOrder` class and writing the O/R mapping document, we can now persist instances of the `PendingOrder` class and the tests that we wrote earlier pass. Let's now see how to implement a repository class using Hibernate.

6.4 *Implementing a repository using Hibernate*

In the previous section we looked at how to persist a domain model class using Hibernate. The other part of implementing a persistent domain model is to implement the repositories, which define methods for creating, finding, and deleting persistent objects. In this section, we'll show you how to use a test-driven approach to implement a repository that uses the Hibernate APIs to manipulate persistent objects. We'll use the `RestaurantRepository.findAvailableRestaurants()` method, which finds the restaurants that serve a given delivery address and time, as an example. We'll first write some mock object tests for the `RestaurantRepository`, and then we'll write the method. After that, we'll write some database tests for the Hibernate query that is executed by the repositories to find the restaurants.

6.4.1 *Writing a mock object test for a repository method*

Mock object tests are a very effective way to directly test the functionality implemented by the repository independently of the persistence framework and the database. The `findAvailableRestaurants()` method retrieves the available restaurants by executing a query; therefore, a mock object test for this method must invoke it with a delivery time and address and verify that it calls the Hibernate APIs to execute the expected query with the expected parameters. As you will see, the test is easy to write and executes extremely quickly.

To write the mock object test, we must decide how the repository executes the query. One easy decision to make is to use named queries. Rather than embed the Hibernate query string in the code, it makes more sense to use a named query and store the query string in the O/R mapping document. This makes the query easier to read and change and also simplifies the code.

Another decision is which API to use. The repository could use the Hibernate `Session` and `Query` APIs directly. However, a better approach—one that requires fewer lines of code and that is easier to mock—is Spring's `HibernateTemplate` class. It provides a number of convenience methods that wrap the Hibernate API. In particular, it provides a `HibernateTemplate.findByNamedQueryAndNamedParam()` method that takes three parameters: the query name, parameter names, and parameter values.

Using `HibernateTemplate.findByNamedQueryAndNamedParam()` makes testing `findAvailableRestaurants()` very straightforward. A test can use a mock `HibernateTemplate` that verifies that `findByNamedQueryAndNamedParam()` is called with the correct arguments. It can pass the mock `HibernateTemplate` to the repository using constructor injection. Listing 6.4 shows the test for this method.

Listing 6.4   HibernateRestaurantRepositoryImplMockTest

```
public class HibernateRestaurantRepositoryImplMockTest extends
    MockObjectTestCase {

  private Mock mockHibernateTemplate;
  private HibernateTemplate hibernateTemplate;
  private HibernateRestaurantRepositoryImpl repository;

  public void setUp() {
    mockHibernateTemplate =
        new Mock(HibernateTemplate.class);
    hibernateTemplate = (HibernateTemplate)
      mockHibernateTemplate.proxy();


    repository =
      new HibernateRestaurantRepositoryImpl(
            hibernateTemplate);



  }

  public void testFindAvailableRestaurants() {
    Restaurant restaurant = new Restaurant();
    int EXPECTED_MINUTE = 6;
    int EXPECTED_HOUR = 5;
    int EXPECTED_DAY_OF_WEEK = 3;
    List expectedRestaurants =
      Collections.singletonList(restaurant);

    Address deliveryAddress =
        new Address("1 somewhere", null,
                Oakland", "CA", "94619");

    Date deliveryTime =
        makeDeliveryTime(EXPECTED_DAY_OF_WEEK,
            EXPECTED_HOUR, EXPECTED_MINUTE);

    Object[] expectedValues =
      new Object[] {
        deliveryAddress.getZip(),
        new Integer(EXPECTED_DAY_OF_WEEK),
        new Integer(EXPECTED_HOUR),
        new Integer(EXPECTED_MINUTE) };
    String[] expectedNames = { "zipCode",
            "dayOfWeek", "hour",
            "minute" };

    mockHibernateTemplate.expects(once())
      .method("findByNamedQueryAndNamedParam")
```

❶ Creates mock HibernateTemplate

❷ Creates repository

❸ Creates test data

❹ Configures mock HibernateTemplate

```
        .with(eq("findAvailableRestaurants"),
            eq(expectedNames),
              eq(expectedValues)))
      .will(returnValue(expectedRestaurants)));
```
❹ **Configures mock
   HibernateTemplate**

```
    List foundRestaurants =
      repository.findAvailableRestaurants(
        deliveryAddress, deliveryTime);
```
❺ **Calls
   findAvailableRestaurants()**

```
    assertEquals(expectedRestaurants,
              foundRestaurants);
  }

  private Date makeDeliveryTime(int dayOfWeek, int hour,
      int minute) {
    Calendar c = Calendar.getInstance();
    c.set(Calendar.DAY_OF_WEEK, dayOfWeek);
    c.set(Calendar.HOUR_OF_DAY, hour);
    c.set(Calendar.MINUTE, minute);
    return c.getTime();
  }
}
```
❻ **Verifies
   the return value**

Let's look at the details:

❶ The setUp() method creates the mock HibernateTemplate.

❷ The setUp() method creates the HibernateRestaurantRepositoryImpl, passing the mock HibernateTemplate to its constructor.

❸ The test creates some test data, including the parameters that are passed to HibernateRestaurantRepository.findAvailableRestaurants() and the parameters that are expected to be passed to HibernateTemplate.findByNamedQueryAndNamedParam().

❹ The test configures the mock HibernateTemplate to expect its findByNamedQueryAndNamedParam() method to be called with particular arguments.

❺ The test calls findAvailableRestaurants()

❻ The test verifies that it returns list of restaurants that was returned by the mock HibernateTemplate.

As you can see, mock objects enable you to test the repositories without calling Hibernate or the database. The tests are easy to write and execute very quickly. Of course, the mock tests are only one part of the test suite; later on we will write the tests for the query. But now let's write the code to get this test to compile and pass.

6.4.2 *Implementing HibernateRestaurantRepositoryImpl*

`HibernateRestaurantRepositoryImpl` is the Hibernate implementation of the `RestaurantRepository` interface. It retrieves restaurants by using a Spring `HibernateTemplate` to execute an HQL query. Listing 6.5 shows part of the source code of this class.

Listing 6.5   HibernateRestaurantRepositoryImpl

```
public class HibernateRestaurantRepositoryImpl extends
    HibernateDaoSupport implements RestaurantRepository {

  public HibernateRestaurantRepositoryImpl(
      HibernateTemplate template) {                    ❶ Creates a
    setHibernateTemplate(template);                      HibernateRestaurant
  }                                                      RepositoryImpl

  public List findAvailableRestaurants(Address deliveryAddress,
      Date deliveryTime) {
    String[] paramNames = {"zipCode",
                           "dayOfWeek",
                           "hour",                      ❷ Creates array
                           "minute" };                    of parameter values
    Object[] paramValues =
      makeParameterValues(deliveryAddress,
                          deliveryTime);

    return getHibernateTemplate()
        .findByNamedQueryAndNamedParam(                 ❸ Executes
            "findAvailableRestaurants",                   named query
            paramNames,
            paramValues);
  }

  Object[] makeParameterValues(Address deliveryAddress,
      Date deliveryTime) {
    Calendar c = Calendar.getInstance();
    c.setTime(deliveryTime);
    int dayOfWeek = c.get(Calendar.DAY_OF_WEEK);
    int hour = c.get(Calendar.HOUR_OF_DAY);
    int minute = c.get(Calendar.MINUTE);
    String zipCode = deliveryAddress.getZip();

    Object[] values = new Object[] { zipCode,
        new Integer(dayOfWeek), new Integer(hour),
        new Integer(minute) };
    return values;
  }

}
```

`HibernateRestaurantRepositoryImpl` extends `HibernateDaoSupport`, which provides convenience methods such as `setHibernateTemplate()` and `getHibernateTemplate()`. Let's look at the details:

❶ Its constructor takes a `HibernateTemplate` as a parameter and calls `setHibernateTemplate()`, which is defined by its superclass.

❷ The `findAvailableRestaurants()` method calls `makeParameterValues()` to create the array of parameters. The `makeParameterValues()` uses a `Calendar` to extract the components of the delivery time and returns them in an array along with the delivery ZIP code.

❸ It executes the named query by calling `HibernateTemplate.findByNamedQueryAndNamedParam()`.

Once we write this method, the test we created earlier compiles and passes. Because the test uses mock objects, it is not calling the real Hibernate APIs to execute a query. To complete the implementation, we must write the query.

6.4.3 *Writing the query that finds the restaurants*

The `HibernateRestaurantRepositoryImpl` retrieves the available restaurants by executing a named Hibernate query, which is stored in the Hibernate mapping document. The query finds all restaurants whose service area contains the specified ZIP code and that have a `TimeRange` that matches the specified time:

```
<hibernate-mapping>
...
<query name="findAvailableRestaurants">
  <![CDATA[
select r
from Restaurant r
 inner join r.openingHours.timeRanges tr
 where :zipCode in elements(r.serviceArea) and
(tr.dayOfWeek = :dayOfWeek
and
(tr.openHour < :hour
OR (tr.openHour = :hour and tr.openMinute <= :minute))
and
(tr.closeHour > :hour
OR (tr.closeHour = :hour and tr.closeMinute > :minute)))
]]></query>
...
</hibernate-mapping>
```

The query consists of a join between the restaurant and its time ranges. A restaurant is selected if its `serviceArea` field contains the `zipCode` and it has a `TimeRange` that matches the specified time.

6.4.4 *Writing tests for a query*

At this point, you were probably hoping to be done, but alas there is one more set of tests that we must write. The `where` clause of the query we just wrote contains several relational operators. As you saw in chapter 4, it's a good idea to test it with various combinations of data. Each of the tests for this query, some of which are shown in listing 6.6, initializes the database with test data, invokes the query with a particular set of arguments, and verifies that it returns the expected results. The test class extends the ORMUnit class `HibernatePersistenceTests` and uses the `RestaurantMother` helper class to construct a test restaurant in the database.

Listing 6.6 HibernateRestaurantRepositoryQueryTests

```
public class HibernateRestaurantRepositoryQueryTests extends
    HibernatePersistenceTests {

  private static final String GOOD_ZIP_CODE = "94619";

  private static final String BAD_ZIP_CODE = "94618";

  protected void setUp() throws Exception {      ◁———❶ Initializes database
    super.setUp();
    delete(Restaurant.class);
    Restaurant r = RestaurantMother
        .makeRestaurant(GOOD_ZIP_CODE);
    save(r);
  }

  private void findAvailableRestaurants(              ❷ Executes query
                ➥ int dayOfWeek, int hour,  ◁—————┘
     int minute, String zipCode, boolean expectRestaurants)
     throws Exception {
    String[] paramNames = { "zipCode", "dayOfWeek", "hour",
        "minute" };
    Object[] paramValues = new Object[] { zipCode,
        new Integer(dayOfWeek), new Integer(hour),
        new Integer(minute) };
    List availableRestaurants = getHibernateTemplate()
        .findByNamedQueryAndNamedParam(
            "findAvailableRestaurants", paramNames,
            paramValues);
    if (expectRestaurants)
      assertFalse(availableRestaurants.isEmpty());
```

```
        else
          assertTrue(availableRestaurants.isEmpty());
      }


      public void
          testFindAvailableRestaurants_good()     ◁──────❸ Tests with good
                  throws Exception {                        delivery info
        findAvailableRestaurants(Calendar.TUESDAY,
          RestaurantMother.GOOD_HOUR, 0, GOOD_ZIP_CODE, true);
      }


      public void
        testFindAvailableRestaurants_badZipCode()  ◁──────❹ Tests with bad
                  throws Exception {                        delivery info
        findAvailableRestaurants(Calendar.TUESDAY,
          RestaurantMother.GOOD_HOUR, 0, BAD_ZIP_CODE, false);
      }
    }
```

Let's examine `HibernateRestaurantRepositoryQueryTests`:

❶ The `setUp()` method initializes the database by deleting existing restaurants and inserting a restaurant that serves the 94619 ZIP code.

❷ `findAvailableRestaurants()`, which is a helper method called by the tests, executes the query with the parameters and verifies the result.

❸ `testFindAvailableRestaurants_good()` executes the query with delivery information that is served by a restaurant.

❹ `testFindAvailableRestaurants_badZipCode()` executes the query with a ZIP code that is not served by any restaurants.

This class would also define tests for various boundary conditions, such as a delivery time that is equal to the opening time of a restaurant.

Although these tests can be time consuming to write and execute, they verify that the query behaves correctly and are thus extremely useful.

6.5 *Hibernate performance tuning*

Chapter 4 described how eager loading and process-level caching can be used to significantly improve performance. You can determine which relationships to eagerly load by analyzing the application and then identify the relationships that are traversed when handling each request. If the application always traverses a relationship, you might want to configure it to be always eagerly loaded. Conversely, you might want to dynamically configure eager loading for relationships that are only traversed by the application when handling particular requests.

Whereas eager loading improves performance by loading related objects with a single SELECT statement, process-level caching improves performance by eliminating some SELECT statements. Instead of retrieving objects from the database, the application retrieves them from the process-level cache. Keep in mind that objects that are stored in a process-level cache should not be eagerly loaded because that would bypass the cache.

In this section, you will learn how to improve performance of a Hibernate application. We describe how to configure eager loading in Hibernate and examine some of the ways Hibernate's eager loading features interact with each other and other Hibernate features. We also explain how to use process-level caching and query caching, and we use the Place Order use case as an example. (We aren't going to discuss how to disable lazy loading for a class or how to use the lazy property mechanism we saw in section 6.2.2 because they are rarely used and have some significant limitations.)

6.5.1 *Using eager loading*

One important way to improve the performance of a Hibernate application is to use eager loading. By default, Hibernate lazily loads objects and collections and uses a separate SQL SELECT statement for each object or collection. By enabling eager loading, you can configure Hibernate to load related objects with a single SQL SELECT. You can enable eager loading for a relationship either statically in the O/R mapping or dynamically in a query by using what is called a fetch join. You can use both approaches simultaneously, although Hibernate HQL queries ignore the static settings.

Statically configuring eager loading

One way to configure eager loading for a relationship is in the O/R mapping. In the mapping for a relationship, you can specify that Hibernate should always eagerly load the related object or objects when the referencing object is loaded. You configure eager loading for a relationship by specifying a value for the fetch attribute of the relationship's mapping element. This attribute can have one of two values:

- select: Lazily load the referenced object or collection with a separate SQL SELECT statement. This is the default.

- join: Eagerly load the referenced object or collection using an outer join.

You can, for example, configure the PendingOrder-Restaurant and PendingOrder-
LineItem-MenuItem relationships to be eagerly loaded with an order as follows:

```
<hibernate-mapping>

  <class name="PendingOrder"
    table="PLACED_ORDER">
...
      <many-to-one name="restaurant"
            fetch="join"
            column="RESTAURANT_ID"
...
    />
  </class>

  <class name="PendingOrderLineItem"
    table="PLACED_ORDER">
...
      <many-to-one name="MenuItem"
            fetch="join"
            column="RESTAURANT_ID"
    />
...
  </class>

</hibernate-mapping>
```

The fetch="join" attribute of the mapping element for the PendingOrder-Restaurant relationship tells Hibernate to load a PendingOrder by executing a SQL
SELECT statement that does an outer join between the PENDING_ORDER and RES-
TAURANT tables to retrieve both the pending order and its restaurant. The
fetch="join" attribute for the PendingOrderLineItem-MenuItem has a similar
effect. With this configuration, calling Session.load() with the PendingOrder
class and a pending order id will load a pending order, its restaurant, its line
items, and their menu items using two SELECT statements. The first loads the
pending order and the restaurant, and the second loads the line items and their
menu items.

Although using the fetch attribute to configure eager loading for a relationship might appear to be straightforward, there are a couple of important things to
remember. First, the fetch attribute only affects how objects are loaded by:

- get() and load()
- Navigation from one object to another
- Criteria queries, which are described in detail in chapter 11

The fetch attribute does not affect the behavior of HQL queries. HQL queries that need to eagerly load objects must use fetch joins, which are described next.

Second, for one-to-many and many-to-many relationships the fetch attribute works in conjunction with the lazy attribute to determine how and when the related objects are loaded. The collection mapping elements such as <list> and <map> also have a lazy attribute, which determines how the collection is loaded if fetch="select". If lazy="true" then the collection is loaded when it is accessed by the application, but if lazy="false" then Hibernate loads the collection immediately using a separate SQL SELECT statement. Table 6.2 summarizes this behavior.

Table 6.2 How the fetch and lazy attributes control the loading of collection

	fetch=select (default)	fetch=join
lazy=true (default)	Load collection when accessed by application	Eagerly load collection using an outer join
lazy=false	Eagerly load collection using a separate SELECT statement	Eagerly load collection using an outer join

One limitation of Hibernate is that a class can only have at most one collection loaded using an outer join. This is to prevent inefficient queries that return the Cartesian product of two large collections. However, this does mean that if you want to load multiple collections then you have to write the extra code to load them rather than relying on Hibernate to do it for you.

Dynamically configuring eager loading using fetch joins

Sometimes statically configuring eager loading in the O/R mapping works quite well. If a relationship is always traversed, then it can be configured to use eager loading in its mapping element. However, different requests often require different objects to be eagerly loaded. For example, in chapter 4 we saw how the *update quantities* request requires the pending order, its restaurant, and its restaurant menu items to be loaded whereas the *update payment information* request requires the pending order, its restaurant, its line items, and their menu items to be loaded. To accomplish this, you must dynamically control eager loading by using queries with fetch joins.

A fetch join is a query construct that identifies a relationship to eagerly load. When the application executes a query containing one or more fetch joins, Hibernate executes a SQL SELECT that retrieves the related objects using joins. One thing to remember is that HQL queries ignore the fetch join attribute specified in the O/R mapping and only uses SQL joins for those relationships specified by fetch joins.

Let's look at how the code for the Place Order use case can use fetch joins. Instead of loading the `PendingOrder` by calling `Session.load()`, the `PendingOrder-Repository` methods called by `PlaceOrderService` method must load the `Pending-Order` and the required related objects by executing a query that uses fetch joins. When updating the payment information, the `PlaceOrderService` would call the following method to load the pending order:

```
public class HibernatePendingOrderRepositoryImpl {
...

  public PendingOrder
     findPendingOrderWithRestaurantLineItemsAndMenuItems(
                                     String pendingOrderId) {
    return (PendingOrder) getHibernateTemplate()
        .findByNamedQuery(
          "PendingOrder.
        ➥ findPendingOrderWithRestaurantLineItemsAndMenuItems",
          new Integer(pendingOrderId))
        .get(0);
  }

}


<hibernate-mapping>
...
<query name="PendingOrder.
           ➥ findPendingOrderWithRestaurantLineItemsAndMenuItems">
  <![CDATA[
from PendingOrder po
 left outer join fetch po.restaurant
 left outer join fetch po.lineItems as lineItem
 left outer join fetch lineItem.menuItem
 where po.id = ?
]]></query>
...
</hibernate-mapping>
```

This code executes the named query, which uses fetch joins to eagerly load the pending order's restaurant and its line item. Similarly, when updating the quantities the `PlaceOrderService` must call this method to load the pending order:

```
public class HibernatePendingOrderRepositoryImpl {
...
  public PendingOrder findPendingOrderWithRestaurantAndMenuItems(
       String pendingOrderId) {
    return (PendingOrder) getHibernateTemplate()
        .findByNamedQuery(
```

```
            "PendingOrder.
     ⇨ findPendingOrderWithRestaurantAndMenuItems",
            new Integer(pendingOrderId))
        .get(0);
  }
}

<hibernate-mapping>
...
<query name="PendingOrder.
          ⇨ findPendingOrderWithRestaurantAndMenuItems">
    <![CDATA[
from PendingOrder po
 left outer join fetch po.restaurant as r
 left outer join fetch r.menuItems
 where po.id = ?
]]></query>
...
</hibernate-mapping>
```

This code executes the named query, which eagerly loads the pending order's restaurant and its menu items. In each case, Hibernate loads all the required objects using a single SQL SELECT statement that does a multiway join between the required tables.

Things to remember when using fetch joins

Fetch joins are a simple and concise way to eagerly load objects dynamically. But there are several things you need to remember when using them. First, if you retrieve a collection using a fetch join, then the ResultSet returned by the SELECT statement might contain duplicate data. In the previous example, which retrieves the line items, columns from the PLACED_ORDER and RESTAURANT tables are duplicated in every row. This can impact performance if the query returns a large number of rows and columns.

Second, a query can only use a fetch join on a single collection. The other collections will have to be loaded using separate queries or lazily. This prevents performance problems caused by Hibernate executing a SQL SELECT statement that returns the Cartesian product of two or more large collections.

Finally, it is important to use a fetch join for all references to nonlazy objects and collections in order to prevent performance problems caused by Hibernate loading those objects using additional SQL SELECT statements. This is a variation of the $N+1$ query problem because if a query returns N objects, Hibernate will execute N additional queries to load the related objects.

A significant limitation of Hibernate's fetch join mechanism is that the application must have multiple versions of a query if different requests load different objects eagerly, which can make the code more complicated. Instead of defining a single `findPendingOrder()` method, the `PendingOrderRepository` must define multiple methods for retrieving `PendingOrders`, such as `findPendingOrderWith-RestaurantAndLineItems()` and `findPendingOrderWithRestaurantAndMenuItems()`. This complicates the design of the domain model and makes it more difficult to design a reusable domain model because you must anticipate how it will be used. In comparison, JDO configures eager loading using fetch groups, which are defined declaratively and are separate from the code. They also have the added benefit of controlling eager loading during navigation, which is a feature that Hibernate lacks.

Now that you have seen how to optimize database accesses by using eager loading, let's look at how to reduce database accesses by using a process-level cache.

6.5.2 *Using a process-level cache*

By default, Hibernate caches objects in `Session`, which typically means that objects are cached for the duration of the request. A Hibernate application can also use a process-level cache that caches objects across sessions and hence requests. Before accessing the database to load an object, Hibernate will first look in the `Session` cache and then in the process-level cache. A process-level cache can significantly reduce database accesses if the application accesses the same date repeatedly. The process-level cache is best used to store objects that change relatively infrequently.

Hibernate has a pluggable caching architecture that supports a variety of different caching frameworks, which have varying capabilities. For example, Hibernate ships with Ehcache [EHCache], which is a simple and efficient cache for use in nonclustered environments. Examples of caching frameworks that work in a clustered environment are SwarmCache [SwarmCache] and JBoss Cache [JBoss-Cache]. For more information on how to configure these classes, please consult the Hibernate documentation.

In Hibernate, caching is configured on a per-class and per-collection basis. Hibernate supports a variety of caching strategies including:

- *read-only*—For read-only objects that are never modified by the application

- *read/write*—For objects that are modified by the application

In this example, the restaurant-related classes—`Restaurant`, `MenuItem`, and `Time-Range`—are rarely updated and thus are good candidates for process-level caching. To cache these classes in the process-level cache, we must use the `<cache>` element in the O/R mapping. For example, we would configure process-level caching for the Restaurant class as follows:

```
<class    name="Restaurant"
      table="RESTAURANT">
    <cache usage="read-write"/>
...
</class>
```

The usage="read-write" attribute specifies that instances of this class are sometimes updated by the application. As we saw in chapter 4, cached classes that are updated by the application should almost always use optimistic locking in order to prevent the application from updating the database with stale data. To ensure that the application uses the cache, you must also enable lazy loading for relationships that are from objects that are not cached to objects that are. For example, you must arrange for the PendingOrder-Restaurant relationship to use lazy loading to ensure that restaurants are loaded from the cache.

In this example, by caching the restaurants and menu items and by configuring only the PendingOrder-PendingOrderLineItem to be eagerly loaded, the application will load the pending order, its restaurant, its line items, and its menu items using a single SQL SELECT statement.

6.5.3 *Using a query cache*

So far, we have optimized the loading of a pending order and its related objects by caching the restaurants and using queries with fetch joins. We also need to consider improving the performance of the query that finds the available restaurants. By default, executing a Hibernate query causes the execution of a SQL SELECT statement even if the application uses a process-level cache. Some applications can benefit from the Hibernate query cache, which caches the results of a query and eliminates the need to access the database. To enable the query cache, the application must set the property hibernate.cache.use_query_cache to true; to cache a particular query, the application must call Query.setCacheable(true).

Caching a query only improves performance if it is executed frequently, and the application rarely updates the tables referenced by the query because that causes Hibernate to remove the query from the cache. Caching the query that finds available restaurants might improve performance. However, because there are potentially many combinations of values for the query's parameters—ZIP code and delivery time—it is unclear whether there would be any advantage, and we would have to analyze the running application to determine that.

6.6 *Summary*

Hibernate provides mostly transparent persistence for POJO classes. It provides a rich ORM mechanism that makes it quite easy to persist a domain model such as the one for the Place Order use case. Its features include embedded value objects, inheritance, and automatic deletion of orphaned children in a parent/child relationship.

Despite its power, Hibernate has several important limitations that can impact the design of an application. One limitation is inefficient handling of unidirectional one-to-many relationships that are mapped using a foreign key. Another limitation is that lazily loaded objects do not support `instanceof` and downcasting. In addition, recovering from an error when a `HibernateException` was thrown can be difficult. Another challenge is dynamically configuring eager loading on a per-request basis.

You can use a test-driven approach to develop a Hibernate persistence layer. There are three different kinds of tests you can write for each persistent class. First, you can write a test that uses the Hibernate metadata APIs to verify that the XML mapping document correctly implements the O/R mapping for the class. Second, you can write persistence tests that verify that instances of the class can be saved, updated, and deleted. Finally, you can write a test that that verifies that the schema matches the O/R mapping. For each repository, you write mock object tests that verify that the repository calls the Hibernate/Spring APIs correctly. You can also write database tests for the queries that are called by the repositories.

Now that we have looked at how to use Hibernate and JDO to persist a domain model, the next step is to decide what kind of interface the business logic exposes to the presentation. One option is to encapsulate the domain model with a POJO façade that uses Spring for transaction management, as you'll see in the next chapter.

7

Encapsulating the business logic with a POJO façade

This chapter covers

- Determining when to use a POJO façade
- Designing a POJO facade
- Managing transactions with Spring
- Detaching persistent objects

When I started using EJB, I enthusiastically embraced the J2EE patterns for encapsulating the business logic: the Session Facade pattern and the DTO pattern. I dutifully wrote the session beans and DTOs and patiently waited for the application to deploy in the EJB container. But as the applications I developed became more complex, my frustration with this approach grew. Even though session beans provide declarative transaction management and security, I found that the price for using them was too high. I had to write large amounts of DTO code and session bean boilerplate methods that did very little of value. More important, development was painfully slow because of the long build times and the lengthy edit-compile-debug cycles. I was ready for a different approach.

After spending three days at The ServerSide Java Symposium 2004 learning about such concepts as dependency injection and AOP, I decided it was time to try the Spring framework. Spring offers many of the services provided by the EJB framework but in a much more developer-friendly form. For example, with Spring you just need to write a few lines of XML to make a POJO transactional. Spring enables you to encapsulate your business logic with a POJO façade that you can quickly and easily test within your IDE using regular JUnit tests. I discovered that using the Spring framework dramatically increased my productivity.

Of course, if you are familiar with EJB then you might have a few questions. How exactly are transactions managed? What about remote clients? How does security work? In this chapter you will learn the answers to these and other questions. We examine the benefits and drawbacks of using a POJO façade and show you when to use it to encapsulate a domain model. We also describe how to use Spring to manage transactions and persistence framework connections. Finally, you'll learn how to design, implement, and test a POJO façade using an example façade from the Food to Go application.

7.1 Overview of a POJO façade

The modern car is a complex piece of machinery. It contains mechanical things like pistons, cylinders, gaskets, and probably more computing power than was used to send Neil Armstrong to the moon. Yet for the most part all of this complexity is hidden from us. To make it go, all we interact with are a key, a steering wheel, some pedals, and the gearshift lever. Those simple controls encapsulate the complexity that is under the hood and elsewhere and make driving a car as simple as possible.

For the same kinds of reasons that we must encapsulate the internal mechanisms of a car, we often need to hide the complexity of the business logic from its client, the presentation tier. The EJB way of encapsulating the business logic is to use a session façade, and the POJO approach is to use a POJO façade. We saw in chapter 1 that the concept of a POJO façade is very straightforward. Rather than encapsulating your business logic with heavyweight session beans, you simply use a POJO in conjunction with a lightweight container such as the Spring framework. Like an EJB session façade, a POJO façade exposes a coarse-grained interface to the presentation tier. It handles requests from the presentation tier by delegating to the business logic.

One key difference between a POJO façade and an EJB session façade is that instead of using services provided by the EJB container, the POJO façade uses an AOP framework such as Spring AOP to manage transactions and persistence framework connections. The AOP interceptors automatically begin and commit transactions and open and close persistence framework connections. The POJO façade's client—i.e., the presentation tier—simply gets the façade from the lightweight container, which instantiates the façade and applies the necessary interceptors.

Another key difference is that the POJO façade returns domain objects instead of DTOs to the presentation tier. For example, as you will see a bit later, the POJO façade that implements the Place Order use case returns the `PendingOrder` domain object instead of a DTO containing a copy of its data. This simplifies the façade considerably because you do not have to define a DTO for each domain object and write the code to construct it, which in some applications is as much as 10 percent of the code.

In this section you will learn about the benefits and drawbacks of using a POJO façade and when to use one. But let's first look at an example.

7.1.1 *An example POJO façade*

To see how a POJO façade works, let's look at the `PlaceOrderFacade`. The `Place-OrderFacade` handles requests from the presentation tier components that implement the Place Order use case and invokes the domain model that was developed earlier in chapter 3. For example, one of its methods is `updateDeliveryInfo()`, which is invoked by the presentation tier when the user enters the delivery address and time. This method calls the `PlaceOrderService` to create or update the `PendingOrder`. The `PlaceOrderFacade` also invokes the `RestaurantRepository` to get the available restaurants. The `PlaceOrderFacade` returns the detached `PendingOrder` and `Restaurant` objects to the presentation tier, which displays them to the user. Figure 7.1 shows the structure of the `PlaceOrderFacade` and its relationship with the presentation tier and the domain model.

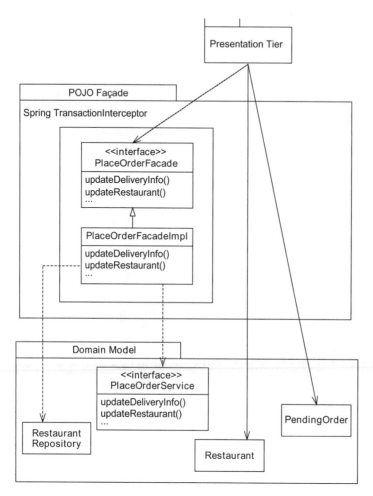

Figure 7.1 The structure of a typical POJO façade

The POJO façade consists of the following types:

- `PlaceOrderFacade` is the interface that specifies the methods that can be called by the presentation tier.

- `PlaceOrderFacadeImpl` implements the `PlaceOrderFacade` interface by calling the `PlaceOrderService` and other domain objects such as `Restaurant-Repository`

- Spring `TransactionInterceptor` is an AOP interceptor that manages transactions and persistence framework connections.

These classes work together as follows. When the presentation tier calls the `Place-OrderFacade`, the Spring `TransactionInterceptor` begins a transaction and opens a persistence framework connection for use by the repositories. The `PlaceOrder-FacadeImpl` invokes the domain model classes to validate the input and perform computations. When the `PlaceOrderFacade` returns, the `TransactionInterceptor` closes the persistence framework connection and commits the transaction.

In section 7.3 we will dive into details of this design. But first, let's review when it is appropriate to use a POJO façade and its benefits and drawbacks.

7.1.2 Benefits of a POJO façade

A POJO façade has several benefits. Let's look at each one in turn.

Faster and easier development

It is a lot easier and faster to develop and test business logic that is encapsulated with a POJO façade. Unlike an EJB façade, the POJO façade can be developed and tested outside of the application server, and there is no need to develop and maintain DTOs for the domain objects.

Potentially eliminates need to use an EJB container

Another benefit of using POJO façades instead of EJB façades is that it can sometimes remove the requirement for the application to use EJBs. In many applications EJBs are only used to encapsulate the business logic. If the EJB session façades are replaced with POJO façades, then the application often no longer needs to use EJBs and can be deployed in a cheaper and simpler web container.

Simplified presentation tier

The *Exposed Domain Model* pattern, which is described in the next chapter, uses a servlet filter to manage persistence framework connections. In comparison, when using a POJO façade all transaction management and database access happens within the façade and the Spring-supplied interceptors. The presentation tier is completely unaware of those mechanisms.

Consistent view of the database

Because each call to the façade consists of a single database transaction, the application can have a consistent view of the database by using the appropriate transaction isolation level (see chapter 12). In comparison, the Exposed Domain Model pattern potentially uses multiple database transactions per request and cannot obtain a consistent view of the database.

More flexible AOP-based design

Whereas an EJB 2 façade can only use the services provided by the EJB container, a Spring AOP-based design has a lot of flexibility. For example, the application can use its own custom interceptors to automatically retry transactions and implement audit logging. It can also use a more flexible exception handling mechanism since the application has greater control over which exceptions cause transaction rollbacks and can use unchecked exceptions more easily. EJB 3 provides some of this flexibility by letting you define interceptors, but Spring is much more flexible.

7.1.3 Drawbacks of a POJO façade

This approach has several drawbacks as well. Let's look at each one of them in turn.

No support for transactions initiated by a remote client

One of the strengths of EJB is that it supports distributed transactions. A remote client can initiate a transaction and invoke one or more EJBs, which then automatically participate in the transaction. Any updates made by those EJBs are applied atomically when the client commits the transactions. If your application has a requirement to use this kind of distributed transaction, then you must use EJB. As you will see in section 7.2.6, POJO façades can be invoked remotely but they cannot participate in transactions that are initiated by a remote caller. However, this is rarely an issue because very few applications actually use this kind of distributed transaction.

No equivalent to message-driven beans

Message-driven beans are a convenient way for an application to consume JMS messages. The EJB container automatically invokes the message-driven bean when a JMS message arrives and takes care of managing transactions. Unfortunately, as of this writing Spring lacked support for the POJO equivalent of message-driven beans. This means that you should most likely use message-driven beans if your application uses JMS extensively. You can make developing with message-driven beans more palatable by writing message-driven beans that delegate to POJO business logic, which, of course, is easier to develop and test.

Nonstandard security

When implementing EJBs, you can use the EJB container's security mechanism to control access to them. Not only is this a well-tried and -tested mechanism, but some application servers are also integrated with other security products that provide more elaborate capabilities. For example, IBM WebSphere is integrated with other IBM products such as Tivoli Access Manager, which provides centralized access control throughout an organization. Obviously, only EJBs can use the EJB container to provide security, so if you want to secure your POJO façade what can you do?

As you would expect, the open source community has responded to this need and developed Acegi Security. Acegi Security [Acegi] is an open source security framework for Spring. It uses Spring AOP to provide security for Spring beans. However, one drawback of using something like Acegi Security is that it is potentially less mature than the security framework provided by the application server. Moreover, while Acegi Security is integrated with some other security products, it might not be integrated with the same ones that are available via the application server.

Client must be able to get the façade from the container

Because a POJO façade relies on AOP interceptors to manage transactions and connections, its client must get the façade from the lightweight container. This isn't a problem for a web-based presentation tier, which might even be tightly integrated with the lightweight container. But some clients might not be able to call the lightweight container. For example, a web services code generator, which generates code that exposes the façade as a web service, needs to know how to instantiate the façade. If the code generator has no knowledge of the lightweight container, which is responsible for creating the façade and applying AOP interceptors, it would not be able to generate code that obtains the correct reference to the façade.

Detaching objects is potentially complex and fragile

Detached objects and POJO façades can be used independently. A POJO façade can return DTOs, and a session façade can return detached objects. But since POJOs and ORM frameworks that support detached objects go hand in hand, you will most likely use them with a POJO façade. The façade must detach all of the objects that the presentation tier will potentially access, which, as you will see later, can require careful coding and is potentially error-prone.

To see why, consider the following example. To enable the presentation tier to render a page that displays a `PendingOrder` and its line items, the business tier must detach those objects. But a developer easily could change that screen to display the restaurant's name in some situations without changing the business tier. Because it is not possible to catch this problem at compile time, this can all too easily cause hard-to-reproduce runtime errors. Although later on I describe ways to minimize this problem, you often have to rely on extensive testing to catch bugs.

Lack of encapsulation of the domain model

In a design that uses DTOs, the presentation tier simply has no access to the domain objects and so cannot bypass the EJB façade and call them directly. Furthermore, the structure of the DTOs does not have to mirror the structure of the domain objects. As a result, the business tier can be changed without impacting the presentation tier. You could even replace a domain model with transaction scripts without affecting the presentation tier. In comparison, when using a POJO façade the presentation tier accesses the domain objects directly and so there is an increased risk of it being affected by changes to the business tier. Later in this chapter I'll show you how to partially encapsulate the domain objects and minimize the impact of changes by using interfaces.

Some domain object methods cannot be called by the presentation tier

Another limitation of detached objects is that some methods cannot be called by the presentation tier. Although many domain object methods return the value of a field or perform simple calculations, others are much more complicated. For example, a `PendingOrder` method could define a `getDiscount()` method that retrieves a discount schedule from the database. If the presentation tier invoked one of these methods, the persistence framework would throw an exception because the connection is closed when the POJO façade returns. To avoid this problem, the POJO façade must call those methods while the database connection is open and return a DTO-like object that stores the computed values.

7.1.4 When to use a POJO façade and detached domain objects

The POJO façade should be used when:

- The business logic does not participate in transactions initiated by remote clients.
- The application uses a lightweight container.
- The client can get the façade from the lightweight container.
- The business logic requires a consistent view of the database.
- The domain objects can be easily detached and can be invoked by the presentation tier.

Now that we have looked at the benefits and drawbacks of a POJO façade, let's look at various design decisions that you must make when using one.

7.2 POJO façade design decisions

When designing a POJO façade, you must decide how to encapsulate and detach domain objects, manage transactions, and support remote clients. Let's look at each one of these issues in turn.

7.2.1 Encapsulating the domain objects

We have seen that one potential drawback of returning domain objects to the presentation tier is that it could call methods to update the domain objects without going via the façade or service. It could also call methods that try to access an external resource such as the database, which would throw an exception because the database connection was closed. For example, a JSP page that displays a Pending-Order could call methods such as updateDeliveryInformation() or update-Restaurant() that update the pending order.

For some applications, the best way to deal with these problems is to simply rely on the presentation tier developers to do the right thing. This can work quite well for smaller projects, especially when the presentation logic and the business logic are implemented by the same developer. But with other applications it's important to encapsulate the domain objects and prevent them from being used inappropriately.

One option is to use Java's visibility rules and define only those methods that are callable by the presentation tier to be public. But since the business logic usually consists of multiple packages, we can rarely use this approach. We must instead encapsulate the domain objects behind interfaces that define read-only views of domain objects. The presentation tier is written in terms of these interfaces rather than the domain model classes. These interfaces can either be implemented by the corresponding domain objects or by an adapter, which is a class that delegates to the domain object. Let's look at how these two approaches work.

Implementing the interfaces with domain objects

Imagine that you want to implement a JSP page that displays a PendingOrder, its restaurant, and its line items. If the JSP page accessed those classes directly, it could call several methods that should only be called by the business tier. A better approach is to define an interface that specifies the methods that are available to the JSP page. The JSP page is written in terms of this interface, which is implemented by the PendingOrder class:

```
interface PendingOrderDetail {
  public Address getDeliveryAddress();
```

```
   public Date getDeliveryTime();
   public RestaurantDetail getRestaurantDetail();
   public double getTotal();
   ...
}

public class PendingOrder implements PendingOrderDetail {
...
   public .. updateDeliveryInfo(..) {…}
}
```

The JSP page that displays the PendingOrder would use the PendingOrderDetail rather than PendingOrder.

Read-only interfaces are mostly straightforward to implement. One problem with using interfaces in JDK 1.4 and earlier is that because the return types are different, a getter that returns a view interface must have a different name than the getter that returns the real object. For example, PendingOrderDetail defines getRestaurantDetail(), which PendingOrder must implement as follows:

```
class PendingOrder implements PendingOrderDetail {
   public RestaurantDetail getRestaurantDetail() {
      return getRestaurant();
   }

   public Restaurant getRestaurant() {
      ...
   }
...
```

It is tedious to write these methods and they clutter the code. Fortunately, Java 5 eliminates the need to write these extra methods by supporting covariant return types. A subclass can define an overloaded method whose return type is a subtype of the return type specified in the inherited method. This means, for example, that the following code is legal:

```
interface PendingOrderView { RestaurantView getRestaurant(); }

class PendingOrder implements PendingOrderDetail {
   public Restaurant getRestaurant() { … };
...
```

Getters that return collections do not have this problem in JDK 1.4 because collections are untyped. The presentation tier can cast each element to the view interface. For example, the presentation tier can cast each element of the List returned by PendingOrderDetail.getLineItems() to a PendingOrderLineItem-Detail. A Java 5 application can use typed collections with wildcards to enable a subclass to override a method with a different return type.

Another drawback of using view interfaces is that they do not help when the presentation tier needs a value that is computed by a method that can only be called by the business tier. In this situation, the business tier must call the method and return the result to the presentation tier using either a DTO, which we are trying to avoid using, or an adapter, which we will discuss next.

Implementing the interfaces with adapters

For example, suppose that the presentation tier could call any of the PendingOrder's getters except for the getTotal() method, which retrieves the pricing and discount information from the database. We can encapsulate the PendingOrder using the interface we saw earlier, except that the interface is implemented by a Pending-OrderAdapter class, which stores a reference to the real PendingOrder and the total computed by the business tier. All of its methods delegate to the PendingOrder except for the getTotals() method, which returns the total stored in the field:

```
public class PendingOrderAdapter implements PendingOrderDetail {

    private PendingOrder pendingOrder;
    private double total;

    public PendingOrderAdapter(PendingOrder pendingOrder,
                    double total, …) {
      this.pendingOrder = pendingOrder;       ❶ Stores
      this.total = total;                         PendingOrder and total
      …
    }

    public Coupon getCoupon() {
      return pendingOrder.getCoupon();
    }

    public Address getDeliveryAddress() {       ❷ Delegates to
      return pendingOrder.                          PendingOrder
            ➥ getDeliveryAddress();
    }

    public RestaurantDetail getRestaurant() {
      return pendingOrder.getRestaurant();
    }

    public double getTotal() {     ⟵  ❸ Returns value
       return total;                     from total field
    }
    …
}
```

Let's look at the details:

❶ The constructor takes the real `PendingOrder` and the total computed by the business tier as parameters and stores them in fields.

❷ Most methods delegate to the `PendingOrder`.

❸ The `getTotal()` method returns the value stored in a field.

Adapters are somewhat similar to DTOs except that they do not involve copying as much data because they delegate to the domain object. They are useful when some values must be computed by the business tier. However, one downside of using adapters is that you have to write more code than you would if the domain object implemented an interface. In the extreme case, an adapter could store so many values that it would effectively be a DTO.

7.2.2 Detaching objects

Another important POJO façade design issue is how to detach the domain objects that are returned to the presentation tier. Each POJO façade method must ensure that the object graph it returns to the presentation tier contains all of the required objects. Otherwise, an exception will be thrown when the presentation tier tries to access a missing object or collection. For example, if the presentation tier displays the `PendingOrder` and its restaurant's menu items, the business tier must load those objects from the database and detach them. Let's look at the details of how to do this with JDO and Hibernate.

Using JDO detached objects

JDO will throw an exception if the application tries to access the field of an object after its `PersistenceManager` is closed. In order to return JDO objects to the presentation tier, the façade must first call JDO to detach the object graph from a `PersistenceManager`. Later on, it can call JDO to reattach the object graph to a new `PersistenceManager`.

A JDO application detaches objects by calling either `Persistence-Manager.detachCopy()`, which returns detached copy of the specified object, or `PersistenceManager.detachCopyAll()`, which returns a list of detached copies of the specified objects. By default, these methods will detach only the objects that are passed to them and not any referenced objects. For example, if you call `detachCopy()` with a `PendingOrder`, its default behavior is to return a copy of the `PendingOrder` whose line items, restaurant, and coupon fields are not initialized—a `JDODetachedObjectAccessException` will be thrown if the application tries to access them.

If you want to detach one or more related objects such as a PendingOrder's restaurant and its menu items, then you must configure JDO fetch groups, which you first saw in chapter 5. Not only can fetch groups be used to configure eager loading but you can also use them to configure detachment. An application uses a fetch group to define the object graph to detach.

There are a couple of ways to configure fetch groups to detach related objects. One is to add the reference fields such as PendingOrder.restaurant and Restaurant.menuItems to their class's default fetch group. Alternatively, the application can use custom fetch groups to specify which related objects should be detached. Once the fetch groups have been configured correctly, detachCopy() returns a graph of objects. In section 7.5.2 you will see an example of how to use fetch groups to detach multiple objects.

An important benefit of JDO fetch groups is that because they are a declarative mechanism you do not have to hardwire knowledge of the object structure into the façade's code as you do when using Hibernate. This simplifies the design of the façade and improves maintainability.

Later we will look at some sample JDO code, but now let's look at detached objects in Hibernate.

Using Hibernate detached objects

Because Hibernate objects are automatically detached when the session is closed, the application only has to ensure that the objects required by the presentation tier are loaded. The business tier will load some of those objects while handling the request. But there will often be other objects required by the presentation tier that will need to be loaded as well. For example, the business logic for the Place Order use case might load the PendingOrder and its Restaurant in the course of handling a request in order to invoke their methods. However, it's possible that it would not access the restaurant's menu items, which because of lazy loading would never be loaded. The POJO façade or the business logic must somehow ensure that those objects are loaded in order to make them accessible to the presentation tier.

For some applications, the simplest option is to configure Hibernate to use one of the eager loading mechanisms I described in chapter 6. Hibernate will eagerly load the objects required by the presentation tier when it loads the objects that the business tier needs. You could, for example, load a PendingOrder with a query that used a fetch join to load the restaurant and its menu items. No additional code is required, and the POJO façade can simply return the domain objects back to the presentation tier. Unfortunately, one limitation of this approach is that, as you saw in chapter 6, it can be difficult to configure Hibernate to eagerly load the optimal set of objects for each request.

The other option is for each POJO façade method to make sure that the objects required by the presentation tier are loaded by either navigating to them or by calling `Hibernate.initialize()`. The `initialize()` method takes either an object or a collection as a parameter and ensures that it is loaded. A POJO method façade could, for example, force the pending order's restaurant and its menu items to be loaded using code such as this:

```
Hibernate.initialize(pendingOrder.getRestaurant().getMenuItems());
```

A benefit of this approach is that a POJO façade method knows precisely what objects will be needed by the presentation tier and can ensure that they are loaded. The drawback is that it requires code, which must sometimes contain conditional logic to handle null references and polymorphic references. For example, if the reference to a restaurant could be null, you need to write code such as this to avoid `NullPointerExceptions`:

```
Restaurant r = pendingOrder.getRestaurant();
if (r != null)
  Hibernate.initialize(r.getMenuItems());
```

This code can sometimes get quite complicated. Moreover, it can be difficult to maintain because the structure of the object graph is hardwired into the façade.

7.2.3 *Exceptions versus status codes*

Another decision you need to make is whether the facade should use exceptions or status codes to communicate errors to its caller. There are often many possible outcomes of calling a façade method. For example, `PlaceOrderFacade.update-DeliveryInfo()` normally updates the `PendingOrder`, but several things could go wrong. There are, for instance, various application-level errors, such as delivery information that is not served by any restaurants or a delivery time that is not far enough in the future. Various infrastructure-level errors can also occur, including database crashes or deadlocks. A POJO façade should certainly report an infrastructure error to its caller by throwing an exception, but what about application-level errors?

One option is to return a DTO for the "normal" outcome and to throw an exception for the other outcomes. One appealing feature of exceptions is that the Spring `TransactionInterceptor` can be configured to automatically roll back the transaction when an exception is thrown (as you will see later in this section). The code does not have to programmatically roll back the transaction, which would have the undesirable side effect of coupling the code to the Spring framework.

However, one issue with using exceptions is that calling a façade method can have several equally valid outcomes. Even validation errors such as invalid delivery information can be considered normal. This means that choosing the "normal" outcome is somewhat arbitrary. Another issue is that the exception will typically need to contain the data that the presentation tier displays to the user, so throwing an exception is not that straightforward.

Because of these shortcomings, my preference is to use exceptions only for truly exceptional conditions (such as database connection failures) and to use status codes to signal application-level errors. However, if the transaction needed to be rolled back, then I would throw an exception for an application-level error in order to decouple the business logic from the Spring framework.

7.2.4 *Managing transactions and connections*

A POJO façade method must usually be executed within a transaction in order to ensure that it updates the database atomically. The application must start a transaction when the POJO façade method is invoked and either commit or roll back the transaction when it returns. In addition, when the POJO façade method is invoked the application must open a connection (a JDBC connection, a Hibernate session, or a JDO `PersistenceManager`) and close it after the method returns.

The Spring framework has an AOP-based transaction and connection management mechanism. You define Spring beans that wrap your application code with AOP interceptors that manage transactions and connections. Spring transaction management, like EJB container-managed transactions, is declarative; you do not have to write any code.

A valuable feature of Spring transaction management is that although EJB container-managed transactions require the application to use JTA transactions, Spring also provides the option of local transactions, which are lighter weight and don't require an application server to manage transactions. Furthermore, switching to JTA transactions (which are only required if an application needs to update multiple resources such as a database and JMS) is simply a matter of reconfiguring a Spring bean.

Configuring the Spring TransactionInterceptor

Declaratively managing transactions with Spring is remarkably easy. You simply have to use a `TransactionInterceptor`, which is a Spring AOP interceptor. It intercepts calls to the POJO façade and ensures that each one executes in the transaction. In addition, depending on how you have configured the `TransactionInterceptor` it will also open and close a database or persistence framework connection.

To see how to configure a `TransactionInterceptor`, let's imagine that the `TransferFacade` from chapter 1 has the following interface:

```
public interface TransferFacade {

    public BankingTransaction transfer(
        String fromAccountId, String toAccountId,
        double amount)
        throws MoneyTransferException;

    public void getBalance(String accountId);

}
```

The `transfer()` method transfers money from one account to another and throws a `MoneyTransferException` if the transfer fails. We want this method to be executed within a transaction that is rolled back if the `MoneyTransferException` is thrown. The `getBalance()` method returns the balance of the specified account. It doesn't need to be executed within a transaction because it does not update the database.

Here is the definition of a `TransactionInterceptor` that manages transactions for the `TransferFacade`:

```
<beans>

<bean id="ExampleTransactionInterceptor"
    class="org.springframework.transaction.interceptor.
    ➥ TransactionInterceptor">
  <property name="transactionAttributeSource">
    <value>net.chrisrichardson.bankingExample.facade.
      ➥ TransferFacade.transfer=PROPAGATION_REQUIRED,
        ➥ net.chrisrichardson.bankingExample.facade.
        ➥ MoneyTransferException
    net.chrisrichardson.bankingExample.facade.TransferFacade.get*=
      ➥ PROPAGATION_SUPPORTS, readOnly
    </value>
  </property>
  <property ref="transactionManager"/>
</bean>
...
</beans>
```

The `transactionAttributesSource` property specifies the transaction attribute for each method. In this example, the transaction attributes for the `transfer()` method are

```
PROPAGATION_REQUIRED,-net.chrisrichardson.bankingExample.facade.
        ➥ MoneyTransferException
```

A value of `PROPAGATION_REQUIRED` indicates this method must be executed in a transaction. The `TransactionInterceptor` will start a transaction if one is not already in progress.

The `-net.chrisrichardson.bankingExample.facade.MoneyTransferException` entry is an example of a Spring rollback rule and tells the `TransactionInterceptor` to roll back the transaction if the `MoneyTransferException` is thrown. By default, Spring behaves like EJB and only rolls back a transaction if an unchecked exception is thrown, but you can override this behavior by configuring rollback rules. This example uses a rollback rule that tells the `TransactionInterceptor` to roll back when a checked exception is thrown, but you can also write rollback rules that commit transactions when unchecked exceptions are thrown. An important benefit of rollback rules is that they enable the application to roll back a transaction without calling a Spring API. This is yet another example of how Spring does not intrude on your application's code.

The transaction attributes for the `getBalance()` method, which matches the `get*` wildcard, are

```
PROPAGATION_SUPPORTS, readOnly
```

The `PROPAGATION_SUPPORTS` value indicates that this method can be executed in a transaction but does not require one. The `readOnly` value indicates that this method does not update the database, which allows some database systems, to optimize the transaction.

In addition to specifying the transaction attributes of each method, you must specify the `PlatformTransactionManager` used by the `TransactionInterceptor`. The `PlatformTransactionManager` is a Strategy (as in the Strategy pattern) that is used by the `TransactionInterceptor` to begin, commit, and roll back transactions. Figure 7.2 shows some of the different implementations of `PlatformTransactionManager`.

The `PlatformTransactionManager` interface specifies three methods: `getTransaction()`, which begins a transaction; `commit()`, which commits a transaction; and `rollback()`, which roll backs a transaction. Which kind of `PlatformTransactionManager` you use depends on whether you are using local transactions or JTA transactions. All of the examples in this book use local transactions but can easily be enhanced to use JTA transactions by simply reconfiguring the `TransactionInterceptor`.

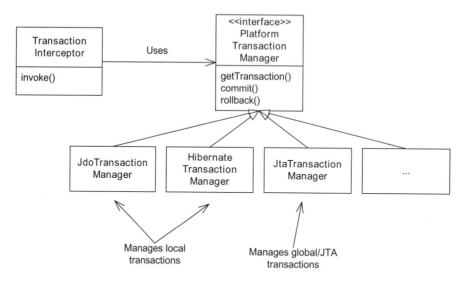

Figure 7.2   **The different implementations of the** `PlatformTransactionManager` **interface**

Using local transactions

A local transaction involves only a single database, and can be started, committed, and rolled back using the JDBC or persistence framework APIs directly. Spring provides several `PlatformTransactionManager` implementations for managing local transactions; which one you use depends on how the application accesses the database. A JDO application uses a `JdoTransactionManager`, which manages transactions using the JDO `Transaction` interface, and a Hibernate application uses a `HibernateTransactionManager`, which manages transactions using the Hibernate `Transaction` interface. In addition, a JDBC application uses a `Data-SourceTransactionManager`, which manages transactions using the JDBC `Connection` interface (this is described in more detail in chapter 9).

As well as managing transactions, these `PlatformTransactionManager` implementations manage a connection that can be used by the repositories that are called during the transaction. Behind the scenes, they use a `ThreadLocal` to bind the connection to the thread. Before starting the transaction, the `JdoTransactionManager` opens a `PersistenceManager`, which can be obtained by the repositories using `PersistenceManagerFactoryUtils.getPersistenceManager()`. It closes the `PersistenceManager` after the transaction ends. Similarly, a `HibernateTransactionManager` manages a `Session`, which the repositories can access by calling `SessionFactoryUtils.getSession()`. Spring's ORM template classes use these methods to get a persistence framework connection.

An application can use local transactions if it only updates a single database via JDBC, JDO, or Hibernate. However, applications that update multiple databases or update a database and use JMS must use JTA.

Using JTA transactions

A JTA (or global) transaction is a transaction that involves multiple databases and/or resources such as a JMS. An application uses JTA transaction either by using the JTA APIs directly or by using EJB container-managed transactions that call the JTA APIs internally. The JTA APIs call the transaction manager (not to be confused with the Spring `PlatformTransactionManager` interface), which is typically provided by the application server. The transaction manager coordinates the atomic commit and rollback of the multiple resources.

To use a JTA transaction in a Spring application, you simply configure the `TransactionInterceptor` with a `JtaTransactionManager`, which is a `PlatformTransactionManager` that manages the transaction using the JTA APIs. However, one important difference between the `JtaTransactionManager` and the `PlatformTransactionManagers` that manage local transactions is that it does not manage a persistence framework connection. You can either let the ORM template class open the connection, or you can use a persistence framework-specific interceptor. For example, a `HibernateInterceptor` binds a Hibernate `Session` to the thread and a `JdoInterceptor` binds a JDO `PersistenceManager` to the thread.

7.2.5 Implementing security

In the film *The Lord of the Rings*, the town of Bree has a gatekeeper who decides who can enter the town. At night, when the gate is closed he looks through a peephole to make sure that the visitor is not an enemy of the town. A façade that encapsulates the business logic often plays the role of gatekeeper. It verifies that the caller has permission to invoke a particular façade method. Hopefully, the façades in your application will fare better than Bree's gatekeeper. Shortly after he let in Frodo and his companions, the Black Riders sent the town's gate crashing down on top of him.

An EJB can use the declarative security mechanism provided by the EJB container, which verifies that the user has permission to execute a business method. It also can call the `EJBContext` to get the identity of the caller and determine whether the caller is in a particular role. A POJO façade does not use the EJB container and so must adopt a different approach to security. It can either rely on the presentation tier to provide security or, if the POJO façade must enforce security, it can use a framework such as Acegi Security.

Using web tier security

Some applications can get away with only enforcing security in the presentation tier. The POJO façade assumes that any security checks have been done by the presentation tier and does not do any itself. The presentation tier can use the security mechanisms provided by the web container to control access to web pages based on the user's identity or role. It can, for example, declaratively specify that a user must be in a particular role to access a URL. Also, the presentation tier can call HttpServletRequest methods that return the identity of the user and test whether the user is in a particular role.

Implementing security with Acegi Security

Although web tier-only security is adequate for some applications, many applications require security to be handled in the business tier. For example, an application with more stringent security requirements might not be able to assume that the presentation tier will do the right thing. Alternatively, it might have business logic that does different things depending on the caller's identity. One way to implement security with POJO business logic is to use Acegi Security, which provides security for Spring applications. We're only going to briefly describe a few of the features of this comprehensive framework, so for more information see the reference [Acegi].

Acegi Security provides the several options for storing the users and their roles. You can configure it to use the security infrastructure provided by the underlying web container or application. Alternatively, Acegi Security can maintain the user and role information itself—in a database, for example. One key thing to remember is that Acegi Security has a very flexible architecture that enables it to support a wide range of applications.

Acegi Security has an AOP-based mechanism that can be used to verify that the caller has permission to invoke a POJO façade method. You can, for example, use the MethodSecurityInterceptor class, which is a Spring AOP interceptor, to intercept calls to a POJO and throw an exception if the caller is not authorized. You configure MethodSecurityInterceptor as a Spring bean in almost the same way you would configure a Spring TransactionInterceptor. As part of its definition in the XML configuration file, you specify the roles that are allowed to invoke each method. You would also use a Spring AOP proxy creator such as BeanNameProxy-Creator to apply the MethodSecurityInterceptor to a particular POJO façade.

Acegi Security also has a SecurityContextHolder class, which defines static methods for obtaining the caller's identity and roles. In the same way that an EJB can get information about the caller from the EJBContext, POJO business logic that does different things depending on the identity of the caller can call the `SecurityContextHolder`.

Security is one of the issues you must address when developing a POJO façade. Another is remoting.

7.2.6 *Supporting remote clients*

In many applications, the business tier is invoked by a presentation tier that runs within the same JVM. However, in some applications the business tier is invoked by a client running on a different machine. For example, an application running on a cell phone that enables a customer to order dinner on the way home would invoke the `PlaceOrderFacade` remotely. Supporting remote clients with EJBs is easy because remote invocation is built in. It even allows EJBs to participate in transactions that are initiated by remote clients. If we want a POJO façade to support remote clients, then we have to use a separate remoting technology.

Once again the Spring framework comes to the rescue. It supports several methods of exposing a POJO façade to a remote client:

- Standard Java RMI
- Hessian, an open source binary HTTP protocol that uses its own serialization mechanism for Java objects
- Burlap, an open source XML over HTTP protocol that uses its own serialization mechanism for Java objects
- Spring HTTP, an HTTP protocol provided by Spring that uses standard Java serialization
- Web services using the Java API for XML-based RPC (JAX-RPC) and Axis

Please note, however, that none of these technologies allows a POJO façade to participate in a transaction initiated by a remote client. If that is one of your requirements, then you must use EJBs.

Spring makes it remarkably easy to expose a POJO façade to a remote client using RMI, Hessian, Burlap, or the Spring HTTP invoker. You configure an "exporter" Spring bean such as `RMIServiceExporter`, or `HessianServiceExporter` takes care of the infrastructure magic required to map requests from remote clients into calls to POJO façade methods. Exposing a POJO façade as a web service is not quite as easy because you do need to write some code, but it is still very straightforward. For more information on using these remoting technologies with Spring, see the Spring documentation or *Spring in Action* [Walls 2005].

7.3 *Designing a POJO façade's interface*

The process of implementing a POJO façade consists of the following steps:

1   Design the POJO façade's public interface.
2   Implement the POJO façade's methods, which call the domain model objects and the result object factory.
3   Implement the result object factory that is called by the POJO façade to detach the domain objects.
4   Configure the Spring framework's AOP interceptors, which provide services such as transaction management.

In this section, you will learn how to design the POJO façade's public interface. We describe how to identify the methods and the parameters, and how to return values. You will also see examples of how to encapsulate the domain objects to prevent the presentation tier from calling methods that it should not. We use the PlaceOrderFacade, which we introduced earlier, as an example. Later sections in this chapter describe the other steps in the process.

7.3.1 *Determining the method signatures*

The design of a POJO façade is driven by the needs of the presentation tier. Each POJO façade method corresponds to a request handled by the presentation tier. The method's parameters correspond to user input, and its return values include data that is displayed by the presentation in response to the request. Consequently, in order to design a POJO façade, we need to understand the presentation tier's requirements.

The presentation tier in a web application handles HTTP requests and generates HTTP responses. An HTTP request is sent by the browser when the user clicks on a link or submits a form. Some HTTP requests might be handled entirely by the presentation tier, but most requests result in a call to the business tier to update the database or to retrieve data. The HTTP response is typically an HTML page but could also be data for a rich client using a technology such as Ajax [Crane 2005] that runs in the browser.

To determine the methods that a POJO façade must provide, you need to know the requests that are handled by the presentation tier. The presentation tier calls a POJO façade method, passing as arguments the user's input and any session state stored in the presentation tier or the browser. The POJO façade must return the data that the presentation tier needs to display the page along with any updated session state. As you can see, in order to define the POJO façade you must have some understanding of the presentation tier.

Consider the following example. The UI for the Place Order use case consists of several web pages. Two of these pages are shown in figure 7.3 and figure 7.4. Figure 7.3 shows the Restaurant List page, which displays the list of available restaurants for the delivery information entered by the user. This page displays information obtained by a previous request to the façade. Each restaurant name is a link whose URL has the restaurant ID as a parameter.

Figure 7.4 shows the Order page, which is displayed when the user selects a restaurant. This page displays the selected restaurant's menu items and lets the user enter quantities for each one.

When the user selects a restaurant, their browser sends an HTTP request containing a parameter that specifies the ID of the selected restaurant. The application must update the `Pending-Order` with the selected restaurant, retrieve the restaurant's menu items,

Select Restaurant		
Name	Type	Description
Ajanta	Indian	Fine Indian dining
XYZ Pizza	Pizza	Excellent Pizza
...		

<table>
<tr><td>Back</td><td>Cancel</td></tr>
</table>

Figure 7.3   Restaurant List page

Delivering to: 100 Some Street	Order When: 8.30pm	From: Ajanta
Name	Quantity	Price
Meat Samosas	1	$3.75
Kima Curry	1	$9.75
Ginger Chicken	1	$10.75
Naan Bread	1	$3.75
Chapati	1	$2.75
Mango Lassi	1	$1.75
	Total	$32.50

<table>
<tr><td>Update</td><td>Checkout</td></tr>
</table>

Figure 7.4   Order page

and display the Order page. Figure 7.5 shows how the various components handle the request.

In order for the presentation tier to handle this request, the `PlaceOrderFacade` must provide an `updateRestaurant()` method:

```
public interface PlaceOrderFacade {

  public PlaceOrderFacadeResult updateRestaurant(
     String pendingOrderId, String restaurantId);

  ...
```

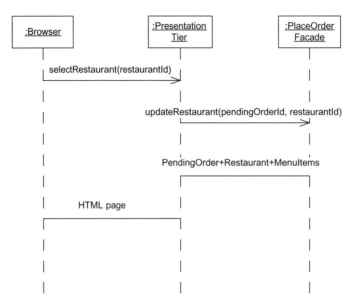

Figure 7.5 Handling the request that selects a restaurant

This method takes as parameters the `pendingOrderId`, which is stored in the `HttpSession`, and the restaurant ID from the HTTP request. It returns a `PlaceOrderFacadeResult`, which consists of a status code, and the `PendingOrder`, which contains the delivery information and a reference to the selected restaurant and its menu items:

```
public class PlaceOrderFacadeResult {

  private int statusCode;
  private PendingOrderDetail pendingOrder;

  public PlaceOrderFacadeResult(
    int statusCode,
    PendingOrderDetail pendingOrder) {
    this.statusCode = statusCode;
    this.pendingOrder = pendingOrder;
  }
  ...
```

The status code indicates the outcome of calling the method. A façade method can often have several expected outcomes, and a status code is a good way to communicate the outcome along with the data to display to the caller. `PendingOrderDetail`, which we first saw in section 7.2.1, is a view interface that provides a read-only view of pending orders and is implemented by the `PendingOrder` class.

In this example the presentation tier accesses the objects it needs to generate the response, such as the restaurant and its menu items, by navigating from the PendingOrder. However, a POJO façade method often returns multiple domain objects to the presentation tier. For example, the PlaceOrderFacade defines an updateDeliveryInfo() method, which returns the PendingOrder and a list of available restaurants. Consequently, façade methods typically return a DTO-like object that aggregates several detached domain objects.

We would identify the other POJO façade methods by looking at each transition between pages in the UI and defining a corresponding POJO façade method. See this book's online source code for the complete PlaceOrderFacade.

7.4 Implementing the POJO façade

Once you have identified the methods and defined the POJO façade's interface, the next step is to develop the POJO façade class that implements the interface. This class in our example façade implements the PlaceOrderFacade interface and is called PlaceOrderFacadeImpl. Each POJO façade method defined by this class is usually quite simple because it does not contain any significant business logic. Instead, as figure 7.6 shows, it delegates to domain model classes. It also calls the persistence framework to detach the domain objects required by the presentation tier.

A good way to implement a POJO façade's methods is to use a test-driven approach that mocks the objects that it calls. This enables you to test only the simple logic implemented by the façade without worrying about the complex business logic implemented by the domain model or, worse, the database. To see how this is done, let's implement the updateRestaurant() method, which we identified earlier in section 7.3.1. We will first write some tests and then write the method.

7.4.1 Writing a test for a POJO façade method

Because we are using test-driven development, we first need to write a test for the updateRestaurant() method. As figure 7.6 shows, this method calls the PlaceOrderService to update the PendingOrder with the selected restaurant. It returns the PlaceOrderFacade result object, which contains the detached PendingOrder. Unlike some of the other methods defined by PlaceOrderFacadeImpl, updateRestaurant() doesn't invoke any repositories.

The updateRestaurant() method returns a PlaceOrderFacadeResult that contains a status code and the detached PendingOrder. The PlaceOrderFacadeImpl could detach the objects by calling the persistence framework APIs directly. However, this would complicate development and testing because it would be directly

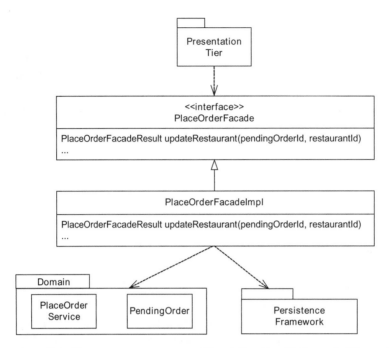

Figure 7.6 The `PlaceOrderFacade` and its relationship with the rest of the application

coupled to the persistence framework and the database. A better design, which simplifies testing, is to encapsulate the detachment logic behind what I call a result factory.

The result factory interface in this particular example is called `PlaceOrder-FacadeResultFactory`. It defines a `make()` method that takes a status code and `Pend-ingOrder` as parameters. This method detaches the `PendingOrder` and returns a `PlaceOrderFacadeResult`. `PlaceOrderFacadeResultFactory` provides an easy-to-mock interface that makes testing the `PlaceOrderFacade` simpler. It also improves reusability by decoupling the `PlaceOrderFacade` from the persistence framework.

Now that we have figured out how this method works, let's write a test. Listing 7.1 shows a test that uses JMock to verify that this method behaves as expected. The test case class extends `MockObjectTestCase` and creates mock implementations of the `PlaceOrderService` and the `PlaceOrderFacadeResultFactory`.

Listing 7.1   PlaceOrderFacadeMockTests

```
public class PlaceOrderFacadeMockTests extends MockObjectTestCase {

    private Mock mockPlaceOrderService;
    private Mock mockResultFactory;
```

...

```
public void setUp() {
  mockPlaceOrderService =
      new Mock(PlaceOrderService.class);

  mockResultFactory =
   new Mock(PlaceOrderFacadeResultFactory.
        ➡ class);

  placeOrderService =
    (PlaceOrderService)
        mockPlaceOrderService.proxy();
  resultFactory =
    (PlaceOrderFacadeResultFactory)
      mockResultFactory.proxy();

  placeOrderFacade =
    new PlaceOrderFacadeImpl(
      placeOrderService,
      resultFactory);
  ...
}

public void testUpdateRestaurant() throws Exception {
  String restaurantId = "restaurantId";

  PlaceOrderServiceResult
      placeOrderServiceResult
        = new PlaceOrderServiceResult(
          PlaceOrderStatusCodes.OK,
          pendingOrder);

  PlaceOrderFacadeResult
      resultFactoryResult
          = new PlaceOrderFacadeResult(
                PlaceOrderStatusCodes.OK,
                pendingOrder,
                availableRestaurants);

  mockPlaceOrderService
    .expects(once())
    .method("updateRestaurant")
    .with(eq(pendingOrderId),
          eq(restaurantId))
    .will(returnValue(
      ➡ placeOrderServiceResult));

  mockResultFactory
    .expects(once())
    .method("make")
```

❶ Creates mocks

❷ Creates façade

❸ Creates objects returned by mocks

❹ Defines expectations for mocks

```
      .with(eq(PlaceOrderStatusCodes.OK),
            eq(pendingOrder))
        .will(returnValue(
              ⇒ resultFactoryResult));
```
❹ **Defines expectations for mocks**

```
    PlaceOrderFacadeResult result =
      placeOrderFacade
        .updateRestaurant(pendingOrderId,
                          restaurantId);
```
❺ **Calls façade**

```
    assertSame(resultFactoryResult, result);
  }
  ...
```
❻ **Verifies result**

Let's look at the details:

❶ The setUp() method creates the mock implementations of the RestaurantRepository, PlaceOrderService, and PlaceOrderFacadeResultFactory classes.

❷ The setUp() method creates the PlaceOrderFacade, passing the mock PlaceOrderService and PlaceOrderFacadeResultFactory to its constructor.

❸ The testUpdateRestaurant() method configures the expectations of each mock object and the return value of each method. For example, it specifies that the PlaceOrderService is called once with the same parameters that were passed to the PlaceOrderFacade and that it should return an UpdateDeliveryResult indicating a successful outcome.

❹ The test then calls the PlaceOrderFacade.

❺ The test verifies that it returns the result of the PlaceOrderFacadeResultFactory.

❻ The MockObjectTestCase automatically verifies that the mockPlaceOrderService and mockPlaceOrderFacadeResultFactory are called as expected.

The next step is to write the method.

7.4.2 *Implementing updateRestaurant()*

In order for this test to compile and run successfully, we have to define the PlaceOrderFacadeImpl class and implement its constructor and the updateRestaurant() method. The constructor stores its parameters in fields, and the updateRestaurant() method calls PlaceOrderService and the PlaceOrderFacadeResultFactory. Here is an excerpt of the source code for PlaceOrderFacadeImpl:

```
public class PlaceOrderFacadeImpl implements PlaceOrderFacade {

    private PlaceOrderFacadeResultFactory resultFactory;
```

```
    private PlaceOrderService service;

    public PlaceOrderFacadeImpl(
        PlaceOrderService service,
        PlaceOrderFacadeResultFactory resultFactory) {
      this.service = service;
      this.resultFactory = resultFactory;
    }

    public PlaceOrderFacadeResult updateRestaurant(
        String pendingOrderId, String restaurantId) {
      PlaceOrderServiceResult result = service.updateRestaurant(
          pendingOrderId, restaurantId);
      return resultFactory.make(PlaceOrderStatusCodes.OK, result
          .getPendingOrder());

    }
    ...
  }
```

The updateRestaurant() method first calls PlaceOrderService.updateRestaurant(). It then calls the PlaceOrderFacadeResultFactory to create a return value containing a SUCCESS status code and the PendingOrder. The other PlaceOrderFacade methods are similar to updateRestaurant(). Each one calls the corresponding PlaceOrderService method. Some of these methods also call repositories to retrieve additional data needed by the presentation tier. For example, updateDeliveryInfo() calls RestaurantRepository to find the available restaurants.

PlaceOrderFacadeImpl is a pretty simple class, and so you might be wondering, why not simplify the design and implement its functionality as part of the PlaceOrderService? One good reason to have a POJO façade is that it enables the domain model services to focus on the core business logic. They can be developed independently of the presentation tier because they are not responsible for gathering data for the presentation tier of the domain model services. Another benefit of using a POJO façade is that it enables the same domain model services to work with multiple presentation tiers and other kinds of business-tier clients. While merging the POJO façade and the domain services might make sense for some applications, many applications will benefit from keeping them separate.

As well as invoking the domain model services and repositories, a POJO façade must detach the domain objects that it returns to the presentation tier. To ensure that the POJO façade is easy to test, the detachment code, which must sometimes call the persistence framework, is encapsulated within a result factory class.

7.5 *Implementing a result factory*

The third step in the process of implementing a POJO façade is writing the result factory that is called by the POJO façade to detach the domain objects that it returns to the presentation tier. In a JDO application, the result factory must call the JDO detachment APIs, which return detached copies of the persistent objects. In a Hibernate application, the result factory simply has to make sure the required objects are loaded because detachment is automatic. In both cases, the POJO façade must make sure that the object graph contains all of the objects required by the presentation tier.

The set of objects that need to be detached is primarily determined by the data that is displayed by the presentation tier. For example, in the Place Order use case, the Order page displays data from several objects, including the delivery information from the `PendingOrder`, the quantities from the pending order's line items, and the menu items from the selected restaurant. Consequently, the `PlaceOrderFacade` must return an object graph containing the `PendingOrder`, its line items, its restaurant, and its restaurant's menu items. Figure 7.7 shows the object graph starting from the `PendingOrder` that needs to be returned to the presentation tier.

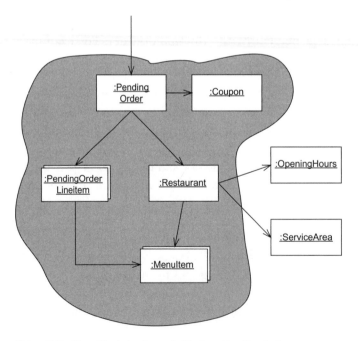

Figure 7.7 The object graph reachable from `PendingOrder`

The `PlaceOrderFacade` must return to the presentation tier all of the objects reachable from the `PendingOrder` except for the restaurant's opening hours and the service area.

The `PlaceOrderFacade` uses the `PlaceOrderFacadeResultFactory` to detach the persistent objects and create a `PlaceOrderFacadeResult` object returned by the façade. As figure 7.8 shows, there are two implementations of this interface: a Hibernate version and a JDO version.

The Hibernate version ensures that all the necessary domain objects are loaded, and the JDO version loads the domain objects and detaches them from the `PersistenceManager`. Let's look at their implementation.

7.5.1 *Implementing a Hibernate result factory*

The `HibernatePlaceOrderFacadeResultFactory` is the Hibernate implementation of the `PlaceOrderFacadeResultFactory` interface. It makes sure that the `Pending-Order`'s line items are loaded, and if the `PendingOrder` has a restaurant, it also ensures that the restaurant's menu items are loaded.

Earlier we saw that a Hibernate application can force an object or collection to be loaded by calling `Hibernate.initialize()`. However, instead of calling that

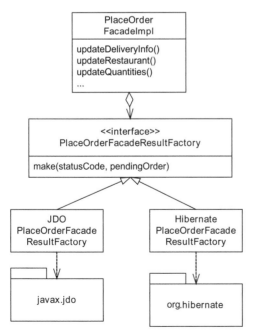

Figure 7.8
Design of the
`PlaceOrderFacadeResultFactory`

method directly, `HibernatePlaceOrderFacadeResultFactory` calls `HibernateTemplate.initialize()`, which is a convenience method that calls `Hibernate.initialize()` and converts `HibernateException` to a Spring data access exception. Using the `HibernateTemplate` simplifies the code and makes testing a lot easier because it can be mocked. In contrast, `Hibernate.initialize()` is a static method and impossible to mock.

The `HibernatePlaceOrderFacadeResultFactory` class extends the Spring class `HibernateDaoSupport` and implements the `PlaceOrderFacadeResultFactory` interface:

```
public class HibernatePlaceOrderFacadeResultFactory extends
    HibernateDaoSupport implements
    PlaceOrderFacadeResultFactory {

  public HibernatePlaceOrderFacadeResultFactory(
      HibernateTemplate hibernateTemplate) {
    setHibernateTemplate(hibernateTemplate);     ⟵——— Saves HibernateTemplate
  }

  public PlaceOrderFacadeResult make(int statusCode,
      PendingOrder pendingOrder) {
    getHibernateTemplate().
        initialize(pendingOrder.          │ Initializes
            ⇢ getLineItems());            │ line items

    Restaurant restaurant =
        pendingOrder.getRestaurant();
    if (restaurant != null) {             │ Initializes optional
      List menuItems =                    │ menu items
          restaurant.getMenuItems();
      getHibernateTemplate().
          ⇢ initialize(menuItems);
    }
    return new PlaceOrderFacadeResult(statusCode, pendingOrder);
  }
}
```

`HibernatePlaceOrderFacadeResultFactory` defines a constructor that takes a `HibernateTemplate` as a parameter and saves it for later. The `make()` method initializes the pending order's line items and the menu items for its restaurant (if it has one). Unlike its JDO equivalent, `HibernatePlaceOrderFacadeResultFactory` needs to have knowledge of the object structure. This isn't a problem in this example since the object structure is so simple, but a factory that detaches a complex object graph could be quite messy because, as we saw earlier, it would need to contain conditional logic to handle null references and polymorphic references.

7.5.2 *Implementing a JDO result factory*

Now that you have seen the Hibernate implementation of the `PlaceOrderResult-Factory`, let's look at the JDO implementation. The `JDOPlaceOrderFacadeResult-Factory` must call the JDO detached object APIs to detach the `PendingOrder` and its related objects. To do this, it must configure the JDO fetch groups to describe the graph of objects to detach. One option is to add the reference and collection fields to each class's default fetch group, as shown in table 7.1

Table 7.1 Configuring the default fetch groups to load the required objects

Class	Fields to add to the default fetch group
PendingOrder	lineItems
restaurant	coupon
PendingOrderLineItem	menuItem
Restaurant	menuItems

This is certainly the easiest approach, but because default fetch groups also affect object loading, it will cause the complete graph of object to be loaded each time a `PendingOrder` is loaded. This is usually not desirable because loading objects unnecessarily can impact performance. A better approach is to use either custom fetch groups or a vendor-specific mechanism such as Kodo JDO's per-field fetch configuration mechanism (described in chapter 5). This approach will not affect object loading elsewhere in the application because only the detachment code activates the custom fetch groups or uses the vendor-specific mechanism.

According to the JDO 2.0 specification, adding the following fetch group to the currently active fetch groups will detach the `PendingOrder` and its related objects:

```
<class name="PendingOrder">

  <fetch-group name="PendingOrder.placeOrderFacade">
<field name="restaurant"/>
<field name="lineItems"/>
<field name="coupon"/>
<field name="restaurant.menuItems"/>
<field name="lineItems#element.menuItem"/>
  </fetch-group>

</class>
```

This fetch group definition lists the names of the fields that reference related objects that must be eagerly loaded. In addition to specifying fields of the Pending-Order class, it specifies the menu items of the pending order's restaurants and the menuItem of each of the pending order's line items. Detaching a pending order when this fetch group is active will result in the JDO implementation detaching those objects as well.

At the time of this writing, however, a JDO implementation that supported this fetch group definition was not available, and in order to have a working example I used Kodo JDO's per-field fetch configuration mechanism, which is used for both eager loading and detachment. To detach the PendingOrder and its related objects, we need to add the corresponding fields to the Kodo JDO's FetchConfiguration before calling KodoPersistenceManager.detach(), which is Kodo JDO's equivalent to PersistenceManager.detachCopy().

Because the JDOPlaceOrderFacadeResultFactory calls the Kodo JDO APIs, it must use a Spring JdoTemplate to execute a callback class, which downcasts the JDO PersistenceManager to KodoPersistenceManager. As a result, the design consists of the classes shown in figure 7.9. JDOPlaceOrderFacadeResultFactory instantiates a KodoJDODetachObjectCallback and executes it using the JdoTemplate.

KodoJDODetachObjectCallback configures the Kodo FetchConfiguration and calls the KodoPersistenceManager to detach the PendingOrder. Let's take a detailed look at these classes.

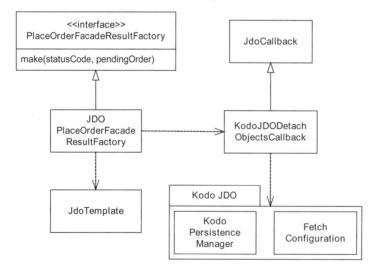

Figure 7.9 The design of the JDOPlaceOrderFacadeResultFactory

JDOPlaceOrderFacadeResultFactory

The JDOPlaceOrderFacadeResultFactory, which is shown in listing 7.2, is a simple class. It uses a Spring JdoTemplate to execute the KodoJDODetachObjectCallback. To completely decouple the code from the object graph that must be detached, we pass in the names of the relationship fields to detach using dependency injection.

Listing 7.2   JDOPlaceOrderFacadeResultFactory

```
public class JDOPlaceOrderFacadeResultFactory implements
    PlaceOrderFacadeResultFactory {

  private final String[] fieldsToDetach;

  public JDOPlaceOrderFacadeResultFactory(
      JdoTemplate jdoTemplate,
      String[] fieldsToDetach) {
    setJdoTemplate(jdoTemplate);
    this.fieldsToDetach = fieldsToDetach;
  }

  public PlaceOrderFacadeResult make(
      int statusCode,
      PendingOrder pendingOrder) {
    PendingOrder detachedPendingOrder =
            detachPendingOrder(pendingOrder);
    return new PlaceOrderFacadeResult(statusCode,
        detachedPendingOrder);
  }

  private PendingOrder detachPendingOrder(
      PendingOrder pendingOrder) {
    return (PendingOrder) getJdoTemplate()
        .execute(
            new KodoJDODetachObjectCallback(
                pendingOrder,
                fieldsToDetach));
  }

}
```

JDOPlaceOrderFacadeResultFactory has a constructor that takes a JdoTemplate and the names of the fields to detach as parameters. It stores the JdoTemplate by calling setJdoTemplate(), which is provided by its superclass. The detachPending-Order() method instantiates the KodoJDODetachObjectCallback with the Pending-Order and field names to detach and passes it to the JdoTemplate.

KodoJDODetachObjectCallback

The KodoJDODetachObjectCallback, which is shown in listing 7.3, is used by the JDOPlaceOrderResultFactory to detach the PendingOrder. Because it's a JdoCallback, it has a doInJdo() method, which is passed a JDO PersistenceManager by the JdoTemplate. This method downcasts the PersistenceManager to a KodoPersistenceManager and configures the FetchConfiguration with the specified fields. After detaching the objects, it undoes the changes it made to the FetchConfiguration so that any other callers of the PersistenceManager can use the default configuration.

Listing 7.3 KodoJDODetachObjectCallback

```
public class KodoJDODetachObjectCallback implements JdoCallback {
  private final String[] fields;

  private final Object object;

  KodoJDODetachObjectCallback(Object object, String[] fields) {
    this.object = object;
    this.fields = fields;
  }

  public Object doInJdo(PersistenceManager pm)
      throws JDOException {
    KodoPersistenceManager kodoPM = (KodoPersistenceManager) pm;

    if (object == null)
      return null;
    FetchConfiguration fc = kodoPM.getFetchConfiguration();
    String[] oldFields = fc.getFields();
    if (fields != null) {
      fc.addFields(fields);
    }
    try {
      return (Object) kodoPM.detach(object);
    } finally {
      if (fields != null) {
        fc.clearFields();
        fc.addFields(oldFields);
      }
    }
  }

}
```

The `KodoJDODetachObjectCallback` calls `FetchConfiguration.getFields()` to get the set of currently active fields and then adds the specified fields. The `finally` clause restores the set of current active fields to its original value.

At this point you know how to detach Hibernate and JDO objects. Next, let's look at how to deploy a POJO façade using the Spring framework.

7.6 *Deploying the POJO façade with Spring*

In the fairytale of Jack and the Beanstalk, Jack traded his cow for some magic beans. That fateful decision was the start of a thrilling adventure that included an encounter with a homicidal giant and eventually led to a life of happiness for Jack and his mother. Now I'm not promising that using Spring beans will result in life-long happiness, but they will certainly make development a lot easier. The final step of implementing a POJO façade is to write the Spring beans that deploy the POJO façade in Spring's lightweight container.

We must write the Spring bean definitions that configure Spring to create the POJO façade and make it transactional by wrapping it with an AOP interceptor. The bean definitions describe how the Spring lightweight container should instantiate the POJO façade and any objects that it requires. Spring's dependency injection mechanism passes the required objects as either constructor arguments or setter arguments. The bean definitions also describe how to apply the AOP interceptors that make the POJO façade transactional.

To deploy the `PlaceOrderFacade`, we must define several kinds of beans. First, we need to define Spring beans that instantiate the `PlaceOrderFacade` and the classes that it needs, such as the `PlaceOrderService` and repositories. Second, we must define beans that instantiate Spring classes such as `TransactionInterceptor`, and a `PlatformTransactionManager` that makes the `PlaceOrderFacade` transactional. Third, we must define Spring beans that instantiate classes that enable the application to access the database, such as an ORM template class and a persistence framework connection factory. Figure 7.10 shows the beans required to deploy the `PlaceOrderFacade`.

Some of those beans, such as the `PlaceOrderFacade`, the `PlaceOrderService`, and the `TransactionInterceptor`, are independent of the persistence framework. Other beans are persistence framework-specific, including the repositories, the `PlaceOrderResultFactory`, the `PlatformTransactionManager`, the ORM template class, and the connection factory. I begin this section by describing the generic bean definitions. After that, I will describe the Hibernate-specific and JDO-specific bean definitions.

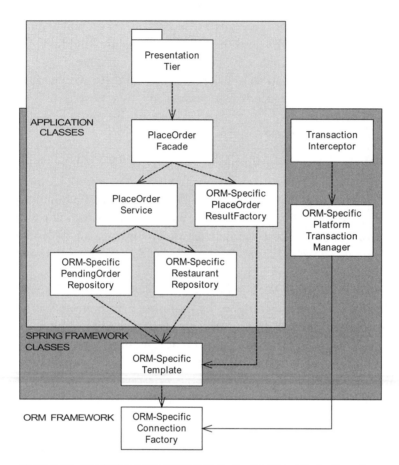

Figure 7.10 The Spring beans required to deploy the `PlaceOrderFacade`

7.6.1 *Generic bean definitions*

The generic Spring beans instantiate the `PlaceOrderFacade` and apply the `TransactionInterceptor`. They also create the `PlaceOrderService`. Because both the `PlaceOrderService` and the `PlaceOrderFacade` use constructor injection, Spring will pass their dependencies to their constructors. The `TransactionInterceptor` and `BeanNameAutoProxyCreator` use setter injection, which means that Spring passes their dependencies as setter arguments. Listing 7.4 shows the generic Spring bean definitions.

Listing 7.4 placeOrderFacade-generic-beans.xml

```xml
<beans>

<bean id="PlaceOrderFacade"                                    ❶
  class="net.chrisrichardson.foodToGo.pojoFacade.
      ➥ PlaceOrderFacadeImpl">
      <constructor-arg ref="PlaceOrderService"/>
      <constructor-arg ref="RestaurantRepositoryImpl"/>
      <constructor-arg ref="ResultFactory"/>
</bean>

<bean id="PlaceOrderService"                                   ❷
  class="net.chrisrichardson.foodToGo.domain.
      ➥ PlaceOrderServiceImpl">
      <constructor-arg ref="RestaurantRepositoryImpl"/>
      <constructor-arg ref="PendingOrderRepositoryImpl"/>
</bean>


<bean id="TransactionInterceptor"                              ❸
  class="org.springframework.transaction.interceptor.
      ➥ TransactionInterceptor">
  <property name="transactionManager" ref="myTransactionManager"/>
  <property name="transactionAttributeSource">
    <value>
    net.chrisrichardson.foodToGo.pojoFacade.PlaceOrderFacade.
          ➥ *=PROPAGATION_REQUIRED
    </value>
  </property>
</bean>

<bean id="BeanNameProxyCreator"                                ❹
  class="org.springframework.aop.framework.autoproxy.
        ➥ BeanNameAutoProxyCreator">
  <property name="beanNames">
      <list>
          <idref bean="PlaceOrderFacade" />
      </list>
  </property>
  <property name="interceptorNames">
    <list>
          <idref bean="TransactionInterceptor" />
    </list>
  </property>
</bean>

</beans>
```

Let's look at the details of each bean definition:

❶ This bean definition creates a `PlaceOrderFacade` and injects the `PlaceOrderService`, and `PlaceOrderFacadeResultFactory`. The `RestaurantRepository` and `PlaceOrder-FacadeResultFactory` beans are defined later in this section because there are separate Hibernate and JDO versions.

❷ This bean definition creates a `PlaceOrderService` and injects the repositories.

❸ This bean definition creates a `TransactionInterceptor` and injects the `Platform-TransactionManager`, which is defined later in this section.

❹ This bean definition defines the `BeanNameAutoProxyCreator`, which applies the `TransactionInterceptor` to all calls to `PlaceOrderFacade`.

All of these beans (except the `BeanNameAutoProxyCreator`) depend on persistence framework-specific classes. For example, the `PlaceOrderService` must be injected with the persistence framework-specific implementations of the repositories. Let's look at the definition of the JDO-specific Spring beans.

7.6.2 *JDO-specific bean definitions*

The JDO bean definitions instantiate the JDO implementations of the repositories and result factory, the `JdoTransactionManager`, the `JdoTemplate`, and the `PersistenceManagerFactory`. Listing 7.5 shows these bean definitions.

Listing 7.5 placeOrderFacade-jdo-beans.xml

```xml
<beans>

  <bean id="myTransactionManager"                    ❶
    class="org.springframework.orm.jdo.JdoTransactionManager">
    <property name="persistenceManagerFactory"
      ref="myPersistenceManagerFactory" />
  </bean>

  <bean id="PendingOrderRepositoryImpl"              ❷
    class="net.chrisrichardson.foodToGo.domain.jdo.
           ⮫ JDOPendingOrderRepositoryImpl">
    <constructor-arg ref="JdoTemplate" />
  </bean>

  <bean id="RestaurantRepositoryImpl"                ❸
    class="net.chrisrichardson.foodToGo.domain.jdo.
        ⮫ JDORestaurantRepositoryImpl">
    <constructor-arg ref="JdoTemplate" />
  </bean>
```

```
<bean id="ResultFactory"                     ④
      <bean id="ResultFactory"
    class="net.chrisrichardson.foodToGo.pojoFacade.jdo.
         ➥ JDOPlaceOrderFacadeResultFactory">
    <constructor-arg ref="JdoTemplate" />
    <constructor-arg>
      <list>
        <value>
          net.chrisrichardson.foodToGo.domain.PendingOrder.
            ➥ restaurant
        </value>
        <value>
          net.chrisrichardson.foodToGo.domain.Restaurant.
            ➥ menuItems
        </value>
        <value>
          net.chrisrichardson.foodToGo.domain.PendingOrder.
            ➥ lineItems
        </value>
        <value>
          net.chrisrichardson.foodToGo.domain.
              ➥ PendingOrderLineItem.menuItem
        </value>
      </list>
    </constructor-arg>
  </bean>

  <bean id="JdoTemplate"                       ⑤
    class="org.springframework.orm.jdo.JdoTemplate">
    <constructor-arg ref="myPersistenceManagerFactory" />
  </bean>

  <bean id="myPersistenceManagerFactory"           ⑥
      class="org.springframework.orm.jdo.
              ➥ LocalPersistenceManagerFactoryBean">
    <property name="configLocation">
      <value>classpath:/kodo.properties</value>
    </property>
</bean>
...
</beans>
```

Here are the details:

① `myTransactionManager` creates a `JdoTransactionManager`, which is configured to use the `PersistenceManagerFactory` and is used by the `TransactionInterceptor`.

② `PendingOrderRepositoryImpl` creates a `JDOPendingOrderRepositoryImpl`, which uses a `JdoTemplate`.

❸ RestaurantRepositoryImpl creates a JDORestaurantRepositoryImpl, which uses a JdoTemplate.

❹ PlaceOrderFacadeResultFactory creates a JDOPlaceOrderFacadeResultFactory, which is injected with the JdoTemplate and the names of the fields to detach.

❺ JdoTemplate creates a Spring JdoTemplate and injects a PersistenceManagerFactory.

❻ myPersistenceManagerFactory creates a Kodo JDO PersistenceManagerFactory from the properties file kodo.properties.

Let's now look at the Hibernate Spring beans, which are quite similar to the JDO Spring beans.

7.6.3 *Hibernate bean definitions*

The Hibernate bean definitions instantiate the Hibernate implementations of the repositories and result factory, the HibernateTransactionManager, the Hibernate-Template, and the SessionFactory. Listing 7.6 shows these bean definitions.

Listing 7.6 placeOrderFacade-hibernate-beans.xml

```
<beans>


<bean id="PendingOrderRepositoryImpl"              ❶
   class="net.chrisrichardson.foodToGo.domain.hibernate.
         ➥ HibernatePendingOrderRepositoryImpl">
   <constructor-arg ref="HibernateTemplate" />
</bean>

<bean id="RestaurantRepositoryImpl"                ❷
   class="net.chrisrichardson.foodToGo.domain.hibernate.
         ➥ HibernateRestaurantRepositoryImpl">
   <constructor-arg ref="HibernateTemplate" />
</bean>

<bean id="ResultFactory"                ❸
class="net.chrisrichardson.foodToGo.pojoFacade.hibernate.
         ➥ HibernatePlaceOrderFacadeResultFactory">
   <constructor-arg ref="HibernateTemplate" />
</bean>


<bean id="HibernateTemplate"              ❹
   class="org.springframework.orm.hibernate3.
          ➥ HibernateTemplate">
```

```
        <property name="sessionFactory" ref="mySessionFactory" />
      </bean>

      <bean id="myTransactionManager"              ❺
        class="org.springframework.orm.hibernate3.
              ➥ HibernateTransactionManager">
        <property name="sessionFactory" ref="mySessionFactory" />
      </bean>

      <bean id="mySessionFactory"                  ❻
       class="org.springframework.orm.hibernate3.
              ➥ LocalSessionFactoryBean">
        <property name="mappingLocations">
          <list>
  <value>classpath:net/chrisrichardson/foodToGo/domain/
  ➥ hibernate/PendingOrder.hbm.xml</value>
          ...
          </list>
        </property>

        <property name="hibernateProperties">
          <props>
            ...
          </props>
        </property>
      </bean>
      ...
    </beans>
```

Here's a closer look:

❶ `PendingOrderRepository` is an instance of `HibernatePendingOrderRepository`, which is injected with the `HibernateTemplate`.

❷ `RestaurantRepository` is an instance of `HibernateRestaurantRepository`, which is injected with the `HibernateTemplate`.

❸ `PlaceOrderFacadeResultFactory` is an instance of the `HibernatePlaceOrderFacade-ResultFactory`.

❹ `HibernateTemplate` is an instance of `HibernateTemplate`, which is injected with a Hibernate `SessionFactory`.

❺ The `myTransactionManager` bean is an instance of `HibernateTransactionManager`, which is configured to use the `SessionFactory`.

❻ `mySessionFactory` creates a Hibernate `SessionFactory` using several mapping files, including PendingOrder.hbm.xml.

As you can see, when using the Spring framework you only need to define a few Spring beans in order to make a POJO façade transactional and integrated with the persistence framework. The only drawback is that the Spring bean definitions can be verbose, especially when compared with EJB 3 annotations. This is, however, an insignificant price to pay for all of the benefits of Spring.

7.7 *Summary*

The traditional approach of encapsulating the business logic in a J2EE application using the Session Façade and DTO patterns has numerous drawbacks. It couples the business logic to the EJB container, which slows down development and testing. It is also time consuming and tedious to develop and maintain the DTOs and the code that creates them.

For many applications, a much better approach is to encapsulate the business logic with a POJO façade. The POJO façade handles requests by calling the underlying domain model classes. The POJO façade is deployed in a lightweight container such as Spring and uses AOP interceptors to manage transactions, persistence framework connections, and security. Development and testing is faster and easier since the POJO façade can run outside the application server. In addition, because the POJO façade returns data using detached domain objects, the only DTOs that need to be written are those that aggregate domain objects. Another benefit is that a POJO façade can be tested with a simple set of tests that use mock objects for the domain objects that it calls.

In the next chapter, we will look at the Exposed Domain Model pattern, which is another lightweight alternative to the Session Façade pattern.

Part 3

Variations

Part 2 described one effective way to design the business and database access tiers. In part 3, you will learn about other approaches. Chapter 8 describes how you can dispense with the façade that encapsulates the business logic. Although exposing the domain model to the presentation tier might sound like heresy, doing so has its benefits. There is less code to write and maintain. It also avoids some of the potential problems with using detached objects. But as you will discover, in order to use this approach you must solve some tricky database connection and transaction management issues.

I'm a great fan of using object-oriented design and ORM frameworks. But sometimes this approach doesn't make sense. In chapter 9 you will learn when you should consider implementing the business logic using a procedural design and accessing the database using iBATIS. This chapter describes how to develop a procedural business logic starting from a use case and how to structure it in a way that makes it easier to maintain. You will learn how to access the database using Spring's iBATIS support classes.

Dissatisfaction with EJB motivated the Java community to adopt alternative frameworks such as Spring, Hibernate, and JDO. In response, EJB has evolved and embraced many POJO and lightweight framework concepts. Chapter 10 examines EJB 3 and compares it to JDO, Hibernate, and Spring. You will learn about the benefits and drawbacks of EJB 3. This chapter describes how to use EJB 3 to persist the domain model developed earlier in chapter 2 and exposes some significant limitations. It also looks at how to implement the session façade developed in chapter 7 as an EJB 3 session bean. You will learn how to use EJB 3 dependency injection to assemble an application. This chapter also describes how to integrate EJB 3 dependency injection with Spring to enable the injection of POJOs.

Using an exposed
domain model

This chapter covers

- Implementing an exposed domain model
- Managing transactions with Spring AOP
- Managing database connections with a servlet filter

In the previous chapter, you saw how encapsulating the business logic with a POJO façade has several benefits, including ease of development and improved maintainability. However, one problem with a POJO façade is that the code that detaches the domain objects returned to the presentation tier is error-prone. When you're making changes to the presentation tier, it is quite easy for the detachment code and the presentation tier to get out of sync and for the POJO façade to only return some of the objects required by the presentation tier. This can cause subtle bugs that can only be detected by thorough testing.

An alternative approach that avoids this problem is to use the Exposed Domain Model pattern, which is also known as the *Open Session in View* pattern [OpenSessionInView] or the *Open PersistenceManager in View* pattern. This pattern exposes the domain model to the presentation tier. The presentation tier calls the domain services and repositories directly without going through a façade. It also accesses the persistent domain objects, which means that as it navigates the object graph, the persistence framework will lazily load any required objects. The business tier is simpler and less error-prone because it does not have to detach objects. However, while this approach avoids the problems of using detached domain objects, some tricky design issues arise from how transactions, persistence frameworks, and the servlet API interact.

In this chapter, you will learn how to solve those design issues for both JDO and Hibernate. We describe how to implement business logic that has an exposed domain model and show you how to use Spring AOP to manage transactions and persistence framework connections. You'll also learn about the drawbacks of using an exposed domain model and when it is not the best solution. Once again, we'll use the business logic for the Place Order use case as an example.

8.1   *Overview of the Exposed Domain Model pattern*

It took me a while to accept the value of the Exposed Domain Model pattern. The first time I heard about this design technique my instant reaction was, "It can't be right! You must use a façade." I had a similar reaction the second and third times. I had become accustomed to encapsulating the business logic with either a session façade or a POJO façade. Eventually, this approach started to make sense. After all, if the presentation tier and business tiers are running in the same machine, then the cost of calls between the tiers is negligible. We do not need to be constrained by a design approach whose main motivation was to minimize the overhead of remote calls. We can eliminate the façade, which is just a middleman, and write less code and not worry about detaching objects. Let's see how this pattern works and why you would want to use it.

8.1.1 *Applying the Exposed Domain Model pattern*

In a design based on this approach, the business tier consists of just the domain model, which is called directly by the presentation tier. The presentation tier calls domain services to update the domain objects, and repositories to query the database. It gets the data to display directly from the persistent domain entities and value objects. For example, if the presentation tier for the Place Order use case is based on the *Model–View-Controller* (MVC) pattern [Buschmann 1996], then the servlets (the controllers) handle requests by calling the `PlaceOrderService` and the `RestaurantRepository` (the model), and the JSP pages (the views) generate the responses using domain objects, such as `PendingOrder` and `Restaurant`. Presentation tiers that use a web framework such as Struts [Husted 2002], JavaServer Faces [Mann 2005], Spring MVC [Walls 2005], or Tapestry [Tapestry] would interact with the domain model in a similar way. The controllers invoke the services and repositories, and the view components access the domain objects.

Because the view components can cause persistent objects to be loaded as they navigate relationships, the JDO `PersistenceManager` or Hibernate `Session` must remain open while the presentation tier handles the request. Consequently, the `PersistenceManager` or `Session` must be managed by the presentation tier instead of by an AOP interceptor in the business tier. The presentation tier can accomplish this by using a servlet filter, which is a web component that intercepts requests before the servlets and JSP pages are invoked. The servlet filter opens a `Persistence-Manager` or `Session`, invokes the servlets and JSP pages, and closes `PersistenceManager` or `Session`.

To see how this pattern works, let's consider how to apply this pattern when writing the code to handle the entry of the delivery information in the Place Order use case. The user enters the delivery information using the form shown in figure 8.1. The application then validates the delivery information and displays a list of available restaurants, as shown in figure 8.2.

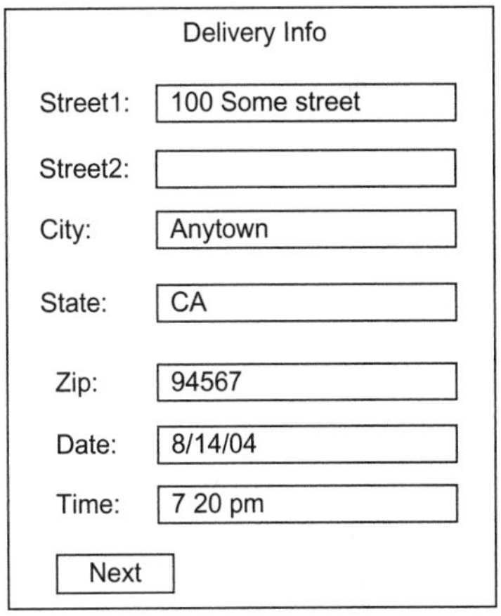

Figure 8.1   Delivery Info screen

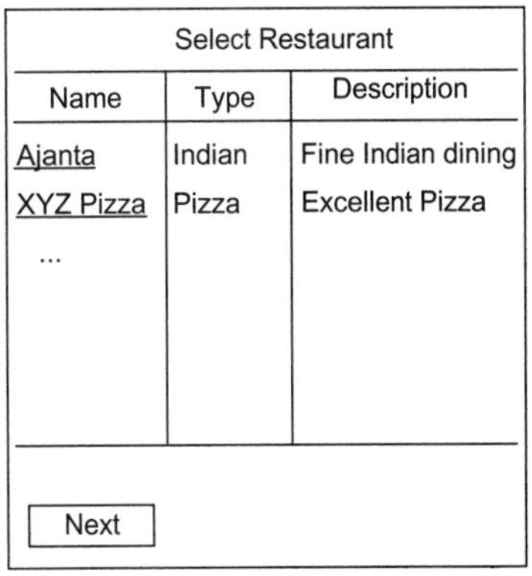

Figure 8.2   Restaurant List screen

Figure 8.3 shows the presentation and business tier components that are responsible for processing the submission of the form and displaying the list of available restaurants. The presentation tier consists of the servlet filter, which opens and closes the JDO `PersistenceManager` or Hibernate `Session`; the `Update-DeliveryInfoServlet`, which handles the form submission; and the restaurants.jsp JSP page, which displays the list of available restaurants. The business logic consists of the domain model classes that we developed in chapter 3.

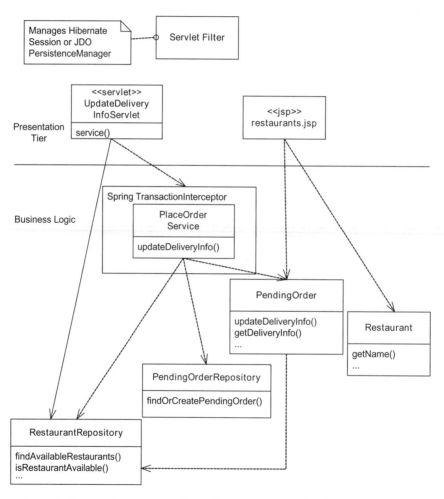

Figure 8.3   An example of the presentation tier accessing the domain objects directly

The servlet and JSP page call the domain model objects directly. `UpdateDelivery-InfoServlet` calls `PlaceOrderService` to update the `PendingOrder` and calls `RestaurantRepository` to retrieve the list of available restaurants. It passes the `PendingOrder` and the restaurants to the JSP page restaurants.jsp, which uses them to generate the HTML page that displays the available restaurants.

In this design, transactions are managed by a Spring `TransactionInterceptor`, which intercepts calls to the `PlaceOrderService`, but another option is to manage transactions using a servlet filter. In section 8.3, we will explain the benefits and drawbacks of these two approaches to transaction management. But first let's look at the overall benefits and drawbacks of using the Exposed Domain Model pattern.

8.1.2 *Benefits and drawbacks of this pattern*

The Exposed Domain Model pattern has several benefits and drawbacks:

- *Faster development*—An important benefit of this pattern is that it accelerates development. There is less code to write because the business tier does not contain façades or error-prone detachment logic. Development is also faster because, unlike an EJB session façade, the business logic uses POJOs and can be developed and tested outside the application server.

- *Potentially eliminates the need for an EJB container*—Many applications use an EJB container only because they encapsulate the business logic with session façade EJBs. Consequently, this pattern potentially eliminates the need to use an EJB container.

- *Less encapsulation*—One problem with this pattern is the lack of encapsulation. Because there isn't a façade to clearly define the API between the presentation and business logic, it is quite easy for business logic to creep into the presentation tier. Consequently, developers using this design approach must periodically review and refactor their code to ensure that the business logic and presentation logic are kept separate. Furthermore, as with the POJO façade approach described in chapter 7, the presentation tier has access to the domain objects. It could, for example, update them directly without going via a domain service. There is also a greater chance of changes to the business logic impacting the presentation tier. Luckily, you can reduce the risk of these problems occurring by encapsulating the domain objects with view interfaces and adapters.

- *More difficult to optimize the business tier*—Ideally, we should be able to optimize the performance of the business and persistence tiers without worrying about the presentation tier. But optimizing those tiers in isolation can be difficult to do when using this pattern. Because the presentation tier freely accesses the domain objects, the interactions between the tiers are less clearly defined and finer-grained. Either you can optimize each fine-grained method in isolation, which provides a lot less opportunity to improve performance, or you have to understand the design of the presentation tier, which complicates the performance-tuning task.

- *More error handling in JSP pages*—Another drawback of exposing the domain model is that JSP pages might have to contain additional code to handle exceptions thrown by domain model classes. In a façade-based design, the façade and servlets handle all exceptions. The JSP pages display the data contained in DTOs or detached objects whose methods are all simple getters (which access fields and do not throw exceptions). When using the Exposed Domain Model pattern, a JSP page must be prepared to handle any exceptions that are thrown by the domain objects that it invokes.

- *No support for remote access*—The business tier must expose a coarse-grained API in order to support remote clients efficiently. It must also return detached objects because it does not make sense to the remote client to use lazy loading. Consequently, it's not possible for an exposed domain model to support remote clients. The interface is too fine-grained and the objects are never detached. If your application must support remote clients, then you must encapsulate the business logic with either a POJO façade or an EJB façade.

The two ways in which you can manage transactions when using this pattern have other potential drawbacks. But first, let's look at when to use this pattern.

8.1.3 *When to use the Exposed Domain Model pattern*

Despite these drawbacks, the Exposed Domain Model pattern is a good way to design certain JDO and Hibernate applications. You should consider using an exposed domain model when:

- The business logic's client can manage the persistent framework connection.
- The business logic does not need to be accessed remotely.

You also need to consider the potentially tricky transaction management issues that are described in section 8.3. But before getting to that, let's first look at the details of managing connections in a Spring application.

8.2 *Managing connections using a Spring filter*

Lazy loading requires the persistence framework connection—JDO `Persistence-Manager` or Hibernate `Session`—used to load the root object to remain open. When the application traverses a relationship to an unloaded object, the persistence framework uses that connection to load it. Consequently, when using the Exposed Domain Model pattern the application must keep the persistence framework connection open while handling a request in order to allow the view components to load objects lazily. We have seen that a good way to accomplish this is to use a servlet filter, which intercepts requests and opens the connection, executes the servlet and the JSP page, and closes the connection. Figure 8.4 shows how a request is handled in an application that uses a servlet filter to manage connections.

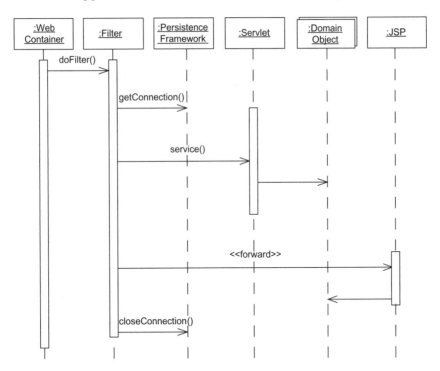

Figure 8.4 Using a servlet filter to handle connections

The sequence of events is as follows:

1   The web container begins the handling of a request by calling a servlet filter.

2   The servlet filter calls a persistence framework API to open a connection.

3   The servlet filter invokes the servlet such as the PlaceOrderService.

4   The servlet invokes the domain objects.

5   The servlet forwards the request to a JSP page.

6   The JSP page generates the response using the domain objects passed by the servlet.

7   The servlet filter closes the connection.

Using the servlet filter to manage connections has a number of benefits. The servlet filter provides a robust way of managing connections because it uses a `try/ finally` block to ensure that the connection is closed. Also, it is reusable because the same filter can be used by multiple applications. Finally, the servlet filter is used declaratively by specifying the requests that it is applied to in the web applications deployment descriptor. The developer doesn't have to remember to write code in order to use it.

You could implement the filter yourself, but it's a lot easier to use the filters provided by the Spring framework. It provides an `OpenSessionInViewFilter`, which is a servlet filter that manages a Hibernate `Session`, and an `OpenPersistenceManagerInViewFilter`, which manages a JDO `PersistenceManager`. Each filter binds the connection object to the executing thread, which makes it available to the `HibernateTemplate` and `JdoTemplate` classes used by the repositories.

The servlet filter is a generic way to manage persistence framework connections, which works in any servlet container. Some web application frameworks have other ways of implementing the same mechanism. For example, Spring Web MVC, which is a web application framework for developing presentation tiers, provides the `OpenSessionInViewInterceptor`, which is an AOP interceptor that wraps Spring's web components. Even though they differ in the details, it is important to remember that the goal is to keep the `Session` or `PersistenceManager` open while the view components generate the response.

8.3 *Managing transactions*

In addition to managing the persistence framework connection, an application must manage transactions in order to ensure atomic and consistent updates. An EJB-based session façade would most likely use container-managed transactions, and a POJO façade would be wrapped with a Spring `TransactionInterceptor`. However, since this design does not have a façade, it must use another approach to transaction management, which turns out to be a tricky problem.

There are two ways to manage transactions. One option is to manage transactions in the presentation tier using a servlet filter. The other option is to manage transactions using a Spring AOP interceptor around the domain model services. Both approaches have their drawbacks, but as you will discover, using an AOP interceptor is the less problematic of the two. In this section you will learn some of the ugly details of how the transactions interact with the presentation tier and the persistence framework.

8.3.1 Managing transactions in the presentation tier

When using this approach, a servlet filter begins the transaction, invokes the servlets and JSP pages, and commits the transaction. Because Spring does not provide such a filter, you must write your own. You could, for example, write a single custom filter that manages both transactions and connections. Alternatively, you could implement a transaction management filter that works with Spring's `OpenSessionInViewFilter` or `OpenPersistenceManagerInViewFilter`. Figure 8.5 shows how the various classes collaborate in a design that uses the latter approach.

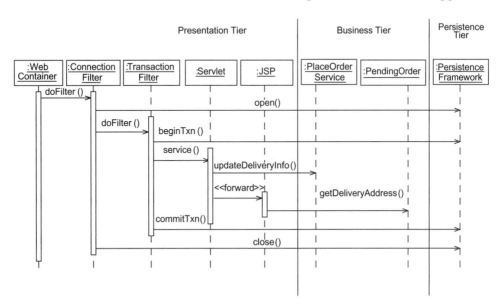

Figure 8.5   Managing transactions with a servlet filter

The sequence of events is as follows:

1. The web container invokes the connection filter (`OpenSessionInViewFilter` or `OpenPersistenceManagerInViewFilter`).

2. The connection filter, which manages connections, calls the persistence framework to open the connection.

3. The connection filter calls the transaction management filter.

4. The transaction management filter begins a transaction.

5. The transaction management filter calls the servlet.

6. The servlet invokes the `PlaceOrderService`.

7. The `PlaceOrderService` is invoked and updates the pending order.

8. The servlet forwards the request to the JSP page.

9. The JSP uses the domain objects such as the `PendingOrder` to generate the response.

10. The transaction management filter commits a transaction.

11. The connection filter calls the persistence framework to close the connection.

This design is extremely simple. The filters manage connections and ensure that the servlet and JSP pages execute within a transaction. In addition, filters can be used with both local transactions and JTA transactions. But one problem with managing transactions in the presentation tier is that handling transaction rollbacks and retries is quite tricky.

Handling transaction retries

In chapter 12, we will see that an application must sometimes roll back and retry a transaction if, for example, a deadlock or an optimistic locking error occurs. The problem with trying to roll back a transaction in the presentation tier is that it is not always possible to undo the side effects of the servlets and JSP pages that were executed as part of the transaction. For example, to roll back a transaction the presentation tier must reset the `HttpServletResponse` and clear any output generated by any JSP pages. To guarantee that this can be done, the application must buffer the output of the JSP pages to ensure that none of it is sent back to the browser, which increases the application's memory usage.

You must also solve the problem of servlet APIs that can only be called once. For example, the input stream of a `ServletRequest` can be read only once, which makes retrying a transaction difficult. To work around this problem, you will need to write extra presentation-tier code.

An even trickier problem to solve is undoing changes made to the `HttpSession` when the transaction is rolled back. For example, after calling `PlaceOrderService.updateDeliveryInfo()` for the first time, the `UpdateDeliveryServlet` will store the ID of the newly created `PendingOrder` in the `HttpSession`. If the transaction is rolled back, the `HttpSession` will contain the ID of a nonexistent order, which will then be passed to the `PlaceOrderService` when the transaction is retried. You will have to write yet more code in either the presentation tier or business tier to solve these kinds of problems.

It's certainly possible to work around these problems by writing extra code. But can you be confident that it works? Rollbacks happen relatively infrequently and writing tests for the rollback scenarios can be difficult, so there is a pretty good chance that bugs will lurk in the code.

Benefits and drawbacks of managing transactions in the presentation tier

Using a servlet filter to manage transactions has these benefits:

- *Enables the presentation tier to have a consistent view of the database*—The servlets and JSP pages execute with a single transaction, which can enable them to have a consistent view of the database.

- *Supports both JTA and local transactions*—An application can use either local transactions or JTA transactions by configuring filters appropriately.

It has these drawbacks:

- *Overhead of buffering the response*—In order to be able to roll back the transaction, the output of the JSP pages must be buffered until the transaction ends, which increases the application's memory usage.

- *Complexity of writing presentation tier code that supports transaction retries*—It can be difficult to develop and test presentation-tier code that supports transaction rollbacks and retries.

Because of these problems, my preference is to manage transactions in the business tier. However, this approach also has its drawbacks, particularly in a Hibernate application.

8.3.2 Managing transactions in the business tier

For many applications, a much better approach is to manage transactions in the business tier by using a Spring `TransactionInterceptor` around the domain model services that are called by the presentation tier. The interceptor begins a transaction when a domain model service is invoked and commits the transaction when it returns. The interceptor might also roll back a transaction if an exception is thrown. Figure 8.6 shows how the various classes collaborate in a design that uses this approach.

The sequence of events is as follows:

1   The web container invokes the connection filter.

2   The connection filter calls the persistence framework to open the connection.

3   The filter calls the servlet.

4   The servlet invokes the `PlaceOrderService`.

5   The `TransactionInterceptor` begins the transaction.

6   The `PlaceOrderService` is invoked and updates the `PendingOrder`.

7   The `TransactionInterceptor` commits the transaction.

8   The servlet forwards the request to the JSP page.

9   The JSP uses the domain objects such as the `PendingOrder` to generate the response.

10 The filter calls the persistence framework to close the connection.

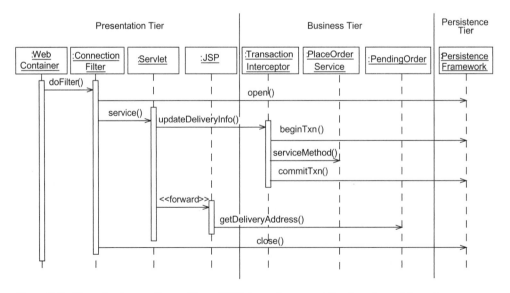

Figure 8.6   Managing transactions with an AOP interceptor around the domain model services

In this design, the domain model service retrieves and updates objects within a transaction. After the transaction commits, the presentation tier navigates the object's graph, which can cause other objects to be loaded lazily. In order for this to work, the persistence framework must support what are called nontransactional reads.

Loading persistent objects outside of a transaction

One key assumption of this design is that the persistence framework allows an application to access persistent objects outside of a transaction, which are also known as nontransactional reads. For example, when a JSP page generates the HTML to display a `PendingOrder`, it must access the pending order's fields and traverse relationships to other objects, such as its line items. Because the `TransactionInterceptor` committed the transaction when the `PlaceOrderService` returned, the persistence framework must allow the JSP page to access the domain objects outside of the transaction, lazily loading them, if necessary.

Nontransactional reads are an optional JDO feature that is supported by most JDO implementations. When nontransactional reads are enabled, the application can perform queries and navigations outside of a transaction. The JDO implementation accesses the database using short database transactions and caches the object graph so that subsequent field accesses and navigations are fast. An application enables nontransactional reads by either creating a `PersistenceManagerFactory` with the `javax.jdo.option.NontransactionalRead` property set to `true` or calling `setNontransactionalRead(true)` on the `PersistenceManagerFactory` or the `Transaction` interface.

Hibernate also supports nontransactional reads. A Hibernate application can perform queries and navigations without beginning a transaction. Hibernate will retrieve objects from the database and cache them. No special configuration is necessary.

Using JTA transactions

This approach works with local JDO and Hibernate transactions. Moreover, a Hibernate application can use JTA transactions because Spring ensures that the Hibernate `Session` participates in the transaction. Spring arranges for any newly created or updated objects in the Hibernate `Session` to be written back to the database before the JTA transaction commit. Unfortunately, Spring does not offer a similar feature for JDO. A JDO `PersistenceManager` can only participate in a JTA transaction if it is opened when the transaction is active. This means that a JDO application that uses JTA transactions must use a POJO façade.

Retrying transactions

Transactions that are rolled back because of a recoverable error such as an optimistic locking failure should be retried. A convenient way to automatically retry a transaction is to use an AOP interceptor that catches exceptions that indicate recoverable errors and then retries the transaction. Figure 8.7 shows what happens when a transaction is retried. In this design, the `PlaceOrderService` is wrapped with the `TransactionRetryInterceptor`, which is a custom AOP interceptor that is described in more detail in chapter 12, and the regular Spring `TransactionInterceptor`.

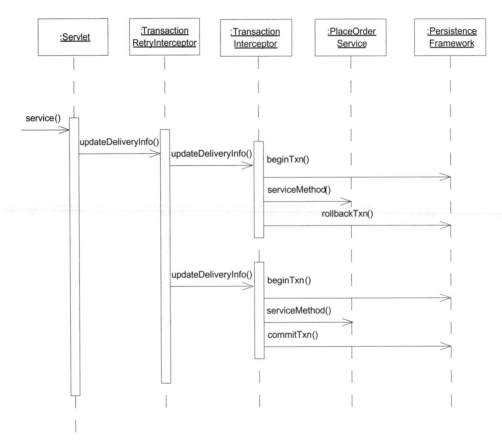

Figure 8.7   Retrying a transaction with an AOP interceptor

The sequence of events is as follows:

1. The servlet calls the `TransactionRetryInterceptor`.
2. The `TransactionRetryInterceptor` calls the `TransactionInterceptor`.
3. The `TransactionInterceptor` begins a transaction.
4. The `TransactionInterceptor` calls the `PlaceOrderService`.
5. The `PlaceOrderService` throws an exception.
6. The `TransactionInterceptor` catches the exception and rolls back the transaction.
7. The `TransactionRetryInterceptor` catches the exception rethrown by the `TransactionInterceptor` and calls the `TransactionInterceptor`.

The second time around, the call to `PlaceOrderService` via the `TransactionInterceptor` succeeds.

Using this interceptor is straightforward in a JDO application because the JDO specification allows a `PersistenceManager` to be reused after an exception is thrown. However, retrying a transaction is a lot more difficult in a Hibernate application because the Hibernate documentation states that the application must close the existing `Session` and open a new one if Hibernate throws an exception.

One solution to this limitation of Hibernate is to use the `OpenSessionInView-Filter` in a mode that uses a separate `Session` for each transaction and data access operation. This mode, which is known as the deferred close method, is enabled by setting the `singleSession` property of the `OpenSessionInViewFilter` to `false`. Each time a transaction is retried a new `Session` will be opened, which avoids the problem of `Session` reuse. Any lazy loading that occurs after the transaction commits will use the `Session` that was opened at the start of the transaction. The `OpenSessionInViewFilter` closes all sessions prior to returning. One drawback with this approach is that each call to a repository outside of the transaction will use its own `Session`, which can be inefficient. In addition to using extra database connections, it will bypass any session-level caching and use extra database accesses. You can also end up with objects belonging to multiple sessions, which can sometimes be confusing.

An alternative approach is to disregard the advice in the Hibernate documentation and to continue to reuse the `Session`. Spring's `HibernateTransactionManager` automatically calls `Session.clear()` when a transaction is rolled back. In the current version of Hibernate, this method clears the session-level cache and ensures that the `Session` is in a pristine state at the start of the next transaction.

The disadvantage of this approach is that a future version of Hibernate could behave differently and break your application. So beware!

Benefits and drawbacks of managing transactions in the business tier

The main benefit of managing transactions in the business tier is that it simplifies the presentation tier. You don't need to write presentation logic that supports retries and buffers the response. However, there are the following drawbacks:

- *Retrying transactions with Hibernate is difficult*—As we described earlier, retrying transactions in a Hibernate application is tricky. Neither of the options we've outlined is ideal. Using multiple sessions per request can be inefficient, and relying on `Session.clear()` to reinitialize the session is a little risky.

- *There is a lack of transactional consistency*—Because a JSP page accesses lazily loaded objects outside of the transaction, it could potentially get an inconsistent view of the database. See chapter 12 for an in-depth discussion of transaction isolation levels.

- *Using JTA transactions in a JDO application isn't possible*—As we explained earlier, a JDO `PersistenceManager` cannot participate in a JTA transaction because it is opened before the transaction begins.

That's it! We have reached the end of a section that covers a fairly difficult topic. As you've learned, there are several tricky issues that you must resolve when using the Exposed Domain Model pattern. When using this pattern, neither Hibernate nor the servlet API handle transactions retries as well as we would like. However, despite these drawbacks it is worthy of consideration for some applications. Let's look at an example.

8.4 An example of the Exposed Domain Model pattern

In this section we'll dive into the details of implementing the Place Order use case with the Exposed Domain Model pattern. You will learn how to implement this pattern with Spring, JDO, and Hibernate. The design, which is shown in figure 8.8, consists of the following components:

- Servlets and JSP pages that handle HTTP requests and generate responses by calling the domain model

- A Spring servlet filter that manages persistence framework connections

- A Spring `TransactionInterceptor`, which wraps the `PlaceOrderService` and manages transactions with the `PlatformTransactionManager`

- A Spring `PlatformTransactionManager`, which manages transactions using the JDO or Hibernate transaction API

- A `TransactionRetryInterceptor`, which is a custom Spring AOP interceptor that automatically retries a transaction if a database concurrency error occurs

- The domain model-based business logic

As you can see, Spring implements the majority of the transaction and connection management logic, including the `TransactionInterceptor` and the servlet filter for managing persistence framework connections. The only custom infrastructure code is the `TransactionRetryInterceptor`.

Let's look at the details. Each servlet handles a request by first invoking the `PlaceOrderService` and calling other domain model classes, such as repositories, to get the data to display. It then forwards the request to a JSP page, which it

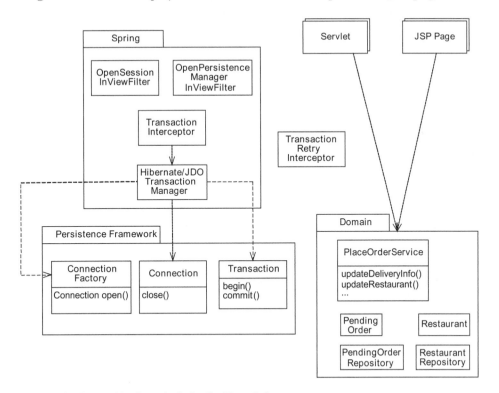

Figure 8.8 Exposed business logic for the Place Order use case

chooses based on the outcome of calling `PlaceOrderService`. A JSP page generates the response using the domain objects passed to them by the servlets.

Persistence framework connections are managed by Spring's `OpenSessionInViewFilter` and `OpenPersistenceManagerInViewFilter` classes. Transactions are managed by Spring's `TransactionInterceptor`, which uses a persistence framework-specific `PlatformTransactionManager` that invokes the persistence framework's transaction management APIs. The Hibernate version uses the `HibernateTransactionManager`, which calls the Hibernate Transaction API, and the JDO version uses `JdoTransactionManager`, which calls the JDO Transaction API. `TransactionRetryInterceptor` is a custom interceptor that automatically retries a transaction that was rolled back because of a database concurrency failure and is described in chapter 12.

In the rest of this section, let's look at the servlets, the JSP pages, and the configuration of the `PlaceOrderService` Spring bean, which are the same regardless of which persistence framework is used. After that, in the following sections we describe the persistence framework-specific parts of the design.

8.4.1   Servlet design

The servlets handle HTTP requests from the user's browser, invoke the business logic, and forward requests to a JSP page, which generates the response. To see how these servlets work, let's look at `UpdateDeliveryInfoServlet`, which handles the submission of the delivery information form. Listing 8.1 shows the source code for `UpdateDeliveryInfoServlet`. The servlet gets the `PlaceOrderService` from the Spring `WebApplicationContext`, a Spring bean factory for the web application. `WebApplicationContext` instantiates `PlaceOrderService`, injects any dependencies, and wraps it with the AOP interceptors that manage transactions. The servlet obtains a `RestaurantRepository` from the `WebApplicationContext`. The servlet calls `PlaceOrderService` and `RestaurantRepository` and forwards the request to a JSP page.

Listing 8.1   UpdateDeliveryInfoServlet

```
public class UpdateDeliveryInfoServlet extends HttpServlet {

    private ServletConfig servletConfig;
    private PlaceOrderService service;
    private RestaurantRepository restaurantRepository;
    public void init(ServletConfig servletConfig)
        throws ServletException {
      super.init(servletConfig);
      this.servletConfig = servletConfig;
```

```
        ServletContext context =
            servletConfig.getServletContext();
        ApplicationContext appContext =
          WebApplicationContextUtils
            .getWebApplicationContext(context);
```
❶ Creates
  PlaceOrderService

```
        service = (PlaceOrderService) appContext.getBean(
          "PlaceOrderService",
          PlaceOrderService.class);
        ...
}

protected void service(
  HttpServletRequest request,
  HttpServletResponse response)
  throws ServletException, IOException {

    if (!validateParameters(request,
                            response))
```
❷ Validates
  parameters

```
       return;

    Address deliveryAddress = makeDeliveryAddress(request);
    Date deliveryTime = makeDeliveryTime(request);

    HttpSession session =
            request.getSession();
    String pendingOrderId =
      (String) session.
              getAttribute("pendingOrderId");
```
❸ Gets pending
  order ID

```
    PlaceOrderServiceResult result =
      service.updateDeliveryInfo(
        pendingOrderId,
        deliveryAddress,
        deliveryTime);
```
❹ Invokes
  PlaceOrderService

```
    PendingOrder pendingOrder = result.getPendingOrder();

    session.setAttribute(
      "pendingOrderId",
          pendingOrder.getId();
```
❺ Stores pending
  order ID

```
    switch (result.getResult()) {
      case PendingOrder.OK :
        displayAvailableRestaurants(
          request,
          response,
          deliveryAddress,
          deliveryTime,
```
❻ Determines JSP
  page to invoke

```
            session,
            pendingOrder);
         break;

      ...
   }

}

   private void displayAvailableRestaurants(
     HttpServletRequest request,
     HttpServletResponse response,
     Address deliveryAddress,
     Date deliveryTime,
     HttpSession session,
     PendingOrder pendingOrder)

   throws ServletException, IOException {

   List restaurants =
     restaurantRepository.findAvailableRestaurants(
       deliveryAddress,
       deliveryTime);

   request.setAttribute("restaurants",
         restaurants);
   request.setAttribute("pendingOrder", pendingOrder);
   request
     .getRequestDispatcher("/domain/availableRestaurants.jsp")
     .forward(request, response);
   ...
   }

   private boolean validateParameters(
     HttpServletRequest request,
     HttpServletResponse response) {
   ...
   }

   private Date makeDeliveryTime(HttpServletRequest request) {
   ...
   }

   private Address
         makeDeliveryAddress(HttpServletRequest request) {
   ...
   }
}
```

7 **Passes data to display**

8 **Forwards request**

Let's look at the details of the servlet:

❶ The servlet's `init()` method creates `PlaceOrderService` and `RestaurantRepository`.

❷ The servlet validates the parameters and creates the delivery address and delivery time objects.

❸ It gets the pending order ID from the `HttpSession`.

❹ The servlet invokes `PlaceOrderService.updateDeliveryInfo()`.

❺ The servlet stores the pending order ID in the `HttpSession`.

❻ It selects the JSP page to use to generate the response based on the outcome of calling the `PlaceOrder`. For example, if the call to `updateDeliveryInfo()` succeeds, the servlet calls `displayAvailableRestaurants()`.

❼ The `displayAvailableRestaurant()` method retrieves the list of available restaurants by calling `RestaurantRepository`.

❽ The `displayAvailableRestaurant()` method forwards the request to the JSP page availableRestaurants.jsp, passing `PendingOrder` and the list of restaurants as `HttpServletRequest` attributes.

The other servlets are similar. They validate the request parameters, invoke the `PlaceOrderService`, and forward the request to a JSP page.

8.4.2 *JSP page design*

The JSP pages generate HTML using the domain objects passed to them by the servlets. Each JSP page navigates the object graph and displays the properties of domain objects. Here is an excerpt of the JSP page that displays the available restaurants:

```
<%@ page import="net.chrisrichardson.foodToGo.domain.*,
                ➥ java.util.*" %>

<%
PendingOrder pendingOrder =
        (PendingOrder)request.getAttribute("pendingOrder");
List restaurants = (List)request.getAttribute("restaurants");
%>
...
```

This excerpt shows how the JSP page gets the `PendingOrder` and the list of restaurants from the `HttpServletRequest`. It then uses them to generate the HTML response. The other JSP pages are similar.

8.4.3 *PlaceOrderService configuration*

The servlets and JSP pages are not the only part of the design that is independent of the persistence framework. There are also the Spring beans that configure the `PlaceOrderService`. The `PlaceOrderService` is wrapped with two interceptors. First is the `TransactionRetryInterceptor`, which retries the transaction if it is rolled back because of a database concurrency failure, and the second is Spring's `TransactionInterceptor`. Listing 8.2 shows the definitions of the `PlaceOrderService`, `TransactionInterceptor`, `TransactionRetryInterceptor`, and `PlaceOrderService-ProxyCreator` beans.

> **Listing 8.2 placeOrderService-exposedDomain-beans.xml**

```xml
<beans>
...
<bean id="PlaceOrderService"
  class="net.chrisrichardson.foodToGo.domain.PlaceOrderServiceImpl">
    <constructor-arg ref="RestaurantRepositoryImpl"/>
    <constructor-arg ref="PendingOrderRepositoryImpl"/>
</bean>


<bean id=" PlaceOrderServiceProxyCreator "
  class="org.springframework.aop.framework.autoproxy.
      ➥ BeanNameAutoProxyCreator">
  <property name="beanNames">
      <list>
          <idref bean="PlaceOrderService" />
      </list>
  </property>
  <property name="interceptorNames">
      <list>
          <idref bean="TransactionRetryInterceptor" />
          <idref bean="TransactionInterceptor" />
      </list>
  </property>
</bean>

<bean id="TransactionInterceptor"
  class="org.springframework.transaction.interceptor.
      ➥ TransactionInterceptor">
  <property name="transactionManager" ref="myTransactionManager"/>
  <property name="transactionAttributeSource">
    <value>
  net.chrisrichardson.foodToGo.domain.PlaceOrderService.*=
      ➥ PROPAGATION_REQUIRED
    </value>
  </property>
```

```
</bean>

<bean id="TransactionRetryInterceptor"
  class="net.chrisrichardson.foodToGo.util.
       ➥ TransactionRetryInterceptor">
    <property name="maxRetryCount" value="5"/>
</bean>
...
<beans>
```

The `PlaceOrderService` bean is implemented by the `PlaceOrderServiceImpl` class and is injected with the `PendingOrderRepository` and the `RestaurantRepository`. The `PlaceOrderServiceProxyCreator` bean wraps the `PlaceOrderService` with the `TransactionRetryInterceptor` and the `TransactionInterceptor`. Let's now look at the persistence framework–specific details of the design, starting with the JDO version.

8.5 *Using JDO with an exposed domain model*

In addition to the persistence framework-independent parts of the design that you have just seen, there are some JDO-specific Spring beans and configuration settings. The JDO-specific Spring beans are the `JdoTransactionManager` that is used by the `TransactionInterceptor`, and the JDO `PersistenceManagerFactory`, which must be configured to support nontransactional reads. We must also configure the web application to initialize the Spring `WebApplicationContext` and to invoke the `OpenPersistenceManagerInViewFilter`, which is the servlet filter that manages the `PersistenceManager`. Let's look at each of these.

8.5.1 *Defining the Spring beans*

Here are the Spring beans that configure the `JdoTransactionManager` and the `PersistenceManagerFactory`:

```
<bean id="myTransactionManager"
  class="org.springframework.orm.jdo.JdoTransactionManager">
  <property name="persistenceManagerFactory"
    ref="myPersistenceManagerFactory"/>
</bean>

<bean id="myPersistenceManagerFactory"
  class="org.springframework.orm.jdo.
      ➥ LocalPersistenceManagerFactoryBean">
  <property name="jdoProperties">
```

```
    <props>
     <prop key="javax.jdo.option.NontransactionalRead">
 ➠ true</prop>
     <prop key="javax.jdo.option.RetainValues">
 ➠ true</prop>
      ...
    </props>
    </property>
     ...
  </bean>
```

The `JdoTransactionManager` is configured to use the `PersistenceManagerFactory` configured by the `myPersistenceManagerFactory` bean. The `myPersistenceManagerFactory` bean configures the `PersistenceManagerFactory` to allow nontransactional reads. Setting the `NontransactionalRead` property to `true` allows the JSP pages to navigate the object graph and perform queries outside of a transaction. Setting the `RetainValues` property to `true` tells the JDO implementation to keep the objects that were accessed during the transaction in the cache after the transaction commits. This improves performance because it ensures that they will not be reloaded when they are accessed by the JSP pages outside of the transaction. Not shown are the JDO implementations of the repositories, which are configured in the same way as in chapter 7.

Now that we have configured the Spring beans, let's configure the web application.

8.5.2 Configuring the web application

To be able to deploy the application in a web container, we must first package the application's components, including the servlets and business logic classes, as a web application. One part of creating the web application is defining some entries in its web.xml file. The web.xml configures the servlets, which handle the HTTP requests, the Spring `WebApplicationContext`, and the `OpenPersistenceManager-InViewFilter`, which is the servlet filter that opens and closes the `PersistenceManager`. Listing 8.3 shows an example configuration.

> **Listing 8.3 web.xml for the Open PersistenceManager in View example**

```
<web-app>

<context-param>              ❶
  <param-name>contextConfigLocation</param-name>
  <param-value>
  classpath:/placeOrderService-exposedDomain-beans.xml
   ...
  </param-value>
</context-param>
```

```
<filter>                    ❷
  <filter-name>OpenPersistenceManagerInViewFilter</filter-name>
  <filter-class>
  org.springframework.orm.jdo.support.
  ➥ OpenPersistenceManagerInViewFilter
  </filter-class>
  <init-param>
    <param-name>persistenceManagerFactoryBeanName</param-name>
    <param-value>myPersistenceManagerFactory</param-value>
  </init-param>
</filter>

<filter-mapping>              ❸
  <filter-name>OpenPersistenceManagerInViewFilter</filter-name>
  <url-pattern>/*</url-pattern>
</filter-mapping>

<servlet>              ❹
  <servlet-name>context</servlet-name>
  <servlet-class>org.springframework.web.context.
    ➥ ContextLoaderServlet</servlet-class>
  <load-on-startup>1</load-on-startup>
</servlet>

<servlet>              ❺
  <servlet-name>UpdateDeliveryInfoServlet</servlet-name>
  <servlet-class>
    net.chrisrichardson.foodToGo.ui.domain.servlets.
  ➥ UpdateDeliveryInfoServlet
  </servlet-class>
</servlet>
...
</web-app>
```

Let's look at the details:

❶ The web application context parameter `contextConfigLocation` lists the XML files that define the Spring beans, including placeOrderService-exposedDomain-beans.xml.

❷ The `OpenPersistenceManagerInViewFilter` is configured to use the session factory named `myPersistenceManagerFactory`, which it retrieves from the web application's `WebApplicationContext`.

❸ The `OpenPersistenceManagerInViewFilter` is configured to be invoked for all requests.

❹ The `ContextLoaderServlet` is a Spring servlet that reads the Spring configure files specified by the `contextConfigLocation` parameter and initializes the `WebApplicationContext`.

❺ The `UpdateDeliveryInfoServlet` is one of the application's servlets.

This file, along with the Spring bean configuration files, the application classes, and the required libraries, would be packaged as a web application and deployed in a web container.

8.6 Using Hibernate with an exposed domain model

The Hibernate-specific Spring beans and configuration settings are similar to the JDO beans and settings you just saw. Let's look at them.

8.6.1 Defining the Spring beans

The Hibernate version of the Spring configuration files defines the `myTransactionManager` Spring bean, which is used by the `TransactionInterceptor`:

```
<bean id="myTransactionManager"
    class="org.springframework.orm.hibernate.
        ↪ HibernateTransactionManager">
    <property name="sessionFactory" ref="mySessionFactory"/>
</bean>
```

The Hibernate repositories and `SessionFactory` are configured in the same way we showed you in chapter 7. Since Hibernate automatically supports nontransactional reads, we do not need to configure the `SessionFactory` in any special way.

8.6.2 Configuring the web application

As with the JDO version, we must configure the web application with some entries in the web.xml. These entries configure Spring, the `OpenSessionInViewFilter`, and the servlets. Listing 8.4 shows an example configuration.

Listing 8.4 web.xml for the Open Session in View example

```
<web-app>

<context-param>
  <param-name>contextConfigLocation</param-name>
  <param-value>
```

```
        classpath:/placeOrderService-exposedDomain-beans.xml
        …
        </param-value>
</context-param>

<filter>
  <filter-name>OpenSessionInViewFilter</filter-name>
  <filter-class>
  org.springframework.orm.hibernate.support.OpenSessionInViewFilter
  </filter-class>
  <init-param>
    <param-name>sessionFactoryBeanName</param-name>
    <param-value>mySessionFactory</param-value>
  </init-param>
</filter>

<filter-mapping>
  <filter-name>OpenSessionInViewFilter</filter-name>
  <url-pattern>/updateDeliveryInfo</url-pattern>
</filter-mapping>


<servlet>
  <servlet-name>context</servlet-name>
  <servlet-class>org.springframework.web.context.ContextLoaderServlet
➥</servlet-class>
  <load-on-startup>1</load-on-startup>
</servlet>


<servlet>
  <servlet-name>UpdateDeliveryInfoServlet</servlet-name>
  <servlet-class>
   net.chrisrichardson.foodToGo.ui.domain.servlets.
    ➥ UpdateDeliveryInfoServlet
   </servlet-class>
</servlet>
…
</web-app>
```

The web.xml in listing 8.4 is quite similar to the JDO version we saw earlier. The main difference is that it uses the Hibernate-specific `OpenSessionInViewFilter`. The `OpenSessionInViewFilter` is configured to use the session factory named `mySessionFactory`, which it retrieves from the web application's `ApplicationContext`. This web.xml file, along with the Spring bean configuration files, the application classes, and the required libraries, would be packaged as a web application and deployed in a web container.

8.7 Summary

One drawback of using a POJO façade is that you must write potentially complex and error-prone code to detach domain objects. A simpler approach, which eliminates the need to detach objects, is to use the Exposed Domain Model pattern. This pattern keeps the persistence framework connection open for the duration of the request, which allows the presentation tier to lazily load objects. The presentation tier calls domain services to update the domain objects, as well as repositories to query the database, and then gets the data to display directly from domain entities and value objects. You no longer have to worry about detaching the objects that it needs.

However, while this approach reduces the amount of code that you must write, there are some tricky design issues because of how transactions, persistence frameworks, and the servlet API interact. Also, the lack of a façade increases the chance that changes to the business tier could affect the presentation tier. There is also the risk of business logic creeping into the presentation tier. Despite these drawbacks, this approach makes sense for many applications and is becomingly increasingly popular.

In the next chapter you'll learn how to implement business logic using a procedural approach.

9

Using the Transaction Script pattern

This chapter covers

- Deciding when to use a procedural approach
- Implementing and testing procedural code
- Accessing the database with iBATIS and Spring

The Domain Model pattern is an excellent way to organize complex business logic. However, there are situations where you might not want to use a domain model, such as when the development team lacks the necessary OO design skills to develop one or the business logic is very simple. It also does not make sense to use a domain model when you cannot use a persistence framework because, for example, the architecture does not include one or the application accesses the database in ways that require it to use SQL directly. In these situations, you should consider writing procedural business logic, an approach also known as the Transaction Script pattern.

In this chapter, we explore the benefits and drawbacks of using the Transaction Script pattern, and describe how to implement this pattern using POJOs and the Spring framework. You'll learn how to implement the procedural business logic and database access logic in a way that makes them easier to develop, test, and maintain. You'll also learn how to develop procedural business logic using a test-driven approach that uses mock objects to implement the tests. We use the Place Order use case as an example.

9.1 *Overview of the Transaction Script pattern*

The law of unintended consequences is that human actions always have unforeseen effects. Sometimes, these consequences are positive, such as the drug aspirin preventing heart attacks. Other unforeseen consequences are negative or a source of further problems, such as drugs with dangerous side effects and wind farms that threaten migrating birds. Software technologies also have unexpected consequences such as Tim Berners-Lee's hypertext system for sharing information with particle physics researchers growing into the World Wide Web.

EJBs are intended to be a framework for building OO business applications. But, ironically, one of its negative unintended consequences is that it has done a lot to encourage procedural programming. As we saw in chapter 1, it's very common for the business logic of a J2EE application to reside in the session beans instead of being distributed among domain objects. Such a design is a perfect example of the Transaction Script pattern. Each session bean method is what this pattern calls a transaction script.

This pattern is widely used mainly because EJB 1 and EJB 2 made it easy to design applications this way while making it difficult to use an OO approach. As a result, the Transaction Script pattern is used even when inappropriate, which has led to all kinds of problems. However, despite its drawbacks there are situations when this pattern is the best choice. Let's investigate when it makes sense to use the Transaction Script pattern and how to implement it using POJOs, iBATIS, and Spring.

9.1.1 Applying the Transaction Script pattern

The Transaction Script pattern organizes the business logic into a set of transaction scripts, each of which is a method that accesses the database and performs computations. Each transaction script handles one request from the presentation tier. They are usually grouped together to form a transaction script class that implements the business logic for one or more use cases. Using the Transaction Script pattern is very straightforward because you do not have to worry about identifying classes and assigning responsibilities as you do when developing a Domain Model pattern-based design. For each request, you simply write one transaction script.

The simplicity of this pattern is also a major limitation. Unlike the Domain Model pattern, which creates a design in which classes typically have both data and behavior, the Transaction Script pattern creates a design in which classes have either data or behavior. The transaction script classes have behavior but no data and manipulate dumb data objects that have data but no behavior. As a result, the business logic is concentrated in a relatively small number of transaction scripts, which can make it difficult to understand and maintain, especially if it is complex.

A transaction script-based design consists of the transaction scripts; the DTOs, which are the dumb data objects; and the DAOs, which are used by the transaction scripts to access the database. Let's look briefly at each part of the design and then explore an example.

Implementing transaction script classes

A transaction script class consists of a set of transaction script methods. It is almost always a stateless class, which means that it does not store any state that relates to its caller. In a traditional J2EE architecture, the transaction script class is implemented as a stateless session bean. When using lightweight technologies such as Spring, the transaction script class is a POJO that uses a Spring AOP interceptor to manage transactions.

Using DTOs

A transaction script manipulates dumb data objects, also known as DTOs, that contain data from the database and that are returned by the transaction script to the presentation tier. A typical transaction script queries the database and creates one or more DTOs that contain the results of the query. The transaction script might then perform computations, change the DTOs, and update the database. It would then return some of the DTOs to the presentation tier, which uses the data within those DTOs to generate the response to the user.

Accessing the database with DAOs

Transaction scripts could access the database by calling JDBC or iBATIS directly. The trouble with this approach is that the transaction scripts will contain a mixture of business logic and database access code, which can make them difficult to maintain and test. It's better to move the database access code into a separate set of DAO classes that encapsulate the database access logic and define methods for creating, reading, deleting, and updating rows in the database tables. There is typically one DAO for each of the main entities in the application. A DAO returns the results of a query as one or more DTOs, and a transaction script passes DTOs to the DAOs in order to insert or update data in the database. As you will see later, using DAOs simplifies the transaction scripts and makes them considerably easier to test.

An example of a transaction script-based design

Let's look at a simple example of a transaction script-based design. The design, which is shown in figure 9.1, uses the Transaction Script pattern to implement the business logic for the Place Order use case. It consists of the following:

- The `PlaceOrderTransactionScripts` class implements the transaction scripts.
- DAOs encapsulate the database access logic.
- DTOs contain data that is retrieved from the database and returned to the presentation tier.
- The Spring `TransactionInterceptor` class ensures that each invocation of a transaction script is transactional.

The `PlaceOrderTransactionScripts` class defines a transaction script for each request that it must handle, including `updateDeliveryInfo()`, which is called when the user enters the delivery information, and `updateRestaurant()`, which is called when the user selects a restaurant.

The transaction scripts access the database by calling the DAOs, which define methods for creating, finding, deleting, and updating pending orders and restaurants in the database. Each DAO consists of an interface, as well as an implementation class that uses either JDBC or iBATIS to access the database. The `PendingOrderDAO` queries and updates the PENDING_ORDER and PENDING _ORDER_LINE_ITEM tables, and the `RestaurantDAO` queries the RESTAURANT and MENU_ITEM tables.

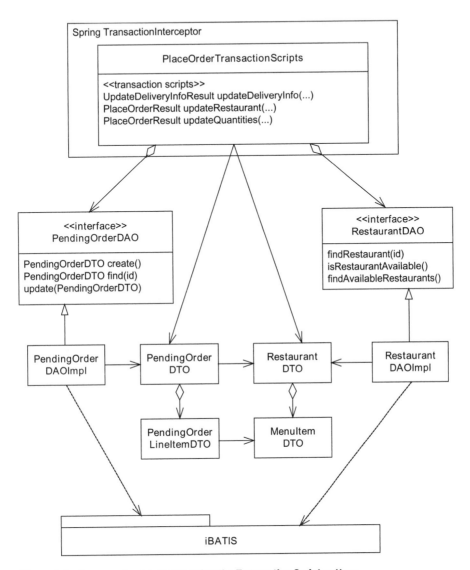

Figure 9.1 An example of a design using the Transaction Script pattern

The transaction scripts use DTOs to exchange data with the DAOs. The DAOs return the results of a query as one or more DAOs, and the transaction scripts pass DTOs to the DAOs in order to insert or update data in the database. For example, PendingOrderDAO defines a findPendingOrder() method, which returns a PendingOrderDTO that contains the pending order from the database, and a savePendingOrder() method, which takes a PendingOrderDTO as a parameter and saves it in the database.

The transaction scripts also return the DTOs, such as PlaceOrderResult and UpdateDeliveryInfoResult, to the presentation tier. These DTOs contain a status code and other DTOs, such as PendingOrderDTO.

This design has a simple structure, which is a distinctive feature of a Transaction Script pattern-based design. The majority of the code is in the transaction scripts and the DAOs. You may have noticed that the names of the DTOs, which are simple data holders, are similar to the names of the domain model classes that we implemented in chapter 3. It is important to remember that they contain only data and do not implement any other behavior. As you will see later, the simplicity of this pattern is both a blessing and a curse.

9.1.2 Benefits and drawbacks of the Transaction Script pattern

The Transaction Script pattern has the following benefits and drawbacks.

Easy to use

One of the most appealing aspects of the Transaction Script pattern is that it is easy to apply because you don't need to have OO design skills. You just have to write a transaction script method to handle each request. Similarly, to implement a new business logic feature you typically have to add some code to an existing transaction script. In comparison, to use the Domain Model pattern you must have object-design skills and know how to identify classes and assign responsibilities to them.

Can use full range of SQL features

Another benefit of the Transaction Script pattern is that it can sometimes improve performance significantly because transaction scripts can access the database using the full range of SQL features. An application can use SQL to efficiently query the database in ways that are not supported by persistence frameworks such as JDO and Hibernate. This can be especially important when you're working with a legacy schema. In addition, SQL's ability to perform bulk updates and deletions is far superior to those capabilities provided by some persistence frameworks. As a result, it's not uncommon to implement some parts of an application using the Transaction Script pattern and SQL.

Code can be difficult to understand and maintain

The simplicity of this pattern is a double-edged sword. Because you do not have to do any OO design, all of the business logic is concentrated in the transaction scripts. This can make the code difficult to understand and maintain, especially if the business logic is complex. This is made worse by the fact that transaction script-based business must explicitly load and save data, whereas in a domain model-based design, many objects are automatically loaded by navigation and changes are automatically written back to the database.

Cost of maintaining handwritten SQL

Another problem with using the Transaction Script pattern is that you have to write all of the SQL yourself. While this gives you a lot of control and makes your SQL available for inspection by the DBAs, it can be difficult and tedious to maintain large amounts of SQL. It is quite common for one small change to a table definition to cause you to update multiple SQL statements and DAOs. For example, if you add a column to the RESTAURANT table, then in addition to changing the `Restaurant-DAO` you might need to change the `PendingOrderDAO` because it executes a SQL statement involving the RESTAURANT table. There are ways of designing the DAO classes that reduces this problem, but they do not prevent it altogether.

Lack of portability of SQL

The problem with developing and maintaining SQL is made even worse by the differences between the SQL dialects supported by the various databases. For example, some databases (such as Oracle) have sequences to generate unique IDs, whereas other databases (such as HSQLDB) have identity columns. Consequently, developing a JDBC application that supports multiple databases is extremely challenging. This can be a problem even if your application is only deployed on a single database because you might want to write tests that use an in-memory database such as HSQLDB.

You could use a persistence framework to avoid these problems. JDO and Hibernate insulate the application from the differences between the various databases and will even generate the DDL that defines the schema from the O/R mapping. In this kind of design, the persistent classes would mirror the database schema rather than implementing a domain model and would not contain any business logic. Of course, this option would only work if an application accessed the database in ways that are supported by the persistence framework, which is often not the case if you are using the Transaction Script pattern. Moreover, if the application can use a persistence framework, then it is not clear why you would not want to go further and implement a complete domain model.

9.1.3 *When to use the Transaction Script pattern*

As you have just seen, business logic organized using the Transaction Script pattern can be hard to maintain because it is procedural and typically uses handwritten SQL to access the database. However, there are four main situations where the Transaction Script pattern is the best choice.

The application must use SQL directly

One common reason to use the Transaction Script pattern is if the application must execute SQL directly because it needs to access the database in ways that are not efficiently supported by the persistence framework. However, it is important to keep in mind that persistence frameworks are constantly improving. JDO and Hibernate have powerful query languages and they both support SQL queries, which means that you can implement more of your business logic with the Domain Model pattern. In addition, Hibernate 3.0 and EJB 3 support bulk updates and deletes, which reduces the need to use SQL. As a result, the need to directly use SQL directly is diminishing

A persistence framework is unavailable

It can also make sense to use the Transaction Script pattern if the application cannot use a persistence framework. Budget issues and preference of the architect or developers are just two reasons why you'd want to take this approach. In this case, the developers must use SQL directly to access the database. In principle, you could write JDBC code to persist a domain model, but this is usually impractical if the domain model is complex.

The business logic is very simple

You might consider using the Transaction Script pattern if the business logic is very simple and developing a domain model is not worthwhile. For example, if the application just queries a database and displays the data, then it could very well be a candidate for the Transaction Script pattern.

The development team doesn't have OO design skills

Developing a domain model requires the development team to have OO design skills, which is not always the case. It is better to succeed with a procedural transaction script-based design rather than fail with a domain model.

Now that we have gotten an overview of the Transaction Script pattern and its benefits and drawbacks, let's see how to develop transaction script-based business logic.

9.2 *Identifying the transaction scripts*

We are now going to take a step back and look at how to develop a transaction script-based design from scratch. We'll describe how to implement transaction script-based business logic using the Place Order use case as an example. You will learn how to develop working and tested transaction scripts and DAOs from the use case and the UI design. We'll also describe how to use Spring for transaction and connection management.

The process of developing Transaction Script pattern-based business logic consists of the following steps:

1   Identify the transaction scripts.

2   Implement and test the transaction scripts using mock DAOs.

3   Implement and test the DAOs.

4   Configure Spring beans to provide JDBC transaction and connection management.

Let's start by identifying the transaction scripts; later sections describe the other steps. The techniques for identifying transaction scripts are similar to the ones used in chapters 3 and 7 to design the domain model service and the POJO façade, but we'll review the basic process here.

9.2.1 *Analyzing the use case*

You can identify the transaction scripts and determine their responsibilities, parameters, and return types by analyzing the use case and the user interface. The transaction scripts typically correspond to the steps of the use case. Consider, for example, the Place Order use case:

> The customer enters the delivery address and time. The system first verifies that the delivery time is in the future and that at least one restaurant serves the delivery information. It then updates the pending order with the delivery information, and displays a list of available restaurants.
>
> The customer selects a restaurant. The system updates the pending order with the restaurant and displays the menu for the selected restaurant.
>
> The customer enters quantities for each menu item. The system updates the pending order with the quantities and displays the updated pending order.

> The customer enters payment information (credit card information and billing address). The system updates the pending order with the payment information and displays the pending order with totals, tax, and charges.
>
> The customer confirms that she wants to place the order. The system authorizes the credit card, creates the order, and displays an order confirmation, which includes the order number.

Each paragraph of this use case suggests several transaction scripts, including:

- `updateDeliveryInfo()`: Validates the delivery information and creates or updates the pending order
- `updateRestaurant()`: Updates the pending order with the selected restaurant
- `updateQuantities()`: Updates the line item quantities of the pending order

You can also determine a transaction script's parameters, which consist of user input, from the use case. For example, the Place Order use case implies that the `updateDeliveryInfo()` transaction takes the delivery address and time entered by the user as parameters. The use case may also reveal additional parameters and return values that hold the session state that is exchanged between the presentation tier and the transaction scripts. See chapter 3, which uses the same techniques to design the domain model service for the Place Order use case, for the details.

9.2.2 *Analyzing the user interface design*

Another way to identify the transaction scripts is by analyzing the UI design and defining a transaction script for each HTTP request. Furthermore, you can analyze the data that is displayed on each screen to determine the data that each transaction script must return and hence the DTOs that you must implement. For example, figure 9.2 shows the first two HTTP requests for the Place Order use case.

The first request is sent by the user's browser when they enter the delivery information. The presentation tier calls a transaction script to update the pending order and displays the list of available restaurants, which must be returned by the transaction script. The second request is sent when the user selects a restaurant. The presentation tier calls another transaction script to update the pending order and displays the menu for the selected restaurant, which must also be returned by the transaction script.

For the details of how to do this and a more in-depth example, see chapter 7, which uses similar techniques to design a POJO façade.

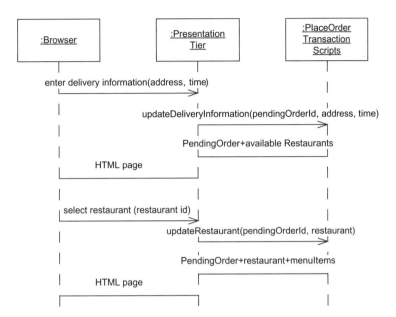

Figure 9.2   Some of the HTTP requests for the Place Order use case

9.2.3   *The PlaceOrderTransactionScripts interface*

Figure 9.3 shows the outcome of analyzing the Place Order use case and the UI. As you might expect, the PlaceOrderTransactionScripts interface is very similar to the PlaceOrderFacade interface developed in chapter 7. After all, they were derived from the same requirements using the same process. But one important difference between the two interfaces is that the transaction scripts return DTOs instead of domain objects. Moreover, as you will see a bit later, their implementations are very different.

The PlaceOrderTransactionScripts interface specifies transaction scripts for each step of the use case including updateDeliveryInfo() and updateRestaurant(). The transaction scripts return DTOs containing data that is displayed by the presentation tier or stored as part of the session state. For example, update-DeliveryInfo() returns an UpdateDeliveryInfoResult, which contains a status code indicating the outcome of calling the transaction script, a PendingOrderDTO containing the attributes of the PendingOrder from the database, and a list of available restaurants. Here is part of the corresponding Java definition of the Place-OrderTransactionScripts interface:

```
public interface PlaceOrderTransactionScripts {

  public UpdateDeliveryInfoResult updateDeliveryInfo(
      String pendingOrderId,
      Address deliveryAddress, Date deliveryTime);

  public PlaceOrderResult updateRestaurant(
      String pendingOrderId, String restaurantId);

  public PlaceOrderResult updateQuantities(
      String pendingOrderId, int[] quantities);
  ...
}
```

Let's now develop the implementation the transaction script's interface.

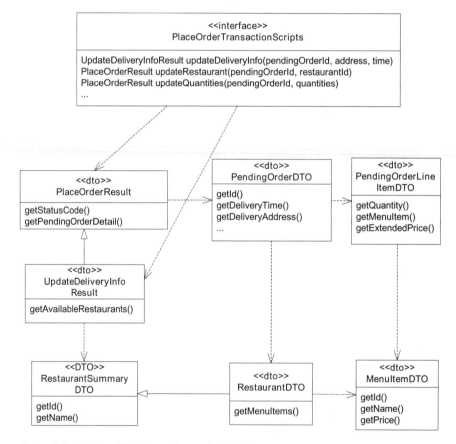

Figure 9.3   Design of the transaction script interface

9.3 *Implementing a POJO transaction script*

Once you have identified the transaction scripts and determined their parameters and return types, the next step in the process is to implement them using a test-driven approach. The `PlaceOrderTransactionScripts` interface is implemented by `PlaceOrderTransactionScriptsImpl`, which is shown in figure 9.4. `PlaceOrderTransactionScriptsImpl` is a POJO and uses Spring AOP for JDBC connection and transaction management. Its constructors take the DAOs that it calls to access the database as parameters. This enables Spring to supply the DAOs to the `PlaceOrderTransactionScriptsImpl` by using constructor injection.

To understand how to implement a transaction script, let's take an in-depth look at one of them: the `updateDeliveryInfo()` transaction script. From analyzing the use case, we determined it has the following responsibilities. It must create the pending order if required, validate the delivery information, and store it in the pending order. In addition, `updateDeliveryInfo()` must return an `UpdateDeliveryInfoResult` containing a successful status code, `PendingOrderDTO`, and the list of available restaurants. As before, we will start by writing a test and using it to drive the design.

9.3.1 *Writing a test for the transaction script*

The `updateDeliveryInfo()` transaction script can be invoked with many different combinations of arguments. For example, the pending order ID can be `null`, which indicates a new pending order, or it can identify an existing pending order.

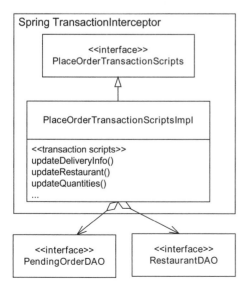

Figure 9.4
Transaction Script–based
business tier design

Similarly, the delivery information parameters can be valid or invalid for a variety of reasons. In order to flesh out and thoroughly test the transaction script, we must write tests for several combinations of arguments. Let's look a test for the scenario where updateDeliveryInfo() is invoked with a null pending order ID and valid delivery information.

In this scenario, updateDeliveryInfo() fulfills its responsibilities as follows:

1   *Creates the* PendingOrder—It can call PendingOrderDAO.createPending-Order().

2   *Verifies that the delivery time in the future*—It can do this with some simple conditional logic.

3   *Finds the available restaurants*—It can retrieve the available restaurants by calling the RestaurantDAO, which defines a findAvailableRestaurants() method. This method returns the list of restaurants that serve the specified delivery information.

4   *Stores the delivery information in the* PendingOrder—updateDeliveryInfo() can do this by simply calling setters on the PendingOrderDTO. Remember that unlike the PendingOrder domain object, the PendingOrderDTO does not implement any business logic and so doesn't validate the data that it contains.

5   *Saves it in the database*—It saves the PendingOrder in the database by calling PendingOrderDAO.savePendingOrder(), which updates the PENDING_ORDER table.

6   *Returns an* UpdateDeliveryInfoResult *that contains the updated* PendingOrder *and the available restaurants*—It creates the UpdateDeliveryInfoResult by calling new.

We can write a test that verifies that updateDeliveryInfo() does this by using mock objects for the PendingOrderDAO, RestaurantDAO, and PendingOrderDTO. The test configures these mock objects to expect particular methods to be called and return test values, and passes the mock DAOs to PlaceOrderTransaction-ScriptsImpl as constructor arguments. It then calls the transaction script and verifies that it returns the expected DTO. Listing 9.1 shows the test method.

Listing 9.1   PlaceOrderTransactionScriptsImplTests

```
public class PlaceOrderTransactionScriptsImplTests
    extends MockObjectTestCase {

  private Mock mockPendingOrderDAO;
```

```
private Mock mockRestaurantDAO;

private PendingOrderDAO pendingOrderDAO;

private RestaurantDAO restaurantDAO;

private PlaceOrderTransactionScripts service;

private Mock mockPendingOrder;

private PendingOrderDTO pendingOrder;

public void setUp() throws Exception {         <----   ❶
  super.setUp();
  mockPendingOrderDAO = new Mock(
      PendingOrderDAO.class);
  mockRestaurantDAO = new Mock(
      RestaurantDAO.class);
  pendingOrderDAO = (PendingOrderDAO) mockPendingOrderDAO
      .proxy();
  restaurantDAO = (RestaurantDAO) mockRestaurantDAO
      .proxy();
  mockPendingOrder = new Mock(
      PendingOrderDTO.class);
  pendingOrder = (PendingOrderDTO) mockPendingOrder
      .proxy();
  service = new PlaceOrderTransactionScriptsImpl(
      pendingOrderDAO, restaurantDAO);
}

public void testUpdateDeliveryInfo_good()
    throws Exception {

  Address deliveryAddress = new Address();
  Date deliveryTime = new Date();
  List availableRestaurants = Collections
      .singletonList(new RestaurantDTO());

  mockPendingOrderDAO.expects(once())
      .method("createPendingOrder")
      .will(eturnValue(pendingOrder));          ❷

  mockPendingOrderDAO.expects(once())
      .method("savePendingOrder")
      .with(eq(pendingOrder));

  mockRestaurantDAO
      .expects(once())                          ❸
      .method("findAvailableRestaurants")
      .with(eq(deliveryAddress),
```

```
            eq(deliveryTime))
        .will(
            returnValue(availableRestaurants));                    ③

mockPendingOrder.expects(once())
    .method("setDeliveryAddress")
    .with(eq(deliveryAddress));
mockPendingOrder.expects(once())
    .method("setDeliveryTime")                    ④
    .with(eq(deliveryTime));
mockPendingOrder
    .expects(once())
    .method("setState")
    .with(eq(PendingOrder.
        ➥ DELIVERY_INFO_SPECIFIED));


UpdateDeliveryInfoResult result =
    service                                       ⑤
    .updateDeliveryInfo(null,
        deliveryAddress, deliveryTime);

assertEquals(
    UpdateDeliveryInfoResult.
        SELECT_RESTAURANT,
    result.getStatusCode());                      ⑥
assertSame(pendingOrder, result
    .getPendingOrder());
assertSame(availableRestaurants, result
    .getAvailableResturants());
    }
}
```

Let's look at the details:

❶ The setup() method creates the mock objects and the PlaceOrderTransaction-ScriptsImpl.

❷ The testUpdateDeliveryInfo_good() method configures the mock PendingOrder-DAO to expect its createPendingOrder() method to be called and to return the blank PendingOrder.

❸ The test configures the mock RestaurantDAO to expect its findAvailableRestaurants() to be called with the delivery information and to return the list of available restaurants.

❹ The testUpdateDeliveryInfo_good() method configures the mock PendingOrder to expect its savePendingOrder() to be called with the updated PendingOrder.

❺ The test calls the transaction script.

❻ The `testUpdateDeliveryInfo_good()` method verifies that the transaction script returns an `UpdateDeliveryInfoResult` containing the expected data.

The tests for the other scenarios are similar. They configure mock objects, call `updateDeliveryInfo()` with other combinations of arguments, and assert that the method returns the expected value. Let's now look at the `updateDeliveryInfo()` method.

9.3.2 Writing the transaction script

Now that we have written a test, the next step is to get it to compile and pass. To do that we must implement the `updateDeliveryInfo()` transaction script, as well as the DTOs. Let's look at how to do that, beginning with the transaction script.

Writing the updateDeliveryInfo() method

The `updateDeliveryInfo()` method is one of the transaction scripts implemented by the `PlaceOrderTransactionScriptsImpl`. Listing 9.2 shows `PlaceOrderTransactionScriptsImpl`'s constructor and the `updateDeliveryInfo()` transaction script. The constructor takes a `PendingOrderDAO` and a `RestaurantDAO` as parameters and stores them in fields for use by the transaction scripts. The `updateDeliveryInfo()` transaction script finds or creates the `PendingOrder`; finds the available restaurants; updates the `PendingOrder` if the delivery information is valid; and returns the `UpdateDeliveryInfoResult`.

Listing 9.2   PlaceOrderTransactionScriptsImpl

```
public class PlaceOrderTransactionScriptsImpl implements
    PlaceOrderTransactionScripts {

  private RestaurantDAO restaurantDAO;

  private PendingOrderDAO pendingOrderDAO;

  public PlaceOrderTransactionScriptsImpl(
      PendingOrderDAO pendingOrderDAO,
      RestaurantDAO restaurantDAO) {
    this.pendingOrderDAO = pendingOrderDAO;
    this.restaurantDAO = restaurantDAO;
  }

  public UpdateDeliveryInfoResult updateDeliveryInfo(
      String pendingOrderId,
      Address deliveryAddress, Date deliveryTime) {
```

```
PendingOrderDTO pendingOrder =          ◄─────── ❶ Finds or creates
   findOrCreatePendingOrder(pendingOrderId);            pending order

Calendar earliestDeliveryTime = Calendar
      .getInstance();
earliestDeliveryTime
         .add(Calendar.HOUR, 1);

if (deliveryTime                                 ❷ Checks
      .before(earliestDeliveryTime                  delivery time
               .getTime())) {
   return new UpdateDeliveryInfoResult(
      UpdateDeliveryInfoResult.
      ➡ INVALID_DELIVERY_INFO,
      pendingOrder, null);
}

List availableRestaurants =               ❸ Finds available
   restaurantDAO                             restaurants
      .findAvailableRestaurants(
          deliveryAddress, deliveryTime);

if (availableRestaurants.isEmpty()) {   ◄────── ❹ Returns error code
   return new UpdateDeliveryInfoResult (         if there are none
      UpdateDeliveryInfoResult.
      ➡ NO_RESTAURANT_AVAILABLE,
      pendingOrder, null);
}

pendingOrder
   .setDeliveryAddress(deliveryAddress);
pendingOrder                                 ❺ Updates
   .setDeliveryTime(deliveryTime);              PendingOrderDTO
pendingOrder
   .setState(PendingOrder.
      ➡ DELIVERY_INFO_SPECIFIED);

pendingOrderDAO                          ❻ Saves PendingOrderDTO
   .savePendingOrder(pendingOrder);         back to database

return new UpdateDeliveryInfoResult(
   UpdateDeliveryInfoResult.              ❼ Creates
   ➡ SELECT_RESTAURANT,                     result object
   pendingOrder,
   availableRestaurants);
}

private PendingOrderDTO findOrCreatePendingOrder(
   String pendingOrderId) {
 if (pendingOrderId == null)
```

```
            return pendingOrderDAO
                .createPendingOrder();
        else
            return pendingOrderDAO
                .findPendingOrder(pendingOrderId);
    }
}
```

Let's look at the details:

❶ The `updateDeliveryInfo()` transaction script finds or creates the pending order by calling the `PendingOrderDAO`.

❷ The script checks that the delivery time is in the future.

❸ The script then calls the `RestaurantDAO` to find the available restaurants for the delivery information.

❹ If the delivery information is not served by any restaurant, `updateDeliveryInfo()` returns a DTO with a status code of `NO_RESTAURANT_AVAILABLE`.

❺ If there are available restaurants, the transaction script updates the `PendingOrder-DTO` with the new delivery information, and changes its state to `DELIVERY_INFO_SPECIFIED`.

❻ The script calls `PendingOrderDAO.savePendingOrder()` to update the database.

❼ The script then returns a DTO that specifies a status code of `SELECT_RESTAURANT`, which indicates that the delivery information was updated successfully, and contains the list of restaurants to display.

Even though we have only implemented one of many tests for the `updateDeliveryInfo()` transaction script, key differences between the Transaction Script pattern and Domain Model pattern are beginning to emerge. The transaction script validates the delivery information itself instead of delegating that responsibility to a domain model. Also, the transaction script must call a DAO to save the changes rather than relying on the persistence framework to do this automatically. The business logic will become only more complex as we implement more tests and flesh out the transaction script.

Implementing the DTOs

Now that we have written the transaction script, let's implement the DTOs that are passed between the transaction scripts and the DAOs and between the transaction scripts and the presentation tier. The DAOs use the DTOs to return data retrieved from the database to the transactions scripts, and the transaction scripts use the

DTOs to pass data to the DAOs in order to update the database. They are also returned by the transactions scripts to the presentation tier.

DTOs are simple data holders and only have fields and getters. The DTOs and their fields can be identified in one of three ways:

- Define a DTO for each database table that has fields corresponding to the table's columns.
- Define a DTO for each screen whose fields contain the data that is displayed on the screen.
- Perform simple OO analysis and design techniques to identify the classes and their fields.

For this particular use case, we can apply a combination of these techniques and get the DTOs shown in figure 9.5.

The names of these DTOs, their fields, and their associations are very similar to the names, fields, and associations of the classes in the domain model described earlier in chapter 3. However, one very important difference is that unlike the domain model classes, they do not implement any business logic. Listing 9.3 shows an excerpt of the source code for the `PendingOrderDTO` that illustrates the simple structure of a DTO.

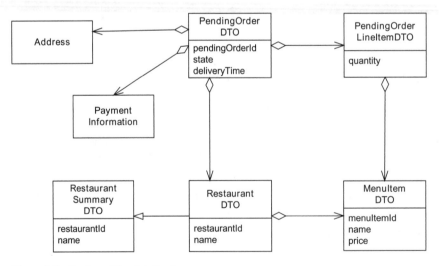

Figure 9.5 Design of the details classes

Listing 9.3 PendingOrderDTO

```
public class PendingOrderDTO {

  private String pendingOrderId;
  private int state;
  private Address deliveryAddress;
  private Date deliveryTime;
  private RestaurantDTO restaurant;
  private List lineItems = new ArrayList();

  public PendingOrderDTO() {
  }

  public String getPendingOrderId() {
    return pendingOrderId;
  }

  public RestaurantDTO getRestaurant() {
    return restaurant;
  }

  public int getState() {
    return state;
  }

  public Address getDeliveryAddress() {
    return deliveryAddress;
  }

  public Date getDeliveryTime() {
    return deliveryTime;
  }
  ...
}
```

It is a simple class that defines some fields and some getters and setters. Let's now look at the DAOs that are used by the transaction scripts to access the database.

9.4 *Implementing the DAOs with iBATIS and Spring*

The phrase "it's turtles all the way down" refers to a myth (or perhaps an urban legend) about the nature of the universe that says that the earth is on the back of a turtle that is standing on the back of a larger turtle, and so on. I sometimes feel the same way about software: one layer after another without end. Fortunately, this really isn't true and in the case of business logic that is designed using the

Transaction Script pattern, there are only three layers: the transaction scripts, the DAOs, and the Spring/iBATIS class.

So far, we have implemented the transaction scripts and tested them using mock DAOs. The next step in the process of implementing the transaction script-based business logic is to implement those DAOs, which include `PendingOrderDAO` and `RestaurantDAO`. As figure 9.6 shows, each DAO consists of an interface and an implementation class. The interface makes it easy to swap implementations. It

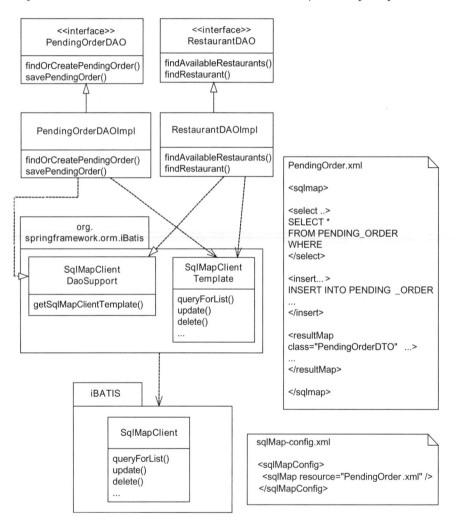

Figure 9.6   iBATIS DAO classes and configuration files

enabled us, for example, to replace the real implementation with a mock implementation when testing the transaction scripts.

The DAO interfaces define the methods that are called by the transaction scripts to insert, find, update, and delete rows in the database. The DAO implementation classes use the Spring iBATIS support classes, which are a convenient way to use the iBATIS framework and mirror the support that Spring provides for JDBC and ORM frameworks such as JDO and Hibernate. These classes integrate iBATIS with Spring's mechanisms for managing JDBC connections and transactions. They allow iBATIS to be configured using Spring beans and enable the iBATIS code to use the same JDBC `DataSource` as the rest of the application.

The two classes used by the DAOs are `SqlMapClientTemplate` and `SqlMapClient-DaoSupport`. The `SqlMapClientTemplate` class provides methods for executing SQL statements and is analogous to the `JdoTemplate` and `HibernateTemplate` classes you have seen earlier in this book. It invokes an iBATIS `SqlClientMap` to execute SQL statements defined in XML descriptor files, and maps any exceptions to Spring data access exceptions. `SqlMapClientDaoSupport` is a convenient base class for iBATIS DAOs and makes a `SqlMapClientTemplate` available to its subclasses.

In this section, we'll look at how to implement DAOs using iBATIS and Spring. You will learn how to develop DAOs using a test-driven approach that uses mock objects for the Spring/iBATIS APIs in order to be able to test the DAOs without a database. We also describe strategies for testing with the database.

9.4.1 *Overview of using iBATIS with Spring*

The iBATIS framework is an open source project that was founded by Clinton Begin with the goal of simplifying database access. The name "iBATIS" is a combination of the letter "i" from the word "Internet" and the letters "b-a-t-i-s" from the word "abatis," which is a defensive barrier formed by cut-down trees with sharpened branches facing the enemy. In case you were wondering who the enemy is, the name reflects the fact that the iBATIS project first developed Internet cryptography software.

Today, the iBATIS project is very much focused on database access software. The iBATIS framework significantly simplifies the task of executing SQL statements. It eliminates the need to write the error-prone and sometimes complex JDBC code that manipulates `PreparedStatements` and `ResultSets` and maps between them and Java objects. iBATIS uses XML descriptor files to map between Java objects and SQL statements and JDBC result sets. It maps the properties of an object to the parameters of a SQL statement and maps the columns of a `ResultSet` to the properties of an object. As a result, DAOs implemented using iBATIS often contain very little code.

Using a Spring SqlMapClientTemplate

Let's imagine, for example, that you had to write a DAO method that finds the restaurants that serve a particular delivery address and time. It takes the delivery address and time as parameters and returns a list of `RestaurantDTO` objects. The DAO would execute this `SELECT` statement:

```
SELECT r.*
  FROM RESTAURANT r,
    RESTAURANT_ZIPCODE rz,
    RESTAURANT_TIME_RANGE tr
  WHERE rz.ZIPCODE = ?
  AND rz.RESTAURANT_ID = r.RESTAURANT_ID
  AND tr.RESTAURANT_ID = r.RESTAURANT_ID
  AND tr.DAY_OF_WEEK = ?
  …
```

If you were using JDBC, then you would have to write the usual boilerplate code to create, initialize, and execute a `PreparedStatement` and iterate through the `ResultSet` creating the DTOs. You would also have to make sure that the `PreparedStatement` and `ResultSet` were closed by using a `try/finally`. In comparison, the iBATIS/Spring version of the DAO method is remarkably simple. It creates a map containing the parameters for the query and executes the query by calling `SqlMapClientTemplate.queryForList()`:

```
public class RestaurantDAOIBatisImpl extends SqlMapClientDaoSupport
    implements RestaurantDAO {

  public RestaurantDAOIBatisImpl(
      SqlMapClientTemplate template) {
    setSqlMapClientTemplate(template);     ⟵——— Saves SqlMapClientTemplate
  }

  public List findAvailableRestaurants(Address deliveryAddress,
      Date deliveryTime) {
    Calendar c = Calendar.getInstance();
    c.setTime(deliveryTime);
    int dayOfWeek =
        c.get(Calendar.DAY_OF_WEEK);
    int hour = c.get(Calendar.HOUR_OF_DAY);      Creates a Map
    int minute = c.get(Calendar.MINUTE);         containing query
    String zipCode =                             parameters
        deliveryAddress.getZip();

    Map deliveryInfo = new HashMap();
    deliveryInfo.put("zipCode", zipCode);
```

```
deliveryInfo.put("dayOfWeek",
                new Integer(dayOfWeek));        Creates a Map
deliveryInfo.put("hour", new Integer(hour));   containing query
deliveryInfo.put("minute",                     parameters
                new Integer(minute));

return getSqlMapClientTemplate()               Executes SELECT
    .queryForList("findAvailableRestaurants",  statement
                deliveryInfo);
  }
  ...
}
```

In this listing, the constructor saves the `SqlMapClientTemplate` for later by calling `setSqlMapClientTemplate()`, which is provided by the superclass. The `findAvailableRestaurants()` method creates a `Map` containing the parameters for the query. It then executes the query by invoking the `SqlMapClientTemplate` and passing it the name of the SQL statement and the map containing the parameters as arguments. iBATIS executes the `SELECT` statement and constructs a list of `RestaurantDTO` objects from the `ResultSet`.

In addition to `queryForList()`, the `SqlMapClientTemplate` interface provides other methods for executing SQL statements, including the following:

- `insert()` executes a SQL `INSERT` statement.
- `update()` executes a SQL `UPDATE` statement.
- `queryForObject()` executes a query that returns a single object.

Each method takes as parameters the name of the SQL statement to execute and the Java object or objects that supply the SQL statement's parameters.

Of course, in order for iBATIS to do its job you must tell it three things: the SQL statement to execute; how to initialize its placeholders; and, if it's a query, how to create Java objects from the result set. To do this, you must write one or more XML descriptor files.

Writing the iBATIS descriptor file

iBATIS uses an XML descriptor file to define statements and result maps. A statement specifies the SQL statement, its parameter map, and the result map to use. The parameter map specifies the mapping between a Java object and the SQL statement's parameters, and the result map specifies the mapping between a `ResultSet`'s columns and Java objects.

Listing 9.4 shows an excerpt of the iBATIS XML file used by the `findAvailableRestaurants()` method. This XML file defines a mapped statement, which queries the RESTAURANT table to find the available restaurants for the specified delivery information, and a result map, which constructs `RestaurantDTO` from each row of the result set.

Listing 9.4 Example iBATIS description file

```
<sqlMap>

<select id="findAvailableRestaurants"
    parameterClass="java.util.Map"
    resultMap="RestaurantResultMap">
  SELECT r.*
  FROM RESTAURANT r,
    RESTAURANT_ZIPCODE rz,
    RESTAURANT_TIME_RANGE tr
  WHERE rz.ZIPCODE = #zipCode#
  AND rz.RESTAURANT_ID = r.RESTAURANT_ID
  AND tr.RESTAURANT_ID = r.RESTAURANT_ID
  AND tr.DAY_OF_WEEK = #dayOfWeek#
...
</select>
...
<resultMap id="RestaurantResultMap"
    class="net.chrisrichardson.foodToGo...details.RestaurantDTO">
    <result property="restaurantId" column="RESTAURANT_ID"/>
    <result property="name" column="NAME"/>
</resultMap>

</sqlMap>
```

The `findAvailableRestaurants` statement takes a `Map` as a parameter and uses its entries in the `WHERE` clause of the `SELECT` statement. The `#propertyName#` notation specifies the property to pass as a parameter.

`RestaurantResultMap` is used by the statement to construct the `RestaurantDTOs` from the `ResultSet`. It maps the columns of the `ResultSet` returned by executing the query to the properties of the `RestaurantDTO`. It constructs a `RestaurantDTO` for each row in the result set.

In addition to mapping columns to properties, a result map can also set a property to the result of executing a nested `SELECT` statement. An application can use this feature to automatically retrieve one or more related objects. Later on you will see some example code that uses this feature.

The iBATIS XML files that define the mapped statements along with an iBATIS configuration file, which lists the map XML files, are deployed in either a class path directory or JAR file and are read by iBATIS on startup. In section 9.5, we will look at how to configure iBATIS using Spring beans.

Even though DAOs written using iBATIS are much simpler than DAOs written using JDBC, it is important to remember that maintaining the XML descriptor files and SQL statements can be a lot of work. For example, let's imagine you need to add a new field to an object. If you are using an ORM framework such as Hibernate or JDO, which maps Java objects to the database schema, you just have to add a single entry to an O/R mapping file. In comparison, if you are using iBATIS, which maps objects to SQL statements, you often need to change multiple statements, including at least one SELECT statement, an INSERT statement, and an UPDATE statement. Keeping multiple statements in sync can be both time-consuming and error-prone. However, if you must execute SQL statements, then iBATIS is an excellent way to do that.

For more detailed information about iBATIS and the Spring support classes, see *iBATIS in Action* [Begin, forthcoming] and *Spring in Action* [Walls 2005]. Let's now look at how to use iBATIS and Spring to implement a DAO and see some examples of how to use the iBATIS and Spring APIs.

9.4.2 *Implementing a DAO method*

Most DAOs are simple wrappers around the database access API, which in this example is iBATIS. Each DAO method performs one or more database operations—executing a query, inserting rows, updating rows, deleting rows, or calling a stored procedure—by executing iBATIS mapped statements.

Because we are using test-driven development, the task of implementing the DAOs begins with writing a test. We could write a test that runs against the database, but that would be slow and complicated. Instead, we will write tests that use mock objects for the Spring and iBATIS APIs. Once those pass, we will write tests that run against the database.

We are going to use the findPendingOrder() method to illustrate how to implement a DAO method with Spring and iBATIS. This method, which is implemented by the PendingOrderDAO, retrieves the pending order, its line items, its restaurant, and its restaurant's menu items from the database and returns a PendingOrderDTO containing this data.

Testing DAOs using mock objects

The first step in the process of implementing a DAO method is to write a mock object test that verifies that the method executes the expected iBATIS statement and returns the correct PendingOrderDTO. The findPendingOrder() method has to execute three SQL statements:

1 Retrieve the `PendingOrder` and restaurant by executing a SQL statement that does an outer join between the PENDING_ORDER and RESTAURANT tables.

2 Retrieve the `PendingOrder`'s line items by executing a SQL `SELECT` statement that queries the PENDING_ORDER_LINE_ITEM table.

3 If the `PendingOrder` has a restaurant, retrieve its menu items by executing a SQL `SELECT` statement that retrieves the menu items from the MENU_ITEM table.

The `findPendingOrder()` method can load a `PendingOrder` by calling `SqlMapClientTemplate.queryForObject()` with the name of the `SELECT` statement that queries the PENDING_ORDER table and the pending order ID arguments. Moreover, because iBATIS can be configured to execute queries that retrieve related objects, that call to `queryForObject()` can execute additional `SELECT` statements that retrieve the line items and menu items. As a result, `findPendingOrder()` only needs a single test.

The test shown in listing 9.5 uses a mock `SqlMapClientTemplate`. It calls `findPendingOrder()` with a pending order ID of `10` and verifies that it calls `queryForObject()` with `findPendingOrder` as the statement name and `10` as arguments. The test also verifies that `findPendingOrder()` returns the object that was returned by `queryForObject()`.

Listing 9.5 PendingOrderDAOIBatisImplMockTests

```
public class PendingOrderDAOIBatisImplMockTests extends
    MockObjectTestCase {

  private Mock mockSqlMapClientTemplate;
  private PendingOrderDAOIBatisImpl dao;
  private PendingOrderDTO pendingOrder;

  protected void setUp() throws Exception {
    super.setUp();
    mockSqlMapClientTemplate =
      new Mock(SqlMapClientTemplate.class);       ◁———❶ Creates mock objects
    SqlMapClientTemplate sqlMapClientTemplate =
        (SqlMapClientTemplate) mockSqlMapClientTemplate.proxy();
    pendingOrder = new PendingOrderDTO();

    dao = new PendingOrderDAOIBatisImpl(sqlMapClientTemplate);
  }

  public void testFindPendingOrder() {
```

```
mockSqlMapClientTemplate.expects(once())
   .method("queryForObject")
   .with(eq("findPendingOrder"),
         eq("10"))
   .will(returnValue(pendingOrder));
```
② **Sets expectations**

```
PendingOrderDTO result =
   dao.findPendingOrder("10");
```
③ **Calls the DAO**

```
assertSame(pendingOrder, result);
}

}
```
④ **Checks return value**

Let's take a closer look at this listing:

① The setUp() method creates a mock SqlMapClientTemplate, a test PendingOrder-DTO, and a PendingOrderDAOIBatisImpl.

② The testFindPendingOrder() method creates an expectation that SqlMapClient-Template.queryForObject() will be called with a statement name of findPending-Order and a parameter with the value 10, and then returns the test PendingOrderDTO.

③ The test calls the findPendingOrder() method.

④ The testFindPendingOrder() method asserts that the findOrderCreatePending-Order() returns the PendingOrderDTO returned by queryForObject().

The test is extremely simple. It requires only a minimal amount of setup and has no external dependencies. It also runs considerably faster than a test that accesses the database.

Writing a DAO method

Now that we have written the test, the next step in the process of implementing the DAO is to write the findPendingOrder() method. The PendingOrderDAO-IBatisImpl class extends Spring's SqlMapClientDaoSupport class and defines a findPendingOrder() method, which uses Spring's SqlMapClientTemplate to execute SQL statements:

```
public class PendingOrderDAOIBatisImpl extends
   SqlMapClientDaoSupport implements PendingOrderDAO {

   public PendingOrderDAOIBatisImpl(
      SqlMapClientTemplate template) {
      setSqlMapClientTemplate(template);   ⟵── Saves SqlMapClientTemplate
   }
```

```
    private PendingOrderDTO
        findPendingOrder(String pendingOrderId) {
      PendingOrderDTO pendingOrderDTO =
        (PendingOrderDTO)
          getSqlMapClientTemplate()
            .queryForObject(              Executes query
              "findPendingOrder",
              pendingOrderId);
      return pendingOrderDTO;
  }
  ...
}
```

In this method, the constructor takes a SQLMapClientTemplate as a parameter and calls the setter defined by SqlMapClientDaoSupport. The findPendingOrder() method uses SqlMapClientTemplate to execute the SQL SELECT statements that load the PendingOrder, its line items, its restaurant, and its restaurant's menu items.

This method is extremely simple because iBATIS does all of the work. Let's look at how it is configured.

Writing the iBATIS SQL maps

After writing a DAO method, the next step is to write the iBATIS mapped statements that are executed by the DAO to query and update the database. The mapped statement that is executed by the findPendingOrder() must retrieve not only the pending order but also its line items, its restaurant, and the restaurant's menu items. One straightforward way to accomplish this is to configure iBATIS to execute the following SQL statements:

```
select *
from PENDING_ORDER o, RESTAURANT r
where
o.pending_order_id = ?
AND r.restaurant_id (+)= o.restaurant_id

select *
from PENDING_ORDER_LINE_ITEM l, MENU_ITEM mi
where
l.pending_order_id = ?
AND mi.menu_item_id = l.menu_item_id

select *
from MENU_ITEM mi
where mi.restaurant_id = ?
```

The first SELECT statement is executed when findPendingOrder() calls iBATIS and retrieves the pending order and its restaurant using an outer join. The other two statements are automatically executed by the first statement's result map when it initializes the PendingOrderDTO and RestaurantDTO objects. The second statement retrieves the line items and their associated menu items. The third statement retrieves the menu items for the restaurant. Figure 9.7 shows the statements and result maps that we must write to execute these statements.

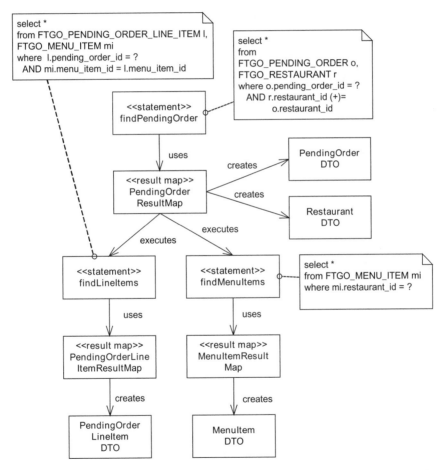

Figure 9.7 Mapped statements and result maps required to load a pending order, its line items, restaurant, and menu items

The statements and result maps shown in this diagram are as follows:

- findPendingOrder is a statement that retrieves the pending order and its restaurant.

- PendingOrderResultMap is the result map for the ResultSet returned find-PendingOrder statement. It maps the columns of this ResultSet to properties of a PendingOrderDTO and RestaurantDTO. It also executes the nested SQL SELECT statements to retrieve the line items and menu items.

- findLineItems is a statement that retrieves the PendingOrder's line items.

- PendingOrderLineItemResultMap maps the columns of the ResultSet returned by findLineItems to properties of the PendingOrderLineItemDTO.

- findMenuItems is a statement that retrieves the restaurant's menu items.

- MenuItemResultMap is a result map that maps the columns of the ResultSet returned by findMenuItems to the properties of the MenuItemDTO.

Listing 9.6 shows an excerpt of the iBATIS XML file that defines these statements and result maps.

Listing 9.6   Excerpt of PendingOrder.xml

```
<sqlMap>

<select id="findPendingOrder"                    ❶
        parameterClass="java.lang.String"
        resultMap="PendingOrderResultMap">
    select *
    from PENDING_ORDER o, RESTAURANT r
    where
    o.pending_order_id = #value#
    AND r.restaurant_id (+)= o.restaurant_id
</select>

<resultMap id="PendingOrderResultMap"            ❷
    class="net.chrisrichardson.foodToGo...PendingOrderDTO">
    <result property="pendingOrderId" column="PENDING_ORDER_ID"/>
    <result property="state" column="STATE"/>
    <result property="deliveryTime" column="DELIVERY_TIME"/>
    <result property="deliveryAddress.street1"
            column="DELIVERY_STREET1"/>
    <result property="deliveryAddress.street2"
            column="DELIVERY_STREET2"/>
    <result property="deliveryAddress.city"
            column="DELIVERY_CITY"/>
    <result property="deliveryAddress.state"
            column="DELIVERY_STATE"/>
```

```xml
            <result property="deliveryAddress.zip" column="DELIVERY_ZIP"/>
            <result property="restaurant.restaurantId"
                    column="RESTAURANT_ID"/>
            <result property="restaurant.name" column="NAME"/>
            <result property="lineItems"
                column="PENDING_ORDER_ID"
                select="findLineItems"/>                          ❸
            <result property="restaurant.menuItems"
                column="RESTAURANT_ID"
                select="findMenuItems"/>
        </resultMap>

        <select id="findLineItems"                                ❹
                parameterClass="java.lang.String"
            resultMap="PendingOrderLineItemResultMap">
            select *
            from PENDING_ORDER_LINE_ITEM l, MENU_ITEM mi
            where
            l.pending_order_id = #value:NUMERIC#
            AND mi.menu_item_id = l.menu_item_id
        </select>

        <resultMap                                                ❺
            id="PendingOrderLineItemResultMap"
            class="net.chrisrichardson…PendingOrderLineItemDTO">
            <result property="quantity" column="QUANTITY"/>
            <result property="index" column="LINE_ITEM_INDEX"/>
            <result property="menuItem.menuItemId" column="MENU_ITEM_ID"/>
            <result property="menuItem.name" column="NAME"/>
            <result property="menuItem.price" column="PRICE"/>
        </resultMap>

        <select id="findMenuItems"                                ❻
                parameterClass="java.lang.String"
            resultMap="MenuItemResultMap">
            select *
            from MENU_ITEM mi
            where mi.restaurant_id = #value:NUMERIC#
        </select>

        <resultMap id="MenuItemResultMap"                         ❼
            class="net.chrisrichardson.foodToGo.placeOrderTransactionScripts.
                ➥ details.MenuItemDTO">
            <result property="menuItemId" column="MENU_ITEM_ID"/>
            <result property="name" column="NAME"/>
            <result property="price" column="PRICE"/>
        </resultMap>

    </sqlMap>
```

Let's look at the details of the top-level mapped statement and its result map:

❶ The findPendingOrder mapped statement defines the SQL SELECT statement that retrieves the pending order and its restaurant. The pending order is specified by a String parameter and the result is constructed using the PendingOrderResultMap result map.

❷ The PendingOrderResultMap result map specifies the mapping between the properties of the PendingOrderDTO and RestaurantDTO beans and columns of the result set returned by the query that finds the pending order.

❸ The result map also specifies that the line items and the restaurant's menu items should be retrieved using other nested mapped statements.

❹ The findLineItems mapped statement defines the SELECT statement that retrieves the pending order's line items.

❺ The PendingOrderLineItemResultMap result map is used by the findLineItems mapped statement to create the PendingOrderLineItemDTOs.

❻ The findMenuItems mapped statement defines the SELECT statement that retrieves the restaurant's menu items.

❼ The MenuItemResultMap result map is used by the findMenuItems mapped statement to create the MenuItemDTOs.

The details of other <select> statements and <resultMap> definitions are similar.

Testing iBATIS maps

The final step in the process of implementing a DAO is to write tests for the iBATIS maps and the SQL statements. Because iBATIS replaces potentially complex DAOs with simple DAOs and XML mapping files, testing the DAOs can be extremely straightforward and can be accomplished with mock objects. However, it is also important to write tests for the iBATIS maps and SQL statements because they implement a lot of functionality. These tests must verify the correctness of three things:

- The iBATIS statements, which specify how object properties map to SQL statement parameters
- The SQL statements, which query and update the database
- The iBATIS result maps, which specify how database columns map to object properties

There are a variety of approaches that you can use to test the iBATIS maps and SQL statements. The most thorough approach is to write to one or more tests for each mapped statement that executes against the database. A test for a SELECT statement populates the database with test data, executes the query, and verifies that it returns the expected result. Similarly, a test for an UPDATE statement populates the database, executes the update, and verifies the contents of the database. A good tool for writing these kinds of tests is DbUnit [DbUnit], which is an extension to JUnit that provides methods for initializing the database and verifying its contents. For example, here is the outline of a test that for the findPendingOrder mapped statement. The test uses the DbUnit method DatabaseOperation.CLEAN_INSERT.execute() to initialize the database with the data from the XML file pending-order-1.xml and executes the query using a SqlMapClientTemplate:

```
public class DBUnitIBatisExampleTests extends TestCase {

    private DatabaseConnection dbUnitConnection;
    private SqlMapClientTemplate sqlMapClientTemplate;

    public void setUp() throws Exception  { … };

    public void test() throws Exception {
      FlatXmlDataSet dataSet = new FlatXmlDataSet(
          getClass().getResourceAsStream(
              "pending-order-1.xml"));
      DatabaseOperation.CLEAN_INSERT.execute(
          dbUnitConnection, dataSet);

      PendingOrderDTO pendingOrder =
        (PendingOrderDTO) sqlMapClientTemplate
          .queryForObject("findPendingOrder", "1");

      assertNotNull(pendingOrder);
      …

    }
    …
    }
```

For more information on how to write these kinds of tests, see the DbUnit documentation and the excellent book *JUnit Recipes* [Rainsberger 2004].

The downside of this approach is that the tests are time consuming to write and execute. Mapped statements often require multiple tests to verify different scenarios. One simplification, which is often a good way to start, is to write tests that execute each SQL statement once without verifying either the return value or the database. This is relatively easy to do and catches many common errors. In addition, the tests will execute fairly quickly.

Another simplification, which lessens the need for the automated tests to verify the SQL statements, is to visually inspect the mapping document and to execute each SQL statement by copying and pasting the SQL statement into a command-line tool such as Oracle SQL*Plus. The trouble with this manual approach is that it will not catch errors caused by changes to the Java code or the database schema. It also relies on the developer to manually retest the mapping documents after making changes. One way to make this testing approach more robust is to use the Gold Master approach described in *JUnit Recipes*. After manually testing the SQL statements, you write tests that fail whenever the SQL statement is changed, which will remind you to recheck the statement. You must still write tests that execute the statements, but they do not need to test the SQL statements as thoroughly.

Tests such as the one for the `findOrder` mapped statement must verify that the result map constructs the objects correctly. The most direct approach is to populate the database with test data, execute the query, and verify that iBATIS returns the correct object. The trouble with this approach is that the tests can be difficult to write and slow to execute. An alternative approach is to write tests that use the iBATIS mapping metadata in a similar way to the tests that we wrote to verify the Hibernate and JDO O/R mapping. As with the JDO and Hibernate tests, the iBATIS tests must use internal APIs. For example, let's look at an example of a test for the `findOrder` mapped statement and its result map. The test gets the metadata describing the mapped statement from the `SqlMapClient` and makes assertions about it:

```
public class IBatisMappingTests extends TestCase {

    private SqlMapClient sqlMapClient;

    public void setUp() throws Exception  { … };

    public void test () throws Exception {
        mappedStatement = ((ExtendedSqlMapClient)sqlMapClient)
            .getMappedStatement("findPendingOrder");

        assertEquals(String.class,
                    mappedStatement
                        .getParameterClass());

        ResultMap resultMap = mappedStatement
            .getResultMap();
        assertEquals(PendingOrderDTO.class,
                    resultMap
                        .getResultClass());

        resultMappings = resultMap.getResultMappings();
```

Verifies parameter type

Verifies result type

```
BasicResultMapping idMapping =
   findBasicResultMapping(
       "pendingOrderId");
assertEquals("PENDING_ORDER_ID",
           idMapping
              .getColumnName());
```
Verifies pendingOrderId property

```
BasicResultMapping lineItemsMapping =
   findBasicResultMapping("lineItems");
assertEquals("PENDING_ORDER_ID",
     lineItemsMapping.getColumnName());
assertEquals("findLineItems",
           lineItemsMapping
              .getStatementName());
}
```
Verifies lineItems property

```
private BasicResultMapping findBasicResultMapping(
    String propertyName) {
  for (int i = 0; i < resultMappings.length; i++) {
    ResultMapping mapping = resultMappings[i];
    if (mapping.getPropertyName().equals(
          propertyName)) {
      return (BasicResultMapping) mapping;
    }
  }
  fail("no mapping for property: "
      + propertyName);
  return null;
}

...

}
```

This test verifies that the findOrders mapped statement takes a string parameter, and then verifies that the result map creates a PendingOrderDTO. Next, it checks that the pendingOrderId property is set to the PENDING_ORDER column, and that the lineItems property is set to the result of executing a nested statement called findLineItems.

These kinds of tests are easy to write and are a good way of testing the result maps. You still need to test the SQL statements and verify that the parameters are substituted correctly into the SQL statement.

Each one of these testing strategies makes different trade-offs between development time, execution time, and effectiveness. Which option you should choose depends primarily on how much time you are willing to invest in testing and the likelihood of bugs. Unfortunately, I've found that writing database-level tests for DAOs that use SQL to be significantly more difficult and time consuming than writing tests for repositories that use an ORM framework. You need to write much more elaborate tests that run against the database—yet another reason to use SQL only if it is absolutely necessary.

Let's now look at how to deploy the transaction scripts.

9.5 Configuring the transaction scripts using Spring

We have almost finished implementing the business logic for this use case. The final step in the process of implementing transaction scripts is to write the Spring bean definitions that wire together the various classes and apply the AOP interceptors that manage transactions and JDBC connections.

9.5.1 How Spring manages JDBC connections and transactions

Spring has an AOP-based mechanism for managing JDBC connections and transactions. It uses the `TransactionInterceptor` class, which you saw earlier in chapter 7, with a `DataSourceTransactionManager`, which is a Spring `Platform-TransactionManager` that manages transactions using JDBC. Figure 9.8 shows these classes and interfaces.

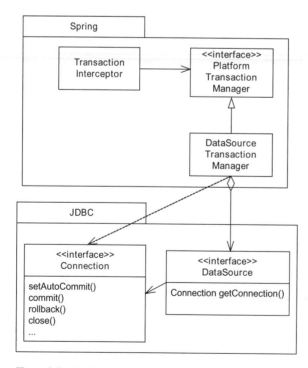

Figure 9.8   Spring classes for managing JDBC connections and transactions

DataSourceTransactionManager is configured with a JDBC DataSource. When called by the TransactionInterceptor to begin a transaction, it gets a connection from the DataSource and ensures that auto-commit is disabled. It also binds the JDBC connection to the thread for use by the SqlMapClientTemplate. Later when it is called by the TransactionInterceptor to commit the transaction, the Data-SourceTransactionManager calls Connection.commit(), closes the connection, and unbinds it from the thread.

Making the transaction scripts transactional is easy. In the Spring bean definitions you configure a TransactionInterceptor to use a DataSourceTransaction-Manager and apply it to the transaction script class. Let's see how to do this.

9.5.2 *The Spring bean definitions*

Figure 9.9 shows the Spring beans that we must define to configure the Place-OrderTransactionScripts class and make it transactional. In addition to configuring the TransactionInterceptor bean, it defines beans for the DAOs and the SqlMapClient and SqlMapClientTemplate classes.

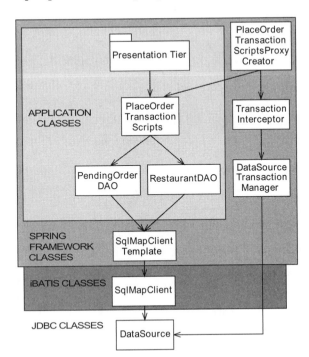

Figure 9.9
The Spring beans required to deploy the
`PlaceOrderTransactionScripts`

These bean definitions instantiate the transaction script class and the DAOs along with the SqlMapClientTemplate and the SqlMapClient. They also apply the TransactionInterceptor to the transaction scripts and create the DataSource. Listing 9.7 shows these Spring bean definitions.

Listing 9.7   placeOrderTransactionScripts-iBatis-beans.xml

```xml
<beans>

  <bean id="SqlMapClient"                      ❶
    class="org.springframework.orm.iBatis.
        ➥ SqlMapClientFactoryBean">
   <property name="configLocation" value="/sqlMap-config.xml" />
   <property name="dataSource" ref="DataSource" />
  </bean>

  <bean id="SqlMapClientTemplate"              ❷
    class="org.springframework.orm.iBatis.SqlMapClientTemplate">
   <property name="exceptionTranslator"
                 ref="ExceptionTranslator" />
   <property name="sqlMapClient" ref="SqlMapClient" />
  </bean>

  <bean id="PendingOrderDAO"                   ❸
    class="net.chrisrichardson.foodToGo.placeOrderTransactionScripts.
          ➥ dao.PendingOrderDAOIBatisImpl">
   <constructor-arg ref="SqlMapClientTemplate" />
  </bean>

  <bean id="RestaurantDAO"                     ❹
    class="net.chrisrichardson.foodToGo.placeOrderTransactionScripts.
        ➥ dao.RestaurantDAOIBatisImpl">
   <constructor-arg ref="SqlMapClientTemplate" />
  </bean>

  <bean id="PlaceOrderTransactionScripts"      ❺
    class="net.chrisrichardson.foodToGo.placeOrderTransactionScripts.
        ➥ PlaceOrderTransactionScriptsImpl">
   <constructor-arg ref="PendingOrderDAO" />
   <constructor-arg ref="RestaurantDAO" />
  </bean>


  <bean id="DataSourceTransactionInterceptor"  ❻
    class="org.springframework.transaction.interceptor.
        ➥ TransactionInterceptor">
   <property name="transactionManager"
     ref="DataSourceTransactionManager" />
   <property name="transactionAttributeSource">
```

```xml
      <value>
        net.chrisrichardson.foodToGo.placeOrderTransactionScripts.
        ➥ PlaceOrderTransactionScriptsImpl.*=PROPAGATION_REQUIRED
      </value>
    </property>
  </bean>

  <bean id="PlaceOrderTransactionScriptsProxyCreator"                    ❼
    class="org.springframework.aop.framework.autoproxy.
        ➥ BeanNameAutoProxyCreator">
    <property name="beanNames">
      <list>
        <idref bean="PlaceOrderTransactionScripts" />
      </list>
    </property>
    <property name="interceptorNames">
      <list>
        <idref bean="DataSourceTransactionInterceptor" />
      </list>
    </property>
  </bean>


  <bean id="DataSourceTransactionManager"                                ❽
    class="org.springframework.jdbc.datasource.
        ➥ DataSourceTransactionManager">
    <property name="dataSource" ref="DataSource" />
  </bean>


  <bean id="DataSource"                          ❾
        class="org.apache.commons.dbcp.BasicDataSource">
    <property name="driverClassName">
      <value>oracle.jdbc.driver.OracleDriver</value>
    </property>
    <property name="url">
      <value>jdbc:oracle:thin:@gringots:1521:db92</value>
    </property>
    <property name="username">
      <value>ftgouser</value></property>
    <property name="password">
      <value>ftgopassword</value>
    </property>
  </bean>

</beans>
```

Here is an explanation of what is happening in this listing:

❶ Create an iBATIS `SqlMapClient` using the iBATIS descriptor files that are listed in the configuration file sqlMap-config.xml:

```
<sqlMapConfig>
  <sqlMap resource="PendingOrder.xml" />
</sqlMapConfig>
```

❷ Create the Spring `SqlMapClientTemplate`.

❸ Create `PendingOrderDAOImpl` and wire it to the `SqlMapClientTemplate`.

❹ Create the `RestaurantDAOImpl` and wire it to the `SqlMapClientTemplate`.

❺ Create the `PlaceOrderTransactionScripts` injecting the `PendingOrderDAO` and `RestaurantDAO`.

❻ Configure the `TransactionInterceptor` to use the `DataSourceTransactionManager`.

❼ Apply the `DataSourceTransactionInterceptor` to the `PlaceOrderTransaction-Scripts`.

❽ Create a `DataSourceTransactionManager` that begins and commits a transaction that uses a JDBC connection that is bound to the thread for use by the DAOs.

❾ Create a JDBC `DataSource` implemented using Database Connection Pool (DBCP), which is an open source connection pool.

When the presentation tier asks the Spring lightweight container for `PlaceOrder-TransactionScripts`, Spring will instantiate all of these components and return a `PlaceOrderTransactionScripts` that is wrapped with a `TransactionInterceptor` that executes each method within a transaction.

The application's classes, along with the Spring bean definitions and the iBATIS configuration files, would then be packaged and deployed as part of a web application in a web container.

9.6 *Summary*

The Transaction Script pattern is a procedural approach that organizes the business logic into a set of transaction scripts. A transaction script is a method that accesses the database and performs computations and updates the database. There is usually one transaction script for each request from the presentation tier, and they are grouped together to form a transaction script class. For example, the transaction script version of the Place Order use case consists of a transaction script class that defines a separate transaction script for each step of the use case.

The Transaction Script pattern concentrates behavior in the transaction scripts rather than distributing it among multiple domain classes. This pattern tends not to work well when the business logic is complex because transaction scripts consist of procedural code, which is usually hard to understand and maintain. You also have to write a lot more database access code when using this pattern. Consequently, this pattern should only be used when either the application's business logic is extremely simple or when it is not possible to efficiently access the database using a persistence framework.

Transaction scripts should not access the database directly because that would mix business logic with database code and make development and testing harder. Instead, they should use DAOs that encapsulate the database access code. The transaction scripts are configured with the DAOs via constructor parameters, which enables them to be developed and tested using mock DAOs.

The DAOs used by the transaction scripts could use JDBC. However, a much better approach is to use the iBATIS framework, which significantly reduces the amount of code required to execute SQL statements. iBATIS takes care of mapping Java objects to SQL statement parameters, calling JDBC to execute the SQL statement, and mapping the ResultSet to one or more Java objects. Therefore, many DAO methods consist of a single line of code that calls an iBATIS method.

When developing an application's business logic, you do not have to exclusively use either the Domain Model pattern or the Transaction Script pattern. You should instead choose the pattern that is most appropriate for each request. You could, for example, implement the first step of a use case using a transaction script that retrieves a list of orders using a complex SQL query and implement the rest of use case using domain model-based business logic that manipulates individual orders.

Now that we have covered the Transaction Script pattern, the next chapter tackles implementing POJOs with EJB 3.

10

Implementing POJOs with EJB 3

Most of this book has focused on implementing POJO business logic using the lightweight alternatives to EJB: Spring, Hibernate, and JDO. So why discuss EJBs? After all, an EJB as defined by the EJB 2 specification is the ultimate anti-POJO. It is a heavyweight object that implements special interfaces and can only run inside the EJB container. To use the valuable features of EJB, which include standardized declarative transaction management, distributed transactions, and persistence, developers had to struggle with excessive complexity and long edit-compile-debug cycles.

However, all of this has changed with EJB 3, which embraces POJOs and is a radical improvement over its predecessor. EJB 3 session beans, entity beans, and message-driven beans are POJOs and do not implement any special interfaces. Deployment and configuration is considerably simpler. In addition, even though entity beans are defined by the EJB expert group, they are intended to be the standard persistence framework for both J2EE and J2SE. As a result, EJB 3 provides the valuable features of EJB 2 but with less complexity and pain. It is destined to be both an important and an effective technology for developing enterprise Java applications. Let's see how EJB 3 works.

10.1 Overview of EJB 3

EJB is intended to be the standard component architecture for building Java business applications. The primary goal of EJB 3, which is part of Java Enterprise Edition 5 (JEE 5), is to make EJB easier to use, and it incorporates some of the lightweight concepts that you encountered earlier in this book. EJB 3 still provides session, message-driven, and entity beans, but how you write them and configure them is very different and a lot simpler. EJB 3 Enterprise JavaBeans are POJOs, which makes them easier to write. You have the choice of using either Java 5 annotations or an XML deployment descriptor to configure an EJB. EJB 3 has sensible defaults for many bean attributes, such as the JNDI name and transactional behavior, which means that you do not have to explicitly specify every aspect of the bean. In addition, session and message-driven beans can use dependency injection instead of JNDI calls to access other beans and resources, which simplifies the code and further decouples it from the EJB container. EJB 3 has a powerful ORM mechanism that incorporates many of the ideas from Hibernate, JDO, and Oracle TopLink. What's more, EJB 3 entity beans can run outside the container, which makes testing much easier.

EJB 3 as defined by the June 2005 public draft [EJB 3 June 2005] also has some significant limitations. The O/R mapping lacks necessary features such as collections of primitive types. Dependency injection only supports injecting JNDI objects into EJBs. In addition, developing EJBs is still more complicated than developing with lightweight technologies. In this section, we provide an overview of EJB 3 as defined by the June 2005 public draft specification and describe the key improvements as well as the remaining limitations and how to work around them.

10.1.1   Key improvements in EJB 3

EJB 3 has several key improvements that address deficiencies in EJB 2. Let's look at each one in turn.

EJBs are POJOs

To implement an EJB 2 bean, you must write classes and interfaces that are coupled to the EJB container. For example, to implement an EJB 2 session bean you must write a bean class that implements the `SessionBean` interface, a home interface that extends `EJBHome`, and a component interface that extends either `EJBObject` or `EJBLocalObject`. Because of the dependency on these interfaces, an EJB 2 bean can only run inside the EJB container. It is anything but a POJO.

Implementing EJB 3 beans is much simpler because EJB 3 eliminates interfaces such as `EJBHome` and `SessionBean`. EJB 3 beans are POJOs that do not extend or implement those EJB-specific interfaces. For example, an EJB 3 session bean consists of a plain old Java interface, which defines its public methods, and a POJO bean class, which implements the interface. A message-driven bean is even simpler and consists of only a POJO bean class.

An entity bean also consists of just the POJO bean class. Unlike EJB 2 it's a concrete class because you don't define abstract accessors for the container-managed fields and relationship. The entity bean's fields or JavaBean-style properties are mapped to the database using annotations or entries in the deployment descriptor. An entity bean is instantiated using the `new` operator and persisted using the EJB `EntityManager`, which is similar to a JDO `PersistenceManager` or Hibernate `Session` and is described a bit later.

Because of these changes in EJB 3, you have to write a lot less code when developing EJB 3. As an added bonus, your code is a lot less dependent on the EJB container. Later in this chapter you will see how POJOs developed earlier in this book can be deployed as EJBs.

Entity beans can run outside the EJB container

EJB 2 entity beans are inherently server-side components and can only run within the EJB container. To test an entity bean, you have to wait for it to deploy in the EJB container, which slows down the edit-compile-debug cycle. One drastic change in the EJB 3 specification is that entity beans are no longer just a server-side technology.

They are intended to be the standard Java object persistence mechanism and can be used both inside and out of the application server. EJB 3 persistence works outside the application server in the same way as JDO and Hibernate. Even if you are only developing server applications, this is an extremely valuable feature because it means that you can test entity beans without deploying them in the EJB container.

Simpler configuration

Another important improvement in EJB 3 is that you are no longer required to write complex XML deployment descriptors to describe a bean's configuration. Instead, EJB 3 lets you configure a bean using Java 5 annotations. An annotation is a Java 5 language feature that associates extra data with a program element such as a class or method. This data can be read by tools and frameworks such as the EJB container. Annotations are often easier to use than an XML deployment descriptor because they are located next to the program element that they describe. What's more, because EJB 3 has sensible defaults for an EJB's properties you often only have to use a few annotations to turn a POJO into an EJB.

For example, the following code fragment shows the annotations on the `PlaceOrderFacade` interface and `PlaceOrderFacadeImpl` class that will deploy the `PlaceOrderFacade` from chapter 7 as a stateless session bean:

```
@Local
public interface PlaceOrderFacade {
...
}

@Stateless
public class PlaceOrderFacadeImpl
  implements PlaceOrderFacade {
...
}
```

The `@Local` annotation specifies that the `PlaceOrderFacade` interface is a local EJB interface, and the `@Stateless` annotation specifies that `PlaceOrderFacadeImpl` is a stateless session bean. By default, its JNDI name is the fully qualified class name of the local EJB interface and the EJB container uses container-managed transactions with a transaction attribute of REQUIRED. If necessary, you can override the defaults by using additional annotations. The EJB container reads the information specified by the annotations and uses it to deploy the EJB.

Configuring an entity bean is equally straightforward. You annotate the POJO class with an `@Entity` annotation and annotate its fields or properties to map them to the database. For example, here is part of the code for the `PendingOrder` EJB:

```
@Entity(access=AccessType.FIELD)
class PendingOrder {

  @Id(generate = GeneratorType.AUTO)
  private int id;

  private int state = PendingOrder.NEW;

  @ManyToOne
  private Restaurant restaurant;

  @OneToMany(cascade = CascadeType.ALL)
  private List<PendingOrderLineItem> lineItems
    = new ArrayList<PendingOrderLineItem>();

  @ManyToOne
  private Coupon coupon;
  ...
```

The @Entity annotation specifies that the PendingOrder class is an entity bean, and the access=AccessType.FIELD member tells the EJB container to map its fields rather than its properties to the database. The @Id annotation identifies the primary key field and tells the EJB container to generate a primary key. The @OneTo-Many annotation specifies that the lineItems field is a one-to-many relationship, and the @ManyToOne annotation specifies that the restaurant and coupon fields are many-to-one relationships. The EJB 3 persistence mechanism uses the information specified by the annotations in the same way that the JDO or Hibernate implementation uses the XML O/R mapping documents.

This example uses the default EJB 3 O/R mapping rules that generate default table and column names and define the mappings for relationships. The PendingOrder class is mapped to the PENDINGORDER table, the id field is mapped to the ID column, and the lineItems field is mapped to a join table called PENDING_ORDER_PENDING_ORDER_LINE_ITEM, which has foreign keys to the PENDINGORDER and PENDINGORDERLINEITEM tables. You can, however, use annotations to specify the names of the tables and columns and change how some relationships are mapped. Later in this chapter you'll see examples of how to do that.

EJB 3 encourages developers to use annotations to define an EJB, but you can still use XML deployment descriptors. Whether you use annotations or deployment descriptors is largely a matter of personal preference, but there are situations in which deployment descriptors are useful. For example, the annotations that define the O/R mapping can be verbose, and it can be easier to use a deployment descriptor instead. Another potential use for a deployment descriptor is to override the annotations for an EJB. You could, for example, use a deployment descriptor to map an entity bean to a different database schema. As of this writing, EJB 3 deployment descriptors are still a work in progress and so we won't discuss them further.

Dependency injection

An EJB rarely works in isolation. It typically uses resources such as JDBC Data-Sources and even other EJBs to fulfill its responsibilities. An EJB 2 bean uses JNDI to look up these resources and EJBs. The problem with using JNDI is that in addition to requiring you to write the lookup code it couples the EJB to the application server environment. EJB 3 fixes this problem for session and message-driven beans by using dependency injection to encapsulate the JNDI lookup. It defines several annotations that you can use to identify a field or setter method as requiring a reference to an EJB or resource. When the EJB container instantiates a session or message-driven bean, it initializes the fields and calls the setters with objects obtained from JNDI. For example, here is how the PlaceOrderFacadeImpl EJB can use field injection to obtain a reference to the PlaceOrderService EJB:

```
@Stateless
class PlaceOrderFacadeImpl implements PlaceOrderFacade {

    @EJB
    PlaceOrderService service;
...
```

The @EJB annotation tells the EJB container to set the service field to a reference to the PlaceOrderService, which is another EJB deployed in the container. By default, EJB 3 derives the JNDI name from the type of the field or setter parameter, but if necessary it can be specified in the annotation.

EJB 3 dependency injection is extremely useful. By eliminating the JNDI lookups, it simplifies session and message-driven beans and reduces their dependency on the application server environment. It is also quite concise, unlike Spring dependency injection, which requires you to write XML to configure the beans. There are, however, some limitations.

Significantly improved O/R mapping

Historically, the EJB CMP, which is the EJB equivalent of persistent objects, has been very weak. For example, EJB 1 CMP did not support relationships and it wasn't until EJB CMP 2.1 that the query language supported sorting! EJB 3 persistence is a huge improvement over EJB 2 CMP. It has many features that were lacking from EJB 2, including the following:

- A standardized O/R mapping mechanism
- Support for inheritance
- Embedded objects whose fields are mapped to the same table as the entity bean's fields
- Optimistic locking with version numbers

EJB 3 also enhances the EJB query language with new features such as Hibernate-style fetch joins for eagerly loading objects and bulk update and delete. In addition, queries can be defined either statically or generated dynamically.

Improved persistence API

As I mentioned earlier, EJB 3 has a new and improved persistence API that is quite similar to the APIs provided by JDO and Hibernate. As figure 10.1 shows, the API consists of interfaces that play the role of connection factory, connection, transaction, and query. There is also a `Persistence` class that provides methods for creating the EJB 3 equivalent of the connection factory.

The `EntityManager` replaces the entity bean home interfaces and is equivalent to the JDO `PersistenceManager` and Hibernate `Session`. It defines methods for creating, deleting, and querying entity beans. For example, the `create()` method

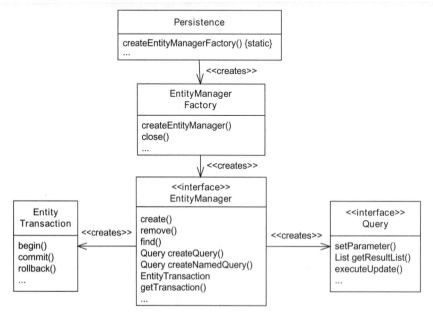

Figure 10.1   The EJB 3 persistence API

makes an entity bean persistent, `remove()` deletes an entity bean, and `find()` retrieves an entity bean by its primary key.

The `Query` interface is equivalent to the Hibernate or JDO `Query` interfaces. It defines methods for executing queries, bulk deletes, and bulk updates. An application creates a `Query` by calling factory methods defined by the `EntityManager` such as `createQuery()`, which creates a `Query` from a query string, and `create-NamedQuery()`, which creates one from a named query. The `Query` interface defines several methods, including `setParameter()`, which sets a query parameter; `get-ResultList()`, which executes a query and returns a list of results; and `execute-Update()`, which executes an update or delete statement. For example, here is a code fragment that shows how an application can execute an EJB 3 named query:

```
EntityManager entityManager = ...;
Query query = entityManager
    .createNamedQuery("Restaurant.findAvailableRestaurants");
...
query.setParameter("dayOfWeek", new Integer(dayOfWeek));
query.setParameter("hour", new Integer(hour));
query.setParameter("minute", new Integer(minute));
query.setParameter("zipCode", new Integer(zipCode));
List result = query.getResultList();
```

The application calls `EntityManager.createNamedQuery()` to create the query, sets some parameters, and executes the query by calling `Query.getResultList()`.

The `EntityManagerFactory` interface is equivalent to a Hibernate `Session-Factory` or a JDO `PersistenceManagerFactory`. It has a `createEntityManager()` method that creates an `EntityManager`. J2EE applications will typically use dependency injection to access an `EntityManager`, but client-side code, most notably test cases, needs to explicitly create an `EntityManager` using the `EntityManager-Factory`. Client-side code creates an `EntityManagerFactory` by calling `Persistence.createEntityManagerFactory()`, which is a static method.

The `EntityTransaction` interface is equivalent to the `Transaction` interfaces provided by Hibernate and JDO. The application gets the `EntityTransaction` from the `EntityManager` and calls its methods to control transactions. J2EE applications will most likely use container-managed transactions, but client-side tests will use `EntityTransaction`.

As you can see, the EJB 3 persistence interface is completely different from the EJB 2 equivalent. It's very similar to JDO and Hibernate APIs. Later in this chapter, you will see examples of how to use it. Let's now look at EJB 3 detached objects.

Detached objects

EJB 2 applications use DTOs to exchange data between the presentation tier and the business tier. Developing and maintaining the DTOs and the code that creates them is often a significant amount of work. It is also quite tedious. EJB 3 eliminates most uses of DTOs by supporting Hibernate-style detached objects. When a transaction ends, all entity beans that were loaded during the transaction are automatically detached and can be returned to the presentation tier. The presentation tier can also modify a detached entity bean and then pass it back to the business tier, which can reattach it to update the database.

So as you can see, EJB 3 is significantly better than EJB 2. If you have never used a lightweight technology such as Spring, Hibernate, or JDO, you will be pleasantly surprised by how easy it is to use. But, as of this writing, when compared to those lightweight technologies EJB 3 still has some significant issues and drawbacks. Let's take a look.

10.1.2   Key limitations of EJB 3

Like every technology, EJB 3 has some limitations and issues that make development more difficult. Some are limitations of the ORM mechanism as described by the June 2005 public draft and will likely be fixed before the final version of the specification. Other issues, such as the development time complexity that lurks beneath the surface, are an inherent part of the EJB concept itself. They are caused by the reliance of session and message-driven beans on the EJB container and application server-side technologies such as JNDI. Let's review each of the issues and drawbacks.

Limited support for collections

In the radio series "Hitchhiker's Guide to Galaxy," Ford Prefect and Arthur Dent get stranded on Earth two million years in the past with the Golgafrinchams. After a year or so, the Golgafrinchams, who are the human race's ancestors, have failed to discover fire or invent the wheel. The development subcommittees responsible for these two inventions cannot decide how people will use fire or what color wheels should be. As you can imagine, Ford and Arthur were very frustrated.

I sometimes feel as frustrated about the collection support in EJB 3. It's certainly much better than what is in EJB 2, but it is still inferior compared to JDO and Hibernate. For example, EJB 3 only supports collections of entities. You cannot, for example, have collections such as `Set<String>` or `Set<Integer>`, which are quite common in a POJO domain model and are supported by Hibernate and JDO. As you will see later, you have to replace these kinds of collections with collections of entity beans that wrap the value, which often requires a lot of extra code.

Another limitation of the EJB 3 O/R mapping is that although it supports lists it does not guarantee to preserve the ordering unless you use the `@OrderBy` annotation. The `@OrderBy` annotation specifies how to sort the list when it is retrieved from the database. You can either sort by the primary key of the element or by a field or property. This means that, for example, in order to persist `Restaurant.menuItems`, which is a list of `MenuItems`, you must add an index field to the `MenuItem` class and write code to maintain it:

```
@Entity(access=AccessType.FIELD)
public class Restaurant {
  ...
  @OneToMany(cascade = CascadeType.ALL, fetch = FetchType.LAZY)
  @OrderBy("index")
  private List<MenuItem> menuItems;
  ...
}

@Entity (access=AccessType.FIELD)
@Table(name="MENU_ITEM")
public class MenuItem implements Serializable {
  ...
  private int index;
  ...
  }
```

In this example, the `@OrderBy` annotation on the `Restaurant.menuItems` specifies that the list should be sorted by the `MenuItem.index` field. This is a minor change, but it's a shame that you need to do this given that Hibernate and JDO will automatically maintain the ordering.

If you are willing to sacrifice portability, then you can use a vendor-specific extension such as JBoss's `@OrderBy` annotation:

```
@Entity(access=AccessType.FIELD)
public class Restaurant {
  @OneToMany(cascade = CascadeType.ALL, fetch = FetchType.LAZY)
  @IndexColumn(name="MENU_ITEM_INDEX")
  private List<MenuItem> menuItems;
  ...
  }
```

The `@IndexColumn` annotation tells JBoss EJB 3 to maintain the index of each `MenuItem` in the MENU_ITEM_INDEX column of the MENU_ITEM table.

Another feature missing from EJB 3 is the ability to automatically delete a child entity when it is removed from its parent's collection. It might sound harsh, but Hibernate and JDO can be configured to automatically delete such orphans. This is essential for relationships such as `PendingOrder-PendingOrderLineItem`, where line items must be deleted when they are no longer associated with the parent.

To correctly implement these kinds of a relationship, a portable EJB 3 application must contain code to explicitly delete orphaned children. For example, the method `PendingOrder.updateQuantities()`, which updates the `lineItems` field, must call `EntityManager.remove()` on each line item it removes from the `lineItems` fields. This potentially impacts several classes in the domain model. First, we have to encapsulate the deletion code in a repository such as the `PendingOrderRepository`. Second, we must change the `PlaceOrderService` to pass the repository to the `PendingOrder`. Finally, we need to change the `PendingOrder` to call the repositories. Lots of little changes—all because EJB 3 lacks a feature that has been in JDO and Hibernate for quite some time.

The alternative, of course, is to use a vendor-specific feature. For example, JBoss EJB 3 supports a nonstandard `@Cascade` annotation that lets you tell the EJB 3 implementation to delete orphaned children:

```
public class PendingOrder implements Serializable {
…
  @OneToMany(cascade = { CascadeType.ALL })
  @OrderBy("index")
  @JoinColumn(name = "PENDING_ORDER_ID")
   @org.hibernate.annotations.Cascade(org.hibernate.annotations.
                                   ➥ CascadeType.DELETE_ORPHAN)
  private List<PendingOrderLineItem> lineItems = new
  ArrayList<PendingOrderLineItem>();
…
}
```

The value of `CascadeType.DELETE_ORPHAN` specifies that the EJB container should delete children when they are removed from the collection.

As you can see, these kinds of limitations force you to make the difficult decision between writing a portable application that requires extra code and using vendor-specific extensions. I hope these problems are addressed before the release of the EJB 3 specification. After all, it's not as if there is anything new to invent or discover.

Limitations of fetch joins

EJB 3's support for eager loading is definitely an improvement over EJB 2, which lacks a mechanism for configuring eager loading and requires you to use a vendor-specific mechanism. EJB 3 lets you statically configure eager loading in the annotations defining the O/R mapping or dynamically by using Hibernate-style fetch joins in queries. However, while fetch joins are a concise and easy-to-use way to dynamically control eager loading, they have some limitations.

As you saw in chapter 6, one important limitation of Hibernate-style fetch joins is that because they are part of the query language they cannot control eager loading when loading an individual object or traversing a relationship. Also, if different use cases need to eagerly load different sets of objects, an application must use multiple variants of a query, each one with a different set of fetch joins. This can make it difficult to implement a repository that is shared by different business logic components because it must provide multiple query methods or a single query method that has a parameter that indicates which fetch joins to use. Consequently, you will encounter the same issues with optimizing an EJB 3 application as you will with a Hibernate application.

Limitations of automatic detachment

Detached objects are another important EJB 3 feature. But the lack of a declarative fetch group mechanism in EJB 3 can make it difficult to detach the necessary objects. In EJB 3, the EJB container automatically detaches all objects that were loaded by the application. Unlike JDO, an application cannot use fetch groups to specify which objects to detach. If different business methods need to return different object graphs, an EJB 3 application has two options. One option is to use multiple queries with different fetch joins, which compounds the problem with eager loading that we described earlier. Another option is to navigate to each of the required objects, which is tedious and error-prone and embeds the object structure in the application's code. In comparison, a JDO 2.0 application can use fetch groups to declaratively specify which objects to return.

Dependency injection can only inject JNDI objects into EJBs

A façade, which is typically implemented as a session or message-driven bean, usually depends on one or more other components, which in turn depend on other components. For example, the `PlaceOrderFacade` depends on components such as the `PlaceOrderService` and the `RestaurantRepository`. Ideally, we should be able to use EJB dependency injection to wire all of these components together. However, one of its big limitations is that it can only inject JNDI objects into EJBs. It will not wire together POJOs such as domain services and repositories and inject their dependencies. Later in this chapter we describe how to solve this problem. It is disappointing, however, that EJB 3 does not support dependency injection of POJOs or provide some kind of integration with a lightweight framework container such as Spring.

Session and message-driven beans must be deployed

Apart from the limitations described earlier, EJB 3 entity beans are fairly easy to use: develop your POJOs and annotate them. However, session and message-driven beans are different beasts entirely. Even though they are POJOs, you must deploy them in the EJB container, which slows down the edit-compile-debug cycle. Furthermore, unless they have a remote interface you must implement the tests using Cactus [Cactus] and deploy them in the application server as well, which is an added source of complexity. In comparison, executing tests in a Spring-based application is convenient and fast.

Development environment complexity

Another drawback of developing with EJB 3 is that you must deal with the added complexity of incorporating a full-blown application server in your development environment even if your application does not use other parts of the J2EE stack such as JMS. EJB 3 shields you from some of the complexity, but it is still there, lurking beneath the surface.

As you can see, even though EJB 3 is definitely much easier to use than EJB 2, it still has some significant limitations. Let's now look at how to use EJB 3 to implement an application. In the next section you will learn how to persist a domain model with EJB 3. After that we describe the different ways to implement a façade in an EJB 3 application.

10.2 Implementing a domain model with EJB 3

In this section you will learn how to use EJB 3 to persist a domain model. We use the domain model for the Place Order use case that was developed in chapter 7 as an example. Figure 10.2 shows the domain model classes that we will be discussing.

You will learn how to define the O/R mapping for the domain model entities, such as `PendingOrder` and `Coupon`. We explain how to implement the `EJB3RestaurantRepository`, and also briefly describe how to write tests for EJB 3 entity beans. You will see examples of how the limitations we discussed earlier in section 10.1.2 can impact the design of even a simple domain model.

10.2.1 Mapping the classes to the database

Let's look at some example classes that show how to configure entities beans and define their O/R mapping. You will see that some aspects of persisting a POJO domain model using EJB 3 are straightforward. You just have to annotate the

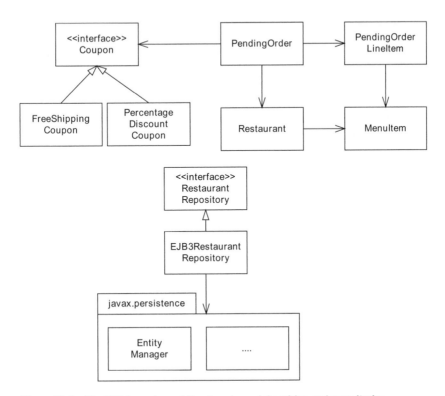

Figure 10.2   The EJB 3 versions of the domain model entities and repositories

POJOs to configure the entity beans and define their O/R mapping. However, the limitations we saw earlier make it more difficult than it should be.

Implementing the PendingOrder entity bean

The first class we'll look at is the PendingOrder class. This class is interesting because it uses several ORM features. It has simple fields, embedded objects, an ordered unidirectional one-to-many-relationship, and two many-to-one relationships, including a polymorphic reference. As you learned in chapters 5 and 6, persisting this class with Hibernate and JDO is very straightforward. So what about when using EJB 3?

It turns out that persisting this class with EJB 3 is not as easy. We can easily map most fields and relationships to the database, but EJB 3 does not make it easy to persist the line items. The two main challenges are how to preserve the ordering of the lineItems collection, which is of type List<PendingOrderLineItem>, and how to delete a line item when it is removed from the lineItems collection. If we stayed within the EJB 3 standard the PendingOrder class, we would have to write extra code to maintain an index field in PendingOrderLineItem and to explicitly delete line items when they are removed from the collection.

The other option is to use the vendor-specific extensions we saw in section 10.1.2. We can use the JBoss-specific @OrderColumn extension to tell JBoss to automatically maintain the index of each line item. We can also use the Cascade-Type.DELETE_ORPHAN extension to specify that a line item should be automatically deleted when it is removed from the lineItems collection. Using these annotations couples the code to the JBoss EJB 3 implementation, but it's better that writing extra code. Listing 10.1 shows part of the source code for the PendingOrder class.

Listing 10.1   PendingOrder entity bean

```
@Entity(access = AccessType.FIELD)              ❶ Defines mapping for class
@Table(name = "PENDING_ORDER")
public class PendingOrder implements Serializable {

    @Id(generate = GeneratorType.AUTO)       ◁──────❷ Configures
    private int id;                                    primary key field

    private int state = PendingOrder.NEW;

    @Column(name="DELIVERY_TIME")     ◁──────❸ Maps deliveryTime field
    private Date deliveryTime;

    @ManyToOne                                  ❹ Maps restaurant field
    @JoinColumn(name = "RESTAURANT_ID")
    private Restaurant restaurant;

    @OneToMany(cascade = { CascadeType.ALL })  ◁──────❺ Maps lineItems
    @JoinColumn(name = "PENDING_ORDER_ID")
    @org.hibernate.annotations.IndexColumn
        ➥ (name="MENU_ITEM_INDEX")
    @org.hibernate.annotations.Cascade(
    ➥ org.hibernate.annotations.CascadeType.DELETE_ORPHAN)
    private List<PendingOrderLineItem>
        lineItems = new ArrayList<PendingOrderLineItem>();

    @ManyToOne(cascade=CascadeType.PERSIST,      ❻ Maps coupon
        targetEntity=AbstractCouponImpl.class)
    @JoinColumn(name = "COUPON_ID")
    private Coupon coupon;
                              ❼ Maps deliveryAddress,
    @Embedded( {          ◁────┘   paymentInformation
      @AttributeOverride(name = "street1",
          column = { @Column(name = "DELIVERY_STREET1") }),
      @AttributeOverride(name = "street2",
```

```
                column = { @Column(name = "DELIVERY_STREET2") }),
          @AttributeOverride(name = "city",
                column = @Column(name = "DELIVERY_CITY")),
          @AttributeOverride(name = "state",
                column = @Column(name = "DELIVERY_STATE")),
          @AttributeOverride(name = "zip",
                column = @Column(name = "DELIVERY_ZIP")) })
    private Address deliveryAddress;

    @Embedded( {
          @AttributeOverride(name = "type",
                column = { @Column(name = "PAYMENT_TYPE") }),
          @AttributeOverride(name = "name",
                column = { @Column(name = "PAYMENT_NAME") }),
          @AttributeOverride(name = "number",
                column = @Column(name = "PAYMENT_NUMBER")),
          @AttributeOverride(name = "month",
                column = @Column(name = "PAYMENT_MONTH")),
          @AttributeOverride(name = "year",
                column = @Column(name = "PAYMENT_YEAR")) })
    private PaymentInformation paymentInformation;
...

    public void updateQuantities(int[] quantities) {
      List<MenuItem> menuItems = restaurant.getMenuItems();

      lineItems.clear();

      Iterator it = menuItems.iterator();
      int index = 0;
      for (int i = 0; i < quantities.length; i++) {
        int quantity = quantities[i];
        MenuItem menuItem = (MenuItem) it.next();
        if (quantity > 0) {
        lineItems
          .add(new PendingOrderLineItem(
          quantity, menuItem));
        }

      }

      setState(meetsMinimumOrder() ? PendingOrder.READY_FOR_CHECKOUT
        : PendingOrder.RESTAURANT_SELECTED);
      }
...
}
```

Let's look at the details:

❶ @Entity annotation specifies that PendingOrder is an entity bean and the access = AccessType.FIELD member specifies that its fields are mapped

❷ The @Id annotation specifies that the id field stores the primary key and that the EJB container should pick the most appropriate primary key generation mechanism for the database.

❸ The @Column annotation for the deliveryTime field specifies that it maps to the DELIVERY_TIME column.

❹ The restaurant field has an @ManyToOne annotation, which specifies that the relationship is many-to-one, and an @JoinColumn, which specifies that the foreign key column in the PENDING_ORDER table is called RESTAURANT_ID.

❺ The lineItems field has two standard annotations: an @OneToMany annotation, which specifies that the relationship is one-to-many, and an @JoinColumn attribute, which specifies that the foreign key in the PENDING_ORDER_LINE_ITEM table is called PENDING_ORDER_ID. It also has two JBoss extensions: @IndexColumn, which automatically maintains the index, and @Cascade, which automatically deletes orphaned children.

❻ The coupon field has an @ManyToOne annotation that specifies that the field is really a reference to an AbstractCouponImpl. You'll learn why in a moment.

❼ The @Embedded and @AttributeOverride annotations for the deliveryAddress and paymentInformation fields define the O/R mapping for the fields of the embedded objects.

Implementing the Restaurant entity bean

The Restaurant class is the next class we are going to examine. We must solve two issues in order to persist this class with EJB 3. The first is how to persist Restaurant.serviceArea, which is of type Set<String> and is not supported by EJB 3. To persist this field we must change the serviceArea field to Set<ZipCode> and define a ZipCode entity, which is a wrapper around a String.

The second problem we must address is how to preserve the ordering of the menuItem field, which is a List<MenuItem>. As with the PendingOrder.lineItem field we have two options. We can either add an index field to the MenuItem class or we can use a vendor-specific extension. Once again I'm going to use the JBoss extensions to avoid writing extra code.

Here is part of the code for the Restaurant class:

```
@Entity (access=AccessType.FIELD)
@Table(name="RESTAURANT")
public class Restaurant  implements Serializable {
  @Id(generate = GeneratorType.AUTO)
  private int id;

  private String name;

  @OneToMany(cascade = CascadeType.ALL,          ◁─────── Maps
            fetch = FetchType.LAZY)                        menuItems
  @JoinColumn(name = "RESTAURANT_ID")
  @org.hibernate.annotations.IndexColumn(name="MENU_ITEM_INDEX")
  private List<MenuItem> menuItems;
                                      Maps serviceArea
  @ManyToMany                  ◁────────┘
  private Set<ZipCode> serviceArea;
                                            Finds
                                            ZipCode entity
  public boolean isInServiceArea(Address   ◁──────┘
                              ⇝ address) {
    for (Iterator it = serviceArea.iterator(); it.hasNext();) {
      ZipCode zipCode = (ZipCode) it.next();
      if (zipCode.getZipCode().equals(address.getZip()))
        return true;
      }
      return false;
  }
```

The menuItems field is a collection of MenuItem objects and is mapped using the @OneToMany annotation. The serviceField is a set of ZipCode entity beans instead of a set of strings, and the isInServiceArea() method looks for a ZipCode entity bean for the specified zipCode. As you can see, this change impacts this class's constructor and the isInServiceArea() method. It also affects the classes that create restaurants.

We must also define the ZipCode entity bean, which wraps the ZIP code:

```
@Entity (access=AccessType.FIELD)
public class ZipCode implements Serializable {

  @Id
  public String zipCode;
  ZipCode() {
  }

  public ZipCode(String zipCode) {
  this.zipCode = zipCode;
  }


  public String getZipCode() {
```

```
       return zipCode;
     }
}
```

It consists of a single `zipCode` field, which is the primary key field. Defining this kind of entity bean to wrap a primitive value is a pretty simple change, but it's a shame that it's necessary. You might be used to doing it when developing with EJB 2, but if you have been using JDO or Hibernate it's an annoying change to make.

Implementing the Coupon entity bean

The final set of types we'll show how to persist is the `Coupon` class hierarchy, which consists of the `Coupon` interface and the concrete subclasses that implement various discount strategies. One of the great features of EJB 3 is that, unlike EJB 2, it supports inheritance. This means that in order to map the `Coupon` class hierarchy to the COUPON table, we must simply introduce an abstract superclass—the same change we made with Hibernate and JDO. This class implements the `Coupon` interface and is extended by the concrete classes such as `FreeShippingCoupon` and `PercentageDiscountCoupon`:

```
@Entity(access = AccessType.FIELD)
@Table(name = "COUPON")
@Inheritance(strategy = InheritanceType.SINGLE_TABLE,
             discriminatorType = DiscriminatorType.STRING)
@DiscriminatorColumn(name = "COUPON_TYPE")
public abstract class AbstractCouponImpl implements Coupon {

  @Id(generate = GeneratorType.AUTO)
  private int id = -1;

  private String code;

  protected AbstractCouponImpl() {

  }

  protected AbstractCouponImpl(String code) {
  this.code = code;
  }

  public String getCode() {
    return code;
  }

  public int getId() {
    return id;
  }
}
```

The @Inheritance annotation defines the inheritance strategy for the Coupon class hierarchy and specifies that the discriminator column, which identifies the type of the instance, stores strings. The @DiscriminatorColumn annotation specifies that the COUPON_TYPE column stores the type of the coupon.

Here is the FreeShippingCoupon class, which now extends AbstractCouponImpl rather than implementing Coupon:

```
@Entity (access=AccessType.FIELD)
@Inheritance(strategy=InheritanceType.SINGLE_TABLE,
   discriminatorValue="FREE_SHIP")
public class FreeShippingCoupon extends Coupon {

   private double minimum;

   public FreeShippingCoupon() {
   }

   public FreeShippingCoupon(String code, double minimum) {
        super(code);
        this.minimum = minimum;
     }

}
```

The discriminatorValue member of the @Inheritance annotation specifies that the value of "FREE_SHIP" in the COUPON_TYPE column indicates that the row represents a FreeShippingCoupon. The other subclasses of Coupon are annotated in a similar way.

Fields such as PendingOrder.coupon, which reference a Coupon, must be annotated with an @ManyToOne annotation that specifies the referenced class as AbstractCouponImpl:

```
Class PendingOrder {
...
   @ManyToOne(cascade = CascadeType.PERSIST,
      targetEntity = AbstractCouponImpl.class)
   @JoinColumn(name = "coupon_id")
   private Coupon coupon;
...
}
```

The targetEntity member specifies that the coupon field is really a reference to an AbstractCouponImpl.

As you can see, entity beans are POJOs, but the limitations of the EJB 3 O/R mapping requires some changes to the domain model and/or the use of vendor-specific extensions. Table 10.1 summarizes these issues.

Table 10.1 Summary of the issues when using EJB 3 to persist the Food to Go domain model

Class	Issue
PendingOrder.lineItems Restaurant.menuItems	Either: Add an index column to the `element` class. Use a JBoss-specific annotation.
Restaurant.serviceArea	Replace the `Set<String>` with a `Set<ZipCode>`.
Coupon class hierarchy	Introduce an `AbstractCouponImpl` superclass.

Each modification is small, but lots of little changes like these accumulate and introduce unnecessary complexity into the domain model. We must also decide between using vendor extensions and making even more changes. Using vendor extensions is appealing because it can reduce the amount of code that must be written. The downside of using them is that the code is no longer portable between EJB 3 implementations. This can sometimes be a difficult decision to make.

As well as defining the O/R mapping for a domain model, we must develop the repositories, which define methods for creating, finding, and deleting persistent objects. The next section shows you how.

10.2.2 Implementing repositories

In an EJB 3 application, the repositories use the `EntityManager` and `Query` interfaces to access the database. For example, listing 10.2 shows the EJB 3 implementation of the `RestaurantRepository`, which find restaurants using these interfaces. It has a `findRestaurant()` method, which loads a single restaurant, and a `findAvailableRestaurants()` method, which finds all restaurants that serve the specified delivery address and time.

Listing 10.2 EJB3RestaurantRepository

```
public class EJB3RestaurantRepository implements
  RestaurantRepository {

  private EntityManager entityManager;

  public EJB3RestaurantRepository(
    EntityManager entityManager) {
      this.entityManager = entityManager;    <——— Saves EntityManager

  }

  public Restaurant findRestaurant(
```

```
      String restaurantId) {
      return entityManager.find(Restaurant.class,        Finds the Restaurant
                                new Integer(restaurantId));
  }

  public List findAvailableRestaurants(        Executes named query
     Address deliveryAddress, Date deliveryTime) {
     Query query = entityManager
       .createNamedQuery("Restaurant.findAvailableRestaurants");
     Calendar c = Calendar.getInstance();
     c.setTime(deliveryTime);
     int dayOfWeek = c.get(Calendar.DAY_OF_WEEK);
     int hour = c.get(Calendar.HOUR_OF_DAY);
     int minute = c.get(Calendar.MINUTE);
     String zipCode = deliveryAddress.getZip();

     query.setParameter("dayOfWeek", new Integer(
       dayOfWeek));
     query.setParameter("hour", new Integer(hour));
     query.setParameter("minute", new Integer(
       minute));
     query.setParameter("zipCode", new Integer(
       zipCode));
     return query.getResultList();

  }

  public boolean isRestaurantAvailable(
     Address deliveryAddress, Date deliveryDate) {
     return !findAvailableRestaurants(
       deliveryAddress, deliveryDate)
       .isEmpty();
  }

}
```

In listing 10.2, the constructor takes the EntityManager as a parameter and stores it in a field. The findRestaurant() method then calls EntityManager.find() to retrieve the specified restaurant. Finally, the findAvailableRestaurants() method uses the EntityManager to execute a named query that finds the available restaurants.

Note that as of the time of this writing, Spring does not yet support EJB 3 and so this repository uses the EJB 3 APIs directly rather than using a Spring ORM template class. It also throws EJB exceptions instead of Spring data access exceptions. Once Spring has an EJB 3 ORM template class, we will be able to simplify the code, which will make it a little easier to test, and use Spring's exception mapping mechanism, which will enable the application to handle data access exceptions uniformly.

The named EJB QL query that is executed by the `EJB3RestaurantRepository` is defined using the `@NamedQuery` annotation of the `Restaurant` entity bean:

```
@Entity(access = AccessType.FIELD)
@NamedQuery(name = "Restaurant.findAvailableRestaurants",
            queryString = "SELECT OBJECT(restaurant) "
  + "FROM  Restaurant as restaurant, "
  + "   IN(restaurant.serviceArea) zip, "
  + "    IN(restaurant.timeRanges) tr "
  + "WHERE zip.zipCode = :zipCode AND tr.dayOfWeek = :dayOfWeek "
  + "   AND (   (tr.openHour < :hour "
  + "     OR (tr.openHour = :hour AND tr.openMinute <= :minute))"
  + "   AND (tr.closeHour > :hour "
  + "     OR (tr.closeHour = :hour AND tr.closeMinute > :minute)
  + "))")
@Table(name = "FTGO_RESTAURANT")
public class Restaurant implements Serializable {
  ...
}
```

This query is pretty similar to the HQL and JDOQL queries you saw earlier in chapters 5 and 6. It finds those restaurants whose `serviceArea` contains a `ZipCode` for the specified for ZIP code and whose `timeRanges` field contains a `TimeRange` for the specified day, hour, and minute. It is interesting to see that the long queries defined in using the `@NamedQuery` annotation have the same readability problems as queries defined in Java code. They must be split up into multiple strings that are concatenated together. In comparison, it's much easier to write a long query in an XML document.

Next let's consider the issue of testing entity beans.

10.2.3 *Testing the persistent EJB domain model*

Naturally, a discussion of EJB 3 persistence would not be complete without a mention of testing. Testing EJB 2 entity beans was quite difficult because they had to be deployed in the EJB container. What's worse, the tests also needed to be deployed in the application server so that they could access the entity beans using their local interface. As well as making testing more complicated, the deployment step slowed down the edit-compile-debug cycle. In comparison, testing an EJB 3 domain model is straightforward because EJB 3 entity beans can run outside the container. We can write and execute persistence tests for persistent objects and repositories in the same way that did in a JDO or Hibernate application. They are regular JUnit-based tests that are easily run from within the IDE.

Listing 10.3 shows an example of such a test. This test creates a `PendingOrder` entity bean and updates its delivery information. The test class has a `setup()`

method that creates the JBoss/Hibernate implementation of an `EntityManager-Factory` and a `tearDown()` method that closes it. Like the JDO and Hibernate tests you have seen earlier, this test uses a `doInTransaction()` method to execute code within a transaction. This method opens an `EntityManager`, begins a transaction, executes the callback, commits the transaction, and closes the `EntityManager`.

Listing 10.3 EJB3PendingOrderPersistenceTests

```
public class EJB3PendingOrderPersistenceTests extends
  TestCase {

  private EntityManager em;
  private EntityTransaction transaction;
  private EntityManagerFactory emf;
  private String poId;

  protected void setUp() throws Exception {
    super.setUp();
    Properties props = new Properties();

    props.setProperty(          ◁────────❶ Specifies persistence provider
    Persistence.PERSISTENCE_PROVIDER,
    HibernatePersistence.class.getName());

    emf = Persistence   ◁────────❷ Creates EntityManagerFactory
      .createEntityManagerFactory(props);
  }

  protected void tearDown() throws Exception {
    super.tearDown();
    if (emf != null)   ◁────────❸ Closes EntityManagerFactory
    emf.close();
  }

  protected void doWithTransaction(TxnCallback cb)
    throws Throwable {

    em = emf   ◁────────❹ Creates EntityManager
      .createEntityManager(PersistenceContextType.EXTENDED);

    transaction = em.getTransaction();        ❺ Begins
    try {                                        transaction
      transaction.begin();

      cb.execute();   ◁────────❻ Executes
                                  callback

      transaction.commit();                   ❼ Commits or rolls back
    } finally {                                  the transaction
      if (transaction != null
        && transaction.isActive())
```

```
          transaction.rollback();

          if (em != null)        ⑧ Closes
          em.close();              the EntityManager
      }

  }

  public void test() throws Throwable {

      doWithTransaction(new TxnCallback() {

          public void execute() throws Exception {

          PendingOrder po = new PendingOrder();   ◁——— ⑨ Creates and persists
          em.persist(po);                                 PendingOrder

          poId = po.getId();
          }
      });

  doWithTransaction(new TxnCallback() {

      public void execute() throws Exception {

      RestaurantRepository rr = new EJB3RestaurantRepository(em);
      Class<PendingOrder> type = PendingOrder.class;
      PendingOrder po = em.find(type, poId);
      assertEquals(
        PlaceOrderStatusCodes.OK,
        po.updateDeliveryInfo(   ◁——— ⑩ Updates PendingOrder's
            rr,                          delivery info
            RestaurantTestData
              .getADDRESS1(),
            RestaurantTestData
              .makeGoodDeliveryTime(),
            false));

      }
  })
  }

}
```

Let's look at the details:

❶ The `setUp()` method creates a `Properties` object that specifies the EJB 3 persistence provider.

❷ It creates the `EntityManagerFactory`.

❸ The `teardown()` method closes the `EntityManagerFactory`.

❹ The `doWithTransaction()` method that executes a callback within a transaction first creates an `EntityManager`.

❺ It then begins a transaction.

❻ The method then executes the callback.

❼ If the callback returns, then `doWithTransaction()` commits the transaction. The `finally` clause roll backs the transaction if it has not been committed.

❽ The `doWithTransaction()` method closes the `EntityManager`.

❾ The test first creates and persists a `PendingOrder`.

❿ It then loads the `PendingOrder` and updates its delivery information.

Once we have persisted the domain model, the next step in the process of implementing the business logic is to encapsulate the domain model with a façade. Let's see how to do this in an EJB 3 application.

10.3 *Implementing a façade with EJB 3*

As we saw in chapter 7, a façade handles requests from the presentation tier by calling the domain model and is responsible for managing transactions. It also detaches the objects that are returned to the presentation tier. One way to implement a façade with EJB 3 is to use a POJO façade and Spring transaction management. I'm not going to describe how to do this because as of the time of this writing Spring doesn't support EJB 3. You would have to write your own interceptors to manage the `EntityManager` and control transactions. However, I expect that by the time you are reading this that the Spring framework will have full support for EJB 3 and you will be able to configure the Spring `TransactionInterceptor` with a `PlatformTransactionManager` that uses the EJB 3 `EntityTransaction` interface to manage transactions.

The other way to implement a façade using EJB 3 is to use a session bean. EJB 3 session beans are certainly a heavyweight approach because they must still be deployed in the EJB container. However, they are certainly worth considering because they are significantly easier to develop than EJB 2 session beans. As you saw earlier in section 10.1, EJB 3 session beans are POJOs instead of classes that implement EJB interfaces. They use dependency injection to obtain their dependencies instead of JNDI. You configure them using simple annotations rather than elaborate deployment descriptors. Moreover, they use transactions, security, and remoting provided by the EJB container, which is extremely convenient.

We use the same techniques that we used in chapter 7 to design a POJO façade to develop an EJB 3 session bean. First, we analyze the UI design to determine the requests that the session bean must handle and the data that it exchanges with the presentation tier. Next, we implement the session bean's methods by calling the domain model classes. Finally, we implement a result factory that detaches the objects required by the presentation tier. The only thing that is different is that the EJB container rather than the Spring framework manages transactions.

We begin this section by describing how to turn the POJO façade such as the one we developed in chapter 7 into an EJB 3 stateless session bean. After that we'll discuss how a façade goes about detaching objects.

10.3.1 *Turning a POJO façade into a session bean*

Turning a POJO façade such as the `PlaceOrderFacade` we developed chapter 7 into an EJB 3 session bean is pretty simple. No code changes are required other than the addition of a public default constructor for use by the EJB container. Apart from that one small change you just have to annotate the façade's interface and implementation class. The interface is annotated with an `@Local` annotation if you want a local interface or `@Remote` annotation if you want a remote interface:

```
@Local
public interface PlaceOrderFacade {
  …
}
```

The implementation class is annotated with the `@Stateless` annotation and has a default constructor:

```
@Stateless
public class PlaceOrderFacadeImpl
  implements PlaceOrderFacade {

  public PlaceOrderFacadeImpl() {
  }
  …
}
```

You can then deploy the bean in the EJB container and all calls to the façade will be transactional. You can also use the EJB container's security mechanism, which provides role-based declarative security. In addition, if the session bean has a remote interface, it can be invoked remotely and participate in distributed transactions.

One drawback, however, of using EJBs is that they are more difficult to test than Spring beans because they must be deployed in the EJB container. For example, in order to test an EJB through its local interface you would have to implement the tests using Cactus [Cactus] and deploy them in the application server as well. In addition, deployment is, as we've mentioned earlier, an extra step that can slow down the edit-compile-debug cycle. In comparison, you don't have jump through these kinds of hoops to test Spring beans.

10.3.2 *Detaching objects*

In addition to managing transactions, a façade is responsible for detaching persistent objects so that they can be used by the presentation tier. EJB 3, like Hibernate, automatically detaches all objects that were loaded during the transaction, and so the façade must simply ensure that all of the objects required by the presentation tier are loaded. Sometimes, the domain model services and repositories called by the façade will load the required objects. However, because of lazy loading those domain model classes often return an incomplete object graph and so a façade must sometimes force objects to be loaded.

A Hibernate application can force an object or collection to be loaded by calling `Hibernate.initialize()`. However, the EJB 3 `EntityManager` does not define the equivalent of `Hibernate.initialize()`, which means the application must traverse the object graph and touch the required objects and collections. As with the POJO façade we saw in chapter 7, we can encapsulate this logic inside a result factory class that loads the required objects and creates the DTO that is returned by the façade.

For example, `PlaceOrderFacade` can use the implementation of the `PlaceOrderFacadeResultFactory` interface shown in listing 10.4 to do this. `EJB3PlaceOrderFacadeResultFactory` ensures that the `PendingOrder`'s line items and restaurant are loaded before creating the `PlaceOrderFacadeResult`.

Listing 10.4 EJB3PlaceOrderFacadeResultFactory

```
public class EJB3PlaceOrderFacadeResultFactory
    implements PlaceOrderFacadeResultFactory {

  public EJB3PlaceOrderFacadeResultFactory() {

  }
```

```
public PlaceOrderFacadeResult make(int statusCode,
  PendingOrder pendingOrder, List restaurants) {
  initializePendingOrder(pendingOrder);
  return new PlaceOrderFacadeResult(statusCode,
                                    pendingOrder, restaurants);
}

public PlaceOrderFacadeResult make(int statusCode,
  PendingOrder pendingOrder) {
  initializePendingOrder(pendingOrder);
  return new PlaceOrderFacadeResult(statusCode,
                                    pendingOrder);
}

private void initializePendingOrder(
  PendingOrder pendingOrder) {
  Restaurant restaurant = pendingOrder
        .getRestaurant();
  if (restaurant != null) {
    MenuItem menuItem = restaurant
      .getMenuItems().get(0);
    menuItem.getName();
  }
  List<PendingOrderLineItem> lineItems = pendingOrder
    .getLineItems();
  if (lineItems != null && !lineItems.isEmpty()) {
    lineItems.get(0);
  }
}
}
```

The make() methods call initializePendingOrder(), which touches the pending order's line items and the restaurant's menu items to ensure that they are loaded. It does not need to touch each line item's menu item because many-to-one relationships are eagerly loaded by default. As with the Hibernate version, this code contains potentially error-prone conditional logic to handle null references and empty collections.

A result factory is just one of the several components that a façade typically needs to fulfill its responsibilities. Let's now look at how to assemble the façade and those components.

10.4 *Assembling the components*

A façade uses several components, including the result factory, the domain services, and repositories. These components can in turn reference other components as well as infrastructure objects such as the EntityManager. For example, the PlaceOrderFacade directly and indirectly requires the components shown in figure 10.3.

The PlaceOrderFacade requires the PlaceOrderService, RestaurantRepository, and the PlaceOrderResultFactory. The PlaceOrderService requires repositories such as the PendingOrderRepository and the RestaurantRepository. The repositories must be configured with the EntityManager.

At runtime, the application must instantiate these components and wire them together. So far, the examples in this book do this using a Spring bean factory. The bean factory uses dependency injection to wire the components together. Each component is passed the components that it needs as either constructor arguments or setter method arguments. Dependency injection is valuable because it eliminates code that looks up dependencies and thus reduces the coupling between components.

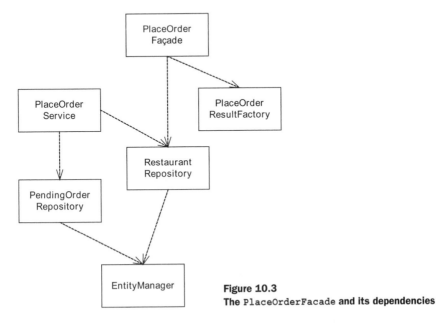

Figure 10.3
The PlaceOrderFacade **and its dependencies**

In an EJB 3 application, there are three ways to use dependency injection. One option is to use EJB 3 dependency injection to wire the components together. The second is to integrate the Spring and EJB dependency injection mechanisms. The third is to only use Spring dependency injection. Let's look at how to use each of these approaches.

10.4.1 Using EJB dependency injection

One of the exciting new features of EJB 3 is dependency injection, which is an easy-to-use mechanism that enables a session or message-driven bean to acquire references to other EJBs and resources without explicit coding. It uses annotations on fields and setters that specify the objects to inject. When the container instantiates a session or message-driven bean, it will initialize the fields and call the setters with the specified objects. However, as you learned in section 10.1.2, a significant limitation of EJB 3 is that the dependencies must be looked up via JNDI and can only be injected into session and message-driven EJBs.

Application components must be EJBs

To use EJB 3 dependency injection to wire together a façade and its components, the components must be available through JNDI lookup. Moreover, if those components use dependency injection, then they must also be EJBs. The simplest approach is to implement the façade's components as stateless session beans. For example, to configure the `PlaceOrderFacade` using EJB dependency injection, all of the classes shown earlier in figure 10.3 must be implemented as session beans.

Fortunately, it is easy to turn POJOs such as domain services and repositories into session beans. As you saw earlier, you just need to annotate the interface with `@Local` and the implementation class with `@Stateless`. However, for this to be practical the overhead of one session bean calling another via a local interface must be low. In addition, the development environment and the EJB container must be able to handle the increased number of EJBs without significantly increasing the deployment time.

Let's now look at the annotations we must use to configure the `PlaceOrder-Facade` and its components.

Annotating a POJO façade

To initialize a POJO façade using dependency injection, we must annotate each field that references an EJB with an `@EJB` annotation in order to tell the EJB container to inject an EJB. Here is an excerpt from the `PlaceOrderFacade` that shows how to do this:

```
@Stateless
public class PlaceOrderFacadeImpl
  implements PlaceOrderFacade {
  @EJB
  private RestaurantRepository restaurantRepository;

  @EJB
  private PlaceOrderFacadeResultFactory resultFactory;

  @EJB
  private PlaceOrderService service;

  public PlaceOrderFacadeImpl() {
  }

  public PlaceOrderFacadeImpl(
    RestaurantRepository restaurantRepository,
    PlaceOrderService service,
    PlaceOrderFacadeResultFactory resultFactory) {
  this.restaurantRepository = restaurantRepository;
  this.service = service;
  this.resultFactory = resultFactory;
  }
...
```

The `restaurantRepository`, `resultFactory`, and `service` fields have an `@EJB` annotation that tells the EJB container to initialize the field with the referenced session bean. Note that even though the EJB container initializes the fields using dependency injection, the bean class must still have a constructor for use by the mock object tests, which cannot access the private fields. As you can see, `PlaceOrder-FacadeImpl` has a constructor that takes the `RestaurantRepository`, `PlaceOrder-ResultFactory`, and `PlaceOrderService` as parameters and initializes the fields.

Annotating the domain service

The `PlaceOrderService`, which is the domain service called by the `PlaceOrder-Facade`, is configured as a session bean using the `@Local` and `@Stateless` annotations. Here is the bean class:

```
@Stateless
public class PlaceOrderServiceImpl implements
  PlaceOrderService {

  @EJB
  private PendingOrderRepository pendingOrderRepository;

  @EJB
  private RestaurantRepository restaurantRepository;

  public PlaceOrderServiceImpl() {
```

```
    }

    public PlaceOrderServiceImpl(
        PendingOrderRepository pendingOrderRepository,
        RestaurantRepository restaurantRepository) {
        this.pendingOrderRepository = pendingOrderRepository;
        this.restaurantRepository = restaurantRepository;
    }
```

The `restaurantRepository` and `pendingOrderRepository` fields have an `@EJB` annotation that tells the EJB container to initialize them. Like the `PlaceOrderFacade`, the `PlaceOrderService` has two constructors: a default constructor for the EJB container to use and another for the mock object tests.

Annotating the repositories

The repositories are also configured as stateless session beans. They are injected with the `EntityManager`. Here is the bean class for the `PendingOrderRepository`:

```
@Stateless
public class EJB3PendingOrderRepository implements
    PendingOrderRepository {

    @PersistenceContext
    private EntityManager entityManager;

    public EJB3PendingOrderRepository() {
    }

    public EJB3PendingOrderRepository(EntityManager entityManager) {
        this.entityManager = entityManager;
    }
```

The `entityManager` field has an `@PersistenceContext` annotation that tells the EJB container to initialize the field with a reference to the `EntityManager`. The other repositories are annotated in a similar fashion. Once we have made these changes, the EJB container will wire together the `PlaceOrderFacade` and its components and configure the repositories with the `EntityManager`.

EJB 3 dependency injection is certainly a simple yet effective mechanism for wiring together components that are implemented as EJBs. Unfortunately, it might not make sense or even be possible to implement all of the components as session beans. Let's look at how to inject POJOs into session beans.

10.4.2 Integrating Spring and EJB dependency injection

The Spring framework has a very powerful dependency injection mechanism. Spring beans are arbitrary POJOs and can be injected with other Spring beans as well as arbitrary values such as strings and integers. There are also other useful features, such as its support for AOP. In comparison, EJB 3 dependency injection is a convenient way for EJBs to access JNDI objects but lacks many of those features provided by Spring dependency injection. Ideally, we should be able to use the two dependency mechanisms together and leverage each of their strengths.

The good news is that there is a way to integrate Spring and EJB 3 dependency injection. We can use Spring's bean factory mechanism to create and wire together POJOs and use EJB 3 dependency injection to inject the POJOs into EJBs. Not only does this let EJB 3 applications take advantage of Spring's dependency injection, but it can also make it easier to incorporate existing Spring code.

We need to do three things to integrate Spring and EJB dependency injection:

1   Expose Spring beans via JNDI when the application is initialized.

2   Annotate the session bean class to bind a JNDI name to the `EntityManager` and annotate its fields to inject the POJOs using JNDI.

3   Configure a Spring `JndiObjectFactoryBean` to look up the `EntityManager` via JNDI so that it can be injected into the repositories.

Let's see how to do approach this task using the `PlaceOrderFacade` EJB as an example. You will learn how to use Spring to create POJOs such as `PlaceOrderService` and `RestaurantRepository` and to then inject them into the `PlaceOrderFacade` EJB. Note that this section describes some aspects of JNDI that you might be unfamiliar with; I had certainly never used these particular JNDI APIs until I tried to do this integration. Please bear with me as I describe all the different pieces.

Exposing Spring beans via JNDI

As you saw in section 10.1, EJB dependency injection is based on JNDI; therefore, if you want to inject a Spring bean into an EJB it must be accessible via JNDI. We can do this by binding a name in the JNDI tree to a JNDI `Reference`. A JNDI `Reference` is an object that tells the JNDI implementation how to find an object that exists outside of JNDI. As figure 10.4 shows, in this particular case the `Reference` acts as a bridge between the EJB container and the Spring bean factory.

To expose a Spring bean via JNDI, we would create a `Reference` that contains the name and type of a Spring bean and the name of a JNDI `ObjectFactory` class that calls Spring to get the bean. When the EJB container does a JNDI lookup, it will find the `Reference` and call the `ObjectFactory` to create the object. The `ObjectFactory` will get the Spring bean by calling `BeanFactory.getBean()`.

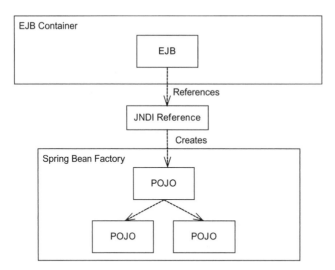

Figure 10.4   Using a JNDI Reference **to a Spring bean**

Here is an example of some code that stores a reference to the PlaceOrderService Spring bean in the JNDI tree:

```
Context ctx = new InitialContext();
Reference reference = new Reference(
    PlaceOrderService.class.getName(),
    new StringRefAddr("beanName", "PlaceOrderService"),
    SpringObjectFactory.class.getName(),
    null);
ctx.bind("PlaceOrderService", reference);
```

This code fragment instantiates a Reference that contains the name of the Place-OrderService class, the name of the Spring bean, and the fully qualified class name of the SpringObjectFactory, which is a JNDI object factory that calls Bean-Factory.getBean(). It then binds the name "PlaceOrderService" to the reference in the JNDI tree.

When the JNDI implementation encounters this reference during a lookup, it calls SpringObjectFactory to create the object. This class defines a getObject-Instance() method that creates a Spring bean by calling a Spring bean factory:

```
public class SpringObjectFactory implements
  ObjectFactory {

  public Object getObjectInstance(Object reference,
    Name name, Context nameCtx,
    Hashtable<?, ?> environment)
```

```
      throws Exception {
    String beanName = (String) ((Reference) reference)
      .get(0).getContent();
    return TheBeanFactory.getBean(beanName,
      Object.class);
    }

  }
```

The `getObjectInstance()` method is called by the JNDI implementation when the EJB container looks up the bean. It gets the bean name from the `Reference` parameter and calls the Spring bean factory.

Binding the references to the Spring beans

One tricky implementation issue is how and when to bind the references to the Spring beans into the JNDI tree. I've rarely had to explicitly call JNDI to bind names to objects because it has always been done automatically by the EJB container when deploying an EJB or by the application server when creating objects such as a JDBC `DataSource`. However, to expose Spring beans via JNDI you must write some initialization code that binds the references.

I originally thought that this could be done by a startup servlet, which is an easy-to-use and portable way to execute initialization code. However, it turns out that some application servers such as JBoss require the JNDI names referenced by an EJB to be bound before the EJB is deployed. This is because when the EJB container deploys an EJB it looks up the JNDI names referenced by the dependency injection annotations. The deployment will fail if the name is not found. Because servlets are usually loaded after the EJBs, you cannot use one to bind the JNDI references. Instead, you must use an application server-specific mechanism.

For example, JBoss Application Server 4.0 has a feature called a service POJO that can be used to execute initialization code. We won't go into the details of how a service POJO works except to say that it can have a `create()` method that is called by the application server when it is deployed and a `destroy()` method that is called when the service POJO is undeployed. You can write a service POJO that has a `create()` method that binds the references to the Spring beans and a `destroy()` method that unbinds the references. Here is an example of a service POJO class that does just that:

```
@Service
@Local(SpringBeanReferenceInitializerLocal.class)
public class SpringBeanReferenceInitializer implements
  SpringBeanReferenceInitializerLocal,
  SpringBeanReferenceInitializerManagement {
```

```
public void create() throws Exception {
  InitialContext ctx = new InitialContext();
  Reference reference = new Reference(
      PlaceOrderService.class.getName(),
      new StringRefAddr("beanName",
        "PlaceOrderService"),
      SpringObjectFactory.class.getName(),
      null);
  ctx.bind("MyTestSpringBean", reference);
}

public void destroy() throws Exception {
  InitialContext ctx = new InitialContext();
  ctx.unbind("MyTestSpringBean");
}

}
```

In this listing, the `@Service` annotation indicates that `SpringBeanReferenceInitializer` is a service POJO. The `create()` method then creates a `Reference` and binds a name to it, and the `destroy()` method unbinds the reference.

As you can see, initializing the JNDI references when using JBoss requires the definition of a simple POJO service. The only other thing we must do is ensure that the `SpringBeanReferenceInitializer` is created before any of the EJBs that reference the Spring beans. Let's look at how to do this.

Annotating the session bean class

The next step is to annotate the session beans to tell the EJB container to inject the Spring beans. There are three different annotations that we must use:

- `@Resource` is used on each field that references a POJO. It tells the EJB container to inject the object bound to the specified JNDI name.

- `@PersistenceContexts` is used on the bean class to bind a JNDI name to the `EntityManager` so that it can be looked up the Spring `JndiObjectFactoryBean`, as we explain a bit later, and injected into the POJO repositories.

- `@Depends` is a JBoss-specific annotation that is used on the bean class to ensure that the `SpringBeanReferenceInitializer` binds the JNDI references before the EJB is deployed.

Here is an example of a stateless bean class that uses these annotations:

```
@Stateless
@Depends("jboss.j2ee:service=EJB3,type=service,
    name=net.chrisrichardson.foodToGo.ejb3.service.
      SpringBeanReferenceInitializerLocal")
```

```
@PersistenceContexts( {
  ➡ @PersistenceContext(name = "EntityManager") })
public class PlaceOrderFacadeUsingIntegratedDependencyInjectImpl
  implements
  PlaceOrderFacadeUsingIntegratedDependencyInject {

  @Resource(name = "RestaurantRepository")
  private RestaurantRepository restaurantRepository;

  @Resource(name = "PlaceOrderFacadeResultFactory")
  private PlaceOrderFacadeResultFactory resultFactory;

  @Resource(name = "PlaceOrderService")
  private PlaceOrderService service;
  ...
}
```

When the EJB container instantiates the `PlaceOrderFacadeUsingIntegratedDependencyInjectImpl` class, it looks up the JNDI names specified by the `@Resource` annotations and retrieves the POJOs. Because those JNDI names are bound to references, the JNDI implementation will end up calling the Spring bean factory, which will create those POJOs and their dependencies. When the Spring bean factory creates the repositories, it will do a JNDI lookup to retrieve the `EntityManager` that is injected into the repositories. Let's take a look.

Injecting the EntityManager into the repositories
The Spring bean factory must inject the `EntityManager` into the repositories. The `@PersistenceContext` annotation on the session bean class binds a JNDI name to the `EntityManager`, and so we just need to use the Spring `JndiObjectFactoryBean`, which is a Spring `FactoryBean` that looks up a JNDI object. One complication, however, is that the `EntityManager` is not bound when the Spring bean factory is called. This means that we must configure the `JndiObjectFactoryBean` to delay looking up `EntityManager` until the first time the application calls it. This is accomplished by using the `JndiObjectFactoryBean`'s `lookupOnStartup` and `proxyInterface` properties. Here are the bean definitions for the `JndiObjectFactoryBean` and an example repository:

```
<beans>
...
<bean id="EntityManager"
      class="org.springframework.jndi.JndiObjectFactoryBean">
  <property name="jndiName">
    <value>java:comp.ejb3/env/         ⟵——— Specifies JNDI name to look up
      ➡ EntityManager</value>
  </property>
  <property name="lookupOnStartup">    ⟵——— Delays lookup until first access
```

```
      <value>false</value>
    </property>
    <property name="proxyInterface">
      <value>javax.persistence.        ◁────── Specifies object's type
           ➥ EntityManager</value>
    </property>
  </bean>


  <bean id="PendingOrderRepositoryImpl"
     class="net.chrisrichardson.foodToGo.ejb3.domain.
        ➥ EJB3PendingOrderRepository">                         Passes EntityManager
      <constructor-arg ref="EntityManager"/>   ◁──────────┘   to constructor
  </bean>
  ...
  </beans>
```

In this listing, the `JndiObjectFactoryBean`'s `jndiName` specifies the JNDI name of the `EntityManager`. The "java:comp.ejb3/env" portion of the name is JBoss-specific, and the "EntityManager" portion corresponds to the name specified by the `@PersistenceContext` annotation on the session bean class.

Next, the `lookupOnStartup` property tells the `JndiObjectFactoryBean` to delay performing the JNDI lookup until the `EntityManager` is first accessed. Then the `proxyInterface` property specifies the type of the object that will be retrieved. Finally, the `<constructor-arg>` element specifies that the `EntityManager` retrieved from JNDI should be passed as a constructor parameter to the `EJB3PendingOrderRepository`.

That's it! We have gotten through all of gory details of using JDNI and JBoss service POJOs. Once you have annotated the session beans, written the service POJO to bind the references, and configured the Spring beans, the EJB and Spring dependency injections can work side by side. Spring takes care of wiring together arbitrary POJOs with their dependencies, and the EJB container injects the POJOs into the EJBs. The main drawback of this approach is that quite a bit of setup is involved, which is typical of EJBs. Instead of a simple lightweight mechanism that Spring provides, we have to resort to the heavyweight JNDI mechanism. It would be much better if EJB 3 was directly integrated with Spring.

10.4.3 Using Spring dependency injection

The third way to wire together the façade and its dependencies is for the session bean to explicitly call the Spring bean factory, as shown in figure 10.5. With this approach, the façade is the only stateless session bean. The other components, such as the domain services and repositories, are POJOs.

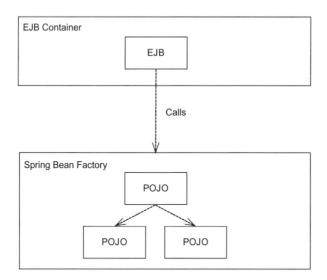

Figure 10.5
Calling the Spring bean
factory directly from an EJB

The façade EJB calls a Spring bean factory, which instantiates the components that it requires and wires them together. Listing 10.5 shows how the `PlaceOrderFacade` EJB can use Spring to construct its dependencies.

Listing 10.5 PlaceOrderFacadeImplUsingSpring

```
@Stateless
public class PlaceOrderFacadeImplUsingSpring
    implements PlaceOrderFacade {
  private RestaurantRepository restaurantRepository;

  private PlaceOrderFacadeResultFactory resultFactory;

  private PlaceOrderService service;

  public PlaceOrderFacadeImplUsingSpring() {
  }

  @PostConstruct
  public void createComponents(
    EntityManager entityManager) {
    this.restaurantRepository =
      (RestaurantRepository) TheBeanFactory
        .getBean("RestaurantRepository",
          RestaurantRepository.class);
    this.resultFactory =
      (PlaceOrderFacadeResultFactory) TheBeanFactory
        .getBean(
          "PlaceOrderFacadeResultFactory",
```

```
                PlaceOrderFacadeResultFactory.class);

        this.service = (PlaceOrderService) TheBeanFactory
          .getBean("PlaceOrderService",
            PlaceOrderService.class);
    }
    ...
```

The `createComponents()` method calls `TheBeanFactory`, which is a helper class that wraps a Spring `BeanFactory`, to create the components that the `PlaceOrderFacade` EJB needs. The `@PostConstruct` annotation specifies that the EJB container must call this method after it has instantiated the EJB. The Spring beans used by the `PlaceOrderFacade` would be configured in the same way as the previous example.

As this example shows, having the session bean call the Spring framework enables the application to use dependency injection with arbitrary objects. The downside is that the EJB must make explicit calls to Spring, which is extra code that must be written and maintained. In addition, the dependency of the EJB on Spring makes it more difficult to test. However, this approach is useful if your application needs to use some functionality that is not provided by the EJB container and that is only available in Spring.

10.5 *Implementing other patterns with EJB 3*

So far in this chapter we have looked at how to use EJB 3 to implement a domain model that is encapsulated by a session façade. There are, of course, other design options, such as the Exposed Domain Model pattern and the Transaction Script pattern. In addition, you must consider other issues when developing the business tier with EJB 3, issues such as database concurrency and efficient database queries.

10.5.1 *Implementing the Exposed Domain Model pattern*

In chapter 8 we described the Exposed Domain Model pattern, in which the presentation tier makes direct calls to the domain model without going through a façade. An application that uses this pattern has a servlet filter that opens and closes the JDO `PersistenceManager` or Hibernate `Session`. Each call to a domain service occurs in a transaction, and when the presentation tier generates the response, it accesses the persistent objects outside of a transaction. This pattern is useful because you don't have to develop a façade or worry about detaching the objects that are required by the presentation tier.

Applications should also be able to able to use this pattern with EJB 3. The servlet filter uses an `EntityManagerFactory` to create an `EntityManager`, and transactions are managed using `EntityTransaction`. Unfortunately, however, at the time of this writing Spring does not yet provide support EJB 3 and so I haven't been able to try it.

10.5.2 *Implementing the Transaction Script pattern*

As you saw in chapter 9, it sometimes makes sense to implement business logic using the Transaction Script pattern instead of the Domain Model pattern. The Transaction Script pattern organizes the business logic as a set of procedural transaction scripts that call DAOs to access the database. The DAOs access the database using either JDBC or a higher level, easier to use API such as Spring's JDBC classes or iBATIS.

There are a couple of ways to implement the transaction scripts in an EJB 3 application. One option is to implement the transaction scripts class and the DAOs as stateless session beans, as shown in figure 10.6. This diagram shows the EJB 3 version of transaction script example from chapter 9.

In this example, `PlaceOrderTransactionScripts`, `PendingOrderDAO`, and `RestaurantDAO` are implemented as stateless session beans. EJB 3 dependency injection is used to wire together these components along with the JDBC `DataSource`.

Using this approach is straightforward if the DAOs use JDBC directly because the EJB container simply has to inject the `DataSource`, which is a standard J2EE resource, into each DAO. However, DAOs often use a higher level, easier to use API such as a Spring `JdbcTemplate` or `SqlMapClientTemplate`. In order for the EJB container to inject these classes into a DAO, the Spring beans must be bound to JNDI, as we described in section 10.4.2.

The other option is to implement the DAOs as POJOs and to create them using Spring. The transaction scripts EJB calls Spring to instantiate the DAOs, which inject the `JdbcTemplate` or `SqlMapClientTemplate` class. The downside of this approach is that the explicit calls to Spring make the transaction scripts more difficult to test.

10.5.3 *Implementing dynamic paged queries*

In chapter 11 we describe how to implement dynamic paged queries, which are used to retrieve data that is displayed on search screens. Search screens allow the user to enter search criteria and view the result set, which is often too large to load into memory, let alone display on a single screen. Consequently, the user must be able to page through the result set. Also, because the database is typically large it's

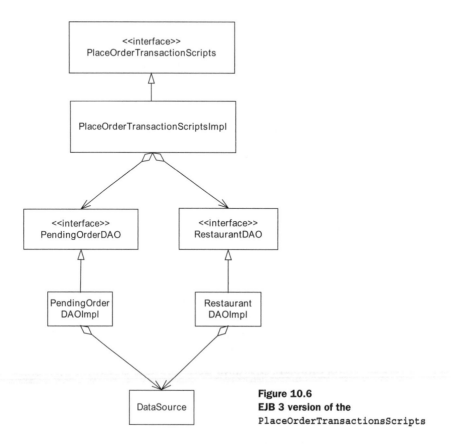

Figure 10.6
EJB 3 version of the
`PlaceOrderTransactionsScripts`

important that the queries be optimized. To implement efficient paged queries, there are several features that a persistence framework must provide. Let's see how EJB 3 does.

First, the persistence framework must allow you to configure eager loading in order for a query to retrieve related objects using a single SQL SELECT statement. In this respect EJB 3 does well because it lets you configure eager loading. The only limitation is that dynamically configuring eager loading can be difficult for the reasons we outlined in section 10.1.2.

Second, the persistence framework should support SQL queries, which are sometimes necessary in order to get good performance. EJB 3 also supports SQL queries, which are useful when a query must use database-specific SQL features to be efficient. SQL queries can be statically defined in the O/R metadata or dynamically created by the application. A query returns a result set that can contain a mixture of entities and scalar values.

Third, the persistence framework must allow the application to efficiently select a range of rows from a large result set without loading it into memory. In EJB 3, executing a query returns a list and you can specify the range of results to return by calling `Query.setFirstResult()` and `Query.setMaxResults()`. However, the specification does not give you any control over how the query is executed. Furthermore, EJB specification does not describe whether the result set is processed lazily or eagerly. Consequently, EJB 3 implementations will vary in how efficiently they can handle large result sets.

Finally, it is extremely helpful if the persistence framework supports Hibernate-style criteria queries, which as you will see in chapter 11, are a good way to construct queries dynamically. Unfortunately, EJB 3 lacks support for criteria queries and the application must dynamically construct a query by concatenating query fragments together, which results in messy code that is difficult to maintain.

10.5.4 *Implementing the concurrency patterns*

As you will see in chapter 12, most enterprise applications have to deal with database concurrency at the database transaction level by using optimistic locking, pessimistic locking, or serializable transactions. Optimistic locking is the only concurrency mechanism currently supported by the EJB 3 specification. However, a note in the specification states that a future version will describe how to control the transaction isolation level. The EJB 3 specification does not mention pessimistic locking, but presumably vendors will provide it as an extension.

In addition to database transaction-level concurrency mechanisms, many applications must also use the offline locking patterns, which are described in chapter 13, to handle concurrency in use cases that consist of multiple transactions. The two patterns are the Pessimistic Offline Lock pattern, which is application-level locking, or the Optimistic Offline Lock pattern, which is an extension of optimistic locking. It is easy to implement the Optimistic Offline Lock pattern using detached entity beans. Similarly, implementing the Pessimistic Offline Lock pattern is also straightforward because it does not rely on any persistence framework features.

10.6 *Summary*

EJB 3 is a tremendous improvement over EJB 2. Because EJB 3 beans do not implement special interfaces, they are POJOs, which makes them much easier to write. EJB 3 entity beans are intended to be the Java persistence standard and can run both inside and outside the EJB container. They can also can be detached and returned to the presentation tier, which eliminates the need to write DTOs. In addition, because EJB 3 provides dependency injection, session and message-driven beans rarely need to call JNDI to access their dependencies. EJB 3 has sensible defaults for many EJB configuration options, which means very little configuration is required. If you are coming to EJB 3 from EJB 2 you will find it considerably easier to use.

But if you are already using lightweight technologies such as Spring, Hibernate, and JDO, you will be disappointed. The O/R mapping defined in the June 2005 public draft had many limitations, including a lack of support for collections of primitive types, and limited support for lists and maps. As a result, you must decide between writing extra code and using vendor-specific features.

Assembling an application's components is a lot more difficult than when using Spring because EJB dependency injection can only inject JNDI objects into EJBs. You must implement all of the components as EJBs, explicitly call the Spring bean factory, or expose Spring beans through JNDI. Furthermore, you have to deal with the complexities of integrating an EJB container into your development environment and live with the overhead of deploying session and message-driven beans. Even though they are POJOs, they must still run in the EJB container.

Despite these problems, EJB 3 will undoubtedly be used widely because it's part of the J2EE standard. However, it is just another implementation option available to enterprise Java developers and, like all options, it has both benefits and drawbacks. It is important to make careful decisions and remain focused on the goal of simpler and faster development rather than being driven by fads and dogma.

Part 4

Dealing with databases and concurrency

Part 4 looks at some important database-related issues that you often encounter when developing an enterprise Java application. Chapter 11 describes how to implement search screens that let the user enter search criteria and page through the matching results. You will learn how to dynamically generate queries in a maintainable way, efficiently query the database, and implement a paging mechanism that allows the user to page through a large result set. This chapter covers how to implement dynamic paged queries using iBATIS, JDO, and Hibernate, and explains when you might want to use Hibernate and JDO native SQL queries.

Enterprise applications invariably have multiple users and background tasks, which means that sometimes multiple database transactions will attempt to access the same data simultaneously. In chapter 12, you will learn how to handle concurrent accesses at the database transaction level. This chapter describes how to handle database concurrency in iBATIS, JDO, and Hibernate applications, and how AOP can provide a simple way to recover from database concurrency failures.

Chapter 13 extends the concepts described in chapter 12 to handle database concurrency across a sequence of transactions. Many web applications have edit-style use cases that allow users to edit data in the database. The code that implements these use cases typically uses one database transaction to read the data and another to update. In this chapter, you will learn how to handle database concurrency in edit-style use cases. You will learn about the various options and their respective benefits and drawbacks.

11

Implementing dynamic paged queries

This chapter covers

- Implementing pagination
- Dynamically generating queries
- Efficiently querying large database
- Using Hibernate and JDO native SQL queries

If an application stores data, then you can be certain that users need to access that data in digestible chunks. All of the enterprise applications that I've developed have featured search screens that allow the user to enter search criteria and page through and sort long lists of items such as orders, mobile devices, and financial transactions. Implementing these search screens was difficult. The applications had to handle result sets consisting of hundreds of thousands of rows that were too large to load into memory and to display on a single screen. They had to dynamically generate database queries from the search criteria entered by the user. These queries had to be carefully optimized in order to achieve acceptable performance because the tables they accessed contained millions of rows.

The burden of implementing efficient paged queries falls on the persistence layer. When entity beans and JDBC were the only available options for accessing the database, I had always implemented them by using JDBC to execute SQL directly. Even though the code was very low-level and pretty messy, using JDBC was easier than using esoteric vendor-specific extensions to EJB 2.0 CMP. However, as you will see in this chapter, you now have more options. You can sometimes implement dynamic paged queries using JDO and Hibernate queries. They allow you to optimize queries and handle large result sets. What's more, if you must resort to SQL you can execute it using Hibernate or JDO. Alternatively, you can use iBATIS, which lets you dynamically generate queries with very little Java code.

In this chapter you will learn how to implement dynamic paged queries using iBATIS, JDO, and Hibernate. We describe a paging mechanism that avoids having to load an entire result set into memory, and provide an overview of the various ways to optimize the performance of SQL queries. In addition, we explain how to configure JDO and Hibernate to use efficient queries. We show how to apply these techniques by implementing the database access code for the View Orders use case using the iBATIS, JDO, and Hibernate persistence mechanisms.

11.1 Key design issues

When you're implementing dynamic paged queries, you must solve a number of design problems. For example, you have to choose from one of several ways of implementing a paging mechanism, each with its own benefits and drawbacks. You must also decide the best way to generate the queries, which can be a maintenance headache. Finally, you should have a good understanding of how to optimize SQL queries because that can dramatically impact the performance of the application. This section provides an overview of these issues, but first let's look at an example.

A good example of a use case that takes advantage of dynamically generated paged queries is the View Orders use case from the Food to Go application. It describes how a customer service representative searches for orders.

> The customer service representative enters one or more of the following search criteria: order number, phone number, email address, and date range. The system displays the orders that match the search criteria.

Figure 11.1 shows the screen for this use case, which consists of a form for entering search criteria and a list of matching orders. The user can page through the list of orders using the Next and Prev (Previous) buttons and can change the sort order by clicking on a column header.

Although the user interface and the underlying business logic for this kind of use case appear to be quite simple, querying a large database has some tricky persistence-tier design issues that must be solved in order for the application to be responsive, scalable, and maintainable:

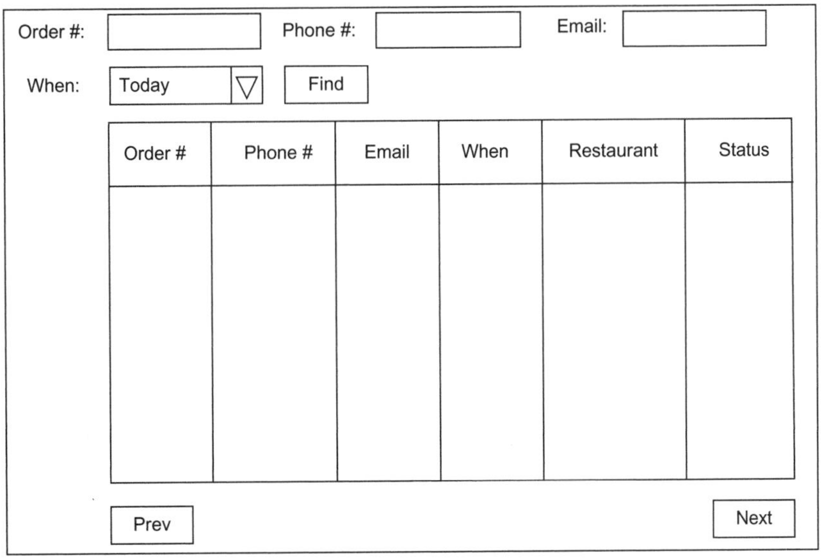

Figure 11.1   The screen for searching for and viewing orders

- A query can return a result set that is too large to display on one page or load into memory. The application must implement a paging mechanism that loads and displays part of the result set.

- There are usually too many permutations of search criteria to use a set of static queries. The application must generate queries dynamically, which requires conditional logic that is messy to write and difficult to maintain.

- Queries can require careful optimization in order to achieve acceptable performance because if the database is large, even simple queries can take many seconds to execute if they are not tuned correctly.

In this section we'll delve into the details of these design issues and describe some solutions that you can use in an application that executes SQL statements directly using either iBATIS or JDBC. In a later section we'll cover the additional problems that must solved when implementing this kind of use case using JDO and Hibernate.

11.1.1 Implementing a paging mechanism

Many applications let the user page backward and forward through a list of results that is too long to display on a single screen. There are several different ways an application can implement a paging mechanism. Table 11.1 lists the options along with their benefits and drawbacks.

Table 11.1 Paging options

Option	Benefits	Drawbacks	When to use it
Retrieve all the rows in one query	Consistent reads Executes a single expensive query	Cost of storing the data Cost of executing the query	Small result sets
Retrieve primary keys	Executes a single expensive query and multiple cheap ones	Inconsistent reads Space overhead of storing the primary keys Cost of executing the query	Modest result sets
Lazily iterate through the JDBC `ResultSet`	Executes a single query Consistent reads Avoids reading a lot of data from the database in one go	Severely limits the scalability of the application Long transaction could lock a large number of rows Long-running serializable transaction could fail	Applications that only have a small number of users
Repeatedly query the database	Stateless Retrieves only the data that will be displayed	Repeatedly querying the database Inconsistent reads	Large result sets Large numbers of users

Let's look at each of these options.

Retrieving all the data using a single query

A simple approach that works well for small amounts of data is to execute a single query and store the entire result set as part of the session state either in the server or the browser.

This approach has the following benefits:

- It can be efficient because the application only executes a single database query.

- The application has a consistent view of the database because it executes a single query.

The main drawback of this approach is that it is only practical when the result set is small. Executing a query that returns a large result set would be too expensive. It would be inefficient and impractical for the application to load a large result set into the application server's memory or send it to the browser. The result set would occupy too much memory and take too much time to transfer over the network. As a result, this approach is rarely useful.

Retrieving the primary keys

A variation on the first approach is for the application to first execute a query that retrieves the primary keys of the matching rows and store them as part of the session state. The application would then use a separate query to retrieve each page of data using the primary keys obtained by the first query.

This approach has a number of benefits:

- The potentially expensive query that finds the matching rows is only executed once.

- It reduces the amount of data that needs to be stored as part of the session state because primary keys are significantly smaller than the data.

It also has several drawbacks:

- The database must find all of the matching rows even though the user might only look at the first few.

- If there are a large number of rows, the session state can be large even though the application only stores the primary keys. The session state will either require a lot of memory on the server or take a long time to transport to the client.

- The application does not have a consistent view of the database because it can change between queries.

This strategy is best used when the queries return only a modest number of rows.

Holding onto database connections

Instead of loading all of the data in one go, another approach is for the application to hold onto a database connection and iterate through the JDBC `ResultSet` as the user pages through the list of orders.

This approach offers these benefits:

- It uses a single query, which is efficient and ensures a consistent view of the database.

- It does not store a large result set in the session state.

- The database doesn't have to find all of the matching rows immediately and so it can execute the query lazily.

as well as the following drawbacks:

- It does not scale to support a large number of users since database connections are a precious resource in a J2EE application.

- The long-running query could potentially lock a large number of rows.

Because of these limitations, this approach is rarely practical.

Using multiple queries

As we have just seen, in most applications the result set is too large to load into memory in its entirety. Furthermore, it's usually impractical for the application to hold onto database connections across user requests. Consequently, a more scalable approach is for the application to repeatedly query the database as the user pages through the list of items. There are a couple of different ways to do this. One option is for each query to return one page of data. Each time the user clicks on the next or previous page button, the application retrieves another page of data from the database. Another option, which reduces the number of database accesses and improves the response time, is for each query to retrieve multiple pages of data, which are then cached by the application as part of the session state.

Here are the benefits of this approach:

- It is scalable because it only uses a database connection for the duration of each HTTP request.

- It uses only a minimal amount of memory because only a subset of the data is loaded.

- It can reduce the load on the database since each query retrieves only a subset of the rows.

There are a couple of drawbacks as well:

- The application potentially executes the same query multiple times, which can be inefficient.

- The user might see an inconsistent view of the database because it could change between queries.

Despite these drawbacks, this approach is the best choice for many applications, and it is the strategy we will adopt for the example application.

11.1.2 *Generating queries dynamically*

Another challenge is how to dynamically generate the SQL SELECT statement. An application must typically generate SQL statements dynamically because there are too many permutations of search criteria to use a static set of statements. For example, the view orders screen allows the user to enter four search criteria, and so we would need to write and maintain 16 (2^4) queries, which would be pretty tedious.

Concatenate SQL fragments

One option is for the DAO to generate the SELECT statement by concatenating fragments of SQL together. The DAO would, for example, construct the WHERE clause of the SELECT statement from the search criteria entered by the user. However, the problem with this approach is that it is not very maintainable. As well as being messy and error prone, it is difficult to locate and change SQL fragments that are embedded in code. It is also difficult to test SQL statements using a tool such as SQL*Plus because only fragments of the SQL exist in the DAO.

Using iBATIS dynamic mapped statements

A better approach is to use the dynamic mapped statement feature of iBATIS. An iBATIS mapped statement can include conditional tags that use the properties of a parameter bean to determine which SQL fragments should be part of the SQL statement. This is an extremely useful feature of iBATIS that significantly reduces the amount of DAO code. It also makes maintaining a SQL query easier because it is stored in its entirety in the mapping file. Section 11.2 describes iBATIS dynamic mapped statements in more detail.

The problem of generating queries dynamically is not confined to applications that use SQL directly. In section 11.3.1 you will see how JDO applications must also generate queries by concatenating query fragments together. Hibernate, on the other hand, has criteria queries that provide an object-oriented API for constructing queries dynamically.

11.1.3 *Improving the performance of SQL queries*

Next, let's look at the techniques you can use to improve query performance of a SELECT statement. If the database is large, some queries—even simple ones—can be expensive to execute. For example, consider the following simple SQL query, which retrieves information about the orders that were placed in the past 30 days and sorts them by external order ID:

```
SELECT o.*, r.name
FROM PLACED_ORDER o, RESTAURANT r
WHERE o.RESTAURANT_ID = r.RESTAURANT_ID
  AND o.DELIVERY_TIME > (SYSDATE - 30)
ORDER BY o.ORDER_EXT_ID DESC
```

Even when the application displays only the first few rows returned by the query, this query can take several seconds to execute against a large database, which is unacceptable for an interactive application. In addition, executing this query consumes excessive database server resources, which limits scalability.

You can improve query performance in several ways. Some performance improvements are done on the database server and do not require code changes. For example, defining the appropriate indexes can improve performance dramatically without having to change the SQL statements. There are, however, other performance optimizations that require the SQL statements to be changed:

- Using query optimizer hints
- Using the ROWNUM pseudo column
- Denormalizing the schema
- Rewriting queries to avoiding inefficient features

If your application uses iBATIS or JDBC, then changing the SQL statements is easy because you have complete control over them. But, as we will see in section 11.3, if the SQL statements are generated by the persistence framework, then implementing these optimizations can be difficult or even impossible. Let's look at each of these query optimization techniques.

Using optimizer hints

One important way to improve the performance of a query is to use optimizer hints, which are a database-specific way of influencing how the database executes a SQL statement. They are useful when the database's query optimizer is unable to automatically determine the best way to execute a query. Using them in a JDBC or iBATIS application is quite straightforward but in section 11.3, we will see that Hibernate and JDO object queries do not support optimizer hints, which can sometimes force you to use SQL queries instead.

Each database has a different way of writing optimizer hints, and we'll provide an overview of how they work in Oracle. An Oracle optimizer hint is a specifically formatted comment in a SQL statement that tells Oracle how to execute the statement. Oracle provides several kinds of optimizer hints. The FIRST_ROWS(N) hint is a good way to improve the performance of queries when the application only displays the first N rows of a result set, as is typically the case with search screens. By default, the Oracle query optimizer assumes that an application wants all of the rows returned by a query and aims to maximize throughput by, for example, minimizing the amount of I/O required to execute the query. Therefore, Oracle will sometimes process the entire result set before returning the first rows back to the application, which can be inefficient if the application only needs the first few rows. It also results in a poor response time. The FIRST_ROWS(N) hint tells Oracle to execute the query in a way that minimizes the time to return the first N rows to the application. This improves the response time and is often more efficient if the application only wants the first N rows. The following query uses this hint to tell Oracle to execute the query in a way that minimizes the time to return the first 20 rows:

```
SELECT /*+  FIRST_ROWS(20)  */ o.*, r.name
FROM PLACED_ORDER o, RESTAURANT r
WHERE o.RESTAURANT_ID = r.RESTAURANT_ID
   AND o.DELIVERY_TIME > (SYSDATE - 30)
   ORDER BY o.ORDER_EXT_ID DESC
```

This query executes considerably faster than the original query shown earlier. However, one downside of using this hint is that sometimes it has the opposite effect and reduces the performance of the query. It is important to experiment.

Denormalizing the schema

If you can change the database schema, then another way to improve query performance is to eliminate expensive joins by denormalizing the schema. For example, we can eliminate the need to use a join between the PLACED_ORDER and RESTAURANT tables by storing the restaurant's name in the PLACED_ORDER table. A database trigger would maintain consistency by updating the RESTAURANT_NAME column in the PLACED_ORDER table whenever RESTAURANT.NAME was updated. Here is the simplified query:

```
SELECT o.order_id, o.restaurant_name, …
FROM PLACED_ORDER o
WHERE o.DELIVERY_TIME > (SYSDATE - 30)
   ORDER BY o.ORDER_EXT_ID DESC
```

The query now just references the PLACED_ORDER table and gets the restaurant's name from the RESTAURANT_NAME column. Because this is a simple query, the benefits of eliminating the join are relatively small. However, for more complex queries the performance gains can be large.

Writing queries that access denormalized columns is straightforward if you are using JDBC or iBATIS, but in section 11.3.4 you will see that mapping denormalized columns to the fields or properties of a domain model can affect it in unpleasant ways.

Using the ROWNUM pseudo column

Normally, you want a query to return all of the matching rows in the database, but search screens are different. They display one page of items at a time, and so the application only wants a particular range of the rows from the database. One way an application that uses JDBC can get a subset of rows is by skipping over the rows in the JDBC ResultSet that it does not want and loading the rows that it does want. Here is an example of JDBC code that does this:

```
PreparedStatement ps = …
ResultSet rs = ps.executeQuery();
rs.absolute(11);
int count = 10;
while (count-- > 0 && rs.next() {
…
}
```

This code uses ResultSet.absolute() to position the cursor on the 11th row and then iterates through the ResultSet, getting the next 10 rows. One potential performance problem with this approach is that the database might find all of the rows when it executes the query even though the application only wants a few of them. Another drawback is that some JDBC drivers will read the rows that are skipped over from the database, which is inefficient because they are transferred from the database and then discarded.

An alternative approach, which avoids this problem, is to use a database-specific SQL feature that restricts the range of rows returned by the query. Only some databases have this feature, and it is implemented differently by each one.

Oracle has the `ROWNUM` pseudo column, whose value is the (1-based) position of a row in the result set. A SQL `SELECT` statement can use the `ROWNUM` column in the `WHERE` clause to control which rows it returns.

A query can use the `ROWNUM` in a couple of ways. Let's first look at the simplest use, which is to return the first *N* rows selected by a query. For example, here is a query that returns first 10 rows:

```
SELECT *
FROM (SELECT O.ORDER_ID, R.NAME, …
 FROM PLACED_ORDER O, RESTAURANT R
 WHERE O.RESTAURANT_ID = R.RESTAURANT_ID
 ORDER BY O.ORDER_EXT_ID
) WHERE ROWNUM < 11
```

This query nests the original query in `SELECT ... WHERE ROWNUM < 11`. Oracle returns the first 10 rows matched by the query. The application could use a query like this one to display the first page of a result set.

A more elaborate use of `ROWNUM` is to select a range of rows. Here is a query that returns rows 11 through 20:

```
SELECT *
FROM
  (SELECT ROWNUM AS RN, XX.*
    FROM
    (SELECT O.ORDER_ID, R.NAME, …
      FROM PLACED_ORDER O, RESTAURANT R
      WHERE O.RESTAURANT_ID = R.RESTAURANT_ID
      ORDER BY O.ORDER_EXT_ID
    ) XX
  WHERE ROWNUM < 21)
WHERE RN > 10
```

The inner query that uses `ROWNUM` returns the first 20 rows and the outer query ignores the first 10 rows. An application could use a query like this one to display all pages of a result set except the first.

Using `ROWNUM` in a query has several benefits:

- An application can ensure that Oracle only returns the rows that it wants.

- It sometimes enables Oracle to execute the query more efficiently.

- It reduces the amount of data transferred over the network.

However, using `ROWNUM` in a query can sometimes cause Oracle to execute the query in a less efficient way, and so you should use it on a case-by-case basis.

In section 11.3.5 you will see that Hibernate and some JDO implementations provide the option of using `ROWNUM`-like features.

Tuning the queries

The fourth and final way to improve the performance of some SQL queries is to rewrite them to use more efficient constructs. This is a complicated topic that is described in numerous books including *SQL Tuning* [Tow 2003]. Examples of what you can do to improve the performance of your query include eliminating SQL functions from the SELECT statement's WHERE clause and replacing a complex SQL statement with the UNION ALL of two simpler ones. Rewriting the SQL statement is only possible if the application executes SQL directly. If it queries the database using the persistence framework's object query mechanism, then you have much less control over the SQL that is generated.

It is also important to take into account database performance issues when designing the UI. Examples of UI features that can cause database performance problems include:

- Case-insensitive substring searches, which, even though they appear to offer the user a lot of flexibility, can be quite inefficient

- Displaying the number of rows that match the query, which requires the database process the entire result set even though only the first few rows are displayed

- An excessively large number of search and sort options, which requires many indexes to be defined

Ideally, the user interface should only support searches that can be implemented using efficient database queries.

Now that we have reviewed the different ways to improve the performance of a SQL SELECT statement, let's look at the implementation of a DAO that uses iBATIS to execute queries.

11.2 *Implementing dynamic paged queries with iBATIS*

The frameworks that you can use to implement the persistence layer include iBATIS, Hibernate, and JDO. In this section you will learn how to implement dynamic paged queries in an application that executes SQL using iBATIS. You will see an example of how using iBATIS to construct the query simplifies the code significantly. In section 11.3 we will see how to use JDO and Hibernate to implement dynamic paged queries.

In an iBATIS application, the query that retrieves the data displayed by the search screen is executed by a DAO. The DAO typically defines a find method that takes parameters that specify the search criteria and the range of rows to return.

The find method executes a query and returns a list of DTOs and a flag that tells the presentation tier whether to display a "next page" button.

For example, the Food to Go application finds the orders using the OrderDAO, which is shown in figure 11.2. The OrderDAO defines a findOrders() method,

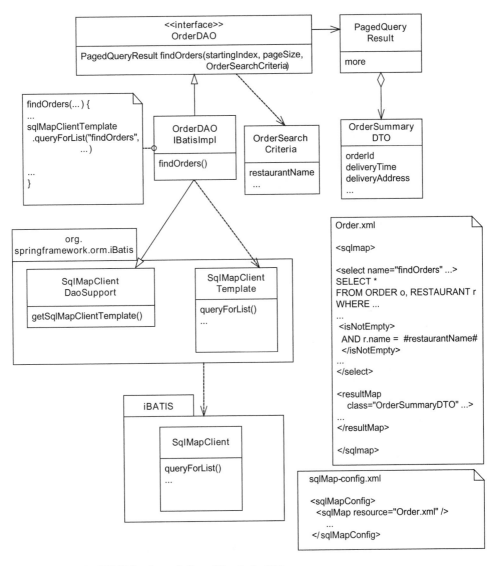

Figure 11.2   The iBATIS implementation of the OrderDAO

which has `startingIndex` and `pageSize` parameters that specify which page of the result set to return, as well as a `OrderSearchCriteria` parameter that contains the search criteria entered by the user and the selected sort order. It has properties that represent the order number, phone number, email address, and date range. The `findOrders()` method returns a `PagedQueryResult` object, which contains the list of `OrderSummaryDTO` objects, and a boolean flag indicating whether there are more orders.

`OrderDAOIBatisImpl`, which implements the `OrderDAO` interface, calls `SqlMap-ClientTemplate` to generate and execute the `findOrders` mapped statement, which is defined in the Order.xml descriptor file. `findOrders` is an iBATIS dynamic mapped statement. It contains conditional XML elements that use the values from the `OrderSearchCriteria` JavaBean to determine whether to include one or more SQL fragments in the statement. Using this mechanism to dynamically generate SQL queries significantly simplifies the DAO by eliminating conditional logic and code that concatenates SQL fragments. In fact, because iBATIS does all of the work, `findOrders()` consists of a few lines of code that call `SqlMapClientTem-plate.queryForList()`, which executes the query and returns a list of beans constructed from the result set.

We have seen earlier that, depending on the query, we will want to select a page of results by either navigating through the result set or by executing a SELECT statement that uses a ROWNUM-like feature. Accordingly, iBATIS defines two versions of the `queryForList()` method. One version takes parameters that specify the range of rows to return. It navigates through the JDBC result to extract the specified rows. The other version of `queryForList()` returns a list containing all of the rows found by the query. It's useful when the SQL query returns just the required rows by using a ROWNUM-like feature. Let's look at how to use each of these methods.

11.2.1 *Using queryForList() to select the rows*

The first version of `queryListForList()` that we will examine is the one that takes parameters specifying the range of rows to return. Here is the implementation of the `OrderDAO.findOrders()` method that executes a mapped statement using this version:

```
public class OrderDAOIBatisImpl extends SqlMapClientDaoSupport
   implements OrderDAO {
   public PagedQueryResult findOrders(int startingIndex,
      int pageSize, OrderSearchCriteria criteria) {
      Map map = new HashMap();
      map.put("pageSize",
            new Integer(pageSize + startingIndex + 1));
      map.put("criteria", criteria);
```

```
List result = getSqlMapClientTemplate().queryForList(
        "findOrders", map, startingIndex, pageSize);
boolean more = result.size() > pageSize;
if (more) {
    result.remove(pageSize);
}
return new PagedQueryResult(result, more);
}
```

This method creates a map containing the OrderSearchCriteria and the number of desired rows. The findOrders() method then invokes queryForList(), passing findOrders, the map, and the desired range of rows to be returned. The findOrders() method retrieves one more row than is actually required in order to determine whether there are more rows. It removes the extra row from the list before returning it.

Listing 11.1 shows the findOrders dynamic mapped statement that is executed by findOrders() and its result map. The mapped statement has conditional XML elements that use the contents of the map, such as the properties of the OrderSearchCriteria object, to dynamically construct the WHERE clause of the SELECT statement. The result map constructs an OrderSummaryDTO from each row of the result set.

Listing 11.1 The findOrders mapped statement and its result set

```
<sqlMap>
...
  <select id="findOrders"
          resultMap="OrderResultMap"
          resultSetType="SCROLL_INSENSITIVE">
  SELECT /*+ FIRST_ROWS($pageSize$) */   ◁——— Specify the number of rows
    O.ORDER_ID, R.NAME AS RESTAURANT_NAME
  FROM FTGO_ORDER O,
     FTGO_RESTAURANT R
  WHERE O.RESTAURANT_ID = R.RESTAURANT_ID

  <isNotEmpty property="criteria.restaurantName">      Conditionally includes
    AND r.name = #criteria.restaurantName#             restaurantName
  </isNotEmpty>

  <isNotEmpty property="criteria.deliveryCity">        Conditionally includes
    AND o.delivery_city                                deliveryCity
          = #criteria.deliveryCity#
  </isNotEmpty>

  <isNotEmpty property="criteria.state">       Conditionally
    AND o.status = #criteria.state#            includes state
  </isNotEmpty>
```

```
        ORDER BY o.ORDER_ID ASC
        </select>


        <resultMap id="OrderResultMap"
            class="net.chrisrichardson.foodToGo.
                    ➥ placeOrderTransactionScripts.details.
                    ➥ OrderSummaryDTO">
          <result property="orderId" column="ORDER_ID" />
          <result property="restaurantName" column="RESTAURANT_NAME" />
          ...
        </resultMap>
      ...
      </sqlMap>
```

The query contains a FIRST_ROWS(N) optimizer hint that tells Oracle how many rows
the application wants. The dynamic mapped statement uses the <isNotEmpty> element to conditionally include SQL fragments based on the properties of an Order-
SearchCriteria object. Each of the <isNotEmpty> elements adds to the SELECT
statement's WHERE clause. For example, <isNotEmpty property="restaurantName">...
</isNotEmpty> adds AND r.name = #restaurantName# to the WHERE clause if the res-
taurantName property is not blank or null.

iBATIS supports many other conditional elements in addition to the
<isNotEmpty> element, including an <iteration> element that iterates through a
list. See the iBATIS documentation for more information.

11.2.2 *Using ROWNUM to select the rows*

For some queries, navigating through the result set is the best approach. For others, a more efficient approach is to use a query that uses a ROWNUM-like feature to
return only the needed rows. To execute this kind of query, the DAO can use the
version of queryForList() that returns the entire result set and pass the starting-
Index and the pageSize as parameters to the mapped statement. One convenient
way to do this is to call queryForList() with a Map containing the startingIndex,
pageSize, and the search criteria. Here is a version of findOrders() that does this:

```
public PagedQueryResult findOrders (int startingIndex,
    int pageSize, OrderSearchCriteria criteria) {
    Map map = new HashMap();
    map.put("startingIndex", new Integer(startingIndex));
    map.put("maxRows", new Integer(pageSize + startingIndex
                    + 2));
    map.put("criteria", criteria);
    List result = getSqlMapClientTemplate().queryForList(
```

```
        "findOrders", map);
    boolean more = result.size() > pageSize;
    if (more) {
      result.remove(pageSize);
    }
    return new PagedQueryResult(result, more);
  }
```

The dynamic mapped statement that is executed by this version of findOrders() is similar to the one we saw earlier and uses the same result map. As well as using the conditional XML tags to construct the WHERE clause, this mapped statement uses them to nest the query inside a SELECT statement that uses ROWNUM to skip over the number of rows specified by the start property.

```
<sqlMap>

  <select id="findOrders" resultMap="OrderResultMap"
      resultSetType="SCROLL_INSENSITIVE">
    <isGreaterThan property=" startingIndex" compareValue="0">
      SELECT * FROM (SELECT XX.*,              Skips over
                     ROWNUM RNXX FROM (        startingIndex rows
    </isGreaterThan>

    SELECT * FROM (  ⟵————  Returns no more
                            than maxRows

      SELECT O.ORDER_ID, R.NAME AS RESTAURANT_NAME FROM FTGO_ORDER O,
        FTGO_RESTAURANT R
      WHERE O.RESTAURANT_ID = R.RESTAURANT_ID

      <isNotEmpty property="criteria.restaurantName">
        AND r.name = #criteria.restaurantName#
      </isNotEmpty>

      <isNotEmpty property="criteria.deliveryCity">
        AND o.delivery_city = #criteria.deliveryCity#
      </isNotEmpty>

      <isNotEmpty property="criteria.state">
        AND o.status = #criteria.state#
      </isNotEmpty>

    ORDER BY o.ORDER_ID ASC

    ) WHERE ROWNUM &lt; #maxRows#   ⟵————  Returns no more
                                            than maxRows

    <isGreaterThan property="start" compareValue="0">
      ) XX ) WHERE RNXX &gt; #startingIndex#   ⟵————  Skips over
    </isGreaterThan>                                   startingIndex rows
  </select>
  ...
</sqlMap>
```

The innermost SELECT statement that uses ROWNUM returns startingIndex+page-Size+1 rows. The outer statement, which is used only if start is greater than 0, skips over the first pageSize rows.

As you can see, you only need to write a few lines of Java code when using iBA-TIS to execute a dynamically constructed query that returns a page of results. Let's now look at how to do the same thing with JDO and Hibernate.

11.3 *Implementing paged queries with JDO and Hibernate*

iBATIS certainly simplifies the task of executing SQL statements. But using an ORM framework such as JDO and Hibernate has many benefits. For example, an ORM framework significantly reduces the amount of database access code you must write and increases your application's portability. Consequently, it's extremely desirable to use one to implement dynamic paged queries. But how well do JDO and Hibernate handle the issues discussed in section 11.1?

As we have seen, when implementing dynamic paged queries in a JDBC or iBA-TIS application, you must do three things. First, you must use carefully tuned SQL SELECT statements that sometimes make use of vendor-specific features such as optimizer hints in order to achieve good performance. Second, you must efficiently select a page of rows by either navigating through the result set or using queries that implement a ROWNUM-like feature. Finally, you must dynamically generate queries in a maintainable way. As you might expect, you have to do similar things when using Hibernate or JDO, but because the persistence framework executes SQL on behalf of the application, implementing dynamic paged queries efficiently with JDO and Hibernate object queries can be tricky.

To see why it can be difficult, let's consider how a repository such as Order-Repository uses the persistence framework to execute a query. As figure 11.3 shows, OrderRepository uses the search criteria entered by the user to generate an object query and calls the persistence framework to execute it. The persistence framework translates the object query into a SELECT statement and calls JDBC to execute it. The persistence framework then iterates through the JDBC ResultSet, creating Java objects

The only control you have over the SQL STATEMENT used by the persistence framework is to use features such as eager loading. You cannot execute object queries that use database-specific features such as optimizer hints. If you need to use these kinds of features to achieve good performance, then you must use SQL native queries instead of object queries. However, the drawback of using native SQL queries is that they don't make full use of the capabilities of the persistence

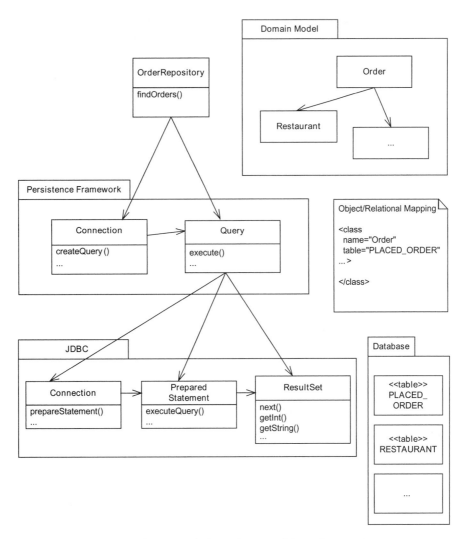

Figure 11.3 How a query is executed when using a persistence framework

framework. Moreover, unlike iBATIS, Hibernate and JDO lack support for dynamically generating SQL statements, which means that you will end up writing some messy query-generation code.

Another potential obstacle to implementing dynamic paged queries with a persistence framework is that you might not be able to control how the persistence framework selects a range of rows from the result set. Hibernate and some JDO implementations such as Kodo JDO let you specify whether it should navigate the result set or use a SELECT statement with a ROWNUM-like feature. However, there is no guarantee that all JDO implementations provide this capability. As a result, you might need to use iBATIS or JDBC instead.

In this section, we provide an overview of how to implement efficient paged queries with Hibernate and JDO object queries. You will learn about what support, if any, Hibernate and JDO provide for dynamically generating object queries. We describe how to persuade the persistence framework to execute an object query using a SELECT statement similar to those that a JDBC or iBATIS application would use. You'll learn how JDO and Hibernate applications can implement pagination. In sections 11.4 and 11.5 you will see how to apply the techniques described here in more detail. In those sections we also describe how to use JDO and Hibernate native SQL queries.

11.3.1 *Generating Hibernate and JDO queries dynamically*

One important aspect of implementing a search screen is generating queries dynamically from the search criteria entered by the user. Ideally, you want to avoid writing messy repository code that generates object queries by concatenating query fragments. Unfortunately, JDO lacks support for dynamically generating queries. Only Hibernate has APIs for dynamically generating object queries. Let's see how JDO and Hibernate repositories dynamically generate queries.

Dynamically generating JDO queries

A JDO application must generate an object query by concatenating fragments of the JDO query language (JDOQL), which makes the code messy and error-prone. Here is an example of a code fragment that constructs the WHERE clause of a query from an OrderSearchCriteria:

```
...
public class JDOOrderRepositoryImpl ... {

  public PagedQueryResult findOrders(int startIndex,
    int pageSize, OrderSearchCriteria criteria) {
    ...
    StringBuffer where = new StringBuffer();
    Map parameters = new HashMap();
    if (criteria.isDeliveryCitySpecified()) {
      if (where.length() != 0)
        where.append(" && ");
        where.append("deliveryAddress.city == :pDeliveryCity");
    }
    if (criteria.isRestaurantSpecified()) {
      if (where.length() != 0)
```

```
        where.append(" && ");
        where.append("restaurant.name == :pRestaurant");
    }
    …
    Query query = pm.createQuery(Order.class, where.toString());
    …
    List orders = (List)query.execute(…);
    …
  }
  …
}
```

The code contains conditional logic that concatenates JDOQL fragments. Section 11.4 shows an in-depth example that uses JDOQL queries.

Using Hibernate criteria queries

Hibernate, on the other hand, has criteria queries, which provide an OO API for constructing object queries dynamically. The application instantiates objects and calls methods instead of concatenating string fragments, which makes the code significantly simpler. Here is a code fragment that shows how to use a Hibernate criteria query:

```
public class HibernateOrderRepositoryImpl … {

  public PagedQueryResult findOrders(int startingIndex,
    int pageSize,
    OrderSearchCriteria searchCriteria) {
    …
    Criteria criteria = session
      .createCriteria(Order.class);
    …
    if (searchCriteria.isDeliveryTimeSpecified())
      criteria.add(Restrictions.ge("deliveryTime",
        searchCriteria.getDeliveryTime()));

    if (searchCriteria.isRestaurantSpecified()) {
      criteria.createCriteria("restaurant").add(
        Restrictions.like("name", searchCriteria
          .getRestaurantName()));

    List orders = criteria.list();
    …
  }
}
```

This code fragment creates a criteria object by calling a `Session.createCriteria()` and then adds restrictions to it based on the properties of the `OrderSearchCriteria`. We must still write conditional logic, but the code is a lot cleaner because it doesn't concatenate query fragments. In section 11.5 you will see an in-depth example that uses criteria queries.

11.3.2 *Loading the data with a single SELECT statement*

Another important aspect of implementing a search screen is querying the database efficiently. As we saw in section 11.1.3, there are a few things that you might need to do to get good performance, but when using a persistence framework the first step is to persuade to retrieve the data using a single SELECT statement. Even though this sounds elementary, a persistence framework might not do this automatically if the search screens display the attributes of multiple related objects. It can, for example, load objects lazily, which requires multiple SELECT statements.

For example, as you can see in figure 11.4, the View Orders screen displays the orderNumber and deliveryTime attributes of an order, the phoneNumber and email attributes of the order's payment information, and the name of the order's restaurant. The presentation tier code that implements the View Orders screen iterates through the list of orders and navigates to each order's payment information and restaurant.

The persistence framework must retrieve this data using a single SELECT statement. It must not, for example, lazily load the restaurants by executing multiple SELECT statements that each loads one restaurant from the RESTAURANT table because that can reduce performance significantly. As we have seen in chapters 4, 5, and 6, you can optimize object loading by eliminating SQL statements by using either process-level cache or eager loading.

We could, for example, improve the performance of the View Orders query by caching the restaurants in the process-level cache, as we saw in chapter 4. Executing a query that retrieves just orders will work just fine. The application will retrieve the restaurants from the process-level cache when it navigates to them.

Alternatively, we can improve the performance of the View Orders query by eagerly loading the restaurants. The persistence framework will then execute a SELECT statement that does a join between the PLACED_ORDER and RESTAURANT tables. The details of how you configure and use eager loading depend on which persistence framework you are using. As we saw in chapter 5, a JDO application uses fetch groups to configure eager loading, and in chapter 6 we saw that a Hibernate application uses queries with fetch joins. Let's see how fetch groups can be used here in the query that retrieves orders.

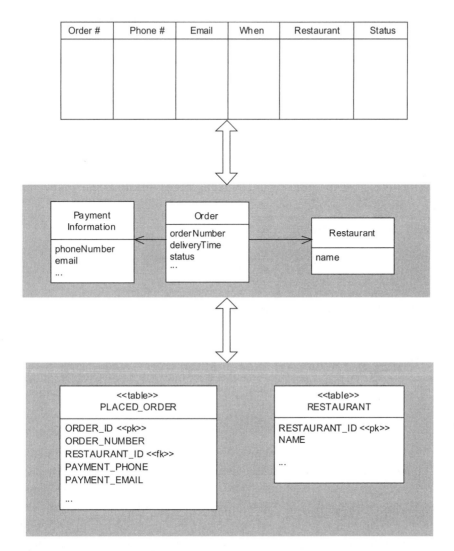

Figure 11.4   The relationship between the View Orders screen, the domain model, and the database schema

Using JDO fetch groups

JDO 2.0 has a powerful fetch group mechanism, which allows the developer to specify a graph of objects to eagerly load. Here is an example of fetch group for the Order class that loads some of its fields and the name field of its restaurant:

```
<class name="Order">

  <fetch-group name="Order.summary">
    <field name="orderId"/>
    <field name="status"/>
    ...
    <field name="restaurant.name"/>
  </fetch-group>

</class>
```

The `<fetch-group>` element defines the `Order.summary` fetch group that consists of fields, including `Order.orderId` and `Order.status`, and the name of the restaurant.

Here is how you would execute a query that uses this fetch group:

```
public class JDOOrderRepositoryImpl ... {

  public PagedQueryResult findOrders(int startIndex,
    int pageSize,
    OrderSearchCriteria searchCriteria) {
    ...
    Query query = pm.newQuery(Order.class, ...);
    FetchPlan fp = query.getFetchPlan();
    fc.addGroup("Order.summary");
    ...
    Collection result = (Collection)query.execute();
    ...
  }

  ...
}
```

This code fragment configures the query to use the `Order.summary` fetch group. The JDO implementation will retrieve the orders and their restaurants by executing this query using a SQL SELECT statement that does a join between the FTO_ORDER and RESTAURANT tables and returns only those columns that correspond to the fields in the fetch group. Note, however, that you might need to configure eager loading using a vendor-specific mechanism such as Kodo JDO 3.3's per-field fetch mechanism if you are using a JDO implementation that does not yet support the JDO 2.0 standard. In section 11.4, we will look at an implementation of the `OrderRepository` that uses Kodo JDO's per-field fetch mechanism to optimize object loading.

Using Hibernate fetch joins

Hibernate provides fetch joins for eagerly loading objects when executing a query. An application uses a fetch join in a criteria query by calling `Criteria.setFetchMode()`. This method takes two parameters that specify the name of the relationship and whether to load it eagerly or lazily. For example, here is a criteria query that finds orders and loads their restaurants eagerly:

```
public class HibernateOrderRepositoryImpl … {

  public PagedQueryResult findOrders(int startingIndex,
    …
    List orders = session
      .createCriteria(Order.class)
      .add(Expression.eq("deliveryAddress.city", "San Francisco"))
      .setFetchMode("restaurant",FetchMode.JOIN)
      .list()
    …
  }
  …
}
```

Hibernate will execute this query using a SELECT statement that does a join between the PLACED_ORDER and RESTAURANT tables.

In addition to eagerly loading the related objects, another way to optimize object loading is to load only those object fields that are required. Let's take a look.

11.3.3 *Loading a subset of an object's fields*

Search screens typically display a subset of each object's fields and require the user to navigate to a details screen to see the rest. For example, as figure 11.1 shows, the View Orders screen only displays the order's number, phone number, email, delivery time and status, and the restaurant's name. We can rely on lazy loading to prevent the query from unnecessarily loading related objects such as the order's line items or the restaurant's menu items. But, by default, JDO and Hibernate will load all of an object's attributes and all of the attributes of its embedded objects.

This means, for example, that the persistence framework will execute a SELECT statement that retrieves the order's delivery address, which is an embedded object, even though it is never displayed. The PLACED_ORDER table only has a few columns; the overhead of loading them all is insignificant. But if a table has many columns or has columns containing large values, then loading only the required objects can often improve performance. Not only does this approach reduce the amount of data that is transferred over the network from the database to the application, but it also reduces the amount of processing that the persistence framework must do to instantiate the Java objects.

As we have seen in chapters 4, 5, and 6, JDO and Hibernate provide various mechanisms for controlling which fields are loaded. The three mechanisms that are particularly useful when implementing dynamic paged queries are JDO fetch groups,

Hibernate projection queries, and JDO projection queries. Hibernate lazily loaded properties are not that useful for the reasons we saw in chapter 6. Let's review how each of these mechanisms can be used to improve the performance of the View Orders query.

Using JDO fetch groups to load a subset of an object's fields

Until now we have used JDO fetch groups to eagerly load objects, but you can also use them to load only a subset of an object's fields. To do that, you must first define a fetch group that specifies the required fields. For example, here is a fetch group containing fields displayed on the view orders screen:

```
<class name="Order">

  <fetch-group name="Order.summary">
    <field name="orderId"/>
    <field name="status"/>
    <field name="paymentInformation.email"/>
    <field name="paymentInformation.phone"/>
    <field name="restaurant.name"/>
  </fetch-group>

</class>
```

The `<fetch-group>` element defines the `Order.summary` fetch group containing several fields, including `Order.orderId` and `Order.status`, and the name of the restaurant.

You then activate the fetch group by replacing the currently active fetch groups with this one fetch group:

```
public class JDOOrderRepositoryImpl … {

  public PagedQueryResult findOrders(int startIndex,
      int pageSize,
      OrderSearchCriteria searchCriteria) {
    Query query = pm.newQuery(Order.class, …);
    FetchPlan fp = query.getFetchPlan();
    fc.setFetchGroup("Order.summary");
    Collection result = (Collection)query.execute();

  …
  }

  …
}
```

This code fragment calls `FetchPlan.setFetchGroup()`, which replaces the currently active fetch groups with the `Order.summary` fetch group. The JDO implementation then executes a SELECT statement that does a join between the PLACED_ORDER and RESTAURANT tables and returns only those columns corresponding to the fields specified in the fetch group.

Using JDO projection queries

Another way a JDO application can load a subset of an object's fields is to use projection queries, which are a new feature of JDO 2.0, and return DTOs containing selected fields. Here is an example of how to use the Kodo JDO 3.*x* extensions to execute a projection query that finds all orders whose delivery date is in the past week. It returns a collection of OrderSummaryDTO objects containing the ID, delivery time, phone number, email, and restaurant name of each order:

```
public class JDOOrderRepositoryImpl extends
    JdoDaoSupport implements OrderRepository {

  ...

  public List findOrdersUsingProjection() {
    return (List) getJdoTemplate().executeFind(
        new ProjectionQueryCallback());
  }

  private final class ProjectionQueryCallback
      implements JdoCallback {
    public Object doInJdo(PersistenceManager pm)
        throws JDOException {
      Calendar c = Calendar.getInstance();
      c.add(Calendar.DAY_OF_WEEK, -7);
      Date deliveryTime = c.getTime();

      String queryString =
          "select id as orderId, deliveryTime, "
          + " paymentInformation.email as email, "
          + " paymentInformation.phoneNumber as phoneNumber, "
          + " restaurant.name as restaurantName "
          + " into " + OrderSummaryDTO.class.getName()
          + " from " + Order.class.getName()
          + " where deliveryTime >= :pDeliveryTime";

      Query query = pm.newQuery(queryString);
      Map map = new HashMap();
      map.put("pDeliveryTime", deliveryTime);
      List result = (List) query
          .executeWithMap(map);
      return result;
    }
  }

  ...

}
```

Kodo JDO executes a SQL SELECT statement that retrieves only the columns corresponding to the fields specified by the query's select clause and returns a collection of OrderSummaryDTO objects. For each row in the result set, Kodo instantiates an OrderSummaryDTO using its default constructor and initializes it by calling setters, including setOrderId(), setDeliveryTime(), and setEmail().

If you do not need the persistent objects, then JDO projection queries are a useful way to retrieve only the required fields without going to the trouble of defining fetch groups.

Using Hibernate projection queries

Hibernate projection queries, like JDO projection queries, return DTOs rather than persistent objects and can be used to load a subset of an object's properties. Here is an example of a criteria query that returns just the ID and deliveryAddress.street1 property of the orders:

```
Criteria x = session.createCriteria(Order.class);
x.setProjection(Projections.projectionList()
    .add(Property.forName("id"))
    .add(Property.forName("deliveryAddress.street1")));
List result = x.list();
Object[] result = x.get(0);
```

Hibernate executes a query that retrieves only the columns corresponding to the specified properties. Each element of the result list is an Object[] containing two elements. Criteria queries that use projections are sometimes useful, but one apparent limitation of criteria projection queries is that they cannot return the property of a related object, such as the name of an order's restaurant. Another limitation of projection queries is that each item in the projection list must map to a single column. This means that you cannot easily retrieve an embedded value object, such as an order's delivery address. Consequently, if you need to retrieve the properties of related objects or embedded value objects, then you have to use a regular criteria query.

11.3.4 Working with a denormalized schema

A common technique for improving performance is to denormalize the schema, which reduces the number of joins that a SQL SELECT statement must use. In order for the denormalized columns to be accessible to an application that uses a persistence framework, they must be mapped to fields or properties in the object model. For example, if we replicated the restaurant name by adding a

RESTAURANT_NAME column to the PLACED_ORDER table, we would have to map that column to a `restaurantName` field in the `Order` class.

Although it is easy to define the O/R mapping for denormalized columns, changing the object model to reflect the denormalized database schema introduces additional complexity and maintenance problems. For example, because the denormalized column is maintained by a trigger, the corresponding field will not have a valid value in a newly created object or during in-memory testing unless the domain model contains extra code to initialize it.

Here is an example of the kind of code you need to write in your domain model objects to support denormalized columns:

```
public class Order {

  private String restaurantName;

  public Order(String externalOrderId, Address address,
      Date date, Restaurant restaurant,
      PaymentInformation information) {
    this.restaurantName = restaurant.getName();
    ...
  }

  public String getRestaurantName() {
    return restaurantName;
  }
  ...
}
```

In this example, the `Order` class has a `restaurantName` field that is initialized by the constructor, which calls `Restaurant.getName()`. Although this is a minor change, lots of little changes such as this can be messy.

11.3.5 *Implementing paging*

The fourth and final part of implementing dynamic paged queries with Hibernate and JDO is handling pagination. A query such as View Orders can potentially return a large number of objects. We definitely do not want Hibernate or JDO to instantiate a list containing the entire result set, especially if the application will only display a subset of the elements. Instead, we must ensure that the persistence framework does one of two things:

- Execute a `SELECT` statement that uses a `ROWNUM`-like feature to return only the required range of rows
- Execute a `SELECT` statement that returns all rows and then navigate the JDBC `ResultSet` selecting the required rows

Sometimes, depending on the query, one of these approaches is significantly more efficient than the other. Let's look at how you can select a page of results using JDO and Hibernate.

Implementing paging in JDO

There are two ways a JDO application can select a page from a result set. It can either specify the required range of objects when it executes the query, or it can pick the required objects out of the collection returned by `Query.execute()`. The application specifies the range of rows by calling `Query.setRange()` with the starting index and page size, or by using the `range <from>,<to>` clause in a JDOQL query string. Here is an example of such a JDOQL query:

```
select from net.chrisrichardson.foodToGo.domain.Order
range 0  to 10
```

The `Query.execute()` method will return a collection containing only the first ten objects.

Alternatively, the application can pick the required objects out of the collection returned by `Query.execute()` by either using an iterator or calling `List.get()`.

A potential problem with both of these approaches is that the JDO specification does not describe how the JDO implementation implements queries. There is no guarantee that the JDO implementation implements JDOQL ranges by executing a SQL `SELECT` statement that has a `ROWNUM`-like construct or will lazily navigate the JDBC `ResultSet` as the application iterates through the collection. The JDO 2.0 specification does not give you a way to control how the JDO implementation executes the query and processes the result set.

Fortunately, some JDO implementations such as Kodo JDO let you choose between navigating the result set and using a `ROWNUM` query. For example, Kodo JDO always uses `ROWNUM` if you specify the range when querying an Oracle database. In addition, Kodo JDO can be configured to process the result set lazily, which enables it to efficiently handle large result sets. As the application accesses the elements of the collection returned by the JDO query, Kodo JDO iterates through the underlying JDBC `ResultSet`, loading objects. Kodo JDO gives you the flexibility you need to efficiently implement paging, but if you are using another JDO implementation you should consult its documentation to determine how it implements ranges and processes result sets.

Implementing paging in Hibernate

Hibernate provides two ways of selecting a range of rows from a result set when executing criteria queries. The easier approach is to tell Hibernate the desired range of rows using the `Criteria.setFirstResult()` and `Criteria.setMax-Results()` methods and then execute the query using `Criteria.list()`, which uses a `ROWNUM SELECT` statement and returns a list containing the specified rows. The other option is to execute the query using `Criteria.scroll()`, which returns a `ScrollableResults` that wraps the JDBC `ResultSet`. The application can then navigate the `ScrollableResults`, selecting the rows that it needs.

Here is an example of a query that uses `Criteria.list()` to retrieve orders 100–199 that are for delivery in San Francisco:

```
List orders = session
    .createCriteria(Order.class)
    .add(Restrictions.eq("deliveryAddress.city", "San Francisco"))
    .setFetchMode("restaurant",FetchMode.JOIN)
    .setFirstResult(100)
    .setMaxResults(100)
    .list()
```

This example calls `setFirstResults()` to specify the first order to return and `set-MaxResults()` to specify how many orders to return. Hibernate retrieves the specified rows in two ways. If supported by the database, Hibernate generates a SQL `SELECT` statement that uses a `ROWNUM`-like feature to return only the specified rows using a database-specific SQL feature. If the database does not support this feature, then Hibernate executes a `SELECT` statement that retrieves all rows and then navigates the JDBC `ResultSet` and picks out the specified rows.

Instead of using `list()`, the application can use `scroll()` and navigate `ScrollableResults` and select the required rows. Here is an example code fragment that uses `scroll()` to retrieve orders 100–199:

```
ScrollableResults results = session
  .createCriteria(Order.class)
  .add(Restrictions.eq("deliveryAddress.city", "San Francisco"))
  .setFetchMode("restaurant", FetchMode.JOIN).scroll();
List orders = new ArrayList();
int pageSize = 100;
if (results.first() && results.scroll(100)) {
  for (int i = 0; i < pageSize; i++) {
      orders.add(results.get(0));
      if (!results.next())break;
  }
}
```

This example calls `ScrollableResults.scroll()` to skip over the first 100 rows and `ScrollableResults.next()` to move through the orders. You need to write more code when using `Criteria.scroll()` than you do when using `list()`, but it is a more efficient way to execute some queries.

At this point you've had an overview of the challenges of implementing efficient dynamic paged queries in a Hibernate or JDO application. Next, let's take an in-depth look at using JDO.

11.4 *A JDO design example*

In a JDO application, queries are typically executed by the domain model's repositories. This means that the code that implements a search screen will ultimately call a repository, which must generate a query and call JDO to execute it. Figure 11.5 shows the JDO version of the `OrderRepository`, which is responsible for retrieving orders from the database.It defines a `findOrders()` method whose signature is similar to the `OrderDAO` method we saw earlier. The `startingIndex` and `pageSize`

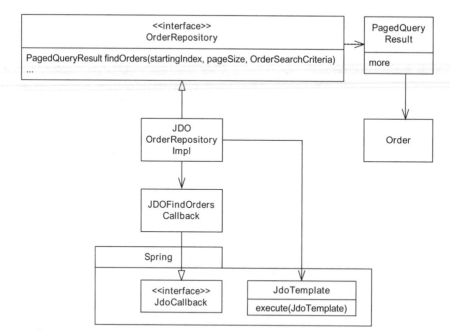

Figure 11.5   The JDO version of the design for finding orders

parameters specify the desired page, and the `OrderSearchCriteria` parameter contains the search criteria entered by the user. It returns a `PagedQueryResult` that contains a list of `Order` objects and a boolean flag indicating whether there are more. The `OrderRepository` interface is implemented by the `JDOOrderRepository-Impl` class. This class generates a query from the `OrderSearchCriteria` and uses a Spring `JdoTemplate` to execute it. Because it uses the JDO APIs to configure the fetch groups, the query is executed using a `JdoCallback` rather than a `JdoTemplate` convenience method. Let's look at the `JDOOrderRepositoryImpl` and `JDOFind-OrdersCallback` classes.

11.4.1 *The JDOOrderRepositoryImpl class*

The biggest challenge when implementing a method such as `findOrders()` is dynamically constructing the query. JDO does not provide any support for generating queries dynamically. The repository must concatenate fragments of JDOQL to create a complete query, which requires some conditional logic. Listing 11.2 shows `findOrders()` and its helper methods, which construct a query using a `StringBuffer`.

Listing 11.2 JDOOrderRepositoryImpl

```
public class JDOOrderRepositoryImpl extends JdoDaoSupport implements
  OrderRepository {

  public JDOOrderRepositoryImpl(JdoTemplate jdoTemplate) {
    setJdoTemplate(jdoTemplate);
  }

  public PagedQueryResult         ◁──────❶ Calls helper methods
      findOrders(int startIndex,           to execute query
          int pageSize,
          OrderSearchCriteria criteria) {

    StringBuffer queryString = makeSelectFrom();
    Map parameters = addWhere(queryString, criteria);
    addOrderBy(queryString, criteria);
    addRange(queryString, startIndex, pageSize);
    return executePagedQuery(pageSize, queryString, parameters);
  }

  private StringBuffer makeSelectFrom() {   ◁──────❷ Creates
    StringBuffer queryString = new StringBuffer();         start of query
    queryString
      .append("select from ")
      .append(Order.class.getName());
    return queryString;
```

```
    }
                              3  Adds where clause
    private Map  ◁──────┘
        addWhere(StringBuffer queryString,
                    OrderSearchCriteria criteria) {
      StringBuffer where = new StringBuffer();
      Map parameters = new HashMap();
      if (criteria.isDeliveryCitySpecified()) {
        if (where.length() != 0)
          where.append(" && ");
          where.append("deliveryAddress.city == :pDeliveryCity");
          parameters.put("pDeliveryCity",
                          criteria.getDeliveryCity());
      }
      if (criteria.isRestaurantSpecified()) {
        if (where.length() != 0)
          where.append(" && ");
        where.append("restaurant.name == :pRestaurant");
        parameters.put("pRestaurant",
                        criteria.getRestaurantName());
      }

      // ...

      if (where.length() != 0)
        queryString.append(" where ").append(where);

      return parameters;
    }


    private void
        addOrderBy(StringBuffer queryString,  ◁──── 4  Adds order by clause
                    OrderSearchCriteria criteria) {
      queryString.append(" order by ");
      queryString.append(getSortField(criteria));
      queryString.append(criteria.isSortAscending() ? " asc "
        : " desc ");
    }

    private void
        addRange(StringBuffer queryString,  ◁──── 5  Adds range clause
                    int startIndex, int pageSize) {
      int endIndex = startIndex + pageSize + 1;
      queryString.append(" range ").append(' ')
        .append(startIndex).append(' ').append(" to ")
        .append(endIndex);
    }

    private PagedQueryResult  ◁──── 6  Executes callback
        executeQuery(int pageSize,
```

```
                    StringBuffer queryString,
                    Map parameters) {
    PagedQueryResult result = (PagedQueryResult) getJdoTemplate()
      .execute(
        new ExecuteFindOrdersQuery(queryString
          .toString(), pageSize, parameters));

    return result;
  }

}
```

Let's look at the details:

❶ The findOrders() method calls a series of helper methods that construct a JDOQL query from the OrderSearchCriteria and execute it.

❷ The makeSelectFrom() method creates the initial part of the query.

❸ The addWhere() method constructs the where clause and appends it to the query.
❹ It has conditional logic that adds an expression to the where clause for each of the search criteria that has been specified in the OrderSearchCriteria object. The addWhere() method returns a map containing the query parameters, which is later passed to Query.executeWithMap().

❺ The addOrderBy() method adds an order by clause to the query.

The addRange() method adds a range clause to the query.

❻ The executeQuery() method executes the query using ExecuteFindOrdersQuery, which is a JdoCallback.

As you can see, we had to write a lot of code to generate a JDO query. Even if some code is refactored into a reusable utility class, the repository would still contain some messy conditional logic and JDOQL fragments, which makes it error-prone and difficult to maintain. But we mostly have to tolerate this problem because of the benefits of JDOQL.

11.4.2 *The ExecuteFindOrdersQuery class*

ExecuteFindOrdersQuery is a JdoCallback that is executed by JDOOrderRepository-Impl. It defines a doInJdo() method, which is called by the JdoTemplate. This method uses the Kodo JDO APIs to configure the object loading and execute the query. Here is the code:

```
class ExecuteFindOrdersQuery implements JdoCallback {
  private final String queryString;

  private final int pageSize;

  private final Map parameters;

  private ExecuteFindOrdersQuery(String queryString,
    int pageSize, Map parameters) {
    this.queryString = queryString;
    this.pageSize = pageSize;
    this.parameters = parameters;
  }

  public Object doInJdo(PersistenceManager pm)
    throws JDOException {
    Query query = pm.newQuery(queryString.toString());
    KodoQuery kquery = (KodoQuery) query;
    FetchConfiguration fc = kquery.getFetchConfiguration();
    fc.addField(Order.class.getName() + ".restaurant");
    List result = new ArrayList((List) query
      .executeWithMap(parameters));

    boolean more = result.size() > pageSize;
    if (more)
    result.remove(pageSize);
    return new PagedQueryResult(result, more);
  }
}
```

The doInJdo() method creates a query, calls configureFetchGroups(), executes the query, and creates the PagedQueryResult containing the list of orders and the more flag.

But sometimes you must execute queries that require the use of SQL features such as optimizer hints in order to achieve good performance. That is when you must use a JDO native SQL query.

11.5 A Hibernate design example

As with JDO, queries in a Hibernate application are typically executed by domain model repositories. The Hibernate version of the OrderRepository, which is pretty similar to the JDO version, is shown in figure 11.6. The OrderRepository interface is implemented by HibernateOrderRepositoryImpl, which uses the Spring HibernateTemplate to construct and execute a Hibernate criteria query.

The OrderRepository interface is implemented by the HibernateOrderRepositoryImpl class. It uses a Spring HibernateTemplate to execute a HibernateCallback

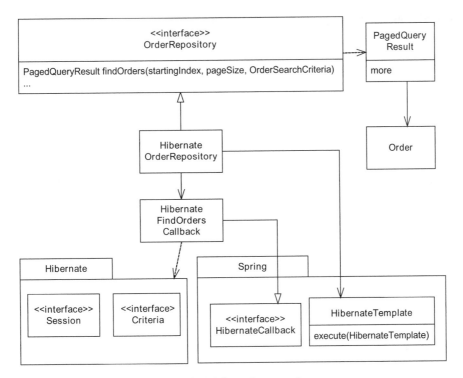

Figure 11.6   Hibernate implementation of the `OrderRepository`

that generates a query from the `OrderSearchCriteria` using the Hibernate `Criteria` API. Let's look at the `HibernateOrderRepositoryImpl` and `HibernateFindOrdersCallback` classes.

11.5.1   The HibernateOrderRepositoryImpl class

The `findOrders()` method is extremely simple. It uses a `HibernateTemplate` to execute a `FindOrdersHibernateCallback`, which does all of the work. Here is the code for `HibernateOrderRepositoryImpl`:

```
public class HibernateOrderRepositoryImpl extends
  HibernateDaoSupport implements OrderRepository {

  public PagedQueryResult findOrders(int startingIndex,
    int pageSize,
    OrderSearchCriteria searchCriteria) {
    return (PagedQueryResult) getHibernateTemplate().execute(
      new FindOrdersHibernateCallback(startingIndex,
        pageSize, searchCriteria));
  }
}
```

The findOrders() method instantiates a FindOrdersHibernateCallback, passing startingIndex, pageSize, and searchCriteria as constructor arguments.

11.5.2 *The FindOrdersHibernateCallback class*

FindOrdersHibernateCallback, which is shown in listing 11.3, is a Spring HibernateCallback and has a doInHibernate() method that constructs and executes a criteria query. It builds the restrictions and sort order for query using the properties of the OrderSearchCriteria.

Listing 11.3 FindOrdersHibernateCallback

```
private final class FindOrdersHibernateCallback implements
    HibernateCallback {
  private final int startingIndex;

  private final int pageSize;

  private final OrderSearchCriteria searchCriteria;

  private FindOrdersHibernateCallback(int startingIndex,
    int pageSize, OrderSearchCriteria searchCriteria) {
    super();
    this.startingIndex = startingIndex;
    this.pageSize = pageSize;
    this.searchCriteria = searchCriteria;
  }
                                  ❶ Creates and executes
  public Object  ⟵──────┘           criteria query
      doInHibernate(Session session)
          throws HibernateException, SQLException {
    Criteria criteria = session.createCriteria(Order.class);
    addCriteria(criteria, searchCriteria);
    addSortBy(criteria, searchCriteria);
    addRange(criteria);
    List result = criteria.list();
    return makePagedQueryResult(result);
  }
                          ❷ Adds
  public void  ⟵──────┘    search criteria
      addCriteria(Criteria criteria,
                    OrderSearchCriteria searchCriteria)
    throws HibernateException {
    if (searchCriteria.isDeliveryTimeSpecified()) {
      criteria.add(Restrictions.ge("deliveryTime",
        searchCriteria.getDeliveryTime()));
    }
    if (searchCriteria.isRestaurantSpecified()) {
      criteria.createCriteria("restaurant").add(
```

```
          Restrictions.like("name", searchCriteria
            .getRestaurantName()));
    } else {
      criteria.setFetchMode("restaurant", FetchMode.JOIN);
    }
    if (searchCriteria.isDeliveryCitySpecified()) {
      criteria.add(Restrictions.eq("deliveryAddress.city",
        searchCriteria.getDeliveryCity()));
    }
    ...

}
                                ❸ Specifies ordering
private void  ◄────────
        addSortBy(Criteria criteria,
                  OrderSearchCriteria searchCriteria) {
    switch (searchCriteria.getSortBy()) {
    case OrderSearchCriteria.SORT_BY_ORDER_ID:
      criteria
        .addOrder(searchCriteria.isSortAscending() ?
          org.hibernate.criterion.Order
          .asc("externalOrderId")
          : org.hibernate.criterion.Order
            .desc("externalOrderId"));
    break;
    ...
    default:
      throw new NotYetImplementedException();
    }
}

private void addRange(Criteria criteria) {   ◄────── ❹ Specifies range
    criteria.setFirstResult(startingIndex);
    criteria.setMaxResults(pageSize + 1);
}
                                ❺ Creates PagedQueryResult
private PagedQueryResult  ◄────────
        makePagedQueryResult(List result) {
    boolean more = result.size() > pageSize;
    if (more) {
      result.remove(pageSize);
    }
    return new PagedQueryResult(result, more);
}

}
```

Let's look at the details:

❶ The `doInJdo()` method creates the criteria query and calls a helper method to add the search criteria, specify the ordering and range, and to create the `PagedQueryResult`.

❷ The `addCriteria()` method adds criteria to the query based on what search criteria are specified in the `OrderSearchCriteria` object. One notable feature of this method is that if the restaurant name is not one of the search criteria, then `addCriteria()` adds a fetch join for `Restaurant`.

❸ The `addSortBy()` method specifies how to sort the results.

❹ The `addRange()` method specifies the range of rows to retrieve.

❺ The `makePagedQueryResult()` method constructs the `PagedQueryResult`.

The Hibernate version of the repository contains some conditional logic, but it's a lot simpler than the JDO version because using criteria queries eliminates the need to concatenate query fragments.

11.6 *Using JDO and Hibernate native SQL queries*

In an ideal world, we would use object queries for all database queries and rely on the persistence framework to generate optimal SQL statements. But as you might expect, in the real world this isn't always possible and sometimes we must use SQL queries that use vendor-specific features such as optimizer hints to achieve the necessary performance. Both JDO and Hibernate support native SQL queries. They give you complete control over the SQL while taking care of the potentially tedious task of constructing Java objects. The only drawback is that neither Hibernate nor JDO provides any support for dynamically generating SQL queries. Consequently, you might want to consider using iBATIS if you are only going to display the results of the query and do not need to manipulate the objects. Let's look at how to use JDO and Hibernate SQL queries.

11.6.1 *Using JDO native SQL queries*

A JDO native SQL query is executed using the JDO `Query` interface but is written in SQL instead of JDOQL. It can return either persistent objects or DTOs. SQL queries that return persistent objects are useful if the application needs to manipulate the persistent objects. However, they are somewhat restrictive because the columns of the result set must map to the fields of a single persistent class. A SQL query cannot, for example, eagerly load related objects such as an order and its restaurant, which makes it impossible to implement the View Orders query.

A SQL query that returns DTOs is also known as a SQL projection query and, if you do not need to load the actual objects, provides more flexibility. The columns of the result set are mapped to the JavaBean-style properties of the result class instead of the fields of a persistent class and can come from multiple tables and denormalized columns. You can, for example, use a SQL projection query to load fields from multiple related objects.

Listing 11.4 shows an example of a SQL projection query that retrieves orders and their restaurants using a SQL SELECT statement that has a FIRST_ROWS optimizer hint. It returns a collection of OrderSummaryDTO objects that contain the order's ID, delivery time, email, and phone number, and the restaurant's name.

Listing 11.4   An example of a JDO SQL projection query

```
public class JDOOrderRepositoryImpl extends
  JdoDaoSupport implements OrderRepository {
...
  public List findOrdersUsingSQL() {
  return (List) getJdoTemplate().executeFind(
    new SQLCallback());
  }

  private final class SQLCallback implements
    JdoCallback {

    public Object doInJdo(PersistenceManager pm)
      throws JDOException {
      String sqlQuery = "SELECT /*+ FIRST_ROWS(20) */ "
        + " o.order_id as orderId, "
        + " o.delivery_time as deliveryTime, "
        + " o.payment_email as email, "
        + " o.payment_phone as phoneNumber, "
        + " r.name as restaurantName   "
        + " from FTGO_ORDER o, FTGO_RESTAURANT r   "
        + " where o.restaurant_id = r.restaurant_id";   Creates SQL query
      Query query = pm.newQuery(
        "javax.jdo.query.SQL", sqlQuery);   Specifies return type
      ((KodoQuery) query)
        .setResultClass(OrderSummaryDTO.class);
      List result = (List) query.execute();   Executes
      return result;                          query
    }

  }
...
}
```

The call to `Query.setResultClass()` specifies that `execute()` should return the results of the query as a list of `OrderSummaryDTO` objects. For each row in the result set returned by the query, Kodo JDO instantiates an `OrderSummaryDTO` and calls its setters.

SQL projection queries enable you to optimize query performance by using database-specific SQL features. There are, however, a number of drawbacks:

- It hardwires knowledge of the database and the schema into the application, which makes porting and maintaining the application more difficult.

- Unless the SQL `SELECT` statement uses `ROWNUM`-like features, you have to rely on the JDO implementation to process the result set lazily.

- You have to write code to generate the SQL `SELECT` statement.

Consequently, if you need to use a SQL query but don't need it to return persistent objects, you should consider using iBATIS mapped statements instead. The iBATIS framework makes it easy to generate SQL `SELECT` statements, and you have control over how it processes the result set.

11.6.2 *Using Hibernate SQL queries*

A Hibernate application creates a SQL query by calling `Session.cre-ateSQLQuery()`, which takes a SQL `SELECT` statement as an argument, or by calling `Session.getNamedQuery()`, which takes the name of a SQL query as an argument. Here is a code fragment that executes a SQL `SELECT` statement to retrieve the orders whose delivery city is Oakland and their associated restaurants:

```
public class HibernateOrderRepositoryImpl extends
  HibernateDaoSupport implements OrderRepository {

  ...
  List findOrdersUsingSQLAndList() {
  List orders = (List) getHibernateTemplate()
    .execute(new SqlUsingListCallback());
  return orders;
  }

  private final class SqlUsingListCallback implements
    HibernateCallback {

    public Object doInHibernate(Session session)
      throws HibernateException,
      SQLException {
      String sqlQuery = "SELECT  {o.*},{r.*} "
        + " FROM FTGO_ORDER o, FTGO_RESTAURANT r "
        + " WHERE r.restaurant_id = o.restaurant_id "
        + "AND o.delivery_city = :name "
```

```
        + " ORDER BY DELIVERY_TIME desc";
    SQLQuery query = session
        .createSQLQuery(sqlQuery);
    query.addEntity("o", Order.class);
    query.addJoin("r", "o.restaurant");
    query.setParameter("name", "Oakland");
    List results = query.list();
    return results;
    }
}
...
}
```

Notice that the SELECT statement uses placeholders such as {o.*} for the column names. Hibernate replaces them with the real column names when it executes the SELECT statement. The call to SQLQuery.addEntity() tells Hibernate that the table alias o refers to the Order class, and the call to SQLQuery.addJoin() tells Hibernate that the table alias r refers to the order's restaurant property. The list() method returns a list of arrays. Each array consists of an Order and its Restaurant. The restaurant is also accessible by calling Order.getRestaurant(). If your application needs to navigate the result set, it can also execute Hibernate SQL queries by calling scroll().

SQL queries enable an application to execute SQL statements while staying within the Hibernate framework. However, they have some drawbacks:

1 You must generate queries by concatenating SQL fragments, which are messy and difficult to maintain.

2 Using SQL directly embeds some knowledge of the database and the schema in the application code.

3 The query must retrieve all the properties of the objects, which might be inefficient.

Therefore, although SQL queries are useful if you need to manipulate the persistent objects, a better approach is to use iBATIS to generate and execute the queries. It requires less code and gives you more control over how the result set is processed.

11.7 Summary

Designing and implementing a search screen that lets the user search for entities that match certain search criteria is challenging. The application must implement a paging mechanism in order to handle result sets that are too large to load entirely into memory or display on a single page. It must generate queries dynamically, which often requires code that is messy and difficult to maintain. In addition, you often need to optimize SQL statements to achieve acceptable performance.

One good solution to this problem is to use the iBATIS framework, which provides a mechanism for generating queries dynamically that requires only a few lines of Java code. The iBATIS framework also keeps the intact SQL statement in an XML file, which makes it easier to test and change. In addition, the framework gives you control over how the result set is processed. You can either execute a query that uses ROWNUM or you can choose rows from the result set. Overall, implementing a DAO for a search screen using iBATIS is very straightforward except for, of course, all the usual issues of maintaining handwritten SQL.

Using JDO or Hibernate avoids the problems associated with using SQL directly, but implementing some search screen queries efficiently can be difficult. Although JDO and Hibernate provide optimizations such as eager loading, you are not always able to get good performance because you cannot use database-specific SQL features such as optimizer hints. Another issue is that while Hibernate and some JDO implementations such as Kodo JDO let you pick the most efficient way to select a page from the result set, others might not. Furthermore, unless you use Hibernate criteria queries you have to write messy query-generation code.

JDO and Hibernate also support native SQL queries, which can use database-specific features such as optimizer hints to improve performance. But, even when using SQL queries, you still need to have control over the processing of the result set. Moreover, both persistence frameworks lack support for generating SQL queries, and so you have to write some potentially messy code. Sometimes, a better approach is to use iBATIS to generate and execute the SQL queries.

In the next chapter, you will learn how to handle database concurrency issues.

12

Database transactions
and concurrency

This chapter covers

- Using optimistic and pessimistic locking
- Handling concurrency in iBATIS, JDO and Hibernate
- Recovering from concurrency failures with Spring

Many enterprise applications store data that is critical to the company and its customers. Consider, for example, how your bank stores your money. Harry Potter's vault at Gringotts bank contains real gold galleons, but your money exists as fragile 1s and 0s in the bank's database. There are many things that your bank must do to safeguard that data, and one of the most important is maintaining the integrity of that data when it is simultaneously updated by multiple database transactions.

Enterprise applications almost always have multiple simultaneous users. Many also have background tasks, which are triggered by schedulers or events received from external systems. As a result, there are usually multiple transactions that are simultaneously reading and updating the database. A major challenge faced by enterprise application developers is that data can become inconsistent when it is updated by multiple transactions simultaneously. Even though you might expect the database to prevent this from happening, it is often the responsibility of the application to maintain the consistency of the data.

This is the first of two chapters that describe how an application can handle concurrent updates. In this chapter you will learn about the basic concurrency mechanisms you can use to handle concurrent updates within a database transaction, which don't involve user interactions. We describe three different concurrency mechanisms and how to use them in iBATIS/JDBC, JDO, and Hibernate applications. In addition, you'll learn how an application can recover from a database concurrency failure. The next chapter shows you how to handle concurrent updates in long-running business transactions, which consist of multiple database transactions and usually involve user interactions.

12.1 *Handling concurrent access to shared data*

The outcome of executing multiple transactions simultaneously must be the same as executing them serially, that is, one after the other, but in random order. Mathematically speaking, if there are N transactions, then there are factorial(N) equally valid outcomes. This means, for example, that in the Food to Go application there are two valid outcomes of executing the Send Orders to Restaurant and Cancel Order use cases simultaneously. One outcome is that the order is sent to the restaurant and not canceled (because it has already been sent). The other outcome is that the order should be canceled and not sent to the restaurant.

If neither the application nor the database ensures that the outcome of executing multiple transactions simultaneously is the same as executing them serially, then the database can become inconsistent and the application can behave incorrectly. One common problem is lost updates, which occur when one transaction blindly overwrites another transaction's changes. Both transactions think they have updated the database even though one transaction's changes have been lost. A lost update in the Food to Go application could, for example, cause a restaurant to prepare an unwanted order. If it were a bank, money could disappear, which is something that couldn't happen to the gold at Gringotts—at least not without magic!

Another common problem are inconsistent reads, which occur when the data being read by one transaction is updated by another transaction. The transaction that is reading the data sees different values at different times, which can result in incorrect behavior. This can potentially happen any time an application queries the same data more than once. It can also happen when a transaction uses multiple queries to load related data, such as an order and its line items. In between two queries another transaction could change the data. For more information about lost updates and inconsistent reads, as well as some more subtle problems, see *Transaction Processing: Concepts and Techniques* [Gray 1993].

There are three main ways to handle concurrent accesses to shared data. Let's look at each one in turn.

12.1.1 *Using fully isolated transactions*

One solution is to use transactions that are fully isolated from one another, which in database-speak are transactions with an isolation level of serializable. The database ensures that the outcome of executing multiple serializable transactions is the same as executing them serially. Serializable transactions prevent such problems as lost updates and inconsistent reads. For more information about serializable transactions and the nuances of how they are supported by different databases, see [Gray 1993] or the documentation for your database.

As you will see later, using serializable transactions is very straightforward. You configure Spring, JDO, or Hibernate, or the JDBC `DataSource`, to use the serializable isolation level. The database tries to execute the transactions serially, and if it cannot because of a problem (such as a deadlock), it will return an error code. The application can then roll back and retry the failed transaction.

Serializable is only one of the transaction isolation levels provided by databases. Some databases also provide a repeatable read isolation level, which, as the name suggests, ensures that a transaction gets the same results each time it reads a row. However, unlike serializable transactions, repeatable read transactions can get inconsistent results when they execute a query because other transactions can insert and delete rows, which are known as phantoms.

The problem with using serialization and repeatable read isolation levels is that they achieve isolation at the expense of system performance and scalability. This is because the database handles concurrent access to shared data using mechanisms such as locking, which reduces the amount of concurrency in the system. As a result, many applications use a third isolation level called read committed to improve performance and scalability. Read committed provides even less isolation than serializable or repeatable read because it does not prevent inconsistent reads or lost updates. Applications make up for this lack of isolation by using it in conjunction with either optimistic or pessimistic locking, which are described later in this section.

Benefits and drawbacks

Fully isolated transactions have two main benefits:

- They are simple to use.
- They prevent many concurrency problems, including lost updates and inconsistent reads.

The main drawback of fully isolated transactions is the high overhead, which can reduce performance and scalability. Also, fully isolated transactions can fail more frequently than less isolated transactions because of deadlocks and other concurrency-related issues.

When to use fully isolated transactions

An application should use fully isolated transactions when:

- Read consistency is essential.
- The overhead of fully isolated transactions is acceptable.

A typical application rarely needs to use fully isolated transactions. Instead, it should use the read committed isolation level in conjunction with either optimistic locking or pessimistic locking.

12.1.2 Optimistic locking

The trouble with fully isolated transactions is that they incur a significant overhead regardless of whether concurrent updates actually occur. Concurrent updates are usually quite rare, and so the mechanism that handles them should ideally impose an overhead on the application only when one happens. A commonly used mechanism that works this way is optimistic locking. Despite its name, optimistic locking doesn't actually lock anything. Instead, when a transaction updates a row it verifies that the row has not been changed or deleted by a different transaction since it was read. If it has, the transaction is typically rolled back and retried. Performing the inexpensive check at update time prevents the other transaction's updates from being lost. Moreover, the overhead of redoing a transaction is only incurred when a concurrent update is detected.

A JDBC/iBATIS application must implement the optimistic locking mechanism itself. But, as you will see later, using optimistic locking in a JDO or Hibernate application is simply a configuration issue. The application loads and updates objects as usual, and JDO and Hibernate take care of all the bookkeeping required to implement optimistic locking.

Tracking changes to data

There are three ways an application or a persistence framework can determine whether a row has been changed since it was read. The first option is to track changes using a version column, which is incremented whenever the application updates a row. The transaction determines whether a row has changed by simply comparing current value of the version column with the value that was originally read from the database. This is usually the best approach since it is relatively simple for the application to check and update a version column.

The second option is to use a timestamp column, which is updated whenever the application updates a row. A transaction determines whether a row has changed by comparing the current value of the timestamp column with the value that was originally read from the database. This scheme is also quite simple to implement, especially since tables often already have a timestamp column in order to record when a user last updated a row. However, one problem with using timestamps is that one transaction might overwrite another if the time interval between the two updates is less than the granularity of the clock. Consequently, an application should only use a timestamp column when working with a legacy schema that already has one and it's not possible to add a version column.

The third option is to compare current values of the columns with their previously read values. The biggest advantage of using this approach is that it can work with an existing legacy schema because it does not require the addition of either a version or timestamp column. One drawback of this approach is that it makes the SQL UPDATE statements more complex since, as we describe later, the WHERE clause will contain a condition for every column. It must also handle null values correctly, which can be complicated. For example, I once discovered that one popular persistence framework could not compare blank strings correctly because in

Oracle, unlike Java, an empty string is considered to be null. We solved this problem by adding a version column to the table.

Another drawback is that floating-point columns cannot be compared precisely and changes to them may not be detected. Because of these issues, an application should only use this approach if it not possible to add a version or timestamp column.

Efficiently implementing the optimistic locking check

A JDBC/iBATIS application or a persistence framework can efficiently implement the optimistic locking check by incorporating it into the UPDATE statement that updates the row. For example, here is an UPDATE statement that updates an order and uses a version column to detect changes:

```
UPDATE PLACED_ORDER
SET VERSION = VERSION + 1,
  STATUS = 'SENT'
WHERE ORDER_ID = ? AND VERSION = ?
```

This UPDATE statement changes the state of the order and increments the version number. Its WHERE clause checks that the version number is unchanged. If another transaction changed or deleted the order, the UPDATE statement would not update any rows and the JDBC PreparedStatement.executeUpdate() method, which executes the UPDATE statement, would return a row count of zero. The application could check this value and roll back the transaction when it is zero. UPDATE statements that used timestamps or compared column values rows would be similar.

Using optimistic locking

Let's look at how optimistic locking can be used to prevent lost updates when one transaction attempts to send an order to a restaurant while another transaction tries to cancel it. Keep in mind that all this applies to read committed or less isolation only. In the scenario shown in figure 12.1, both transactions query the PLACED_ORDER table using a SQL SELECT statement that retrieves the order's version number. When updating the order, they verify that the version number is unchanged.

Transaction A reads the orders and saves the version numbers, and then transaction B does the same. Transaction A then updates an order using an UPDATE statement that checks that the version number is unchanged and increments the version number. When transaction B attempts to update the order, its UPDATE statement fails because the VERSION column has changed and PreparedStatement.executeUpdate() will return zero. At this point transaction B can then do one of two things. It could roll back and start again, or it could reread the

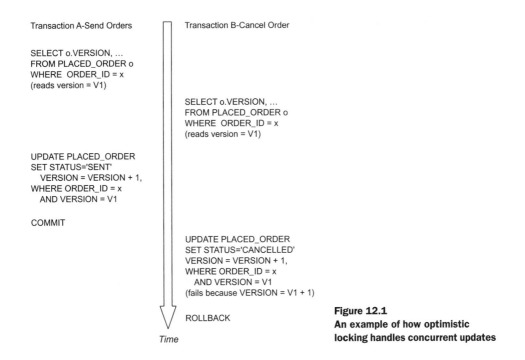

SELECT o.VERSION, ...
FROM PLACED_ORDER o
WHERE ORDER_ID = x
(reads version = V1)

SELECT o.VERSION, ...
FROM PLACED_ORDER o
WHERE ORDER_ID = x
(reads version = V1)

UPDATE PLACED_ORDER
SET STATUS='SENT'
  VERSION = VERSION + 1,
WHERE ORDER_ID = x
  AND VERSION = V1

COMMIT

UPDATE PLACED_ORDER
SET STATUS='CANCELLED'
VERSION = VERSION + 1,
WHERE ORDER_ID = x
  AND VERSION = V1
(fails because VERSION = V1 + 1)

ROLLBACK

Time

Figure 12.1
An example of how optimistic
locking handles concurrent updates

changed row and redo just that part of the computation. In either case, it would
discover that the order had been sent and could not be canceled.

Benefits and drawbacks

Optimistic locking has a couple of advantages:

- It is easy to implement in a JDBC/iBATIS application, and it is supported by
  many persistence frameworks.

- Optimistic locking, unlike pessimistic locking, does not prevent an application from using certain SQL SELECT statement features. As you'll see a bit
  later, some databases have restrictions that prevent pessimistic locking from
  working with some kinds of views and nested SELECT statements, etc.

There are, however, various drawbacks and issues:

- All potentially conflicting transactions must use optimistic locking. Otherwise, errors will occur. Fortunately, this isn't an issue when using a persistence framework because optimistic locking is specified declaratively on a
  per-class basis, which ensures that it will be used consistently.

- The easiest way to implement optimistic locking is to use a version column. But it is not always possible to add a version column to a legacy schema that you have no control over. What's more, you might not be able to modify the legacy applications that also use the schema to increment the version column.

- Optimistic locking does not guarantee that a transaction will be able to update the rows that it read. If those rows have been changed by another transaction, it will have to start over, which can be inefficient.

- Optimistic locking does not prevent inconsistent reads. Fortunately, many applications can tolerate some amount of inconsistency.

When to use it

Despite these drawbacks, optimistic locking is a useful concurrency mechanism. A general recommendation is that an application should use optimistic locking unless:

- The database schema does not support optimistic locking. It's a legacy schema whose tables have columns that contain values such as floating-point values that cannot be compared and you cannot add a version or timestamp column.

- The application must be guaranteed to be able to update the rows that it read.

- The application requires consistent reads.

12.1.3 *Pessimistic locking*

When optimistic locking won't work, another way to handle concurrent updates is by using pessimistic locking. As the name suggests, this mechanism assumes that concurrent updates will occur and so incurs an overhead regardless of whether they do. However, this overhead is much less than with fully isolated transactions. A transaction that uses pessimistic locking locks the rows that it reads, which prevents other transactions from reading and updating them. Other transactions will block until the transaction releases those locks by either committing or rolling back. Pessimistic locking prevents lost updates and provides some degree of read consistency because it prevents the read rows from being changed by other transactions. However, because pessimistic locking does not prevent new rows from being inserted, re-executing the same query might return different results.

How it works

The mechanism for acquiring locks is database specific and not all databases support it. In Oracle, an application uses pessimistic locking by executing a SELECT FOR UPDATE statement, which locks the rows that it selects. The rows remain locked until the transaction either commits or rolls back. Other transactions will be blocked if they update or delete those rows or attempt to retrieve them using a SELECT FOR UPDATE. Here is an example of an SELECT FOR UPDATE statement:

```
SELECT *
FROM PLACED_ORDER o, PLACED_ORDER_LINE_ITEM l
WHERE o.DELIVERY_TIME < SYSDATE
  AND o.STATUS = 'PLACED'
  AND o.ORDER_ID = l.ORDER_ID
FOR UPDATE
```

This SELECT FOR UPDATE statement retrieves and locks all orders whose state is 'PLACED' and whose delivery time is before a certain time.

A transaction that executes a SELECT FOR UPDATE statement will be blocked if another transaction has locked the rows. This will happen if the other transaction has either updated or deleted those rows or locked them using a SELECT FOR UPDATE. The transaction will be blocked until the other transaction commits or rolls back. If a transaction doesn't want to wait, it can use a SELECT FOR UPDATE NO WAIT statement, which returns with an ORA-00054 error if it cannot lock the rows immediately. Alternatively, it can wait for a specified period by using SELECT FOR UPDATE WAIT <n seconds>.

Using pessimistic locking

Let's look at how this application can use a SELECT FOR UPDATE statement to prevent lost updates in the sendOrders/cancelOrder scenario. In the scenario shown in figure 12.2, both transactions query the PLACED_ORDER table using a SELECT FOR UPDATE. In this scenario, transaction A executes the SELECT FOR UPDATE statement first, which locks the row. The SELECT FOR UPDATE executed by transaction B will block until transaction A commits and releases the lock. At this point, transaction B will discover that the order has been sent and cannot be canceled.

A transaction can use pessimistic locking to provide some degree of read consistency. Because rows that are read using SELECT FOR UPDATE are locked, they cannot be changed or deleted by another transaction. If the transaction queries the database again, those rows will be unchanged. However, because pessimistic locking does not prevent another transaction from inserting new rows, a query could return additional rows.

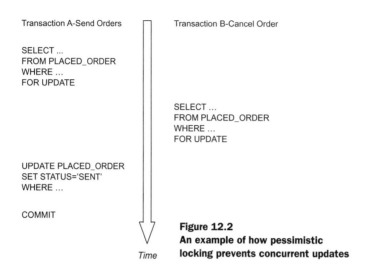

**Figure 12.2
An example of how pessimistic
locking prevents concurrent updates**

Time

Benefits and drawbacks

Pessimistic locking has several advantages:

- Unlike optimistic locking, pessimistic locking does not require any schema changes.

- It prevents a transaction from overwriting another transaction's changes. By locking rows when they are read, a transaction can ensure that when it updates them later it will not overwrite another transaction's changes.

- It can be used to maintain read consistency in scenarios where a transaction reads from one table but updates another. A transaction can use SELECT FOR UPDATE to ensure that rows that it reads but does not update are unchanged when it commits.

- It reduces the probability of deadlocks in databases that implement fully isolated transactions by locking rows when they read.

But again, there are some drawbacks and issues as well:

- All potentially conflicting transactions have to use SELECT FOR UPDATE in order for pessimistic locking to work, which is potentially error-prone. For example, in the sendOrders/cancelOrder scenario, if transaction B used a regular SELECT statement it would not block and would end up overwriting transaction A's changes.

- In databases such as Oracle where SELECT does not normally lock rows, the increased use of locks reduces concurrency and the overhead of maintaining many locks can reduce performance. The increased use of locks also enhances the probability of deadlocks, which occur when two transactions are waiting for locks held by the other. Oracle automatically detects deadlocks and returns an ORA-00060 error to one of the participating transactions, which can either roll back the entire transaction or retry the SQL statement that caused the deadlock. Other databases will signal a deadlock in a similar way.

- Some databases have limitations on how SELECT FOR UPDATE can be used. For example, with Oracle, it can only be used at the top level and cannot be nested within another SQL statement. Also, there are certain SQL features that cannot be used in conjunction with SELECT FOR UPDATE. These features include DISTINCT, aggregate functions, and GROUP BY. It cannot be used on certain types of views and nested SELECTs. This is a particularly important limitation when an application uses a persistence framework since it has no control over the generated SQL.

- An application that accesses the database using a persistence framework can only use pessimistic locking if the persistence framework supports it. An application cannot implement pessimistic locking on top of a persistence framework.

- An application that uses pessimistic locking cannot use a process-level cache because it must access the database in order to lock the rows.

Despite these limitations, pessimistic locking is extremely useful in many situations.

When to use it

Pessimistic locking should be used when:

- The database schema does not support optimistic locking because, for example, the tables do not have a version or timestamp column or contain values such as floats or blobs that cannot be compared.

- The application requires some degree of read consistency.

- You don't want to incur the overhead of serializable transactions.

12.1.4 Using a combination of locking mechanisms

The simplest approach is to use a single concurrency strategy throughout the application, but sometimes you might need to use a combination of concurrency strategies. You could, for example, use optimistic locking for all transactions except those with special requirements. Transactions that access tables that do not support optimistic locking can use pessimistic locking, and transactions that need read consistency can use a serializable isolation level. To determine the right approach, you need to examine the requirements of each use case.

Now that we have gotten an overview of fully isolated transactions, pessimistic locking, and optimistic locking, let's look at how to use them to handle concurrent updates in an enterprise application.

12.2 Handling concurrent updates in a JDBC/iBATIS application

The details of how an application uses each of the three concurrency mechanisms described in the previous section depends on which database access mechanism it uses. We will start by looking at how to use those concurrency options in an application that executes SQL statements directly using either JDBC or iBATIS. This will enable you to learn how the different concurrency mechanisms work at the SQL level, which later sections will build on as they describe how JDO and Hibernate applications use them.

We'll use the business logic for the Send Orders to Restaurant use case as an example. First we provide an overview of a design for the business logic that is based on the Transaction Script pattern and uses an iBATIS/JDBC-based DAO to access the database. After that, you'll learn the details of how each of the concurrency mechanisms is used.

12.2.1 Design overview

The Send Orders to Restaurant use case describes how orders are sent to a restaurant for preparation:

> X minutes before the scheduled delivery time, the system sends (emails or faxes) a placed order to the restaurant.

This use case is driven by a scheduler and has no UI. Figure 12.3 shows the transaction script version of the business logic for this use case. It consists of a transaction script that finds the orders to send, sends them, and then changes each order's status to indicate that it was sent. It uses iBATIS to execute SQL statements that find and update the orders and uses Spring to manage transactions and connections. The transaction script is wrapped with a Spring `TransactionInterceptor`, which manages transactions and a JDBC connection. This design works for serializable transactions, optimistic locking, and pessimistic locking, with only minor changes to the

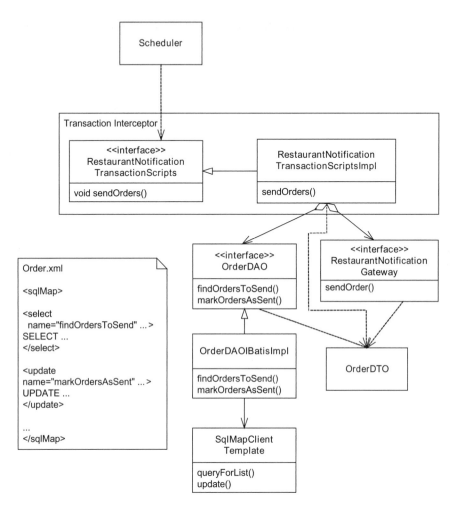

Figure 12.3   Transaction script-based design for the Send Orders to Restaurant use case

SQL statements that are executed by the `OrderDAO` and the configuration of the Spring `TransactionInterceptor` or JDBC `DataSource`.

The key classes in the design are:

- `RestaurantNotificationTransactionScripts`, which `implements` the transaction script
- `Scheduler`, which periodically invokes the `RestaurantNotificationTransactionScripts`

- `RestaurantNotificationGateway`, which encapsulates the mechanism for sending orders to restaurants
- `OrderDAO`, which encapsulates the database access code
- `OrderDAOIBatisImpl`, which implements the `OrderDAO` interface using the Spring `SqlMapClientTemplate`, a wrapper around the iBATIS classes
- `OrderDTO`, which represents an order
- `TransactionInterceptor`, which is the Spring AOP interceptor that manages transactions and JDBC connections

`RestaurantNotificationTransactionScripts` defines the `sendOrders()` method, which is the transaction script that sends the orders to the restaurant. This method first calls the `OrderDAO` to find the orders to send. It then sends each order using the `RestaurantNotificationGateway`. After sending the orders, it calls the `OrderDAO` to mark the orders as having been sent.

The `OrderDAO` defines a `findOrdersToSend()` method, which returns a list of orders, and a `markOrdersAsSent()` method, which updates the orders to indicate that they been sent. The `OrderDAOIBatisImpl` class uses a Spring `SqlMapClientTemplate` to execute the SQL statements that are defined in the iBATIS file Order.xml.

Let's now look at how this business logic can use each of the database concurrency mechanisms. In a real application, the business logic for a use case would only use one concurrency mechanism—most likely optimistic locking—but it is educational to compare the implementations of each one.

12.2.2 Using optimistic locking

The easiest way to implement optimistic locking is to add a version column to the PLACED_ORDER table, which is incremented by the application each time it updates a row:

```
CREATE TABLE PLACED_ORDER (
    ...
    VERSION NUMBER(10) DEFAULT 0 NOT NULL,
    ...
)
```

The version column along with the rest of the data from the PLACED_ORDER table is retrieved by the SQL SELECT statement executed by the `OrderDAO`:

```
SELECT * ... o.VERSION ...
FROM PLACED_ORDER o, RESTAURANT r, PLACED_ORDER_LINE_ITEM l
WHERE
  o.status = 'PLACED' AND DELIVERY_TIME < ?
```

```
        AND
        bbr.restaurant_id = o.restaurant_id
        AND l.order_id = o.order_id
    ORDER BY o.order_id ASC
```

This statement retrieves the order information from the PLACED_ORDER, RES-TAURANT, and PLACED_ORDER_LINE_ITEM tables. The OrderDAO stores the version in the OrderDTO, which is returned to the sendOrders() transaction script.

The OrderDAO updates the Order using the following SQL statement:

```
UPDATE PLACED_ORDER
SET VERSION = VERSION + 1,
    STATUS = 'SENT', MESSAGE_ID = ?, SENT_TIME = ?
WHERE ORDER_ID = ? AND VERSION = ?
```

This UPDATE statement changes the state of a specific order to SENT and updates the MESSAGE_ID, SENT_TIME, and VERSION columns only if the VERSION column is unchanged since it was read.

The markOrderAsSent() method, which executes the UPDATE statement, checks the count of the rows updated and throws an exception if it is zero. It executes the UPDATE statement by calling SqlMapClientTemplate.update():

```
public class OrderDAOIBatisImpl extends SqlMapClientDaoSupport
    implements OrderDAO {

    public OrderDAOIBatisImpl(
        SqlMapClientTemplate sqlMapClientTemplate) {
        setSqlMapClientTemplate(sqlMapClientTemplate);
    }

    void markOrdersAsSent(List orders, …) {

        …
        int rowCount = getSqlMapClientTemplate()
                        .update("markOrderAsSent", …);
        if (rowCount == 0)
            throw new OptimisticLockingFailureException();
        …
    }
    …
```

If the rowCount is zero, this method throws an OptimisticLockingFailureException, which is a Spring framework data access exception that is described in more detail in section 12.2.5. In section 12.4, we describe how the application can catch this exception and retry the transaction.

12.2.3 *Using pessimistic locking*

If you are unable to add a version column to the PLACED_ORDER table, you could use pessimistic locking to handle concurrent updates. When using pessimistic locking, the OrderDAO locks the rows in PLACED_ORDER when it retrieves the orders. It does this using this SQL SELECT FOR UPDATE statement:

```
SELECT *
FROM PLACED_ORDER o, RESTAURANT r, PLACED_ORDER_LINE_ITEM l
WHERE
  order.order_status = 'PLACED' AND DELIVERY_TIME < ? AND
  r.restaurant_id = o.restaurant_id
  and l.order_id = o.order_id
ORDER BY o.order_id ASC
FOR UPDATE OF o.ORDER_ID
```

The FOR UPDATE OF o.ORDER_ID clause tells Oracle to lock the rows in just the PLACED_ORDER table, which is more efficient than locking the rows in all three of the tables. The SELECT FOR UPDATE statement will block if the rows in the PLACED_ORDER table are locked by another transaction. In section 12.2.5, we will look at signaling pessimistic locking failures.

The UPDATE statement is a vanilla update statement:

```
UPDATE PLACED_ORDER
SET STATUS = 'SENT', MESSAGE_ID = ?, SENT_TIME = ?
WHERE ORDER_ID = ?
```

It simply updates the PLACED_ORDER table.

12.2.4 *Using serializable or repeatable read transactions*

Another alternative to pessimistic locking that also leaves the database schema unchanged is to use serializable or repeatable read transactions. When using these isolation levels, the OrderDAO would access the PLACED_ORDER table using the following vanilla SQL statements:

```
SELECT *
FROM PLACED_ORDER o, RESTAURANT r, PLACED_ORDER_LINE_ITEM l
WHERE
  order.order_status = 'PLACED' AND DELIVERY_TIME < ? AND
  r.restaurant_id = o.restaurant_id
  and l.order_id = o.order_id
ORDER BY o.order_id ASC

UPDATE PLACED_ORDER
SET STATUS = 'SENT', MESSAGE_ID = ?, SENT_TIME = ?
WHERE ORDER_ID = ?
```

Because concurrent updates are handled by the database's serializable transaction mechanism, neither statement locks rows or maintains a version number. Instead, you must configure either the Spring `TransactionInterceptor`, which provides transaction management for the transaction script, or the JDBC `DataSource`, which creates JDBC connections.

Configuring the TransactionInterceptor

Here is an example of how to configure a `TransactionInterceptor` Spring bean to use serializable transactions:

```
<bean id="DataSourceTransactionInterceptor"
   class="org.springframework...TransactionInterceptor">
  <property name="transactionManager">
    <ref bean="DataSourceTransactionManager"/>
  </property>
  <property name="transactionAttributeSource">
    <ref bean="MatchAllMethods"/>
  </property>
</bean>

<bean id="MatchAllMethods"
   class="org.springframework...MatchAlwaysTransactionAttributeSource">
   <property name="transactionAttribute">
    <value>PROPAGATION_REQUIRED,ISOLATION_SERIALIZABLE</value>
   </property>
</bean>
```

The `DataSourceTransactionInterceptor` would be applied to the `RestaurantNotificationTransactionScripts` class using a `BeanNameProxyCreator` Spring bean, whose definition is not shown. These bean definitions specify that when any method of the `RestaurantNotificationTransactionScripts` is invoked, the `TransactionInterceptor` will execute that method in a serializable transaction.

Configuring a DataSource

Configuring a transaction interceptor to use a particular isolation level is a flexible solution that enables different methods to use different isolation levels. The other option is to set the isolation level for `DataSource`, which will cause all transactions that use that `DataSource` to use that isolation level. The details of how to configure a `DataSource` to use a particular isolation level are implementation specific. Here is an example of how to configure a Database Connection Pool (DBCP) `DataSource` Spring bean to use serializable transactions:

```
<beans>

  <bean id="DataSource"
     lazy-init="true"
```

```
class="org.apache.commons.dbcp.BasicDataSource">
<property name="driverClassName">
   <value>oracle.jdbc.driver.OracleDriver</value>
 </property>
<property name="defaultTransactionIsolation">
   <value>SERIALIZABLE</value>
</property>
...
```

This bean's definition uses the `defaultTransactionIsolation` property to specify that all connections created by this `DataSource` should use the serializable isolation level. Other `DataSource` implementations typically have an equivalent mechanism.

A DAO that uses serializable transactions, optimistic locking, and pessimistic locking will naturally encounter concurrency failures, which can occur when two transactions try to access the same data simultaneously. It must report the failure by throwing an exception. Let's see how to do this.

12.2.5 *Signaling concurrent update failures*

A concurrency failure occurs when either the DAO or the database determines that two transactions cannot be executed concurrently. If the application is using optimistic locking, the DAO will be unable to update a row because it has been updated or deleted by another transaction. Or, if the application is using serializable transactions or pessimistic locking, the database will detect a deadlock or some other condition and JDBC throws a `SQLException`. A DAO must report a concurrency failure by throwing an exception so that a higher level application component can recover from the error by rolling back or retrying the transaction or by displaying an error message to the user.

A DAO could, for example, allow the JDBC `SQLException` to propagate to its caller, but there are two reasons why this is not a good idea. The first problem with throwing a `SQLException` is that it is JDBC-specific. An application might also be using a persistence framework such as JDO, which throws different exceptions. Ideally, the higher level components of the application should not know how the lower levels access the database. Another problem with `SQLException` is that it is a checked exception, which would require the callers of the DAO to either catch it or declare it as being thrown, which just clutters up the code. It is much better to use unchecked exceptions to report a concurrency failure.

Spring provides a very elegant solution to this problem. It has an unchecked exception class hierarchy for data access errors that enables an application to treat data access errors uniformly regardless of whether it is using JDBC, Hibernate, or JDO. It also has an extensible mechanism for automatically translating exceptions thrown by JDBC, Hibernate, and JDO to database access exceptions. In the next section, we'll see how it can be used to signal concurrent update failures.

Using Spring data access exceptions

The root of the Spring data access exception class hierarchy, part of which is shown in figure 12.4, is `DataAccessException`, which is a `RuntimeException`. There are many subclasses of `DataAccessException`, including `ConcurrencyFailure-Exception`, which is the superclass of exceptions that are thrown when a concurrency error occurs.

Its subclasses include:

- `OptimisticLockingFailureException`, which is thrown when an optimistic locking failure occurs
- `PessimisticLockingFailure`, which is thrown when a pessimistic locking failure occurs
- `CannotAcquireLockException`, which is thrown when a lock could not be acquired
- `CannotSerializeTransactionException`, which is thrown when a transaction could not be serialized

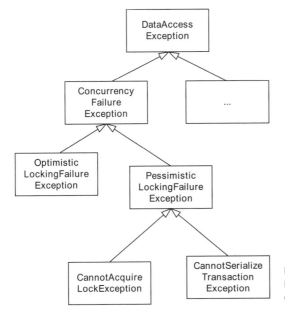

Figure 12.4
Part of the Spring data access exception class hierarchy

A DAO that implements optimistic locking must explicitly throw an Optimistic-LockingFailureException when it fails to update a row. However, Spring's JDBC and iBATIS classes automatically map SQLExceptions to Spring data access exceptions. This means, for example, that if you use a SqlMapClientTemplate to execute a SQL statement that results in an error, Spring will map the SQLException to the appropriate subclass of DataAccessException.

One minor issue with Spring's SQLException mapping mechanism is that it does not recognize all error codes. For example, in the case of Oracle, Spring will map an ORA-00054 error code, which indicates that a row cannot be locked immediately, to a CannotAcquireLockException, but it does not recognize ORA-00060 and ORA-08177 error codes, which indicate other concurrency failures, and maps them to an UncategorizedSQLException. This is a shame because, as I mentioned earlier, an ORA-00060 error code indicates a deadlock and an ORA-08177 error indicates a serialization failure. In order to map those error codes to the appropriate subclass of ConcurrencyFailureException, we must use extend the Spring SQLException mapping mechanism.

Extending Spring's SQLException mapping mechanism

Data access template classes such as SqlMapClientTemplate use a SQLException-Translator to map SQLExceptions to Spring data access exceptions. As figure 12.5 shows, this interface defines a translate() method that takes a SQLException as a

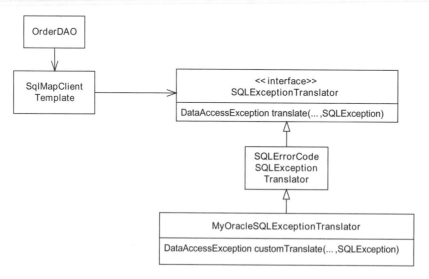

Figure 12.5 Extending the Spring SQLException **mapping mechanism**

parameter and returns a `DataAccessException`.By default, the data access template classes typically use a `SQLErrorCodeSQLExceptionTranslator`. This class implements the `SQLExceptionTranslator` interface and translates a limited number of Oracle error codes to data access exceptions. We can add support for additional error codes by subclassing `SQLErrorCodeSQLExceptionTranslator` and overriding its `customTranslate()` method:

```
public class MyOracleSQLExceptionTranslator extends
    SQLErrorCodeSQLExceptionTranslator {

  protected DataAccessException customTranslate(String task,
      String sql, SQLException sqlex) {
    switch (sqlex.getErrorCode()) {
    case 8177:
      return new CannotSerializeTransactionException(
          "Can't serialize", sqlex);
    case 60:
      return new CannotAcquireLockException(
          "Deadlock", sqlex);
    default:
      return null;
    }
  }
}
```

This class maps ORA-00060 to `CannotAcquireLockException` and ORA-08177 to `CannotSerializeTransactionException`. You would write a similar class for a different database.

Once we have written this class, we must configure the `JdbcTemplate` or `SqlMapClientTemplate` objects, which are used by the application to access the database, to use it. For example, a `SqlMapClientTemplate` is configured as follows:

```
<beans>
...
  <bean id="SqlMapClientTemplate"
    class="org.springframework.orm.iBatis.SqlMapClientTemplate"
    autowire="constructor">
    <property name="exceptionTranslator"
      ref ="ExceptionTranslator"/>
  </bean>

  <bean id="ExceptionTranslator"
    class="net.chrisrichardson.foodToGo.util.spring.
        ⇒ MyOracleSQLExceptionTranslator">
    <property name="dataSource" ref="DataSource"/>
  </bean>
...
</beans>
```

In this example, the SqlMapClientTemplate is configured to use a MyOracleSQL-ExceptionTranslator, which is configured with the DataSource. The DataSource is used by the SQLErrorCodeSQLExceptionTranslator to identify the database and select the default SQLException mapping. Once this is done, any ORA-00060 and ORA-08177 errors that are encountered by the SqlMapClientTemplate will be mapped to the appropriate concurrency exception.

12.3 Handling concurrent updates with JDO and Hibernate

As you might expect, handling concurrent updates in a Hibernate or JDO application is a lot easier than in an iBATIS/JDBC application. For the most part, you simply configure Hibernate or JDO to use a particular concurrency mechanism and it takes care of the rest. With optimistic and pessimistic locking, JDO and Hibernate automatically generate the required SQL statements. And serializable or repeatable read transactions work the same way in Hibernate and JDO applications as they do in iBATIS/JDBC applications.

Hibernate and JDO implement optimistic locking for objects using the same change-tracking mechanisms we described earlier. If the update fails because the version number, timestamp, or column values are different, JDO and Hibernate throw an exception. JDO and Hibernate implement pessimistic locking for objects by loading an object with a SELECT FOR UPDATE statement that locks the corresponding row. In this chapter, it is important to remember that object locking means locking the corresponding database table row or rows.

First we'll examine a domain model-based example that will be used to illustrate how to handle concurrent updates in a JDO or Hibernate application. After that, we'll delve into the details of configuring the JDO and Hibernate to use each concurrency mechanism.

12.3.1 Example domain model design

Using a particular concurrency mechanism in a JDO or Hibernate application is mostly a matter of configuration and requires little or no coding. But it always helps to use an example to make things concrete. Figure 12.6 shows the domain model version of the business logic for the Send Orders to Restaurant use case. It uses JDO or Hibernate to retrieve and update the orders that are ready to be sent to the restaurant.

The key classes are as follows:

- Scheduler, which periodically calls DomainRestaurantNotificationService
- DomainRestaurantNotificationService, the domain model-based implementation of the RestaurantNotificationService
- TransactionInterceptor, the Spring AOP interceptor that manages transactions and the Hibernate Session or JDO PersistenceManager
- Order, which represents an order and defines a noteSent() method that updates the order with the notification details
- RestaurantNotificationGateway, which sends the order to the restaurant
- NotificationDetails, which contains a messageId and timeSent
- OrderRepository, which uses the JDO or Hibernate query APIs to find the orders that are waiting to be sent to the restaurants.

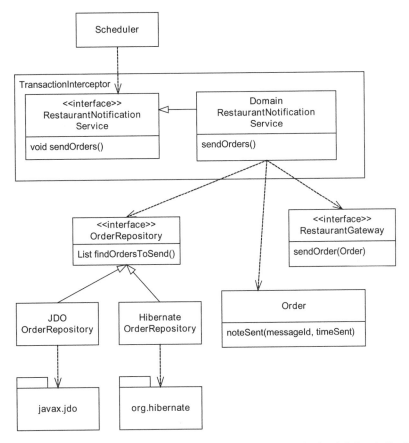

Figure 12.6 Domain model version of the business logic for the Send Orders to Restaurant use case

`DomainRestaurantNotificationService` calls the `OrderRepository` to retrieve the orders that are ready to be sent. It then sends each one using the `RestaurantNotificationGateway`. Finally, `DomainRestaurantNotificationService` marks each order as having been sent by calling `Order.noteSent()`.

This design works for both Hibernate and JDO. The only thing that needs to be changed is the `OrderRepository` class and persistence framework-specific files, such as the O/R mapping. Let's look at the concurrency options provided by JDO and how to configure them.

12.3.2　*Handling concurrent updates with JDO*

JDO supports optimistic locking, pessimistic locking, and serializable transactions. A JDO application uses pessimistic or optimistic locking by specifying the type of the JDO transaction. Let's first explore how this is done and then see how to configure serializable transactions.

Configuring the JDO transaction type

JDO defines two types of transactions: optimistic transactions, which use the optimistic locking, and datastore transactions, which use pessimistic locking or fully isolated transactions. The most common way to specify the JDO transaction type is by configuring the JDO `PersistenceManagerFactory`. The `PersistenceManagerFactory` has a property called `javax.jdo.option.Optimistic`, which specifies whether to use optimistic or datastore transactions. A value of `true` specifies that any `PersistenceManagers` created by the `PersistenceManagerFactory` should use optimistic transactions. A value of `false` specifies that they should use datastore transactions.

There are also a couple of other rarely used ways to programmatically specify the JDO transaction type. You can call `PersistenceManagerFactory.setOptimistic()`, which is equivalent to using the `javax.jdo.option.Optimistic` property. You can also specify the transaction type by calling `Transaction.setOptimistic()`, which specifies the type of the transactions used by that `Transaction` object. However, for most applications, configuring the `PersistenceManagerFactory` declaratively is the easiest approach.

A Spring application sets this property by configuring the Spring bean that creates the `PersistenceManagerFactory`. For example, you can enable optimistic transactions in a Spring application by using the following bean definition:

```
<bean id="myPersistenceManagerFactory"
    lazy-init="true"
    class="org.springframework.orm.jdo.
        ⤷ LocalPersistenceManagerFactoryBean">
  <property name="configLocation">
```

```
        <value>classpath:/kodo.properties</value>
      </property>
      <property name="jdoProperties">
        <props>
          <prop key="javax.jdo.option.Optimistic">true</prop>
        </props>
      </property>
    </bean>
```

The `LocalPersistenceManagerFactoryBean` creates the `PersistenceManagerFactory` that injected into the `JdoTemplate` used by repositories such as `JDOOrderRepositoryImpl`. This bean definition sets the value of `javax.jdo.option.Optimistic` to `true`.

Using a mixture of optimistic and pessimistic transactions in a JDO application is difficult. Using a separate `PersistenceManagerFactory` for each type of transaction is often impractical because you would have to define multiple instances of each Spring bean that depends directly or indirectly on the `PersistenceManagerFactory`. In addition, Spring 1.1.4 does not support declaratively specifying the transaction type. To specify the JDO transaction type on a per-transaction basis, an application would have to use a custom AOP interceptor that calls `Transaction.setOptimistic()`.

Let's see how JDO optimistic transactions and pessimistic transactions work.

Using optimistic transactions

A JDO optimistic transaction uses optimistic locking to handle concurrent updates. When an application commits an optimistic transaction, the JDO implementation verifies that all modified objects are unchanged in the database using one of the three change-tracking mechanisms we described earlier. If any have changed or been deleted, the JDO implementation will roll back the transaction and throw a `JDOOptimisticVerificationFailedException`, which is mapped by Spring's `JdoTemplate` to `OptimisticLockingFailureException`.

JDO 1.0 left the details of the optimistic locking mechanism up to the JDO vendor. However, JDO 1.x implementations such as Versant Open Access JDO (formerly known as JDO Genie) and Kodo JDO implement optimistic locking using all three change-tracking mechanisms. This is an example of how to configure the `Order` class in Kodo JDO 3.0.2 to use a version column:

```
<jdo>
  <package name="net.chrisrichardson.foodToGo.domain">
    <class name="Order" identity-type="datastore">
      <extension vendor-name="kodo" key="table"
            value="PLACED_ORDER" />
      <extension vendor-name="kodo"
            key="jdbc-version-ind"
```

```
            value="version-number">
        <extension vendor-name="kodo"
                key="column" value="VERSION"/>
      </extension>
    ...
```

The XML metadata specifies that the `Order` class be mapped to the PLACED_ORDER table and that the optimistic locking check use the `VERSION` column.

The JDO 2.0 specification, which defines an O/R mapping, requires a JDO implementation to support these three change-tracking mechanisms. This is how you would configure the `Order` class to use a version number in JDO 2.0:

```
<class name="Order"
   table="PLACED_ORDER"
   detachable="true"
   identity-type="application">

   <version strategy="version-number" column="VERSION"/>
   ...
</class>
```

The `<version>` element specifies that the `Order` class should maintain the version number in the `VERSION` column. You could also use a value of `strategy="timestamp"` to implement optimistic locking using a timestamp and `strategy="state-image"` to compare all columns. Note that unlike Hibernate, the timestamp or version number might not be stored in a field. This usually isn't important except when implementing the Optimistic Offline Lock pattern, which is described in the next chapter.

Once the `PersistenceManagerFactory` and the classes have been configured correctly, the JDO implementation will generate the SQL statements that implement optimistic locking. A typical JDO implementation will even perform optimistic lock checks for those classes during a datastore transaction.

Using datastore transactions

Whereas a JDO optimistic transaction uses optimistic locking, a JDO datastore transaction uses either the transaction isolation level or pessimistic locking to handle concurrent updates. No class-level configuration is necessary in order to use datastore transactions. However, the details of how datastore transactions are implemented depends on the JDO implementation and the database. For instance, Versant Open Access JDO and Kodo JDO implement datastore transactions on Oracle by querying the database using `SELECT FOR UPDATE` statements, which lock the rows. With JPOX 1.1, the default is to rely on the isolation level to lock the rows, and you must set a flag in order to use pessimistic locking.

Although this sounds straightforward, there are several issues with JDO data-store transactions. First, JDO datastore transactions potentially lock every row that is retrieved from a set of tables, which can sometimes impact the performance and increase the probability of deadlocks. It can also be unnecessary because many applications only need to lock rows in specific tables. Fortunately, some JDO implementations let the application control which objects are locked. For example, you can configure Versant Open Access JDO to only lock the first object loaded during a transaction, which is sufficient for some transactions.

Second, in order to lock the rows in the database, the JDO implementation (and Hibernate for that matter) must ignore the process-level cache and access the database. In some applications this can reduce performance significantly.

The third issue to consider is that the JDO implementation can translate a JDOQL query into a SQL statement that uses constructs that are incompatible with a `FOR UPDATE` clause. If this happens, you will need to change the query or use a different concurrency mechanism.

Optimistic and pessimistic locking are two of the concurrency mechanisms that a JDO application can use. Isolated database transactions are the third mechanism. Let's explore how to configure the transaction isolation level.

Using serializable or repeatable read transactions

Some JDO implementations provide extensions to the JDO specification for controlling the isolation level of datastore transactions. Examples of the different ways of specifying the transaction isolation level include:

- Setting a `PersistenceManagerFactory` property
- Configuring the isolation level of the `DataSource` that is used by the `PersistenceManagerFactory`, as was shown in section 12.2.4
- Using the `TransactionInterceptor` to specify the isolation level, as was shown in section 12.2.4

Unfortunately, these extensions are specific to the JDO implementation used by your application. You can check your implementation's documentation for more information.

Signaling concurrent update failures

A JDO implementation signals errors by throwing an exception that is an instance of one of the subclasses of `JDOException`. `JDOException`, which is a subclass of `RuntimeException`, has many subclasses, including those shown in figure 12.7.

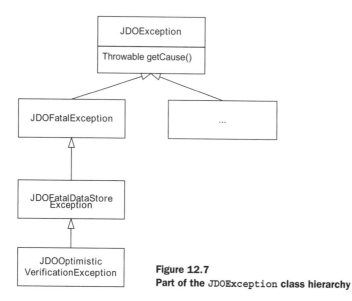

Figure 12.7
Part of the `JDOException` class hierarchy

When an optimistic locking failure occurs, the JDO implementations throws a `JDOOptimisticVerificationException`. The JDO specification does not describe which subclass of `JDOException` the JDO implementation will throw to signal pessimistic locking and serializable transaction failures. However, it's possible that the `JDOException` will contain the underlying `SQLException`, which can be accessed by calling `JDOException.getCause()`. For more information about how errors are reported, consult your JDO implementation's documentation.

The `JdoTemplate` maps the `JDOOptimisticVerificationException` to a Spring `OptimisticLockingFailureException`. In addition, if the `JDOException` contains a `SQLException`, the `JdoTemplate` will convert it to a data access exception using the exception mapping mechanism we saw in section 12.2.5. We can even plug in our own custom `SQLExceptionTranslator`. As a result, it's possible that the `JdoTemplate` will report pessimistic locking and serializable transaction errors correctly. Except for this relatively minor issue and potential problem with using optimistic locking and pessimistic locking in the same application, it is relatively easy to use all three concurrency mechanisms in a JDO application. Next we'll examine how to use optimistic locking, pessimistic locking, and serializable transactions in a Hibernate application.

12.3.3 Handling concurrent updates with Hibernate

Hibernate, like JDO, also supports optimistic locking, pessimistic locking, and serializable transactions. In this section, we use the business logic for the Send Orders to Restaurant use case to illustrate how to use them. The Hibernate version of this business logic is similar to the JDO version you saw in section 12.3.2. The only difference is that the OrderRepository uses Hibernate instead of JDO.

Using optimistic locking

Hibernate supports optimistic locking using a version or a timestamp column or by comparing columns. The version or timestamp column and the corresponding property are specified by using a `<version>` or `<timestamp>` element in a class's ORM document. For example, the following excerpt from the Order class's mapping document configures the class to use a version column:

```
<hibernate-mapping>

<class
 name="net.chrisrichardson.foodToGo.domain.Order"
 table="PLACED_ORDER">
  <id name="id" column="ORDER_ID" unsaved-value="-1">
   <generator class="native"/>
  </id>
  <version name="version" column="VERSION"/>
 ...
</class>
```

This mapping document specifies that the Order class map to the PLACED_ORDER table and use the VERSION column for optimistic locking. A class is configured to use a timestamp in a similar way.

An application can use the `optimistic-lock` attribute of the `<class>` element to specify that Hibernate should implement the optimistic locking check by comparing columns. Hibernate can either check all columns or just the changed columns. Here is an example of how to configure Hibernate to check changed columns:

```
<class
 name="net.chrisrichardson.foodToGo.domain.Order"
 dynamic-update="true"
 optimistic-lock="dirty"
 table="PLACED_ORDER">
 ...
</class>
```

In order for Hibernate to compare columns, the application must also specify `dynamic-update="true"`, which tells Hibernate to generate SQL UPDATE statements that update only changed columns.

Hibernate performs the optimistic locking check when it updates the database to reflect the changes made to the objects, which happens when the application executes a Hibernate query or calls `Session.flush()`, which updates the database with the changes made to objects, before committing the transaction. If Hibernate determines that a row has been updated by another transaction, it throws a `StaleObjectStateException`, which is mapped by Spring's `HibernateTemplate` to `OptimisticLockingFailureException`. An application must handle this exception by first rolling back the transaction and closing the `Session`. It can then open a new `Session` and retry the transaction.

Hibernate's optimistic locking mechanism works quite well. Because it is a declarative mechanism, Hibernate ensures that it is used consistently for all database accesses.

Using pessimistic locking

Hibernate provides a programmatic mechanism for pessimistic locking. An application can lock an object when loading it, and lock objects when executing a query. It can also lock a previously loaded object. An application locks the table rows corresponding to objects by specifying a lock mode when calling the following Hibernate methods: `Session.load()`, `Session.lock()`, and `Query.setLockMode()`. There are several kinds of lock mode, but the values that support pessimistic locking are `LockMode.UPGRADE` and `LockMode.UPGRADE_NO_WAIT`.

The `Session.load()` method, which loads an object, has an optional `lockMode` parameter, which specifies whether to lock the object. When one of these values is specified, `load()` behaves as follows: If the specified object is not loaded, `load()` uses `SELECT FOR UPDATE [NO WAIT]` to retrieve the object. If the object is already loaded with a less restrictive lock, `load()` calls `Session.lock()`.

The method `Session.lock()` is used to lock an already loaded object. When the lock mode is either `UPGRADE` or `UPGRADE_NO_WAIT`, `lock()` does a version check using `SELECT FOR UPDATE [NO WAIT]` and throws a `StaleObjectStateException` if the object is out of date.

The `Query.setLockMode()` method is used to specify whether a query should lock the objects it retrieves. If the application specifies a `lockMode` of either `UPGRADE` or `UPGRADE_NO_WAIT`, Hibernate uses a `SELECT FOR UPDATE [NO WAIT]` query to lock the objects.

Here is how the `HibernateOrderRepositoryImpl` can use pessimistic locking:

```
public class HibernateOrderRepositoryImpl
  …
  public List findOrdersToSend () {
    return getHibernateTemplate().executeFind(
      new HibernateCallback() {

      public Object doInHibernate(Session session)
```

```
        throws HibernateException, SQLException {
    Query query = session.getNamedQuery("findOrdersToSend");
    query.setLockMode("waitingOrder", LockMode.UPGRADE);
    Calendar cutOffTime = Calendar.getInstance();
    cutOffTime.add(Calendar.MINUTE, -timeWindowInMinutes);
    query.setParameter("cutOffTime", cutOffTime.getTime());
    return query.list();
  }});
  }
}
```

The call to `Query.setLockMode()` specifies that the orders identified by the waitingOrder alias should be locked. When Hibernate executes this query, it will use a SELECT FOR UPDATE that locks the rows in the PLACED_ORDER table.

One drawback of how Hibernate implements pessimistic locking is that because it is a programmatic API the developer is responsible for ensuring that it is used consistently. In comparison, JDO's approach of specifying the concurrency mechanism using a `PersistenceManagerFactory` property is easier to use. Fortunately, most of the loads and queries for a class are centralized in its repository, which reduces the chances of forgetting to lock an object.

Another drawback is that pessimistic locking can only be used when the application loads objects by calling one of the methods described earlier. Unlike JDO, Hibernate will not lock a row when the application navigates to object.

The third drawback is that locking objects for only certain transactions is difficult because it must be done programmatically. Either a repository would have to define locking and nonlocking versions of some methods, or its caller would have to tell the repository when to use pessimistic locking

Despite these drawbacks, Hibernate's pessimistic locking mechanism is useful for certain applications. A Hibernate application can also use serializable transactions.

Using serializable or repeatable read transactions

There are three main ways to configure the transaction isolation level in a Hibernate application:

- Using the `TransactionInterceptor` to specify the isolation level on a per-transaction basis, as shown in section 12.2.4

- Configuring the `DataSource`, as shown in section 12.2.4

- Setting the `hibernate.connection.isolation` SessionFactory property to a value of 8 (JDBC `Connection.SERIALIZABLE`)

Using the `TransactionInterceptor` is the most flexible approach since it allows you to specify the isolation level on a per-transaction basis, which is a common requirement. The other two options are useful only if you want to use the serializable isolation level for all transactions.

Signaling concurrent update failures

When Hibernate detects a concurrency failure, it throws one of the subclasses of `HibernateException` that are shown in figure 12.8. If it's an optimistic locking failure, Hibernate throws a `StaleObjectStateException`, which extends `StaleStateException`. Serializable and pessimistic locking failures cause JDBC to throw a `SQLException`, which Hibernate maps to a subclass of `JDBCException`, which contains the `SQLException`.

The `HibernateTemplate` that calls the Hibernate API automatically maps the `HibernateExceptions` to a Spring `DataAccessException`. It maps the `StaleObjectStateException` to a Spring `OptimisticLockingFailureException`. A `HibernateTemplate` maps a `JDBCException` to a `DataAccessException` by mapping the `SQLException` that it contains using the same `SQLExceptionTranslator`-based mechanism used by Spring's JDBC and iBATIS classes. Consequently, the application must use the `MyOracleSQLExceptionTranslator`, which was described in section 12.2.5, to map a `SQLException` to the corresponding data concurrency exception.

In order to do this, you must configure the `HibernateTemplate` with a `MyOracleSQLExceptionTranslator` by setting its `jdbcExceptionTranslator` property:

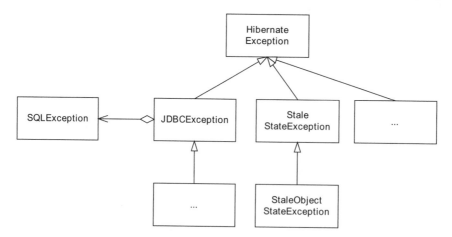

Figure 12.8   Hibernate exceptions that are thrown when a concurrency failure occurs.

```
<beans>
  ...
  <bean id="HibernateTemplate"
    class="org.springframework.orm.hibernate3.HibernateTemplate">
    <property name="sessionFactory">
      <ref bean="mySessionFactory"/>
    </property>
    <property name="jdbcExceptionTranslator">
      <ref bean="ExceptionTranslator"/>
    </property>
  </bean>
  ...
</beans>
```

ExceptionTranslator is the Spring bean that configures the MyOracleSQLExceptionTranslator that we saw earlier. The HibernateTemplate will then map SQLExceptions using the MyOracleSQLExceptionTranslator. Concurrency errors that are reported as JDBC exceptions will automatically be mapped to the appropriate subclass of ConcurrencyFailureException.

Signaling a concurrency failure is just the first step in the process of handling the error. Most of the time an application should attempt to recover from the failure by retrying the transaction; in the next section we'll see how that works.

12.4 *Recovering from data concurrency failures*

I live a few miles from a major earthquake fault, and it's inevitable that the big one will eventually happen. The key to getting through such a disaster is having a seismically retrofitted house along with a plan and supplies. On a much smaller scale, it's inevitable that concurrency failures will occur from time to time in an application. The application must be prepared to handle them in a meaningful way. Ideally, it should do more than simply display an error screen to the user.

As we have seen, the database access layer of a Spring application reports a concurrency failure by throwing a subclass of ConcurrencyFailureException. Because ConcurrencyFailureException is an unchecked exception, in most applications it will propagate to the TransactionInterceptor, which wraps the business logic and makes it transactional. By default, TransactionInterceptor handles an unchecked exception by first making sure that the transaction is rolled back and then rethrowing the exception. However, because data concurrency failures are almost always transient, most applications should retry the transaction again instead of propagating the exception to the presentation tier.

We could place the burden of retrying transactions on the business logic's client. It would wrap each call to the business tier in a try/catch block and retry the call if the exception was recoverable. The trouble with this approach is that it clutters the client code with exception-handling logic. Every call that could potentially throw a recoverable exception would be wrapped with the same code. A much better approach is to centralize the retry logic in a Spring AOP interceptor that retries transactions automatically. Let's take a look.

12.4.1 *Using an AOP interceptor to retry transactions*

A Spring application can use a custom AOP interceptor to catch the Concurrency-FailureException and automatically retry the transaction. Here is a custom Spring AOP interceptor that does this:

```
public class TransactionRetryInterceptor
            implements MethodInterceptor {

  protected int maxRetryCount = 3;

  public void setMaxRetryCount(int maxRetryCount) {
    this.maxRetryCount = maxRetryCount;
  }

  public Object invoke(MethodInvocation invocation)
          throws Throwable {
    int retryCount = 0;
    while (true)
      try {
        ReflectiveMethodInvocation inv =
            (ReflectiveMethodInvocation) invocation;
        MethodInvocation anotherInvocation = inv.invocableClone();
        return anotherInvocation.proceed();
      } catch (ConcurrencyFailureException e) {
        if (retryCount++ > maxRetryCount)
          throw e;
        else {
          continue;
        }
      }
  }

}
```

This class has a maxRetryCount property whose default value is 3. The invoke() method catches the ConcurrencyFailureException and loops at most maxRetryCount times, retrying the transaction. Because proceed() can only be called once, invoke() clones the MethodInvocation before calling it. The TransactionRetryInterceptor is a good example of the power and flexibility of the Spring framework.

The ability to define custom AOP interceptors can be extremely useful and eliminates the need to write the code by hand or use a code generator.

12.4.2 *Configuring the AOP interceptor*

The `TransactionRetryInterceptor` must be configured to intercept calls to transactional classes such as `RestaurantNotificationService` or `RestaurantNotificationTransactionScripts`. Furthermore, it must be applied to the POJO class before the `TransactionInterceptor` so that it is not executed as part of the transaction. In this example, we configured a Spring `BeanNameAutoProxyCreator` to wrap the `RestaurantNotificationService` with a `TransactionRetryInterceptor` and then a `TransactionInterceptor`:

```xml
<beans>
...
<bean id="transactionProxyCreator"
 class="org.springframework.aop.framework.autoproxy.
        ➥ BeanNameAutoProxyCreator">
  <property name="beanNames">
    <idref name="DomainRestaurantNotificationService"/>
  </property>
  <property name="interceptorNames">
    <list>
      <idref name="TransactionRetryInterceptor"/>
      <idref name="TransactionInterceptor"/>
    </list>
  </property>
</bean>

<bean id="DomainRestaurantNotificationService"
  class="net.chrisrichardson.foodToGo.restaurantNotificationService.
        ➥ impl.DomainRestaurantNotificationService">
...
</bean>

<bean id="TransactionRetryInterceptor"
  class="net.chrisrichardson.foodToGo.util.
        ➥ TransactionRetryInterceptor">
  <property name="maxRetryCount"><value>5</value></property>
</bean>

<bean id="TransactionInterceptor"
  class="org.springframework.transaction.interceptor.
        ➥ TransactionInterceptor">
...
</bean>

...
</beans>
```

These bean definitions ensure that any call to RestaurantNotificationService is retried if a ConcurrencyFailureException is thrown. When the RestaurantNotificationService is invoked, the TransactionRetryInterceptor is called first, which then calls the TransactionInterceptor to manage the transactions. The TransactionInterceptor then calls the actual RestaurantNotificationService.

It is important to remember that you can only retry a transaction if all the work done inside the transaction can be undone and repeated. The transaction cannot be automatically rolled back and retried if the application calls nontransactional APIs such as a legacy system, or does things that can't be undone, such as sending email. Recovering from concurrency failures in these kinds of situations can be a challenging problem, one that must be solved by application-level code. Fortunately, rolling back and retrying a transaction isn't a problem if the application only updates the database or calls APIs such as JMS.

12.5 *Summary*

An application can handle concurrent updates to shared data in one of three ways. One option is to use serializable transactions, which are transactions that are completely isolated from one another. Alternatively, you can use pessimistic or optimistic locking. An important benefit of serializable transactions is that each transaction has a consistent view of the data and the database prevents one transaction from overwriting another's changes. Also, they do not involve any extra coding; you just have to configure Spring, the JDBC DataSource, or the persistence framework. However, serializable transactions have a high overhead and thus performance is lower. Furthermore, they are suited to short transactions that update only a few rows.

Because of the overhead of serializable transactions, many applications use a read committed isolation level along with either pessimistic or optimistic locking. A transaction that uses pessimistic locking locks rows when they are read. Other transactions are prevented from updating those rows and, in some cases, from reading them. A transaction that uses optimistic locking doesn't lock the rows but instead verifies that the rows it's about to update are unchanged since they were read. Optimistic locking can detect changes using a version or a timestamp column or by comparing columns.

If you are using iBATIS or JDBC, then you must implement optimistic locking or pessimistic locking yourself. In comparison, JDO and Hibernate have built-in support for optimistic locking and pessimistic locking and automatically generate the required SQL statements. You enable optimistic locking for a class by configuring its

O/R mapping. In a JDO application, you use pessimistic locking by setting a `PersistenceManagerFactory` property; in a Hibernate application, you use pessimistic locking by calling a method when loading an object or executing a query.

The Spring framework has some useful features for signaling and handling concurrency failures. It defines a data access exception hierarchy that hides the mechanism used to access a database. Spring's data access classes automatically map Hibernate, JDO, and JDBC exceptions to Spring data access exceptions, which enables the application to treat them uniformly. An application can use a custom Spring AOP interceptor to automatically retry a transaction that is rolled back because of a database concurrency error.

Handling concurrent updates within a single transaction is only one of the database concurrency problems we need to solve. We must also handle concurrent updates across a sequence of database transactions. The next, and final, chapter shows you how to do that.

13

Using offline
locking patterns

This chapter covers

- Handling concurrency in edit-style use cases
- Extending optimistic locking
- Implementing application-level locks

Users invariably need to edit data that is stored by an enterprise application. For example, let's imagine that you are a Food to Go customer and, just after placing an order for food from your favorite Indian restaurant, you realize that you need to order more. You could phone in and have a customer service representative change an order to add the extra Naan bread, some Tandoori Portobello Mushrooms, and some Ras Malai. But how would you feel if the system mysteriously lost the changes to your order? Most likely, you would be very disappointed that you didn't get all the food you had ordered. What's worse, you might even be discouraged from using Food to Go again. To keep their customers happy, Food to Go must prevent this kind of concurrency problem when users edit data.

Although some use cases, like the one we looked at in the previous chapter, consist of a single database transaction, many others consist of a series of database transactions and involve user input. For example, every enterprise application that I have developed had screens that allow the user to edit data from the database. Because the user could spend a few minutes editing the data, the opportunity exists for concurrent updates. The application must handle the scenario where two users attempt to edit the same data and prevent the same kinds of inconsistencies and problems described in the previous chapter. The challenge is how to handle concurrent access across a sequence of transactions.

Neither serializable transactions nor pessimistic locking can work across a sequence of transactions. Instead, you must either extend the optimistic locking mechanism described in chapter 12 and check that data is unchanged before updating it, or implement an application-level locking mechanism to lock the data at the start of the use case and prevent other users from updating. The first approach is what Fowler calls the Optimistic Offline Lock pattern, and the second approach is what he calls the Pessimistic Offline Lock pattern [Fowler 2002].

In this chapter, we explain why you need to use the Optimistic Offline Lock and Pessimistic Offline Lock patterns. You will learn about the benefits and drawbacks of these two patterns and how to decide which one to use. We show you how to implement these patterns in JDO and Hibernate applications using the Acknowledge Order and Modify Order use cases as examples.

13.1 *The need for offline locking*

To understand why an application must use an offline locking pattern, let's look at an example of an edit-style use case, which is an extremely common kind of use case in which the user edits persistent data. Such a use case begins with the application retrieving data from the database and presenting it to the user. The user then changes the data and the application updates database with their changes.

We'll first describe the example use case and then explain why the concurrency mechanisms we examined in chapter 12 cannot be used to handle the scenario of two users editing the same data simultaneously.

13.1.1 *An example of an edit-style use case*

The Acknowledge Order use case, a typical edit-style use case, describes how the restaurant acknowledges receipt of an order by either accepting or rejecting it. This use case has the following specification:

> The system displays an order that has been sent to the restaurant. The restaurant's order taker accepts or rejects the order. The system displays a confirmation page. The restaurant's order taker confirms that she accepts or rejects the order. The system changes the state of the order to ACCEPTED or REJECTED.

The normal usage scenario for this use case consists of the user selecting the order, accepting it, and confirming that he wants to accept the order. Since this is a web application, each step results in the user's browser sending an HTTP request to the application. The application processes the request, which involves accessing the database, and then generates the HTML for the next page. Figure 13.1 shows these requests and the SQL statements that each one executes.

   The application handles the first request, which is sent when the user begins the use case, by executing a SQL SELECT statement that retrieves the order. The second request, which is sent when the user accepts or rejects the order, is handled by the presentation tier—perhaps within the browser if the application has an Ajax UI, for example—and does not result in any SQL statements being executed. The application handles the third request, which is sent when the user confirms that he wants to accept or reject the order, by executing an UPDATE statement that changes the state of the order to either ACCEPTED or REJECTED and updates the notes.

13.1.2 *Handling concurrency in an edit-style use case*

Because the Food to Go application is a multiuser system, multiple users could attempt to update the same order simultaneously. For example, while the restaurant order taker reviews the order displayed on the Acknowledge Order screen, another user could try to cancel the order. The application must handle this scenario and either prevent the other user from canceling the order or prevent the restaurant order taker from accepting a canceled order. Otherwise, the restaurant would prepare an order that had been canceled.

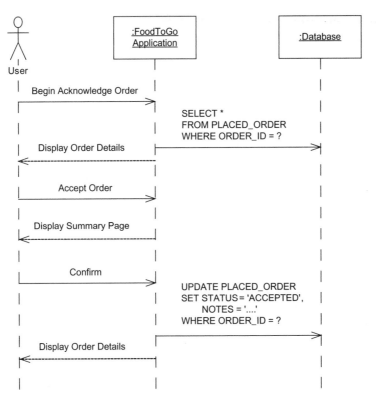

Figure 13.1   Databases accesses during the Acknowledge Order use case

Using a single database transaction

In theory, the application could implement the Acknowledge Order use case using a single database transaction that starts when the user begins the use case and commits after he acknowledges the order. The application prevents concurrent updates by using a serializable transaction or either optimistic locking or pessimistic locking. The problem with this approach is that the database transaction would be long-running because it encompasses multiple web requests and user think time. In addition, the transaction might last until the web session timed out if the user could simply walk away from the browser without completing the use case. Most applications cannot use long-running transactions because they reduce scalability and concurrency. They reduce scalability because database connections, which are a precious resource, would be held for the duration of the transaction and could not be used by other transactions. Long database transactions reduce concurrency because rows in the database are locked for the entire time, which could prevent other users from accessing them. Consequently, a much better approach is to use a separate database transaction for each request.

Using offline locking

When using a separate database transaction for each request, the business logic for the Acknowledge Order use case uses one transaction to retrieve the order and another transaction to update the order. The trouble with this approach is that neither serializable transactions nor pessimistic locking work across multiple transactions. Database-level pessimistic locking cannot be used across a series of transactions because the database releases locks at the end of the each transaction. Similarly, serializable transactions only handle concurrent updates made during their execution because of how they are implemented by the database. Moreover, optimistic locking only works, by default, within a single transaction because Hibernate or JDO only checks objects updated during the transaction. Consequently, the application must handle concurrent updates across a sequence of transactions using a different approach.

There are a couple of different mechanisms that an application can use. One option is the Pessimistic Offline Lock pattern, which implements an application-level locking mechanism that locks data across multiple database transactions (see section 13.5). The other option is the Optimistic Offline Lock pattern, which extends optimistic locking to work across a sequence of database transactions. Whereas regular optimistic locking only detects data that has changed since it was read earlier within the same database transaction, optimistic offline locking determines whether data has changed since the start of the use case, which might have been several database transactions ago. Let's look at how this pattern works.

13.2 Overview of the Optimistic Offline Lock pattern

This pattern detects concurrent updates in the same way as the optimistic locking mechanism described in the previous chapter. When updating the database, it checks that the data is unchanged since it was read. The only difference is that the data is read and updated in two separate transactions. The most common way to implement the Optimistic Offline Lock pattern is for the application to use a version number to detect when a row that was read in a previous transaction has been changed. When the application reads a row from the database, it stores the row's version number as part of the session state, for example, in the HttpSession. Then, when updating a row the application compares its current version number to the one stored in the session state. If they are different, the application does not update the row and instead alerts the user. To see how this pattern works, let's look at an example.

13.2.1 *Applying the Optimistic Offline Lock pattern*

The scenario shown in figure 13.2 illustrates how the Optimistic Offline Lock pattern can be used to handle concurrent updates for the Acknowledge Order use case. In this scenario, user A is attempting to acknowledge the order while user B cancels the order.

The sequence of events is as follows:

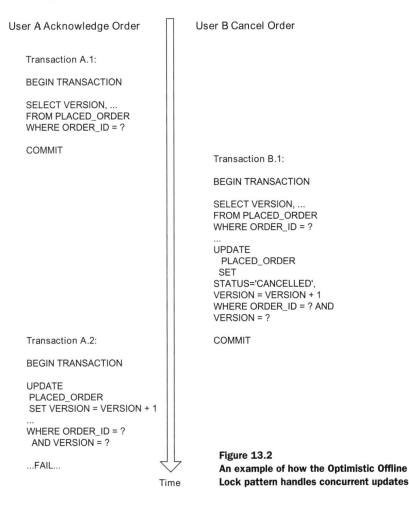

Figure 13.2
An example of how the Optimistic Offline Lock pattern handles concurrent updates

1   Database transaction A.1 retrieves the `Order` and saves its version number as part of the session state.

2   Database transaction B.1 retrieves and cancels the order, which increments the version number.

3   Database transaction A.2 attempts to update the order. Because the version number was incremented by transaction B.1, the `UPDATE` statement does not update any rows and the transaction fails.

As you can see, the Optimistic Offline Lock pattern is very similar to the optimistic locking mechanism described in chapter 12. And, like that mechanism, this pattern can also detect changes using a timestamp or by comparing old and new columns instead of using a version number. What's more, as you will see a bit later, an application that uses a persistence framework typically implements the Optimistic Offline Lock pattern using the persistence framework's optimistic locking mechanism.

13.2.2 *Benefits and drawbacks*

The Optimistic Offline Lock pattern has a couple of advantages:

- It is relatively easy to implement.
- Unlike the Pessimistic Offline Lock pattern, there are no locks to clean up if the user abandons the session, which is not uncommon in a web application.

However, there are the following drawbacks and issues:

- Although the Optimistic Offline Lock pattern prevents changes from being overwritten, it does not prevent two users from attempting to update the same order. In the scenario described earlier, the user of transaction A would not be able to save her work and she would have to start over. In some situations this can be unacceptable—if, for example, a user has invested a lot of time making the changes.
- All transactions that update shared data must increment the version number whenever they update a row, including those that do not use the Optimistic Offline Lock pattern.

13.2.3 *When to use this pattern*

The Optimistic Offline Lock pattern should be used when:

- Data is read in one database transaction and updated in another.
- The probability of conflicts is low and the consequences of redoing the changes are minimal.

- Users regularly abandon sessions and you don't want to implement a lock cleanup mechanism.

Now that you have gotten an overview of this pattern, let's take a detailed look at how to implement it. We're not going to show any JDBC or iBATIS code since it would look similar to the code you saw in the previous chapter. Instead, we'll focus on how to implement this pattern using JDO and Hibernate.

13.3 *Optimistic offline locking with JDO and Hibernate*

One of the benefits of using a persistence framework such as JDO or Hibernate is that it provides an optimistic locking mechanism that typically uses version numbers or timestamps to detect changed objects when it updates the database. In the previous chapter, we described how it is used within a single database transaction to prevent concurrent updates. In this section, you will learn how to use it to implement the Optimistic Offline Lock pattern.

There are two ways you can use a persistence framework's optimistic locking mechanism to implement the Optimistic Offline Lock pattern. You can either store the version number or timestamp of the object being edited in the session state, or you can use detached objects. Let's see how these two approaches work.

13.3.1 *Using version numbers or timestamps*

Implementing the Optimistic Offline Lock pattern with a version number or timestamp is very straightforward. When the application loads an object that it intends to update in a later database transaction, it stores the object's version number or timestamp in the session state in, for example, the `HttpSession`. Then, during the database transaction that updates the object, the application loads the object from the database and verifies that its current version number or timestamp is the same as the one stored in the session state. They will be different if the object was updated since it was originally read and the application will signal an error.

This approach is simple to implement because the persistence framework tracks changes to objects and increments version numbers or updates timestamps. Domain objects just need to define a method that returns the current version number or timestamp. For example, the `Order` class could define a `getVersion()` method, which returns the version number maintained by the persistence framework:

```
class Order {
...
    private int version;
```

```
public int getVersion() {
    return version;
}
```

The O/R mapping for the `Order` class would map the version field to a database column and tell the persistence framework to maintain the version number in the version field. When the code that implements the Acknowledge Order use case loads the object at the start of the use case, it calls `Order.getVersion()` and stores the returned value in the `HttpSession`.

Later on, when the user confirms that she wants to acknowledge the order, the application will execute code that looks something like this:

```
int originalVersion = … // from HttpSession
Order order = orderRepository.findOrder(orderId);
if (order.getVersion() == originalVersion) {
  order.noteAccepted(notes);

  …
} else {
  // fail

  …
}
```

This code fragment loads the order from the database and verifies that its current version is the same as the one that was stored in the `HttpSession` at the beginning of the use case. It only updates the order if it is unchanged. Otherwise, it will return an error code to the caller indicating that the order had been changed by someone else.

Benefits and drawbacks

This approach has the following benefits:

- It is simple to implement.
- It stores only a small amount of data in the session state.
- It provides better encapsulation than using detached objects because the presentation tier can only access the business logic via a façade or service.
- Recovering from offline optimistic locking failures can be more straightforward than with detached objects because the changes are detected by the application instead of the persistence framework.

But keep in mind these drawbacks:

- Some JDO implementations require the application get the version number or timestamp by calling `JDOHelper.getVersion()` instead of simply getting it from a field. This makes the code more complicated and dependent on the JDO APIs.

- Editing a graph of objects requires the application to keep maintain multiple version numbers or timestamps, which can be tricky.

- It is not practical to use this approach when the persistence framework implements optimistic locking using state comparison because you would have to write tedious and error-prone code to store a copy of the object in the session state and perform a field-by-field comparison before updating it.

When to use it

You should this approach when:

- The object that is being updated has an accessible version number or timestamp field.

- The application updates a small number of objects.

- It is important to encapsulate the business logic.

- It is important to minimize the size and complexity of the session state.

We won't show an example of implementing the Optimistic Offline Lock pattern with an object version number because in many Hibernate and JDO applications it's a lot easier to implement this pattern using detached objects.

13.3.2 Using detached objects

A detached object is an object that is no longer persistent but keeps track of its persistent identity and contains data from the database, including references to other detached objects. Because detached objects also keep track of their version number or timestamp, they are a convenient way to implement the Optimistic Offline Lock pattern. When the application loads an object that it will later update, it stores a detached copy of the object as part of the session state. Later, when the user saves the changes the application updates the object and reattaches it. The persistence framework uses its optimistic locking mechanism to verify that the database is unchanged since the object was detached. It will throw an exception if the object has been changed in the database.

Detached objects work well with an edit-style use case such as the Acknowledge Order use case and can make it easier for the presentation tier to pass the user's changes to the business tier. The business tier returns the detached object to the presentation tier, which will store it in the HttpSession or serialize it to the application's client. When the user saves her changes, the presentation tier updates the detached object with those changes and then passes it to the business tier. The business tier then calls the persistence framework to reattach the object and update the database.

Let's briefly review how to detach and attach JDO and Hibernate objects and look at some of the problems with using them.

Detaching and attaching objects in JDO and Hibernate

As we have seen in chapter 7, the details of how you detach and attach objects depend on whether you are using JDO or Hibernate. For example, the JDO version of the business logic for the Acknowledge Order use case attaches and detaches objects as follows. When it loads an Order at the start of the use case, it calls JdoTemplate.detachCopy() to detach it:

```
Order order = orderRepository.findOrder(ordered);
Order detachedOrder = getJdoTemplate().detachCopy(order);
```

It then returns the detached order to the presentation tier, which stores it in the HttpSession. After the user has confirmed that he wants to accept the order, the presentation tier updates the detached order and calls the business logic to attach it. The business tier calls attachCopy():

```
Order order = getJdoTemplate().attachCopy(detachedOrder);
```

When the JDO implementation updates the database, which is typically at commit time, it will throw an exception if the order has been changed in the database by a different user.

The Hibernate version of the business logic would be slightly simpler because Hibernate objects are automatically detached when the Session is closed. It would just have to call HibernateTemplate.update() to attach the acknowledged order:

```
getHibernateTemplate().update(detachedOrder)
```

In section 13.4 we will look at the details of the AcknowledgeOrderService, which uses detached objects.

Benefits of using detached objects

Implementing the Optimistic Offline Lock pattern using detached objects has the following benefits:

- The application is unaware of how the persistence framework implements optimistic locking. It even works with state comparison-based optimistic locking.

- It provides a simple way to lock an entire object graph, such as an order and its line items, without having to explicitly store version numbers for each object in the session state.

- It simplifies the application by enabling the presentation tier to update the detached object directly.

This approach also has drawbacks. As we have seen in chapter 7, the business logic is less encapsulated because the presentation tier has access to the detached objects. In addition, the session state can become bloated with detached objects and recovering from offline optimistic locking failures can be tricky. Let's look at those two problems.

Bloated session state

One potential problem with using detached objects to implement the Optimistic Offline Lock pattern is that the session state can become bloated with graphs of detached objects. Each graph of detached objects consists of detached objects that are directly or indirectly referenced by the objects being edited. In a Hibernate application, the detached object graph will contain all accessible objects that were loaded by the application, including objects that were navigated to by the business tier as well as objects that were eagerly loaded. For example, the business logic for the Acknowledge Order use case must load the order's line items and its restaurant in order to display on the Acknowledge Order screen. As a result, these objects become part of the session state, which significantly increases the amount of memory required to store it.

JDO gives you a lot more control over the structure of the object graph. By defining the appropriate fetch group, you can ensure that the detached object graph contains only the objects being edited. However, this can require the business tier to return at least two object graphs: one that contains the objects to store in the session state and another that contains the data that is displayed to user. Sometimes it is a lot easier to return a single object graph that contains both sets of objects.

Handling optimistic offline locking failures

Another issue is determining when an optimistic offline locking failure has occurred, if the business tier has attached some objects and updated others within the same transaction. The persistence framework throws the same exception regardless of whether an optimistic offline locking failure or a regular optimistic locking failure occurs. Hibernate throws a `StaleObjectStateException` and JDO throws a `JDOOptimisticVerificationException`, which are both mapped by Spring to a subclass of `ObjectOptimisticLockingFailureException`. The presentation tier, which catches the exception, does not immediately know whether it was caused by an optimistic offline locking failure or a regular optimistic offline locking failure.

One solution is to force Hibernate or JDO to verify that the object is unchanged in the database immediately after attaching it. A Hibernate application can do this by calling `Session.lock()`, and a JDO application can call `PersistenceManager.flush()` or `PersistenceManager.checkConsistency()`. If the object has changed in the database since it was detached, the persistence framework will throw an exception. Provided that the application has not updated any other objects, it can assume that the exception is caused by an optimistic offline locking failure. The downside of this approach is that prematurely flushing changes can reduce performance because the persistence framework has less opportunity to optimize database accesses.

The other way to determine whether the exception was caused by an offline locking error is to examine the `ObjectOptimisticLockingFailureException`, which contains the class and ID of the object that failed the optimistic locking. This solution avoids premature and potentially inefficient flushing of changes to the database, but does have the drawback of making the exception-handling logic more complicated.

When to use this approach
An application should use this approach when:

- It simplifies how the presentation tier passes the user's changes to the business tier.

- The persistence framework does not provide access to the version number or timestamp.

- Optimistic locking is implemented using state comparison instead version numbers or timestamps.

- It edits a graph of objects rather than an individual object.

Detached objects are a very convenient way to implement the Optimistic Offline Lock pattern. Let's take an in-depth look at an implementation of the `AcknowledgeOrderService` that uses them.

13.4 Optimistic offline locking with detached objects example

In this section, we will look at a Domain Model pattern–based design for the Acknowledge Order use case that implements the Optimistic Offline Lock pattern using detached objects. At the start of the use case, the business logic detaches the order that is being acknowledged and hands it back to the presentation tier. When the user acknowledges or rejects the order, the presentation tier updates the order and passes it back to the presentation tier, which reattaches it.

The design, which is shown in figure 13.3, consists of several classes, including `AcknowledgeOrderService`, `Order`, and `OrderRepository`.

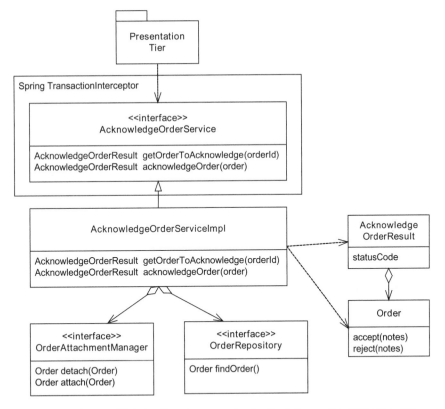

Figure 13.3   Domain Model pattern–based design for the Acknowledge Order use case

Because the business logic in this use case is simple, there isn't a separate POJO façade and the `AcknowledgeOrderService` is called by directly by the presentation tier. A Spring `TransactionInterceptor` ensures that each call to `AcknowledgeOrderService` executes within its own transaction. The same design works with both Hibernate and JDO detached objects because the different APIs for detaching and attach objects are encapsulated behind the `OrderAttachmentManager` interface.The responsibilities of each class are as follows:

- `AcknowledgeOrderService` defines the public interface that encapsulates the business logic.
- `AcknowledgeOrderServiceImpl` implements the business logic.
- `Order` is the domain object.
- `OrderRepository` is used by the `AcknowledgeOrderService` to find the order.
- `OrderAttachmentManager` encapsulates the mechanism for attaching and detaching orders.
- `AcknowledgeOrderResult` is returned by the service and contains a status code and a detached order.

In this design, the presentation tier calls `AcknowledgeOrderService.getOrderToAcknowledge()`, which returns the detached order, including its line items and restaurants. The presentation tier displays the order to the user and stores it in the `HttpSession`. When the user saves their changes, the presentation tier updates the order by calling `Order.accept()` or `Order.reject()`, and then passes it to `AcknowledgeOrderService.acknowledgeOrder()`. This method reattaches the order, which updates the database with the changes. If the order has changed in the database, the persistence framework throws an exception.

13.4.1 *Implementing the domain service*

Most of the business logic for this use case is implemented by `AcknowledgeOrderServiceImpl`, which is shown in listing 13.1. It defines a `getOrderToAcknowledge()` method, which returns the detached order, and an `acknowledgeOrder()` method, which reattaches the updated order. `AcknowledgeOrderServiceImpl` uses an `OrderRepository` to retrieve the order and an `OrderAttachmentManager` to detach and attach the `Order`.

Listing 13.1   AcknowledgeOrderServiceImpl

```
public class AcknowledgeOrderServiceImpl implements
    AcknowledgeOrderService {
```

```
OrderRepository orderRepository;

OrderAttachmentManager attachmentManager;                    ❶ Creates an
                                                                Acknowledge
public void DetachingAcknowledgeOrderServiceImpl(  ◁─────┐      OrderServiceImpl
    OrderRepository orderRepository,
    OrderAttachmentManager attachmentManager) {
  this.orderRepository = orderRepository;
  this.attachmentManager = attachmentManager;
}

public AcknowledgeOrderResult getOrderToAcknowledge(
    String orderId) {
  Order order = orderRepository.findOrder(orderId);
  Order detachedOrder =
        attachmentManager.detach(order);    ◁────────❷ Detaches
  if (order.isAcknowledgable()) {                       order
    return new AcknowledgeOrderResult(
      AcknowledgeOrderResult.OK, detachedOrder);
  } else
    return new AcknowledgeOrderResult(
      AcknowledgeOrderResult.ILLEGAL_STATE,
      detachedOrder);
}

public AcknowledgeOrderResult acknowledgeOrder(
    Order detachedOrder) {
  Order order = attachmentManager.
          ➥ attach(detachedOrder);      ❸ Attaches
  return new AcknowledgeOrderResult(        order
    AcknowledgeOrderResult.OK, detachedOrder);
}

}
```

Let's take a closer look:

❶ AcknowledgeOrderServiceImpl defines a constructor that takes an OrderRepository and an OrderAttachmentManager as parameters, which enables it to be initialized via dependency injection.

❷ The getOrderToAcknowledge() method calls the OrderRepository to retrieve the order. It then detaches the Order. It returns an AcknowledgeOrderResult containing the detached order and status code indicating whether the order can be acknowledged.

❸ The acknowledgeOrder() method attaches the updated detached Order and returns an AcknowledgeOrderResult.

13.4.2 *Implementing the persistent domain class*

The Order class has accept() and reject() methods that update a status field that tracks where the order is in the delivery process:

```
class Order {
    ...
    private int version;  // Hibernate only
    private String state;

    public boolean isAcknowledgable() {
        return state.equals(SENT);
    }

    public void accept(String notes) {
        if (!isAcknowledgable())
            throw new ApplicationError();
        this.state = ACCEPTED;
        this.notes = notes;
    }

    public void reject(String notes) {
        if (!isAcknowledgable())
            throw new ApplicationError();
        this.state = REJECTED;
        this.notes = notes;
    }
    ...
```

The Hibernate version of this class also has a version field, which is optional when using JDO.

The isAcknowledgable() method returns true if the order can be acknowledged. The accept() method updates the order with the notes and changes its state to ACCEPTED. The reject() method is similar—it changes the state to REJECTED. The accept() and reject() methods both throw an exception if the order is in the wrong state to be acknowledged.

Because Order is a persistent class, we also need to define its O/R mapping. Let's see how to do this for JDO and Hibernate.

JDO configuration

In the JDO ORM metadata for the Order class, we must specify that it uses optimistic locking and that it is detachable. In addition, since the line items and restaurants are returned to the presentation tier we must also configure those classes to be detachable. Here is an excerpt of the JDO 2.0 ORM metadata that configures the Order class:

```
<class name="Order"
  table="PLACED_ORDER"
  detachable="true"
  identity-type="application">

  <version strategy="version-number" column="VERSION"/>
  ...
</class>
```

The `detachable="true"` attribute specifies that instances of the `Order` class can be detached. The `<version>` element specifies that the `Order` class should maintain the version number in the `VERSION` column. As described in chapter 5, you can use other optimistic locking strategies such as `strategy="timestamp"`, which uses a timestamp. At the time of this writing, some JDO implementations did not support the JDO 2.0 metadata and required vendor-specific extensions to be used.

Hibernate configuration

In the Hibernate ORM metadata, we just need to configure optimistic locking because Hibernate objects are automatically detached:

```
<hibernate-mapping>
  <class
      name="Order"
      table="PLACED_ORDER">

      <version property="version" column="VERSION" />
  ...
</hibernate-mapping>
```

The `<version>` element specifies that the `Order` class uses the `version` field for optimistic locking and maps it to the `VERSION` column of the PLACED_ORDER table. As we saw in chapter 6, you can also use other optimistic locking strategies such as the `<timestamp>` element to specify a timestamp column.

Now that you know how to configure the O/R mapping, we'll show you how to detach and attach objects.

13.4.3 Detaching and attaching orders

The `AcknowledgeOrderServiceImpl` uses the `OrderAttachmentManager` to detach and attach orders. This interface, which encapsulates the persistence framework–specific detached objects APIs, defines a `detach()` method, which detaches the order, and an `attach()` method, which attaches an order:

```
public interface OrderAttachmentManager {

    Order detach(Order order);
```

```
        Order attach(Order order);
    }
```

In addition to detaching the order, the detach() method also detaches the order's restaurant, its line items, and their menu items so that they can be displayed to the user. There are Hibernate and JDO implementations of this interface.

Using JDO detached objects

Listing 13.2 shows the JDO version of the OrderAttachmentManager. It detaches orders by using a JdoTemplate to execute a KodoJDODetachObjectCallback, which is the class we first saw in chapter 7 that uses the Kodo JDO detachment API. Order-AttachmentManager attaches orders by executing a KodoJDOAttachObjectCallback that is similar to a KodoJDODetachObjectCallback. The list of fields to detach is passed into the JDOOrderAttachmentManager using dependency injection.

Listing 13.2   JDOOrderAttachmentManager

```
public class JDOOrderAttachmentManager implements
    OrderAttachmentManager {
  private String[] fieldsOrFetchGroups;

  private JdoTemplate jdoTemplate;

  public JDOOrderAttachmentManager(
      JdoTemplate jdoTemplate,
      String[] fieldsOrFetchGroups) {
    this.jdoTemplate = jdoTemplate;
    this.fieldsOrFetchGroups = fieldsOrFetchGroups;
  }

  public Order detach(Order order) {
    return (Order) jdoTemplate
        .execute(new KodoJDODetachObjectCallback(
            order, fieldsOrFetchGroups));
  }

  public Order attach(Order order) {
    return (Order) jdoTemplate
        .execute(new KodoJDOAttachObjectCallback(
            order));
  }

}
```

Both the detach() and attach() methods instantiate and execute a JdoCallback that calls Kodo JDO.

Using Hibernate detached objects

The HibernateOrderAttachmentManager does not need to detach orders, but it does need to make sure they are loaded. Here is HibernateOrderAttachmentManager, which calls HibernateTemplate.initialize() to ensure that the required objects are loaded and calls HibernateTemplate.update() to reattach the order:

```
public class HibernateOrderAttachmentManager extends
    HibernateDaoSupport implements OrderAttachmentManager {

  public HibernateOrderAttachmentManager(
      HibernateTemplate hibernateTemplate) {
    setHibernateTemplate(hibernateTemplate);
  }

  public Order detach(Order order) {
    HibernateTemplate template = getHibernateTemplate();
    template.initialize(order);
    template.initialize(order.getLineItems());
    for (Iterator it = order.getLineItems().iterator();
          it.hasNext();) {
      OrderLineItem lineItem = (OrderLineItem) it.next();
      MenuItem menuItem = lineItem.getMenuItem();
      template.initialize(menuItem);
    }
    return order;
  }

  public Order attach(Order order) {
    getHibernateTemplate().update(order);
    return order;
  }

}
```

Because the Hibernate objects are automatically detached when the session is closed, the detach() method just calls HibernateTemplate.initialize() to ensure that the order, its line items, and their menu items are loaded. An alternative approach would be for the AcknowledgeOrderService to load the order by executing a query that uses fetch joins to eagerly load the objects. This simplifies the code by eliminating the need to call HibernateTemplate.initialize() and would improve performance by reducing the number of database accesses. However, because a Hibernate application cannot always eagerly load all of the objects that it must return to the presentation tier, it is worthwhile looking at an example that uses Hibernate.initialize().

The attach() method calls HibernateTemplate.update() to attach the order. This method reassociates the order with the Session, which does not involve any database accesses. Later, at commit time, when Hibernate tries to update the order it will throw an exception if the order has changed in the database since it was first loaded.

As you can see, implementing the Optimistic Offline Lock pattern is relatively straightforward because you can leverage the optimistic locking and detached object mechanisms provided by JDO or Hibernate. However, for some use cases it is not enough to prevent one user from overwriting another's changes and you must use the Pessimistic Offline Lock pattern, which prevents two users from editing the same data simultaneously.

13.5 *The Pessimistic Offline Lock pattern*

We have seen that the Optimistic Offline Locking pattern is a partial solution to the problem described at the start of this chapter. It prevents changes made to an order from mysteriously disappearing. The application will display a message telling the customer service representative to start over. This is certainly better than losing the changes, but it's still pretty irritating. We need a way of guaranteeing that users can save their changes. To do that, we need to use the Pessimistic Offline Lock pattern.

The Pessimistic Offline Lock pattern prevents concurrent updates by locking the shared data while it is being edited. It is similar to pessimistic locking where the transaction locks the data when it is read, which prevents others from accessing it, and releases the locks when it commits or rolls back. However, the key difference is that the Pessimistic Offline Lock pattern is an application-level mechanism that works over multiple database transactions and the locks are implemented by the application rather than the database. The application locks the data when reading and displaying it to the user, and unlocks the data when the user saves her changes.

13.5.1 *Motivation*

In order to understand why the Pessimistic Offline Lock pattern is necessary, let's look at the Modify Order use case. This use case, which is more elaborate than the Acknowledge Order use case, describes how a customer service representative can change an order. It has the following specification:

The user can potentially take several minutes to change the order, and so like the Acknowledge Order use case, this use case consists of multiple database transactions. The first transaction loads the order from the database so that it can be

> The user (customer service representative) selects the order to edit. The system displays the order. The user updates the quantities, the delivery address and time, and the payment information. The system displays the updated order. The user saves his changes. The system updates the order.

displayed to the user, one or more other transactions read data to validate the user's input, and the last transaction updates the order with the user's changes.

Although you could handle concurrent updates by using the Optimistic Offline Lock pattern, this pattern only detects concurrent updates when the user saves the order. While a user would only be mildly irritated if he had to reenter changes during the Acknowledge Order use case, which involves only a small amount of user input, it is not acceptable for the Modify Order use case. A customer service representative could spend several minutes on the phone with a customer changing the order only to discover that she could not save her changes. Telling the customer to start over would be extremely frustrating for everyone concerned.

13.5.2 Using the Pessimistic Offline Lock pattern

In use cases such as this where the probability of concurrent updates is high or the consequences are severe, a better approach is to use the Pessimistic Offline Lock pattern, which implements an application-level locking mechanism that allows only one user to edit a particular piece of data at a time. Typically, either domain model services or transaction scripts are responsible for locking and unlocking the data because they are aware of when the use case begins and ends. The transaction script or service method that is called at the start of the use case to load the data being edited would lock the data. The transaction script or service method that is called at the end of the use case unlocks the data.

Figure 13.4 shows how the business logic for the Modify Order use case can use the Pessimistic Offline Lock pattern to ensure that only one user can edit the order at a time.

The first transaction, which loads the order to display to the user, locks the order and the last transaction unlocks the order after updating with the user's changes. If another user tried to edit the order, they would not be able to do so because they could not claim the lock. In section 13.7 we will see that an application typically claims and releases locks by inserting and deleting rows in an application-level lock table.

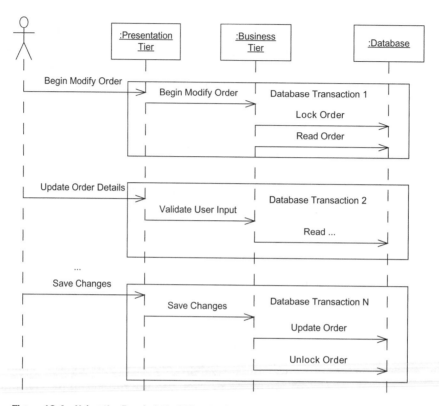

Figure 13.4   Using the Pessimistic Offline Lock pattern

13.5.3   *Benefits and drawbacks*

Let's look at the benefits and drawbacks of the Pessimistic Offline Lock pattern.

Ensures that a user can save changes

The main benefit of the Pessimistic Offline Lock pattern is that it prevents concurrent updates by locking shared data when it is read. It ensures that users will be able to save their changes and will not be required to start over. As a result, the usability of the application is improved.

Impacts the application globally

An unfortunate drawback of this pattern is that if you decide to use it in your application, then all of the business logic that updates the shared data must be aware of the pattern. Unfortunately, this can be error-prone because it can be difficult to use the pattern consistently. When you start using this pattern in your application, it is all too easy to miss existing code that must be modified. Similarly, when writing new code you might forget to use the pattern. One potential solution is the *Implicit Lock* pattern [Fowler 2002], which automates the lock management. However, implementing this pattern can be difficult because the business logic determines when you must lock and unlock data. As a result, you often have to rely on careful coding and lots of testing.

Requires a mechanism to forcibly release locks

In addition to globally impacting the application, this pattern requires you to implement a mechanism to release the locks when a user abandons her session. One solution is to implement a timeout mechanism. The application could release the locks held by a user when the `HttpSession` times out. Alternatively, the application could release locks that have been held for too long. However, the trouble with timeouts is that if they are too long, users are prevented from getting work done and if they are too short, users risk being timed out by accident.

For many applications, a better approach is to let users steal locks after warning them that the data they want to edit is locked by someone else. For example, if a user attempts to edit an order that is locked by someone else, the application can ask them to confirm that they really want to edit the order. Another possibility is to only let users with administrative privileges steal locks. Which option is better depends on the specific requirements of an application.

13.5.4 *When to use this pattern*

Because the Pessimistic Offline Lock guarantees that the user who edits the data can save the changes, this pattern should be used when:

- Data is read in one database transaction and updated in another.
- The probability of conflicts is high.
- The consequences of conflicts are severe.
- Users typically do not abandon their sessions or it's feasible to implement a lock cleanup mechanism.

Let's now look at the different decisions you must make when implementing this pattern.

13.6 *Pessimistic offline locking design decisions*

When using database-level pessimistic locking, the database is responsible for the implementation of the locking mechanism. The only thing that you get to decide is what to lock and perhaps the kind of lock to use. But because the Pessimistic

Offline Lock pattern is an application-level locking mechanism, you have to make several other design decisions, including how to lock it, when to lock it, and where to store the locks. Let's look at each of the decisions you must make in turn.

13.6.1 Deciding what to lock

One decision that you must make is what to lock. In many use cases, there is a class that obviously needs to be locked. For example, in the Modify Order use case it's the order that must be locked because it is the object being edited. Sometimes, however, the class that must be locked is less obvious. Consider, for example, a use case that edits only the order's line items. You could lock the individual line items but this would require locking multiple objects, which is messy to implement. A better approach is to lock a group of related objects using a single lock—the so-called *Coarse-Grained Lock* pattern [Fowler 2002]. In this example, you would lock the order instead of the individual line items. As well as being easier to implement, it avoids the problem of locking multiple objects individually, which can lead to deadlocks. See [Fowler 2002] for a discussion of the details of using this pattern.

13.6.2 Determining when to lock and unlock the data

In addition to deciding what to lock, you must identify which domain service methods and transaction scripts must lock and unlock data. The method or methods that lock the data are those that are called to start the use case and load the data that is being edited. Similarly, the data must be unlocked by those methods that are called at the end of the use case. Methods that are called during the use case can verify that the lock is still held but are not required to do so.

13.6.3 Choosing the type of lock

Another decision you must make when implementing this pattern is which type of lock to use. The simplest kind of lock is an *exclusive write lock*. A transaction that wants to update the data claims the lock and prevents others from editing it. Transactions that only read the data do not have to claim the lock and are not blocked waiting for the owner of the lock to finish editing the data. Exclusive write locks work well for many use cases, so they are the only kind of lock we'll describe in detail.

There are, however, other kinds of locks that are useful in some situations. Let's suppose that the data being edited can become inconsistent during the use case. The application could, for example, apply the user's changes immediately rather than saving them until the end and applying them in a final transaction. One way to prevent other transactions from reading the inconsistent data is to use an exclusive lock. All transactions that read and write the shared data must claim an exclusive lock, which allows only one transaction at a time to access the data. This ensures that transactions only see consistent data and that only one transaction can update the data at a time.

The trouble with using an exclusive read lock is that it can reduce performance. A transaction that only reads the data will block other transactions that also want to only read the data. A more sophisticated approach is to use *read/write locks*. Transactions that read the data claim read locks and transactions that update the data claim write locks. The shared data can have multiple read locks or one write lock. This allows multiple transactions to read the data but only one transaction to edit it. Furthermore, it prevents the data from being read and edited at the same time. This approach preserves data consistency without reducing performance as much as an exclusive read lock, but can be complicated to implement.

13.6.4 *Identifying the lock owner*

The fourth decision you must make when implementing the Pessimistic Offline Lock pattern is what to use as the identity of the lock owner. In a web application, one option is to use the HttpSession ID as the lock owner. The presentation tier passes the HttpSession ID to the business tier as part of each request. This approach is useful if, for example, users are accessing the application anonymously. One limitation of using the session ID is that, because it is a cryptic string, it cannot be used to determine the person who owns the lock.

Another option is to use the user ID as the lock owner. The presentation tier could pass the user ID as a parameter when it calls the business tier. Alternatively, the business tier can call a security framework-specific API such as Acegi Security's SecurityContextHolder to get the identity of the user, which is more secure and eliminates the need for the presentation tier to provide it. One limitation of using the user ID is that users must be logged in, which means this approach cannot be used in applications that have anonymous users. In addition, portability can be an issue because how you get the user ID depends on the security framework. Despite these drawbacks, it is a useful approach.

For simplicity, the example that you will see later in this chapter has the presentation tier pass in the user ID.

13.6.5 *Maintaining the locks*

You must also decide how to maintain the locks. An application that runs on a single application server can implement an in-memory locking mechanism such as a singleton hash table. However, because most enterprise applications are clustered, the locks must usually be stored in the database. There are two different ways an application can store locks in the database. One option is to store locks in a separate table that is managed by a lock manager. The other option is to store locks in the same table as the data.

Lock managers

A lock manager provides an API for acquiring, verifying, and releasing locks based on the object's identity or the row's primary key. Here is an example of a lock manager API:

```
public interface LockManager {
    public boolean acquireLock(String classId, String pk,
                               String owner);

    public boolean verifyLock(String classId, String pk,
                              String owner);

    public void releaseLock(String classId, String pk,
                            String owner);
}
```

The `LockManager` interface defines three methods: `acquireLock()`, which acquires a lock; `verifyLock()`, which verifies that the lock exists; and `releaseLock()`, which releases a lock. All three methods take the same three parameters:

- `classId` is the type of the data, such as the class name.
- `pk` is the identity or primary key of the data.
- `owner` represents the identity of the entity claiming the lock and is usually either the user or session ID.

Together, the `classId` and the `pk` identify the data being locked or unlocked. The `acquireLock()` returns a boolean value indicating whether the object was locked, and `verifyLock()` returns a boolean indicating whether the specified data was locked. The `releaseLock()` method throws an exception if the object was not locked by the caller.

The lock manager stores locks in a database table. Each row in the table stores the type and identity of the entity (object or row) that is locked and the identity of the owner of the lock. The table's primary key consists of the identity of the entity, which means that an entity can have at most one lock. The lock manager acquires a lock by inserting a row into the table and releases the lock by deleting the row.

Using a lock manager

The simplest way to use a lock manager is for the database transaction that reads the data to first lock the data before reading it. This ensures that the data that is read is up to date because once it is locked no other transactions can update it. You can do this if, for example, you are loading an object by its primary key because the transaction can call the lock manager before calling the repository or persistence framework API. However, if a transaction obtains the object by executing a query or by navigation, it does not know the object's primary key until after it has been loaded. It is possible that in between the transaction loading the object and locking it another transaction changes the object, which causes the first transaction to use stale data and potentially overwrite those changes. To see why, consider the scenario shown in figure 13.5, which shows two database transactions accessing the same data. In this example, transaction A reads the data at the start of one use case and transaction B updates the data at the end of another use case.

In this scenario, transaction A reads an order that is locked by transaction B. Transaction B then updates the order and releases the lock, which enables transaction A to acquire it. As a result, transaction A has stale data and would subsequently overwrite the changes made by transaction B.

One solution to this problem is to use database-level pessimistic locking and prevent another transaction from changing the data before the lock is claimed. In the scenario in figure 13.5, transaction A would claim the database-level pessimistic lock, which would block B from updating it and releasing the offline lock. Transaction A would then discover that the order had an offline lock and would roll back.

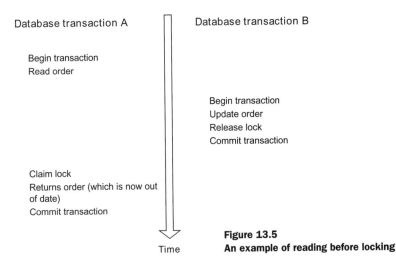

Figure 13.5
An example of reading before locking

The other option is to use database-level optimistic locking. After claiming the lock, transaction A performs an optimistic locking check to verify that the order was unchanged. How this is done depends on the persistence framework. A Hibernate application can call `Session.lock()` with a lock mode of `LockMode.READ` to verify that an object is unchanged in the database. A JDO application would have to make a possibly dummy modification to the object in order to cause the JDO implementation to perform the check at commit time.

Implementing a lock manager

Because of the benefits of using a persistence framework, you might expect to implement the lock manager with a persistence framework. You could map a `Lock` class to the OFFLINE_LOCK table and claim and release locks by creating and deleting objects. However, this approach is not as simple as it might appear. It can be impossible for the business tier to handle locking errors because they will be reported as commit-time exceptions by those persistence frameworks that do not insert objects until commit time. In addition, the application must, as we just saw, use a database transaction-level concurrency mechanism because data is read before the lock is claimed at commit time.

Consequently, the easiest way to implement a lock manager is to use SQL directly. The lock manager can use iBATIS or JDBC to atomically claim a lock by executing an `INSERT` statement and release one or more locks by executing a `DELETE` statement. In addition to being simple and easy to understand, a JDBC/iBATIS lock manager is more reusable because it is not coupled to any particular persistence framework. In 13.7.1, we will look at an iBATIS implementation of a `LockManager`.

Benefits and drawbacks of using a lock manager

Implementing the Pessimistic Offline Lock pattern with a lock manager approach has a number of benefits:

- An application can lock an object using only its ID, which means that it can first lock the object and then read it, which avoids the problem of stale data. In addition, the application can lock entities that have been deleted or not yet inserted.

- Lock management is centralized. The lock management code is only in the lock manager rather than in every class. The locks are stored in a single database table, which makes it easy to see which objects are locked and by whom.

- This approach is also more flexible. We don't have to build the locking strategy into the domain model classes ahead of time. The lock management can be handled by the service classes instead.

- The mechanism for claiming a lock is simple and easy to understand since a lock manager can atomically claim a lock using an INSERT statement.

There are, however, a couple of drawbacks and issues to consider when using a lock manager:

- Using a lock manager makes the design more complicated. All business transactions, even ones that consist of a single database transaction, must claim and release locks. Also, determining whether an object is locked involves a database query rather than simply checking a flag field.

- Locking objects that are retrieved using a query or by navigation is tricky because the application must execute the query in order to know which objects to lock and consequently loads the objects before locking. As we described earlier, an application must use either pessimistic or optimistic locking to ensure that it uses the current version of the data and to prevent lost updates. Or, the application must reread the data after locking it to verify that it hasn't changed.

There are also some additional issues to consider when using a JDBC/iBATIS-based lock manager with a persistence framework:

- Sometimes an application must execute a query that includes or excludes locked data. For example, the query that is used in the Send Orders use case to find orders that are ready to send should ideally ignore locked orders. A SQL query can ignore locked orders by simply doing a join with the lock table. However, if the application uses a persistence framework query, then the lock table must be mapped to a class in order for it to be referenced by the query.

- Enabling JDBC/iBATIS code and JDO code to share a lock manager is tricky if the JDO code uses datastore identity. As described in chapter 5, the JDO code does not have access to the object's primary key and the JDBC code does not have access to the object's JDO identity. In order to lock data that is accessed by both JDBC and JDO code, the application must use some other unique identifier to lock the data.

A lock manager is a centralized and reusable mechanism for implementing the Pessimistic Offline Lock pattern. However, as you have seen, you need to address some tricky implementation issues when using one. Consequently, you might want to consider storing locks in the objects themselves.

Storing locks in objects

Instead of using a centralized lock manager, an application can store a lock in each object. Each class that supports pessimistic offline locking has a lock field, which stores the identity of the lock's owner. The transaction script or domain service method claims the lock by setting this field and releasing this lock by setting it to null.

A JDBC or iBATIS application can atomically claim a lock by executing a SQL UPDATE statement, but an application that uses a persistence framework must load an object in order to determine whether it is locked, set the lock field, and write it back to the database. This means that acquiring a lock is not an atomic action and the application must instead use database-level optimistic or pessimistic locking or a serializable transaction in order to detect concurrent updates. However, because an application is likely to already be using one of these mechanisms, this is usually not a problem.

Benefits and drawbacks of storing locks in objects

This approach has some benefits:

- The application doesn't have to implement an additional mechanism for persisting locks.

- It is easy for an application to determine whether an object is locked—it simply checks the lock field. Business transactions that consist of a single database transaction can verify that an object is unlocked by checking the lock field rather than claiming and releasing a lock. Also, queries can find locked or unlocked objects by including the lock field in the query's where clause.

- It avoids the problem encountered when using a lock manager and implementing locks in an application that uses iBATIS/JDBC and JDO objects that use datastore identity.

There are, however, a number of drawbacks and issues with this approach:

- The decision as to whether a class supports locking must be done up front. There is more code to maintain because lock management code is duplicated in every class that can be locked.

- Existing tables must be changed to add a lock column, which might not be possible when working with a legacy schema. Alternatively, each class could be mapped to the original table and a lock table. However, the overhead of reading and updating the extra table could reduce performance.

- The application must query multiple tables to determine which entities are locked by a user.

- Determining whether an object is locked can be tricky in an application that uses a process-level cache because the in-memory object might not be up to date. The application might have to somehow force the latest copy of an object to be loaded.

Despite these drawbacks, however, storing locks in objects is sometimes the simplest way to implement the Pessimistic Offline Lock pattern.

13.6.6 *Handling locking failures*

The sixth and final decision you must make when implementing the Pessimistic Offline Lock pattern is what to do when one user tries to access (typically edit) data that is locked by another user. When this happens, the attempt to claim the lock will fail. For example, the `acquireLock()` method defined by the `LockManager` you saw earlier will return `false`. The simplest and most effective way to handle locking failures is for the business tier to return a status code or throw an exception indicating that the data could not be locked. Unlike when using database transaction-level concurrency mechanisms, there is little point in having the business tier automatically try again to claim the lock because locks are typically held for a long time.

The presentation tier can then display an error message telling the user to try again later or perhaps give the user the opportunity to steal the lock. A rich client such as an Ajax UI running in the user's browser could, however, periodically re-send the request that claims the lock.

In theory, deadlocks can occur if use cases lock multiple objects. Each user would be waiting for the other to release locks. The simplest way to prevent deadlocks is for the application to release all locks when it fails to claim a lock and require the user to start over from the beginning. Of course, whether this is possible depends on the details of the use case.

Now that we have explored the various design issues you must address when using the Pessimistic Offline Lock pattern, let's learn how to implement it in a domain model-based design.

13.7 Using pessimistic offline locking in a domain model

In this section you will learn how to implement the Pessimistic Offline Lock pattern with a lock manager. First we show the implementation of a simple lock manager; after that we describe the business logic that uses it. For brevity, we'll just discuss the domain model version of the business logic because transaction scripts would call the lock manager in the same way.

13.7.1 Implementing a lock manager with iBATIS

The LockManager interface, which you saw earlier in section 13.6.5, defines methods for acquiring, verifying, and releasing locks. It is called by the transaction scripts and domain service methods to lock and unlock objects. For the reasons outlined earlier, the implementation of the lock manager maintains locks in the database. It claims locks by inserting a row into the OFFLINE_LOCK table and releases a lock by deleting a row:

```
create table OFFLINE_LOCK (
   CLASS_ID VARCHAR2(100) NOT NULL,
   PK VARCHAR2(100) NOT NULL,
   OWNER VARCHAR2(100) NOT NULL,
   CONSTRAINT OFFLINE_LOCK_PK
   PRIMARY KEY (CLASS_ID, PK)
)
```

This table defines the following three columns:

- CLASS_ID identifies the type of the object being locked.
- PK is the primary key of the locked object.
- OWNER is the owner of the lock.

Its primary key consists of the CLASS_ID and PK columns.

The LockManager, which is shown in listing 13.3, is implemented using iBATIS and uses the Spring SqlMapClientTemplate class to access the OFFLINE_LOCK table.

Listing 13.3   LockManagerIBatisImpl

```
public class LockManagerIBatisImpl implements LockManager {

   private final SqlMapClientTemplate template;

   public LockManagerIBatisImpl(
       SqlMapClientTemplate sqlMapClientTemplate) {
     this.template = sqlMapClientTemplate;
   }

   private Map makeParameterMap(String classId,
```

```java
                                    String pk,
                                    String owner) {
    Map map = new HashMap();
    map.put("classId", classId);
    map.put("pk", pk);
    map.put("owner", owner);
    return map;
}

public boolean acquireLock(String classId, String pk,
        String owner) {
    Map map = makeParameterMap(classId, pk, owner);
    try {
        template.insert("acquireLock", map);
        return true;
    } catch (DataIntegrityViolationException e) {
        return false;

    }
}

public boolean verifyLock(String classId, String pk,
        String owner) {
    Map map = makeParameterMap(classId, pk, owner);
    return new Integer(1).equals(template.queryForObject(
        "verifyLock", map));
}

public void releaseLock(String classId,
                        String pk,
                        String owner) {
    Map map = makeParameterMap(classId, pk, owner);
    int count = template.delete("releaseLock", map);
    if (count != 1)
        throw new ApplicationRuntimeException(
            "Count should ==1 " + count);
}
}
```

The `acquireLock()` method acquires a lock by inserting a row into the OFFLINE_LOCK table using the following SQL statement:

```sql
INSERT INTO OFFLINE_LOCK(CLASS_ID, PK, OWNER) VALUES(?,?,?)
```

It executes the `INSERT` statement by calling `SqlMapClientTemplate.insert()`. It then catches the `DataIntegrityViolationException`, which is thrown if the lock already exists, and maps it to a `LockManagerException`.

The verifyLock() method verifies that the caller owns the lock by executing the following SQL statement:

```
SELECT count(*)
FROM OFFLINE_LOCK
WHERE CLASS_ID = ? AND PK = ? AND OWNER = ?
```

It executes the SQL SELECT by calling SqlMapClientTemplate.select(). It throws a LockManagerException if the lock does not exist or is owned by someone else.

The releaseLock() method releases a lock by executing the following SQL statement:

```
DELETE FROM OFFLINE_LOCK WHERE CLASS_ID = ? AND PK = ? AND OWNER = ?
```

It executes this DELETE statement by calling SqlMapClientTemplate.delete(). It throws a LockManagerException if the lock does not exist or is owned by someone else.

This is a very simple implementation of the lock manager. A more elaborate implementation could, for example, track when locks are acquired and allow for old locks to be stolen.

13.7.2 *Implementing the domain service*

Now that you have seen how to implement a lock manager, let's look at an example of business logic that uses it. The business logic of the Modify Order use case is implemented by the ModifyOrderService. The ModifyOrderService is a domain model service that is invoked by either a POJO façade or the presentation tier. It calls various other domain objects, including Order and OrderRepository, and uses the LockManager to lock and unlock orders.

ModifyOrderService defines several methods that handle requests from the presentation tier, including:

- getOrderToModify() is called at the start of the use case when the user decides to edit an order. It verifies that the order can be edited and then locks it.

- updateQuantities() is called when the user changes the line item quantities. It verifies that the order is still locked and saves the new quantities.

- saveChangesToOrder() is called when the user saves her changes. It verifies that the order is still locked, updates it, and then unlocks it.

- cancelModifyOrder() is called when the user gives up editing the order. It unlocks the order.

Because the process of editing an order is similar to the process of placing an order, the ModifyOrderService uses a PendingOrder to keep track of the changes made by the user. At the start of the process, it creates a `PendingOrder` from the `Order` and stores it in the database. When the user saves his changes, the `Modify-OrderService` updates the `Order` with the changes. Figure 13.6 shows the design,

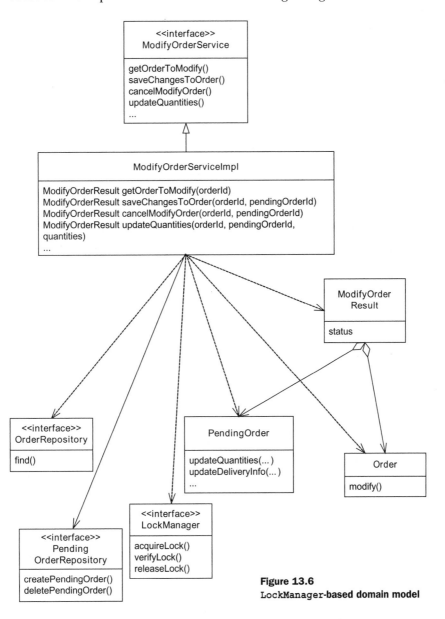

Figure 13.6
LockManager-based domain model

which consists of the `ModifyOrderService`, `ModifyOrderServiceImpl` (which implements the `ModifyOrderService` interface), and the classes that it calls.In addition to the `ModifyOrderService` and `ModifyOrderServiceImpl`, the design consists of these other classes:

- `OrderRepository` loads the `Order`.
- `PendingOrderRepository` creates, loads, and deletes the `PendingOrder`.
- `LockManager` maintains the locks in the database.
- `PendingOrder` stores the changes made to the `Order`.
- `Order` is the order being edited.
- `ModifyOrderResult` is returned by the `ModifyOrderService`.

There are lots of details of the business logic that you do not need to know about to understand how the Pessimistic Offline Lock pattern works, so we'll focus just on the `ModifyOrderService` class and how it interacts with the lock manager. Check out the online source code if you want to see the details of the other classes. `ModifyOrderService` is an interface that specifies the methods that can be invoked by the POJO façade or the presentation tier:

```
public interface ModifyOrderService {
  public ModifyOrderServiceResult getOrderToModify(String caller,
      String orderId);

  public ModifyOrderServiceResult updateDeliveryInfo(
      String caller, String orderId, String pendingOrderId,
      Address deliveryAddress, Date deliveryTime);

  public ModifyOrderServiceResult updateQuantities(String caller,
      String orderId, String pendingOrderId, int[] quantities)
      throws InvalidPendingOrderStateException;

  public ModifyOrderServiceResult saveChangesToOrder(
      String caller, String orderId, String pendingOrderId);

  public ModifyOrderServiceResult cancelModifyOrder(
      String caller, String orderId, String pendingOrderId);
}
```

Each method has a caller parameter, which is used as the lock owner. It could be the `HttpSession` ID or the user ID. The other method parameters include the IDs of orders and pending orders as well as values entered by the user, such as the delivery time and the line item quantities.

The `ModifyOrderService` interface is implemented by the `ModifyOrderServiceImpl` class, which is shown in listing 13.4. `ModifyOrderServiceImpl` fulfills its responsibilities by calling various classes such as `Order`, `OrderRepository`, `PendingOrder`, and `PendingOrderRepository`. Each of its methods also calls the `LockManager` to acquire locks, to verify that locks are still held, and to release locks. They pass the name of the `Order` class, order ID, and the caller as arguments to the `LockManager`.

Listing 13.4 ModifyOrderServiceImpl

```
public class ModifyOrderServiceLockManagerImpl implements
    ModifyOrderService {

  private PendingOrderRepository pendingOrderRepository;

  private OrderRepository orderRepository;

  private LockManager lockManager;

  private RestaurantRepository restaurantRepository;

  public ModifyOrderServiceLockManagerImpl(       ❶ Creates
      OrderRepository orderRepository,               ModifyOrderServiceLock
      PendingOrderRepository pendingOrderRepository, ManagerImpl
      RestaurantRepository restaurantRepository,
      LockManager lockManager) {
    this.pendingOrderRepository = pendingOrderRepository;
    this.orderRepository = orderRepository;
    this.restaurantRepository = restaurantRepository;
    this.lockManager = lockManager;
  }

  public ModifyOrderServiceResult getOrderToModify(String caller,
      String orderId) {
    if (lockManager
        .acquireLock(Order.class.getName(),     ❷ Locks
                orderId,                           Order
                caller)) {
      Order order = orderRepository.findOrder(orderId);
      PendingOrder pendingOrder =
              createPendingOrder(order);       ❸ Creates
      return new ModifyOrderServiceResult(        PendingOrder
        ModifyOrderServiceResult.OK,
        pendingOrder);                         ❹ Returns
    } else {                                      ModifyOrderServiceResult
      return new ModifyOrderServiceResult(
        ModifyOrderServiceResult.ALREADY_LOCKED);

    }
  }
```

```
protected PendingOrder createPendingOrder(Order order) {
  Address deliveryAddress = order.getDeliveryAddress();
  Date deliveryTime = order.getDeliveryTime();
  Restaurant restaurant = order.getRestaurant();
  List orderLineItems = order.getLineItems();
  PendingOrder pendingOrder = pendingOrderRepository
      .createPendingOrder(deliveryAddress, deliveryTime,
          restaurant, orderLineItems);
  return pendingOrder;
}

public ModifyOrderServiceResult updateDeliveryInfo(
    String caller, String orderId, String pendingOrderId,
    Address deliveryAddress, Date deliveryTime) {

  if (lockManager
      .verifyLock(Order.class.getName(),          ❺ Verifies
                orderId,                             Order is locked
                caller)) {

    PendingOrder pendingOrder
      = pendingOrderRepository                     ❻ Updates
        .findPendingOrder(pendingOrderId);           delivery info

    int result =
      pendingOrder.updateDeliveryInfo(
        restaurantRepository,                      ❼ Returns
        deliveryAddress,                             ModifyOrderServiceResult
        deliveryTime,
        false);

    return new ModifyOrderServiceResult(
        ModifyOrderServiceResult.OK, pendingOrder);
  } else {
    return new ModifyOrderServiceResult(
        ModifyOrderServiceResult.NOT_LOCKED);

  }
}

public ModifyOrderServiceResult updateQuantities(String caller,
    String orderId, String pendingOrderId, int[] quantities)
    throws InvalidPendingOrderStateException {
  if (lockManager.verifyLock(Order.class.getName(), orderId,
        caller)) {
    PendingOrder pendingOrder = pendingOrderRepository
        .findPendingOrder(pendingOrderId);
    pendingOrder.updateQuantities(quantities);
    return new ModifyOrderServiceResult(
        ModifyOrderServiceResult.OK, pendingOrder);
  } else {
```

```
        return new ModifyOrderServiceResult(
            ModifyOrderServiceResult.NOT_LOCKED);

    }
}

public ModifyOrderServiceResult saveChangesToOrder(
    String caller, String orderId, String pendingOrderId) {
  if (lockManager
        .verifyLock(Order.class.getName(),
                    orderId,
                    caller)) {
    Order order = orderRepository.findOrder(orderId);
    PendingOrder pendingOrder = pendingOrderRepository
        .findPendingOrder(pendingOrderId);

    order.modify(pendingOrder
                    .getDeliveryAddress(),
                pendingOrder
                 .getDeliveryTime(),
                pendingOrder
                 .getRestaurant(),
                pendingOrder
                 .getPaymentInformation(),
                pendingOrder.getLineItems());

    lockManager
      .releaseLock(Order.class.getName(),
                   orderId,
                   caller);
    return new ModifyOrderServiceResult(
        ModifyOrderServiceResult.OK, order);
  } else {
    return new ModifyOrderServiceResult(
        ModifyOrderServiceResult.NOT_LOCKED);

  }
}

public ModifyOrderServiceResult cancelModifyOrder(
    String caller, String orderId, String pendingOrderId) {
  if (lockManager
        .verifyLock(Order.class.getName(),
                    orderId,
                    caller)) {
    Order order = orderRepository.findOrder(orderId);
    lockManager
      .releaseLock(Order.class.getName(),
                   orderId,
                   caller);
    return new ModifyOrderServiceResult(
```

8 **Verifies Order is locked**

9 **Updates Order**

10 **Unlocks Order**

11 **Verifies Order is locked**

12 **Unlocks Order**

```
            ModifyOrderServiceResult.OK, order);
      } else {
        return new ModifyOrderServiceResult(
            ModifyOrderServiceResult.NOT_LOCKED);

      }
    }

  }
```

Let's look at the details:

❶ The constructor takes a `PendingOrderRepository`, an `OrderRepository`, a `RestaurantRepository`, and a `LockManager` as parameters and stores them in fields.

❷ The `getOrderToModify()` method first locks the `Order` by calling `LockManager.acquireLock()`.

❸ The method then finds the `Order` by calling the `OrderRepository` and creates a `PendingOrder`.

❹ `getOrderToModify()` returns a `ModifyOrderServiceResult`.

❺ The `updateDeliveryInfo()` method first verifies that the order is still locked by calling `LockManager.verifyLock()`.

❻ The method finds the `PendingOrder` and calls `PendingOrder.updateDeliveryInfo()`.

❼ `updateDeliveryInfo()` returns a `ModifyOrderServiceResult`.

❽ The `saveChangesToOrder()` method first verifies that the order is still locked.

❾ The method updates the `Order` with the changes made by the user.

❿ It then unlocks the `Order` and returns a `ModifyOrderServiceResult`.

⓫ The method `cancelModifyOrder()` verifies that the `Order` is still locked.

⓬ It then unlocks the `Order` by calling `LockManager.releaseLock()`.

As you can see, the business logic implemented by the domain model service makes calls to the `LockManager`. The `getOrderToModify()` method, which is called at the start of the use case, attempts to lock the order. If it cannot, then it returns a status code indicating that the order is locked by another user. The user interface can then display an error message to the user telling them to try again later.

Methods such as `updateDeliveryInfo()` and `updateQuantities()`, which are called during the use case, verify that the order is still locked. The `saveChanges-ToOrder()` and `cancelModifyOrder()`, which are called at the end of the use case, first verify that the order is still locked and then unlock it.

Let's now see how using the Pessimistic Offline Lock pattern to implement the Modify Order use case affects the implementation of other use cases.

13.7.3 Adapting the other use cases

We saw in section 13.5.3 that one consequence of using the Pessimistic Offline Lock pattern is that all use cases that update the same shared data must lock and unlock objects. In the Food to Go application, this means that if the implementation of the Modify Order use case uses a `LockManager`, then the other use cases that update orders must do so as well. This section examines the impact that this has on the Send Orders to Restaurant and Acknowledge Order use cases.

Changing the Send Orders to Restaurant use case

Even though the Send Orders to Restaurant use case consists of a single database transaction, it must use the `LockManager` to lock the orders before sending them and unlock them afterward. Listing 13.5 shows the domain model version of the business logic that does this.

Listing 13.5 DomainRestaurantNotificationService

```
public class DomainRestaurantNotificationService

  public boolean sendOrders(String caller) {
    Collection orders =orderRepository.findOrdersToSendToRestaurant();
    Collection lockedOrders = new ArrayList();
    for (Iterator it = orders.iterator(); it.hasNext();) {
      Order order = (Order) it.next();      Locks the order
      if(!lockOrder(caller,order))          Skips already locked orders
        continue;

      lockedOrders.add(order);              Remembers locked order

      Restaurant restaurant = order.getRestaurant();
      NotificationDetails notificationDetails = notificationGateway
          .sendOrder(order);
      Date timestamp = notificationDetails.getTimestamp();
      String messageId = notificationDetails.getMessageId();
      order.noteSent(messageId, timestamp);
    }
    unlockOrders(lockedOrders);             Unlocks previously
    return !orders.isEmpty();               locked orders
  }
```

```
    private boolean lockOrder(String caller, Order order) {
      return lockManager.acquireLock(Order.class.getName(),
                                     order.getId(), caller);
    }

    private void unlockOrders(String caller, Collection orders) {
      for (Iterator it = orders.iterator(); it.hasNext();) {
        Order order = (Order) it.next();
        lockManager.releaseLock(Order.class.getName(), order.getId(),
                                caller);
      }
    }

    ...
}
```

The sendOrders() method iterates through the result of the query and tries to
lock each order. It ignores orders that cannot be locked. After locking the order,
it sends it to the restaurant and updates it. Before returning, this method unlocks
all of the locked orders. The code reads objects before locking and so could
potentially read stale data and overwrite changes made by other transactions. It
must, for the reasons we saw in section 13.6.5, use one of the database transaction-
level concurrency mechanisms such as optimistic locking to avoid doing this.

One way to improve this code is to retrieve the orders with a query that ignores
the ones that are locked. The application must still lock the orders it retrieves to
prevent another transaction from attempting to update them, but excluding the
locked orders from the query prevents the application from loading them unnecessarily. The transaction script-based implementation of the Send Orders to Restaurant use case can use a SQL query that does a join between the
PLACED_ORDER and OFFLINE_LOCK tables. The domain model version would
need to map the OFFLINE_LOCK table to a class so that it can use a persistence
framework query that excludes locked orders.

Changing the Acknowledge Order use case

The Acknowledge Order use case is another use case that updates orders. There
are a couple of different ways we can change the Acknowledge Order use case
code to work with pessimistic offline locking. One option is to implement this use
case using the Pessimistic Offline Locking pattern instead of the Optimistic
Offline Locking pattern. Doing this is easy, but it means that another set of users
(i.e., restaurants) will hold locks on orders. Furthermore, because unlike customer
service representatives they are outside of the direct control of the company, these

users might be less diligent in exiting the application gracefully and unlocking orders. As a result, there is an increased chance of orders remaining locked.

An alternative approach is for the implementation of the Acknowledge Order use case to continue to use the Optimistic Offline Lock pattern with some minor enhancements. The `AcknowledgeOrderService` verifies that the order is unlocked at the start of the use case and locks the order in the final database transaction while updating it. The Optimistic Offline Lock pattern detects when an order was changed by another transaction, and locking the order while updating it ensures that it is safe to do so. This approach avoids having the restaurant user holding onto long-term pessimistic offline locks but does make the code a little more complex. Here is an excerpt of the code for the `AcknowledgeOrderService`, which implements the business logic for this use case. The changes to the `getOrderToAcknowledge()` and `acknowledgeOrder()` methods appear in bold.

```
public class DetachingAcknowledgeOrderServiceWithLockImpl implements
    DetachingAcknowledgeOrderService {

  public AcknowledgeOrderResult getOrderToAcknowledge(
      String orderId) {
    Order order = orderRepository.findOrder(orderId);
    Order detachedOrder = attachmentManager.detach(order);
    if (order.isAcknowledgable()) {
      if (lockManager                          Verifies order
            .isLocked(Order.class,             not locked
                      order.getId()))
        return new AcknowledgeOrderResult(
          AcknowledgeOrderResult.LOCKED,
          detachedOrder);
      else
        return new AcknowledgeOrderResult(
          AcknowledgeOrderResult.OK, detachedOrder);
    } else
      return new AcknowledgeOrderResult(
        AcknowledgeOrderResult.ILLEGAL_STATE,
        detachedOrder);
  }


  public AcknowledgeOrderResult acknowledgeOrder(
      Order detachedOrder, String owner) {
    if (!lockManager
          .acquireLock(Order.getName(),
                       detachedOrder          Locks order
                         .getId(),
                       owner))
      return new AcknowledgeOrderResult(
        AcknowledgeOrderResult.LOCKED, detachedOrder);
```

```
try {
  Order order = attachmentManager.attach(detachedOrder);
  return new AcknowledgeOrderResult(
      AcknowledgeOrderResult.OK, detachedOrder);
} finally {
  lockManager
    .releaseLock(Order.class.getName(),
                 detachedOrder.getId(),              Unlocks order
                 owner);
}
}
```

...

The getOrderToAcknowledge() method calls the LockManager to verify that the order is unlocked. The isLocked() method is a new LockManager method, which returns true if the specified object is locked by anyone. The acknowledgeOrder() method has an owner parameter, which is passed to the LockManager. It calls acquireLock() to lock the order before attaching the order. Afterwards, it calls releaseLock() to unlock the order. If either method fails to acquire the lock, it returns a status code of AcknowledgeOrderResult.LOCKED, which tells the presentation tier that the order is locked and cannot be changed.

As you can see, using the Pessimistic Offline Lock pattern in one use case requires the other use cases that access the same data to use it as well. You might even have to change existing code to call the lock manager if you implement a new use case that requires the Pessimistic Offline Lock pattern. Although these code changes can be substantial, they are unavoidable if you must prevent two users from editing the same data simultaneously.

Using the Pessimistic Offline Lock pattern ensures that changes made to an order will not be lost. The customer service representative will be able to save the changes requested by the customer—and another happy customer will enjoy a delicious meal.

13.8 Summary

There are two ways to handle concurrent updates in edit-style use cases that read data in one database transaction and update it in another. One option is to use the Optimistic Offline Lock pattern, which verifies that the data in the database is unchanged since it was first read at the start of a use case. One way to implement this pattern is to store the original version number or timestamp of the data being edited as part of the session state and to verify that it is unchanged when updating it.

Another way to implement the Optimistic Offline Lock pattern in a JDO or Hibernate application is to use detached objects. The business tier detaches the object being edited and returns it to the presentation tier, which stores it as part of the session state. Later, the presentation tier updates the detached object with the user's changes and passes it back to the business tier, which attaches it. Hibernate and JDO verify that the rows in the database corresponding to the object are unchanged when saving it.

One drawback of the Optimistic Offline Lock pattern is that, although it prevents concurrent updates, it does not prevent to users from editing the same data at the same time. One user will succeed and the other will have to start over. Consequently, if the probability of conflicts is high or the cost of redoing the work is large, then you should use the Pessimistic Offline Lock pattern. This pattern locks the data being edited for the duration of the use case and prevents it from being updated by other users, which guarantees that users can save their changes. The Pessimistic Offline Lock pattern uses application-level style locks, which are stored in the database in either a separate table or in the same table as the data. There is one challenge with using this pattern: if one use case uses it, then all others that update the same data must also use it, which is potentially error-prone. But this is something you just have to deal with if you want to have a usable application.

references

[Acegi] Acegi Security System for Spring. http://acegisecurity.sourceforge.net.

[Alur 2003] Alur, D., Crupi, J., and Malks, D. 2003. *Core J2EE Patterns: Best Practices and Design Strategies*, 2nd ed. Upper Saddle River, NJ: Prentice Hall PTR.

[Bauer 2005] Bauer, C. and King, G. 2004. *Hibernate in Action*. Greenwich, CT: Manning.

[Beck 2002] Beck, K. 2002. *Test-Driven Development: By Example*. Boston: Addison-Wesley Professional.

[Begin, forthcoming] Begin, C. Forthcoming. *iBATIS in Action*. Greenwich, CT: Manning.

[Buschmann 1996] Buschmann, F., Meunier, R., Rohnert, H., Sommerlad, P., and Stal, M. 1996. *Pattern-Oriented Software Architecture, Volume 1: A System of Patterns*. New York: John Wiley & Sons.

[Cactus] Jakarta Cactus. http://jakarta.apache.org/cactus/.

[Crane 2005] Crane, D., and Pascarello, E. 2005. *Ajax in Action*. Greenwich, CT: Manning.

[DBCP] Apache Jakarta project. http://jakarta.apache.org/commons/dbcp/.

[DbUnit] DbUnit project. http://dbunit.sourceforge.net.

[EasyMock] EasyMock project. www.easymock.org/.

[Eclipse] Eclipse Foundation. www.eclipse.org.

[EHCache] Ehcache project. http://ehcache.sourceforge.net/.

[EJB 3 June 2005] EJB3 Expert Group. JSR 220: Enterprise JavaBeans 3.0. www.jcp.org/en/jsr/detail?id=220.2005.

[Evans 2003] Evans, E. 2003. *Domain-Driven Design: Tackling Complexity in the Heart of Software.* Boston: Addison-Wesley Professional.

[Fowler 1999] Fowler, M. 1999. *Refactoring: Improving the Design of Existing Code.* Boston: Addison-Wesley Professional.

[Fowler 2002] Fowler, M. 2002. *Patterns of Enterprise Application Architecture.* Boston: Addison-Wesley Professional.

[Fowler Anemic] Fowler, M. www.martinfowler.com/bliki/AnemicDomainModel.html.

[Fowler POJO] Fowler, M. www.martinfowler.com/bliki/POJO.html.

[Gang of Four] Gamma, E., Helm, R., Vlissides, J., and Johnson, R. 1995. *Design Patterns – Elements of Reusable Object-Oriented Software.* Boston: Addison-Wesley Professional.

[Gray 1993] Gray, J. and Reuter, A. 1993. *Transaction Processing: Concepts and Techniques.* San Mateo, CA: Morgan Kaufmann.

[Hibernate injection] Hibernate community. http://hibernate.org/182.html.

[HSQLDB] HSQL database engine. www.hsqldb.org.

[Husted 2002] Husted, T. Dumoulin, C., Franciscus, G., Winterfeldt, D., and McClanahan, C. 2002. *Struts in Action: Building Web Applications with the Leading Java Framework.* Greenwich, CT: Manning.

[JBossCache] JBoss Cache. www.jboss.org/products/overview/jbosscache.

[jMock] jMock project. www.jmock.org/.

[JPOX] JPOX project. www.jpox.org/index.jsp.

[JSR12] JSR 12, Java Data Objects (JDO) Specification. www.jcp.org/en/jsr/detail?id=12.

[JSR243] JSR 243: Java Data Objects 2.0 – An Extension to the JDO Specification. www.jcp.org/en/jsr/detail?id=243.

[JUnit] JUnit.org. www.junit.org/index.htm.

[Laddad 2003] Laddad, R. *AspectJ in Action.* 2003. Greenwich, CT: Manning.

[Larman 2004] Larman, C. 2004. *Applying UML and Patterns: An Introduction to Object-Oriented Analysis and Design and Iterative Development,* 3rd ed. Upper Saddle River, NJ: Prentice Hall PTR.

[Mann 2005] Mann, K. 2005. *JavaServer Faces in Action.* Greenwich, CT: Manning.

[Marinescu 2002] Marinescu, F. 2002. *EJB Design Patterns: Advanced Patterns, Processes and Idioms.* Hoboken, NJ: John Wiley and Sons, Inc.

[Massol 2003] Massol, V. *JUnit in Action.* 2003. Greenwich, CT: Manning.

[OpenSessionInView] Hibernate community. www.hibernate.org/43.html.

[PicoContainer] PicoContainer project. www.picocontainer.org/.

[Rainsberger 2004] 2004. Rainsberger, J. B. *JUnit Recipes: Practical Methods for Programmer Testing*. Greenwich, CT: Manning.

[Russell 2003] Russell, C. 2003. *Java Data Objects*. Sebastopol, CA: O'Reilly Media.

[SwarmCache] SwarmCache project. http://swarmcache.sourceforge.net/.

[Tapestry] Jakarta Tapestry. http://jakarta.apache.org/tapestry.

[Tate 2003] 2003. Tate, B., Clark, M., Lee, B., and Linskey, P. *Bitter EJB*. Greenwich, CT: Manning.

[TORPEDO] Torpedo Group. www.torpedo-group.org.

[Tow 2003] Tow, D. 2003. *SQL Tuning*. Sebastopol, CA: O'Reilly Media.

[Walls 2005] Walls, C. and Breidenbach, R. 2005. *Spring in Action*. Greenwich, CT: Manning.

[Wirfs-Brock 2002] Wirfs-Brock, R. and McKean, A. 2002. *Object Design: Roles, Responsibilities, and Collaborations*. Boston: Addison-Wesley Professional.

[XmlUnit] XMLUnit project. http://xmlunit.sourceforge.net.

index